Beginning ASP.NET E-Commerce in C#

From Novice to Professional

Cristian Darie and Karli Watson

D0814086

Apress®

Beginning ASP.NET E-Commerce in C#: From Novice to Professional

Copyright © 2009 by Cristian Darie and Karli Watson

All rights reserved. No part of this work may be reproduced or transmitted in any form or by any means, electronic or mechanical, including photocopying, recording, or by any information storage or retrieval system, without the prior written permission of the copyright owner and the publisher.

ISBN-13 (pbk): 978-1-4302-1074-0

ISBN-10 (pbk): 1-4302-1074-5

ISBN-13 (electronic): 13: 978-1-4302-1073-3

ISBN-10 (electronic): 1-4302-1073-7

Printed and bound in the United States of America 9 8 7 6 5 4 3 2 1

Trademarked names may appear in this book. Rather than use a trademark symbol with every occurrence of a trademarked name, we use the names only in an editorial fashion and to the benefit of the trademark owner, with no intention of infringement of the trademark.

Lead Editor: Matthew Moodie
Technical Reviewer: Andrei Rinea
Editorial Board: Clay Andres, Steve Anglin, Mark Beckner, Ewan Buckingham, Tony Campbell,
    Gary Cornell, Jonathan Gennick, Michelle Lowman, Matthew Moodie, Jeffrey Pepper,
    Frank Pohlmann, Ben Renow-Clarke, Dominic Shakeshaft, Matt Wade, Tom Welsh
Project Manager: Tracy Brown Collins
Copy Editor: Damon Larson
Associate Production Director: Kari Brooks-Copony
Production Editor: Ellie Fountain
Compositor: Susan Glinert
Proofreader: Linda Seifert
Indexer: Broccoli Information Management
Artist: Kinetic Publishing Services, LLC
Cover Designer: Kurt Krames
Manufacturing Director: Tom Debolski

Distributed to the book trade worldwide by Springer-Verlag New York, Inc., 233 Spring Street, 6th Floor, New York, NY 10013. Phone 1-800-SPRINGER, fax 201-348-4505, e-mail orders-ny@springer-sbm.com, or visit http://www.springeronline.com.

For information on translations, please contact Apress directly at 2855 Telegraph Avenue, Suite 600, Berkeley, CA 94705. Phone 510-549-5930, fax 510-549-5939, e-mail info@apress.com, or visit http://www.apress.com.

Apress and friends of ED books may be purchased in bulk for academic, corporate, or promotional use. eBook versions and licenses are also available for most titles. For more information, reference our Special Bulk Sales–eBook Licensing web page at http://www.apress.com/info/bulksales.

The information in this book is distributed on an "as is" basis, without warranty. Although every precaution has been taken in the preparation of this work, neither the author(s) nor Apress shall have any liability to any person or entity with respect to any loss or damage caused or alleged to be caused directly or indirectly by the information contained in this work.

The source code for this book is available to readers at http://www.apress.com.

Contents at a Glance

About the Authors xvii
About the Technical Reviewer xviii
Acknowledgments xix
Introduction xxi

PART 1 ■■■ Phase 1 of Development: Getting a Web Store Up and Running, Fast

■CHAPTER 1   Starting an E-Commerce Site 3
■CHAPTER 2   Laying Out the Foundations 13
■CHAPTER 3   Starting the BalloonShop Project 29
■CHAPTER 4   Creating the Product Catalog: Part 1 55
■CHAPTER 5   Creating the Product Catalog: Part 2 115
■CHAPTER 6   Product Attributes 181
■CHAPTER 7   Search Engine Optimization 197
■CHAPTER 8   Searching the Catalog 225
■CHAPTER 9   Improving Performance 257
■CHAPTER 10   Receiving Payments Using PayPal 267
■CHAPTER 11   Catalog Administration: Departments and Categories 279
■CHAPTER 12   Catalog Administration: Products 331

PART 2 ■■■ Phase 2 of Development: Selling More and Increasing Profits

■CHAPTER 13 Creating Your Own Shopping Cart 367
■CHAPTER 14 Accepting and Processing Customer Orders 403
■CHAPTER 15 Product Recommendations 447
■CHAPTER 16 Creating Customer Accounts 465

PART 3 ■■■ Phase 3 of Development: Advanced E-Commerce

■CHAPTER 17 Storing Customer Orders 531
■CHAPTER 18 Implementing the Order Pipeline, Part 1 563
■CHAPTER 19 Implementing the Order Pipeline, Part 2 589
■CHAPTER 20 Credit Card Transactions 637
■CHAPTER 21 Product Reviews 667
■CHAPTER 22 Integrating Amazon Web Services 675

■INDEX 693

Contents

About the Authors xvii

About the Technical Reviewer xviii

Acknowledgments xix

Introduction xxi

PART 1 ▪▪▪ Phase 1 of Development: Getting a Web Store Up and Running, Fast

▪CHAPTER 1   **Starting an E-Commerce Site** 3

The Balloon Shop 3

Deciding Whether to Go Online 4

Getting More Customers 5

Making Customers Spend More 6

Reducing the Costs of Fulfilling Orders 6

Making Money 7

Considering the Risks and Threats 8

Designing for Business 9

Knowing the Client 9

Phase 1 of Development: Getting a Web Store Up and
Running, Fast 10

Phase 2 of Development: Increasing Customer Satisfaction and
Conversion Rate 10

Phase 3 of Development: Advanced E-Commerce 11

Summary 12

■CHAPTER 2   **Laying Out the Foundations** 13

Designing for Growth 13
   Meeting Long-Term Requirements with Minimal Effort 14
Using a Three-Tier Architecture 15
   A Simple Scenario 16
   What's in a Number? 17
   The Right Logic for the Right Tier 18
   A Three-Tier Architecture for BalloonShop 19
   Why Not Use More Tiers? 19
Choosing Technologies and Tools 20
   Using ASP.NET 20
   Using C# and VB .NET 24
   Using Visual Web Developer 2008 Express Edition............. 24
   Using SQL Server 2008 25
Following Coding Standards 26
Summary 27

■CHAPTER 3   **Starting the BalloonShop Project** 29

Preparing the Development Environment 29
   Installing Visual Web Developer 2008 Express Edition.......... 30
   Installing SQL Server 2008 Express Edition................... 31
   Installing IIS... 32
   Preparing the BalloonShop Web Site 33
Creating the BalloonShop Web Application 35
Creating the BalloonShop SQL Server Database 39
Implementing the Site Skeleton 45
   Building the First Page.................................... 47
Downloading the Code 53
Summary 53

■CHAPTER 4   **Creating the Product Catalog: Part 1** 55

Showing Your Visitor What You've Got 55
   What Does a Product Catalog Look Like? 56
   Previewing the Product Catalog 56
Roadmap for This Chapter 59
Storing Catalog Information 61
   Understanding Data Tables 61
   Creating the Department Table............................. 69

Communicating with the Database 72

    Speaking the Database Language 73

    Creating Stored Procedures. 76

Adding Logic to the Site 79

    Connecting to SQL Server 79

    Issuing Commands and Executing Stored Procedures. 81

    Implementing Generic Data Access Code 83

    Catching and Handling Exceptions 85

    Sending Emails 88

    Writing the Business Tier Code 89

Displaying the List of Departments 97

    Preparing the Field: Themes, Skins, and Styles 98

Building a Link Factory 102

    Displaying the Departments 104

Adding a Custom Error Page 110

Summary 113

■CHAPTER 5   **Creating the Product Catalog: Part 2** 115

Storing the New Data 115

    What Makes a Relational Database 116

    Enforcing Table Relationships with the
        FOREIGN KEY Constraint 120

Adding Categories and Products to the Database 121

    Adding Categories. 121

    Adding Products 126

Querying the New Data 133

    Retrieving Short Product Descriptions 133

    Joining Data Tables 134

    Showing Products Page by Page 136

Writing the New Stored Procedures 139

    CatalogGetDepartmentDetails 140

    CatalogGetCategoryDetails 140

    CatalogGetProductDetails 141

    CatalogGetCategoriesInDepartment 141

    CatalogGetProductsOnFrontPromo 141

    CatalogGetProductsInCategory 142

    CatalogGetProductsOnDeptPromo 143

Using ADO.NET with Parameterized Stored Procedures 145

    Using Input Parameters 145

    Using Output Parameters. 146

    Stored Procedure Parameters Are Not Strongly Typed. 146

    Getting the Results Back from Output Parameters 146

Completing the Business Tier Code 147

    GetDepartmentDetails 149

    GetCategoryDetails 151

    GetProductDetails 152

    GetCategoriesInDepartment 154

    GetProductsOnFrontPromo 154

    GetProductsOnDeptPromo 156

    GetProductsInCategory. 157

    Completing the Link Factory 158

Implementing the Presentation Tier 159

    Displaying the List of Categories. 159

    Displaying Department and Category Details 163

    Displaying Product Lists. 167

    Displaying Product Details. 177

Summary 180

■CHAPTER 6   **Product Attributes** 181

Implementing the Data Tier 182

Implementing the Business Tier 188

Implementing the Presentation Tier 189

Summary 196

■CHAPTER 7   **Search Engine Optimization** 197

Optimizing BalloonShop 197

Supporting Keyword-Rich URLs 198

    UrlRewriter.NET and ISAPI_Rewrite 199

    Keyword-Rich URLs for BalloonShop 200

    Adding Keyword-Rich URL Support to BalloonShop 200

URL Rewriting and Regular Expressions 205

    .NET Regular Expressions 208

    The Keyword-Rich URL Factory. 211

Using the 301 and 302 HTTP Status Codes 216

Correctly Signaling 404 and 500 Errors 220

The Short UrlRewriter.NET Reference 222

Summary 224

■CHAPTER 8   Searching the Catalog 225

Choosing How to Search the Catalog 225

Teaching the Database to Search Itself 226

    Installing SQL Server's Full-Text Feature.................... 227

    Creating the FULLTEXT Catalog and Indexes................ 229

    Sorting by Relevance 232

    Improving Relevance 236

    Creating the SearchCatalog Stored Procedure 238

Implementing the Business Tier 243

Implementing the Presentation Tier 246

    Creating the Search Box 246

    Displaying the Search Results............................ 250

Summary 255

■CHAPTER 9   Improving Performance 257

Handling Postback 258

Managing ViewState 260

Using Output Cache 263

Summary 265

■CHAPTER 10   Receiving Payments Using PayPal 267

Considering Internet Payment Service Providers 267

Getting Started with PayPal 268

Integrating the PayPal Shopping Cart and Checkout 270

Summary 277

■CHAPTER 11   Catalog Administration: Departments
and Categories 279

Preparing to Create the Catalog Administration Page 280

Authenticating Administrators 284

Administering Departments 299

Styling the Department Administration Grid 317

Administering Categories 320

Summary 330

■**CHAPTER 12 Catalog Administration: Products** 331

Chapter Roadmap 331
Administering Products 333
Administering Product Details 348
Summary 364

PART 2 ■■■ Phase 2 of Development: Selling More and Increasing Profits

■**CHAPTER 13 Creating Your Own Shopping Cart** 367

Designing the Shopping Cart 368
Storing Shopping Cart Information 370
Implementing the Data Tier 372
    ShoppingCartAddItem 373
    ShoppingCartRemoveItem 373
    ShoppingCartUpdateItem 374
    ShoppingCartGetItems 374
    ShoppingCartGetTotalAmount 375
Implementing the Business Tier 375
    Generating Shopping Cart IDs 375
    What If the Visitor Doesn't Like Cookies? 379
    Implementing the Shopping Cart Access Functionality 379
Implementing the Presentation Tier 383
    Updating the Add to Cart Buttons 384
    Showing the Shopping Cart Summary 384
    Displaying the Shopping Cart 388
    Editing Product Quantities 393
Administering the Shopping Cart 396
    Deleting Products that Exist in Shopping Carts 396
    Removing Old Shopping Carts 396
Summary 402

■**CHAPTER 14 Accepting and Processing Customer Orders** 403

Implementing an Order-Placing System 403
    Storing Orders in the Database 405
    Creating Orders in the Database 409
    Updating the Business Layer 410
    Adding the Checkout Button 411

Administering Orders 413
   Client-Side Validation and Using the ASP.NET
      Validator Controls 415
   Displaying Existing Orders................................ 418
Administering Order Details 430
Summary 445

CHAPTER 15   Product Recommendations 447

Increasing Sales with Dynamic Recommendations 447
Implementing the Data Tier 449
   Adding Product Recommendations......................... 453
   Adding Shopping Cart Recommendations 455
Implementing the Business Tier 457
Implementing the Presentation Tier 458
Summary 461

PART 3 ▪▪▪ Phase 3 of Development: Advanced E-Commerce

CHAPTER 16   Creating Customer Accounts 465

Storing Customer Accounts 466
Creating a BalloonShop Customer Account Scheme 466
   The SecurityLib Classes................................. 467
   Customer Logins.. 495
   Customer Details 502
   The Checkout Page...................................... 520
Setting Up Secure Connections 525
   Obtaining an SSL Certificate from VeriSign 526
   Enforcing SSL Connections 526
   Including Redirections to Enforce Required SSL Connections.... 527
Summary 529

CHAPTER 17   Storing Customer Orders 531

Adding Orders to Customer Accounts 531
   Placing Customer Orders................................ 532
   Accessing Customer Orders 536

Handling Tax and Shipping Charges 546
    Tax Issues 546
    Shipping Issues 547
    Implementing Tax and Shipping Charges 547
Summary 561

■CHAPTER 18   **Implementing the Order Pipeline, Part 1** 563

What Is an Order Pipeline? 564
Understanding the BalloonShop Order Pipeline 564
Building the Order Pipeline 568
    The Basic Order Pipeline 568
    Adding More Functionality to OrderProcessor 583
Summary 587

■CHAPTER 19   **Implementing the Order Pipeline, Part 2** 589

Implementing the Pipeline Sections 589
    Business Tier Modifications 589
    Presentation Tier Modifications 602
Administering BalloonShop Orders 607
    Database Modifications 608
    Business Tier Modifications 611
    Presentation Tier Modifications 621
    Testing the Order Administration Page 633
Summary 635

■CHAPTER 20   **Credit Card Transactions** 637

Credit Card Transaction Fundamentals 637
    Working with Credit Card Payment Gateways 638
    Understanding Credit Card Transactions 639
Working with DataCash 639
    Preauthentication Request 640
    Response to Preauthentication Request 641
    Fulfillment Request 642
    Fulfillment Response 643
    Exchanging XML Data with DataCash 643

Integrating DataCash with BalloonShop 659
    Business Tier Modifications. 659
    Testing the Pipeline 664
    Going Live 666
Summary 666

CHAPTER 21   **Product Reviews** 667

Planning the Product Reviews Feature 667
Implementing Product Reviews 669
Summary 673

CHAPTER 22   **Integrating Amazon Web Services** 675

Introducing Web Services 675
    Creating Your Amazon.com Web Services Account 677
    Obtaining an Amazon.com Associate ID 678
    Accessing the Amazon.com E-Commerce Service
        Using REST. 678
    Accessing the Amazon.com E-Commerce Service
        Using SOAP. 681
Integrating AWS with BalloonShop 682
    Writing the Amazon Access Code. 682
    Implementing the Presentation Tier 688
Summary 691

INDEX 693

About the Authors

CRISTIAN DARIE is a software engineer who specializes in project management and web development, currently studying distributed application architectures for his PhD. Cristian has published several technical books with Apress, Packt Publishing, Wrox, and Sitepoint, and he is the manager and the former technical architect of OKazii.ro (www.okazii.ro), the largest e-commerce web site in Romania. You can reach Cristian through his personal web site at www.cristiandarie.ro.

KARLI WATSON is a technology architect at Boost.net (www.boost.net), as well as a freelance IT specialist, author, developer, and consultant. For the most part, he immerses himself in .NET (in particular, C#), and has written numerous books in the field for several publishers. He specializes in communicating complex ideas in a way that is accessible to anyone with a passion to learn, and spends much of his time playing with new technology to find new things to teach people about.

During those (seemingly few) times where he isn't doing the above, Karli will probably be wishing he was hurtling down a mountain on a snowboard. Or possibly trying to get his novel published. Either way, you'll know him by his brightly colored clothes.

About the Technical Reviewer

ANDREI RINEA is a senior .NET developer reaching into the architect league. He works mainly in the web development arena, but his area of expertise goes beyond that. Coming from a desktop application development background, Andrei was able to easily understand the ASP.NET paradigm, and in the end settled on MVC architectures such as Microsoft ASP.NET MVC. Andrei enjoys feedback from readers and is always glad to help you on any questions you may have regarding this book's code. He can be reached via andrei@rinea.ro or at his own site at http://andrei.rinea.ro.

Acknowledgments

The authors would like to thank the following people for their invaluable assistance with the production of this book:

Tracy Brown Collins, our project manager, for guiding everyone through the process of building this book. The challenges we've faced during the past year of work turned this book into an organizational nightmare at times, but Tracy kept us on track, helping us make the project a success.

Damon Larson, for his wonderful edits, which somehow made our copy sound like it was written by someone who actually knows English (and knows it well!).

Ellie Fountain and the production team for transforming the documents we've written and the graphics we've submitted into the book that you hold in your hands right now.

Andrei Rinea, for testing the code and verifying the technical accuracy of this book.

Family and friends of both Cristian and Karli for the fantastic emotional support they've offered during the writing of this book.

Introduction

Welcome to *Beginning ASP.NET E-Commerce in C#: From Novice to Professional*!

This book is a practical, step-by-step ASP.NET and SQL Server tutorial that teaches you real-world development practices. Guiding you through every step of the design and build process, this tutorial will teach you how to create high-quality, full-featured, extensible e-commerce web sites.

Over the course of the book, you will develop the necessary skills to get your business up on the Web and available to a worldwide audience. In each chapter, you will implement and test new features of your e-commerce web site, and you will learn the theoretical foundations required to understand the implementation details. The features are presented in increasing complexity as you advance throughout the book, so that your journey will be as pleasant and painless as possible. By the end of the book, you'll understand the concepts and have the knowledge to create your own powerful web sites.

Owners of previous editions of this book will find that a large part of it has been rewritten and many features have been added, as a result of the developments in the web development scene, and as a result of the extensive feedback we've received from the readers of the previous editions. Now you'll find the book teaches you how to implement search engine optimization, how to implement product attributes, how to use SQL Server's full-text searching, and many other exciting features.

The case study in this book is presented in three phases of development. The first phase focuses on getting the site up and running as quickly as possible, and at a low cost. Although not yet full-featured, at the conclusion of this phase your site will have a fully functional, searchable product catalog, and will be capable of accepting PayPal payments, enabling you to begin generating revenue immediately.

Phase 2 concentrates on increasing revenue by improving the shopping experience. In this phase, you'll learn how to encourage customers to buy more by implementing a dynamic product recommendation mechanism. You'll also implement your own custom shopping cart, replacing that provided by PayPal.

In the third phase, we'll show you how to increase your profit margins by reducing costs through automating and streamlining order processing and administration, and by handling credit card transactions yourself. You'll also learn how to integrate external functionality through web services (with a practical example of integrating Amazon.com products in your site), and improve your customer's shopping experience by adding product review functionality.

We hope you'll enjoy reading our book, and that you'll find it useful and relevant to your development projects!

Who This Book Is For

This book is aimed at developers looking for a tutorial approach to building a full e-commerce web site from design to deployment. The book teaches most of the necessary concepts and guides you through all the implementation steps, but it assumes that you have some basic knowledge of building web sites with ASP.NET and SQL Server. To get this basic knowledge, we recommend one of these books:

- *Beginning ASP.NET 3.5 in C# 2008: From Novice to Professional, Second Edition*, by Matthew MacDonald (Apress, 2007)

- *Build Your Own ASP.NET 3.5 Website Using C# & VB, Third Edition*, by Cristian Darie (Sitepoint, 2008)

How This Book Is Structured

This book is divided into three parts consisting of 22 chapters. We cover a wide variety of topics, showing you how to

- Build a product catalog that can be browsed and searched

- Design relational databases, and write SQL Server queries and stored procedures

- Use the SQL Server full-text search feature to implement product searching

- Implement search engine optimization features

- Implement the catalog administration pages that allow adding, modifying, and removing products, categories, and departments

- Create your own shopping basket and checkout mechanism

- Increase sales by implementing product recommendations and product reviews

- Handle payments using PayPal and DataCash

- Implement a customer account system

- Integrate Amazon.com web services to sell Amazon.com items through your web site

The following brief roadmap highlights how we'll take you from novice to professional regarding each of these topics.

Part 1: Phase 1 of Development: Getting a Web Store Up and Running, Fast

The first phase of development, which encompasses the first 12 chapters of the book, focuses on the basics of getting your site up and running quickly.

Chapter 1: Starting an E-Commerce Site

In this chapter, we'll introduce some of the principles of e-commerce in the real world. You'll see the importance of focusing on short-term revenue and keeping risks down. We'll look at the three basic ways in which an e-commerce site can make money. We'll then apply those principles to a three-phase plan that provides a deliverable, usable site at each phase of this book.

Chapter 2: Laying Out the Foundations

The first chapter offered an overview of e-commerce in the real world. Now that you've decided to develop a web site, we'll start to look in more detail at laying down the foundations for its future. We'll talk about what technologies and tools you'll use, and even more importantly, how you'll use them.

Chapter 3: Starting the BalloonShop Project

In this chapter, you'll prepare the groundwork for developing the BalloonShop project—the e-commerce web site you'll be creating throughout the book. You'll be guided through installing and configuring the necessary software on your development machine, including Visual Web Developer 2008 and SQL Server 2008. You'll also write a bit of code for the foundations of your project, and you'll create the SQL Server database that will store the web site's data.

Chapter 4: Creating the Product Catalog: Part 1

After learning about three-tier architecture and implementing a bit of your web site's main page, it's time to continue your work by starting to create the BalloonShop product catalog. Because the product catalog is composed of many components, you'll create it over two chapters. In Chapter 4, you'll create the first database table, create the first stored procedure, implement generic data access code, learn how to handle errors and email their details to the administrator, and finally use data gathered from the database to compose dynamic content for your visitor.

Chapter 5: Creating the Product Catalog: Part 2

In Chapter 4, you'll create a selectable list of departments for BalloonShop. However, a product catalog is much more than a list of departments. In Chapter 5, you'll add the rest of the product catalog features, creating category pages, product lists, and product details pages. While designing the data structure that supports these features, you'll learn how to implement relationships between data tables, and how to use parameterized SQL Server stored procedures.

Chapter 6: Product Attributes

Many online stores allow shoppers to customize the products they buy. For example, when selling balloons (as BalloonShop does), it's recommended to let your customer choose the color of the balloon. In this chapter, you'll implement the product attributes feature in BalloonShop.

Chapter 7: Search Engine Optimization

Search engine optimization, or simply SEO, refers to the practices employed to increase the number of visitors a web site receives from organic (unpaid) search engine result pages. Today, the search engine is the most important tool people use to find information and products on the Internet. Needless to say, having your e-commerce web site rank well for the relevant keywords will help drive visitors to your site and increase the chances that visitors will buy from you and not the competition! In this chapter, we'll update BalloonShop so that its core architecture will be search engine–friendly, which will help marketers in their efforts.

Chapter 8: Searching the Catalog

In the preceding chapters, you will have implemented a functional product catalog for Balloon-Shop. However, the site still lacks the all-important search feature. The goal in this chapter is to allow the visitor to search the site for products by entering one or more keywords. You'll learn how to implement search result rankings, and how to browse through the search results page by page. You'll see how easy it is to add new functionality to a working site by integrating the new components into the existing architecture.

Chapter 9: Improving Performance

Why walk when you can run? No, we won't talk about sports cars in this chapter. Instead, we'll analyze a few possibilities to improve the performance of the BalloonShop project.

Chapter 10: Receiving Payments Using PayPal

Your e-commerce web site needs a way to receive payments from customers. The preferred solution for established companies is to open a merchant account, but many small businesses choose to start with a solution that's simpler to implement, where they don't have to process credit card or payment information themselves.

A number of companies and web sites exist to help individuals or small businesses that don't have the resources to process credit card and wire transactions, and can be used to process the payment between companies and their customers. In this chapter, we'll demonstrate some of the functionality provided by one such company, PayPal.

Chapter 11: Catalog Administration: Departments and Categories

The final detail to take care of before launching a web site is to create its administrative interface. Although this is a part visitors will never see, it's still key to delivering a quality web site to your client. In this chapter and the following one, you'll implement a catalog administration page. This chapter deals specifically with administering departments and categories.

Chapter 12: Catalog Administration: Products

This chapter completes the catalog administration features by implementing product management features. Once this chapter is complete, your site administrators will be able to create products, assign products to new departments or categories, and so on.

Part 2: Phase 2 of Development: Selling More and Increasing Profits

In Part 2, you enter the second phase of development, where you start improving and adding new features to the already existing, fully functional e-commerce site.

Chapter 13: Creating Your Own Shopping Cart

With this chapter, you'll implement the custom shopping cart, which stores its data in the local database. This provides you with more flexibility than the PayPal shopping basket, over which you have limited control and that you can't save into your database for further processing and analysis.

Chapter 14: Accepting and Processing Customer Orders

The good news is that the brand new shopping cart implemented in Chapter 13 looks good and is fully functional. The bad news is that it doesn't allow the visitor to place an order yet, making it totally useless in the context of a production system. As you have probably already guessed, you'll deal with that problem in Chapter 14, in two separate stages. In the first part of the chapter, you'll implement the client-side part of the order-placing mechanism. In the second part of the chapter, you'll implement a simple order administration page where the site administrator can view and handle pending orders.

Chapter 15: Product Recommendations

One of the most important advantages of an Internet store, compared to a brick-and-mortar location, is the capability to customize the web site for each visitor based on his or her preferences or preferences based on data gathered from similar visitors. If your web site knows how to suggest additional products to your visitors in a clever way, they might end up buying more than initially planned. You have undoubtedly already seen this strategy in action on many successful e-commerce sites, and there is a reason for that—it increases profits. In this chapter, you'll implement a simple but efficient dynamic product recommendation system in your BalloonShop web store.

Part 3: Phase 3 of Development: Advanced E-Commerce

In the first two stages of development, you'll have built a basic (but functional) site, and you'll have hooked it into PayPal for taking payments and confirming orders. In the third section of the book, you'll take things a little further. By cutting PayPal out of the ordering process, you can gain better control as well as reduce overhead. This isn't as complicated as you might think, but you must be careful to do things right.

Chapter 16: Creating Customer Accounts

Chapter 16 lays the groundwork by implementing a customer account system, as well as looking into the security aspects of exchanging and storing customer and credit card details.

Chapter 17: Storing Customer Orders

In Chapter 16, we added customer account management capabilities, and we're keeping track of customer addresses and credit card information, which are stored in a secure way. However, we're not currently using this information in our order tracking system, which was created in phase 2 of development. We currently don't associate an order with the account of the customer that placed that order.

In this chapter, we'll make the modifications required for customers to place orders that are associated with their user profiles. The main modification here is that the customer associated with an order will be identified by a new piece of information in the orders table, and much of the rest of the modifications will be made to use this information.

These changes will allow us to track into our database the orders placed by a particular customer, and represent a base for implementing the order pipeline and credit card transactions in the following chapters.

Chapter 18: Implementing the Order Pipeline, Part 1

Order pipeline functionality is an extremely useful capability for an e-commerce site. Order pipeline functions let us keep track of orders at every stage in the process and provide auditing information that we can refer to later or if something goes wrong during the order processing. We can do all this without relying on a third-party accounting system, which can also reduce costs.

Implementing the order pipeline is the first step we're making for creating a professional order management system. In this and the next chapter, we'll build our own order-processing pipeline that deals with credit card authorization, stock checking, shipping, email notification, and so on. We'll leave the credit card–processing specifics for Chapter 20, but in this chapter, we'll show you where this process fits into the picture.

Chapter 19: Implementing the Order Pipeline, Part 2

In this chapter, you'll add the required pipeline sections so that you can process orders from start to finish, although you won't be adding full credit card transaction functionality until the next chapter. We'll also look at the web administration of orders by modifying the order admin pages added earlier in the book to take into account the new order-processing system.

Chapter 20: Credit Card Transactions

The last thing you need to do before launching the e-commerce site is enable credit card processing. In this chapter, we'll look at how you can build this into the pipeline you created in Chapters 18 and 19 by using the DataCash service. By the end of this chapter, BalloonShop will be a fully functioning, secure, and usable e-commerce application.

Chapter 21: Product Reviews

At this point, you have a complete and functional e-commerce web site. However, this doesn't stop you from adding even more features to it, making it more useful and pleasant for visitors. By adding a product reviews system to your web site, you increase the chances that visitors will get back to your site, either to write a review for a product they bought, or to see what other people think about that product.

Chapter 22: Integrating Amazon Web Services

So far in this book, you've learned how to integrate external functionality provided by PayPal and DataCash to process payments from your customers. In this chapter, you'll learn new possibilities for integrating features from external sources through web services. Knowing how to interact with third-party web services can offer you an important advantage over your competitors. In Chapter 22, you'll learn how to use Amazon.com functionality from and through web services.

Downloading the Code

The code for this book can be downloaded in ZIP file format from the Source Code section of the Apress web site. You can also find the code, errata, and other resources related to the book on Cristian Darie's web site, at `www.cristiandarie.ro/asp35-sql-server-ecommerce`.

PART 1

Phase 1 of Development: Getting a Web Store Up and Running, Fast

■■■

CHAPTER 1

Starting an E-Commerce Site

During the course of this book, you'll write the code for a full-featured online store. You'll learn how to design and implement the most important features of such a project, which include a product catalog, a shopping cart, and an administrative control panel.

We plan to be very practical and concise in this book, but before moving on to writing some code, it's worth taking a little step back to make sure we're all on the same page regarding the project we're about to implement. In this chapter, we'll discuss the project as a whole and a few of the business aspects to consider before launching such a project:

- Deciding whether to go online

- Considering risks and threats

- Planning the project development

The Balloon Shop

For the purposes of this book, we'll assume that the client for whom we create this site sells themed balloons, and the company already exists as a mail-order company with a good network of customers. The web site we'll create is named BalloonShop, and it will look like that shown in Figure 1-1.

The company is not completely new to the business and wants the site to make it easier and more enjoyable for its existing customers to buy—with the goal that they'll end up buying more.

■**Tip** You can preview the online version of BalloonShop at `http://www.cristiandarie.ro/BalloonShop`. Many thanks go to the Balloon Shop (`http://www.balloon-shop.com/`) for allowing us to use some of their products to populate our virtual BalloonShop store.

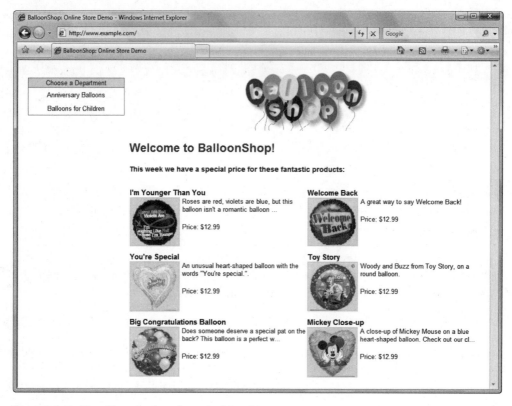

Figure 1-1. *BalloonShop during phase 2 of development*

Deciding Whether to Go Online

Creating and maintaining an e-commerce web site is less expensive than creating and maintaining a brick-and-mortar store, but it still implies a significant financial and time investment. While the risk management strategy is not your primary concern as a developer, understanding the economics of starting such a project will certainly prove helpful sooner or later.

If you want to build an e-commerce site today, you must answer some tough questions. The good news is these questions do have answers, and we're going to have a go at answering them in this chapter:

- So many big e-commerce sites have failed. What can e-commerce possibly offer me in today's tougher environment?

- Most e-commerce companies seemed to need massive investment. How can I produce a site on my limited budget?

- Even successful e-commerce sites expect to take years before they turn a profit. My business can't wait that long. How can I make money now?

Although there are hundreds of possible reasons for an offline business to go online, they tend to fall into the following motivations:

- Getting more customers

- Making customers spend more

- Reducing the costs of fulfilling orders

We'll look at each of these in the following sections.

Getting More Customers

Getting more customers is immediately the most attractive reason. With an e-commerce site, even small businesses can reach customers all over the world. This reason can also be the most dangerous because many people set up e-commerce sites assuming that the site will reach customers immediately. *It won't.*

In the offline world, you need to know a shop exists before you can go into it. This is still true in the world of e-commerce—people must know your site exists before you can hope to get a single order.

Making a web site popular is a much more complex task than it may appear to the uninitiated—and it requires extensive efforts and investment in areas such as web marketing and public relations (PR), search engine optimization (SEO), web analytics, pay-per-click campaigns, usability and accessibility research, customer support, and so on. We'll touch on some of these issues while implementing our virtual store, but we also recommend that you consult additional references if you're interested in deepening your knowledge in any of these fields.

Here are a few books that we recommend you read when you have a bit of spare time:

- *The New Rules of Marketing and PR: How to Use News Releases, Blogs, Podcasting, Viral Marketing and Online Media to Reach Buyers Directly* (Wiley, 2007)

- *Web Design and Marketing Solutions for Business Websites* (friends of ED, 2007)

- *Prioritizing Web Usability* (New Riders Press, 2006)

- *Don't Make Me Think: A Common Sense Approach to Web Usability* (New Riders Press, 2005)

- *Professional Search Engine Optimization with ASP.NET: A Developer's Guide to SEO* (Wrox, 2007)

- Web Analytics: An Hour a Day (Sybex, 2007)

- Designing Interfaces: Patterns for Effective Interaction Design (O'Reilly, 2005)

Admittedly, being a web developer, addressing these issues is not your direct concern, but widening your knowledge on collateral aspects of your day job will certainly not hurt.

Making Customers Spend More

Assuming your brick-and-mortar store already has customers, you probably wish that they bought more. What stops them? If the customers don't want any more of a certain product, there's not a lot that e-commerce can do, but chances are there are other reasons, too:

- Getting to the shop/placing an order by mail is a hassle.

- Some of the things you sell can be bought from more convenient places.

- You're mostly open while your customers are at work.

- Buying some products just doesn't occur to your customers.

An e-commerce site can fix those problems. In many cases, people with Internet access will find placing an order online far easier than any other method—meaning that when the temptation to buy strikes, it will be much easier for them to give in. Of course, the convenience of being online also means that people are more likely to choose your site over other local suppliers.

Because your site is online 24 hours a day, rather than the usual 9 to 5, your customers can shop at your store outside of their working hours. Having an online store brings a double blessing to you if your customers work in offices because they can indulge in retail therapy directly from their desks.

Skillful e-commerce design can encourage your customers to buy things they wouldn't usually think of. You can easily update your site to suggest items of particular seasonal interest or to announce interesting new products.

Many of the large e-commerce sites encourage shoppers to buy useful accessories along with the main product or to buy a more expensive alternative to the one they're considering. Others give special offers to regular shoppers or suggest impulse purchases during checkout. You'll learn how to use some of these methods in later chapters, and by the end of the book, you'll have a good idea of how to add more features for yourself.

Finally, it's much easier to learn about your customers via e-commerce than in face-to-face shops, or even through mail order. Even if you just gather email addresses, you can use these to send out updates and news. More sophisticated sites can automatically analyze a customer's buying habits to suggest other products the customer might like to buy.

Another related benefit of e-commerce is that you can allow people to browse without buying at no real cost to you. In fact, getting people to visit the site as often as possible can be valuable. You should consider building features into the site that are designed purely to make people visit regularly; for example, you might include community features such as forums or free content related to the products you're selling. Although we won't cover these features explicitly, by the end of the book you will have learned enough to easily add them for yourself.

Reducing the Costs of Fulfilling Orders

A well-built e-commerce site will be much cheaper to run than a comparable offline business. Under conventional business models, a staff member must feed an order into the company's order-processing system. With e-commerce, the customer can do this for you—the gateway between the site and the order processing can be seamless.

Of course, after your e-commerce site is up and running, the cost of actually taking orders gets close to zero—you don't need to pay for checkout staff, assistants, security guards, or rent in a busy shopping mall.

If you have a sound business idea, and you execute the site well, you can receive these benefits without a massive investment. It's important to always focus on the almighty dollar: Will your site, or any particular feature of it, help you get more customers, get customers to spend more, or reduce the costs and therefore increase your profit margins?

Now it's time to introduce the site we'll be using as the example in this book, and see just how all these principles relate to your own shop.

Making Money

In this book, we're going to build an online balloon shop. On all the e-commerce sites we've worked on, there's been a great deal of tension between wanting to produce an amazing site that everybody will love and needing to create a site with a limited budget that will make money. Usually, we're on the trigger-happy, really-amazing-site side, but we're always grateful that our ambitions are reined in by the actual business demands. If you're designing and building the site for yourself and you are the client, then you have a challenge: keeping your view realistic while maintaining your enthusiasm for the project.

This book shows you a logical way to build an e-commerce site that delivers what it needs to be profitable. However, when designing your own site, you need to think carefully about exactly who your customers are, what they need, how they want to place orders, and what they are most likely to buy. Most important of all, you need to think about how they will come to your site in the first place. You should consider the following points before you start to visualize or design the site, and certainly before you start programming:

- *Getting customers*: How will you get visitors to the site in the first place?

- *Offering products*: What will you offer, and how will you expect customers to buy? Will they buy in bulk? Will they make a lot of repeat orders? Will they know what they want before they visit, or will they want to be inspired? These factors will influence how you arrange your catalog and searching, as well as what order process you use. A shopping basket is great if people want to browse. If people know exactly what they want, then they may prefer something more like an order form.

- *Processing orders*: How will you turn a customer order into a parcel ready for mailing? How will you ship the products (for example, FedEx, UPS, or DHL)? Your main consideration here is finding an efficient way to process payments and deliver orders to whoever manages your stocks or warehouse. You must give your customers confidence in your ability to protect their data and deliver their purchases on time.

- *Servicing customers*: Will customers require additional help with products that they buy from you? Do you need to offer warranties, service contracts, or other support services?

- *Bringing customers back*: How will you entice customers back to the site? Are they likely to only visit the site to make a purchase, or will there be e-window shoppers? Are your products consumables, and can you predict when your customers will need something new?

After you've answered these questions, you can start designing your site, knowing that you're designing for your customers—not just doing what seems like a good idea. Determining the answers to these questions also helps ensure that your design covers all the important areas, without massive omissions that will be a nightmare to fix later.

The example presented in this book takes a deliberate generic approach to show you the most common e-commerce techniques. To really lift yourself above the competition, however, you don't need fancy features or Flash movies—you just need to understand, attract, and serve your customers better than anybody else. Think about this before you launch into designing and building the site itself.

Considering the Risks and Threats

All this might make it sound as if your e-commerce business can't possibly fail. Well, it's time to take a cold shower and realize that even the best-laid plans often go wrong. Some risks are particularly relevant to e-commerce companies, such as

- Hacking and identity theft

- Credit card scams

- Hardware failures

- Unreliable shipping services

- Software errors

- Changing laws

You can't get rid of these risks, but you can try to understand them and defend yourself from them. The software developed in this book goes some way toward meeting these issues, but many of the risks have little to do with the site itself.

An important way to defend your site from many risks is to keep backups. You already know backups are important; however, if you're anything like us, when it gets to the end of the day, saving five minutes and going home earlier seems even more important. When you have a live web site, this simply isn't an option. Coding with security in mind is also essential. In this book, you'll learn how to protect yourself by implementing a good error-handling strategy and validating user input. Using SSL (Secure Sockets Layer) connections is vital for securing sensible pages, such as the ones that contain credit card data, and we'll cover this as well.

We haven't talked much about the legal side of e-commerce in this book because we're programmers, not lawyers. However, if you're setting up an e-commerce site that goes much beyond an online garage sale, you'll need to look into these issues before putting your business online.

While we're on the subject of risks and threats, one issue that can really damage your e-commerce site is unreliable order fulfillment. An essential part of the processes is getting the products delivered. To do this, you need a good logistics network set up before launching your shop. If your store doesn't deliver the goods, customers won't come back or refer their friends.

Designing for Business

Building an e-commerce site requires a significant investment. If you design the site in phases, you can reduce the initial investment, and therefore cut your losses if the idea proves unsuccessful. You can use the results from an early phase to assess whether it's worthwhile to add extra features, and even use revenue from the site to fund future development. If nothing else, planning to build the site in phases means that you can get your site online and receive orders much earlier than if you build every possible feature into the first release.

Even after you've completed your initial planned phases, things may not end there. Whenever you plan a large software project, it's important to design in a way that makes unplanned future growth easy. In Chapter 2, where we'll start dealing with the technical details of building e-commerce sites, you'll learn how to design the web site architecture to allow for long-term development flexibility and scalability.

If you're building sites for clients, they will like to think their options are open. Planning the site, or any other software, in phases will help your clients feel comfortable doing business with you. They will be able to see that you are getting the job done, and they can decide to end the project at the end of any phase if they feel—for whatever reason—that they don't want to continue to invest in development.

Knowing the Client

As specified earlier, the client already exists as a mail-order company and has a good network of customers. The company is not completely new to the business and wants the site to make it easier and more enjoyable for its existing customers to buy—with the goal that they'll end up buying more.

Additional business requirements to take into consideration are

- The company is unlikely to get massive orders initially, so you should keep the initial cost of building the web site down as much as possible.

- The company is accustomed to manually processing mail orders, so manually processing orders emailed by a third-party payment processor such as PayPal will not introduce many new problems.

- The company doesn't want to invest all of its money in a massive e-commerce site only to find that people actually prefer mail order after all! Or, after phase 1, the company might realize that the site already meets its needs and there's no reason to expand it further. Either way, you hope that offering a lower initial cost gives your bid the edge. (It might also mean you can get away with a higher total price.)

- Because this company is already a mail-order business, it probably already has a merchant account and can process credit cards. Thus, moving away from PayPal and implementing a custom credit card–processing mechanism as soon as possible would be best for this company so it can benefit from the preferential card-processing rates.

To best address the business requirements of our client, we come up with a plan that consists of three large development and deployment cycles. The first stage will focus on getting the web store up and running as fast as possible. Only the essential features will be included.

In the second stage of development, you'll implement additional features that should increase the customer satisfaction while interacting with your site, and increase the conversion rate from its visitors.

Finally, in the third (and last) stage of development, you'll implement advanced e-commerce features such as storing your customers' confidential information securely and processing credit card payments yourself.

Let's see what you'll learn (and do) in each of these stages.

Phase 1 of Development: Getting a Web Store Up and Running, Fast

Chapters 1 through 12 concentrate on planning the project, establishing the basic framework for a site, and putting a product catalog online. You'll learn how to

- Design a database for storing a product catalog containing categories, products, and product attributes.

- Write the SQL (Structured Query Language) code and C# code for accessing and manipulating that data.

- Build a simple and usable catalog, with an internal searching feature, that makes it easy for visitors to find the products they're looking for.

- Implement SEO techniques to make your web site friendly to both search engines and human visitors.

- Implement an efficient error-reporting system that notifies the administrator in case the site runs into trouble and displays a friendly "Oops" message to the visitor when a critical error occurs.

- Integrate an external payment processor (with examples for PayPal) to allow visitors to order your products.

- Give the site's administrators a private section of the site where they can modify the catalog online.

After you've built this catalog, you'll see how to offer the products for sale by integrating it with PayPal's *Website Payments Standard* feature—a simple shopping cart and order-processing system that will handle credit card transactions for you and email you with details of orders. These orders will be processed manually because in the early stages of an e-commerce site, the time you lose processing orders will be less than the time it would have taken to develop an automated system.

Phase 2 of Development: Increasing Customer Satisfaction and Conversion Rate

The second stage of development is the optimization stage. You won't create new significant pages in your site, but you'll make great improvements to what you've already created.

First, you'll replace the shopping cart provided by PayPal's Website Payments Standard with your own. Having your own shopping cart is desirable because you can totally control its look and feel, you can better integrate it with your web site, and you can customize it by adding features such as product recommendations.

While creating your shopping cart, you will also start keeping track of your orders using your own database instead of PayPal's, and then use that data to learn about your customers. The first feature you'll implement using the new collected data is a product recommendations feature, similar to the one popularized by Amazon ("Customers who bought this product also bought . . ."). Showing these recommendations in product pages and in the shopping cart transforms these pages into a platform for selling even more products. How often have you been tempted by impulse purchases near the checkout of your local store? Well, this also works with e-commerce.

The second stage of development is covered in Chapters 13 through 15, and it takes you through

- Building your own ASP.NET shopping cart

- Passing a complete order through to PayPal for credit card processing

- Creating an order administration page

- Implementing a product recommendation system

Once again, at the end of phase 2, your site will be fully operational. If you want, you can leave it as it is or add features within the existing PayPal-based payment system. When the site gets serious, however, you'll want to start processing orders and credit cards yourself, and add more advanced features to your site.

Phase 3 of Development: Advanced E-Commerce

The core of e-commerce, and the bit that really separates it from other web development projects, is handling orders and credit cards. PayPal has helped you put this off, but there are a few reasons why—eventually—you'll want to part company with PayPal's Website Payments Standard:

- *Marketing*: The larger your business grows, the less appropriate it becomes to send your customers to a third-party web site that processes your payments for you. Imagine what you would think if Amazon sent you to PayPal when you bought a book, and you'll know what I mean.

- *Advanced payment options*: When you have direct control over performing transactions for your clients, you can start offering advanced payment options such as automatic subscription renewal or one-click payments.

- *Cost*: PayPal is not expensive, but moving to a simpler credit card–processing service may lead to lower transaction costs, although developing your own system will obviously incur up-front costs.

- *Easier integration*: If you deal with transactions and orders using your own system, you can integrate your store and your warehouse to whatever extent you require. You could even automatically contact a third-party supplier that ships the goods straight to the customer.

- *Information*: When you handle the whole order yourself, you can record and collate all the information involved in the transaction—and then use it for marketing and research purposes. You could, for example, gather statistical data based on your customers' demographics and personal data.

By integrating the order processing with the warehouse, fulfillment center, or suppliers, you can reduce costs significantly. This might mean that it reduces the need for staff in the fulfillment center, or at least that the business can grow without requiring additional staff.

Acquiring information about customers can feed back into the whole process, giving you valuable information about how to sell more. At its simplest, you could email customers with special offers, or just keep in touch with a newsletter. You could also analyze buying patterns and use that data to formulate targeted marketing campaigns.

During phase 3, which is covered in Chapters 16 through 21, you will learn how to

- Build a customer accounts module so that customers can log in and retrieve their details every time they make an order.

- Allow customers to add product reviews.

- Establish secure connections using SSL so that data sent by users is encrypted on its travels across the Internet.

- Authenticate and charge credit cards using third-party companies such as DataCash and their XML web services.

- Store credit card numbers securely in a database.

- Learn how to integrate the Amazon E-Commerce Service (ECS) into your web site.

This third phase is the most involved of all and requires some hard and careful work. By the end of phase 3, however, you will have an e-commerce site with complete user account and order-processing system mechanisms.

Summary

In this chapter, we've covered some of the principles of e-commerce in the real, hostile world where it's important to focus on short-term revenue and keep risks down. We've discussed the three basic motivations for taking your business online:

- Acquiring more customers

- Making customers spend more

- Reducing the costs of fulfilling orders

We've shown you how to apply those principles to a three-phase plan that provides a deliverable, usable site at each stage. We'll continue to expand on this plan throughout the book.

At this point, you've presented your plan to the owners of the balloon shop. In the next chapter, you'll put on your programming hat, and start to design and build your web site (assuming you get the contract, of course).

CHAPTER 2

■ ■ ■

Laying Out the Foundations

Now that you've convinced the client that you can create a cool web site to complement his or her activity, it's time to stop celebrating and start thinking about how to put into practice all the promises you've made. As usual, when you lay down on paper the technical requirements you must meet, everything starts to seem a bit more complicated than initially anticipated.

To ensure this project's success, you need to come up with a smart way to implement what you agreed to when you signed the contract. You want to develop the project smoothly and quickly, but the ultimate goal is to make sure the client is satisfied with your work. Consequently, you should aim to provide your site's increasing number of visitors with a positive web experience by creating a pleasant, functional, and responsive web site.

The requirements are high, but this is normal for an e-commerce site today. To maximize the chances of success, we'll analyze and anticipate as many of the technical requirements as possible and implement solutions in a way that supports changes and additions with minimal effort. Your goals for this chapter are to

- Analyze the project from a technical point of view

- Analyze and choose the architecture for your application

- Decide which technologies, programming languages, and tools to use

- Consider naming and coding conventions

Designing for Growth

The word *design* in the context of a web application can mean many things. Its most popular usage probably refers to the visual and user interface design of a web site.

This aspect is crucial because, let's face it, the visitor is often more impressed with how a site looks and how easy it is to use than about which technologies and techniques are used behind the scenes or what operating system the web server is running. If the site is slow, hard to use, or easy to forget, it just doesn't matter what rocket science was used to create it.

Unfortunately, this truth makes many inexperienced programmers underestimate the importance of the way the invisible part of the site is implemented—the code, the database, and so on. The visual part of a site gets visitors interested to begin with, but its functionality makes them come back. A web site can sometimes be implemented very quickly based on certain initial requirements, but if not properly architected, it can become difficult, if not impossible, to change.

For any project of any size, some preparation must be done before starting to code. Still, no matter how much preparation and design work is done, the unexpected does happen, and hidden catches, new requirements, and changing rules always seem to work against deadlines. Even without these unexpected factors, site designers are often asked to change or add functionality many times after the project is finished and deployed. This will also be the case for BalloonShop, which will be implemented in three separate stages, as discussed in Chapter 1.

You'll learn how to create the web site so that the site (or you) will not fall apart when functionality is extended or updates are made. Because this is a programming book, it doesn't address important aspects of e-commerce, such as designing the UI, marketing techniques, or legal issues. You'll need additional material to cover that ground. Instead, in this book, we'll pay close attention to constructing the code that makes the site work.

The phrase "designing the code" can have different meanings; for example, we'll need to have a short talk about naming conventions. Still, the most important aspect that we need to look at is the architecture to use when writing the code. The architecture refers to the way you split the code for a simple piece of functionality (for example, the product search feature) into smaller, interconnected components. Although it might be easier to implement that functionality as quickly and as simply as possible, in a single component, you gain great long-term advantages by creating more components that work together to achieve the desired result.

Before considering the architecture itself, you must determine what you want from this architecture.

Meeting Long-Term Requirements with Minimal Effort

Apart from the fact that you want a fast web site, each of the phases of development we talked about in Chapter 1 brings new requirements that must be met.

Every time you proceed to a new stage, you want to *reuse* most of the already existing solution. It would be very inefficient to redesign the site (not just the visual part, but the code as well!) just because you need to add a new feature. You can make it easier to reuse the solution by planning ahead so that any new functionality that needs to be added can slot in with ease, rather than each change causing a new headache.

When building the web site, implementing a *flexible architecture* composed of pluggable components allows you to add new features—such as the shopping cart, the departments list, or the product search feature—by coding them as separate components and plugging them into the existing application. Achieving a good level of flexibility is one of the goals regarding the application's architecture, and this chapter shows how you can put this into practice. You'll see that the level of flexibility is proportional to the amount of time required to design and implement it, so we'll try to find a compromise that provides the best gains without complicating the code too much.

Another major requirement that is common to all online applications is to have a *scalable architecture*. Scalability is defined as the capability to increase resources to yield a linear increase in service capacity. In other words, in a scalable system, the ratio (proportion) between the number of client requests and the hardware resources required to handle those requests is constant, even when the number of clients increases (ideally). An unscalable system can't deal with an increasing number of clients, no matter how many hardware resources are provided. Because we're optimistic about the number of customers, we must be sure that the site will be able to deliver its functionality to a large number of clients without throwing out errors or performing sluggishly.

Reliability is also a critical aspect for an e-commerce application. With the help of a coherent error-handling strategy and a powerful relational database, you can ensure data integrity and ensure that noncritical errors are properly handled without bringing the site to its knees.

Using a Three-Tier Architecture

Generally, the architecture refers to splitting each piece of the application's functionality into separate components based on what they do and grouping each kind of component into a single logical tier.

The three-tier architecture has become very popular because it answers many of the problems discussed so far by splitting an application's functionality unit into three logical tiers:

- The presentation tier

- The business tier

- The data tier

The **presentation tier** contains the UI elements of the site, and includes all the logic that manages the interaction between the visitor and the client's business. This tier makes the whole site feel alive, and the way you design it is crucially important to the site's success. Because your application is a web site, its presentation tier is composed of dynamic web pages.

The **business tier** (also called the *middle tier*) receives requests from the presentation tier and returns a result to the presentation tier depending on the business logic it contains. Almost any event that happens in the presentation tier results in the business tier being called (except events that can be handled locally by the presentation tier, such as simple input data validation). For example, if the visitor is doing a product search, the presentation tier calls the business tier and says, "Please send me back the products that match this search criterion." Almost always, the business tier needs to call the data tier for information to respond to the presentation tier's request.

The **data tier** (sometimes referred to as the *database tier*) is responsible for storing the application's data and sending it to the business tier when requested. For the BalloonShop e-commerce site, you'll need to store data about products (including their categories and their departments), users, shopping carts, and so on. Almost every client request finally results in the data tier being interrogated for information (except when previously retrieved data has been cached at the business tier or presentation tier levels), so it's important to have a fast database system. In Chapters 3 and 4, you'll learn how to design the database for optimum performance.

These tiers are purely logical—there is no constraint on the physical location of each tier. In theory, you are free to place all of the application, and implicitly all of its tiers, on a single server machine, or you can place each tier on a separate machine if the application permits this. Chapters 20 and 22 explain how to integrate functionality from other web sites using XML web services. XML web services permit easy integration of functionality across multiple servers without the hassle of customized code.

An important constraint in the three-tier architecture model is that information must flow in sequential order among tiers. The presentation tier is only allowed to access the business tier, and it can never directly access the data tier. The business tier is the brain in the middle that communicates with the other tiers and processes and coordinates all the information flow. If the presentation tier directly accessed the data tier, the rules of three-tier architecture programming would be broken.

These rules may look like limitations at first, but when utilizing an architecture, you need to be consistent and obey its rules to reap the benefits. Sticking to the three-tier architecture ensures that your site remains easily updated or changed and adds a level of control over who or what can access your data. This may seem to be unnecessary overhead for you right now; however, there is a substantial future benefit of adhering to this system whenever you need to change your site's functioning or logic.

Figure 2-1 is a simple representation of how data is passed in an application that implements the three-tier architecture.

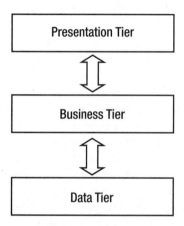

Figure 2-1. *Simple representation of the three-tier architecture*

A Simple Scenario

It's easier to understand how data is passed and transformed between tiers if you take a closer look at a simple example. To make the example even more relevant to the project, let's analyze a situation that will actually happen in BalloonShop. This scenario is typical for three-tier applications.

Like most e-commerce sites, BalloonShop will have a shopping cart, which we'll discuss later in the book. For now, it's enough to know that the visitor will add products to the shopping cart by clicking an Add to Cart button. Figure 2-2 shows how the information flows through the application when that button is clicked.

At step 1, the user clicks the Add to Cart button for a specific product. At step 2, the presentation tier (which contains the button) forwards the request to the business tier: "Hey, I want this product added to my shopping cart!" At step 3, the business tier receives the request, understands that the user wants a specific product added to the shopping cart, and handles the request by telling the data tier to update the visitor's shopping cart by adding the selected product. The data tier needs to be called because it stores and manages the entire web site's data, including users' shopping cart information.

At step 4, the data tier updates the database and eventually returns a success code to the business tier. At step 5, the business tier handles the return code and any errors that might have occurred in the data tier while updating the database, and then returns the output to the presentation tier.

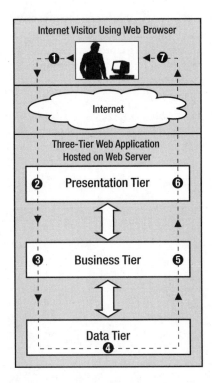

Figure 2-2. *Internet visitor interacting with a three-tier application*

At step 6, the presentation tier generates an updated view of the shopping cart. At step 7, the results of the execution are wrapped up by generating a Hypertext Markup Language (HTML) web page that is returned to the visitor where the updated shopping cart can be seen in the visitor's web browser.

Note that, in this simple example, the business tier doesn't do a lot of processing, and its business logic isn't very complex. However, if new business rules appear for your application, you would change the business tier. If, for example, the business logic specified that a product could be added to the shopping cart only if its quantity in stock was greater than zero, an additional data tier call would have been made to determine the quantity. The data tier would be requested to update the shopping cart only if products are in stock. In any case, the presentation tier is informed about the status and provides human-readable feedback to the visitor.

What's in a Number?

It's interesting to note how each tier interprets the same piece of information differently. For the data tier, the numbers and information it stores have no significance because this tier is an engine that saves, manages, and retrieves numbers, strings, or other data types—not product quantities or product names. In the context of the previous example, a product quantity of 0 represents a simple, plain number without any meaning to the data tier (it is simply 0, a 32-bit integer).

The data gains significance when the business tier reads it. When the business tier asks the data tier for a product quantity and gets a "0" result, this is interpreted by the business tier as

"Hey, no products in stock!" This data is finally wrapped in a nice visual form by the presentation tier—for example, a label reading "Sorry, at the moment the product cannot be ordered."

Even if it's unlikely that you want to forbid a customer from adding a product to the shopping cart if the product isn't in stock, the example (described in Figure 2-3) is good enough to present in yet another way how each of the three tiers has a different purpose.

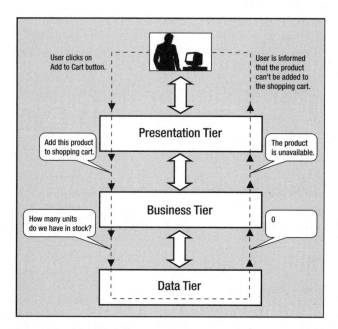

Figure 2-3. *Internet visitor interacting with a three-tier application*

The Right Logic for the Right Tier

Because each layer contains its own logic, sometimes it can be tricky to decide where exactly to draw the line between the tiers. In the previous scenario, instead of reading the product's quantity in the business tier and deciding whether the product is available based on that number (resulting in two data tier, and implicitly database, calls), you could have a single data tier method named AddProductIfAvailable that adds the product to the shopping cart only if it's available in stock.

In this scenario, some logic is transferred from the business tier to the data tier. In many other circumstances, you might have the option to place the same logic in one tier or another, or maybe in both. In most cases, there is no single best way to implement the three-tier architecture, and you'll need to make a compromise or a choice based on personal preference or external constraints.

Furthermore, there are occasions in which even though you know the *right* way (in respect to the architecture) to implement something, you might choose to break the rules to get a performance gain. As a general rule, if performance can be improved this way, it is OK to break the strict limits between tiers *just a little bit* (for example, add some of the business rules to the data tier or vice versa), *if* these rules are not likely to change in time. Otherwise, keeping all the business rules in the middle tier is preferable, because it generates a cleaner application that is easier to maintain.

Finally, don't be tempted to access the data tier directly from the presentation tier. This is a common mistake that is the shortest path to a complicated, hard-to-maintain, and inflexible system. In many data access tutorials or introductory materials, you'll be shown how to perform basic database operations using a simple user interface application. In these kinds of programs, all the logic is probably written in a short, single file, instead of separate tiers. Although the materials might be very good, keep in mind that most of these texts are meant to teach you how to do different individual tasks (for example, access a database), and not how to correctly create a flexible and scalable application.

A Three-Tier Architecture for BalloonShop

Implementing a three-tier architecture for the BalloonShop web site will help you achieve the goals listed at the beginning of the chapter. The coding discipline imposed by a system that might seem rigid at first sight allows for excellent levels of flexibility and extensibility in the long run.

Splitting major parts of the application into separate, smaller components also encourages reusability. More than once when adding new features to the site you'll see that you can reuse some of the already existing bits. Adding a new feature without needing to change much of what already exists is, in itself, a good example of reusability. Also, smaller pieces of code placed in their correct places are easier to document and analyze later.

Another advantage of the three-tier architecture is that, if properly implemented, the overall system is resistant to changes. When bits in one of the tiers change, the other tiers usually remain unaffected, sometimes even in extreme cases. For example, if for some reason the backend database system is changed (say, the manager decides to use Oracle instead of SQL Server), you only need to update the data tier. The existing business tier should work the same with the new database.

Why Not Use More Tiers?

The three-tier architecture we've been talking about so far is a particular (and the most popular) version of the *n*-Tier architecture, which is a commonly used buzzword these days. *n*-Tier architecture refers to splitting the solution into a number (*n*) of logical tiers. In complex projects, sometimes it makes sense to split the business layer into more than one layer, thus resulting in an architecture with more than three layers. However, for this web site, it makes most sense to stick with the three-layer design, which offers most of the benefits while not requiring too many hours of design or a complex hierarchy of framework code to support the architecture.

Maybe with a more involved and complex architecture, you would achieve even higher levels of flexibility and scalability for the application, but you would need much more time for design before starting to implement anything. As with any programming project, you must find a fair balance between the time required to design the architecture and the time spent to implement it. The three-tier architecture is best suited to projects with average complexity, like the BalloonShop web site.

You also might be asking the opposite question, "Why not use fewer tiers?" A two-tier architecture, also called client-server architecture, can be appropriate for less complex projects. In short, a two-tier architecture requires less time for planning and allows quicker development in the beginning, although it generates an application that's harder to maintain and extend in the long run. Because we're expecting to extend the application in the future, the client-server architecture isn't appropriate for this application, so it won't be discussed further in this book.

Now that you know the general architecture, let's see what technologies and tools you'll use to implement it. After a brief discussion of the technologies, you'll create the foundation of the presentation and data tiers by creating the first page of the site and the backend database. You'll start implementing some real functionality in each of the three tiers in Chapter 3 when you start creating the web site's product catalog.

Choosing Technologies and Tools

No matter which architecture is chosen, a major question that arises in every development project is which technologies, programming languages, and tools are going to be used, bearing in mind that external requirements can seriously limit your options.

In this book, we're creating a web site using Microsoft technologies. Keep in mind, however, that when it comes to technology, problems often have more than one solution, and rarely is there only a single best way to solve the problem. Although we really like the technologies presented in this book, it doesn't necessarily mean they're the best choice for any kind of project, in any circumstances. Additionally, in many situations, you must use specific technologies because of client requirements or other external constraints. The **system requirements** and **software requirements** stages in the software development process will determine which technologies you must use for creating the application.

This book is about programming e-commerce web sites with **ASP.NET 3.5** (Active Server Pages .NET 3.5) and **C#**. The tools you'll use are **Visual Web Developer 2008 Express Edition** and **SQL Server 2008 Express Edition**, which are freely available from Microsoft's web site, and are free for both personal and commercial use. Although the book assumes a little previous experience with each of these, we'll take a quick look at them and see how they fit into the project and into the three-tier architecture.

■**Note**   This book builds on *Beginning ASP.NET 2.0 E-Commerce in C# 2005: From Novice to Professional* (Apress, 2004), which used ASP.NET 2.0, Visual Studio .NET 2005, and SQL Server 2005. If you're an open source fan, you might also want to check out *Beginning PHP and MySQL E-Commerce, Second Edition: From Novice to Professional* (Apress, 2008).

Using ASP.NET

ASP.NET 3.5 is Microsoft's technology set for building dynamic, interactive web content. Because it is a complex technology, in this book we'll only cover a subset of its vast feature set. Therefore, you will need additional ASP.NET 3.5 books to complete your knowledge on theory issues that didn't make it into this book. Other ASP.NET 3.5 resources that we recommend you check out include:

- Build Your Own ASP.NET 3.5 Web Site Using C# & VB *(Sitepoint, 2008)*: If you're new to the world of ASP.NET or web development, this should be your first book to read. It assumes only minimal previous programming knowledge.

- Beginning ASP.NET 3.5 in C# 2008: From Novice to Professional, Second Edition *(Apress, 2007)*. This is the book that prepares the foundational principles assumed by the book you're currently reading. It assumes moderate web development skills.

- Pro ASP.NET 3.5 in C# 2008: Includes Silverlight 2, Third Edition *(Apress, 2008)*: This is a comprehensive reference that touches on all the significant theory of ASP.NET 3.5 and the .NET 3.5 Framework. I highly recommend keeping this book close for whenever you need a quick answer to any question you may have while developing ASP.NET projects.

Of course, ASP.NET is not the only server-side technology around for creating professional e-commerce web sites. Among its most popular competitors are PHP (PHP Hypertext Preprocessor), JSP (JavaServer Pages), ColdFusion, and even the outdated ASP 3.0 and CGI (Common Gateway Interface). Among these technologies are many differences, but also some fundamental similarities. For example, pages written with any of these technologies are composed of basic HTML, which draws the static part of the page (the template), and code that generates the dynamic part.

Web Clients and Web Servers

You probably already know the general principles about how dynamic web pages work. However, as a short recap, Figure 2-4 shows what happens to an ASP.NET web page from the moment the client browser (no matter if it's Internet Explorer, Mozilla Firefox, or any other web browser) requests it to the moment the browser actually receives it.

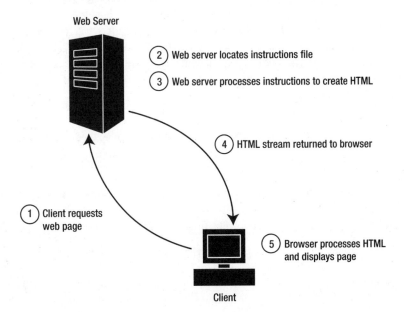

Figure 2-4. *Web server processing client requests*

After the request, the page is first processed at the server before being returned to the client (this is the reason ASP.NET and the other mentioned technologies are called server-side technologies). When an ASP.NET page is requested, its underlying code is first executed on the server. After the final page is composed, the resulting HTML is returned to the visitor's browser.

The returned HTML can optionally contain client-side script code, which is directly interpreted by the browser. The most popular client-side scripting technologies are JavaScript and VBScript. JavaScript is usually the better choice because it has wider acceptance, whereas only Internet Explorer recognizes VBScript. Other important client-side technologies are Adobe Flash, Java applets, and Microsoft's Silverlight, but these are somewhat different because the web browser does not directly parse them—Flash requires a specialized plug-in and Java applets require a JVM (Java Virtual Machine). Internet Explorer also supports ActiveX controls and .NET assemblies.

The Code Behind the Page

From its first version, ASP.NET encouraged (and helped) developers to keep the code of a web page physically separated from the HTML layout of that page. Keeping the code that gives life to a web page in a separate file from the HTML layout of the page was an important improvement over other server-side web-development technologies whose mix of code and HTML in the same file often led to long and complicated source files that were hard to document, change, and maintain. Also, a file containing both code and HTML is the subject of both programmers' and designers' work, which makes team collaboration unnecessarily complicated and increases the chances of the designer creating bugs in the code logic while working on cosmetic changes.

ASP.NET 1.0 introduced a **code-behind** model, used to separate the HTML layout of a web page from the code that gives life to that page. Although it was possible to write the code and HTML in the same file, Visual Studio .NET 2002 and Visual Studio .NET 2003 always automatically generated two separate files for a Web Form: the HTML layout resided in the .ASPX file and the code resided in the code-behind file. Because ASP.NET allowed the developer to write the code in the programming language of his or her choice (such as C# or VB .NET), the code-behind file's extension depended on the language it was written in (such as .aspx.cs or .aspx.vb).

ASP.NET 2.0 introduced a refined code-behind model, which is still present in ASP.NET 3.5. Although the new model is more powerful, the general principles (to help separate the page's looks from its brain) are still the same.

Before moving on, let's summarize the most important general features of ASP.NET:

- The server-side code can be written in the .NET language of your choice. By default, you can choose from C#, VB .NET, and J#, but the whole infrastructure is designed to support additional languages. These languages are powerful and fully object oriented.

- The server-side code of ASP.NET pages is fully compiled and executed—as opposed to being interpreted line by line—which results in optimal performance and offers the possibility to detect a number of errors at compile-time instead of runtime.

- The concept of code-behind files helps separate the visual part of the page from the (server-side) logic behind it. This is an advantage over other technologies, in which both the HTML and the server-side code reside in the same file (often resulting in what we call "spaghetti code").

- Visual Web Developer 2008 is an excellent and complete visual editor that represents a good weapon in the ASP.NET programmer's arsenal (although you don't need it to create ASP.NET web applications). Visual Web Developer 2008 Express Edition is free, and you can use it to develop the examples in this book.

ASP.NET Web Forms, Web User Controls, and Master Pages

ASP.NET web sites are developed around ASP.NET **Web Forms**. ASP.NET Web Forms have the `.aspx` extension and are the standard way to provide web functionality to clients. Usually, the ASPX file has an associated code-behind file, which is also considered part of the Web Form. A request to an ASPX resource, such as `http://www.cristiandarie.ro/BalloonShop/default.aspx`, results in the `default.aspx` file being executed on the server (together with its code-behind file) and the results being composed as an HTML page that is sent back to the client.

Web User Controls and **Master Pages** are similar to Web Forms in that they are also composed of HTML and code (they also support the code-behind model), but they can't be directly accessed by clients. Instead, they are used to compose the content of the Web Forms.

Web User Controls are files with the `.ascx` extension that can be included in Web Forms, with the parent Web Form becoming the container of the control. Web User Controls allow you to easily reuse pieces of functionality in a number of Web Forms.

Master Pages were a new feature in ASP.NET 2.0. A Master Page is a template that can be applied to a number of Web Forms in a site to ensure a consistent visual appearance and functionality throughout the various pages of the site. Updating the Master Page has an immediate effect on every Web Form built on top of that Master Page.

Web User Controls, Web Server Controls, and HTML Server Controls

It's worth taking a second look at Web User Controls from another perspective. Web User Controls are a particular type of server-side control. Server-side controls generically refer to three kinds of controls: Web User Controls, Web Server Controls, and HTML Server Controls. All these kinds of controls can be used to reuse pieces of functionality inside Web Forms.

As stated in the previous section, Web User Controls are files with the `.ascx` extension that have a structure similar to the structure of Web Forms, but they can't be requested directly by a client web browser; instead, they are meant to be included in Web Forms or other Web User Controls.

Web Server Controls are compiled .NET classes that, when executed, generate HTML output (eventually including client-side script). You can use them in Web Forms or in Web User Controls. The .NET Framework ships with a large number of Web Server Controls, including simple controls such as `Label`, `TextBox`, or `Button`, and more complex controls, such as validation controls, data controls, the famous `GridView` control, and so on. Among other features, you can programmatically declare and access their properties, make these properties accessible through the Visual Web Developer designer, and add the controls to the toolbox, just as in Windows Forms applications or old VB6 programs.

HTML Server Controls allow you to programmatically access HTML elements of the page from server-side code. You transform an HTML control to an HTML Server Control by adding the `runat="server"` attribute to it and assigning an ID to it, which makes it accessible just like a regular variable or object in your C# code. Most HTML Server Controls are doubled by Web Server Controls (such as labels, buttons, and so on). For consistency, we'll stick with Web Server Controls most of the time, but you'll need to use HTML Server Controls in some cases.

For the BalloonShop project, you'll use all kinds of controls, and you'll create a number of Web User Controls.

Because you can develop Web User Controls independently of the main web site and then just plug them in when they're ready, having a site structure based on Web User Controls provides an excellent level of flexibility and reusability.

ASP.NET and the Three-Tier Architecture

The collection of Web Forms, Web User Controls, and Master Pages form the presentation tier of the application. They are the part that creates the HTML code loaded by the visitor's browser.

The logic of the UI is stored in the code-behind files of the Web Forms, Web User Controls, and Master Pages. Note that although you don't need to use code-behind files with ASP.NET (you're free to mix code and HTML), we'll exclusively use the code-behind model for the presentation-tier logic.

In the context of a three-tier application, the logic in the presentation tier usually refers to the various event handlers, such as `Page_Load` and `someButton_Click`. As you learned earlier, these event handlers should call business tier methods to get their jobs done (and never call the data tier directly).

Using C# and VB .NET

C# and VB .NET are languages that can be used to code the Web Forms' code-behind files. In this book, we're using C#. ASP.NET even allows you to write the code for various elements inside a project in different languages, but we won't use this feature in this book. Separate projects written in different .NET languages can freely interoperate, as long as you follow some basic rules.

■**Note** Just because you *can* use multiple languages in a single language, doesn't mean you *should* overuse that feature, if you have a choice. Being consistent is more important than playing with diversity if you care for long-term ease of maintenance and prefer to avoid unnecessary headaches (which is something that most programmers do).

In this book, apart from using C# for the code-behind files, you'll use the same language to code the middle-tier classes. You'll create the first classes in Chapter 3 when building the product catalog.

Using Visual Web Developer 2008 Express Edition

Visual Studio 2008 is by far the most powerful tool you can find to develop .NET applications. It is a complete programming environment capable of working with many types of projects and files, including Windows and web projects, setup and deployment projects, and many others. Visual Studio also can be used as an interface to the database to create tables and stored procedures, visually design database structures, and so on.

Visual Web Developer 2008 Express Edition is a free version of Visual Studio 2008, focused on developing web applications with ASP.NET 3.5. It includes features such as IntelliSense

(Microsoft's code auto-completion technology), code formatting, database integration with the ability to design databases visually, debugging, and much more.

For developing BalloonShop, we'll use Visual Web Developer 2008 Express Edition, which contains all the features you'll need, but you can use Visual Studio if you have it. In the latter case, you may find that a few menu options are named differently than what is presented in the book, but you'll find all the necessary features in the expected places.

The typical web server used to run ASP.NET applications is IIS (Internet Information Services), but Visual Web Developer 2008 and Visual Studio 2008 include an integrated web server so that you can run your ASP.NET applications even if you don't have IIS installed on your development machine. This is good news for users of the Home editions of Windows XP and Windows Vista, who can't install IIS on their machines because it isn't supported by the operating system.

Although we'll use Visual Web Developer 2008 Express Edition for writing the BalloonShop project, it's important to know that you don't have to. ASP.NET and the C# and VB .NET compilers are available as free downloads at http://www.microsoft.com as part of the .NET Framework .SDK (software development kit), and a simple editor such as Notepad is enough to create any kind of web page.

Using SQL Server 2008

Along with Visual Studio 2008, Microsoft also released a new version of its player in the Relational Database Management Systems (RDBMS) field—SQL Server 2008. This complex software program's purpose is to store, manage, and retrieve data as quickly and reliably as possible. You'll use SQL Server to store all the information regarding your web site, which will be dynamically placed on the web page by the application logic. Simply said, all data regarding the products, departments, users, shopping carts, and so on will be stored and managed by SQL Server.

The good news is that a lightweight version of SQL Server 2008, named SQL Server 2008 Express Edition, is freely available. Unlike the commercial versions, SQL Server 2008 Express Edition doesn't ship by default with any visual-management utilities. However, a very nice tool called SQL Server Management Studio Express is also freely available.

The first steps in interacting with SQL Server will come in Chapter 3 when you will create the BalloonShop database.

SQL Server and the Three-Tier Architecture

It should be clear by now that SQL Server is somehow related to the data tier. However, if you haven't worked with databases until now, it might be less than obvious that SQL Server is more than a simple store of data. Apart from the actual data stored inside, SQL Server is also capable of storing logic in the form of stored procedures, maintaining table relationships, ensuring that various data integrity rules are obeyed, and so on.

You can communicate with SQL Server through a language called T-SQL (Transact-SQL), which is the SQL dialect recognized by SQL Server. SQL, or Structured Query Language, is the language used to interact with the database. SQL is used to transmit to the database instructions such as "Send me the last ten orders" or "Delete product #123."

Although it's possible to compose T-SQL statements in your C# code and then submit them for execution, this is generally considered a *bad practice* because it usually leads to hard-to-maintain code, and if not done correctly it can incur security and performance penalties. In our solution, we'll store all data tier logic using **stored procedures**.

The stored procedures are stored internally in the database and can be called from external programs. In your architecture, the stored procedures will be called from the business tier. The stored procedures in turn manipulate or access the data store, get the results, and return them to the business tier (or perform the necessary operations).

Figure 2-5 shows the technologies associated with every tier in the three-tier architecture. SQL Server contains the data tier of the application (stored procedures that contain the logic to access and manipulate data) and also the actual data store.

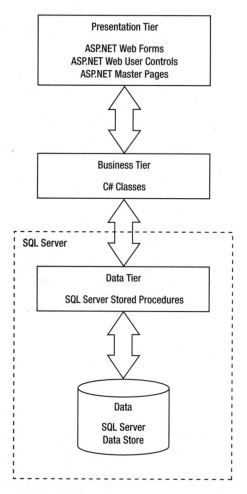

Figure 2-5. *Using Microsoft technologies and the three-tier architecture*

Following Coding Standards

Although coding and naming standards might not seem that important at first, they definitely shouldn't be overlooked. Not following a set of rules for your code almost always results in code that's hard to read, understand, and maintain. On the other hand, when you follow a consistent way of coding, you can say your code is already half documented, which is an important contribution toward the project's maintainability, especially when many people are working on the same project at the same time.

■**Tip** Some companies have their own policies regarding coding and naming standards, whereas in other cases you'll have the flexibility to use your own preferences. In either case, the golden rule to follow is *be consistent in the way you code*.

Naming conventions refer to many elements within a project, simply because almost all of a project's elements have names: the project itself, namespaces, Web Forms, Web User Controls, instances of Web User Controls and other interface elements, classes, variables, methods, method parameters, database tables, database columns, stored procedures, and so on. Without some discipline when naming all those elements, after a week of coding, you won't understand a line of what you've written. This book tries to stick to Microsoft's recommendations regarding naming conventions. We'll talk more about naming conventions while building the site.

Summary

Hey, we covered a lot of ground in this chapter, didn't we? We talked about the three-tier architecture and how it helps you create great flexible and scalable applications. We also saw how each of the technologies used in this book fits into the three-tier architecture.

If you feel overwhelmed, please don't worry. In the next chapter, we will begin to create the first part of our site. We will explain each step as we go, so you will have a clear understanding of each element of the application.

CHAPTER 3

∎∎∎

Starting the BalloonShop Project

Now that the theoretical foundations of the project have been laid, it's time to start putting them to work. In this chapter, we'll implement the first page for the BalloonShop web site. In this chapter, you will

- Install and configure the necessary software on your development machine

- Create the basic structure of the web site

- Set up the database that will be used to store catalog data, customer orders, and so on

Subsequent chapters will build on this foundation to create the product catalog with department and category navigation, product lists, product details pages, and much more.

Preparing the Development Environment

It's time to prepare your machine for developing BalloonShop. The installation procedure shouldn't pose any difficulties, but we'll list all the steps for completeness. We'll walk you through installing:

- Visual Web Developer 2008 Express Edition

- SQL Server 2008 Express Edition

- SQL Server Management Studio Express

SQL Server Management Studio Express is a free SQL Server management interface. Although you can also interact with your databases using Visual Web Developer, using SQL Server Management Studio Express is preferable because its interface has been built solely for the purpose of working with SQL Server databases.

After installing the necessary software, you'll configure the web server—IIS (Internet Information Services)—create the BalloonShop project, set up the BalloonShop database, and create a simple test page in this application to ensure that your machine has been installed and configured properly.

Installing Visual Web Developer 2008 Express Edition

Install Visual Web Developer 2008 Express Edition by following these simple steps:

1. Browse to http://www.microsoft.com/express/vwd/.

2. Click the Download Now! link.

3. Under the Web Install section, click the Download link for Visual Web Developer 2008 Express Edition.

4. Execute the downloaded file, vwdsetup.exe.

5. After you accept the terms and conditions, you're offered a number of additional optional products. I recommend that you check MSDN Express Library, which contains the product and framework documentation. Preferably, you should not check SQL Server 2008 Express Edition: we prefer to install it separately afterward, because the default installation that you can get here doesn't include the Full-Text Search services that you'll need in Chapter 8.

6. On the next setup screen you'll be informed of the products and components you're about to install. Click Next, and wait for the installer to download and install the software (the setup window looks like Figure 3-1).

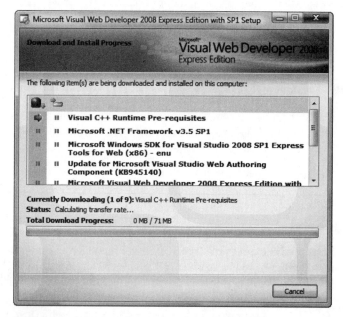

Figure 3-1. *Installing Visual Web Developer 2008 Express Edition*

7. Start Visual Web Developer to ensure it installed correctly. Its welcome screen should look similar to Figure 3-2.

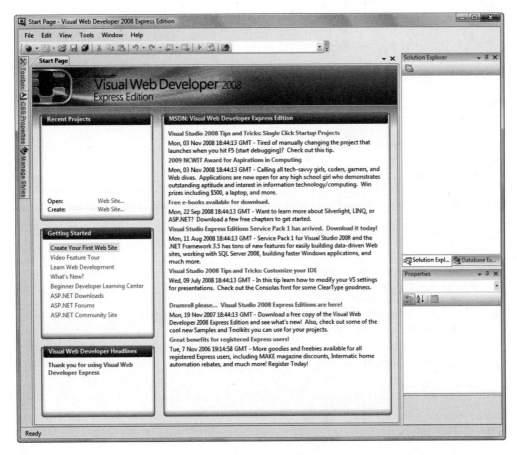

Figure 3-2. *The Start Page of Visual Web Developer 2008 Express Edition*

Installing SQL Server 2008 Express Edition

Installing SQL Server 2008 Express Edition separately allows us to install its version that contains the Full-Text Search feature, which we'll need when implementing the catalog search feature, in Chapter 8. If you already have SQL Server 2008 Express Edition installed, then you can skip this section—in Chapter 8 we'll teach you how to add the Full-Text Search feature to your existing SQL Server 2008 instance.

Install SQL Server 2008 Express Edition by following these simple steps:

1. Browse to `http://www.microsoft.com/express/vwd/`.

2. Click the Download Now! link.

3. Under the Web Install section, click the Download link for SQL Server 2008 Express Edition.

4. Here you'll find a link to the real download page, where you can choose between the various product editions. Choose SQL Server 2008 Express with Advanced Services, which (among other features) includes the Full-Text Search feature mentioned earlier. The file you'll download is SQLEXPRADV_x86_ENU.exe or SQLEXPRADV_x64_ENU.exe, depending on your hardware platform (if in doubt, choose the x86 version).

5. Execute the downloaded file, and select Planning ➤ System Configuration Checker to make sure you have all the necessary software components installed on your machine.

6. Select Installation ➤ New SQL Server stand-alone installation or add features to an existing installation.

7. Go through the standard setup steps to install SQL Server Express with Advanced Services. When asked for the product components you want to install, choose

   - **Full-Text Search**: You'll need this feature when implementing the product search feature in Chapter 8.

   - **Management Tools—Basic**: This option includes SQL Server Management Studio Express Edition, the tool you'll use to connect to your SQL Server instance.

8. Leave the default options in the following setup screens. If asked for an account name for running the database engine, it's safe to choose the system account on your development machine. When asked to specify a SQL Server administrator, it's safe to click Add Current User to add your current Windows account as the database administrator.

■**Note** SQL Server Management Studio is also available as a stand-alone package. The simplest way to get to Microsoft's download page is to search the Internet for "Download SQL Server Management Studio Express."

Installing IIS

IIS is the web server included by Microsoft in its server-capable Windows versions. These are Windows Vista Business, Windows Vista Home Premium, Windows XP Professional, Windows XP Media Center Edition, Windows 2000 Professional, Server, Advanced Server, and Windows Server 2003—but it's not installed automatically in all versions. IIS isn't available (and can't be installed) with Windows XP Home Edition or Windows Vista Home Basic.

To follow the examples in the book, you can use either IIS or the web server included in Visual Web Developer 2008—**Cassini**. Using Cassini, you can run the ASP.NET Web Application from any physical folder on your disk. For example, when creating the Web Site project, you can specify as destination a folder such as C:\BalloonShop.

Whenever possible, we suggest that you use IIS, because this resembles more accurately the deployment environment in which the ASP.NET application will ultimately run on.

To install IIS under Windows Vista, follow these steps:

1. In the Control Panel, select Programs ➤ Programs and Features.

2. Choose Turn Windows features on or off.

3. In the list of components, check Internet Information Services. Then select the following options, which are necessary for developing web applications with Visual Web Developer with IIS:

- World Wide Web Services ➤ Application Development Features ➤ ASP.NET (this automatically selects .NET Extensibility, ISAPI Extensions, and ISAPI Filters)

- World Wide Web Services ➤ Security ➤ Windows Authentication

- Web Management Tools ➤ IIS 6 Management Compatibility ➤ IIS Metabase and IIS 6 configuration compatibility

4. Click OK to finish the process.

To install IIS under Windows XP, follow these steps:

1. In the Control Panel, select Add or Remove Programs.

2. Choose Add/Remove Windows Components.

3. In the list of components, select Internet Information Services, and then click the Details button and make sure the IIS Frontpage Extensions node is checked.

4. Click Next or OK. Windows may prompt you to insert the Windows CD or DVD.

5. The final step involves configuring ASP.NET with IIS. Start a command-line console (go to Start ➤ Run, and type **cmd** at the prompt), and type the following commands:

```
cd C:\Windows\Microsoft.NET\Framework\v2.0.50727
aspnet_regiis.exe -i
```

Preparing the BalloonShop Web Site

To keep your hard drive tidy, we'll use a single web application for all the exercises in this book, which will be located in the C:\BalloonShop\ folder. (Of course, you can use a different folder or location if you prefer.) We'll cover the web application setup steps for Windows Vista.

IIS 7 in Windows Vista supports multiple root web sites on the same web server, so we'll create a web site called http://www.example.com/, which will point to the C:\BalloonShop\ folder that you create for your application. This way, your new web site will not interfere with the existing http://localhost/.

IIS 5 and 6 don't support multiple root web sites, so if you have Windows XP, just stick to http://localhost/ and skip the following exercise—don't worry, the whole application functionality will remain the same, except the URL you'll use to access BalloonShop during development.

Follow these steps to prepare your BalloonShop web site in Windows Vista:

1. First, you need to add the www.example.com host to the Windows hosts file. This will tell Windows that all domain name resolution requests for www.example.com should be handled by the local machine instead of your configured DNS. Open the hosts file, which is located by default in C:\Windows\System32\drivers\etc\hosts, and add this line to it:

```
127.0.0.1        localhost
::1              localhost
127.0.0.1        www.example.com
```

Note If you have User Account Control in Vista enabled, your editor must run with administrative privileges. The easiest way to edit the hosts file is to right-click Notepad, select Run as administrator, and open `C:\Windows\System32\drivers\etc\hosts` from there.

2. Next, create a folder named `BalloonShop` in `C:\`.

3. Open the IIS Manager tool from the Administrative Tools section of the Control Panel. Browse to the Default Web Site by navigating in the Connections tab, or by clicking the View Sites link in the Actions tab—see Figure 3-3.

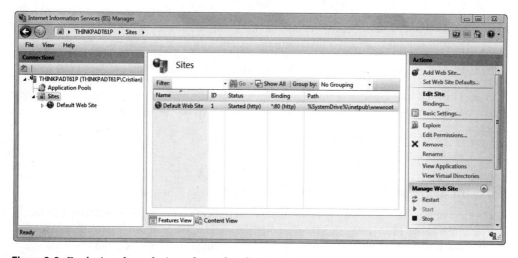

Figure 3-3. *Exploring the web sites of your local IIS server*

4. Right-click the Sites node and select Add Web Site . . . from the context menu, or click Add Web Site . . . in the Actions tab.

5. Type **BalloonShop** for the site name, **www.example.com** for the host name, and **C:\BalloonShop** for its physical path. In the end, the Add Web Site dialog should look like Figure 3-4. Then click OK.

6. The `http://www.example.com` web site will show up as a child node under the Sites node.

Congratulations. Your work is now done here. Feel free to close IIS Manager.

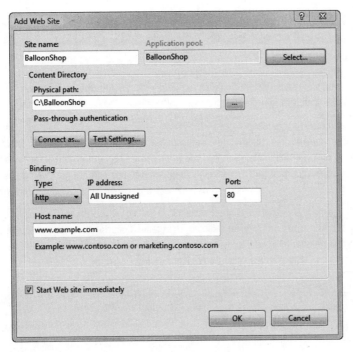

Figure 3-4. *Creating the BalloonShop site*

Creating the BalloonShop Web Application

We'll now go back to our favorite toy, which is, of course, Visual Web Developer. It allows you to create all kinds of development projects, including Web Site projects. The other favorite toy is SQL Server, which will hold your web site's data. We'll deal with it a bit later in this chapter.

The first step toward building the BalloonShop site is to open Visual Web Developer and create a new ASP.NET Web Site project. You'll create the BalloonShop project step-by-step in the exercise that follows. To ensure that you always have the code we expect you to have and to eliminate any possible frustrations or misunderstandings, we'll always include the steps you must follow to build your project in separate exercise sections. We know it's very annoying when a book tells you something, but the computer's monitor shows you something else, so we'll try to avoid this kind of problems.

■**Note** You can always contact the Apress customer support team, or even us, Cristian and Karli, if you run into trouble with this book's code.

Exercise: Creating the BalloonShop Project

Here we'll create the BalloonShop web application at `http://www.example.com/`.

1. Start Visual Web Developer as Administrator, and choose **File ➤ New Web Site**. In the dialog box that opens, select **ASP.NET Web Site** from the Templates panel.

2. In the Location combo box, you can choose from File System, HTTP, and FTP, which determine where your project is loaded from and how it is executed. If you choose to install the project on the file system, you need to choose a physical location on your disk, such as `C:\BalloonShop\`. In this case, the web application is executed using Visual Web Developer's integrated web server (Cassini). If you choose an HTTP location (such as `http://www.example.com`), the web application will be executed through IIS.

3. For the purpose of this exercise, we're creating the project in the `http://www.example.com` location. Leave the default **ASP.NET Web Site** template selected, change the **Location** to **HTTP**, and set the web location to `http://www.example.com`. In this book we'll use Visual C# for the language, so be sure the language option is correctly selected, as shown in Figure 3-5.

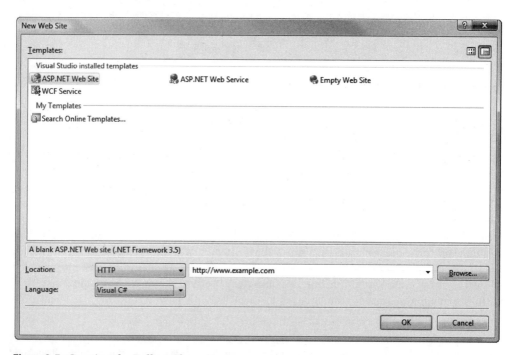

Figure 3-5. *Creating the BalloonShop site*

4. After you click **OK**, Visual Web Developer will create a new project at the selected location. The initial window looks like that shown in Figure 3-6.

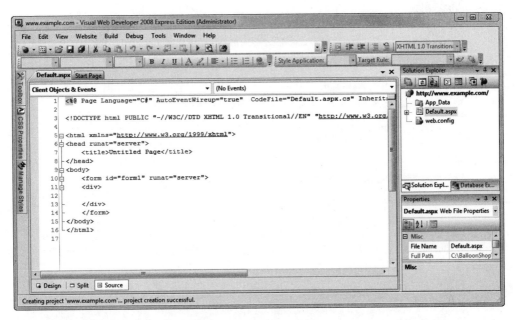

Figure 3-6. *The BalloonShop project in Visual Web Developer*

5. Modify the default content of `Default.aspx` like this:

```
<%@ Page Language="C#" AutoEventWireup="true" CodeFile="Default.aspx.cs" ➡
Inherits="_Default" %>

<!DOCTYPE html PUBLIC "-//W3C//DTD XHTML 1.0 Transitional//EN" ➡
"http://www.w3.org/TR/xhtml1/DTD/xhtml1-transitional.dtd">

<html xmlns="http://www.w3.org/1999/xhtml">
<head runat="server">
    <title>Untitled Page</title>
</head>
<body>
    <form id="form1" runat="server">
    <div>
        Welcome to Beginning ASP.NET 3.5 E-Commerce in C# 2008: ➡
From Novice to Professional
    </div>
    </form>
</body>
</html>
```

6. To ensure your system is properly configured to run and debug your project, press **F5**. This is the default keyboard shortcut for the **Start Debugging** command, which means it starts your project in debug mode. The first time you start the project with debugging, Visual Web Developer will offer to enable debugging for you by setting the necessary options in the configuration file (`web.config`)—see Figure 3-7.

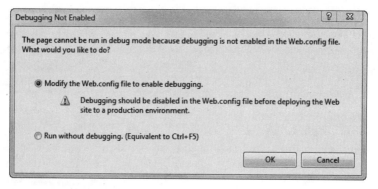

Figure 3-7. *Enabling debugging in* `web.config`

7. After you click **OK**, you will also be asked if you want to enable script debugging in Internet Explorer, if it's not already enabled (see Figure 3-8). This is useful for debugging JavaScript code. Choose **Yes**.

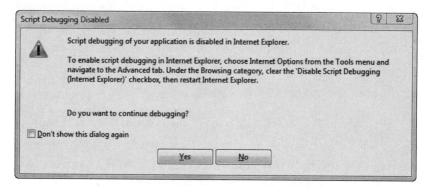

Figure 3-8. *Enabling JavaScript debugging in Internet Explorer*

8. After you click **OK**, the default browser of your system will be launched to load your web application at `http://www.example.com/`, as shown in Figure 3-9.

■**Note** When executing the project, the web site is loaded in your system's default web browser. For the purposes of debugging your code, we recommend configuring Visual Web Developer to use Internet Explorer, even if your system's preferred browser is, for example, Mozilla Firefox. We recommend using Internet Explorer when you need to debug ASP.NET applications because it integrates better with Visual Web Developer's .NET and JavaScript debugging features. (For example, Visual Web Developer knows to automatically stop debugging the project when the Internet Explorer window is closed.) To change the default browser to be used by Visual Web Developer, right-click the root node in **Solution Explorer**, choose **Browse With**, select a browser from the Browsers tab, and click **Set as Default**.

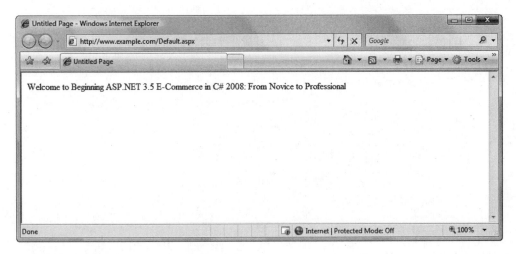

Figure 3-9. *Loading your first BalloonShop page*

How It Works: Your Visual Web Developer Project

Congratulations. If your page loaded successfully, you're ready to move on. If you encountered any errors, verify that you have correctly followed all the steps of the exercises, and that your machine is configured correctly.

At this moment your project contains three files:

- `Default.aspx` is your Web Form.
- `Default.aspx.cs` is the code-behind file of the Web Form.
- `web.config` is the project's configuration file.

We'll have a closer look at these files later.

Creating the BalloonShop SQL Server Database

You'll now create the SQL Server database for your project, although you won't get to effectively use it until the next chapter. This database will store all the information in your site, such as data about products, customers, and so on.

As mentioned earlier, it is possible to use Visual Web Developer to connect to your SQL Server 2008 instance. However, we prefer to use SQL Server Management Studio Express, because it's more powerful and better suited for usual database operations.

Exercise: Creating the BalloonShop Database

1. Start SQL Server Management Studio Express. When executed, it will first ask for your credentials, as shown in Figure 3-10.

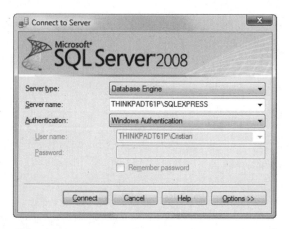

Figure 3-10. *Starting SQL Server Management Studio*

2. By default, when installed, SQL Server 2008 will only accept connections through Windows Authentication, meaning that your Windows user account will be used for logging in. Because you're the user that installed SQL Server 2008, you will already have full privileges to the instance. Click **Connect** to connect to your SQL Server 2008 instance. After connecting to SQL Server, you'll be shown an interface that offers you numerous ways to manage your server and databases—see Figure 3-11.

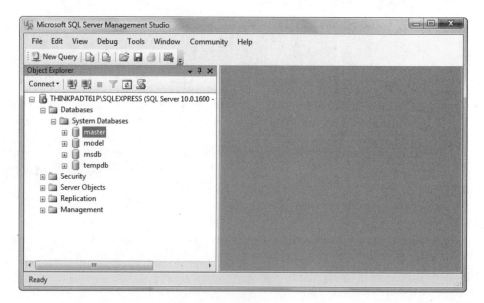

Figure 3-11. *SQL Server Management Studio Express*

3. In most real-world scenarios, you'll connect to the database using a SQL Server user ID and password, rather than Windows Authentication, and we'll use this method in our examples as well. To enable SQL Server authentication, right-click the root node in the Object Explorer window and select **Properties**. In the dialog that appears, select the **Security** page, and select **SQL Server and Windows Authentication mode**, as shown in Figure 3-12.

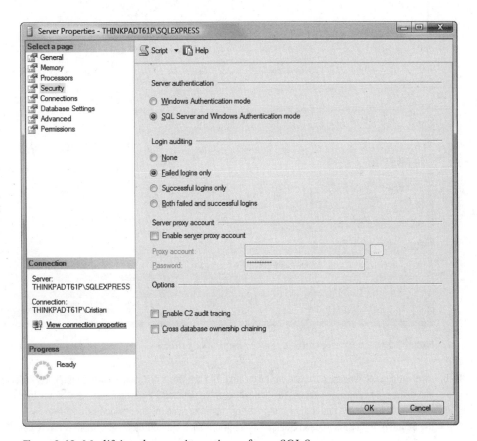

Figure 3-12. *Modifying the security options of your SQL Server*

4. Click **OK** to save the change. You'll be notified that you may need to restart SQL Server in order for the change to take effect. You can do so now by right-clicking the server node (the root node) in the Object Explorer pane and selecting **Restart**. (This action will be allowed if you started SQL Server Management Studio as Administrator.) Alternatively, you can choose Control Panel ➤ Administrative Tools ➤ Services, and restart the SQL Server service from there.

5. Let's create the BalloonShop database now. Right-click the **Databases** node and choose **New Database....** Type **BalloonShop** for the name of the new database, and leave all the options as their defaults, as shown in Figure 3-13.

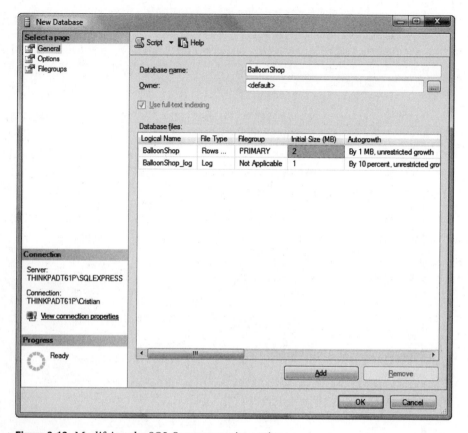

Figure 3-13. *Modifying the SQL Server security options*

6. After clicking **OK**, the new database will be created. The last task for this exercise is to create a SQL Server username, which will have access to our newly created database. We'll then use this account to access the database, which is better than using the administrator account (for obvious safety reasons). Expand the **Security ➤ Logins** node in Object Explorer, right-click the **Logins** node, and select **New Login...**.

7. In the dialog that shows up, select **SQL Server authentication**, and type **balloonshop** for the username and **ecommerce** for the password. Unselect the **Enforce password policy** check box. This will make your way through the book easier, but it's obvious that you shouldn't do the same in a production environment. Finally, change the default database to **BalloonShop**. The required settings are described in Figure 3-14.

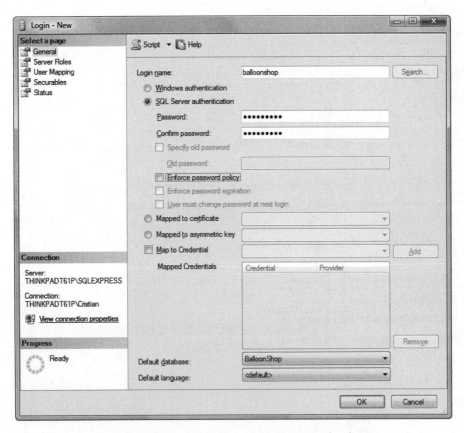

Figure 3-14. *Creating the balloonshop user in the SQL Server database*

8. We want our new user to have full access to the `BalloonShop` database. You can modify the user permission when creating the user or afterward. To make the balloonshop user the owner of the BalloonShop
database in the New Login window (Figure 3-14), select **User Mapping** from the **Select a page** pane,
check the **BalloonShop** table from the list, and check the **db_owner** role, as shown in Figure 3-15.
(After creating the user, you can get to this page by right-clicking the balloonshop user in SQL Server
Management Studio and selecting **Properties**.)

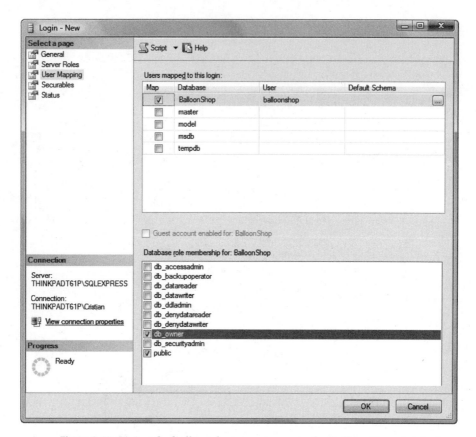

Figure 3-15. *Giving the balloonshop user access to the BalloonShop database*

9. Click **OK**, and wait for your user to be created.

How It Works: The SQL Server Database

You've just created a new SQL Server database. That's it for now. To test that your new user was created success-fully, you can restart SQL Server Management Studio, and log in using SQL Server authentication and the balloonshop login name with the ecommerce password. This time you won't be allowed to create new users or perform other administrative tasks—instead, you'll have full privileges only to the BalloonShop database, which is exactly what you want.

As mentioned earlier, you can also use Visual Web Developer to access your database. We'll do this in the following chapters, but if you're too impatient you can always check the Database Explorer (View ➤ Database Explorer) panel in Visual Web Developer.

Implementing the Site Skeleton

The visual design of the site is usually agreed upon after a discussion with the client, in collaboration with a professional web designer. Alternatively, you can buy a web site template from one of the many companies that offer this kind of service for a reasonable price.

Because this is a programming book, we won't discuss web design issues. Furthermore, we want a simple design that allows you to focus on the technical details of the site. A simplistic design will also make your life easier if you'll need to apply your layout on top of the one we're creating here.

All pages in BalloonShop, including the first page, will have the structure shown in Figure 3-16. In later chapters, you'll add more components to the scheme (such as the login box or shopping cart summary box), but for now, these are the pieces we're looking to implement in the next few chapters.

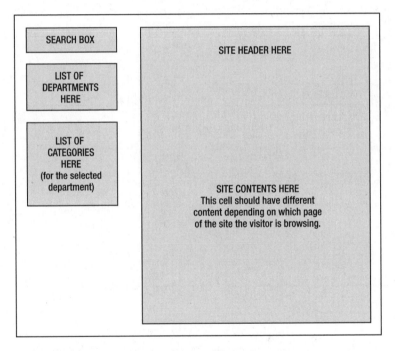

Figure 3-16. *Structure of web pages in BalloonShop*

Although the detailed structure of the product catalog is covered in the next chapter, right now you know that the main list of departments needs to be displayed on every page of the site. You also want the site header to be visible in any page the visitor browses.

You'll implement this structure by creating the following:

- A Master Page containing the general structure of all the web site's pages, as shown in Figure 3-16

- A number of Web Forms that use the Master Page to implement the various locations of the web site, such as the main page, the department pages, the search results page, and so on

- A number of Web User Controls to simplify reusing specific pieces of functionality (such as the departments list box, the categories list box, the search box, the header, and so on)

In Figure 3-17, you can see some of the components you'll build in the next few chapters. The site contents box will be generated by the Master Page that you'll build later in this chapter. In Chapter 4, you'll extend it by adding controls that generate dynamic content, most often by reading it from the SQL Server database.

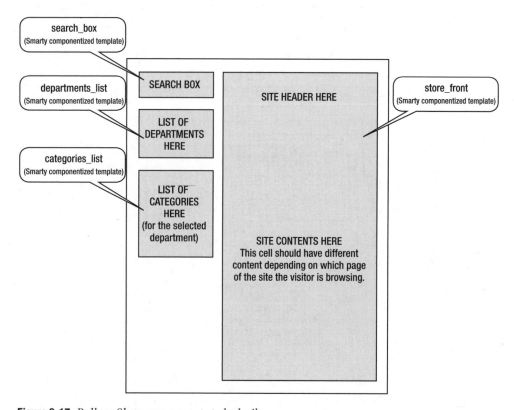

Figure 3-17. *BalloonShop components to be built*

Figure 3-18 shows these elements in action.

Using Web User Controls to implement different pieces of functionality has many long-term advantages. Logically separating different, unrelated pieces of functionality from one another gives you the flexibility to modify them independently and even reuse them in other pages without having to write HTML code and the supporting code-behind file again. It's also extremely easy to extend the functionality or change the place of a feature implemented as a user control in the parent web page; changing the location of a Web User Control is anything but a complicated and lengthy process.

In the remainder of this chapter, we'll write the Master Page of the site, a Web Form for the first page that uses the Master Page, and the Header Web User Control. We'll deal with the other user controls in the following chapters.

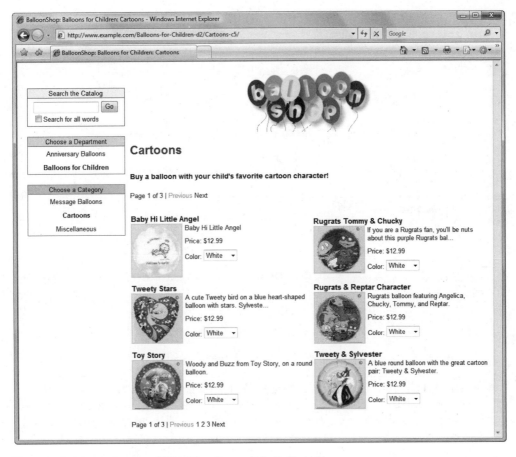

Figure 3-18. *Master Page and Web User Controls in BalloonShop*

Building the First Page

At the moment, you have a single Web Form in the site, `Default.aspx`, which Visual Web Developer automatically created when you created the project. By default, Visual Web Developer didn't generate a Master Page for you, so you'll do this in the following exercise.

Exercise: Creating the Main Web Page

1. Open the `http://www.example.com` project in Visual Web Developer. Then click **Website ➤ Add New Item** (or press **Ctrl+Shift+A**). In the dialog box that opens, choose **Master Page** from the Visual Studio Installed Templates list.

2. Choose **Visual C#** for the language, check the **Place code in a separate file** check box, and change the page name to `BalloonShop.master` (the default name `MasterPage.master` isn't particularly expressive). The Add New Item dialog box should now look like Figure 3-19.

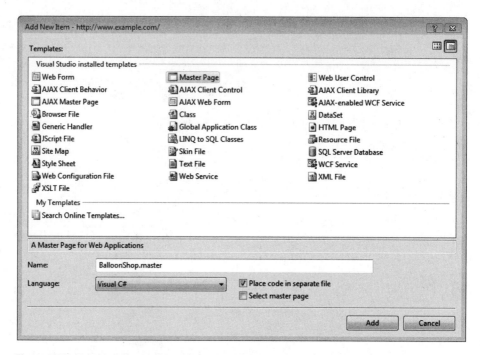

Figure 3-19. *Creating the BalloonShop Master Page*

3. Click **Add** to add the new Master Page to the project. The new Master Page will be opened with some default code in Source View. If you switch to Design View, you'll see the `ContentPlaceHolder` object that it contains. While in Source View, update the code of the page like in the following code snippet. We're setting a page title and we're replacing the `ContentPageFolder` object and its parent `div` element with the code that we need.

```
<%@ Master Language="C#" AutoEventWireup="true" CodeFile=➥
"BalloonShop.master.cs"
Inherits="BalloonShop" %>

<!DOCTYPE html PUBLIC "-//W3C//DTD XHTML 1.0 Transitional//EN" ➥
"http://www.w3.org/TR/xhtml1/DTD/xhtml1-transitional.dtd">
```

```
<html xmlns="http://www.w3.org/1999/xhtml">
<head runat="server">
  <title>BalloonShop: Online Store Demo</title>
  <asp:ContentPlaceHolder id="head" runat="server">
  </asp:ContentPlaceHolder>
</head>
<body>
  <form id="form1" runat="server">
    <div class="Window">
      <div class="Main">
        <div class="Left">
          <div class="Container">
            Place list of departments here
          </div>
        </div>
        <div class="Right">
          <div class="Header">
            <asp:HyperLink ID="HeaderLink"
                    ImageUrl="~/Images/BalloonShopLogo.png" runat="server"
                    NavigateUrl="~/" ToolTip="BalloonShop Logo" />
          </div>
          <div class="Contents">
            Place contents here
            <asp:ContentPlaceHolder ID="ContentPlaceHolder1"
runat="server">
            </asp:ContentPlaceHolder>
          </div>
        </div>
      </div>
    </div>
  </form>
</body>
</html>
```

4. Download the code for this book from the Source Code page of the Apress web site, at http://
   www.apress.com, or from the book's dedicated page at http://www.cristiandarie.ro, unzip it
   somewhere on your disk, and copy only the Images folder to your project's directory (which will be
   C:\BalloonShop\ if you created the project as directed in this chapter). The Images folder contains,
   among other files, a file named BalloonShopLogo.png, which is the logo of your web site. Now, if
   you right-click the root item in Solution Explorer and select **Refresh Folder**, the Images folder will show
   up in the tree, as shown in Figure 3-20.

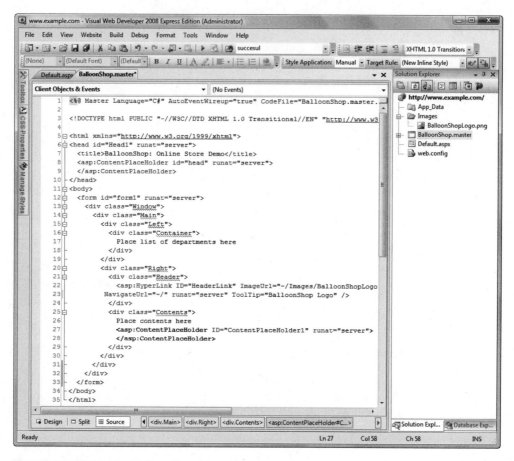

Figure 3-20. *Editing the BalloonShop Master Page*

5. Now switch again to Design View; you should see something like Figure 3-21. (You may need to reload or refresh the project in order for the BalloonShop image to show up.)

6. Master Pages are not meant to be accessed directly by clients, but to be implemented in Web Forms. You'll use the Master Page you've just created to establish the template of the Default.aspx Web Form. Because the Default.aspx page that Visual Web Developer created for you was not meant to be used with Master Pages (it contains code that should be inherited from the Master Page), it's easier to delete and re-create the file. Right-click Default.aspx in Solution Explorer and choose **Delete**. Confirm the deletion.

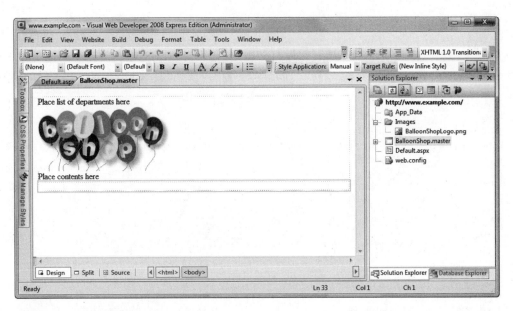

Figure 3-21. *BalloonShop.master in Design View*

7. Right-click the project root in Solution Explorer and select **Add New Item**. Choose the Web Form template, leave its name as Default.aspx, uncheck **Place code in separate file** (you don't need a code-behind file for that form), check **Select master page**, verify that the language is Visual C#, and click **Add**. When asked for a Master Page file, choose BalloonShop.master and click **OK**. Your new page will be created with just a few lines of code, all the rest being inherited from the Master Page:

```
<%@ Page Title="" Language="C#" MasterPageFile="~/BalloonShop.master" %>

<script runat="server">

</script>

<asp:Content ID="Content1" ContentPlaceHolderID="head" Runat="Server">
</asp:Content>
<asp:Content ID="Content2" ContentPlaceHolderID="ContentPlaceHolder1" ➥
Runat="Server">
</asp:Content>
```

When you switch to Design View, Default.aspx will look like Figure 3-22.

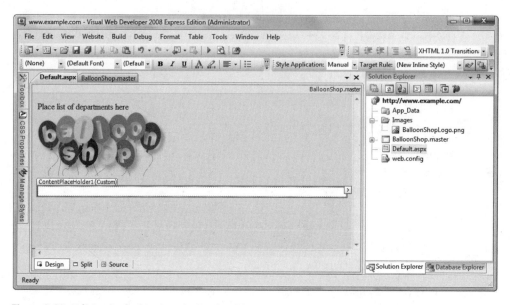

Figure 3-22. *Editing* `Default.aspx` *in Design View*

8. Change the title of the page from "Untitled Page" to "BalloonShop: Online Store Demo" by editing the code in Source View like this:

```
<%@ Page Title="BalloonShop: Online Store Demo" ➥
Language="C#" MasterPageFile="~/BalloonShop.master" %>
```

9. Press **F5** to execute the project. You should get a page similar to the one in Figure 3-23.

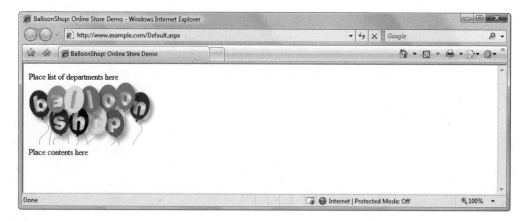

Figure 3-23. *Loading BalloonShop*

How It Works: The Front Page

Right now you have the skeleton of the first BalloonShop page in place. Perhaps it's not apparent right now, but working with Master Pages will save you a lot of headaches later on when you extend the site.

The Master Page establishes the layout of the pages that implement it, and these pages have the freedom to update the contents of the `ContentPlaceHolder` elements. In our case, the header, the list of departments, and the list of categories are standard elements that will appear in every page of the web site (although the list of categories will have blank output in some cases and will appear only when a department is selected—you'll see more about this in the next chapter). For this reason, we included these elements directly in the Master Page, and they are not editable when you're designing `Default.aspx`. The actual contents of every section of the web site (such as the search results page, the department and category pages, and so on) will be generated by separate Web Forms that will be differentiated by the code in the `ContentPlaceHolder` object.

The list of departments and the list of categories will be implemented as Web User Controls that generate their output based on data read from the database. You'll implement this functionality in Chapters 4 and 5.

Downloading the Code

The code you have just written is available in the Source Code area of the Apress web site at http://www.apress.com or at the author's web site at http://www.CristianDarie.ro. It should be easy for you to read through this book and build your solution as you go; however, if you want to check something from our working version, you can. Instructions on loading the chapters are available in the Welcome.html document in the download. You can also view the online version of BalloonShop at http://www.cristiandarie.ro/BalloonShop.

Summary

It's time to put your feet up on your desk and admire your work. In this chapter, you learned about the benefits of using the right architecture for an application. So far, we have a very flexible and scalable application (mostly because it doesn't do much yet), but you'll feel the real advantages of using a disciplined way of coding in the next chapters.

In this chapter, you have prepared your working environment and have coded the basic, static part of the presentation tier, and created the BalloonShop database, which is the support for the data tier. In the next chapter, you'll start implementing the product catalog and learn a lot about how to dynamically generate visual content using data stored in the database with the help of the middle tier and with smart and fast controls and components in the presentation tier.

■ ■ ■

CHAPTER 4

Creating the Product Catalog: Part 1

After learning about the three-tier architecture and implementing a bit of your web site's main page, you're ready to start creating the BalloonShop product catalog. Because the product catalog is composed of many components, you'll create it over two chapters. In this chapter you'll create the first database table, create the first stored procedure, implement generic data access code, learn how to handle errors and email their details to the administrator, and finally use data gathered from the database to compose dynamic content for your visitor.

The main topics we'll touch on in this chapter are:

- Analyzing the structure of the product catalog and the functionality it should support

- Creating the database structures for the catalog and the data tier of the catalog

- Implementing the business tier objects required to make the catalog run, and putting a basic but functional error-handling strategy in place

- Implementing a functional UI for the product catalog

Showing Your Visitor What You've Got

One of the essential features required in any e-store is to allow the visitor to easily browse through the products. Just imagine what Amazon.com would be like without its excellent product catalog!

Whether your visitors are looking for something specific or just browsing, it's important to make sure their experience with your site is a pleasant one. After all, you want your visitors to find what they are looking for as easily and painlessly as possible. This is why you'll want to add search functionality to the site and also find a clever way of structuring products into categories so they can be quickly and intuitively accessed.

Depending on the size of the store, it might be enough to group products under a number of categories, but if there are a lot of products, you'll need to find even more ways to categorize them.

Determining the structure of the catalog is one of the first tasks to accomplish in this chapter. Keep in mind that using a professional approach, these details would have been established before starting to code, when building the requirements document for the project. However, for the purposes of this book, we prefer to deal with things one at a time.

After the structure of the catalog is established, you'll start writing the code that makes the catalog work as planned.

What Does a Product Catalog Look Like?

Today's web surfers are more demanding than they used to be. They expect to find information quickly on whatever product or service they have in mind, and if they don't find it, they are likely to go to the competition before giving the site a second chance. Of course, you don't want this to happen to *your* visitors, so you need to structure the catalog to make it as intuitive and helpful as possible.

Because the e-store will start with around 100 products and will probably have many more in the future, it's not enough to just group them in categories. The store has a number of departments, and each department will contain a number of categories. Each category can then have any number of products attached to it.

■**Note**   Later in the book, you'll also create the administrative part of the web site, often referred to as the *Control Panel*, which allows the client to update department, category, and product data. Until then, you'll manually fill in the database with data (or you can "cheat" by using the SQL scripts provided in the Source Code area on the Apress web site [http://www.apress.com], as you'll see).

Another particularly important detail that you need to think about is whether a category can exist in more than one department, and whether a product can exist in more than one category. As you might suspect, this is the kind of decision that has implications on the way you code the product catalog, so you need to consult your client on this matter.

For the BalloonShop product catalog, each category can exist in only one department, but a product can exist in more than one category. For example, the product "Today, Tomorrow & Forever" will appear in both the "Love & Romance" and "Birthdays" categories. (Not that the authors are very romantic by nature, but the example is good enough to illustrate the idea.)

Finally, apart from having the products grouped in categories, we also want to have featured products. For this web site, a product can be featured either on the front page or in the department pages. Let's look at a few screenshots that explain this.

Previewing the Product Catalog

Although we'll have the fully functional product catalog finished by the end of Chapter 5, look at it now to help you get a better idea about where you're heading. In Figure 4-1, you can see the BalloonShop front page and four of its featured products.

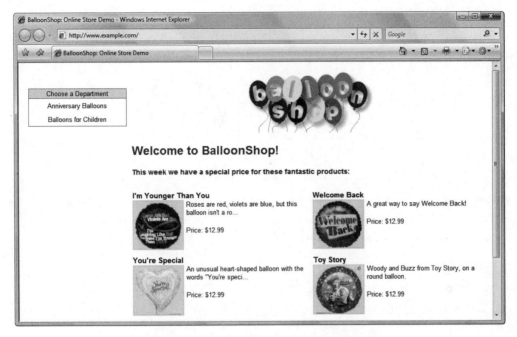

Figure 4-1. *The BalloonShop front page and some of its featured products*

Note the Choose a Department list in the upper-left corner of the page. The list of departments is dynamically generated with data gathered from the database; you'll implement the list of departments in this chapter.

When site visitors click a department in the departments list, they go to the main page of the specified department. This replaces the store's list of catalog-featured products with a page containing information specific to the selected department—including the list of featured products for that department. In Figure 4-2, you see the page that will appear when the "Anniversary Balloons" department is clicked.

Under the list of departments, you can now see the Choose a Category list of categories that belong to the selected department. In the right side of the screen, you can see the name, description, and featured products of the selected department. We decided to list only the featured products in the department page, in part because the complete list would be too long. The text above the list of featured products is the description for the selected department, which means you'll need to store in the database both a name and a description for each department.

In this page, when a particular category from the categories list is selected, all of its products are listed, along with updated title and description text. In Figure 4-3, you can see how that page appears when selecting the "Birthdays" category. Also note the paging controls, which appear in any product listings that contain more than an established number of products.

Figure 4-2. *The "Anniversary Balloons" department and four of its featured products*

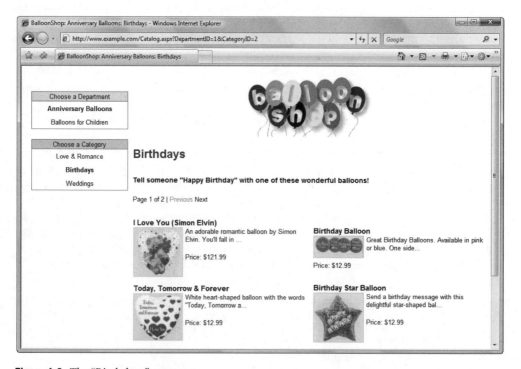

Figure 4-3. *The "Birthdays" category*

In any page that displays products, you can click the name or the picture of a product to view its product details page (see Figure 4-4). In later chapters, you'll add more functionality to this page, such as product recommendations.

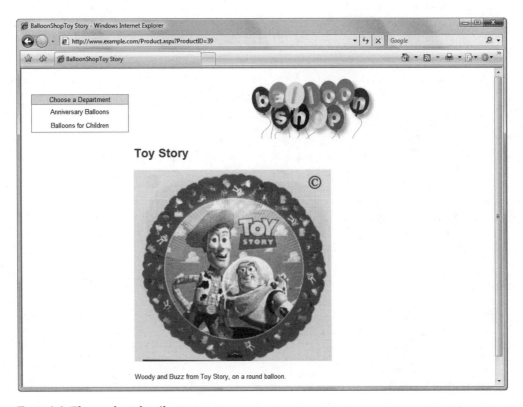

Figure 4-4. *The product details page*

Roadmap for This Chapter

We'll cover a lot of ground in this chapter. To make sure you don't get lost on the way, let's have a look at the big picture.

The departments list will be the first dynamically generated data in your site, as the names of the departments will be extracted from the database. We cover just the creation of the department list in this chapter, in the form of a Web User Control, because we'll also take a closer look at the mechanism that makes the control work. After you understand what happens behind the list of departments, you'll quickly implement the other components in Chapter 5.

In Chapter 2, we discussed the three-tiered architecture that you'll use to implement the web application. The product catalog part of the site makes no exception to the rule, and its components (including the departments list) will be spread over the three logical layers. Figure 4-5 previews what you'll create at each tier in this chapter to achieve a functional departments list.

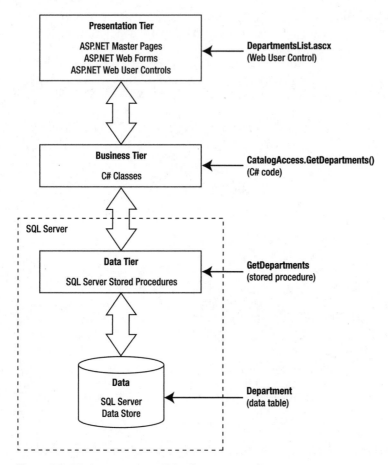

Figure 4-5. *The components of the departments list*

To implement the departments list, you'll start with the database and make your way to the presentation tier:

1. You'll create the Department table in the database. This table will store data regarding the store's departments. Before adding this table, you'll learn the basic concepts of working with relational databases.

2. You'll add the GetDepartments stored procedure to the database, which (like all the other stored procedures you'll write) is logically located in the data tier part of the application. At this step, you'll learn how to speak with relational databases using SQL.

3. You'll create the business tier components of the departments list. You'll learn how to communicate with the database by calling the stored procedure and sending the results to the presentation tier.

4. Finally, you'll implement the DepartmentsList.ascx Web User Control to display a dynamic list of departments for your visitor, which is the goal of this chapter.

You'll implement the rest of the product catalog in Chapter 5. So, let's start with the database.

Storing Catalog Information

The vast majority of web applications, e-commerce web sites being no exception, live around the data they manage. Analyzing and understanding the data you need to store and process is an essential step in successfully completing your project.

The typical data storage solution for this kind of application is a relational database. However, this is not a requirement—you have the freedom to create your own data access layer and have whatever kind of data structures to support your application.

■**Note** In some particular cases, it may be preferable to store your data in plain text files or XML files instead of databases, but these solutions are generally not suited for applications like BalloonShop, so we won't cover them in this book. However, it's good to know there are options.

Although this is not a book about databases or relational database design, you'll learn all you need to know to understand the product catalog and make it work. For more information about database programming using SQL Server, you should read a SQL Server book such as *Beginning SQL Server 2008 Express for Developers* (Apress, 2008) or *Beginning SQL Server 2008 for Developers* (Apress, 2008).

Essentially, a relational database is made up of data tables and the relationships that exist between them. Because in this chapter you'll work with a single data table, we'll cover only the database theory that applies to the table as a separate, individual database item. In the next chapter, when you add the other tables to the picture, we'll take a closer look at more theory behind relational databases by analyzing how the tables relate to each other and how SQL Server helps you deal with these relationships.

■**Note** In a real-world situation, you would probably design the whole database (or at least all the tables relevant to the feature you build) from the start. However, we chose to split the development over two chapters to maintain a better balance of theory and practice.

So, let's start with a little bit of theory, after which you'll create the Department data table and the rest of the required components.

Understanding Data Tables

This section is a quick database lesson that covers the essential information you need to know to design simple data tables. We'll briefly discuss the main parts that make up a database table:

- Primary keys
- UNIQUE columns
- SQL Server data types

- Nullable columns and default values

- Identity columns

- Indexes

■**Note** If you have enough experience with SQL Server, you might want to skip this section and go directly to the "Creating the Department Table" section.

A data table is made up of columns and rows. Columns are also referred to as **fields**, and rows are sometimes called **records**. Still, in a relational database, a good deal of hidden logic exists behind a simple list of data rows.

Because this chapter covers only the departments list, you'll only need to create one data table: the Department table. This table will store your departments' data and is one of the simplest tables you'll work with.

With the help of tools such as Visual Studio or Visual Web Developer, it's easy to create a data table in the database if you know what kind of data it will store. When designing a table, you must consider which fields it should contain and which data types should be used for those fields. Besides a field's data type, there are a few more properties to consider; we'll learn about them in the following pages.

To determine which fields you need for the Department table, write down a few examples of records that would be stored in that table. Remember from the previous figures that there isn't much information to store about a department—just the name and description for each department. The table containing the departments' data might look like Figure 4-6.

Name	Description
Anniversary Balloons	These sweet balloons are the perfect gift for someone you love.
Balloons for Children	The colorful and funny balloons will make any child smile!

Figure 4-6. *Data from the Department table*

From a table like this, the names would be extracted to populate the list in the upper-left part of the web page, and the descriptions would be used as headers for the featured products list.

Primary Keys

The way you work with data tables in a relational database is a bit different from the way you usually work on paper. A fundamental requirement in relational databases is that each data row in a table must be *uniquely identifiable*. This makes sense because you usually save records into a database so that you can retrieve them later; however, you can't do that if each row isn't uniquely identifiable. For example, suppose you add another record to the Department table shown previously in Figure 4-6, making it look like the table shown in Figure 4-7.

Name	Description
Anniversary Balloons	These sweet balloons are the perfect gift for someone you love.
Balloons for Children	The colorful and funny balloons will make any child smile!
Balloons for Children	Totally different department... oops!

Figure 4-7. *Two departments with the same name*

Now look at this table, and tell me the description of the "Balloons for Children" department. Yep, we have a problem! The problem arises because there are two departments with this name. If you queried the table using the Name column and wanted to add new products to the "Balloons for Children" department, to change the department's name, or to do literally anything, you would get two results!

This problem is addressed, in the world of relational database design, using the concept of the *primary key*, which allows you to uniquely identify a specific row out of many rows. Technically, the primary key is not a column itself. Instead, PRIMARY KEY is a *constraint* that when applied on a column guarantees that the column will have unique values across the table.

■**Note** Applying a PRIMARY KEY constraint on a field also generates a unique index by default. Indexes are objects that improve the performance of many database operations, speeding up your web application (you'll learn more about indexes a bit later).

Constraints are rules that apply to data tables and make up part of the *data integrity* rules of the database. The database takes care of its own integrity and makes sure these rules aren't broken. If, for example, you try to add two identical values for a column that has a PRIMARY KEY constraint, the database refuses the operation and generates an error. We'll do some experiments later in this chapter to show this.

■**Note** A primary key is not a column but a constraint that applies to that column; however, from now on and for convenience, when referring to the primary key, we'll be talking about the column that has the PRIMARY KEY constraint applied to it.

Back to the example, setting the Name column as the primary key of the Department table would solve the problem because two departments would not be allowed to have the same name. If Name is the primary key of the Department table, searching for a row with a specific Name will always produce exactly one result if the name exists, or no results if no records have the specified name.

■**Tip** This is common sense, but it has to be said: a primary key column will never accept NULL values.

An alternative solution, and usually the preferred one, is to have an additional column in the table, called an ID column, to act as its primary key. With an ID column, the Department table would look like Figure 4-8.

DepartmentID	Name	Description
1	Anniversary Balloons	These sweet balloons are the perfect gift for someone you love.
2	Balloons for Children	The colorful and funny balloons will make any child smile!

Figure 4-8. *Adding an ID column as the primary key of Department*

The primary key column is named DepartmentID. We'll use the same naming convention for primary key columns in the other data tables we'll create.

There are two main reasons why it's better to create a separate numerical primary key column than to use Name (or another existing column) as the primary key:

- *Performance*: The database engine handles sorting and searching operations much faster with numerical values than with strings. This becomes even more relevant in the context of working with multiple related tables that need to be frequently joined (you'll learn more about this in Chapter 5).

- *Department name changes*: If you need to rely on the ID value being stable in time, creating an artificial key (in the form of an additional ID column) solves the problem because it's unlikely you'll ever need to change the ID.

In Figure 4-8, the primary key is composed of a single column, but this is not a requirement. If the primary key is composed of more than one column, the group of primary key columns (taken as a unit) is guaranteed to be unique (but the individual columns that form the primary key can have repeating values in the table). In Chapter 5, you'll see an example of a multivalued primary key. For now, it's enough to know that they exist.

Unique Columns

UNIQUE is yet another kind of constraint that can be applied to table columns. This constraint is similar to the PRIMARY KEY constraint because it doesn't allow duplicate data in a column. Still, there are differences. Although there is only one PRIMARY KEY constraint per table, you are allowed to have as many UNIQUE constraints as you like.

Columns with the UNIQUE constraint are useful when you already have a primary key, but you still have columns for which you want to have unique values. You can set Name to be unique in the Department table if you want to forbid repeating values, when the DepartmentID column is the primary key. (We won't use the UNIQUE constraint in this book, but we mention it here for completeness.) We decided to allow identical department names because only site administrators will have the privileges to modify or change department data.

The facts that you need to remember about UNIQUE constraints are

- The UNIQUE constraint forbids having identical values on the field.

- You can have more than one UNIQUE field in a data table.

- Unlike with primary keys, a UNIQUE constraint can't apply to more than one field.

- A UNIQUE field is allowed to accept NULL values, in which case it can only accept one NULL value.

- Indexes are automatically created on UNIQUE and PRIMARY KEY columns.

Columns and Data Types

Each column in a table has a particular data type. By looking at the previously shown Figure 4-8 with the Department table, it's clear that DepartmentID has a numeric data type, whereas Name and Description contain text.

It's important to consider the many data types that SQL Server supports so that you can make correct decisions concerning how to create your tables. Table 4-1 isn't an exhaustive list of SQL Server data types, but it focuses on the main types you might come across in your project. Refer to SQL Server 2008 Books Online, which can be freely accessed and downloaded from http://msdn.microsoft.com/sql, for a more detailed list.

■**Note** Table 4-1 was created with SQL Server 2008 in mind, but these data types exist in older versions of SQL Server as well. The differences between SQL Server versions are reflected in details such as the maximum size for character data.

To keep Table 4-1 short, under the Data Type heading we've listed only the most frequently used types, while similar data types are explained under the Description and Notes heading. You don't need to memorize the list, but you should get an idea of which data types are available.

Table 4-1. *SQL Server Data Types*

Data Type	Size in Bytes	Description and Notes
Int	4	Stores whole numbers from –2,147,483,648 to 2,147,483,647. You'll use them for ID columns and in other circumstances that require integer numbers. Related types are SmallInt and TinyInt. A Bit data type is able to store values of 0 and 1.
Money	8	Stores monetary data with values from -2^{63} to $2^{63} - 1$ with a precision of four decimal places. You'll use this data type to store product prices, shopping cart subtotals, and so on. SQL Server also supports the Float data type, which holds floating-point data, but Float is not recommended for storing monetary information because of its lack of precision. A variation of Money is SmallMoney, which has a smaller range, but the same precision.
DateTime	8	Supports date and time data from January 1, 1753 through December 31, 9999 with an accuracy of three hundredths of a second. A SmallDateTime type has a range from January 1, 1900 to June 6, 2079 with an accuracy of one minute. You'll use this data type to store information such as order shipping dates.

Table 4-1. *SQL Server Data Types (Continued)*

Data Type	Size in Bytes	Description and Notes
UniqueIdentifier	16	Stores a numerical Globally Unique Identifier (GUID). A GUID is guaranteed to be unique; this property makes it very useful in certain situations. In this book, we prefer to generate unique identifiers using other methods, but it's good to know there are options.
VarChar, NVarChar	Variable	Stores variable-length character data. NVarChar stores Unicode data with a maximum length of 4,000 characters, and VarChar stores non-Unicode data with a maximum length of 8,000 characters. This data type is best used for storing short strings (note their length limitations) without fixed lengths.
Char, NChar	Fixed	Stores fixed-length character data. Values shorter than the declared size are padded with spaces. NChar is the Unicode version and goes to a maximum of 4,000 characters, whereas Char can store 8,000 characters. When the size of the strings to be stored is fixed, it's more efficient to use Char than VarChar.
Text, NText	Fixed	Stores large character data. NText is the Unicode version and has a maximum size of 1,073,741,823 characters. Text has double this maximum size. Using these data types can slow down the database, and it's generally recommended to use Char, VarChar, NChar, or NVarChar instead. When adding Text or NText fields, their length is fixed to 16, which represents the size of the pointer that references the location where the actual text is stored—not the size of the text itself. The Text data type can be used to store large character data such as paragraphs, long product descriptions, and so on. We won't use this data type in this book.
Binary, VarBinary	Fixed/variable	Stores binary data with a maximum length of 8,000 bytes.
Image	Variable	Stores binary data of maximum $2^{31} - 1$ bytes. Despite its name, this field can store any kind of binary data, not just pictures. In most circumstances, it's easier and faster to store the files in the OS file system and store only their names in the database, but there are situations when it makes more sense to use the database for storing binary data. For BalloonShop, you'll store the product images in the file system.

Note The names of the SQL Server data types are not case sensitive, and most programmers write them either in full uppercase or lowercase. We've cased them properly in the table for readability.

Now let's get back to the Department table and determine which data types to use. Don't worry that you don't have the table yet in your database, you'll create it a bit later. For now, you just need to understand how data types work with SQL Server.

If you know what these data types mean, Figure 4-9 is self-explanatory. DepartmentID is an Int, and Name and Description are VarChar data types. The little golden key at the left of DepartmentID specifies that the column is the primary key of the Department table.

Column Name	Data Type	Allow Nulls
🔑 DepartmentID	int	☐
Name	nvarchar(50)	☐
Description	nvarchar(1000)	☑

Figure 4-9. *Designing the Department table*

You can also see the length of the VarChar fields. Note that "length" means different things for different data types. For numerical data types, the length is usually fixed (so it doesn't show up in some designers, such as the one in Figure 4-9), and it specifies the number of bytes it takes to store one record; whereas for string data types (excluding Text and NText), the length specifies the number of characters that can be stored in a record. This is a subtle but important difference because for Unicode text data (NChar, NVarChar, NText), the actual storage space needed is 2 bytes per character.

We choose to have 50 characters available for the department's name and 1,000 for the description. Some prefer to use NVarChar instead of VarChar—this is actually a requirement when you need to store Unicode characters (such as when storing Chinese text).

Nullable Columns and Default Values

Observe the Allow Nulls column in the design window of the Department table—some fields have this check box checked, but others don't. If the check box is checked, the column is allowed to store the NULL value.

The best and shortest definition for NULL is "undefined." In your Department table, only DepartmentID and Name are required, so Description is optional—meaning that you are allowed to add a new department without supplying a description for it. If you add a new row of data without supplying a value for columns that allow nulls, NULL is automatically supplied for them.

Especially for character data, a subtle difference exists between the NULL value and an "empty" value. If you add a product with an empty string for its description, this means that you actually set a value for its description; it's an empty string, not an undefined (NULL) value.

The primary key field never allows NULL values. For the other columns, it's up to you to decide which fields are required and which are not.

In some cases, instead of allowing NULLs, you'll prefer to specify default values. This way, if the value is unspecified when creating a new row, it will be supplied with the default value. The default value can be a literal value (such as 0 for a Salary column or "Unknown" for a Description column), or it can be a system value (such as the GETDATE function, which returns the current date).

Identity Columns

Identity columns are auto-numbered columns. This behavior is similar to AutoNumber columns in Microsoft Access. When a column is set as an identity column, SQL Server automatically provides values for it when inserting new records into the table; by default, the database doesn't permit manually specified values for identity columns.

SQL Server guarantees that the generated values are always unique, which makes them especially useful when used in conjunction with the PRIMARY KEY constraint. You already know that primary keys are used on columns that uniquely identify each row of a table. If you set a primary key column to also be an identity column, SQL Server automatically fills that column with values when adding new rows (in other words, it generates new IDs), ensuring that the values are unique.

■**Note** After making a column an identity column, SQL Server will not allow you, by default, to add values to that column manually. This is why you'll find, typically in SQL table creation scripts, commands like the following, which are used to temporarily enable inserting custom data to the identity column:

```
SET IDENTITY_INSERT Departments ON
```

When setting an identity column, you can specify an identity seed, which is the first value that SQL Server provides for that column, and an identity increment value, which specifies the number of units to increase between two consecutive records. By default, identity seed and identity increment values are both set to 1, meaning that the first value will be 1 and the following ones will be generated by adding 1 to the last created value. You don't need to specify other values because you don't care what values are generated anyway.

Although it wasn't shown in the earlier Figure 4-9, DepartmentID in your Department table is an identity column. You'll learn how to set identity columns a bit later, when creating the Department table.

■**Note** The generated values for identity columns are unique over the life of your table. A value that was generated once will never be generated again, even if you delete all the rows from the table. If you want SQL Server to restart numbering from the initial value, you need to either delete and re-create the table or *truncate* the table using the TRUNCATE SQL command. Truncating a table has the same effect as deleting and creating it again.

Indexes

Indexes are database objects meant to increase the overall speed of database operations. They work by maintaining a special structure of data that reflects the contents of the indexed table, which enables very fast searches on the table.

In consequence, indexes speed up table reads, but they slow down insert, delete, and update operations—because on those operations, the database server needs to alter not only the table, but also the additional structures created by its index (or indexes). In most real-world applications, the vast majority of database operations are read operations, and the presence of indexes leads to significant overall performance improvements.

On a table, you can create one or more indexes, with each index working on one column or on a set of columns. When a table is indexed on a specific column, its rows are either indexed or physically arranged based on the values of that column and the type of index. This makes search operations on that column very fast. If, for example, an index exists on DepartmentID, and then you do a search for department 934, the search is performed very quickly.

You should keep the following in mind about indexes:

- Indexes greatly increase search operations on the database, but they slow down operations that change the database (delete, update, and insert operations).

- Having too many indexes can slow down the general performance of the database. The general rule is to set indexes on columns frequently used in WHERE, ORDER BY, and GROUP BY clauses, used in table joins, or having foreign-key relationships with other tables.

- Indexes are automatically created on primary key and unique table columns.

You can use dedicated tools to test the performance of a database under stress conditions with and without particular indexes; in fact, a serious database administrator will want to make some of these tests before deciding on a winning combination for indexes. You can also use the Database Engine Tuning Advisor, which can be accessed through SQL Server Management Studio (the tuning advisor doesn't ship with Express Edition, however). Consult a specialized SQL Server book for more details on these subjects.

In your application, you'll rely on the indexes that are automatically created on the primary key columns, which is a safe combination for our kind of web site.

Creating the Department Table

You created the BalloonShop database in Chapter 3. In the following exercise, you'll add the Department table to it.

We recommend that you create the Department table by following the steps in the exercise. Alternatively, you can use the SQL scripts for this book in the Source Code area of the Apress web site (http://www.apress.com) to create and populate the Department table. You can execute the SQL script files using the SQL Server Management Studio Express utility.

Exercise: Creating the Department Table

1. As mentioned in Chapter 3, you can interact with your SQL Server database using both Visual Web Developer and SQL Server Management Studio—when it comes to creating data tables, stored procedures, and so on, their interfaces are almost identical.

2. We used SQL Server Management Studio in Chapter 3. Let's use Visual Web Developer this time. Start by opening the Database Explorer pane using **View ➤ Database Explorer**, or using the default shortcut **Ctrl+Alt+S**.

3. Since this is the first time we're connecting to our database using Visual Web Developer, we need to configure a connection. Right-click the **Data Connections** entry in Database Explorer and select **Add Connection**.

4. In the Add Connection dialog, type **localhost\SQLExpress** for the server name (feel free to use the name of your machine instead of localhost), select **SQL Server Authentication**, and type the username and password you created in Chapter 3 (**balloonshop/ecommerce**, if you followed our instructions). Check the **Save my password** check box, and type **BalloonShop** in the **Select or enter a database name** box. Click **Test Connection** to make sure you've typed everything correctly, and finally click **OK** to close the window and save your new connection.

■**Note** Your SQL Server instance must be configured to accept connections using SQL Server authentication—you did this in Chapter 3.

5. In Database Explorer, expand the **BalloonShop** database connection node, right-click the **Tables** node, and select **Add New Table** from the context menu. Alternatively, after expanding the BalloonShop node, you can choose **Data ➤ Add New ➤ Table**.

6. A form appears where you can add columns to the new table. Using this form, add three columns, with the properties described in Table 4-2.

Table 4-2. *Designing the Department Table*

Field Name	Data Type	Other Properties
DepartmentID	int	Primary Key and Identity column
Name	nvarchar(50)	Don't allow NULLs
Description	nvarchar(1000)	Allow NULLs

■**Note** You set a column to be the primary key by right-clicking it and clicking the **Set Primary Key** item from the context menu. You set a column to be an identity column by expanding the **Identity Specification** item from its Column Properties window, and setting the **(Is Identity)** node to **Yes**. You can also access the Identity Increment and Identity Seed values, if you should ever want to use values other than the defaults.

7. After adding these fields, the form should look like Figure 4-10 in Visual Studio.

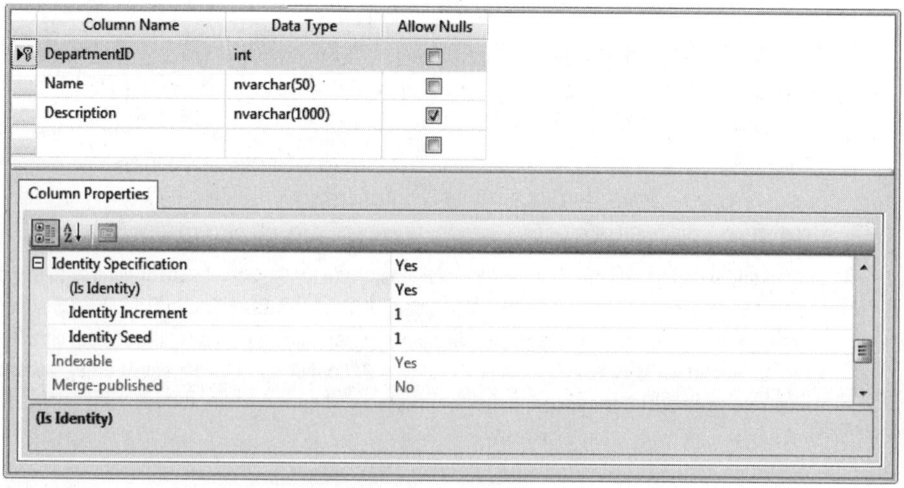

Figure 4-10. *The three fields of the Department table*

8. Now that everything is in place, you need to save the newly created table. Press **Ctrl+S** or select **File ➤ Save Table1**. When asked, type **Department** for the table name.

9. After creating the table in the database, you can open it to add some data. To open the `Department` table for editing, right-click it in Database Explorer and select **Show Table Data** from the context menu. (Alternatively, you can choose **Database ➤ Show Table Data** after selecting the table in Database Explorer.) Using the integrated editor, you can start adding rows. Because `DepartmentID` is an identity column, you cannot manually edit its data—SQL Server automatically fills this field, depending on the identity seed and identity increment values that you specified when creating the table.

10. Add two departments, as shown in Figure 4-11.

	DepartmentID	Name	Description
▶	1	Anniversary Balloons	These sweet balloons are the perfect gift for someone you love.
	2	Balloons for Children	The colorful and funny balloons will make any child smile!
*	NULL	NULL	NULL

`|◀  ◀  |1      of 2 | ▶  ▶|  ▶≡ | ⊚ | Cell is Read Only.`

Figure 4-11. *Adding two sample rows to the Department table*

■**Note** To ensure consistency with the scripts in the Source Code area on the Apress web site (and to make your life easier), make sure the department IDs are 1 and 2, as shown in Figure 4-11. Because `DepartmentID` is an identity column, an ID value is generated only once, even if you remove records from the table in the meantime. The only way to reset the identity values generator is to delete and re-create the table, or truncate the table. The easiest way to truncate the table is to start SQL Server Express Manager, log in to your local SQL Server Express instance (by default, named `localhost\SqlExpress`), and execute the following SQL commands:

```
USE BalloonShop
TRUNCATE TABLE Department
```

After truncating the table, the first row you add to the table will get the ID 1. (Experienced developers can also use `SET IDENTITY_INSERT` to set the values for the identity columns manually, but we'll leave this kind of experimentation for you as an exercise.)

How It Works: The Department Table

You have just created your first database table! You also set a primary key and an identity column, and then filled the table with some data. As you can see, as soon as you have a clear idea about the structure of a table, Visual Web Developer and SQL Server make it very easy to implement.

Let's continue by learning how to programmatically access and manipulate this data with SQL code.

Communicating with the Database

Now that you have a table filled with data, let's do something useful with it. The ultimate goal with this table is to get the list of department names from the database using C# code.

To get data from a database, you first need to know how to communicate with the database. SQL Server understands a language called Transact-SQL (T-SQL). The usual way of communicating with SQL Server is to write a T-SQL command, send it to SQL Server, and get the results back. However, these commands can either be sent directly from the business tier to SQL Server (without having an intermediary data tier) or centralized and saved as stored procedures as part of the database.

Stored procedures are database objects that store programs written in T-SQL. Much like normal functions, stored procedures accept input and output parameters and have return values.

■Note As mentioned in Chapter 2, SQL Server offers, since its 2005 version, managed stored procedures, which are programs written in a .NET language that execute inside SQL Server. Writing managed stored procedures is an advanced topic outside the scope of this book, but it's good to know that they exist.

You don't need to use stored procedures if you want to perform database operations. You can directly send the SQL commands from an external application to SQL Server. When using stored procedures, instead of passing the SQL code you want executed, you just pass the name of the stored procedure and the values for any parameters it might have. Using stored procedures for data operations has the following advantages:

- Storing SQL code as a stored procedure usually results in better performance because SQL Server generates and caches the stored procedure execution plan when it's first executed.

- Using stored procedures allows for better maintainability of the data access and manipulation code, which is stored in a central place, and permits easier implementation of the three-tier architecture (the stored procedures forming the data tier).

- Security can be better controlled because SQL Server permits setting different security permissions for each individual stored procedure.

- SQL queries created ad hoc in C# code are more vulnerable to SQL injection attacks, which is a major security threat. Many Internet resources cover this security subject, such as the article at http://www.sitepoint.com/article/sql-injection-attacks-safe.

- This might be a matter of taste, but having the SQL logic separated from the C# code keeps the C# code cleaner and easier to manage; it looks better to call the name of a stored procedure than to join strings to create a SQL query to pass to the database.

Your goal for this section is to write the GetDepartments stored procedure; but first, let's take a quick look at SQL.

Speaking the Database Language

SQL (Structured Query Language) is the language used to communicate with modern Relational Database Management Systems (RDBMSs). Most database systems support a particular dialect of SQL, such as T-SQL for SQL Server and PL/SQL (Procedural Language extensions to SQL) for Oracle. Because T-SQL is a big subject when analyzed in detail, we'll briefly introduce it and cover just enough so you'll understand the code in your stored procedures.

■**Tip** For further SQL reference, we also recommend *Beginning SQL Queries* (Apress, 2008).

The basic and most important SQL commands are SELECT, INSERT, UPDATE, and DELETE. Their names are self-explanatory, and they allow you to perform basic operations on the database.

You can use SQL Server Management Studio Express to test these commands with your newly created Department table. Start SQL Server Management Studio Express, log in to your local SQL Server Express instance (by default, named localhost\SqlExpress), and then execute the following command, which connects you to the BalloonShop database. (To execute the command, click New Query to open a new query window, type the command you want to execute, and finally use the Execute button on the toolbar. Alternatively, choose Query ➤ Execute, or press the F5 shortcut key.)

```
USE BalloonShop
```

After executing this command, you should get a "Command(s) completed successfully" message. After you connect to the database, you're ready to test the SQL commands you're about to learn.

Be aware that each SQL command has many optional arguments, and they can become more complex than those presented here. Still, to keep the presentation short and simple, you'll learn the most important and frequently used parameters, and we'll get into more details later in the book.

SELECT

The SELECT statement is used to query the database and retrieve selected data that match the criteria you specify. Its basic structure is

```
SELECT <column list>
FROM <table name(s)>
[WHERE <restrictive condition>]
```

■**Note** Although SQL is not case sensitive, in this book the SQL commands and queries appear in uppercase for consistency and clarity. The WHERE clause appears in brackets because it's optional.

The simplest SELECT command you can execute on your BalloonShop database is

```
SELECT * FROM Department
```

If you've created and populated the Department table as described in the exercises, you should get the results shown in Figure 4-12.

The "*" wildcard you used in the SQL query means "all columns." Most of the time, unless you have a serious reason to use it, it's good to avoid using this wildcard, instead specifying the columns you want returned manually, like this:

```
SELECT DepartmentID, Name, Description
FROM Department
```

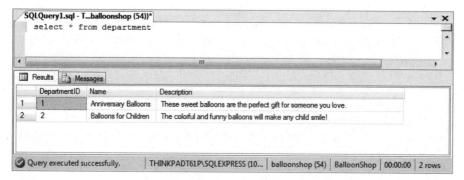

Figure 4-12. *Executing a simple SQL command using SQL Server Management Studio*

The following command returns the name of the department that has the DepartmentID of 1. In your case, the returned value is "Anniversary Balloons", but you would receive no results if there were no departments with an ID of 1.

```
SELECT Name FROM Department WHERE DepartmentID = 1
```

INSERT

The INSERT statement is used to insert or add a row of data into the table. Its syntax is as follows:

```
INSERT [INTO] <table name> (column list) VALUES (column values)
```

The following INSERT statement adds a department named "Mysterious Department" to the Department table:

```
INSERT INTO Department (Name) VALUES ('Mysterious Department')
```

■**Tip** The INTO keyword is optional, but including it makes the statement easier to read.

We didn't specify any value for the Description field because it was marked to allow NULLs in the Department table. This is why you can omit specifying a value, if you want to. (You can also omit specifying values for columns that have default values defined.) However, the Name field is required, so if you tried, for example, to specify a description without specifying a name, you would get an error:

```
INSERT INTO Department (Description) VALUES ('Some Description Here')
```

The error message specifies

```
.Net SqlClient Data Provider: Msg 515, Level 16, State 2, Line 1
Cannot insert the value NULL into column 'Name',
table 'balloonshop.dbo.Department'; column
does not allow nulls. INSERT fails.
The statement has been terminated.
```

Also note that you didn't specify a DepartmentID. Because DepartmentID was set as an identity column, you're not allowed to manually specify values for this column. SQL Server can guarantee this has unique values, but only if you don't interfere with it.

So, if you can't specify a value for DepartmentID, how can you determine which value was automatically supplied by SQL Server? For this, you have a special variable named @@IDENTITY. You can type its value by using the SELECT statement. The following two SQL commands add a new record to Department and return the DepartmentID of the row just added:

```
INSERT INTO Department (Name) Values ('Some New Department')
SELECT @@IDENTITY
```

UPDATE

The UPDATE statement is used to modify existing data and has the following syntax:

```
UPDATE <table name>
SET <column name> = <new value> [, <column name> = <new value> ...]
[WHERE <restrictive condition>]
```

The following query changes the name of the department with the ID of 43 to Cool Department. If there were more departments with that ID, all of them would be modified, but because DepartmentID is the primary key, you can't have more departments with the same ID.

```
UPDATE Department SET Name='Cool Department' WHERE DepartmentID = 43
```

Be careful with the UPDATE statement, because it makes it easy to mess up an entire table. If the WHERE clause is omitted, the change is applied to every record of the table, which you usually don't want to happen. SQL Server will be happy to change all your records, without any warning; even if all departments in the table would have the same name and description, they would still be perceived as different entities because they have DepartmentIDs.

DELETE

The syntax of the DELETE command is actually very simple:

```
DELETE [FROM] <table name>
[WHERE <restrictive condition>]
```

The FROM keyword is optional and can be omitted. We generally use it because it makes the query sound more like normal English.

Most times, you'll want to use the WHERE clause to delete a single row:

```
DELETE FROM Department
WHERE DepartmentID = 43
```

As with UPDATE, be careful with this command, because if you forget to specify a WHERE clause, you'll end up deleting all the rows in the specified table. The following query deletes all the records in Department. The table itself isn't deleted by the DELETE command.

```
DELETE FROM Department
```

■**Tip** As with INSERT [INTO], the FROM keyword is optional. Add it if you feel it makes the statement easier to understand.

Creating Stored Procedures

You need to create the GetDepartments stored procedure, which returns department information from the Department table. This stored procedure is part of the data tier and will be accessed from the business tier. The final goal is to have this data displayed in the user control.

The SQL code that retrieves the necessary data and that you need to save to the database as the GetDepartments stored procedure is the following:

```
SELECT DepartmentID, Name, Description FROM Department
```

This command returns all the department information.

■**Caution** Unless you have a specific reason to do so, never ask for all columns (using the * wildcard) when you only need a part of them. This generates more traffic and stress on the database server than necessary and slows down performance. Moreover, even if you do need to ask for all columns in the table, it's safer to mention them explicitly to protect your application in case the number or order of columns change in future.

Saving the Query As a Stored Procedure

As with data tables, after you know the structure, implementing the stored procedure is a piece of cake. Now that you know the SQL code, the tools will help you save the query as a stored procedure easily.

The syntax for creating a stored procedure that has no input or output parameters is as follows:

```
CREATE PROCEDURE <procedure name>
AS
  <stored procedure code>
```

If the procedure already exists and you just want to update its code, use ALTER PROCEDURE instead of CREATE PROCEDURE.

Stored procedures can have input or output parameters. Because GetDepartments doesn't have any parameters, you don't have to bother about them right now. You'll learn how to use input and output parameters in Chapter 5.

In the following exercise, you'll add the GetDepartments stored procedure to your database.

■**Note** Alternatively, you can execute the GetDepartments.sql script file in the BalloonShop database, which creates the GetDepartments stored procedure.

Exercise: Writing the Stored Procedure

1. Make sure the data connection to the BalloonShop database is expanded and selected in Database Explorer. Choose **Data ➤ Add New ➤ Stored Procedure**. Alternatively, you can right-click the **Stored Procedures** node in Database Explorer and select **Add New Stored Procedure**.

2. Replace the default text with your GetDepartments stored procedure:

```
CREATE PROCEDURE GetDepartments AS
    SELECT DepartmentID, Name, Description
    FROM Department
```

3. Press **Ctrl+S** to save the stored procedure. Unlike with the tables, you won't be asked for a name because the database already knows that you're talking about the GetDepartments stored procedure.

■**Note** Saving the stored procedure actually executes the SQL code you entered, which creates the stored procedure in the database. After saving the procedure, the CREATE keyword becomes ALTER, which is the SQL command that changes the code of an existing procedure.

---

4. Now test your first stored procedure to see that it's actually working. Navigate to the GetDepartments stored procedure node in Database Explorer and select **Execute**, as shown in Figure 4-13.

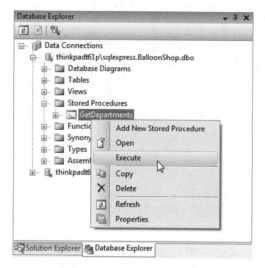

Figure 4-13. *Executing a stored procedure from Visual Web Developer*

5. After running the stored procedure, you can see the results in the Output window (see Figure 4-14). You can open the Output window by choosing **View ➤ Other Windows ➤ Output**, or by pressing **Ctrl+Alt+O**.

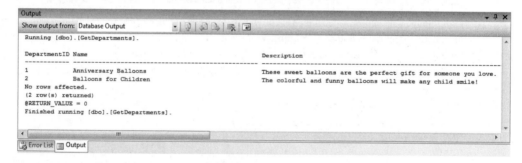

Figure 4-14. *The Output window shows the results.*

How it Works: The GetDepartments Stored Procedure

You've just finished coding the data tier part that reads the departments list!

The results in the Output window confirm your stored procedure works as expected. You can also test the stored procedure by using SQL Server Management Studio Express and executing the stored procedure from there:

```
USE BalloonShop
EXEC GetDepartments
```

Adding Logic to the Site

The business tier (or middle tier) is said to be the brains of the application because it manages the application's business logic. However, for simple tasks such as getting a list of departments from the data tier, the business tier doesn't have much logic to implement. It just requests the data from the database and passes it to the presentation tier.

For the business tier of the departments list, you'll implement three classes:

- GenericDataAccess implements common functionality that you'll then reuse whenever you need to access the database. Having this kind of generic functionality packed in a separate class saves keystrokes and avoids bugs in the long run.

- CatalogAccess contains product catalog–specific functionality, such the GetDepartments method that will retrieve the list of departments from the database.

- BalloonShopConfiguration and Utilities contain miscellaneous functionality such as sending emails, which will be reused in various places in BalloonShop.

In Chapter 5, you'll keep adding methods to these classes to support the new pieces of functionality.

Connecting to SQL Server

The main challenge is to understand how the code that accesses the database works. The .NET technology that permits accessing a database from C# code is called **ADO.NET**. ADO.NET groups all .NET classes that are related to database access.

ADO.NET is a complex subject that requires a separate book by itself, so we'll cover just enough to help you understand how your business tier works. For more information about ADO.NET, refer to *Beginning C# 2008 Databases: From Novice to Professional* (Apress, 2008).

The data access class named GenericDataAccess that you'll write will make extensive use of many ADO.NET features. The GenericDataAccess class deals with accessing the database, executing stored procedures, and returning the retrieved data. This class will provide generic data access functionality for the business tier classes, which need to read or manipulate that data.

Each database operation always consists of three steps:

1. Open a connection to the SQL Server database.

2. Perform the needed operations with the database and get back the results.

3. Close the connection to the database.

Before you implement the GenericDataAccess class itself, which implements all these steps, we'll have a quick look at each step individually.

■Tip Always try to make the second step (executing the commands) as fast as possible. Keeping a data connection open for too long or having too many database connections open at the same time is expensive for your application's performance. The golden rule is to open the connection as late as possible, perform the necessary operations, and then close it immediately.

The class used to connect to SQL Server is SqlConnection. When creating a new database connection, you always need to specify at least three important pieces of data:

- The name of the SQL Server instance you're connecting to

- The authentication information that will permit you to access the server

- The database you want to work with

This connection data is grouped in a connection string, which needs to be passed to the SqlConnection object. The following code snippet demonstrates how to create and open a database connection. (You don't need to type anything just yet—here we're just explaining the theory, and we'll put it into practice in a step-by-step exercise just a little bit later.)

```
// Create the connection object
SqlConnection connection = new SqlConnection();
// Set the connection string
connection.ConnectionString = "Server=(local)\SqlExpress; " +
                              "User ID=balloonshop; Password=ecommerce;" +
                              "Database=BalloonShop";
// Open the connection
connection.Open();
```

The code is fairly straightforward: you first create a SqlConnection object, then set its ConnectionString property, and finally open the connection. A connection needs to be opened before it is used for any operations.

Understanding the connection string is important—if your program has problems connecting to the database, these problems likely can be solved by fixing the connection string (assuming that SQL Server is properly configured and that you actually have access to it).

The connection string contains the three important elements. The first is the name of the SQL Server instance you're connecting to. For SQL Server 2008 Express Edition, the default instance name is (local)\SqlExpress. You'll want to change this if your SQL Server instance has another name. You can use your computer name instead of (local). Of course, if you connect to a remote SQL Server instance, you'll need to specify the complete network path instead of (local).

After specifying the server, you need to supply security information needed to log in to the server. You can log in to SQL Server either by using SQL Server Authentication (in which case you need to supply a SQL Server username and password as shown in the code snippet) or by using Windows Authentication (also named Windows Integrated Security). With Windows Integrated Security, you don't have to supply a username and password, because SQL Server uses the Windows login information of the currently logged-in user.

To log in using Windows Authentication, you'll need to supply `Integrated Security=True` (or `Integrated Security=SSPI`) instead of `User ID=username; Password=password`. The final part of the connection string specifies the database you'll be working with.

Instead of setting the connection string after creating the `SqlConnection` object, you can provide the connection string right when creating the `SqlConnection` object:

```
// Create the connection object and set the connection string
SqlConnection connection = new SqlConnection("... connection string ...");
// Open the connection
connection.Open();
```

A final note about the connection string is that several synonyms can be used inside it; for example, instead of `Server`, you can use `Data Source` or `Data Server`, and instead of `Database`, you can use `Initial Catalog`. The list is much longer, and the complete version can be found in SQL Server Books Online.

Issuing Commands and Executing Stored Procedures

After you have an open connection to the database, you usually need to create a `SqlCommand` object to perform operations. Because there are more tricks you can do with the `SqlCommand` object, we'll take them one at a time.

Creating a SqlCommand Object

`SqlCommand` will be your best friend when implementing the data access code. This class is capable of storing information about what you want to do with the database—it can store a SQL query or the name of a stored procedure that needs to be executed. The `SqlCommand` is also aware of stored procedure parameters—you'll learn more about these in Chapter 5, because the stored procedure you work with in this chapter (`CatalogGetDepartments`) doesn't have any parameters.

Following is the standard way of creating and initializing a `SqlCommand` object:

```
// Create the command object
SqlCommand command = new SqlCommand();
command.Connection = connection;
command.CommandText = "CatalogGetDepartments";
command.CommandType = CommandType.StoredProcedure;
```

Once again, there's no mystery about the code. You first create a `SqlCommand` object and then set some of its properties. The most important property that needs to be set is `Connection`, because each command needs to be executed on a specific connection. The other important property is `CommandText`, which specifies the command that needs to be executed. This can be a SQL query such as `SELECT * FROM Department`, but in your application this will always be the name of a stored procedure.

By default, the `CommandText` property receives SQL queries. Because you are supplying the name of a stored procedure instead of a SQL query, you need to inform the `SqlCommand` object about this by setting its `CommandType` property to `CommandType.StoredProcedure`.

The previous code snippet shows a simple and structured way to create and configure the `SqlCommand` object. However, it's possible to achieve the same result using less code by passing some of the information when creating the command object:

```
// Create the command object
SqlCommand command = new SqlCommand("GetDepartments", connection);
command.CommandType = CommandType.StoredProcedure;
```

Executing the Command and Closing the Connection

This is the moment of glory—finally, after creating a connection, creating a `SqlCommand` object, and setting various parameters, you're ready to execute the command. It is important always to close the connection as soon as possible—immediately after the necessary database operation has been performed—because open connections consume server resources, which finally results in poor performance if not managed carefully.

You can execute the command in many ways, depending on the specifics. Does it return any information? If so, what kind of information, and in which format? You'll analyze the various scenarios later, when you actually put the theory into practice, but for now let's take a look at the three `Execute` methods of the `SqlCommand` class: `ExecuteNonQuery`, `ExecuteScalar`, and `ExecuteReader`.

`ExecuteNonQuery` is used to execute a SQL statement or stored procedure that doesn't return any records. You'll use this method when executing operations that update, insert, or delete information in the database. `ExecuteNonQuery` returns an integer value that specifies how many rows were affected by the query—this proves useful if you want to know, for example, how many rows were deleted by the last delete operation. Of course, in case you don't need to know that number, you can simply ignore the return value. Here's a simple piece of code that shows how to open the connection, execute the command using `ExecuteNonQuery`, and immediately close the connection afterward:

```
connection.Open();
command.ExecuteNonQuery();
command.Close();
```

`ExecuteScalar` is like `ExecuteNonQuery` in that it returns a single value, although it returns a value that has been read from the database instead of the number of affected rows. It is used in conjunction with `SELECT` statements that select a single value. If `SELECT` returns more rows and/or more columns, only the first column in the first row is returned. A typical SQL query that should be executed using `ExecuteScalar` is `SELECT COUNT(*) FROM Department`—which returns the number of rows in the `Department` table.

`ExecuteReader` is used with `SELECT` statements that return multiple records (with any number of fields). `ExecuteReader` returns a `SqlDataReader` object, which contains the results of the query. A `SqlDataReader` object reads and returns the results one by one, in a forward-only and read-only manner. The good news about the `SqlDataReader` is that it represents the fastest way to read data from the database, and the bad news is that it needs an open connection to operate—no other database operations can be performed on that connection until the reader is closed. In our solution, you'll load all the data returned by the SqlDataReader into a DataTable object (which is capable of storing the data offline without needing an open connection), which will allow you to close the database connection very quickly.

The DataTable class can store a result set locally without needing an open connection to SQL Server, and it isn't data provider–specific, like the other ADO.NET objects mentioned so far (whose names begin with Sql because they're SQL Server–specific).

■Tip A "parent" of the DataTable object is the DataSet, which is a very smart object that represents something like an in-memory database. DataSet is capable of storing data tables, their data types, relationships between tables, and so on. Because of their complexity, DataSets consume a lot of memory, so it's good to avoid them when possible. We won't use any DataSets when building BalloonShop.

Here's a simple example of reading some records from the database and saving them to a DataTable:

```
// Open the connection
conn.Open();
// Create the SqlDataReader object by executing the command
SqlDataReader reader = comm.ExecuteReader();
// Create a new DataTable and populate it from the SqlDataReader
DataTable table = new DataTable();
table.Load(reader);
// Close the reader and the connection
reader.Close();
conn.Close();
```

Implementing Generic Data Access Code

So far in the examples, we've used classes whose names start with Sql: SqlConnection, SqlCommand, and SqlDataReader. These objects and all the others whose names start with Sql are specifically created for SQL Server, and are part of the **SQL Server Managed Data Provider**. The SQL Server Managed Data Provider is the low-level interface between the database and your program. The ADO.NET objects that use this provider are grouped in the System.Data.SqlClient namespace, so you need to import this namespace when you need to access these classes directly.

The .NET Framework ships with managed data providers for SQL Server (System.Data. SqlClient namespaces), Oracle (System.Data.Oracle), OLE DB (System.Data.OleDb), and ODBC (System.Data.Odbc).

To keep your application as independent as possible to the backend database, we'll use a trick to avoid using database-specific classes, such as SqlConnection. Instead, we'll let the application decide at runtime which provider to use, depending on the connection string provided.

■Tip If you're familiar with object-oriented programming (OOP) theory, you'll find it interesting to hear this extra bit of information. In our code, we'll use database-agnostic classes, such as `DbConnection` and `DbCommand`, instead of `SqlConnection` and `SqlCommand`. At execution time, objects of these classes will contain instances of their database-specific variants, through polymorphism. As a result, for example, calling a method on the `DbConnection` class will have the similar method from `SqlConnection` executed. Using this trick, if you change the backend database, the compiled code keeps working with absolutely no changes, as long as the stored procedures are implemented the same under the new database. You can download some free material on OOP with C# from my personal web site, at `http://www.cristiandarie.ro`.

Although using SQL Server–specific classes was better for the sake of keeping examples simple, in practice we'll use a method that doesn't make the C# code depend (in theory, at least) on a specific database server product.

The new ADO.NET classes that allow for generic data access functionality—such as `DbConnection`, `DbCommand`, and so on—are grouped under the `System.Data.Common` namespace.

The first step in implementing database-agnostic data access is to use the `DbProviderFactory` class to create a new database provider factory object:

```
// Create a new database provider factory
DbProviderFactory factory =
                DbProviderFactories.GetFactory("System.Data.SqlClient");
```

This piece of code, because of the `System.Data.SqlClient` parameter passed, will have the factory object contain a SQL Server database provider factory (the term *factory* generally refers to a class that builds class instances, or objects, for you). In practice, the `System.Data.SqlClient` string parameter is kept in a configuration file, allowing you to have C# code that really doesn't know what kind of database it's dealing with.

The database provider factory class is capable of creating a database-specific connection object through its `CreateConnection` method. However, you'll keep the reference to the connection object stored using the generic `DbConnection` reference:

```
// Obtain a database-specific connection object
DbConnection conn = factory.CreateConnection();
```

So, in practice, the connection object will actually contain a `SqlConnection` object if the backend database is SQL Server, an `OracleConnection` if the backend database is Oracle, and so on. However, instead of working with `SqlConnection` or `OracleConnection` objects, we simply use `DbConnection` and let it decide at runtime what kind of object to create in the background.

After you have a connection object, you can simply set its properties the familiar way, just as you would with a "normal" connection object:

```
// Set the connection string
conn.ConnectionString = "... connection string ...";
```

Okay, so you have the connection, but what about executing the command? Well, it just so happens that the connection object has a method named `CreateCommand` that returns a database command object. Just like with the connection object, `CreateCommand` returns a database-specific command object, but you'll keep the reference stored using a database-neutral object: DbCommand. Here's the line of code that does the job:

```
// Create a database specific command object
DbCommand comm = conn.CreateCommand();
```

Now that you have a connection object and a command object, you can play with them just like the good old days. Here's a fairly complete (and almost working) ADO.NET code listing that loads the list of departments into a DataTable without knowing what kind of database it's working with:

```
// Create a new database provider factory
DbProviderFactory factory =
                DbProviderFactories.GetFactory("System.Data.SqlClient");
// Create the connection object
DbConnection conn = factory.CreateConnection();
// Initialize the connection string
conn.ConnectionString = "... connection string ...";
// Create the command object and set its properties
DbCommand comm = conn.CreateCommand();
comm.CommandText = "CatalogGetDepartments";
comm.CommandType = CommandType.StoredProcedure;
// Open the connection
conn.Open();
// Execute the command and save the results in a DataTable
DbDataReader reader = comm.ExecuteReader();
DataTable table = new DataTable();
table.Load(reader);
// Close the reader and the connection
reader.Close();
conn.Close();
```

Catching and Handling Exceptions

Although ideally our code will run without any unpleasant surprises, there's always a possibility that something might go wrong when processing client requests. In the context of a live web application, errors can happen unexpectedly for various reasons, such as software failures (operating system or database server crashes, viruses, and so on), hardware failures, or even bad or unexpected input user data.

The best strategy to deal with these unexpected problems is to implement error-handling mechanisms that intercept the errors and handle them appropriately. And here we'll meet **exceptions**.

Exceptions represent the modern way of intercepting and handling runtime errors in object-oriented languages—such as C#. When a runtime error occurs in your code, the execution is interrupted, and an exception is generated (or **raised**). If the exception is not handled by the local code that generated it, the exception goes up through the methods in the stack trace. If it isn't handled anywhere, it's finally caught by the .NET Framework, which generates an error message. If the error happens in an ASP.NET page during a client request, ASP.NET displays an error page, eventually including debugging information, to the visitor. (The good news in this scenario is that ASP.NET can be instructed to display a custom error page instead of the default one—you'll do that by the end of the chapter.)

On the other hand, if the exception is dealt with in the code, execution continues normally, and the visitor will never know a problem ever happened when handling the page request.

The general strategy to deal with runtime exceptions is as follows:

- If the error is not critical, deal with it in code, allowing the code to continue executing normally, and the visitor will never know an error happened.

- If the error is critical, handle it partially with code to reduce the negative effects as much as possible, and then let the error propagate to the presentation tier that will show the visitor a nice-looking "Houston, we have a problem" page.

- For the errors that you can't anticipate, the last line of defense is still the presentation tier, which logs the error and politely asks the visitor to come back later.

For any kind of error, it's good to let the site administrator (or the technical staff) know about the problem. Possible options include sending details about the error to a custom database table, to the Windows Event log, or by email. At the end of this chapter, you'll learn how to send an email to the site administrator with detailed information when an error happens.

In our data access code, you'll consider any error as critical. As a result, you'll minimize potential damage by closing the database connection immediately, logging the error, and then letting it propagate to the business tier.

■Note   The business logic you see in the business tier code can control which exceptions pass through it. Any exception generated by the data access code can be caught and handled by the business tier. In case the business tier doesn't handle it, the exception propagates to the presentation tier, where it's logged once again (so the administrator will know it was a critical error), and the visitor is shown a nice error message asking him to come back later.

So, in our approach, data access errors that are handled somewhere before getting to the visitor are logged only once (in the data access code). Critical errors that affect the visitor's browsing experience (by displaying the error message) are logged twice—the first time when they are thrown by the data access code and the second time when they display the error message for the visitor.

The theory sounds good enough, but how do we put it into practice? First, you need to learn how to work with exceptions. Exceptions are dealt with in C# code using the try-catch-finally construct, whose simple version looks something like

```
try
{
  // code that might generate an exception
}
catch (Exception ex)
{
  // code that is executed only in case of an exception
```

```
  // (exception's details are accessible through the ex object)
}
finally
{
  // code that executes at the end, no matter if
  // an exception was generated or not
}
```

You place inside the try block any code that you suspect might possibly generate errors. If an exception is generated, the execution is immediately passed to the catch block. If no exceptions are generated in the try block, the catch block is bypassed completely. In the end, no matter whether an exception occurred or not, the finally block is executed.

The finally block is important because it's guaranteed to execute no matter what (it executes even if a return statement is executed inside the try block!). If any database operations are performed in the try block, it's a standard practice to close the database connection in the finally block to ensure that no open connections remain active on the database server. This is useful because open connections consume resources on the database server and can even keep database resources locked, which can cause problems for other concurrently running database activities.

Both the finally and catch blocks are optional, but (obviously) the whole construct only makes sense if at least one of them is present. If no catch block exists (and you have only try and finally), the exception is not handled; the code stops executing, and the exception propagates to the higher levels in the class hierarchy, but not before executing the finally block (which, as stated previously, is guaranteed to execute no matter what happens).

Runtime exceptions propagate from the point they were raised through the call stack of your program. So, if an exception is generated in the database stored procedure, it is immediately passed to the data access code. If the data tier handles the error using a try-catch construct, then everything's fine, and the business tier and the presentation tier will never know that an error occurred. If the data tier doesn't handle the exception, the exception is then propagated to the business tier, and if the business tier doesn't handle it, the exception then propagates to the presentation tier. If the error isn't handled in the presentation tier either, the exception is finally propagated to the ASP.NET runtime that will deal with it by presenting an error page to the visitor.

There are cases when you want to catch the exception, respond to it somehow, and then allow it to propagate through the call stack anyway. This will be the case in the BalloonShop data access code, where we want to catch the exceptions to log them, but afterward we let them propagate to higher-level classes that know better how to handle the situation and decide how critical the error is. To rethrow an error after you've caught it in the catch block, you use the throw statement:

```
try
{
  // code that might generate an exception
}
catch (Exception ex)
{
  // code that is executed only in case of an exception
  throw;
}
```

As you can see in the code snippet, exceptions are represented in .NET code by the Exception class. The .NET Framework contains a number of specialized exception classes that are generated on certain events, and you can even create your own. However, these topics are out of the scope of this book.

See the C# language reference for complete details about using the try-catch-finally construct. In this chapter, you'll see it in action in the data access code, where it catches potential data access errors to report them to the site administrator.

Sending Emails

Speaking of reporting errors, in BalloonShop you'll report errors by emailing them to the site administrator (or to the person you designate to handle them). Alternatives to this solution consist of using the Windows Event log, saving the error to the database, or even saving to a text file.

To send emails, you need the SmtpClient and MailMessage classes from the System.Net.Mail namespace.

MailMessage has four important properties that you set before sending an email: From, To, Subject, and Body. These properties can also be set through MailMessage's constructor, which accepts them as parameters. After the MailMessage object is properly set up, you send it using the SmtpClient class.

When working with SmtpClient, you can set its Host property to the address of an external SMTP (Simple Mail Transfer Protocol) server; otherwise, the mail is sent through the local SMTP service in Windows. Note that the local SMTP service must be installed in Windows before you can use it.

Note Unlike Windows XP, Windows Vista doesn't ship with an SMTP server. If your Windows version doesn't include an SMTP server and you still want to use a local SMTP server for testing, try searching the Web for "free SMTP server"—we've successfully used such free servers in the past for testing purposes.

The standard code that sends an email looks like the following code snippet (you need to replace the text in italics with your own data):

```
// Configure mail client
SmtpClient smtpClient = new SmtpClient("SMTP server address");
smtpClient.Credentials = new System.Net.NetworkCredential("SMTP user name", ➥
"SMTP password");
// Create the mail message
MailMessage mailMessage = new MailMessage("from", "to", "subject", "body");
// Send mail
smtpClient.Send(mailMessage);
```

If you're having problems, before trying a web search, first look at http://www. systemnetmail.com—this site may contain the solution to your problem.

Writing the Business Tier Code

It's time to upgrade your BalloonShop solution with some new bits of code. The following exercise uses much of the theory presented so far, while implementing the data access code. You'll add the following C# classes to your application:

- GenericDataAccess contains the generic database access code, implementing basic error-handling and logging functionality.

- CatalogAccess contains the product catalog business logic.

- BalloonShopConfiguration provides easy access to various configuration settings (that are generally read from web.config), such as the database connection string, and so on.

- Utilities contains miscellaneous functionality such as sending emails, which will be used from various places in BalloonShop.

Follow the steps of the exercise to add these classes to your project.

Exercise: Implementing the Data Access Code

1. Open the web.config configuration file (double-click its name in Solution Explorer) and update the `<connectionStrings>` element like this:

```
<configuration>
    <appSettings/>
    <connectionStrings>
      <add name="BalloonShopConnection" connectionString="Server=(local)\➥
SqlExpress; Database=BalloonShop; User=balloonshop;Password=ecommerce"➥
providerName="System.Data.SqlClient" />
    </connectionStrings>
    <system.web>
    <!--
```

■**Note** You might need to adapt the connection string to match your particular SQL Server configuration. Also, you should type the `<add>` element on a single line, not split in multiple lines as shown in the previous code snippet.

2. Find the `<appSettings/>` element in web.config and alter it by adding the other necessary configuration data:

```
<appSettings>
    <add key="MailServer" value="mail server address" />
    <add key="MailUsername" value="mail username " />
    <add key="MailPassword" value="mail password" />
    <add key="MailFrom" value="mail address" />
    <add key="EnableErrorLogEmail" value="true" />
```

```
        <add key="ErrorLogEmail" value="errors@example.com" />
    </appSettings>
```

■Note Make sure you include a working server address and a valid email account, if you intend to use the
email logging feature. Otherwise, just set `EnableErrorLogEmail` to false.

---

3. Right-click the project's name in Solution Explorer and choose **Add New Item** from the context menu.

4. Choose the **Class** template, and set its name to BalloonShopConfiguration.cs. Click **Add**.

   You'll be asked about creating a new folder named App_Code and adding your class to that folder. This
   is a special folder in ASP.NET. Choose **Yes**.

5. Modify the BalloonShopConfiguration class like this:

```
using System.Configuration;

    /// <summary>
    /// Repository for BalloonShop configuration settings
    /// </summary>
    public static class BalloonShopConfiguration
    {
      // Caches the connection string
      private static string dbConnectionString;
      // Caches the data provider name
      private static string dbProviderName;

      static BalloonShopConfiguration()
      {
        dbConnectionString = ConfigurationManager.ConnectionStrings ➡
    ["BalloonShopConnection"].ConnectionString;
        dbProviderName = ConfigurationManager.ConnectionStrings ➡
    ["BalloonShopConnection"].ProviderName;
      }

      // Returns the connection string for the BalloonShop database
      public static string DbConnectionString
      {
        get
        {
          return dbConnectionString;
        }
      }

      // Returns the data provider name
      public static string DbProviderName
      {
        get
        {
          return dbProviderName;
```

```
    }
  }


  // Returns the address of the mail server
  public static string MailServer
  {
    get
    {
      return ConfigurationManager.AppSettings["MailServer"];
    }
  }

  // Returns the email username
  public static string MailUsername
  {
    get
    {
      return ConfigurationManager.AppSettings["MailUsername"];
    }
  }

  // Returns the email password
  public static string MailPassword
  {
    get
    {
      return ConfigurationManager.AppSettings["MailPassword"];
    }
  }

  // Returns the email password
  public static string MailFrom
  {
    get
    {
      return ConfigurationManager.AppSettings["MailFrom"];
    }
  }

  // Send error log emails?
  public static bool EnableErrorLogEmail
  {
```

```
    get
    {
      return bool.Parse(ConfigurationManager.AppSettings
      ["EnableErrorLogEmail"]);
    }
  }

  // Returns the email address where to send error reports
  public static string ErrorLogEmail
  {
    get
    {
      return ConfigurationManager.AppSettings["ErrorLogEmail"];
    }
  }
}
```

6. Right-click the **App_Code** folder in Solution Explorer and choose **Add New Item** from the context menu.

7. Choose the **Class** template and set the new class name to Utilities.cs. Click **Add**.

8. Write the following code into Utilities.cs.

■**Tip** Note that we've removed the unnecessary using statements. Visual Web Developer can help you clean them up if you right-click the editing window and choose **Organize Usings ➤ Remove Unused Usings**.

```
using System;
  using System.Net;
  using System.Net.Mail;

  /// <summary>
  /// Class contains miscellaneous functionality
  /// </summary>
  public static class Utilities
  {
    static Utilities()
    {
      //
      // TODO: Add constructor logic here
      //
    }

    // Generic method for sending emails
    public static void SendMail(string from, string to, string subject,
    string body)
    {
      // Configure mail client
      SmtpClient mailClient = new
SmtpClient(BalloonShopConfiguration.MailServer);
```

```
      // Set credentials (for SMTP servers that require authentication)
      mailClient.Credentials = new NetworkCredential(BalloonShopConfigurati➡
on.MailUsername, BalloonShopConfiguration.MailPassword);
      // Create the mail message
      MailMessage mailMessage = new MailMessage(from, to, subject, body);
      // Send mail
      mailClient.Send(mailMessage);
    }

    // Send error log mail
    public static void LogError(Exception ex)
    {
      // get the current date and time
      string dateTime = DateTime.Now.ToLongDateString() + ", at "
                   + DateTime.Now.ToShortTimeString();
      // stores the error message
      string errorMessage = "Exception generated on " + dateTime;
      // obtain the page that generated the error
      System.Web.HttpContext context = System.Web.HttpContext.Current;
      errorMessage += "\n\n Page location: " + context.Request.RawUrl;
      // build the error message
      errorMessage += "\n\n Message: " + ex.Message;
      errorMessage += "\n\n Source: " + ex.Source;
      errorMessage += "\n\n Method: " + ex.TargetSite;
      errorMessage += "\n\n Stack Trace: \n\n" + ex.StackTrace;
      // send error email in case the option is activated in web.config
      if (BalloonShopConfiguration.EnableErrorLogEmail)
      {
        string from = BalloonShopConfiguration.MailFrom;
        string to = BalloonShopConfiguration.ErrorLogEmail;
        string subject = "BalloonShop Error Report";
        string body = errorMessage;
        SendMail(from, to, subject, body);
      }
    }
  }
}
```

9. Right-click the **App_Code** folder in Solution Explorer and choose **Add New Item** from the context menu. Choose the **Class** template and set its name to GenericDataAccess.cs. Click **Add**.

10. Write the following code into GenericDataAccess.cs:

```
using System;
using System.Data;
using System.Data.Common;

/// <summary>
/// Class contains generic data access functionality to be accessed from
/// the business tier
/// </summary>
```

```csharp
public static class GenericDataAccess
{
  // static constructor
  static GenericDataAccess()
  {
    //
    // TODO: Add constructor logic here
    //
  }

  // executes a command and returns the results as a DataTable object
  public static DataTable ExecuteSelectCommand(DbCommand command)
  {
    // The DataTable to be returned
    DataTable table;
    // Execute the command, making sure the connection gets closed in the
    // end
    try
    {
      // Open the data connection
      command.Connection.Open();
      // Execute the command and save the results in a DataTable
      DbDataReader reader = command.ExecuteReader();
      table = new DataTable();
      table.Load(reader);

      // Close the reader
      reader.Close();
    }
    catch (Exception ex)
    {
      Utilities.LogError(ex);
      throw;
    }
    finally
    {
      // Close the connection
      command.Connection.Close();
    }
    return table;
  }

  // creates and prepares a new DbCommand object on a new connection
  public static DbCommand CreateCommand()
  {
    // Obtain the database provider name
    string dataProviderName = BalloonShopConfiguration.DbProviderName;
```

```
// Obtain the database connection string
string connectionString = BalloonShopConfiguration.DbConnectionString;
// Create a new data provider factory
DbProviderFactory factory = DbProviderFactories.
GetFactory(dataProviderName);
// Obtain a database-specific connection object
DbConnection conn = factory.CreateConnection();
// Set the connection string
conn.ConnectionString = connectionString;
// Create a database-specific command object
DbCommand comm = conn.CreateCommand();
// Set the command type to stored procedure
comm.CommandType = CommandType.StoredProcedure;
// Return the initialized command object
return comm;
  }
}
```

11. In Solution Explorer, right-click the **App_Code** folder and choose **Add New Item.** Using the window that appears, create a new class named CatalogAccess (which would reside in a file named CatalogAccess.cs). Add the new code to the file:

```
using System;
using System.Data;
using System.Data.Common;

/// <summary>
/// Product catalog business tier component
/// </summary>
public static class CatalogAccess
{
  static CatalogAccess()
  {
    //
    // TODO: Add constructor logic here
    //
  }

  // Retrieve the list of departments
  public static DataTable GetDepartments()
  {
    // get a configured DbCommand object
    DbCommand comm = GenericDataAccess.CreateCommand();
    // set the stored procedure name
    comm.CommandText = "GetDepartments";
    // execute the stored procedure and return the results
    return GenericDataAccess.ExecuteSelectCommand(comm);
  }
}
```

How It Works: The Business Tier

Let's take some time to understand the code you just wrote.

First, you added some configuration settings to the `web.config` configuration file. `web.config` is an external configuration XML file managed by ASP.NET. This complex and powerful file can include many options regarding the application's security, performance, behavior, and so on.

Saving data to `web.config` is beneficial because you can change it independently of your C# code, which now doesn't need to be recompiled when you change the address of the mail server or the database connection string. This detail, combined with the fact that the data access code is written to be database-independent, makes the whole data access code powerful.

Then, you added the `BalloonShopConfiguration` class, which is simply a collection of static properties that return data from `web.config`. Using this class instead of needing to read `web.config` all the time will make your life easier in the long run. The performance is improved as well because the class can cache the values read from `web.config` instead of reading them on every request. The first place you use the `BalloonShopConfiguration` class is the `Utility` class, which for now only contains code that sends emails.

Next, you implemented the `GenericDataAccess` class, whose purpose is to store a series of common database access operations, to avoid typing it all over again in other places. The two methods it contains now are

- `CreateCommand`, which creates a `DbCommand` object, sets some standard properties to it, and returns the configured object. If you preferred to use a database-specific command object, such as `SqlCommand`, the code would have been a bit simpler, but in this case we prefer to have database-independent access code, as explained earlier in this chapter. The `CreateCommand` method uses the steps presented earlier in this chapter to create a command object specific to the database implementation you're working with, wrap that instance into a generic `DbCommand` reference, and return this reference. This way, external classes will be able to call `CreateCommand` to get an already configured—with a prepared connection—`DbCommand` object.

- `ExecuteSelectCommand`, which is essentially a wrapper for `DbCommand`'s `ExecuteReader` method, except it returns the results as a `DataTable` instead of a `DataReader`. Using the `DataTable` ensures that the database connection is kept open as short as possible. In this method, you implement an error-handling technique that guarantees that in case of an exception, the administrator is informed by email (if the application is configured to do so), the database connection is properly closed, and the error is rethrown. We decided to let the error propagate because this class is at too low a level to know how to properly handle the errors. At this point, we're only interested in keeping the database safe (by closing the connection) and reporting any eventual error. The best example of how a client class can use `GenericDataAccess` to work with the `BalloonShop` database is the `GetDepartments` method in the `CatalogAccess` class.

All the classes you've added are static classes, which are composed exclusively of static members. Note that some understanding of basic OOP terminology—such as classes, objects, constructors, methods, properties, fields, instance members and static members, public data and private data, and so on—is an important prerequisite for this book. These topics are covered in many articles on the Internet, such as the ones you can find for free download at `http://www.cristiandarie.ro/downloads.html`.

■**Note** As opposed to instance class members, which always belong to a class instance (an object, that is), static class members belong to the class as a whole. Static members can only be accessed through the class name—such as in `Math.Sin()`—and are typically used when creating generic functionality that isn't tied to a particular instance. A class can contain both static and instance members, but a class that is declared static can only contain static members. The static class fields can be initialized in the static constructor, which is executed only once in the application lifetime— just before the first static field, property, or method of the class is accessed. Under the hood, the static class members are called on a global instance of that class, which is not destroyed by the GC (garbage collector) after execution.

Because the static constructor is called only once per application lifetime, and the global instance is never destroyed, we can ensure that any initializations performed by the static constructor (such as reading the database connection string) are performed only once, and the values of any static members are persisted. A static class member can call or access another static class member directly. However, if you needed to access an instance class member (nonstatic class member) from a static class member, you had to create an instance of the class, even from a method of that class, to access that member. For more information about static class members, please read an OOP C# tutorial, such as the one available for download from Cristian Darie's web site, at `http://www.cristiandarie.ro/downloads/`.

We've chosen to use static members mainly to improve performance. Because static classes and static members are initialized only once, they don't need to be reinstantiated each time a new visitor makes a new request; instead, their global instances are used. In the presentation tier, you'll display your list of departments with a call like this:

```
list.DataSource = CatalogAccess.GetDepartments();
```

If `GetDepartments` is an instance method, you need to create a separate instance of the `CatalogAccess` class instead of using the static instance, which would have had, obviously, a bigger performance impact:

```
CatalogAccess catalogAccess = new CatalogAccess();
list.DataSource = catalogAccess.GetDepartments();
```

In `BalloonShopConfiguration`, you've implemented an additional trick to improve performance by caching connection string data using static fields (`dbConnectionString` and `dbProviderName`), whose data is read in from `web.config` in the class's static constructor. The static class constructor is called only once per application's life cycle, so the `web.config` file won't be read on every database operation, but just once when the class is initialized.

Displaying the List of Departments

Now that everything is in place in the other tiers, all you have to do is create the presentation tier—the final goal you've been working toward from the beginning. As you saw in the figures at the beginning of this chapter, the departments list needs to look something like Figure 4-15 when the site is loaded in the web browser.

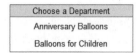

Figure 4-15. *The departments list when loaded in the web browser*

You'll implement this as a separate Web User Control named `DepartmentsList`, and then you'll add the user control to the Master Page to make it available to all the site's pages.

The list of departments needs to be dynamically generated based on what you have in the database. Fortunately, the .NET Framework provides a few useful web controls that can help you solve this problem without writing too much code. For example, the `DataList` control can be set to simply take a `DataTable` object as input and generate content based on it.

Before actually writing the user control, let's prepare the BalloonShop CSS file.

Preparing the Field: Themes, Skins, and Styles

Cascading Style Sheets (CSS) files are a standard repository for font and formatting information that can be easily applied to various parts of the site. For example, instead of setting fonts, colors, and dimensions for a `Label` control, you can set its `CssClass` property to one of the existing styles. The CSS file is applied at the client side and doesn't imply any server-side processing on the ASP.NET application. A typical CSS style definition looks like this:

```
.AdminButtonText
{
  color: Black;
  font-family: Verdana, Helvetica, sans-serif;
  font-size: 12px;
}
```

ASP.NET, since version 2.0, brings in the notions of themes and skins. **Skins** are like CSS files in that they contain various properties, but they do this on a control-type basis, they allow setting properties that aren't accessible through CSS (such as an image's `src` property), and they are applied on the server side. Skin definitions are saved in files with the `.skin` extension (these files can store one or more skin definitions) and look much like the definition of an ASP.NET control. A typical skin definition looks like this:

```
<asp:Image runat="server" SkinID="BalloonShopLogo" src="/Images/BalloonShop.png"/>
```

This skin entry is a named skin because it has a `SkinID`. In this case, when adding images you want to implement this skin, you need to set their `SkinID` properties to `BalloonShopLogo`. If you don't specify a `SkinID` when creating the skin, that skin becomes the default skin for its control type.

Just as with CSS files, you use skins when you want to reuse a particular control format in more controls. However, your `DepartmentsList.ascx` Web User Control and its contents will be one-of-a-kind, and using a skin for just one instance of a control wouldn't bring much of a benefit. As a result, we won't build any skins in this chapter, but you'll meet them later in the book, where it makes more sense to use them.

A **theme** is a collection of CSS files, skins, and images. You can add more themes to a web site and allow for easily changing the look of your site by switching the active theme at design time or even at runtime.

In the exercise, you'll create a new theme called BalloonShopDefault, and you'll add a CSS file to it, which will be then used to display the list of departments.

Exercise: Preparing the Styles

1. Right-click the root entry in Solution Explorer, and then choose **Add ASP.NET Folder ➤ Theme**. Set the name of the new folder to **BalloonShopDefault**, as shown in Figure 4-16.

Figure 4-16. *Adding a new theme folder to the BallonShop project*

2. Right-click the **BalloonShopDefault** entry in Solution Explorer and then choose **Add New Item**. From the **Templates** window, choose **Style Sheet** and name it BalloonShop.css. Click **Add**.

3. Open BalloonShop.css, delete its default contents, and add these styles to it:

```
body {
    font-family:Arial;
    font-size:10pt;
    color: Black;
}
a {
    text-decoration: none;
    color:black;
}
a:hover {
    text-decoration: underline;
}

.Window {
    width: 100%;
}
```

```css
.Window .Main {
  width: 950px;
  margin: auto;
}
.Window .Main .Left {
  width: 220px;
  float: left;
}
.Window .Main .Left .Container {
  margin: 0px 0px 10px 10px;
  float: left;
}
.Window .Main .Right {
  width: 730px;
  float: left;
}
.Window .Main .Right .Header{
  margin: 5px 5px 5px 0px;
  width: 100%;
  text-align: center;
}
.Window .Main .Right .Contents{
  margin: 5px 5px 5px 0px;
  width: 100%;
  float: left;
}

.DepartmentsList{
  border: #01a647 1px solid;
  text-align: center;
  margin-top: 20px;
}
.DepartmentsListHead
{
  border: #01a647 1px solid;
  background-color: #99FFCC;
}
a.DepartmentUnselected {
  line-height: 25px;
  text-decoration: none;
  color: Black;
}
a.DepartmentUnselected:hover {
  text-decoration: underline;
}
a.DepartmentSelected {
  line-height: 25px;
  font-weight: bold;
  text-decoration: none;
  color: Black;
}
```

4. Finally, open `web.config` to enable the default theme:

```
<system.web>
    ...
        <pages theme="BalloonShopDefault" />
        ...
```

How It Works: Using Themes

Having a central place to store style information helps you to easily change the look of the site without changing a line of code.

At this moment, `BalloonShop.css` contains a few styles you'll need for displaying the departments list. These styles refer to the way department names should look when they are unselected, unselected but with the mouse hovering over them, or selected. The CSS file and skin file are added to the default theme, which is enabled in `web.config`, so they'll be accessible from any page of the site.

While you're here, it's worth noticing the built-in features Visual Web Developer has for editing CSS files. While `BalloonShop.css` is open in edit mode, right-click one of its styles and click the **Build Style** menu option. You'll get a dialog box such as the one in Figure 4-17, which permits editing the style visually.

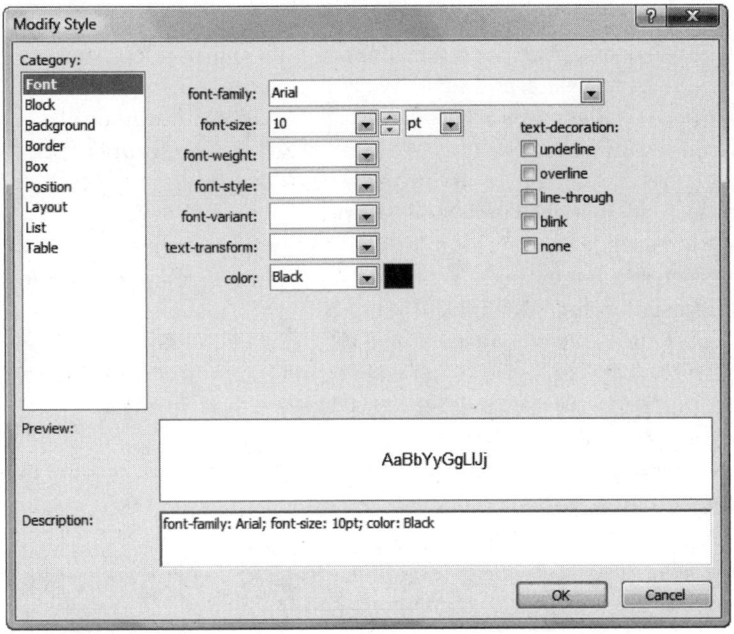

Figure 4-17. *Editing a style in Visual Web Developer*

Building a Link Factory

Creating the list of departments is the first occasion when we need to dynamically generate links in our site—clicking the name of a department needs to take the visitor to the page of that department in our site.

With this occasion, we'll also start preparing a simple class named Link, which we'll call our "link factory" because its sole purpose will be to generate links for us. We want to implement this feature because it's important that all links in BalloonShop have the same form.

For example, in ASP.NET, you read query string parameters by name rather than ordinal, so the following two links would normally have the same output:

- http://www.example.com/Catalog.aspx?DepartmentID=1&CategoryID=2

- http://www.example.com/Catalog.aspx?CategoryID=2&DepartmentID=1

Using the Link class will avoid having different URLs that deliver the same content and help us with URL maintenance. For example, in Chapter 7, we'll update the URLs in our web site to be more friendly to search engines and human visitors browsing your site. Having a central place that generates links will make this feature easy to implement.

Also, at some point in the development process, you'll want certain pages of your site to be accessible only through secured HTTPS connections to ensure the confidentiality of the data passed from the client to the server and back. Such sensitive pages include user login forms, pages where the user enters credit card data, and so on. We don't get into much detail here. However, what you need to know is that pages accessed through HTTPS occupy much of a server's resources, and we only want to use a secure connection when visiting secure pages. Once again, the link factory can come in handy, as it can be configured to generate HTTPS links only for the sections of the web site that need increased security.

Our link factory will always generate absolute links. Most of the time, it's more comfortable to use relative links inside the web site. For example, it's typical for the header image of a site to contain a link to Catalog.aspx rather than the full URL, such as http://www.example.com/Catalog.aspx. In this case, clicking the header image from a secured page would redirect the user to https://www.example.com/Catalog.aspx, so the visitor would end up accessing through a secure connection a page that isn't supposed to be accessed like that (and, in effect, consumes much more server resources than necessary).

To avoid this problem and other similar ones, we'll write a bit of code that makes sure all the links in the web site are absolute links.

Exercise: Creating the Link Class

1. Right-click the **App_Code** folder, select **Add New Item**, select the **Class** template, and type **Link** for the name. Then type the following code for the class:

```
using System;
using System.Web;

/// <summary>
/// Link factory class
/// </summary>
```

```
public class Link
{
  // Builds an absolute URL
  private static string BuildAbsolute(string relativeUri)
  {
    // get current uri
    Uri uri = HttpContext.Current.Request.Url;
    // build absolute path
    string app = HttpContext.Current.Request.ApplicationPath;
    if (!app.EndsWith("/")) app += "/";
    relativeUri = relativeUri.TrimStart('/');
    // return the absolute path
    return HttpUtility.UrlPathEncode(
      String.Format("http://{0}:{1}{2}{3}",
      uri.Host, uri.Port, app, relativeUri));
  }

  // Generate a department URL
  public static string ToDepartment(string departmentId, string page)
  {
    if (page == "1")
      return BuildAbsolute(String.Format("Catalog.aspx?DepartmentID=➥
{0}", departmentId));
    else
      return BuildAbsolute(String.Format("Catalog.aspx?DepartmentID=➥
{0}&Page={1}", departmentId, page));
  }

  // Generate a department URL for the first page
  public static string ToDepartment(string departmentId)
  {
    return ToDepartment(departmentId, "1");
  }
}
```

How It Works: The Link Factory

The link factory contains two public static methods that generate department links. The first of the two methods generates links for department subpages, such as, for example, the second page of products in the "Balloons for Children" category. Calling Link.ToDepartment("2", "3") returns

    http://www.example.com:80/Catalog.aspx?DepartmentID=2&Page=3

The second ToDepartment method is doesn't take the page parameter, and we've included it for those cases when we want to easily obtain the URL of the first page. Calling Link.ToDepartment("2") returns

    http://www.example.com:80/Catalog.aspx?DepartmentID=2

Displaying the Departments

Now everything is in place, the only missing part being the DepartmentsList user control itself. You'll create a folder named UserControls that will hold this user control and the others you will create for BalloonShop.

This user control will contain a DataList control that generates the list of departments. In this exercise, you'll implement most functionality by using the Design View of Visual Web Developer, and you'll see the HTML code that it generates. In other exercises, you'll work directly in Source View mode.

Exercise: Creating DepartmentsList.ascx

1. Make sure that the project isn't currently running (if it is, the editing capabilities are limited), and that the Solution Explorer window is visible (if it isn't, choose **View ➤ Solution Explorer** or use the default **Ctrl+Alt+L** shortcut). Right-click the root entry and select **New Folder**. Enter **UserControls** as the name of the new folder, as shown in Figure 4-18.

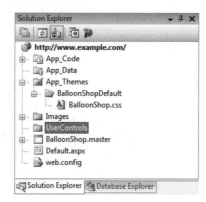

Figure 4-18. *Creating the UserControls folder*

2. Let's now create a new Web User Control in the UserControls folder. Right-click the **UserControls** folder and then choose **Add New Item**. Select the **Web User Control** template and name it DepartmentsList.ascx (or simply DepartmentsList). Check the **Place code in separate file** check box, make sure the language is **Visual C#**, and click **Add**.

3. Switch DepartmentsList.ascx to Design View. Make sure the toolbox is visible (**Ctrl+Alt+X**), open the **Data** tab, and double-click the **DataList** entry. This will add a DataList control to DepartmentsList.ascx.

4. Use the **Properties** window (see Figure 4-19) to change the properties of your DataList, as shown in Table 4-3. (If the **Properties** window is not visible, press **F4** to activate it.)

Table 4-3. *Setting the DataList Properties*

Property Name	Value
(ID)	list
Width	200px
CssClass	DepartmentsList
HeaderStyle-CssClass	DepartmentsListHead

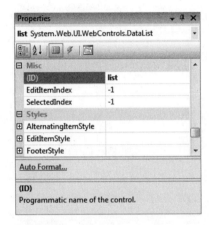

Figure 4-19. *Changing the name of the DataList control*

5. Open DepartmentsList.ascx in Design View, right-click the **DataList** control, and select **Edit Template ➤ Header and Footer Templates**.

6. Type **Choose a Department** in the header template (see Figure 4-20).

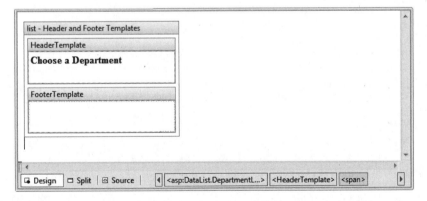

Figure 4-20. *Editing the header template of the DataList control*

7. Right-click the **DataList** and select **Edit Template ➤ Item Templates**.

8. Drag a HyperLink control from the Standard tab of the toolbox to the ItemTemplate.

9. Set the Text property of the HyperLink to an empty string. The list control should then look like Figure 4-21.

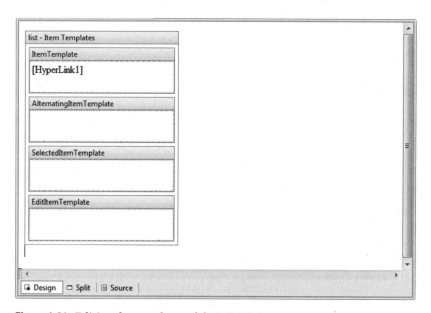

Figure 4-21. *Editing the templates of the DataList*

10. Switch to Source View, where you need to make few changes to the HyperLink control, as shown in the following code snippet of the DataList control. Note that in your case, the order of the elements of the DataList control may be different.

```
<asp:DataList ID="list" runat="server" Width="200px">
    <HeaderStyle CssClass="DepartmentListHead" />
    <HeaderTemplate>
      Choose a Department
    </HeaderTemplate>
    <ItemTemplate>
      <asp:HyperLink
ID="HyperLink1"
Runat="server"
NavigateUrl='<%# Link.ToDepartment(Eval("DepartmentID").ToString())%>'
Text='<%# HttpUtility.HtmlEncode(Eval("Name").ToString()) %>'
ToolTip='<%# HttpUtility.HtmlEncode(Eval("Description").ToString()) %>'
CssClass='<%# Eval("DepartmentID").ToString() ==
Request.QueryString["DepartmentID"] ? "DepartmentSelected" :
"DepartmentUnselected" %>'>
      </asp:HyperLink>
    </ItemTemplate>
</asp:DataList>
```

■**Tip** For the CssClass properties, you will get a warning that says "The class or CssClass value is not defined." This happens because the location of the CSS class is altered at runtime, so the IDE doesn't pick up the styles from the theme, but the code does when it runs.

11. Now open the code-behind file of the user control (DepartmentsList.ascx.cs) and modify the Page_Load event handler function like this:

```
// Load department details into the DataList
    protected void Page_Load(object sender, EventArgs e)
    {
        // CatalogAccess.GetDepartments returns a DataTable object containing
        // department data, which is read in the ItemTemplate of the DataList
        list.DataSource = CatalogAccess.GetDepartments();
        // Needed to bind the data bound controls to the data source
        list.DataBind();
    }
```

12. Open BalloonShop.master in Design View. Drag DepartmentsList.ascx from Solution Explorer and drop it near the "Place list of departments here" text. Delete the text from the cell, so that only the user control is there, as shown in Figure 4-22.

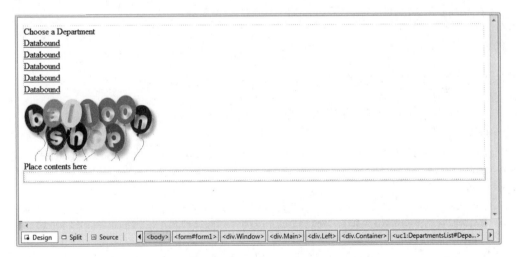

Figure 4-22. *Adding the list of departments to the Master Page*

13. Finish the exercise by creating Catalog.aspx, the page that is referenced by the departments list links. Right-click the name of the project in Solution Explorer and select **Add New Item**. Choose the **Web Form** template, set its name to Catalog.aspx, make sure both check boxes **Place code in separate file** and **Select Master Page** are checked, and click **Add**. When asked for a Master Page file, choose BalloonShop.master.

14. Open `Catalog.aspx` in Source View and change its title to **BalloonShop: Catalog**, like so:

```
<%@ Page Title="BalloonShop: Catalog" Language="C#" MasterPageFile= ➥
    "~/BalloonSho p.master"
    AutoEventWireup="true" CodeFile="Catalog.aspx.cs"
    Inherits="Catalog" %>
```

15. Press **F5** to execute the project. Then select one of the departments (see Figure 4-23).

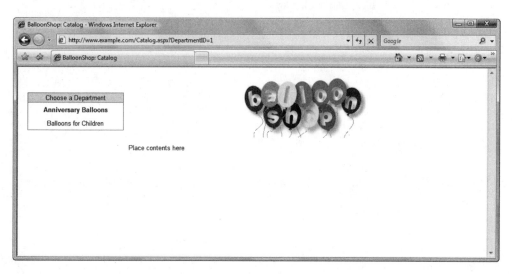

Figure 4-23. *Executing the BalloonShop project*

How It Works: The DepartmentsList User Control

The heart of the `DepartmentsList` Web User Control is its `DataList` control, which generates the list of departments. To make a `DataList` work, you need to edit its `ItemTemplate` property at the least. You also edited its `HeaderTemplate`.

The templates can be edited either in Design View mode or in Source View mode. It's easier to work with the designer, but editing the HTML directly is more powerful and allows some tweaks that aren't always possible with the designer.

The `DataList` control, which generates the list of departments, is flexible and configurable. The most important step for configuring this control is to set its `ItemTemplate` property. When the `DataList` is bound to a data source, the `ItemTemplate` generates a new data list entry for each row of the data source. In our case, the `DataList` object contains a `HyperLink` control in its `ItemTemplate`, so we'll have one hyperlink for each record returned from the database. It's important to understand how the data-binding process works. Let's have another look at the code of the `HyperLink`:

```
<asp:HyperLink
    ID="HyperLink1"
    Runat="server"
    NavigateUrl='<%# Link.ToDepartment(Eval("DepartmentID").ToString())%>'
```

```
    Text='<%# HttpUtility.HtmlEncode(Eval("Name").ToString()) %>'
    ToolTip='<%# HttpUtility.HtmlEncode(Eval("Description").ToString()) %>'
    CssClass='<%# Eval("DepartmentID").ToString() ==
    Request.QueryString["DepartmentID"] ? "DepartmentSelected" :
    "DepartmentUnselected" %>'>
</asp:HyperLink>
```

Basically, this piece of code uses Link.ToDepartment to generate a link of the form http://*webserver*/
Catalog.aspx?DepartmentID=XXX for each row retrieved from the data source. In our case, the data source
is a DataTable that contains this information about each department: the DepartmentID, the Name, and the
Description. These details are extracted using the Eval function. For example, Eval("Name") will return the
Name field of the row being processed by the DataList.

Perhaps the most interesting detail about the piece of code that creates the hyperlinks is the way you set CssClass. The
code should make sense if you're familiar with the ternary operator. The expression assigned to the CssClass property
returns "DepartmentSelected" if the DepartmentID from the query string is the same as the DepartmentID of the
row being read from the data source, and "DepartmentUnselected" otherwise. This ensures that after the visitor
clicks a department and the page gets reloaded with a new query string, the selected department is painted using
a different style than the other departments in the list.

■**Tip** The ternary operator has the form condition ? value1 : value2. If the condition is true, value1
is returned; otherwise, value2 is returned. The expression could be rewritten as

if (condition) return value1 else return value2;

Back to the DataList, it's important to know that it accepts more templates that can be used to customize its
appearance, using a schema like the following:

```
<asp:DataList id="list" runat="server">
    <HeaderTemplate>
      <!- contents -->
    </HeaderTemplate>
    <SelectedItemTemplate>
      <!- contents -->
    </SelectedItemTemplate>
    <ItemTemplate>
      <!- contents -->
    </ItemTemplate>
    <AlternatingItemTemplate>
      <!- contents -->
    </AlternatingItemTemplate>
    <FooterTemplate>
      <!- contents -->
    </FooterTemplate>
</asp:DataList>
```

The last piece of the puzzle that makes the list of departments work is the C# code you wrote in DepartmentsList.
ascx.cs. The Page_Load event is fired when loading the data list, with which you ask for the list of departments
from the business tier, and bind that list to the DataList:

```
// Load department details into the DataList
   protected void Page_Load(object sender, EventArgs e)
   {
      // CatalogAccess.GetDepartments returns a DataTable object containing
      // department data, which is read in the ItemTemplate of the DataList
      list.DataSource = CatalogAccess.GetDepartments();
      // Needed to bind the data bound controls to the data source
      list.DataBind();
}
```

It's exciting how the full power of the business tier code you implemented earlier can now be used to populate a DataList control with just a couple of lines of code, isn't it? Keep in mind that you're working on the presentation tier right now. It doesn't matter how the CatalogAccess class or the GetDepartments method is implemented. You just need to know that GetDepartments returns a list of (DepartmentID, Name) pairs. While you are on the presentation tier, you don't really care how Catalog.GetDepartments does what it's supposed to do.

Adding a Custom Error Page

Now, at the final bit of this chapter, you complete the last piece of error-handling functionality for BalloonShop.

At this point, the single piece of error handling that you've implemented is in the data access code. The data access code can't know if an error is serious or if it can simply be ignored, so the only purposes are to make sure the database connection is closed properly and to report the error to the administrator. The exception is rethrown, and it's up to the upper layers of the architecture to decide what to do next with the exception.

The problem is, if the error isn't properly handled anywhere, it generates an ugly error message that your visitors will see—you don't want this to happen.

In the next exercise you will

- Add a custom error page to your site that your visitor will see in case an unhandled error happens. That page will politely ask the visitor to come back later.

- Report the error once again, so the administrator knows that this serious error gets to the visitor and needs to be taken care of as soon as possible.

Adding the custom error page is a very simple task, consisting of building a simple Web Form and configuring it as the default error page in web.config. Reporting unhandled errors is equally simple, by using a class named the Global Application Class. Follow the steps in the exercise to apply all this in practice.

Exercise: Adding a Custom Error Page and Reporting Unhandled Errors

1. Right-click the project entry in Solution Explorer and then select **Add New Item**.

2. Choose the **Global Application Class** template and click **Add**.

3. Modify Application_Error like this:

```
void Application_Error(Object sender, EventArgs e)
  {
    // Log all unhandled errors
    Utilities.LogError(Server.GetLastError());
  }
```

4. In Solution Explorer, double-click **web.config** and add the following element as a child of the `<system.web>` element:

```
<customErrors mode="RemoteOnly" defaultRedirect="Oops.aspx" />
```

Note After this change, remote clients will be forwarded to Oops.aspx when unhandled exceptions are thrown; however, on the local machine, you'll still receive detailed error information. If you want to see the same error message as your visitors, set mode to On instead of RemoteOnly.

5. Add a new Web Form to your application's root, named Oops.aspx. This form *should not* use a Master Page, to make sure nothing gets in the way of displaying our simple error. The page also doesn't need a code-behind file.

6. While in Source View, modify its contents like this:

```
<!DOCTYPE html PUBLIC "-//W3C//DTD XHTML 1.0 Transitional//EN" ➥
    "http://www.w3.org/TR/xhtml1/DTD/xhtml1-transitional.dtd">
    <html xmlns="http://www.w3.org/1999/xhtml">
    <head runat="server">
        <title>BalloonShop: Oops!</title>
    </head>
    <body>
      <form id="form1" runat="server">
        <asp:HyperLink ID="HeaderLink" ImageUrl="~/Images/BalloonShopLogo.png"
    NavigateUrl="~/" ToolTip="BalloonShop logo" Text="BalloonShop logo"
    runat="server" />
        <p>Your request generated an internal error!</p>
        <p>We apologize for the inconvenience. The error has been reported and will
           be fixed as soon as possible. Thank you!</p>
        <p>The <b>BalloonShop</b> team</p>
      </form>
    </body>
    </html>
```

7. Finally, let's remove the text "Place contents here" from BalloonShop.master so that we can test our newly created error page.

How It Works: Error Reporting

Right now, your web site, no matter what happens, will look good. In case of an error, instead of displaying the default error message (which is, of course, not colorful enough for our customers' tastes), it will display a nice-looking error message page.

For a short test, open `web.config` and edit the database connection password from the connection string. Now, trying to load BalloonShop without debugging (Ctrl+F5) generates a runtime exception. Have a look at the custom error page in Figure 4-24.

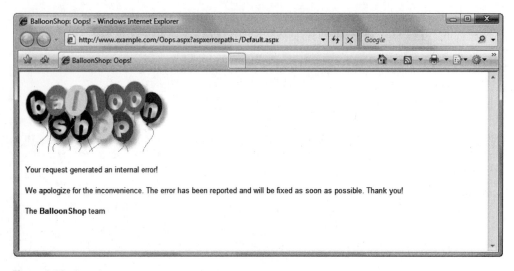

Figure 4-24. *Oops!*

First, this exception is caught in the data access tier, which simply reports it and then rethrows it. The report from the data tier generates an email with contents like shown in Figure 4-25.

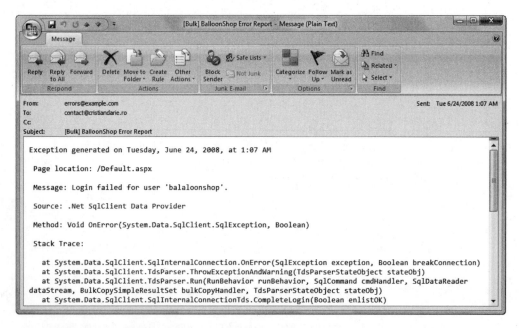

Figure 4-25. *Example of BalloonShop error email report*

This email contains all the significant details about the error. However, the error is rethrown, and because it isn't handled anywhere else, it's finally caught by the presentation tier, which displays the nice error page. A second email is generated, which should be taken seriously because the error caused the visitor to see an error message:

```
Exception generated on Tuesday, June 24, 2008, at 1:07 AM
    Page location: /Default.aspx
    Message: Exception of type 'System.Web.HttpUnhandledException' was thrown.
    Source: System.Web
    Method: Boolean HandleError(System.Exception)
    Stack Trace:
      at System.Web.UI.Page.HandleError(Exception e)
      at System.Web.UI.Page.ProcessRequestMain(Boolean
includeStagesBeforeAsy➡
    ncPoint, Boolean includeStagesAfterAsyncPoint)
      at System.Web.UI.Page.ProcessRequest(Boolean
includeStagesBeforeAsyncPo➡
    int, Boolean includeStagesAfterAsyncPoint)
      at System.Web.UI.Page.ProcessRequest()
      at System.Web.UI.Page.ProcessRequestWithNoAssert(HttpContext context)
      at System.Web.UI.Page.ProcessRequest(HttpContext context)
      at ASP.default_aspx.ProcessRequest(HttpContext context) in ➡
    c:\Windows\M➡icrosoft.NET\Framework\v2.0.50727\Temporary ASP.NET ➡
    Files\root\0a7ff8cb\7bc2fe51\App_Web_tvdzzowf.2.cs:line 0
      at
System.Web.HttpApplication.CallHandlerExecutionStep.System.Web.HttpA➡
    pplication.IExecutionStep.Execute()
      at System.Web.HttpApplication.ExecuteStep(IExecutionStep step,
Boolean&➡
    completedSynchronously)
```

Summary

This long chapter was well worth the effort when you consider how much theory you've learned and applied to the BalloonShop project! In this chapter, you accomplished the following:

- You created the Department table and populated it with data.

- You added a stored procedure to the database and added code to access this stored procedure from the middle tier using a special data access class.

- You added a number of configuration options to web.config, such as the database connection string, to make things easier if you need to change these options.

- You wrote error-handling and reporting code to keep the administrator notified of any errors that happen to the web site.

- You added the DepartmentsList Web User Control to the site.

In the next chapter, you'll continue building the site to include even more exciting functionality!

■ ■ ■

Creating the Product Catalog: Part 2

In the previous chapter, you implemented a selectable list of departments for the BalloonShop web site. However, a product catalog is much more than that list of departments. In this chapter, you'll add many new product catalog features, including displaying product lists and product details.

Review Figures 4-1, 4-2, and 4-3 to get a feel for the new functionality you'll implement in this chapter. More specifically, in this chapter, you will

- Learn about relational data and the types of relationships that occur between data tables, and then create the new data structures in your database.

- Understand how to join related data tables, how to use subqueries, how to implement paging at the data tier level, and even more theory about T-SQL functions and techniques.

- Complete business tier functionality to work with the new stored procedures, including stored procedures with input and output parameters, and use simple data structures to pass requested data to the presentation tier.

- Create new Web Forms and Web User Controls to show your visitors details about your categories, your products, and more.

Yep, that's a lot of material to get through! Take a deep breath, and let's get started!

Storing the New Data

Given the new functionality you are adding in this chapter, it's not surprising that you need to add more data tables to the database. However, this isn't just about adding new data tables. You also need to learn about relational data and the relationships that you can implement between the data tables, so that you can obtain more significant information from your database.

What Makes a Relational Database

It's no mystery that a database is something that stores data. However, today's modern relational database management systems (RDBMSs), such as MySQL, PostgreSQL, SQL Server, Oracle, DB2, and others, have extended this basic role by adding the capability to store and manage relational data.

So what does *relational data* mean? It's easy to see that every piece of data ever written in a real-world database is somehow related to some already existing information. Products are related to categories and departments, orders are related to products and customers, and so on. A relational database keeps its information stored in data tables but is also aware of the relations between them.

These related tables form the relational database, which becomes an object with a significance of its own, rather than simply being a group of unrelated data tables. *Data* becomes *information* only when we give significance to it, and establishing relations with other pieces of data is a good means of doing that.

Look at the product catalog to see what pieces of data it needs and how you can transform this data into information. For the product catalog, you'll need at least three data tables: one for departments, one for categories, and one for products. It's important to note that physically each data table is an independent database object, even if logically it's part of a larger entity—in other words, even though we say that a category *contains* products, the table that contains the products is not inside the table that contains categories. This is not in contradiction with the relational character of the database. Figure 5-1 shows a simple representation of three data tables, including some selected sample data.

When two tables are related, this more specifically means that the *records* of those tables are related. So, if the products table is related to the categories table, this translates into each product record being somehow related to one of the records in the categories table.

Figure 5-1 doesn't show the physical representation of the database, so we didn't list the table names there. Diagrams like this are used to decide *what* needs to be stored in the database. After you know *what* to store, the next step is to decide *how* the listed data is related, which leads to the physical structure for the database. Although Figure 5-1 shows three kinds of data that you want to store, you'll learn later that to implement this structure in the database, you'll actually use four tables.

So, now that you know the data you want to store, let's think about how the three parts relate to each other. Apart from knowing that the records of two tables are related *somehow*, you also need to know *the kind of relationship* between them. Let's now take a closer look at the different ways in which two tables can be related.

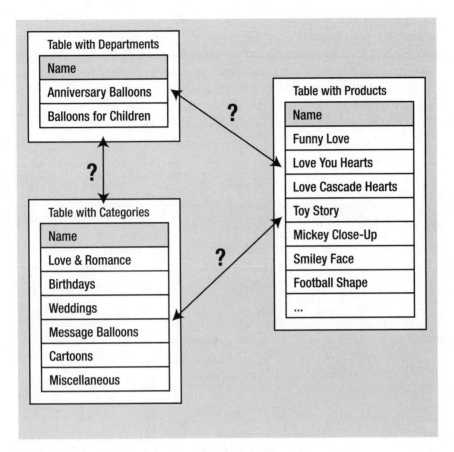

Figure 5-1. *Unrelated departments, categories, and products*

Relational Data and Table Relationships

To continue exploring the world of relational databases, let's further analyze the three logical tables we've been looking at so far. To make life easier, let's give them names now: the table containing products is Product, the table containing categories is Category, and the last one is our old friend, Department. No surprises here! These tables implement the most common kinds of relationships that exist between tables, the **One-to-Many** and **Many-to-Many** relationships, so you have the chance to learn about them.

> ■**Note** Some variations of these two relationship types exist, as well as the less popular One-to-One relationship. In the One-to-One relationship, each row in one table matches exactly one row in the other. For example, in a database that allowed patients to be assigned to hospital beds, you would hope that there would be a One-to-One relationship between patients and beds! Database systems don't support enforcing this kind of relationship, because you would have to add matching records in both tables at the same time. Moreover, two tables with a One-to-One relationship can be joined to form a single table. No One-to-One relationships are used in this book.

One-to-Many Relationships

The One-to-Many relationship happens when one record in a table can be associated with multiple records in the related table, but not vice versa. In our catalog, this happens for the Department-Category relation. A specific department can contain any number of categories, but each category belongs to exactly one department. Figure 5-2 better represents the One-to-Many relationship between departments and categories.

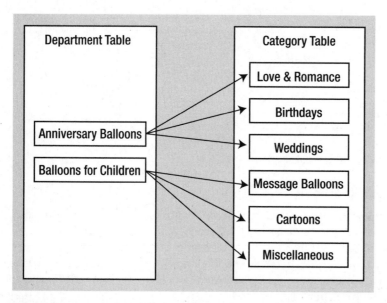

Figure 5-2. *A One-to-Many relationship between departments and categories*

Another common scenario in which you see the One-to-Many relationship is with the Order–Order Details tables, where Order contains general details about the order (such as date, total amount, and so on) and Order Details contains the products related to the order.

Many-to-Many Relationships

The other common type of relationship is the Many-to-Many relationship. This kind of relationship is implemented when records in both tables of the relationship can have multiple matching records in the other. In our scenario, this happens between the Product and Category tables, because a product can exist in more than one category (*one* product—*many* categories), and also a category can have more than one product (*one* category—*many* products).

This happens because we decided earlier that a product could be in more than one category. If a product belonged to a single category, you would have another One-to-Many relationship, just like that between departments and categories (where a category can't belong to more than one department).

If you represent this relationship with a picture as shown previously in Figure 5-2, but with generic names this time, you get something like what is shown in Figure 5-3.

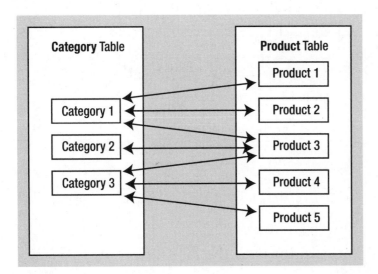

Figure 5-3. *The Many-to-Many relationship between categories and products*

Although logically the Many-to-Many relationship happens between two tables, databases don't have the means to physically implement this kind of relationship by using just two tables, so we cheat by adding a third table to the mix. This third table, called a junction table (also known as a **linking table** or **associate table**) and two One-to-Many relationships will help achieve the Many-to-Many relationship.

The junction table is used to associate products and categories, with no restriction on how many products can exist for a category or how many categories a product can be added to. Figure 5-4 shows the role of the junction table.

Note that each record in the junction table links one category with one product. You can have as many records as you like in the junction table, linking any category to any product. The linking table contains two fields, each one referencing the primary key of one of the two linked tables. In our case, the junction table will contain two fields: a `CategoryID` field and a `ProductID` field.

Each record in the junction table will consist of a (`ProductID`, `CategoryID`) pair, which is used to associate a particular product with a particular category. By adding more records to the junction table, you can associate a product with more categories or a category with more products, effectively implementing the Many-to-Many relationship.

Because the Many-to-Many relationship is implemented using a third table that makes the connection between the linked tables, there is no need to add additional fields to the related tables in the way that you added `DepartmentID` to the `category` table for implementing the One-to-Many relationship.

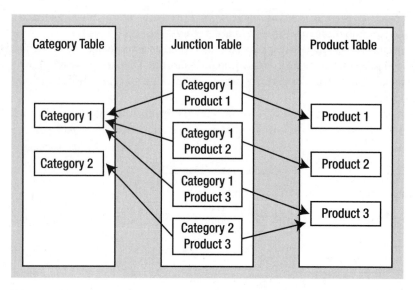

Figure 5-4. *Implementing a Many-to-Many relationship using a junction table*

There's no definitive naming convention to use for the junction table. Most of the time it's okay to just join the names of the two linked tables—in this case, our junction table will be named ProductCategory.

Enforcing Table Relationships with the FOREIGN KEY Constraint

Relationships between tables are physically enforced in the database using FOREIGN KEY constraints, or simply **foreign keys**. You learned in the previous chapter about the PRIMARY KEY and UNIQUE constraints. We covered them there because they apply to the table as an individual entity. Foreign keys, on the other hand, always occur between two tables: the table in which the foreign key is defined (the referencing table) and the table the foreign key references (the referenced table).

■**Tip** Actually, the referencing table and the referenced table can be one and the same. You won't see this too often in practice, but it's not unusual, either. For example, you can have a table with employees, where each employee references the employee that is their boss (in this case, the big boss would probably reference itself).

SQL Server Books Online defines a foreign key as a column or combination of columns used to establish or enforce a link between data in two tables (usually representing a One-to-Many relationship). Foreign keys are used both to ensure data integrity and to establish a relationship between tables.

To enforce database integrity, the foreign keys, like the other types of constraints, apply certain restrictions. Unlike PRIMARY KEY and UNIQUE constraints that apply restrictions to a single table, the FOREIGN KEY constraint applies restrictions on both the referencing and referenced tables. For example, when enforcing a One-to-Many relationship between the Department table and the Category table by using a FOREIGN KEY constraint, the database includes this relationship as part of its integrity. The foreign key won't allow you to add a category to a nonexistent department, and it won't allow you to delete a department if categories belong to it.

You now know the general theory of foreign keys. You'll implement them in the following exercise, where you'll have the chance to learn more about how foreign keys work. A bit later, you'll learn how to visualize and implement foreign keys using the integrated diagramming feature in Visual Web Developer.

Adding Categories and Products to the Database

In the following exercises, you'll put into practice the new theory you learned on table relationships by creating and populating these tables:

- Category

- Product

- ProductCategory

Adding Categories

The process of creating the Category table is pretty much the same as for the Department table you created in Chapter 3. The Category table will have four fields, as described in Table 5-1.

Table 5-1. *Designing the Category Table*

Field Name	Data Type	Other Properties
CategoryID	int	Primary key and identity column
DepartmentID	int	Doesn't allow NULLs
Name	nvarchar(50)	Doesn't allow NULLs
Description	nvarchar(1000)	Allows NULLs

Exercise: Creating the Category Table and Relating It to Department

Essentially, creating the Category table is pretty much the same as the Department table you've already created, so we'll move pretty quickly. What makes this exercise special is that you'll learn how to implement and enforce the One-to-Many relationship between the Category and Department tables.

1. Using Database Explorer (**Ctrl+Alt+S**), open the data connection to the BalloonShop database. When the database is selected, choose **Data ➤ Add New ➤ Table**. Alternatively, you can right-click the **Tables** node under BalloonShop and select **Add New Table**.

2. Add the columns shown in Table 5-1. The table should look as shown in Figure 5-5.

■**Tip** A quick reminder from the previous chapter: You set a column to be the primary key by right-clicking on it and clicking the **Set Primary Key** item from the context menu. You set it to be an identity column by expanding the **Identity Specification** item from its Column Properties window, and setting the **(Is Identity)** node to **Yes**. At this moment the form should look like Figure 5-5.

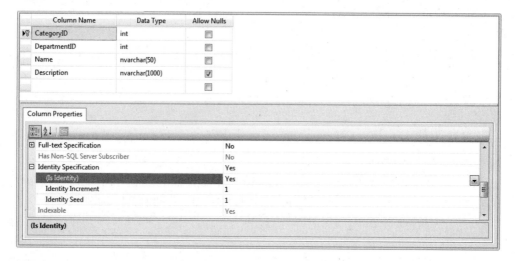

Figure 5-5. *Creating the Category table*

3. Press **Ctrl+S** to save the table. When asked, type **Category** for the table's name.

4. While the Category table is still selected, click **Table ➤ Designer ➤ Relationships**. Here is where you specify the details for the foreign key. This works by relating a column of the referencing table (Category) to a column of the referenced table (Department). You need to relate the DepartmentID column in Category with the DepartmentID column of the Department table.

5. In the dialog box that appears, click **Add**.

6. Select the **Tables and Columns Specifications** entry and click the "..." button that appears. In the dialog box that opens (see Figure 5-6), choose **Department** for the **Primary key table** and **DepartmentID** for the column on both tables.

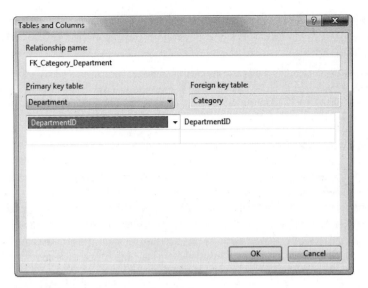

Figure 5-6. *Creating a new foreign key*

7. Click **OK** and then **Close** to save the relationship.

■**Tip** If anything goes wrong, delete the relationship, and then create it again.

---

8. Press **Ctrl+S** to save the table again. You'll be warned about the Category and Department tables being updated and asked for confirmation. This confirms again that a foreign-key relationship affects both tables that take part in the relationship. Click **Yes**.

How It Works: The One-to-Many Relationship

Okay, so you created and then enforced a relationship between the Category and Department tables. But how does it work, and how does it affect your work and life? Let's study how you implemented this relationship.

In the Category table, apart from the primary key and the usual CategoryID, Name, and Description columns, you added a DepartmentID column. This column stores the ID of the department the category belongs to. Because the DepartmentID field in Category doesn't allow NULLs, you must supply a department for each category. Furthermore, because of the foreign-key relationship, the database won't allow you to specify a nonexistent department.

Actually, you can ask the database not to enforce the relationship. In the Foreign Key Relationships dialog box where you created the relationship, you can set a number of options for your foreign key. We left them with the default value, but let's see what they do:

- *Check Existing Data On Creation*: If you set this to Yes, it doesn't allow the creation of the relationship if the existing database records don't comply with it. In other words, the relationship can't be created if orphaned categories are in the database (you have categories with a DepartmentID that references a nonexistent department).

- *Enforce For Replication*: This option applies to database replication, which is beyond the scope of this book. Replication is a technology that allows the synchronization of data between multiple SQL Servers situated at different locations.

- *Enforce Foreign Key Constraint*: This is probably the most important of the options. It tells SQL Server to make sure that database operations on the tables involved in the relationship don't break the relationship. When this option is selected, by default SQL Server won't allow you to add categories to nonexistent departments or delete departments that have related categories.

- INSERT *and* UPDATE *specification*: These options allow you to fine-tune the way SQL Server behaves when you delete or update data that would break data integrity. For example, if you set the Update Rule to Cascade, changing the ID of an existing department would cause the change to propagate to the Category table to keep the category-department associations intact. This way, even after you change the ID of the department, its categories would still belong to it (you can leave this option set to No Action because you won't need to change departments IDs.) Setting the Delete Rule to Cascade is a radical solution for keeping data integrity. If this is selected and you delete a department from the database, SQL Server automatically deletes all the department's related categories. This is a sensitive option and you should be very careful with it. You won't use it in the BalloonShop project.

In the One-to-Many relationship (and implicitly the FOREIGN KEY constraint), you link two columns from two different tables. One of these columns is a primary key, and it defines the One part of the relationship. In our case, DepartmentID is the primary key of Department, so Department is the one that connects to many categories. A primary key must be on the One part to ensure that it's unique—a category can't be linked to a department if you can't be sure that the department ID is unique. You must ensure that no two departments have the same ID; otherwise, the relationship wouldn't make much sense.

Now that you've created the Category table, you can populate it with some data. We'll also try to add data that would break the relationship that you established between the Department and Category tables.

Exercise: Adding Categories

1. Open the Category table for editing (right-click the table in Database Explorer and select **Show Table Data**).

2. Using the editor integrated with Visual Web Developer, you can start adding rows. Because CategoryID has been set as an identity column, you cannot manually edit its data—SQL Server automatically fills this field for you. However, you'll need to manually fill the DepartmentID field with ID values of existing departments. Alternatively, you can populate the Category table using the scripts from the code archive of this book (which can be downloaded from the Source Code section of the Apress web site, at http://www.apress.com). Add categories as shown in Figure 5-7.

3. Now try to break the database integrity by adding a category to a nonexistent department (for example, set the DepartmentID to 500). After filling the new category data, try to move to the next row. At this point, Visual Web Developer submits the newly written data to SQL Server. If you've created the relationship properly, an error should occur (see Figure 5-8). For more detailed information about the error, click the **Help** button.

	CategoryID	DepartmentID	Name	Description
▶	1	1	Love & Romance	Here's our collection of balloons with romantic messages.
	2	1	Birthdays	Tell someone "Happy Birthday" with one of these wonderful balloons!
	3	1	Weddings	Going to a wedding? Here's a collection of balloons for that special event!
	4	2	Message Balloons	Why write on paper, when you can deliver your message on a balloon?
	5	2	Cartoons	Buy a balloon with your child's favorite cartoon character!
	6	2	Miscellaneous	Various baloons that your kid will most certainly love!
*	NULL	NULL	NULL	NULL

◀◀ ◀ 1   of 6 ▶ ▶▶ ▶▪ ⦿ | Cell is Read Only.

Figure 5-7. *Populating the Category table*

■**Tip** Keep the CategoryID numbers in sequential order to make your life easier when associating them with product IDs later in this chapter. Remember that you can use the TRUNCATE TABLE command to empty the table's contents and reset the identity value.

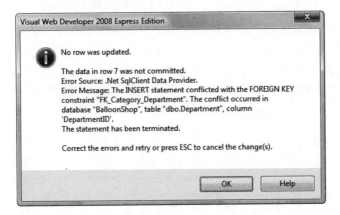

Figure 5-8. *The foreign key in action*

How It Works: Populating the Categories Table

Visual Web Developer makes it very easy to add new records to a data table. The only trick is to keep the generated CategoryID numbers in sequential order, as shown earlier in Figure 5-7. Otherwise, you won't be able to use the SQL scripts from the book's code archive to populate the tables that relate to Category.

This can be tricky if you delete and add records in the table, because the auto-generated number keeps increasing, and you can't specify the ID manually. Erasing all the records of the table doesn't reset the auto-increment number. Instead, you need to truncate the table, or delete and re-create it. Another solution is to temporarily disable the (Is Identity) option, change the IDs manually, and then activate the option again. Finally, you can use the SET IDENTITY_INSERT command that we used in the SQL scripts in the code archive to populate the data table.

Adding Products

Now that you've added categories and departments to the database, the next logical step is to add products. This is different from what you did when adding categories, because between Product and Category, you must implement a Many-to-Many relationship.

Here you'll create the Product and ProductCategory tables. The Product table contains a few more fields than the usual ProductID, Name, and Description. Most of them are pretty self-explanatory, but for completeness, let's look at each of them:

- ProductID uniquely identifies a product. It's the primary key of the table.

- Name stores the product's name.

- Description stores the product's description.

- Price stores the product's price.

- Thumbnail stores the name of the product's thumbnail file name. SQL Server can store binary data, including pictures, directly in the database, but we chose to store only the file names in the database and the actual picture files in the Windows file system. This method also allows you to save the images in a separate physical location (for example, another hard disk), further improving performance for high-traffic web sites.

- Image stores the name of the product's large picture file, which is displayed on the product details page.

- PromoFront is a bit field (can be set to either 0 or 1) that specifies whether the product is featured on the front page of the web site. The main page of the site will list the products that have this bit set to 1. This field doesn't accept NULLs and has a default value of 0.

- PromoDept is a bit field that specifies whether the product is featured on the department pages. When visiting a department, the visitor is shown only the featured products of that department. If a product belongs to more than one department (remember, it can belong to more than one category), it will be listed as featured on all those departments. This field doesn't accept NULLs and has a default value of 0.

Using those bit fields allows you to let the site administrators highlight a set of products that are particularly important at a specific time (for example, before Valentine's Day they will draw attention to the pink balloons, and so on).

Okay, enough talk; let's add the Product table to the database.

Exercise: Creating the Product Table and Relating It to Category

1. Using the steps that you already know, create a new Product table with the fields shown in Table 5-2.

Table 5-2. *Designing the* Product *Table*

Field Name	Data Type	Other Properties
ProductID	int	Primary key and identity column
Name	nvarchar(50)	Doesn't allow NULLs
Description	nvarchar(max)	Doesn't allow NULLs
Price	money	Doesn't allow NULLs
Thumbnail	nvarchar(50)	Default value is GenericThumb.png
Image	nvarchar(50)	Default value is GenericImage.png
PromoFront	bit	Doesn't allow NULLs and has a default value of 0
PromoDept	bit	Doesn't allow NULLs and has a default value of 0

■**Tip** You set a column's default value from the Default Value or Binding property in its Column Properties window.

After adding the fields, your table window will look like Figure 5-9.

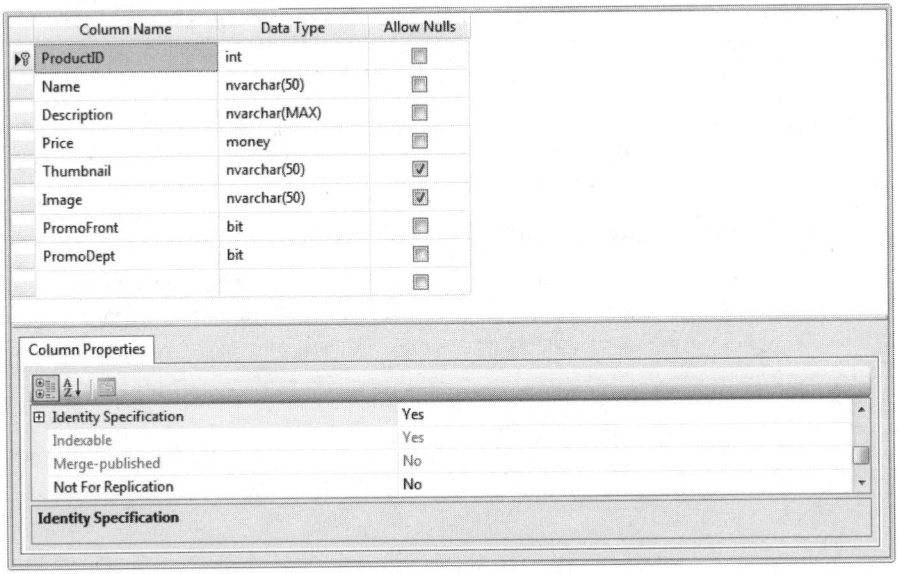

Figure 5-9. *Creating the* Product *table*

■Important nvarchar(max) is a SQL Server data type that was introduced in SQL Server 2005. If your server is running SQL Server 2000 or older, use nvarchar(4000), which limits the size of the description to 4,000 characters, or varchar(8000). Alternatively, you can use text or ntext, which don't have the size limitations of varchar and nvarchar. Unfortunately, text and ntext are a bit more difficult to work with (not all string manipulation functions can work with them), using them incurs performance penalties, they cannot be indexed, and they will be declared obsolete in future versions of SQL Server.

---

2. Press **Ctrl+S** to save the table and type **Product** for its name. Now you have a brand new Product table!

3. Because there are many products, populate this table by executing the 05_04_insert_products.sql script from the book's code archive.

4. Now let's create the junction table to associate products to categories (implementing the Many-to-Many relationship between Product and Category). Create a new table with two fields, as shown in Figure 5-10.

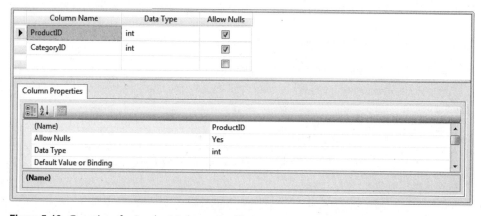

Figure 5-10. *Creating the ProductCategory table*

5. Now select both fields, ProductID and CategoryID, and click **Table ➤ Designer ➤ Set Primary Key**. Two golden keys appear on the left side, and the Allow Nulls check boxes are automatically unchecked (see Figure 5-11).

6. Press **Ctrl+S** to save the newly created table. Its name is ProductCategory.

7. Expand your database node in Database Explorer, right-click the **Database Diagrams** node, and select **Add New Diagram** from the context menu (alternatively, you can choose **Data ➤ Add New ➤ Diagram**). If a dialog box that asks about creating database objects required for diagramming shows up, click **Yes**.

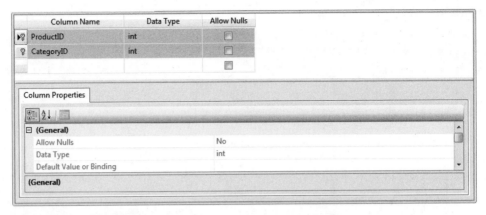

Figure 5-11. *Setting the primary key of the ProductCategory table*

8. You'll see a dialog box as shown in Figure 5-12. Click **Add** four times to add all your tables to the diagram, and then click **Close**.

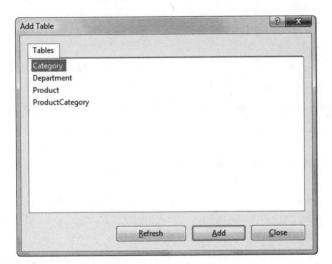

Figure 5-12. *Adding tables to the diagram*

9. Feel free to zoom the window and rearrange the tables on the diagram to fit nicely on the screen. With the default options, your diagram will look like Figure 5-13.

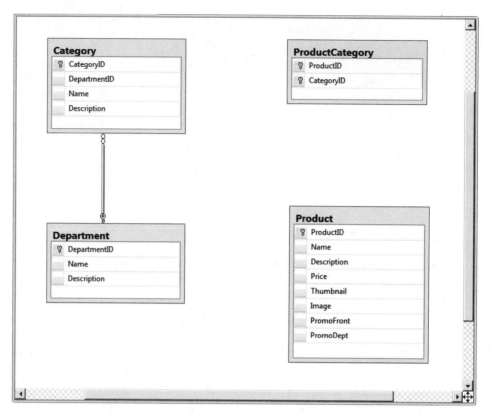

Figure 5-13. *BalloonShop database diagram*

To enforce the Many-to-Many relationship between Category and Product, you need to add two FOREIGN KEY constraints. In this exercise, you'll create these constraints visually.

10. Click the ProductID key in the ProductCategory table and drag it over the ProductID column of the Product table. The dialog box that adds a new foreign-key relationship shows up, already filled with the necessary data (see Figure 5-14).

11. Click **OK** to confirm adding the foreign key, and then click **OK** again to close the Foreign Key Relationship dialog box.

12. Create a new relationship between the Category and ProductCategory tables on their CategoryID columns in the same way you did in steps 10 and 11. The diagram now reflects the new relationships (see Figure 5-15).

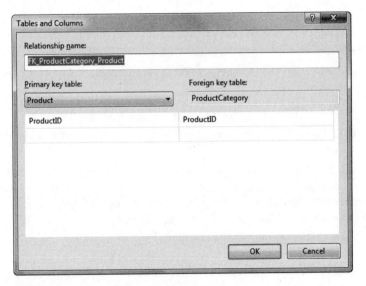

Figure 5-14. *Creating a new foreign key*

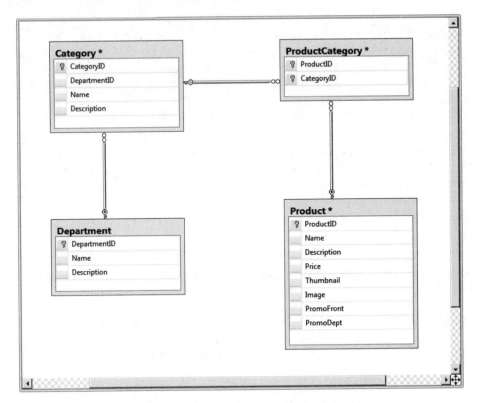

Figure 5-15. *Viewing tables and relationships using the database diagram*

Press **Ctrl+S** to save your diagram and the changes you made to your tables. When asked for a diagram name, type **CatalogDiagram**. You'll be warned that Product, Category, and ProductCategory will be saved to the database. Click **Yes** to confirm.

13. Populate the ProductCategory table by running the 05_06_populate_productcategory.sql script from the code archive.

How It Works: Many-to-Many Relationships and Database Diagrams

In this exercise, you created the Product table and implemented (and enforced) a Many-to-Many relationship with Category.

Many-to-Many relationships are created by adding a third table, called a junction table, which is named ProductCategory in this case. This table contains (ProductID, CategoryID) pairs, and each record in the table associates a particular product with a particular category. So, if you see a record such as (1,4) in ProductCategory, you know that the product with ProductID 1 belongs to the category with CategoryID 4.

The Many-to-Many relationship is physically enforced through two FOREIGN KEY constraints—one that links Product to ProductCategory, and the other that links ProductCategory to Category. In English, this means, "One product can be associated with many product-category entries, each of those being associated with one category." The foreign keys ensure that the products and categories that appear in the ProductCategory table actually exist in the database and won't allow you to delete a product if you have a category associated with it and vice versa.

This is also the first time that you set a primary key consisting of more than one column. The primary key of ProductCategory is formed by both its fields: ProductID and CategoryID. This means that you won't be allowed to have two identical (ProductID, CategoryID) pairs in the table. However, it's perfectly legal to have a ProductID or CategoryID appear more than once, as long as it's part of a unique (ProductID, CategoryID) pair. This makes sense, because you don't want to have two identical records in the ProductCategory table. A product can be associated with a particular category, or not; it cannot be associated with a category multiple times.

At first, all the theory about table relationships can be a bit confusing, until you get used to them. To understand the relationship more clearly, you can get a picture by using database diagrams like the ones you worked with in this exercise. Database diagrams are very useful. If, until now, you could only imagine the relationships between the different tables, the diagram allows you to see what actually happens. The diagram you created shows your three One-to-Many relationships.

The diagram also shows the type and direction of the relationships. Note that a key symbol appears at the One part of each relationship and an infinity symbol appears at the Many side of the relationship. The table whose whole primary key is involved in the relationship is at the One side of the relationship and is marked with the little golden key.

One of the most useful things about diagrams is that you can edit database objects directly from the diagram. If you right-click a table or a relationship, you'll see a lot of features there. Feel free to experiment a bit to get a feeling for the features available. Not only can you create foreign keys through the diagram, you can also create new tables, or design existing ones, directly within the diagram. To design one of the existing tables, you must switch the table to normal mode by right-clicking the table, and then choosing Table View ➤ Standard. When the table is in Standard View mode, you can edit it directly in the diagram, as shown in Figure 5-16.

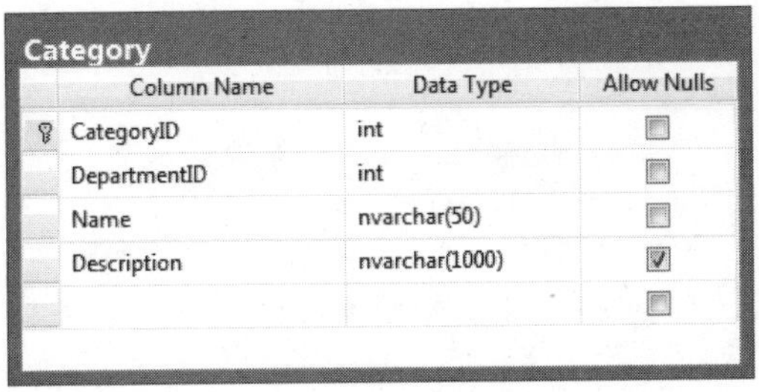

Figure 5-16. *Editing the table directly in the diagram*

Querying the New Data

Now you have a database with a wealth of information just waiting to be read by somebody. However, the new elements bring with them a set of new things you need to learn.

For this chapter, the data tier logic is a little bit more complicated than in the previous chapter, because it must answer to queries like "Give me the second page of products from the 'Cartoons' category," or "Give me the products on promotion for department X." Before moving on to writing the stored procedures that implement this logic, let's first cover the theory about

- Retrieving short product descriptions

- Joining data tables

- Implementing paging

Let's deal with these monsters one by one.

Retrieving Short Product Descriptions

In our web site, product lists don't display complete product descriptions, but only a portion of them (the full descriptions are shown only in the product details pages). In T-SQL, you get the first characters of a string using the LEFT function. After extracting a part of the full description, you append "..." to the end using the + operator.

The following SELECT query returns all product's descriptions trimmed at 60 characters, with "..." appended:

```
SELECT LEFT(Description, 60) + '...' AS 'Short Description'
FROM Product
```

The new column generated by the (LEFT(Description, 60) + '...') expression doesn't have a name, so we created an alias for it using the AS keyword. With your current data, this query would return something like this:

```
Short Description
-----------------------------------------------------------------
An adorable romantic balloon by Simon Elvin. You'll fall in ...
A heart-shaped balloon with the great Elvis on it and the wo...
A red heart-shaped balloon with "I love you" written on a wh...
White heart-shaped balloon with the words "Today, Tomorrow a...
Red heart-shaped balloon with a smiley face. Perfect for say...
A red heart-shaped balloon with "I Love You" in script writi...
Red heart-shaped balloon with a smiley face and three kisses...
...
```

To make sure we add the trailing "..." only when the product description is longer than the maximum allowed size, we use the CASE keyword, which has the following basic syntax:

```
CASE
     WHEN expression THEN result
     [ WHEN expression2 THEN result2 ]
     [ ... ]
     [ ELSE else_result_expression ]
END
```

In practice, our SELECT statement will look something like this:

```
SELECT
     CASE WHEN LEN(Description) <= 60 THEN Description
          ELSE LEFT(Description, 60) + '...' END
     AS 'Short Description'
FROM Product
```

Joining Data Tables

Because the data is stored in several tables, you'll frequently run into situations in which not all the information you want is in one table. Take a look at the following list, which contains data from both the Department and Category tables:

```
Department Name                         Category Name
-------------------------------------   ---------------------------------------
Anniversary Balloons                    Love & Romance
Anniversary Balloons                    Birthdays
Anniversary Balloons                    Weddings
Balloons for Children                   Message Balloons
Balloons for Children                   Cartoons
Balloons for Children                   Miscellaneous
```

In other cases, all the information you need is in just one table, but you need to place conditions on it based on the information in another table. You cannot get this kind of result set with simple queries such as the ones you've used so far. Needing a result set based on data from multiple tables is a good indication that you might need to use **table joins**.

When extracting the products that belong to a category, the SQL query isn't the same as when extracting the categories that belong to a department. This is because products and categories are linked through the ProductCategory junction table.

To get the list of products in a category, you first need to look in the ProductCategory table and get all the (ProductID, CategoryID) pairs where CategoryID is the ID of the category you're looking for. That list contains the IDs of the products in that category. Using these IDs, you can generate the required product list. Although this sounds complicated, it can be done using a single SQL query. The real power of SQL lies in its capability to perform complex operations on large amounts of data using simple queries.

You'll learn how to make table joins by analyzing the Product and ProductCategory tables and by analyzing how to get a list of products that belong to a certain category. Tables are joined in SQL using the JOIN clause. Joining one table with another table results in the columns (not the rows) of those tables being joined. When joining two tables, there must be a common column on which the join will be made.

Suppose you want to get all the products in the category where CategoryID = 5. The query that joins the Product and ProductCategory tables is as follows:

```
SELECT ProductCategory.ProductID, ProductCategory.CategoryID, Product.Name
FROM ProductCategory INNER JOIN Product
ON Product.ProductID = ProductCategory.ProductID
```

The result will look something like this (to save space, the listing doesn't include all returned rows:

ProductID	CategoryID	Name
1	1	I Love You (Simon Elvin)
1	2	I Love You (Simon Elvin)
2	1	Elvis Hunka Burning Love
2	4	Elvis Hunka Burning Love
2	6	Elvis Hunka Burning Love
3	1	Funny Love
3	3	Funny Love
3	4	Funny Love
...		

The resultant table is composed of the requested fields from the joined tables synchronized on the ProductID column, which was specified as the column to make the join on. You can see that the products that exist in more categories are listed more than once—once for each category they belong in—but this problem will go away after we filter the results to get only the products for a certain category.

Note that in the SELECT clause, the column names are prefixed by the table name. This is a requirement if columns exist in more than one table participating in the table join, such as ProductID in our case. For the other column, prefixing its name with the table name is optional, although it's a good practice to avoid confusion.

The query that returns only the products that belong to category 5 is

```
SELECT Product.ProductID, Product.Name
FROM ProductCategory INNER JOIN Product
ON Product.ProductID = ProductCategory.ProductID
WHERE ProductCategory.CategoryID = 5
```

The results are

ProductID	Name
21	Baby Hi Little Angel
25	Tweety Stars
39	Toy Story
40	Rugrats Tommy & Chucky
41	Rugrats & Reptar Character
42	Tweety & Sylvester
43	Mickey Close-up
44	Minnie Close-up
45	Teletubbies Time
46	Barbie My Special Things
47	Paddington Bear
48	I Love You Snoopy
49	Pooh Adult
50	Pokemon Character
51	Pokemon Ash & Pikachu
53	Smiley Face
54	Soccer Shape
55	Goal Ball

A final thing worth discussing here is the use of **aliases**. Aliases aren't necessarily related to table joins, but they become especially useful (and sometimes necessary) when joining tables, and they assign different (and usually shorter) names for the tables involved. Aliases are necessary when joining a table with itself, in which case you need to assign different aliases for its different instances to differentiate them. The following query returns the same products as the query before, but it uses aliases:

```
SELECT p.ProductID, p.Name
FROM ProductCategory pc INNER JOIN Product p
ON p.ProductID = pc.ProductID
WHERE pc.CategoryID = 5
```

Showing Products Page by Page

If certain web sections need to list large numbers of products, it's useful to let the visitor browse them page by page, with a predefined (or configurable by the visitor) number of products per page. Depending on the tier on your architecture where paging is performed, there are two main ways to implement paging:

- *Paging at the database level*: In this case, the database returns only the page of products the visitor wants to see.

- *Paging at the application level*: In this scenario, the data tier always returns the complete list of products for a certain section of the site, and the presentation tier objects (such as the `GridView` control) extract the requested page of products from the complete list. This method has potential performance problems especially when dealing with large result sets, because it transfers unnecessarily large quantities of data from the database to the presentation tier. Additional data also needs to be stored on the server's memory, unnecessarily consuming server resources.

In our web site, we'll implement paging at the data tier level, not only because of its better performance, but also because it allows you to learn some tricks about database programming that you'll find useful when developing your web sites.

You'll write stored procedures that take as parameter a page number, and return only the products that appear in that page. This technique is powerful because of flexibility and performance reasons.

In the following pages, you'll learn how to write smart stored procedures that return a specific page of records. Say, the first time the visitor searches for something, only the first *n* matching products are retrieved from the database. Then, when the visitor clicks Next page, the next *n* rows are retrieved from the database, and so on.

■**Tip** We'll cover this theory for SQL Server 2005 and 2008. If you happen to be working with an older version, check the code archive for an alternate implementation.

Implementing Paging Using SQL Server 2008

With some relational database systems, result sets are always perceived as a group, and individual rows of the set aren't numbered (ranked) in any way. As a consequence, there was no straightforward way to say "I want the sixth to the tenth records of this list of products," because the database actually didn't know which those records were.

■**Note** The problem was sometimes even more serious because unless some sorting criteria was implemented, the database didn't (and doesn't) guarantee that if the same `SELECT` statement is run twice, you get the resulted rows in the same order. Therefore, you couldn't know for sure that after the visitor sees the first five products and clicks Next, products six to ten returned by the database are the ones you would expect.

To demonstrate the paging feature, we'll use the `SELECT` query that returns all the products of the catalog:

```
SELECT Name
FROM Product
```

Now, how do you take just one portion from this list of results, given that you know the page number and the number of products per page? (To retrieve the first *n* products, the simple answer is to use the TOP keyword in conjunction with SELECT, but that wouldn't work to get the *next* page of products.)

SQL Server 2008 (and 2005) has a ROW_NUMBER function that assigns consecutive row numbers, starting with 1, for each row returned by a SELECT statement. Because numbering can only be guaranteed to be consistent if a sorting criterion applies to the query, when using ROW_NUMBER, you also need to specify a column on which the rows are ordered prior to being numbered:

```
SELECT ROW_NUMBER() OVER (ORDER BY ProductID) AS Row, Name
FROM Product
```

This query will have a list of results such as the following:

Row	Name
1	I Love You (Simon Elvin)
2	Elvis Hunka Burning Love
3	Funny Love
4	Today, Tomorrow & Forever
5	Smiley Heart Red Balloon
6	Love 24 Karat
7	Smiley Kiss Red Balloon
8	Love You Hearts
9	Love Me Tender
10	I Can't Get Enough of You Baby
...	

To retrieve five products, namely the sixth to the tenth products of the list, you transform the previous query into a subquery and filter the results on the WHERE clause of the main query. The results of a subquery can be interpreted as a separate table on which the main query applies (the AS keyword that follows the subquery assigns a name to this virtual table). The following T-SQL code returns the specified list of products:

```
SELECT Row, Name
FROM(
     SELECT ROW_NUMBER() OVER (ORDER BY ProductID) AS Row, Name
     FROM Product
     ) AS ProductsWithRowNumbers
WHERE Row >= 6 AND Row <= 10
```

Using Table Variables

If you get a set of data that you need to make further operations on, you're likely to need to save it either as a temporary table or in a TABLE variable. Both temporary tables and TABLE variables can be used just like normal tables, and are very useful for storing temporary data within the scope of a stored procedure.

In the stored procedures that return pages of products, you'll save the complete list of products in a TABLE variable, allowing you to count the total number of products (so you can tell the visitor the number of pages of products) before returning the specified page.

The code listing that follows shows you how to create a TABLE variable named @Products:

```
-- declare a new TABLE variable
DECLARE @Products TABLE
(RowNumber INT,
 ProductID INT,
 Name NVARCHAR(50),
 Description NVARCHAR(MAX))
```

After creating this variable, you'll populate it with data using INSERT INTO:

```
-- populate the table variable with the complete list of products
INSERT INTO @Products
SELECT ROW_NUMBER() OVER (ORDER BY Product.ProductID) AS Row,
       ProductID, Name, Description
FROM Product
```

You can then retrieve data from this table object like this:

```
-- extract the requested page of products
SELECT Name, Description FROM @Products
WHERE RowNumber >= 6 AND RowNumber <= 10
```

Writing the New Stored Procedures

It's time to add the new stored procedures to the BalloonShop database, and then you'll have the chance to see them in action. For each stored procedure, you'll need its functionality somewhere in the presentation tier. You may want to refresh your memory by having a look at the first four figures in Chapter 3.

In this chapter, the data you need from the database depends on external parameters (such as the department selected by a visitor, the number of products per pages, and so on). You'll send this data to your stored procedures in the form of stored procedure parameters.

The syntax used to create a stored procedure with parameters is

```
CREATE PROCEDURE <procedure name>
[(
    <parameter name> <parameter type> [=<default value>] [INPUT|OUTPUT],
    <parameter name> <parameter type> [=<default value>] [INPUT|OUTPUT],
    ...
    ...
)]
AS
    <stored procedure body>
```

The portions between the square brackets are optional. Specifying parameters is optional, but if you specify them, they must be within parentheses. For each parameter, you must supply at least its name and data type.

You can optionally supply a default value for the parameter. In this case, if the calling function doesn't supply a value for this parameter, the default value will be used instead. Also you can specify whether the parameter is an input parameter or output parameter. By default, all parameters are input parameters. The value of output parameters can be set in the stored procedure and then read by the calling function after the stored procedure executes.

Stored procedure parameters are treated just like any other SQL variables, and their names start with @, as in @DepartmentID, @CategoryID, @ProductName, and so on. The simplest syntax for setting the value of an output parameter, inside the stored procedure, is as follows:

```
SELECT @DepartmentID = 5
```

Because you already know how to add stored procedures, we won't go through an exercise this time. Add the stored procedures discussed in the following sections to the BalloonShop database.

CatalogGetDepartmentDetails

The CatalogGetDepartmentDetails stored procedure is needed when the user selects a department in the product catalog. When this happens, the database must be queried again to find out the name and the description of the particular department.

The stored procedure receives the ID of the selected department as a parameter and returns its name and description. A bit later, when you create the business tier, you'll learn how to extract these values into individual variables after executing the stored procedure.

The code for CatalogGetDepartmentDetails is as follows:

```
CREATE PROCEDURE CatalogGetDepartmentDetails
(@DepartmentID INT)
AS
SELECT Name, Description
FROM Department
WHERE DepartmentID = @DepartmentID
```

CatalogGetCategoryDetails

The CatalogGetCategoryDetails stored procedure is called when the visitor selects a category and wants to find out more information about it, such as its name and description. Here's the code:

```
CREATE PROCEDURE CatalogGetCategoryDetails
(@CategoryID INT)
AS
SELECT DepartmentID, Name, Description
FROM Category
WHERE CategoryID = @CategoryID
```

CatalogGetProductDetails

The CatalogGetProductDetails stored procedure is called to display a product details page. The information it needs to display is the name, description, price, and the second product image.

```
CREATE PROCEDURE CatalogGetProductDetails
(@ProductID INT)
AS
SELECT Name, Description, Price, Thumbnail, Image, PromoFront, PromoDept
FROM Product
WHERE ProductID = @ProductID
```

CatalogGetCategoriesInDepartment

When the visitor selects a particular department, apart from showing the department's details, you also want to display the categories that belong to that department. This is done using the CatalogGetCategoriesInDepartment procedure, which returns the list of categories in a department.

CatalogGetCategoriesInDepartment returns the IDs, names, and descriptions for the categories that belong to the department mentioned by the @DepartmentID input parameter:

```
CREATE PROCEDURE CatalogGetCategoriesInDepartment
(@DepartmentID INT)
AS
SELECT CategoryID, Name, Description
FROM Category
WHERE DepartmentID = @DepartmentID
```

CatalogGetProductsOnFrontPromo

CatalogGetProductsOnFrontPromo returns a page of products that are on catalog promotion (have the PromoFront bit field set to 1). This stored procedure employs much of the theory presented earlier in this chapter:

- The stored procedure saves the total number of products into the @HowManyProducts variable.

- A TABLE variable holds the complete list of products.

- The ROW_NUMBER function implements paging.

  ```
  CREATE PROCEDURE CatalogGetProductsOnFrontPromo
  (@DescriptionLength INT,
  @PageNumber INT,
  @ProductsPerPage INT,
  @HowManyProducts INT OUTPUT)
  AS
  ```

```
-- declare a new TABLE variable
DECLARE @Products TABLE
(RowNumber INT,
 ProductID INT,
 Name NVARCHAR(50),
 Description NVARCHAR(MAX),
 Price MONEY,
 Thumbnail NVARCHAR(50),
 Image NVARCHAR(50),
 PromoFront bit,
 PromoDept bit)


-- populate the table variable with the complete list of products
INSERT INTO @Products
SELECT ROW_NUMBER() OVER (ORDER BY Product.ProductID),
       ProductID, Name,
       CASE WHEN LEN(Description) <= @DescriptionLength THEN Description
            ELSE SUBSTRING(Description, 1, @DescriptionLength) + '...' END
       AS Description, Price, Thumbnail, Image, PromoFront, PromoDept
FROM Product
WHERE PromoFront = 1

-- return the total number of products using an OUTPUT variable
SELECT @HowManyProducts = COUNT(ProductID) FROM @Products

-- extract the requested page of products
SELECT ProductID, Name, Description, Price, Thumbnail,
       Image, PromoFront, PromoDept
FROM @Products
WHERE RowNumber > (@PageNumber - 1) * @ProductsPerPage
  AND RowNumber <= @PageNumber * @ProductsPerPage
```

CatalogGetProductsInCategory

When a visitor selects a particular category from a department, you'll want to list all the products that belong to that category. For this, you'll use the CatalogGetProductsInCategory stored procedure. This stored procedure is much the same as CatalogGetProductsOnFrontPromo, except the actual query is a bit more complex (it involves a table join to retrieve the list of products in the specified category):

```
CREATE PROCEDURE CatalogGetProductsInCategory
(@CategoryID INT,
@DescriptionLength INT,
@PageNumber INT,
@ProductsPerPage INT,
@HowManyProducts INT OUTPUT)
AS
```

```
-- declare a new TABLE variable
DECLARE @Products TABLE
(RowNumber INT,
 ProductID INT,
 Name NVARCHAR(50),
 Description NVARCHAR(MAX),
 Price MONEY,
 Thumbnail NVARCHAR(50),
 Image NVARCHAR(50),
 PromoFront bit,
 PromoDept bit)


-- populate the table variable with the complete list of products
INSERT INTO @Products
SELECT ROW_NUMBER() OVER (ORDER BY Product.ProductID),
       Product.ProductID, Name,
       CASE WHEN LEN(Description) <= @DescriptionLength THEN Description
            ELSE SUBSTRING(Description, 1, @DescriptionLength) + '...' END
       AS Description, Price, Thumbnail, Image, PromoFront, PromoDept
FROM Product INNER JOIN ProductCategory
  ON Product.ProductID = ProductCategory.ProductID
WHERE ProductCategory.CategoryID = @CategoryID

-- return the total number of products using an OUTPUT variable
SELECT @HowManyProducts = COUNT(ProductID) FROM @Products

-- extract the requested page of products
SELECT ProductID, Name, Description, Price, Thumbnail,
       Image, PromoFront, PromoDept
FROM @Products
WHERE RowNumber > (@PageNumber - 1) * @ProductsPerPage
  AND RowNumber <= @PageNumber * @ProductsPerPage
```

CatalogGetProductsOnDeptPromo

When the visitor selects a particular department, apart from needing to list its name, description, and list of categories (you wrote the necessary stored procedures for these tasks earlier), you also want to display the list of featured products for that department.

CatalogGetProductsOnDeptPromo needs to return all the products that belong to a department and have the PromoDept bit set to 1. In CatalogGetProductsInCategory, you needed to make a table join to find out the products that belong to a specific category. Now that you need to do this for departments, the task is a bit more complicated because you can't directly know which products belong to which departments.

You know how to find categories that belong to a specific department (you did this in CatalogGetCategoriesInDepartment), and you know how to get the products that belong to a specific category (you did that in CatalogGetProductsInCategory). By combining this information, you can determine the list of products in a department. For this, you need two table joins. You'll also filter the final result to get only the products that have the `PromoDept` bit set to 1.

You'll also use the `DISTINCT` clause to filter the results to make sure you don't get the same record multiple times. This can happen when a product belongs to more than one category and these categories are in the same department. In this situation, you would get the same product returned for each of the matching categories, unless you filter the results using `DISTINCT`. (Using `DISTINCT` also implies using a `SELECT` subquery that doesn't return row numbers when populating the `@Products` variable, because the rows would become different and using `DISTINCT` would make no more difference.)

```
CREATE PROCEDURE CatalogGetProductsOnDeptPromo
(@DepartmentID INT,
@DescriptionLength INT,
@PageNumber INT,
@ProductsPerPage INT,
@HowManyProducts INT OUTPUT)
AS

-- declare a new TABLE variable
DECLARE @Products TABLE
(RowNumber INT,
 ProductID INT,
 Name NVARCHAR(50),
 Description NVARCHAR(MAX),
 Price MONEY,
 Thumbnail NVARCHAR(50),
 Image NVARCHAR(50),
 PromoFront bit,
 PromoDept bit)

-- populate the table variable with the complete list of products
INSERT INTO @Products
SELECT ROW_NUMBER() OVER (ORDER BY ProductID) AS Row,
     ProductID, Name, SUBSTRING(Description, 1, @DescriptionLength)
+ '...' AS Description,
     Price, Thumbnail, Image, PromoFront, PromoDept
FROM
(SELECT DISTINCT Product.ProductID, Product.Name,
     CASE WHEN LEN(Product.Description) <= @DescriptionLength
          THEN Product.Description
          ELSE SUBSTRING(Product.Description, 1, @DescriptionLength) + '...' END
     AS Description, Price, Thumbnail, Image, PromoFront, PromoDept
  FROM Product INNER JOIN ProductCategory
                    ON Product.ProductID = ProductCategory.ProductID
              INNER JOIN Category
                    ON ProductCategory.CategoryID = Category.CategoryID
  WHERE Product.PromoDept = 1
  AND Category.DepartmentID = @DepartmentID
```

```
) AS ProductOnDepPr

-- return the total number of products using an OUTPUT variable
SELECT @HowManyProducts = COUNT(ProductID) FROM @Products

-- extract the requested page of products
SELECT ProductID, Name, Description, Price, Thumbnail,
       Image, PromoFront, PromoDept
FROM @Products
WHERE RowNumber > (@PageNumber - 1) * @ProductsPerPage
  AND RowNumber <= @PageNumber * @ProductsPerPage
```

Using ADO.NET with Parameterized Stored Procedures

In this section, you'll learn a few more tricks for ADO.NET, mainly regarding dealing with stored procedure parameters. Let's start with the usual theory part, after which you'll write the code.

The ADO.NET class that deals with input and output stored procedure parameters is DbCommand. This shouldn't come as a big surprise—DbCommand is responsible for executing commands on the database, so it makes sense that it should also deal with their parameters. (Remember that DbCommand is just a base class for "real" command objects, such as SqlCommand.)

Using Input Parameters

When adding an input parameter to a command object, you need to specify the parameter's name, data type, and value. The DbCommand object stores its parameters in a collection named Parameters, which contains DbParameter objects. Each DbParameter instance represents a parameter.

Given that you have a DbCommand object named comm, the following code snippet creates a DbParameter object for the command using the CreateParameter method, sets its properties, and adds the parameter to the command's Parameters collection.

```
// create a new parameter
DbParameter param = comm.CreateParameter();
param.ParameterName = "@DepartmentID";
param.Value = value;
param.DbType = DbType.Int32;
comm.Parameters.Add(param);
```

The command's CreateParameter method always returns a parameter object type specific to the data provider you're using, so the DbParameter object will actually reference a SqlParameter instance if you're using SQL Server, and so on.

Another important property of DbParameter is size, which is good to set for data types that don't have fixed values, such as VarChar. For numerical columns, specify the parameter size in bytes. For columns that store strings (such as Char, VarChar, or even Text), specify the size in number of characters. Longer strings are automatically truncated to the size specified for the parameter.

Using Output Parameters

Output stored procedure parameters behave like Out parameters in C#. They are much like return values, in that you set their value in the stored procedure and read it from the calling function after executing the procedure. Output parameters are especially useful when you have more return values, when you want to return non-integer data, or when you prefer to keep using the return value for indicating executing success (or for some other purpose).

The code that creates an output parameter is as follows:

```
// create a new parameter
param = comm.CreateParameter();
param.ParameterName = "@HowManyProducts";
param.Direction = ParameterDirection.Output;
param.DbType = DbType.Int32;
comm.Parameters.Add(param);
```

This is almost the same as the code for the input parameter, except instead of supplying a value for the parameter, you set its Direction property to ParameterDirection.Output. This tells the command that @HowManyProducts is an output parameter.

Stored Procedure Parameters Are Not Strongly Typed

When adding stored procedure parameters, you should use exactly the same name, type, and size as in the stored procedure. You don't always have to do it, however, because SQL Server is very flexible and automatically makes type conversions. For example, you could add @DepartmentID as a VarChar or even NVarChar, as long as the value you set it to is a string containing a number.

We recommend always specifying the correct data type for parameters, however, especially in the business tier. The DbParameter object will always check the value you assign to see if it corresponds to the specified data type, and if it doesn't, an exception is generated. This way, you can have the data tier check that no bogus values are sent to the database to corrupt your data.

The C# methods in the business tier (the CatalogAccess class) always take their parameters from the presentation tier as strings. We chose this approach for the architecture to keep the presentation tier from being bothered with the data types; for example, it simply doesn't care what kind of product IDs it works with (123 is just as welcome as ABC). It's the role of the business tier to interpret the data and test for its correctness.

Getting the Results Back from Output Parameters

After executing a stored procedure that has output parameters, you'll probably want to read the values returned in those parameters. You can do this by reading the parameters' values from the DbParameter object after executing it and closing the connection.

In your business tier code, you'll have a line like this, which will retrieve the value of the @HowManyProducts output parameter:

```
int howManyProducts =
 Int32.Parse(comm.Parameters["@HowManyProducts"].Value.ToString());
```

In this example, ToString is called to convert the returned value to a string, which is then parsed and transformed into an integer.

Completing the Business Tier Code

Most of your business tier code will consist of the new code you'll add to the CatalogAccess class. That code will use a few new configuration settings that you'll add to web.config:

- ProductsPerPage stores the maximum number of products to list on a page of products. If the entire list contains more items, the paging controls (next page/previous page) appear.

- ProductDescriptionLength stores the length of the product descriptions to be used in product lists. The entire description is shown only in the product details page.

- SiteName stores the name of your store, which will be used to compose catalog page names.

Let's add these settings in a short exercise.

Exercise: Adding New Configuration Settings

1. Open web.config and add the following entries to the <appSettings> node:

```
<appSettings>
    <add key="MailServer" value="mail server address" />
    <add key="MailUsername" value="mail username " />
    <add key="MailPassword" value="mail password" />
    <add key="MailFrom" value="mail address" />
    <add key="EnableErrorLogEmail" value="true" />
    <add key="ErrorLogEmail" value="errors@example.com" />
    <add key="ProductsPerPage" value="6"/>
    <add key="ProductDescriptionLength" value="60"/>
    <add key="SiteName" value="BalloonShop"/>
</appSettings>
```

2. Open the BalloonShopConfiguration class and add two fields, whose values are loaded once by the static constructor of the class:

```
public static class BalloonShopConfiguration
{
    // Caches the connection string
    private static string dbConnectionString;
    // Caches the data provider name
    private static string dbProviderName;
    // Store the number of products per page
    private readonly static int productsPerPage;
    // Store the product description length for product lists
    private readonly static int productDescriptionLength;
    // Store the name of your shop
    private readonly static string siteName;
```

```
    // Initialize various properties in the constructor
    static BalloonShopConfiguration()
    {
      dbConnectionString =
ConfigurationManager.ConnectionStrings["BalloonShopConnection"].
ConnectionString;
      dbProviderName =
ConfigurationManager.ConnectionStrings["BalloonShopConnection"].ProviderName;
      productsPerPage =
System.Int32.Parse(ConfigurationManager.AppSettings["ProductsPerPage"]);
      productDescriptionLength =
System.Int32.Parse(ConfigurationManager.AppSettings
["ProductDescriptionLength"]);
      siteName = ConfigurationManager.AppSettings["SiteName"];
    }
```

3. Also in the BalloonShopConfiguration class, add the corresponding properties to return the values of the fields you've added in the previous step:

```
// Returns the maximum number of products to be displayed on a page
public static int ProductsPerPage
{
  get
  {
    return productsPerPage;
  }
}
```

```
// Returns the length of product descriptions in products lists
public static int ProductDescriptionLength
{
  get
  {
    return productDescriptionLength;
  }
}
```

```
// Returns the length of product descriptions in products lists
public static string SiteName
{
  get
  {
    return siteName;
  }
}
```

How It Works: Read-Only Fields and Constants

The productsPerPage and productDescriptionLength fields are marked as readonly. This mainly means that after setting their values in the class constructor, you can't change their values any more in any method. If you're curious to find more details about readonly and how readonly is different from const, read on.

The major similarity between the readonly and const fields is that you aren't allowed to change their values inside class methods or properties. The main difference is that whereas for constants you need to set their value at the time you write the code (their values must be known at compile-time), with readonly fields you are allowed to dynamically set their values in the class constructor.

Constant values are always replaced with their literal values by the compiler. If you look at the compiled code, you'll never know constants were used. You can use the const keyword only with value types (the primitive data types: Int, Char, Float, Bool, and so on), but not with reference types (such as the classes you're creating).

readonly fields are handled differently. They don't have to be value types, and they can be initialized in the class constructor. Static readonly fields can be initialized only in the static class constructor, and instance readonly fields can be initialized only in the instance class constructor.

Note that in case of readonly fields of reference types, only the reference is kept read-only. The inner data of the object can still be modified. A good example is an array, whose elements can be modified even if the array itself is read-only.

Let's now implement the business tier methods. Each method calls exactly one stored procedure, and the methods are named exactly like the stored procedures they are calling. In Visual Studio, open the CatalogAccess.cs file you created in the previous chapter, and prepare to fill it with business logic.

GetDepartmentDetails

GetDepartmentDetails is called from the presentation tier when a department is clicked to display its name and description. The presentation tier passes the ID of the selected department, and you need to send back the name and the description of the selected department.

The GetDepartmentDetails method of the business tier uses the GenericDataAccess. CreateCommand method to get a DbCommand object and execute the CatalogGetDepartmentDetails stored procedure. The business tier wraps the returned data into a separate object and sends this object back to the presentation tier.

What object, you say? The technique is to create a separate class (or **struct**, in our case) for the particular purpose of storing data that you want to pass around. This struct is named DepartmentDetails and looks like this:

```
public struct DepartmentDetails
{
  public string Name;
  public string Description;
}
```

STRUCTS

A struct is a user-defined data type that is very similar to a class; it can contain constructors, fields, methods, and properties. Structs are declared using the `struct` keyword instead of `class`. As a quick reference, here are the notable differences between structs and classes:

- A struct is a value type, whereas classes are reference types. Internally, structs are implicitly derived from `System.ValueType`.

- Inheritance doesn't work with structs. A struct cannot derive from a class or from another struct; a class cannot derive from a struct.

- Structs always contain by default a parameterless, default constructor, which does nothing. You're allowed to add more overloads, but you can't add a parameterless constructor.

- Although structs are very powerful, they are mainly designed to act as containers for data rather than as fully featured objects. Because they are value types (and are stored on the stack), passing them around can be very fast. MSDN says that data structures smaller than 16 bytes may be handled more efficiently as structs than as classes.

You wrap the department's name and description into one `DepartmentDetails` object and send it back to the presentation tier. The `DepartmentDetails` class can be added in a separate file in the `App_Code` folder or added to one of the existing files. Most of the time, you'll want to create a separate file for each class, but because in this case `DepartmentDetails` is more like a tool for the `CatalogAccess` class, we chose to add it to `CatalogAccess.cs`.

Add the `DepartmentDetails` class at the beginning of `CatalogAccess.cs` (but not inside the `CatalogAccess` class) like this:

```
using System;
using System.Data;
using System.Data.Common;

/// <summary>
/// Wraps department details data
/// </summary>
public struct DepartmentDetails
{
  public string Name;
  public string Description;
}

/// <summary>
/// Product catalog business tier component
/// </summary>
public static class CatalogAccess
```

Now add the GetDepartmentDetails method to the CatalogAccess class. The exact location doesn't matter, but to keep the code organized, add it just after the GetDepartments method:

```
// get department details
public static DepartmentDetails GetDepartmentDetails(string departmentId)
{
  // get a configured DbCommand object
  DbCommand comm = GenericDataAccess.CreateCommand();
  // set the stored procedure name
  comm.CommandText = "CatalogGetDepartmentDetails";
  // create a new parameter
  DbParameter param = comm.CreateParameter();
  param.ParameterName = "@DepartmentID";
  param.Value = departmentId;
  param.DbType = DbType.Int32;
  comm.Parameters.Add(param);
  // execute the stored procedure
  DataTable table = GenericDataAccess.ExecuteSelectCommand(comm);
  // wrap retrieved data into a DepartmentDetails object
  DepartmentDetails details = new DepartmentDetails();
  if (table.Rows.Count > 0)
  {
    details.Name = table.Rows[0]["Name"].ToString();
    details.Description = table.Rows[0]["Description"].ToString();
  }
  // return department details
  return details;
}
```

You know what happens in this function fairly well because we analyzed portions of it in the first part of the chapter. Its main purpose is to send back the name and description of the relevant department. To do this, it calls the CatalogGetDepartmentDetails stored procedure, supplying it with a department ID. After execution, the function reads the @DepartmentName and @DepartmentDescription output parameters, saves them into a DepartmentDetails object, and sends this object back to the calling function.

GetCategoryDetails

History repeats itself in this section. Just as you needed to return a name and description for the selected department, now you need to do the same thing for the categories. You'll use the same technique here and wrap the data into a separate class.

Add the CategoryDetails struct at the beginning of CatalogAccess.cs, just after DepartmentDetails. Don't place it inside the CatalogAccess class!

```
/// <summary>
/// Wraps category details data
/// </summary>
public struct CategoryDetails
{
  public int DepartmentId;
  public string Name;
  public string Description;
}
```

Next, add the GetCategoryDetails method to the CatalogAccess class. Except for the fact that it calls another stored procedure and uses another class to wrap the return information, it is identical to GetDepartmentDetails:

```
// Get category details
public static CategoryDetails GetCategoryDetails(string categoryId)
{
  // get a configured DbCommand object
  DbCommand comm = GenericDataAccess.CreateCommand();
  // set the stored procedure name
  comm.CommandText = "CatalogGetCategoryDetails";
  // create a new parameter
  DbParameter param = comm.CreateParameter();
  param.ParameterName = "@CategoryID";
  param.Value = categoryId;
  param.DbType = DbType.Int32;
  comm.Parameters.Add(param);

  // execute the stored procedure
  DataTable table = GenericDataAccess.ExecuteSelectCommand(comm);
  // wrap retrieved data into a CategoryDetails object
  CategoryDetails details = new CategoryDetails();
  if (table.Rows.Count > 0)
  {
    details.DepartmentId = Int32.Parse(table.Rows[0]["DepartmentID"].ToString());
    details.Name = table.Rows[0]["Name"].ToString();
    details.Description = table.Rows[0]["Description"].ToString();
  }
  // return department details
  return details;
}
```

GetProductDetails

Let's do the same with the product details now. Add the ProductDetails struct at the beginning of CatalogAccess.cs. Don't place it inside the CatalogAccess class!

```
/// <summary>
/// Wraps product details data
/// </summary>
public struct ProductDetails
{
  public int ProductID;
  public string Name;
  public string Description;
  public decimal Price;
  public string Thumbnail;
  public string Image;
  public bool PromoFront;
  public bool PromoDept;
}
```

Add the GetProductDetails method to the CatalogAccess class:

```
// Get product details
public static ProductDetails GetProductDetails(string productId)
{
  // get a configured DbCommand object
  DbCommand comm = GenericDataAccess.CreateCommand();
  // set the stored procedure name
  comm.CommandText = "CatalogGetProductDetails";
  // create a new parameter
  DbParameter param = comm.CreateParameter();
  param.ParameterName = "@ProductID";
  param.Value = productId;
  param.DbType = DbType.Int32;
  comm.Parameters.Add(param);

  // execute the stored procedure
  DataTable table = GenericDataAccess.ExecuteSelectCommand(comm);
  // wrap retrieved data into a ProductDetails object
  ProductDetails details = new ProductDetails();
  if (table.Rows.Count > 0)
  {
    // get the first table row
    DataRow dr = table.Rows[0];
    // get product details
    details.ProductID = int.Parse(productId);
    details.Name = dr["Name"].ToString();
    details.Description = dr["Description"].ToString();
    details.Price = Decimal.Parse(dr["Price"].ToString());
    details.Thumbnail = dr["Thumbnail"].ToString();
    details.Image = dr["Image"].ToString();
```

```
    details.PromoFront = bool.Parse(dr["PromoFront"].ToString());
    details.PromoDept =
bool.Parse(dr["PromoDept"].ToString());
  }
  // return department details
  return details;
}
```

GetCategoriesInDepartment

The GetCategoriesInDepartment method is called to retrieve the list of categories that belong to a department. Add this function to the CatalogAccess class:

```
// retrieve the list of categories in a department
public static DataTable GetCategoriesInDepartment(string departmentId)
{
  // get a configured DbCommand object
  DbCommand comm = GenericDataAccess.CreateCommand();
  // set the stored procedure name
  comm.CommandText = "CatalogGetCategoriesInDepartment";
  // create a new parameter
  DbParameter param = comm.CreateParameter();
  param.ParameterName = "@DepartmentID";
  param.Value = departmentId;
  param.DbType = DbType.Int32;
  comm.Parameters.Add(param);
  // execute the stored procedure
  return GenericDataAccess.ExecuteSelectCommand(comm);
}
```

GetProductsOnFrontPromo

The methods that return products (GetProductsOnFrontPromo, GetProductsOnDeptPromo, GetProductsInCategory) are a bit more complex because they need to manage paging. This implies adding three parameters to the command objects: @PageNumber, @ProductsPerPage, and @HowManyProducts. The latter is an output parameter, which will be set by the stored procedure to the total number of products for the section (so you can calculate and tell the visitor the number of pages of products). Another new parameter is @DescriptionLength, which specifies how many characters the product's description should be trimmed down to (remember that we don't show full product descriptions in product lists).

   The GetProductsOnFrontPromo method gets the list of products featured on the main page of the site. It has two parameters: pageNumber and howManyPages. The latter parameter, howManyPages, is an out parameter. The values for the other two parameters needed for the CatalogGetProductsOnFrontPromo stored procedure (@DescriptionLength and @ProductsPerPage) are taken from the productsPerPage and productDescriptionLength class fields that you added earlier to the class.

When the presentation tier calls GetProductsOnFrontPromo, you send back the requested list of products in the form of a DataTable and the number of product subpages using the howManyPages out parameter.

Add this method to the CatalogAccess class:

```
// Retrieve the list of products on catalog promotion
public static DataTable GetProductsOnFrontPromo(string pageNumber, out int
howManyPages)
{
  // get a configured DbCommand object
  DbCommand comm = GenericDataAccess.CreateCommand();
  // set the stored procedure name
  comm.CommandText = "CatalogGetProductsOnFrontPromo";
  // create a new parameter
  DbParameter param = comm.CreateParameter();
  param.ParameterName = "@DescriptionLength";
  param.Value = BalloonShopConfiguration.ProductDescriptionLength;
  param.DbType = DbType.Int32;
  comm.Parameters.Add(param);
  // create a new parameter
  param = comm.CreateParameter();
  param.ParameterName = "@PageNumber";
  param.Value = pageNumber;
  param.DbType = DbType.Int32;
  comm.Parameters.Add(param);
  // create a new parameter
  param = comm.CreateParameter();
  param.ParameterName = "@ProductsPerPage";
  param.Value = BalloonShopConfiguration.ProductsPerPage;
  param.DbType = DbType.Int32;
  comm.Parameters.Add(param);
  // create a new parameter
  param = comm.CreateParameter();
  param.ParameterName = "@HowManyProducts";
  param.Direction = ParameterDirection.Output;
  param.DbType = DbType.Int32;
  comm.Parameters.Add(param);

  // execute the stored procedure and save the results in a DataTable
  DataTable table = GenericDataAccess.ExecuteSelectCommand(comm);
  // calculate how many pages of products and set the out parameter
  int howManyProducts = Int32.Parse(comm.Parameters
["@HowManyProducts"].Value.ToString());
  howManyPages = (int)Math.Ceiling((double)howManyProducts /
                 (double)BalloonShopConfiguration.ProductsPerPage);
  // return the page of products
  return table;
}
```

GetProductsOnDeptPromo

The GetProductsOnDeptPromo function returns the list of products featured for a particular department. The department's featured products must be displayed when the customer visits the home page of a department.

```
// retrieve the list of products featured for a department
public static DataTable GetProductsOnDeptPromo
(string departmentId, string pageNumber, out int howManyPages)
{
  // get a configured DbCommand object
  DbCommand comm = GenericDataAccess.CreateCommand();
  // set the stored procedure name
  comm.CommandText = "CatalogGetProductsOnDeptPromo";
  // create a new parameter
  DbParameter param = comm.CreateParameter();
  param.ParameterName = "@DepartmentID";
  param.Value = departmentId;
  param.DbType = DbType.Int32;
  comm.Parameters.Add(param);
  // create a new parameter
  param = comm.CreateParameter();
  param.ParameterName = "@DescriptionLength";
  param.Value = BalloonShopConfiguration.ProductDescriptionLength;
  param.DbType = DbType.Int32;
  comm.Parameters.Add(param);
  // create a new parameter
  param = comm.CreateParameter();
  param.ParameterName = "@PageNumber";
  param.Value = pageNumber;
  param.DbType = DbType.Int32;
  comm.Parameters.Add(param);
  // create a new parameter
  param = comm.CreateParameter();
  param.ParameterName = "@ProductsPerPage";
  param.Value = BalloonShopConfiguration.ProductsPerPage;
  param.DbType = DbType.Int32;
  comm.Parameters.Add(param);
  // create a new parameter
  param = comm.CreateParameter();
  param.ParameterName = "@HowManyProducts";
  param.Direction = ParameterDirection.Output;
  param.DbType = DbType.Int32;
  comm.Parameters.Add(param);
  // execute the stored procedure and save the results in a DataTable
  DataTable table = GenericDataAccess.ExecuteSelectCommand(comm);
  // calculate how many pages of products and set the out parameter
  int howManyProducts = Int32.Parse
```

```
(comm.Parameters["@HowManyProducts"].Value.ToString());
  howManyPages = (int)Math.Ceiling((double)howManyProducts /
                 (double)BalloonShopConfiguration.ProductsPerPage);
  // return the page of products
  return table;
}
```

GetProductsInCategory

GetProductsInCategory returns the list of products that belong to a particular category. Add the following method to the CatalogAccess class:

```
// retrieve the list of products in a category
public static DataTable GetProductsInCategory
(string categoryId, string pageNumber, out int howManyPages)
{
  // get a configured DbCommand object
  DbCommand comm = GenericDataAccess.CreateCommand();
  // set the stored procedure name
  comm.CommandText = "CatalogGetProductsInCategory";
  // create a new parameter
  DbParameter param = comm.CreateParameter();
  param.ParameterName = "@CategoryID";
  param.Value = categoryId;
  param.DbType = DbType.Int32;
  comm.Parameters.Add(param);
  // create a new parameter
  param = comm.CreateParameter();
  param.ParameterName = "@DescriptionLength";
  param.Value = BalloonShopConfiguration.ProductDescriptionLength;
  param.DbType = DbType.Int32;
  comm.Parameters.Add(param);
  // create a new parameter
  param = comm.CreateParameter();
  param.ParameterName = "@PageNumber";
  param.Value = pageNumber;
  param.DbType = DbType.Int32;
  comm.Parameters.Add(param);
  // create a new parameter
  param = comm.CreateParameter();
  param.ParameterName = "@ProductsPerPage";
  param.Value = BalloonShopConfiguration.ProductsPerPage;
  param.DbType = DbType.Int32;
  comm.Parameters.Add(param);
  // create a new parameter
  param = comm.CreateParameter();
  param.ParameterName = "@HowManyProducts";
  param.Direction = ParameterDirection.Output;
```

```
  param.DbType = DbType.Int32;
  comm.Parameters.Add(param);
  // execute the stored procedure and save the results in a DataTable
  DataTable table = GenericDataAccess.ExecuteSelectCommand(comm);
  // calculate how many pages of products and set the out parameter
  int howManyProducts = Int32.Parse
(comm.Parameters["@HowManyProducts"].Value.ToString());
  howManyPages = (int)Math.Ceiling((double)howManyProducts /
                (double)BalloonShopConfiguration.ProductsPerPage);
  // return the page of products
  return table;
}
```

Completing the Link Factory

Add the two ToCategory, ToProduct, and ToProductImage methods to your Link class, in Link.cs:

```
public static string ToCategory(string departmentId, string categoryId, string
page)
{
  if (page == "1")
    return BuildAbsolute(String.Format(
"Catalog.aspx?DepartmentID={0}&CategoryID={1}",
departmentId, categoryId));
  else
    return BuildAbsolute(String.Format(
"Catalog.aspx?DepartmentID={0}&CategoryID={1}&Page={2}",
departmentId, categoryId, page));
}

public static string ToCategory(string departmentId, string categoryId)
{
  return ToCategory(departmentId, categoryId, "1");
}

public static string ToProduct(string productId)
{
  return BuildAbsolute(String.Format("Product.aspx?ProductID={0}", productId));
}

public static string ToProductImage(string fileName)
{
  // build product URL
  return BuildAbsolute("/ProductImages/" + fileName);
}
```

Implementing the Presentation Tier

Once again, it's time to see some colors! Believe it or not, right now the data and business tiers of the product catalog are complete for this chapter (finally!). All you have to do is use their functionality in the presentation tier. In this final section, you'll create a few Web Forms and Web User Controls and integrate them into the existing project.

If you now execute the BalloonShop project and click one of the departments, you are redirected to Catalog.aspx, with a DepartmentID parameter in the query string that specifies the ID of the selected department:

```
http://www.example.com/Catalog.aspx?DepartmentID=1
```

In the following sections, you'll write code that makes the catalog more friendly by actually responding when the visitor clicks on those links. In the following sections, you will

- Write the CategoriesList.ascx control, which will display the list of categories for the selected department. This new control is similar to DepartmentsList.ascx that you wrote in the previous chapter.

- Complete the functionality in Catalog.aspx, making it display the name and description of the selected department or category.

- Implement ProductsList.ascx, which will display the products for the currently visited page (the main page, a department page, or a category page).

- Implement Product.aspx, which will be the product details page. When visitors click on a product in the products list, they will be taken to a product details page at a URL such as http://www.example.com/Product.aspx?ProductID=1.

Displaying the List of Categories

CategoriesList is similar to the DepartmentsList Web User Control. It consists of a DataList control that is populated with data retrieved from the business tier. The DataList control will contain links to Catalog.aspx, but this time the query string will also contain a CategoryID parameter, showing that a category has been clicked, like this:

```
http://localhost/BalloonShop/Catalog.aspx?DepartmentID=1&CategoryID=2
```

The steps in the following exercise are similar to the steps you followed to create the DepartmentsList user control, so we'll move a bit more quickly this time.

Exercise: Creating the CategoriesList Web User Control

1. Create a new Web User Control in the UserControls folder. In Solution Explorer, right-click the UserControls folder, and then choose **Add New Item**. Select the **Web User Control** template, and set CategoriesList.ascx (or simply CategoriesList) as its name. Make sure **Place code in separate file** is checked, and click **Add**.

2. In Design View, open the toolbox and double-click the **DataList** entry on the **Data** tab to add a DataList control to your Web User Control.

3. Set the properties on the `DataList` object as shown in Table 5-3.

Table 5-3. *Setting the DataList Properties*

Property Name	Value
(ID)	list
Width	200px
CssClass	CategoriesList
HeaderStyle-CssClass	CategoriesListHead

4. Right-click the `DataList` and select **Edit Template ➤ Header and Footer Templates**. Type **Choose a Category** in the **Header** template.

5. Right-click the `DataList` and select **Edit Template ➤ Item Templates**. Add a `HyperLink` control from the Standard tab of the toolbox to the **ItemTemplate**. Set the **Text** property of the `HyperLink` to an empty string.

6. Switch to Source View. The code auto-generated by Visual Studio for the hyperlink should look like this:

```
<asp:DataList ID="list" runat="server" CssClass="CategoriesList"
Width="200px">
  <HeaderTemplate>
    Choose a Category
  </HeaderTemplate>
  <HeaderStyle CssClass="CategoriesListHead" />
  <ItemTemplate>
    <asp:HyperLink ID="HyperLink1" runat="server"></asp:HyperLink>
  </ItemTemplate>
</asp:DataList>
```

7. Modify the code of the `<ItemTemplate>` element like this:

```
<ItemTemplate>
  <asp:HyperLink ID="HyperLink1" Runat="server"
    NavigateUrl='<%# Link.ToCategory(Request.QueryString["DepartmentID"],
Eval("CategoryID").ToString()) %>'
    Text='<%# HttpUtility.HtmlEncode(Eval("Name").ToString()) %>'
    ToolTip='<%# HttpUtility.HtmlEncode(Eval("Description").ToString()) %>'
    CssClass='<%# Eval("CategoryID").ToString() ==
            Request.QueryString["CategoryID"] ?
            "CategorySelected" : "CategoryUnselected" %>'>>
  </asp:HyperLink>
</ItemTemplate>
```

8. Switching to Design View should reveal a window such as the one in Figure 5-17.

Figure 5-17. *CategoriesList.ascx in Design View*

9. Add the following styles to BalloonShop.css:

```css
.CategoriesList {
  border: #ea6d00 1px solid;
  text-align: center;
  margin-top: 20px;
}
.CategoriesListHead {
  border: #ea6d00 1px solid;
  background-color: #f8c78c;
}
a.CategoryUnselected {
  line-height: 25px;
  text-decoration: none;
  color: Black;
}
a.CategoryUnselected:hover {
  text-decoration: underline;
}
a.CategorySelected {
  line-height: 25px;
  font-weight: bold;
  text-decoration: none;
  color: Black;
}
```

10. Now open the code-behind file of the user control (CategoriesList.ascx.cs) and modify the Page_Load event handler like this:

```csharp
protected void Page_Load(object sender, EventArgs e)
{
  // Obtain the ID of the selected department
  string departmentId = Request.QueryString["DepartmentID"];
  // Continue only if DepartmentID exists in the query string
```

```
if (departmentId != null)
{
  // Catalog.GetCategoriesInDepartment returns a DataTable
  // object containing category data, which is displayed by the DataList
  list.DataSource =
     CatalogAccess.GetCategoriesInDepartment(departmentId);
  // Needed to bind the data bound controls to the data source
  list.DataBind();
}
}
```

11. Open BalloonShop.master in Design View. Drag CategoriesList.ascx from Solution Explorer and drop it near the list of departments.

12. Execute the project, select a department, and then select a category. You should see something like Figure 5-18.

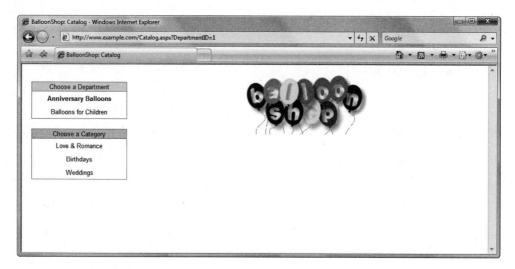

Figure 5-18. *BalloonShop with a brand new list of categories*

How It Works: The CategoriesList User Control

The important detail to know about CategoriesList is what happens when you click a category link: Catalog.aspx is reloaded, but this time, CategoryID is appended to the query string. In some of the other controls you'll create, you'll check for CategoryID in the query string—when it's present, this indicates that the visitor is browsing a category.

CategoriesList works like DepartmentsList—they are both used in the Master Page, and they both get loaded at the same time. However, when CategoriesList gets loaded and its Page_Load function executes, the code checks to determine whether a department was selected:

```
void Page_Load(object sender, EventArgs e)
{
    // Obtain the ID of the selected department
    string departmentId = Request.QueryString["DepartmentID"];
    // Continue only if DepartmentID exists in the query string
    if (departmentId != null)
    {
...
...
...
```

If the DataList isn't populated with data, it doesn't show at all. This is important, because if the visitor is on the main page and a department was not selected, no categories should show up.

On the other hand, if a department was selected, the business tier GetCategoriesInDeparment method of the CatalogAccess class is called to obtain the list of categories in that department:

```
    // Continue only if DepartmentID exists in the query string
    if (departmentId != null)
    {
        // Catalog.GetCategoriesInDepartment returns a DataTable object
        // containing category data, which is displayed by the DataList
        list.DataSource =
    CatalogAccess.GetCategoriesInDepartment(departmentId);
        // Needed to bind the data bound controls to the data source
        list.DataBind();
    }
```

■Note A final note about CategoriesList.ascx is that you're free to use it in other pages or even for other user controls. For example, you might want to add CategoriesList inside the SelectedItemTemplate element of the DataList in the DepartmentsList instead of placing it directly on the Master Page. Feel free to experiment and see how easy it is to change the look of the web site with just a few clicks!

Displaying Department and Category Details

Now the visitor can visit the main web page and select a department or a category. In each of these cases, your page contents cell must update itself with data about the selected department or category.

The good thing is that category and department pages have similar structure: they display the name of the selected category or department on the top, then the description, and finally a list of products. You'll use a single Web Form named Catalog.aspx, which handles generating both category and department pages. The list of products in those pages is generated by a separate Web User Control that you'll implement later.

In the following exercise, you implement Catalog.aspx, which hosts the details of the selected department or category.

Exercise: Displaying Department and Category Data

1. Open Catalog.aspx in Source View. You need to add two labels, named catalogTitleLabel and catalogDescriptionLabel, to the content part of the page. Feel free to use Design View to add them the way you like. Alternatively, use Source View to add the following HTML code, which also contains the mentioned labels:

```
<%@ Page Language="C#" MasterPageFile="~/BalloonShop.master"
AutoEventWireup="true" CodeFile="Catalog.aspx.cs" Inherits="Catalog"
Title="BalloonShop: Catalog" %>

<asp:Content ID="Content1" ContentPlaceHolderID="head" runat="Server">
</asp:Content>
<asp:Content ID="Content2" ContentPlaceHolderID="ContentPlaceHolder1"
runat="server">
    <h1>
      <asp:Label ID="catalogTitleLabel" CssClass="CatalogTitle"
runat="server" />
    </h1>
    <h2>
      <asp:Label ID="catalogDescriptionLabel" CssClass="CatalogDescription"
runat="server" />
    </h2>
    [Place List of Products Here]
</asp:Content>
```

2. Open Default.aspx in Source View and edit the content placeholder like this:

```
<asp:Content ID="Content2" ContentPlaceHolderID="ContentPlaceHolder1"
runat="server">
    <h1>
      <span class="CatalogTitle">Welcome to BalloonShop!</span>
    </h1>
    <h2>
      <span class="CatalogDescription">This week we have a special price
for these fantastic products: </span>
    </h2>
    [Place List of Products Here]
</asp:Content>
```

3. Add the following styles to BalloonShop.css:

```
.CatalogTitle {
  color: red;
  font-size: 24px;
  font-weight: bold;
}
```

```
.CatalogDescription {
  color: Black;
  font-weight: bold;
  font-size: 14px;
}
```

4. It's time to write the code that populates the two labels with data from the database. Add the following
   code to the Catalog class, in Catalog.aspx.cs:

```
public partial class Catalog : System.Web.UI.Page
{
  protected void Page_Load(object sender, EventArgs e)
  {
    PopulateControls();
  }

  // Fill the page with data
  private void PopulateControls()
  {
    // Retrieve DepartmentID from the query string
    string departmentId = Request.QueryString["DepartmentID"];
    // Retrieve CategoryID from the query string
    string categoryId = Request.QueryString["CategoryID"];
    // If browsing a category...
    if (categoryId != null)
    {
      // Retrieve category and department details and display them
      CategoryDetails cd = CatalogAccess.GetCategoryDetails(categoryId);
      catalogTitleLabel.Text = HttpUtility.HtmlEncode(cd.Name);
      DepartmentDetails dd =
CatalogAccess.GetDepartmentDetails(departmentId);
      catalogDescriptionLabel.Text =
HttpUtility.HtmlEncode(cd.Description);
      // Set the title of the page
      this.Title = HttpUtility.HtmlEncode(BalloonShopConfiguration.SiteName +
              ": " + dd.Name + ": " + cd.Name);
    }
    // If browsing a department...
    else if (departmentId != null)
    {
      // Retrieve department details and display them
      DepartmentDetails dd =
CatalogAccess.GetDepartmentDetails(departmentId);
      catalogTitleLabel.Text = HttpUtility.HtmlEncode(dd.Name);
      catalogDescriptionLabel.Text =
HttpUtility.HtmlEncode(dd.Description);
      // Set the title of the page
      this.Title = HttpUtility.HtmlEncode(BalloonShopConfiguration.SiteName +
  ": " + dd.Name);
    }
  }
}
```

5. Execute the project and click one of the departments, and then click one of the categories. You should get something like Figure 5-19.

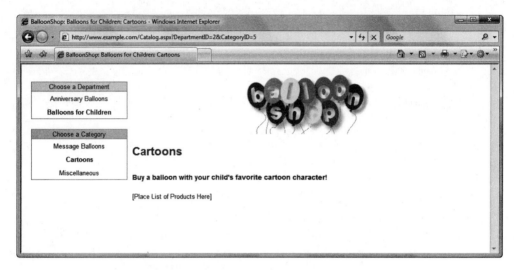

Figure 5-19. *Displaying category and department details*

How It Works: Displaying Department and Category Data

BalloonShop started looking almost like a real web site, didn't it? In this exercise you started by adding some controls to `Catalog.aspx` that display the name and description of the selected department or category. You also added some text to `Default.aspx` that gets displayed on the main page of your catalog. Both `Catalog.aspx` and `Default.aspx` contain the `[Place list of products here]` text; you'll replace this text with the actual list of products in the next section.

The work of displaying department and category data is done in the `PopulateControls` method in `Catalog.aspx.cs`. To determine whether the visitor is browsing a department or a category, the method needs to check out the values of `CategoryID` and `DepartmentID` in the query string, so it saves the values of these parameters as local variables:

```
// Retrieve DepartmentID from the query string
string departmentId = Request.QueryString["DepartmentID"];
// Retrieve CategoryID from the query string
string categoryId = Request.QueryString["CategoryID"];
```

Next it determines whether a value has been supplied for `CategoryID`, in which case we pass this value to `CatalogAccess.CatalogGetCategoryDetails`, which returns the details of that category in the form of a `CategoryDetails` object:

```
// If browsing a category...
if (categoryId != null)
{
  // Retrieve category and department details and display them
  CategoryDetails cd = CatalogAccess.GetCategoryDetails(categoryId);
  catalogTitleLabel.Text = cd.Name;
```

```
DepartmentDetails dd = CatalogAccess.GetDepartmentDetails(departmentId);
catalogDescriptionLabel.Text = cd.Description;
// Set the title of the page
this.Title = BalloonShopConfiguration.SiteName +
            ": " + dd.Name + ": " + cd.Name;
}
```

If CategoryId is NULL, you could assume the visitor is browsing a department and display the department's data (Catalog.aspx is loaded only if the visitor has clicked on a department or a category). However, for safety, we verify that a department ID has actually been supplied, and if this turns out to be so, we load the department's data using CatalogAccess.GetDepartmentDetails:

```
// If browsing a department...
else if (departmentId != null)
{
  // Retrieve department details and display them
  DepartmentDetails dd = CatalogAccess.GetDepartmentDetails(departmentId);
  catalogTitleLabel.Text = dd.Name;
  catalogDescriptionLabel.Text = dd.Description;
  // Set the title of the page
  this.Title = BalloonShopConfiguration.SiteName +
              ": " + dd.Name;
}
```

Displaying Product Lists

So where's the meat? Your web site will display product lists using a Web User Control named ProductsList.ascx. In theory, this control is very much like CategoriesList.ascx and DepartmentsList.ascx, in that it uses a DataList control to generate a list of items. In practice, implementing this control is a little bit more complicated because there's more code to write.

This control also needs to support the paging feature offered by the business tier. It needs to display controls to allow the visitor to move forward and backward between pages of products. We'll encapsulate the paging feature in a separate Web User Control, Pager.ascx.

Let's go.

Exercise: Creating the Pager and ProductsList Web User Controls

This exercise is made up of two parts. First, we'll create the Pager Web User Control. Then we'll create the ProductsList Web User Control.

Creating the Pager Web User Control

1. Copy the ProductImages folder from the book's code archive to your BalloonShop folder.

2. Add a new Web User Control named Pager to the UserControls folder, with a code behind file.

3. While in Source View, write the pager template code:

```
<%@ Control Language="C#" AutoEventWireup="true" CodeFile="Pager.ascx.cs"
Inherits="UserControls_Pager" %>

<p>
Page
<asp:Label ID="currentPageLabel" runat="server" />
of
<asp:Label ID="howManyPagesLabel" runat="server" />
|

<asp:HyperLink ID="previousLink" Runat="server">Previous</asp:HyperLink>

<asp:Repeater ID="pagesRepeater" runat="server">
  <ItemTemplate>
    <asp:HyperLink ID="hyperlink" runat="server" Text='<%# Eval("Page") %>'

NavigateUrl='<%# Eval("Url") %>' />
  </ItemTemplate>
</asp:Repeater>

<asp:HyperLink ID="nextLink" Runat="server">Next</asp:HyperLink>
</p>
```

4. Switch to Design View. Your control should look like Figure 5-20.

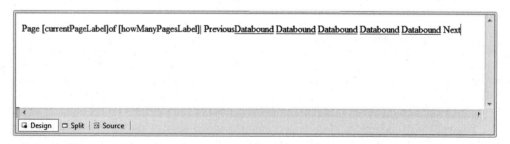

Figure 5-20. *The Pager Control*

5. Switch to the code-behind file, and update it as shown in the following code snippet:

```
// simple struct that represents a (page number, url) association
public struct PageUrl
{
  private string page;
  private string url;
```

```csharp
  // Page and Url property definitions
  public string Page
  {
    get
    {
      return page;
    }
  }
  public string Url
  {
    get
    {
      return url;
    }
  }

  // constructor
  public PageUrl(string page, string url)
  {
    this.page = page;
    this.url = url;
  }
}

// the Pager control
public partial class UserControls_Pager : System.Web.UI.UserControl
{
  // show the pager
  public void Show(int currentPage, int howManyPages, string firstPageUrl,
string pageUrlFormat, bool showPages)
  {
    // display paging controls
    if (howManyPages > 1)
    {
      // make the pager visible
      this.Visible = true;

      // display the current page
      currentPageLabel.Text = currentPage.ToString();
      howManyPagesLabel.Text = howManyPages.ToString();

      // create the Previous link
      if (currentPage == 1)
      {
        previousLink.Enabled = false;
      }
```

```
            else
            {
              previousLink.NavigateUrl = (currentPage == 2) ?
                firstPageUrl : String.Format(pageUrlFormat, currentPage - 1);
            }

            // create the Next link
            if (currentPage == howManyPages)
            {
              nextLink.Enabled = false;
            }
            else
            {
              nextLink.NavigateUrl = String.Format(pageUrlFormat, currentPage + 1);
            }

            // create the page links
            if (showPages)
            {
              // the list of pages and their URLs as an array
              PageUrl[] pages = new PageUrl[howManyPages];
              // generate (page, url) elements
              pages[0] = new PageUrl("1", firstPageUrl);
              for (int i = 2; i <= howManyPages; i++)
              {
                pages[i - 1] =
                  new PageUrl(i.ToString(), String.Format(pageUrlFormat, i));
              }
              // do not generate a link for the current page
              pages[currentPage - 1] = new PageUrl((currentPage).ToString(), "");
              // feed the pages to the repeater
              pagesRepeater.DataSource = pages;
              pagesRepeater.DataBind();
            }
        }
    }

    protected void Page_Load(object sender, EventArgs e)
    {
    }
}
```

6. Before proceeding to implementing the ProductsList Web User Control, press **Ctrl+Shift+B** (**Build Solution**) to make sure the code compiles. This will make debugging easier in case an error occurs.

Creating the ProductsList Web User Control

1. Add a new Web User Control named ProductsList to the UserControls folder. You'll use a code-behind file as well.

2. Open the control in Design View, and drag a Pager from Solution Explorer to your ProductsList control.

3. Continue by dragging a DataList control from the toolbox to ProductsList.

4. Finally, drag another Pager control from Solution Explorer to ProductsList. It should now look as shown in Figure 5-21.

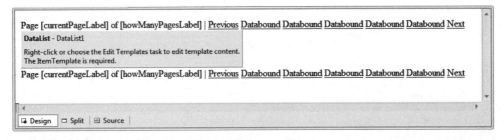

Page [currentPageLabel] of [howManyPagesLabel] | Previous Databound Databound Databound Databound Databound Next

DataList - DataList1

Right-click or choose the Edit Templates task to edit template content. The ItemTemplate is required.

Page [currentPageLabel] of [howManyPagesLabel] | Previous Databound Databound Databound Databound Databound Next

◻ Design   ◻ Split   ◻ Source

Figure 5-21. *Displaying category and department details*

5. Change the ID of the top pager control to topPager, and the ID of the bottom pager control to bottomPager.

6. Set the Visible property of both topPager and bottomPager to **False**. (You want the pager to show up only when there is more than one page of products, so you don't make it visible by default.)

7. Rename the ID of the DataList to list, and set its RepeatColumns property to 2 (specifies the number of products to be displayed per row).

8. Edit the DataList's code directly in Source View:

```
<asp:DataList ID="list" runat="server" RepeatColumns="2"
CssClass="ProductList">
    <ItemTemplate>
      <h3 class="ProductTitle">
        <a href="<%# Link.ToProduct(Eval("ProductID").ToString()) %>">
          <%# HttpUtility.HtmlEncode(Eval("Name").ToString()) %>
        </a>
      </h3>
      <a href="<%# Link.ToProduct(Eval("ProductID").ToString()) %>">
        <img width="100" border="0"
src="<%# Link.ToProductImage(Eval("Thumbnail").ToString()) %>"
alt='<%# HttpUtility.HtmlEncode(Eval("Name").ToString())%>' />
      </a>
      <%# HttpUtility.HtmlEncode(Eval("Description").ToString()) %>
      <p>
        Price:
        <%# Eval("Price", "{0:c}") %>
      </p>
    </ItemTemplate>
</asp:DataList>
```

9. Add these styles to `BalloonShop.css`:

```css
.ProductList img {
  border: 2px solid #c6e1ec;
  float: left;
  margin-right: 5px;
  vertical-align: top;
}
.ProductTitle {
  font-size: 15px;
  font-weight: bold;
  margin: 10px 1px 0 0;
}
```

10. The way ASP.NET outputs product prices to the visitor depends on the culture settings of the computer running the site. You told ASP.NET which numbers represent prices by using the `{0:C}` formatting parameter in the `Eval` expression. For example, if the default culture is set to `fr-FR`, instead of $1.23 you would see 1,23EUR. (For more information on internationalization issues, consult an advanced ASP.NET book.) For now, to make sure the prices are expressed in the same currency (US dollars for this example), double-click `web.config` in Solution Explorer and add the `<globalization>` element under `<system.web>`, like this:

```
...
    <globalization requestEncoding="utf-8" responseEncoding="utf-8"
culture="en-US"/>
  </system.web>
</configuration>
```

This ensures that no matter how the development (or production) machine is set up, your prices will always be expressed in the same currency.

11. Modify the `ProductsList` class in `ProductsList.ascx.cs` like this:

```csharp
public partial class UserControls_ProductsList : System.Web.UI.UserControl
{
  protected void Page_Load(object sender, EventArgs e)
  {
    PopulateControls();
  }

  private void PopulateControls()
  {
    // Retrieve DepartmentID from the query string
    string departmentId = Request.QueryString["DepartmentID"];
    // Retrieve CategoryID from the query string
    string categoryId = Request.QueryString["CategoryID"];
    // Retrieve Page from the query string
    string page = Request.QueryString["Page"];
```

```csharp
    if (page == null) page = "1";
    // How many pages of products?
    int howManyPages = 1;
    // pager links format
    string firstPageUrl = "";
    string pagerFormat = "";

    // If browsing a category...
    if (categoryId != null)
    {
      // Retrieve list of products in a category
      list.DataSource =
      CatalogAccess.GetProductsInCategory(categoryId, page, out howManyPages);
      list.DataBind();
      // get first page url and pager format
      firstPageUrl = Link.ToCategory(departmentId, categoryId, "1");
      pagerFormat = Link.ToCategory(departmentId, categoryId, "{0}");
    }
    else if (departmentId != null)
    {
      // Retrieve list of products on department promotion
      list.DataSource = CatalogAccess.GetProductsOnDeptPromo
      (departmentId, page, out howManyPages);
      list.DataBind();
      // get first page url and pager format
      firstPageUrl = Link.ToDepartment(departmentId, "1");
      pagerFormat = Link.ToDepartment(departmentId, "{0}");
    }
    else
    {
      // Retrieve list of products on catalog promotion
      list.DataSource =
      CatalogAccess.GetProductsOnFrontPromo(page, out howManyPages);
      list.DataBind();
      // have the current page as integer
      int currentPage = Int32.Parse(page);

    }

    // Display pager controls
    topPager.Show(int.Parse(page), howManyPages, firstPageUrl, pagerFormat,
false);
    bottomPager.Show(int.Parse(page), howManyPages, firstPageUrl,
pagerFormat,
true);
  }
}
```

12. Open `Catalog.aspx` in Design View. Drag `ProductsList.ascx` from Solution Explorer, drop it near the **[Place List of Products Here]** text, and then delete the text, as shown in Figure 5-22.

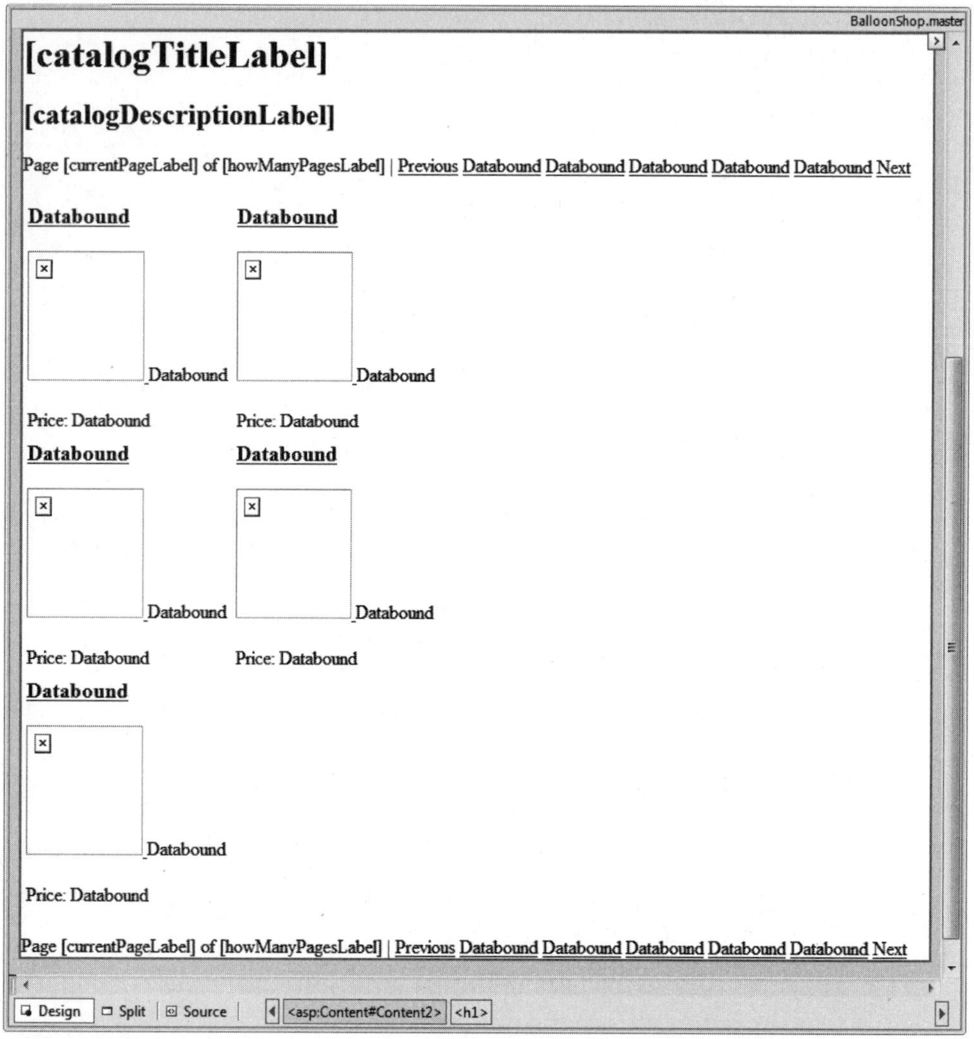

Figure 5-22. *Adding* `ProductsList.ascx` *to* `Catalog.aspx`

13. Now do the same in `Default.aspx`.

14. Press **F5** to execute the project. The main page should now be populated with its featured products (see Figure 5-23).

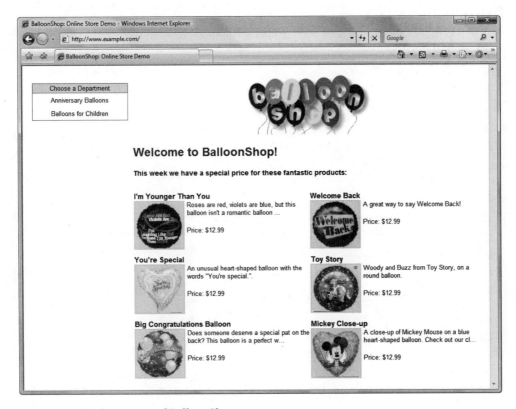

Figure 5-23. *The front page of BalloonShop*

15. Now click a department to see the department's featured products, and then click a category to see all the products in that category. Figure 5-24 shows the paging feature in action.

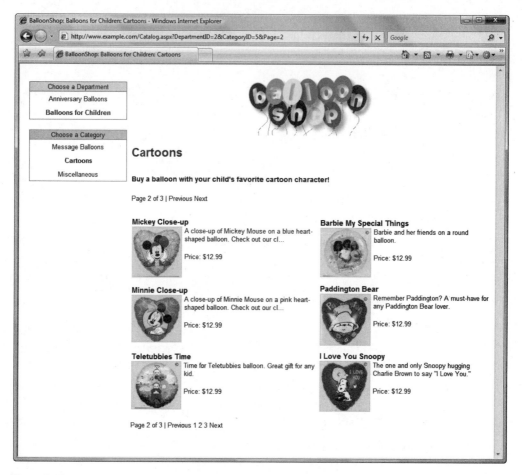

Figure 5-24. *Paging in action*

How It Works: The ProductsList Web User Control

ProductsList.ascx, just like CategoriesList.ascx and DepartmentsList.ascx, uses a DataList to paint a list of items. Because ProductsList.ascx will be reused in both Default.aspx and Catalog.aspx, you can't know beforehand exactly what it needs to display. Is it the list of products on catalog promotion, or is it the list of products in a particular category? In the usual style, ProductsList decides what it needs to display by analyzing the query string parameters. The logic is simple, so we won't go through it again here.

The first two new issues you played with in this exercise are the globalization setting and the paging controls. Setting the application to use the en-US culture ensures that monetary data (product prices) will always be displayed using the dollar symbol, no matter the settings of the computer that hosts the application.

Paging works through a query string parameter named Page. When a list of products is to be displayed and Page doesn't show up in the query string, the code automatically assumes the visitor is on the first page. For example, both these links would forward the visitor to the first page of products for the main page of the catalog:

```
http://localhost/BalloonShop/Catalog.aspx?DepartmentID=1
http://localhost/BalloonShop/Catalog.aspx?DepartmentID=1&Page=1
```

The Previous and Next links have the simple role of incrementing or decrementing the value of the Page query string parameter. Note that the paging controls only appear if there's more than one subpage of products. You find out this detail from the business tier GetProducts... functions, which return the total number of subpages through the howManyPages out parameter:

```
// If browsing a category...
if (categoryId != null)
{
  // Retrieve list of products in a category
  list.DataSource =
CatalogAccess.CatalogGetProductsInCategory(categoryId, page, out
howManyPages);
  list.DataBind();
}
```

You make the paging controls visible only if the number of subpages is greater than 1:

```
// display paging controls
  if (howManyPages > 1)
```

When making the paging controls visible, the main challenge is to build the links for Previous and Next. For example, the Next link should be the same as the currently loaded page, except the Page value in the query string should be incremented by one, but it shouldn't be enabled if the visitor is on the last page. You do this by browsing through the collection of query string parameters and reconstructing the complete query string:

```
// create the Next link
if (currentPage == howManyPages)
  nextLink.Enabled = false;
else
{
  NameValueCollection query = Request.QueryString;
  string paramName, newQueryString = "?";
  for (int i = 0; i < query.Count; i++)
    if (query.AllKeys[i] != null)
      if ((paramName = query.AllKeys[i].ToString()).ToUpper() != "PAGE")
        newQueryString += paramName + "=" + query[i] + "&";
  nextLink.NavigateUrl = Request.Url.AbsolutePath +
newQueryString + "Page=" + (currentPage + 1).ToString();
}
```

The logic that builds the Previous link is similar to the code for the Next link.

Displaying Product Details

This is the last bit of the UI for this chapter. Product lists contain links to the product details pages, which is dealt with by a Web Form named Product.aspx that you'll write in the following exercise.

Exercise: Displaying Product Details

1. Add a new Web Form named `Product.aspx` to your project, based on the `BalloonShop.master` Master Page. Also make sure you create it with a code-behind file.

2. The Web Form opens by default in Source View. The product details page needs to display the product's name in a `Label` control named `titleLabel`, the product's description in a `Label` named `descriptionLabel`, the price in a `Label` named `priceLabel`, and the image in an `Image` control named `productImage`. Feel free to arrange these items in any way you like. Here's how we placed them in `Product.aspx` (note their `CssLabel` property as well):

```
<%@ Page Language="C#" MasterPageFile="~/BalloonShop.master"
AutoEventWireup="true" CodeFile="Product.aspx.cs" Inherits="Product"
Title="BalloonShop: Product Details Page" %>

<asp:Content ID="Content1" ContentPlaceHolderID="head" runat="Server">
</asp:Content>
<asp:Content ID="Content2"
ContentPlaceHolderID="ContentPlaceHolder1" runat="Server">
  <p>
    <asp:Label CssClass="CatalogTitle" ID="titleLabel" runat="server"
Text="Label"></asp:Label>
  </p>
  <p>
    <asp:Image ID="productImage" runat="server" />
  </p>
  <p>
    <asp:Label ID="descriptionLabel" runat="server" Text="Label"></asp:Label>
  </p>
  <p>
    <b>Price:</b>
    <asp:Label CssClass="ProductPrice" ID="priceLabel" runat="server"
Text="Label"></asp:Label>
  </p>
</asp:Content>
```

3. Let's now read the necessary data from the database to set up the labels and the image. Add the following code to the page's `Page_Load` event handler method in `Product.aspx.cs`:

```
public partial class Product : System.Web.UI.Page
{
  protected void Page_Load(object sender, EventArgs e)
  {
    // Retrieve ProductID from the query string
    string productId = Request.QueryString["ProductID"];
    // Retrieves product details
    ProductDetails pd = CatalogAccess.GetProductDetails(productId);
```

```
      // Does the product exist?
      if (pd.Name != null)
      {
        PopulateControls(pd);
      }
    }

    // Fill the control with data
    private void PopulateControls(ProductDetails pd)
    {
      // Display product details
      titleLabel.Text = pd.Name;
      descriptionLabel.Text = pd.Description;
      priceLabel.Text = String.Format("{0:c}", pd.Price);
      productImage.ImageUrl = "ProductImages/" + pd.Image;
      // Set the title of the page
      this.Title = BalloonShopConfiguration.SiteName + pd.Name;
    }
  }
```

4. Congratulations, you've finished! Execute the project to ensure everything works as expected (Figure 5-25).

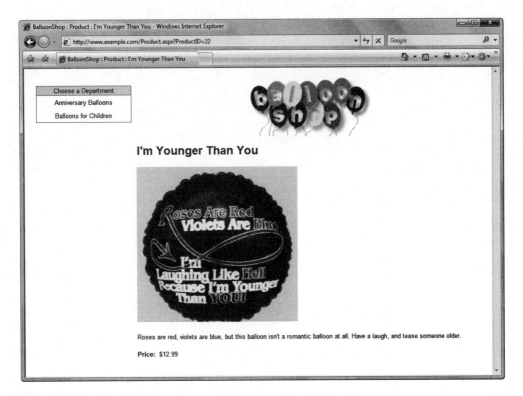

Figure 5-25. *Product details*

Summary

You've done a lot of work in this chapter. You finished building the product catalog by implementing the necessary logic in the data, business, and presentation tiers. On the way, you learned about many new theory issues, including

- Relational data and the types of relationships that can occur between tables

- How to obtain data from multiple tables in a single result set using JOIN and how to implement paging at the data tier level

- How to work with stored procedure input and output parameters

Chapter 6 will be at least as exciting as this one, because you'll learn how to add a dynamic site map to your web site!

Product Attributes

Many online stores allow shoppers to customize the products they buy. For example, when selling balloons, it's common to let your customer choose the color of the balloon—sparing them the fashion risk of one-color-fits-all.

In this chapter, we'll implement the product attributes feature in BalloonShop, assuming that our client lets its customers choose the color of their balloons when placing an order.

We'll do this starting with the data tier, where you'll create data tables and a stored procedure, then write the business tier code that calls that procedure, and finally use this functionality to update the presentation tier components. At the end of this chapter, our catalog will allow customers to choose the color of the balloon, as shown in Figure 6-1. Since the attribute data is stored in the database, you can easily add your own attributes and attribute values.

Figure 6-1. *Products with attributes*

Note that at this moment, these attributes don't make much of a difference for a potential customer, because the products can't be ordered yet—but that detail will be taken care of in the next chapters.

Implementing the Data Tier

The data tier components that support the product attributes feature include three data tables (Attribute, AttributeValue, and ProductAttributeValue) and a stored procedure named GetProductAttributeValues.

The three data tables follow:

- Attribute stores the name of the attributes, such as Size or Color.

- AttributeValue contains the possible attribute values for each attribute group. There is a One-to-Many relationship between Attribute and AttributeValue. Each attribute—take Color, for example—can have several values associated with it—Red, Orange, Yellow, and so on. We need this table to help us to link the AttributeID (like 1 for Color) to AttributeValueIDs for its possible values (Red, Orange, Yellow, and so on). So, it will contain three columns: AttributeID, which is found in the Attribute table and tells us what kind of attribute we are talking about (for example, a color or a size); AttributeValueID, the integer we assign to uniquely identify the items in the AttributeValue table itself; and Value, which will hold the text description, like "Orange," "Red," "Small," "Large," and so on.

- ProductAttributeValue is an associate table implementing a Many-to-Many relationship between the Product and AttributeValue tables, with (ProductID, AttributeValueID) pairs (the AttributeValue table will allow us to quickly and easily populate this table).

■**Note** The system you're implementing doesn't permit an attribute to affect the price of the product. For example, a white balloon will always have the same price as a black balloon. If you need to have different product prices, you need to create different products. If you need to support attributes that affect the product price, one option would be to extend the ProductAttributeValue table by including data about the change in the product price and making many other changes and additions to the business tier and presentation tier code. We advise you not to make any changes at this time, as they would propagate to the following chapters as well, making the task of following the book more difficult.

You learned in Chapter 5 that database diagrams can help in understanding the relationships among data tables. A visual representation of these tables and of the relationships among the attribute tables can be seen in Figure 6-2. If you are new to databases, you should take a moment to study this diagram so that the following code is easier for you to negotiate and understand.

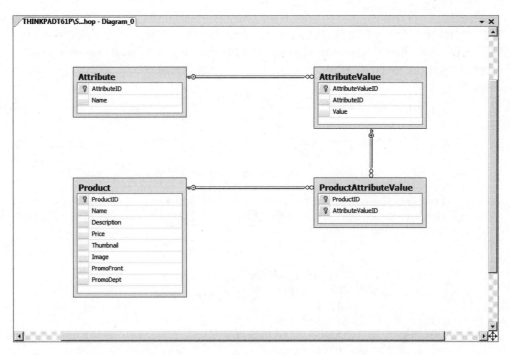

Figure 6-2. *Diagram describing the relationships among the data tables required to implement product attributes*

Let's start by updating the BalloonShop database and then implementing the new stored procedure `catalog_get_ProductAttributeValues` in the following exercise.

Exercise: Creating the Data Tier Functionality for Product Attributes

1. Open SQL Server Management Studio and execute the following code, which creates and populates the `Attribute` table. (You can also use Visual Web Developer to create the stored procedure, if you prefer.)

```
-- Connect to the BalloonShop database
USE BalloonShop

-- Create attribute table (stores attributes such as Size and Color)
CREATE TABLE Attribute (
  AttributeID INT IDENTITY(1,1) NOT NULL PRIMARY KEY,
  Name NVARCHAR(100) NOT NULL -- e.g. Color, Size
)

-- Populate Attribute table
SET IDENTITY_INSERT Attribute ON

INSERT INTO Attribute (AttributeID, Name)
VALUES (1, 'Color');

SET IDENTITY_INSERT Attribute OFF
```

■**Note** We use SET IDENTITY INSERT ON when adding values to the tables to make sure the IDs you create in your own database match those assumed by the scripts in the book's code archive. Apart from this particular scenario, when a column is an IDENTITY column, it makes sense to let the database generate the unique IDs for you.

---

   2. Continue by creating and populating the AttributeValue table, using the following SQL code:

```
-- Create AttributeValue table (stores values such as Yellow or XXL)
CREATE TABLE AttributeValue (
  AttributeValueID INT IDENTITY(1,1) NOT NULL PRIMARY KEY,
  AttributeID INT NOT NULL, -- The ID of the attribute
  Value NVARCHAR(100) NOT NULL -- E.g. Yellow
)

-- Set the IDENTITY INSERT option for AttributeValue
SET IDENTITY_INSERT AttributeValue ON;

-- Populate AttributeValue table
INSERT INTO AttributeValue (AttributeValueID, AttributeID, Value)
SELECT 1, 1, 'White' UNION ALL
SELECT 2, 1, 'Black' UNION ALL
SELECT 3, 1, 'Red' UNION ALL
SELECT 4, 1, 'Orange' UNION ALL
SELECT 5, 1, 'Yellow' UNION ALL
SELECT 6, 1, 'Green' UNION ALL
SELECT 7, 1, 'Blue' UNION ALL
SELECT 8, 1, 'Indigo' UNION ALL
SELECT 9, 1, 'Purple';

-- Set the IDENTITY INSERT option for AttributeValue
SET IDENTITY_INSERT AttributeValue OFF;
```

   3. Create and populate the ProductAttributeValue table using the code in the following listing:

```
-- Create ProductAttributeValue table (associates attribute values to
products)
CREATE TABLE ProductAttributeValue (
  ProductID INT NOT NULL,
  AttributeValueID INT NOT NULL,
  PRIMARY KEY (ProductID, AttributeValueID)
)

-- Populate ProductAttributeValue table
INSERT INTO ProductAttributeValue (ProductID, AttributeValueID)
SELECT p.ProductID, av.AttributeValueID
FROM product p, AttributeValue av;
```

4. Execute the following code, which creates the foreign keys that establish the table relationships that were described earlier in Figure 6-2:

```
-- Create the foreign keys
ALTER TABLE AttributeValue
ADD CONSTRAINT FK_AttributeValue_Attribute
FOREIGN KEY(AttributeID)
REFERENCES Attribute (AttributeID)
GO
ALTER TABLE ProductAttributeValue
ADD CONSTRAINT FK_ProductAttributeValue_AttributeValue
FOREIGN KEY(AttributeValueID)
REFERENCES AttributeValue (AttributeValueID)
GO
ALTER TABLE ProductAttributeValue WITH CHECK
ADD CONSTRAINT FK_ProductAttributeValue_Product
FOREIGN KEY(ProductID)
REFERENCES Product (ProductID)
GO
```

5. Execute the following SQL code, which creates the CatalogGetProductAttributeValues stored procedure. This stored procedure will associate the attributes assigned to a product.

```
-- Create CatalogGetProductAttributeValues stored procedure
CREATE PROCEDURE CatalogGetProductAttributeValues
(@ProductId INT)
AS
SELECT a.Name AS AttributeName,
       av.AttributeValueID,
       av.Value AS AttributeValue
FROM AttributeValue av
INNER JOIN attribute a ON av.AttributeID = a.AttributeID
WHERE av.AttributeValueID IN
  (SELECT AttributeValueID
   FROM ProductAttributeValue
   WHERE ProductID = @ProductID)
ORDER BY a.Name;
```

How It Works: Data Logic for Product Attributes

We'll now discuss the code used to populate the AttributeValue and ProductAttributeValue tables and the CatalogGetProductAttributeValues stored procedure. Before proceeding, please make sure you understand the purpose of each field of the Attribute, AttributeValue, and ProductAttributeValue tables and the code used to populate these tables. It may take a while to understand the table structure exactly. We will not reiterate the theory here, but feel free to refer to Chapters 4 and 5, where we've discussed the major concepts of relational database design.

In this exercise we've used quite a few SQL tricks and syntactic sugar that we need to talk about. Let's first look at the AttributeValue table. To populate it, instead of using multiple INSERT statements, we've used the INSERT...SELECT version of the command, which allows us to insert the data returned by a SELECT statement.

However, instead of using a single SELECT statement to get the data, we've joined the data from multiple SELECT statements using UNION ALL.

All in all, we've replaced this:

```
-- Populate AttributeValue table
INSERT INTO AttributeValue (AttributeValueID, AttributeID, Value)
VALUES (1, 1, 'White');
INSERT INTO AttributeValue (AttributeValueID, AttributeID, Value)
VALUES (2, 1, 'Black');
INSERT INTO AttributeValue (AttributeValueID, AttributeID, Value)
VALUES (3, 1, 'Red'); ...
```

with this:

```
-- Populate AttributeValue table
INSERT INTO AttributeValue (AttributeValueID, AttributeID, Value)
SELECT 1, 1, 'White' UNION ALL
SELECT 2, 1, 'Black' UNION ALL
SELECT 3, 1, 'Red' UNION ALL ...
```

If you run SQL Server 2008, you can use an even cooler way to insert multiple values into a table. Here's the syntactic sugar that SQL Server 2008 introduced:

```
-- Populate AttributeValue table -- SQL SERVER 2008 syntax
INSERT INTO AttributeValue (AttributeValueID, AttributeID, value)
VALUES (1, 1, 'White'), (2, 1, 'Black'), (3, 1, 'Red'), ...
```

When populating ProductAttributeValue, the goal is to associate all the existing attribute values (via the AttributeValueID field) to each of our products (via the ProductID field). In our site, our products are balloons, and we want to sell each of them in all possible colors. The code that populates the ProductAttributeValue table uses the INSERT INTO command to insert a number of records produced by a SELECT query:

```
INSERT INTO ProductAttributeValue (ProductID, AttributeValueID)
```

In our case, the SELECT query that generates the data to be inserted into ProductAttributeValue is a **cross join**. This type of join makes a Cartesian product between two data sets. The result is a list that contains all the possible combinations between the records of the first data set and the records of the second data set.

For example, the Cartesian product between {1, 2, 3} and {a, b, c}, which is mathematically written as {1, 2, 3} × {a, b, c}, is the following set of data: { {1, a}, {1, b}, {1, c}, {2, a}, {2, b}, {2, c}, {3, a}, {3, b}, {3, c} }.

In our case, if we make a Cartesian product between the IDs of the existing products and the IDs of the existing attribute values, we obtain a list formed of (ProductID, AttributeValueID) elements, which is exactly the list we want to add to the ProductAttributeValue table. The syntax to implement this cross-join operation with SQL Server is

```
INSERT INTO ProductAttributeValue (ProductID, AttributeValueID)
        SELECT p.ProductID, av.AttributeValueID
        FROM    product p, AttributeValue av;
```

This is certainly a nice way of creating many records in our database with minimal effort. The sample data of our database contains 9 possible attribute values and 62 products. The cross-join operation that associates all attribute values to all products generates 558 (which is 9 multiplied by 62) records in the ProductAttributeValue table.

Note that the use of SELECT to create the cross join is not standard SQL, although its form is commonly accepted by the major database servers. The "official" syntax to implement cross joins specifies the use of the CROSS JOIN syntax:

```
INSERT INTO ProductAttributeValue (ProductID, AttributeValueID)
       SELECT p.ProductID, av.AttributeValueID
       FROM   product p CROSS JOIN AttributeValue av;
```

Instead of using a cross join, we could use the UNION method described earlier. UNION sums up the results of multiple SELECT statements into a single result set. For example, if you use UNION for two queries that return five records each, you get a result set of ten records. Of course, for UNION to work, all the queries involved must return the same number of columns of compatible data types. We won't go into more details about UNION, but if you're curious to see the UNION-based implementation of the cross join, here it is. It necessitates more keystrokes, but the query offers you more flexibility; for example, using UNION, you could add only certain attribute values to your products.

```
-- Populate ProductAttributeValue table
INSERT INTO ProductAttributeValue (ProductID, AttributeValueID)
SELECT ProductID, 1 AS AttributeValueID FROM product
UNION ALL SELECT ProductID, 2  AS AttributeValueID FROM product
UNION ALL SELECT ProductID, 3  AS AttributeValueID FROM product
UNION ALL SELECT ProductID, 4  AS AttributeValueID FROM product
UNION ALL SELECT ProductID, 5  AS AttributeValueID FROM product
UNION ALL SELECT ProductID, 6  AS AttributeValueID FROM product
UNION ALL SELECT ProductID, 7  AS AttributeValueID FROM product
UNION ALL SELECT ProductID, 8  AS AttributeValueID FROM product
UNION ALL SELECT ProductID, 9  AS AttributeValueID FROM product;
```

Finally, let's take a look at the CatalogGetProductAttributeValues stored procedure. This stored procedure receives as a parameter the ID of a product and returns a list of that product's attributes. This is the handy little device that the business tier will call to get the list of attributes for our products so our customers can choose a color for each balloon:

```
-- Create CatalogGetProductAttributeValues stored procedure
CREATE PROCEDURE CatalogGetProductAttributeValues
(@ProductId INT)
AS
```

The SQL code in this procedure returns a list with the AttributeName, AttributeValueID, and AttributeValue for all the attributes of the mentioned product:

```
SELECT a.Name AS AttributeName,
       av.AttributeValueID,
       av.Value AS AttributeValue
FROM AttributeValue av
```

```
    INNER JOIN attribute a ON av.AttributeID = a.AttributeID
    WHERE av.AttributeValueID IN
      (SELECT AttributeValueID
       FROM ProductAttributeValue
       WHERE ProductID = @ProductID)
    ORDER BY a.Name;
```

To test that the procedure works as it should, you can execute the code of the stored procedure using SQL Server Management Studio, replacing the parameter names with their values. For example, you could take the preceding SQL code, replace @ProductId with the ID of a product, and then execute the code.

Alternatively, you can call the stored procedure itself using the EXEC command in SQL Server Management Studio (such as shown in the following code snippet), or even right-clicking the stored procedure in either Visual Web Developer or SQL Server Management Studio, and selecting Execute Stored Procedure from the contextual menu.

```
    EXEC CatalogGetProductAttributeValues 1
```

Executing this command will return the attributes of the product with the ID of 1. (However, since all our products have the same possible attributes, you'll get the same results no matter what product ID you use.)

```
AttributeName              AttributeValueID    AttributeValue
---------------------      -------------------  ----------------------------------
Color                      1                    White
Color                      2                    Black
Color                      3                    Red
Color                      4                    Orange
Color                      5                    Yellow
Color                      6                    Green
Color                      7                    Blue
Color                      8                    Indigo
Color                      9                    Purple

(9 row(s) affected)
```

Implementing the Business Tier

The business tier bit of the product attributes feature is very straightforward—we only need to write the code that calls the CatalogGetProductAttributeValues stored procedure. Add the following code to the CatalogAccess class, in App_Code/CatalogAccess.cs:

```
  // Retrieve the list of product attributes
  public static DataTable GetProductAttributes(string productId)
  {
    // get a configured DbCommand object
    DbCommand comm = GenericDataAccess.CreateCommand();
```

```
    // set the stored procedure name
    comm.CommandText = "CatalogGetProductAttributeValues";
    // create a new parameter
    DbParameter param = comm.CreateParameter();
    param.ParameterName = "@ProductID";
    param.Value = productId;
    param.DbType = DbType.Int32;
    comm.Parameters.Add(param);
    // execute the stored procedure and return the results
    return GenericDataAccess.ExecuteSelectCommand(comm);
}
```

Implementing the Presentation Tier

Creating the presentation tier implies adding controls that allow users to choose a value from the list of product attribute values. As you will see, attributes are not hard-coded in the templates. Instead, the attributes (Color in our case) and their values (White, Green, and so on) are read from the database.

You can already see how managing attributes for your products is far easier in the long term this way, than hard-coding the attributes in the presentation tier. You simply change the data in the attribute tables and voilà—the changes are automatically reflected on your site!

Let's implement the presentation code, and we'll discuss it afterward. To aid comprehension, remember to correlate the code you're typing now with the results you expect from the CatalogGetProductAttributeValues stored procedures. You saw some sample output of this procedure a little earlier in this chapter.

Exercise: Implementing the Product Attributes Presentation

1. Alter the code in ProductsList.ascx as highlighted:

   ```
   <p class="DetailSection">
     Price:
     <%# Eval("Price", "{0:c}") %>
   </p>
   <asp:PlaceHolder ID="attrPlaceHolder" runat="server"></asp:PlaceHolder>
   ```

2. Add the following style to BalloonShop.css:

   ```
   .DetailSection {
     margin-top: 10px;
     margin-bottom: 10px;
   }
   ```

3. Switch ProductsList.ascx to Design View, select the DataList control, and open its **Properties** window (using **F4**). There, switch the view to Events by clicking the little lightning symbol, and finally double-click the ItemDataBound entry. This will have Visual Web Developer generate the event handler for the ItemDataBound event in the form of a method named list_ItemDataBound.

4. Add the following code to `list_ItemDataBound`. (Note that you may also need to import the `System.Data` namespace, at the beginning of the file, if you haven't referenced it already.)

```
// Executed when each item of the list is bound to the data source
protected void list_ItemDataBound(object sender, DataListItemEventArgs e)
{
  // obtain the attributes of the product
  DataRowView dataRow = (DataRowView) e.Item.DataItem;
  string productId = dataRow["ProductID"].ToString();
  DataTable attrTable = CatalogAccess.GetProductAttributes(productId);

  // get the attribute placeholder
  PlaceHolder attrPlaceHolder = (PlaceHolder)e.Item.FindControl➥
("attrPlaceHolder");

  // temp variables
  string prevAttributeName = "";
  string attributeName, attributeValue, attributeValueId;

  // current DropDown for attribute values
  Label attributeNameLabel;
  DropDownList attributeValuesDropDown = new DropDownList();

  // read the list of attributes
  foreach (DataRow r in attrTable.Rows)
  {
    // get attribute data
    attributeName = r["AttributeName"].ToString();
    attributeValue = r["AttributeValue"].ToString();
    attributeValueId = r["AttributeValueID"].ToString();

    // if starting a new attribute (e.g. Color, Size)
    if (attributeName != prevAttributeName)
    {
      prevAttributeName = attributeName;
      attributeNameLabel = new Label();
      attributeNameLabel.Text = attributeName + ": ";
      attributeValuesDropDown = new DropDownList();
      attrPlaceHolder.Controls.Add(attributeNameLabel);
      attrPlaceHolder.Controls.Add(attributeValuesDropDown);
    }

    // add a new attribute value to the DropDownList
    attributeValuesDropDown.Items.Add(new ListItem(attributeValue, ➥
attributeValueId));
  }
}
```

5. Load a list of products to make sure your attributes show up fine (see Figure 6-3).

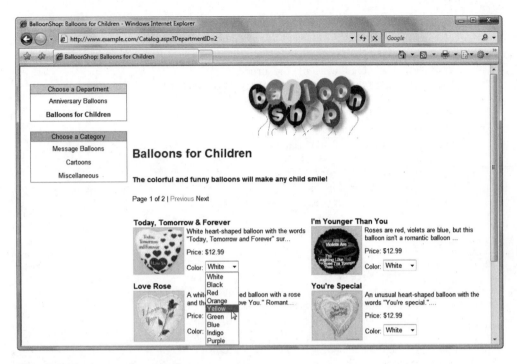

Figure 6-3. *Testing product attributes*

6. Let's now display the list of attributes in the product details page as well. Open `Product.aspx` and add a placeholder at the end of the control:

```
<p>
  <b>Price:</b>
  <asp:Label CssClass="ProductPrice" ID="priceLabel" runat="server"
            Text="Label"></asp:Label>
</p>
<p>
  <asp:PlaceHolder ID="attrPlaceHolder" runat="server"></asp:PlaceHolder>
</p>
</asp:Content>
```

7. Switch to `Product.aspx.cs`, make sure the `System.Data` namespace is referenced at the beginning of the file, and then modify `PopulateControls` by adding the following code at the end of the method:

```
// Fill the control with data
private void PopulateControls()
{
...
...

    // obtain the attributes of the product
    DataTable attrTable = CatalogAccess.GetProductAttributes(productId);

    // temp variables
    string prevAttributeName = "";
    string attributeName, attributeValue, attributeValueId;

    // current DropDown for attribute values
    Label attributeNameLabel;
    DropDownList attributeValuesDropDown = new DropDownList();

    // read the list of attributes
    foreach (DataRow r in attrTable.Rows)
    {
      // get attribute data
      attributeName = r["AttributeName"].ToString();
      attributeValue = r["AttributeValue"].ToString();
      attributeValueId = r["AttributeValueID"].ToString();

      // if starting a new attribute (e.g. Color, Size)
      if (attributeName != prevAttributeName)
      {
        prevAttributeName = attributeName;
        attributeNameLabel = new Label();
        attributeNameLabel.Text = attributeName + ": ";
        attributeValuesDropDown = new DropDownList();
        attrPlaceHolder.Controls.Add(attributeNameLabel);
        attrPlaceHolder.Controls.Add(attributeValuesDropDown);
      }

      // add a new attribute value to the DropDownList
      attributeValuesDropDown.Items.Add(new ListItem(attributeValue, ➥
  attributeValueId));
    }
}
```

8. Load BalloonShop (by loading either Default.aspx or Catalog.aspx) and select a product. You should now see its list of attributes in its details page, as shown in Figure 6-4.

Figure 6-4. *Product details page with attributes*

How It Works: Presenting Product Attributes

The mechanism that generates the list of attributes is not trivial, so let's take a close look at it to make sure you fully understand how it works. You've added the list of attributes to both `ProductsList.ascx` and `Product.aspx`; we'll look at the former because it's the more complex of the two.

To understand the reasoning behind the code of `ProductsList.ascx`, you need to keep the following in mind:

- `ProductsList.ascx` displays a list of products using a `DataList`, and the attributes need to be added to each item generated by the `DataList`.

- Each product can have its own distinct set of attributes, so (unless caching techniques are used) you need to do a database request to obtain the list of attributes for each product.

So basically, what we needed to do was create a piece of code that executes for each displayed product and fetches the list of attributes for that product. Fortunately, the DataList control, which displays our products, makes this task pretty easy: it fires the ItemDataBound event after each displayed item is bound to its data source. So all we had to do was to handle this event by creating the list_ItemDataBound event handler:

```
// Executed when each item of the list is bound to the data source
protected void list_ItemDataBound(object sender, DataListItemEventArgs e)
{
```

The event handler starts by obtaining the DataRowView item that contains the data row from the original data source. This is necessary to get the ID of the product that is displayed in that DataList cell, so that we know for which product to obtain the list of attributes.

```
// obtain the attributes of the product
DataRowView dataRow = (DataRowView) e.Item.DataItem;
string productId = dataRow["ProductID"].ToString();
```

Then we executed CatalogAccess.GetProductAttributes to get the list of attributes for the product:

```
DataTable attrTable = CatalogAccess.GetProductAttributes(productId);
```

We continued by obtaining a reference to the PlaceHolder control from inside the DataList item. Remember that the PlaceHolder control isn't directly accessible because the form doesn't actually contain such an object. Instead, it's part of the ItemTemplate of the DataList and in consequence it's generated for each item of the DataList. Getting the object isn't hard though—all we needed to do was use FindControl over the current list item, represented by the parameter e:

```
// get the attribute placeholder
PlaceHolder attrPlaceHolder =
  (PlaceHolder)e.Item.FindControl("attrPlaceHolder");
```

Next, we defined a number of objects and local variables to help with generating the list of attributes:

```
// temp variables
string prevAttributeName = "";
string attributeName, attributeValue, attributeValueId;

// current DropDown for attribute values
Label attributeNameLabel;
DropDownList attributeValuesDropDown = new DropDownList();
```

To understand the next piece of code, you need to recall what kind of values our stored procedure, CatalogGetProductAttributeValues, returns. (This data is at this point stored by the attrTable DataTable object.) To make things more obvious, we'll just assume that one of our balloons—the one with the ID of 1—has another attribute named Size with the possible values of Small and Large. Executing the stored procedure for this would return the following:

AttributeName	AttributeValueID	AttributeValue
Color	1	White
Color	2	Black
Color	3	Red
Color	4	Orange
Color	5	Yellow
Color	6	Green
Color	7	Blue
Color	8	Indigo
Color	9	Purple
Size	10	Small
Size	11	Large

Back to our code in ProductsList.ascx.cs, we can see the technique used to transform the preceding data to a couple of labels (Color and Size) and a couple of DropDown lists (one with the colors, and the other with sizes). Basically, the data in the attrTable is read row by row, and each time a new AttributeName is met, the code creates a new Label and a new DropDownList control, and it starts adding attribute values to the new DropDownList:

```
// read the list of attributes
foreach (DataRow r in attrTable.Rows)
{
  // get attribute data
  attributeName = r["AttributeName"].ToString();
  attributeValue = r["AttributeValue"].ToString();
  attributeValueId = r["AttributeValueID"].ToString();

  // if starting a new attribute (e.g. Color, Size)
  if (attributeName != prevAttributeName)
  {
    prevAttributeName = attributeName;
    attributeNameLabel = new Label();
    attributeNameLabel.Text = attributeName + ": ";
    attributeValuesDropDown = new DropDownList();
    attrPlaceHolder.Controls.Add(attributeNameLabel);
    attrPlaceHolder.Controls.Add(attributeValuesDropDown);
  }

  // add a new attribute value to the DropDownList
  attributeValuesDropDown.Items.Add(new ListItem(attributeValue, ➥
attributeValueId));
  }
}
```

If you're curious how the product with two attributes looks, you can check Figure 6-5. Note that the database scripts in the code archive only contain the `Color` attribute, but as you can see, our code has been designed to support any number of attributes.

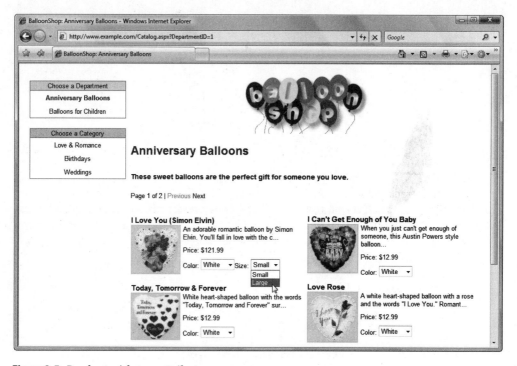

Figure 6-5. *Product with two attributes*

The rest of the code follows along the same lines. Take a few minutes to make sure you understand it all, and then congratulate yourself for completing yet another important feature of your BalloonShop web site!

Summary

In this little chapter, we've added attributes to our products! From now on, our customers will be able to choose the colors of their balloons. Also, it's very easy to add your own attribute groups and attribute values as you see fit.

Our balloon shop is really shaping up! But we won't compete well on the Internet if the search engines have a hard time understanding and ranking our site. Worse, if we don't carefully craft our site for search engines, we could actually lose ranking instead of gaining it! Because it can be very difficult to retrofit a site for search engine optimization, it's important that we begin addressing it early on in our design and development. In some cases, trying to retrofit a site is so difficult that developers decide to simply start again from scratch! But we know that we need to plan from the beginning, so let's proceed to improving our catalog for search engine optimization right now!

CHAPTER 7

■■■

Search Engine Optimization

After adding product attributes to your site, you're probably eager to add new features as well, such as accepting user payments, product searching, or the shopping cart. We'll do that soon, we promise! Before that, there's one detail to take care of: we need to prepare the web site foundation to support our **search engine optimization** efforts. This is an important topic, because it *directly affects the profitability* of a web site. So let's get started!

Search engine optimization, or simply SEO, refers to the practices employed to increase the number of visitors a web site receives from organic (unpaid) search engine result pages. Today, the search engine is the most important tool people use to find information and products on the Internet. Needless to say, having your e-commerce web site rank well for the relevant keywords will help drive visitors to your site and increase the chances that visitors will buy from you and not the competition!

Although not (yet) rocket science, SEO is a complex subject in the even larger subject of search engine marketing. In this chapter, we'll update BalloonShop so that its core architecture will be search engine friendly, which will help marketers in their efforts.

■**Note** If you're serious about SEO—and you should be!—we recommend that you continue your studies with more detailed books on this subject, because this single chapter cannot cover it in much depth. *Search Engine Optimization For Dummies* (For Dummies, 2004) and *Search Engine Optimization: An Hour a Day* (Sybex, 2006) are two excellent resources that will teach you more about the basics of SEO. *Professional Search Engine Optimization with ASP.NET: A Developer's Guide to SEO* (Wrox, 2007) is your comprehensive guide into the world of SEO with ASP.NET and explains, with many more details, all the topics covered in this chapter. Reading usability and user psychology books, such as *Prioritizing Web Usability* (New Riders Press, 2006) and *Don't Make Me Think: A Common Sense Approach to Web Usability* (New Riders Press, 2005), is highly recommended as well; they will help you understand the fine balance between SEO, accessibility, and usability.

Optimizing BalloonShop

So what can be improved in BalloonShop to make it more search engine friendly? Well, it may come as a surprise to you to hear this, since BalloonShop is so small and young, but there's a lot to improve about it already! Fortunately, we've designed its structure in such a way that adding the new features will be painless, and the newly created structure will be there to last.

In this chapter, we will

- Implement keyword-rich URLs through URL rewriting. This way, instead of requesting `default.aspx` or `catalog.aspx` using various query string parameters, our site will support URLs that look better both to humans and to search engines, such as `http://www.example.com/toy-story.html`. At this step, the web site must be updated to use the new links internally.

- Properly redirect old URLs or mistyped URLs to the correct URLs. This is particularly important if your old URLs have been online for a while, and they have pages linking to them. This step will help to ensure that you don't lose any rankings that the pages on your old site may have already gained (their link equity) nor incur penalties for false duplicate pages on your new site. This process of converting various forms of a URL to a standard form is called **URL canonicalization**, and we will talk more about it later.

- Redirect requests to `default.aspx` and `index.html` to `/`. This is important, because we don't want the same content duplicated in different URLs of your web site. As you'll learn, this can lead to implicit or explicit search engine penalties.

- Use the 404 (page not found) and 500 (server error) status codes correctly to reflect problems with pages in the site.

We will make more SEO-related efforts in later parts of the book, but with these changes, we'll have the basics covered. The fact that the site is already structured properly certainly helps. The following SEO-related details have already been implemented:

- We correctly used page headings and other markup, so that search engines will be able to identify the page's important copy.

- We don't have duplicate content. The catalog doesn't contain identical pages or page fragments, which can incur search engine penalties.

- The product, department, and category pages are easily reachable.

- Each page has its own title that reflects its contents.

- Product lists are paginated with links to all the subpages, not only Previous and Next links. This makes pages of products easier to access by both search engines and humans.

- Product images have relevant `alt` attributes.

- We didn't use (and will not use) technologies such as Flash and Ajax, whose content is unreadable by search engines, to generate content. Later in this book, you'll see an example of using Ajax in a way that doesn't affect search engine visibility.

Supporting Keyword-Rich URLs

Have a look at the following URLs, and choose the one you like better:

- `http://www.example.com/Catalog.aspx?DepartmentID=2&CategoryID=5`

- `http://www.example.com/Balloons-for-Children-d2/Cartoons-c5/`

Of course, you want to have URLs such as the second one in your web site. Not only do they contain keywords that are relevant for the content of the page, which can have an impact on search engine rankings, but they're also more appealing to a human visitor. We'll call the first URL a **dynamic URL** and the second a **keyword-rich URL**.

The technical detail that makes the real difference between the keyword-rich URL and the dynamic URL is that the keyword-rich URL doesn't point to an existing physical file or folder in your site. On the other hand, the dynamic URL points to an actual file that can be executed or loaded by your web server—such as Catalog.aspx in the preceding example.

In practice, to support keyword-rich URLs you need to write code that intercepts URLs that follow a certain pattern and **rewrite** the requests to another URL that can be processed by your application. This process is called **URL rewriting**. When implementing URL rewriting, you allow your application to continue working with its "normal," dynamic URLs, while adding support for a new set of URLs (typically keyword-rich URLs) that point to the original dynamic URLs.

Figure 7-1 shows a simple example of URL rewriting. As you can see, the URL rewriting module intercepts the URL requested by the visitor and rewrites it to a dynamic URL that your application can understand. The ASP.NET script executes, and the results are sent back to our users, who are (obviously) very happy to get the content they want.

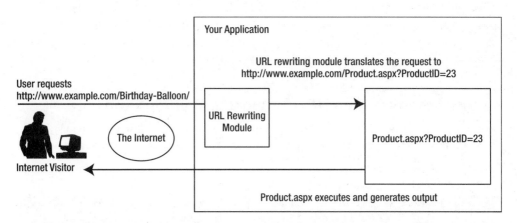

Figure 7-1. *A URL rewriting example*

UrlRewriter.NET and ISAPI_Rewrite

Writing your own URL rewriting code is a complex task that is not worth pursuing unless you need to create your own customized URL rewriting solution. For typical URL rewriting scenarios, it makes sense to use one of the existing URL rewriting products—such as ISAPI_Rewrite by Helicon Tech (http://www.isapirewrite.com/) or UrlRewriter.NET (http://urlrewriter.net). Both products, and even techniques for creating your own URL rewriting code, are covered in *Professional Search Engine Optimization with ASP.NET* (Wrox Press, 2007).

For the purposes of developing BalloonShop, we'll use UrlRewriter.NET. This tool is an open-source component that implements URL rewriting at the ASP.NET level, and for this reason it's very easy to integrate into your project. ISAPI_Rewrite, on the other hand, is implemented as an ISAPI filter and it performs the rewrite at the IIS level. This offers great performance but it also requires access to the server machine in order to install it.

Keyword-Rich URLs for BalloonShop

There are several ways to assign keyword-rich URLs to their dynamic versions. In BalloonShop, we'll apply a technique that is both effective and simple to implement: we'll hide the item ID in the keyword-rich version of the URLs, such as in `http://www.example.com/Birthday-Balloon-p23/`. This keyword-rich URL contains the product ID hidden inside in a way that doesn't hinder its readability for humans and search engines alike.

In this chapter, we'll implement the support for the URL types listed in Table 7-1. In each case, "X" is used as placeholder for department, category, and product ID, and "P" is a page number.

Table 7-1. *URL Formats Supported by BalloonShop*

URL Type	URL Format
Front page URL	`http://www.example.com/`
Department URL	`http://www.example.com/department-name-dX/`
Department URL if paginated	`http://www.example.com/department-name-dX/page-P/`
Category URL	`http://www.example.com/dept-name-dX/cat-name-cX/`
Category URL if paginated	`http://www.example.com/dept-name-dX/cat-name-cX/page-P/`
Product URL	`http://www.example.com/product-name-pX/`

Adding Keyword-Rich URL Support to BalloonShop

There are more details you need to learn to fully support such URLs, but we're taking things one at a time. Follow the exercise to implement support for keyword-rich URLs, and we'll discuss the details afterward.

Exercise: Supporting Keyword-Rich URLs

1. Visit `http://www.urlrewriter.net`, click the **Download** button, and download the latest release of the product.

2. The product package contains a folder named `UrlRewriterV2`. Unzip the package to a folder on your hard disk, different than your `BalloonShop` web site folder. For the purposes of this exercise I'll assume you've extracted `UrlRewriterV2` in `C:\`.

3. Open the `www.example.com` project in Visual Web Developer.

4. Add a reference to the `Intelligencia.UrlRewriter` assembly. To do this, right-click the root entry of your project in Solution Explorer (the entry should read `http://www.example.com/`), and choose **Add Reference....** In the dialog that opens, click the **Browse** tab, and browse to `UrlRewriterV2\bin\Release\Intelligencia.UrlRewriter.dll`. Select the file and click **OK**.

5. Open your `web.config` file in your web project and add the following configuration section handler that enables UrlRewriter.NET to read its configuration from a configuration node named `rewriter`:

```xml
<?xml version="1.0"?>
<configuration>
  <configSections>
    <section name="rewriter" requirePermission="false"
type="Intelligencia.UrlRewriter.Configuration.➥
RewriterConfigurationSectionHandler,Intelligencia.UrlRewriter" />
...
  </configSections>
...
```

■**Important** The `<configSections>` element must be the first child of the `<configuration>` element.

---

6. Now configure the UrlRewriter HTTP module, which allows UrlRewriter.NET to intercept incoming requests (and rewrite them):

```xml
<system.web>
...
  <httpModules>
    <add name="ScriptModule" type="System.Web.Handlers.ScriptModule, ➥
System.Web.Extensions, Version=3.5.0.0, Culture=neutral, ➥
PublicKeyToken=31BF3856AD364E35"/>
    <add type="Intelligencia.UrlRewriter.RewriterHttpModule,
Intelligencia.UrlRewriter" name="UrlRewriter" />
  </httpModules>
...
```

7. Finally, we must make sure UrlRewriter.NET is configured to receive all requests to nonexistent files or folders. If you use IIS 7 (in Windows Vista), you need to add the following highlighted line to your web.config file:

```xml
<system.webServer>
  <validation validateIntegratedModeConfiguration="false"/>
  <modules>
    <add name="UrlRewriter" type="Intelligencia.UrlRewriter. ➥
RewriterHttpModule" />
    <remove name="ScriptModule"/>
    <add name="ScriptModule" preCondition="managedHandler" ...
  </modules>
```

For older versions of IIS (in Windows XP, Windows 2000 Server, or Windows 2003 Server), you need to open the IIS Manager tool, and navigate to the Home Directory tab in the properties window of your web site. There you need to select **Configuration** and click **Add** or **Insert** to add the path to aspnet_isapi.dll (it should be C:\WINDOWS\Microsoft.NET\Framework\v2.0.50727\aspnet_isapi.dll). On Windows XP and Windows 2000 Server, also type .* for the file extension and unselect the **Check that file exists** check box. Finally, click **OK** to close all the dialog boxes.

8. Excellent, now UrlRewriter.NET is ready to use! In our first test, let's have it rewrite incoming requests for `/my-super-product.aspx` to `/Product.aspx?ProductID=1`. Add the highlighted configuration elements in the `<configuration>` section of `web.config`:

```
<configuration>
  <configSections>
    ...
  </configSections>

  <rewriter>
    <rewrite url="/my-super-product.aspx" to="~/Product.aspx?ProductID=1" />
  </rewriter>
  ...
```

9. Load `http://www.example.com/my-super-product.aspx`. You should get the product with the ID of 1, as shown in Figure 7-2.

Figure 7-2. *A URL rewriting example*

10. Now that you've tested that your URL rewriting feature works fine, add the real URL rewriting rules for products, categories, and departments:

```
<rewriter>
  <!-- Rewrite department pages -->
  <rewrite url="^.*-d([0-9]+)/?$" to="~/Catalog.aspx?DepartmentID=$1" ➥
processing="stop" />
  <rewrite url="^.*-d([0-9]+)/page-([0-9]+)/?$" ➥
to="~/Catalog.aspx?DepartmentID=$1&amp;Page=$2" processing="stop" />

  <!-- Rewrite category pages -->
  <rewrite url="^.*-d([0-9]+)/.*-c([0-9]+)/?$" ➥
to="~/Catalog.aspx?DepartmentId=$1&amp;CategoryId=$2" processing="stop" />
  <rewrite url="^.*-d([0-9]+)/.*-c([0-9]+)/page-([0-9]+)/?$" ➥
to="~/Catalog.aspx?DepartmentId=$1&amp;CategoryId=$2&amp;Page=$3" ➥
processing="stop" />

  <!-- Rewrite product details pages -->
  <rewrite url="^.*-p([0-9]+)/?$" to="~/Product.aspx?ProductId=$1" ➥
processing="stop" />
</rewriter>
```

11. At this moment, your web site should correctly support keyword-rich URLs, in the form described prior to starting this exercise. For example, try loading http://www.example.com/ Anniversary-Balloons-d1/. The result should resemble the page shown in Figure 7-3.

Figure 7-3. *Testing keyword-rich URLs*

How It Works: Supporting Keyword-Rich URLs

At this moment, you can test all kinds of keyword-rich URLs that are currently known by your web site: department pages and subpages, category pages and subpages, the front page and its subpages, and product details links. Note, however, that the links currently generated by your web site are still old, dynamic URLs. Updating the links in your site will be the subject of the next exercise.

The core of the functionality you've just implemented lies in the rewriting rules you've added to the `<rewriter>` element in `web.config`. The first rewrite rule you've written is also the simplest:

```
<rewrite url="^.*-d([0-9]+)/?$" to="~/Catalog.aspx?DepartmentID=$1"
         processing="stop" />
```

As you can see, the rule is expressed by an element with three attributes:

- `url` describes the incoming URLs that should be rewritten.

- `to` represents the rewritten URL.

- `processing` is an optional parameter that makes the parser stop reading further rewrite rules in case this one matches.

The `url` attribute contains a **regular expression** that describes the URLs the rewrite rule should match. We'll discuss regular expressions in a second—for now, let's just assume that the regular expression from the rule above—`^.*-d([0-9]+)/?$`—matches strings of the following form, where N is a number:

```
Some-text-here-dN/
```

You can see the resemblance between this string and the URL of a keyword-rich department page:

```
http://www.example.com/Balloons-for-Children-d2/
```

The rewrite rule extracts the matched number N and saves it to a variable named `$1`, which is then used in the `to` part of the rewrite rule to compose the rewritten URL. The `to` part looks like this:

```
to="~/Catalog.aspx?DepartmentID=$1"
```

When `$1` is replaced by the ID of the Balloons for Children department, which is 2, `to` becomes the dynamic URL of the department:

```
~/Catalog.aspx?DepartmentID=2
```

ASP.NET interprets the `~` as the root of your project, so this link will point to the `Catalog.aspx` file, located in your project's root folder.

Admittedly this was a very superficial description of how URL rewriting works—but we'll get back to it soon, after we talk a little bit about regular expressions.

URL Rewriting and Regular Expressions

Regular expressions are one of those topics that programmers tend to either love or hate. A regular expression, commonly referred to as **regex**, is a text string that uses a special format to describe a **text pattern**. Regular expressions are used to define rules that match or transform groups of strings, and they represent one of the most powerful text manipulation tools available today. Find a few details about them at the Wikipedia page at `http://en.wikipedia.org/wiki/Regular_expression`.

Regular expressions are particularly useful in circumstances when you need to manipulate strings that don't have a well-defined format (as XML documents have, for example) and cannot be parsed or modified using more specialized techniques. For example, regular expressions can be used to extract or validate e-mail addresses, find valid dates in strings, remove duplicate lines of text, find the number of times a word or a letter appears in a phrase, find or validate IP addresses, and so on.

In the previous exercise, you used URL rewriting rules, using regular expressions, to match incoming keyword-rich URLs and obtain their rewritten, dynamic versions. A bit later in this chapter, we'll use a regular expression that prepares a string for inclusion in the URL, by replacing unsupported characters with dashes and eliminating duplicate separation characters.

Regular expressions are supported by many languages and tools, including the .NET languages and the URL rewriting tools. A regular expression that works in C# will work in Java or PHP without modifications most of the time. When you want to do an operation based on regular expressions, you usually must provide at least three key elements:

- The source string that needs to be parsed or manipulated

- The regular expression to be applied on the source string

- The kind of operation to be performed, which can be either obtaining the matching substrings or replacing them with something else

Regular expressions use a special syntax based on literal characters, which are interpreted literally, and metacharacters, which have special matching properties. A literal character in a regular expression matches the same character in the source string, and a sequence of such characters matches the same sequence in the source string. This is similar to searching for substrings in a string. For example, if you match "or" in "favorite color," you'll find two matches for it.

Metacharacters have special properties, and it's their power and flexibility that makes regular expressions so useful. For example, the question mark (?) metacharacter specifies that the preceding character is optional. So if you want to match "color" and "colour," your regular expression would be `colou?r`.

As pointed out earlier, regular expressions can become extremely complex when you get into their more subtle details. In this section, you'll find explanations for the regular expressions we're using, and we suggest that you continue your regex training using a specialized book or tutorial.

Table 7-2 contains the description of the most common regular expression metacharacters. You can use this table as a reference for understanding the rewrite rules.

Table 7-2. *Metacharacters Commonly Used in Regular Expressions*

Metacharacter	Description
^	Matches the beginning of the line. In our case, it will always match the beginning of the URL. The domain name isn't considered part of the URL, as far the URL the rewriting engine is concerned. It is useful to think of ^ as anchoring the characters that follow to the beginning of the string—that is, asserting that they are the first part.
.	Matches any single character.
*	Specifies that the preceding character or expression can be repeated *zero* or more times.
+	Specifies that the preceding character or expression can be repeated *one* or more times. In other words, the preceding character or expression must match at least once.
?	Specifies that the preceding character or expression can be repeated *zero or one* time. In other words, the preceding character or expression is optional.
{m,n}	Specifies that the preceding character or expression can be repeated between m and n times; m and n are integers, and m needs to be lower than n.
( )	The parentheses are used to define a captured expression. The string matching the expression between parentheses can then be read as a variable. The parentheses can also be used to group the contents therein, as in mathematics, and operators such as *, +, or ? can then be applied to the resulting expression.
[ ]	Used to define a character class. For example, [abc] will match any of the characters a, b, or c. The hyphen character (-) can be used to define a range of characters. For example, [a-z] matches any lowercase letter. If the hyphen is meant to be interpreted literally, it should be the last character before the closing bracket,]. Many metacharacters lose their special function when enclosed between brackets and are interpreted literally.
[^]	Similar to [ ], except it matches everything except the mentioned character class. For example, [^a-c] matches all characters except a, b, and c.
$	Matches the end of the line. In our case, it will always match the end of the URL. It is useful to think of it as anchoring the previous characters to the end of the string—that is, asserting that they are the last part.
\	The backslash is used to escape the character that follows. It is used to escape metacharacters when you need them to be taken for their literal value, rather than their special meaning. For example, \. will match a dot, rather than any character (the typical meaning of the dot in a regular expression). The backslash can also escape itself—so if you want to match C:\Windows, you'll need to refer to it as C:\\Windows.

To understand how these metacharacters work in practice, let's analyze another of the rewrite rules in BalloonShop: the one that rewrites category page URLs. Just as for rewriting department pages, for rewriting category pages we have two rules—one that handles paged categories and one that handles nonpaged categories. The following rule rewrites categories with pages, and the regular expression is highlighted:

```
<rewrite
  url="^.*-d([0-9]+)/.*-c([0-9]+)/page-([0-9]+)/?$"
  to="/Catalog.aspx?DepartmentId=$1&amp;CategoryId=$2&amp;Page=$3"
  processing="stop" />
```

This regular expression is intended to match URLs such as `http://www.example.com/Balloons-for-Children-d2/Cartoons-c5/Page-2` and extract the ID of the department, the ID of the category, and the page number from these URLs. In plain English, the rule searches for strings that start with some characters followed by `-d` and a number (which is the department ID); followed by a forward slash, some other characters, `-c`, and another number (which is the category ID); followed by `/page-` and a number, which is the page number.

Using Table 7-2 as reference, let's analyze the regular expression technically. The expression starts with the `^` character, matching the beginning of the requested URL (the URL doesn't include the domain name). The characters `.*` match any string of zero or more characters, because the dot means any character, and the asterisk means that the preceding character or expression (which is the dot) can be repeated zero or more times.

The next characters, `-d([0-9]+)`, extract the ID of the department. The `-d` part is interpreted literally—the string must contain a dash followed by the letter *d*. The `[0-9]` bit matches any character between 0 and 9 (that is, any digit), and the `+` that follows indicates that the pattern can repeat one or more times, so you can have a multidigit number rather than just a single digit. The enclosing parentheses around `[0-9]+` indicate that the regular expression engine should store the matching string (which will be the department ID) inside a variable called $1. You'll need this variable to compose the rewritten URL.

The same principle is used to save the category ID and the page number into the $2 and $3 variables. Finally, you have `/?`, which specifies that the URL can end with a slash, but the slash is optional. The regular expression ends with `$`, which matches the end of the string.

■**Note** When you need to use symbols that have metacharacter significance as their literal values, you need to escape them with a backslash. For example, if you want to match `Catalog.aspx`, the regular expression should read `Catalog\.aspx`. The `\` is the escaping character, which indicates that the dot should be taken as a literal dot, not as any character (which is the significance of the dot metacharacter).

The second argument of the rewriting rule plugs in the variables that you extracted using the regular expression into the rewritten URL:

```
/Catalog.aspx?DepartmentId=$1&amp;CategoryId=$2&amp;Page=$3
```

The $1, $2, and $3 variables are replaced by the values supplied by the regular expression, and the URL is loaded by our application. Note that the ampersand character (&) is written as `&amp;` because of the convention of the XML format. When using URL rewriting tools that don't keep the rewriting rules in XML files, you don't need to encode the & character.

Rewriting rules are processed in sequential order as they are written in the configuration file. If you want to make sure that a rule is the last one processed when a match is found for it, you need to use the `processing="stop"` attribute. Alternative values for this attribute are `continue` (the default) and `restart`.

This attribute is particularly useful when you have a long list of rewriting rules; setting its value to `stop` improves performance and prevents the rewriting engine from processing all the rules that follow once a match is found. This is usually what you want regardless.

.NET Regular Expressions

The rewriting rules you've just added to `web.config` aren't the only place where we use regular expressions in BalloonShop. As hinted earlier, regular expressions come in very handy whenever complex text manipulation is necessary. In the next exercise where we expand BalloonShop, we'll need to programmatically create keyword-rich URLs for department, category, and product names using their names and IDs.

The problem with department, category, and product names is that they usually can't be included in URLs as they are. These names contain special characters (such as spaces, commas, and so on), which need to be escaped for inclusion in URLs. Luckily, the .NET Framework contains the very useful method `HttpUtility.UrlEncode`, which does exactly that—it prepares a string for inclusion in an URL by escaping all its special characters. Using this method, we could create the following URL for the Love & Romance category located in the Anniversary Balloons department:

`http://www.example.com/Anniversary+Balloons-d1/Love+%26+Romance-c1/`

This URL isn't ideal for two reasons. First, it looks ugly. It's not the kind of URL that you can easily remember or communicate over the phone. Secondly, IIS may, depending on its security settings, reject the request for security reasons, with an error message that reads:

```
The request filtering module is configured to deny a request that contains a double
escape sequence.
```

As you probably suspect, we'll make use of regular expressions—in C# this time—to generate friendly URLs for our site. We'll use regular expressions to exclude all special characters from these names and replace them with dashes. This way, for the category Love & Romance we'll generate a much nicer URL:

`http://www.example.com/Anniversary-Balloons-d1/Love-Romance-c1/`

You can find a quick and useful introduction to regular expressions in C# at `http://www.regular-expressions.info/dotnet.html`. Andrew Watt's *Beginning Regular Expressions* also contains detailed coverage of .NET's regular expressions implementation. Here we'll only cover the necessary bit of theory required for the exercises in this book.

Microsoft .NET packs all its regular expressions functionality into six classes and one delegate, which are described in Table 7-3. All these classes are part of the `System.Text.RegularExpressions` namespace.

Table 7-3. *Regular Expressions Classes*

Class	Description
Regex	Class that performs regular expression operations. It can be instantiated to represent a compiled instance of a regular expression, or its static methods can be used to perform the same actions.
Capture	Represents the result of a single match.
CaptureCollection	Represents a collection of Capture objects.
Group	Represents the results of a capturing group (an expression written between parentheses in the regular expression), in the form of a CaptureCollection object.
GroupCollection	Represents a collection of Group objects.
Match	Represents the result of a single regular expression match. The captures are available via the Captures member, which returns a CaptureCollection object, and the captured groups are available via the Groups member, which is a GroupCollection object.
MatchCollection	Represents a collection of Match objects.
MatchEvaluator	A delegate that can be used during regular expression–based text replacement operations. A delegate represents a reference to a method, and you can use delegates to pass method references as parameters. This particular delegate helps in replacement operations, when the replacement string for each match must be calculated using C# code depending on the match. In those cases, instead of providing a simple replacement string, you pass an instance of MatchEvaluator.

When instantiating the `Regex` class, you get an object that represents a regular expression. That object can then be used to perform matches or string replacement operations. Here's a simple example of using `Regex`, `Match`, and `Group`:

```
Regex regex = new Regex("^/(.*)-d([0-9]+)/.*-c([0-9]+)/?$");
Match match = regex.Match("/Anniversary-Balloons-d1/Love-Romance-c1/");
Group group = match.Groups[1];
string deptUrlName = group.Value;
```

After this code executes, `deptUrlName` will contain `Anniversary-Balloons`. The `Groups` collection contains the matching strings. In our case this collection has three members, whose values are `Anniversary-Balloons`, 1, and 1.

The captured groups—the expressions written between parentheses—are accessible via the Groups collection. The first element of the collection contains the entire matching string (/Anniversary-Balloons-d1/Love-Romance-c1/). For retrieving the department name, which is captured by the (.*) expression, we've read the second group from the Match object—match.Groups[1]. To read the ID of the department and the ID of the category, we'd need to read match.Groups[2] and match.Groups[3], respectively.

When creating a Regex object, the object stores the regular expression internally in a specific, "compiled" format, which helps improve the performance for any subsequent operations the object will perform. When a certain match or replace operation is performed only once, you can use the static methods of Regex, which create a Regex object for you, use it to perform the required operation, and destroy it afterward. Here's an example:

```
Match match = Regex.Match("/Anniversary-Balloons-d1/Love-Romance-c1/",
                    "^/(.*)-d([0-9]+)/.*-c([0-9]+)/?$");
Group group = match.Groups[1];
string deptUrlName = group.Value;
```

In practice, when needing to extract data from matching groups, instead of accessing the groups by index, we prefer using named groups. In the following example you can see how we've given a name to the group that captures the product's name, and then we accessed the group by its name:

```
Match match = Regex.Match("/Anniversary-Balloons-d1/Love-Romance-c1/",
                    "^/(?<DEPTNAME>.*)-d([0-9]+)/.*-c([0-9]+)/?$");
Group group = match.Groups["DEPTNAME"];
string deptUrlName = group.Value;
```

Table 7-4 describes the most frequently used methods of Regex.

Table 7-4. *Methods of the Regex Class*

Regex Method	Description
Match	Searches for a regular expression in a string and returns the first match in the form of a Match object.
Matches	Searches for a regular expression in a string and returns a MatchCollection object that contains all matches.
IsMatch	Returns a Boolean value indicating whether a match has been found.
Replace	Performs a regular expression string replacing operation. The replacement text can contain variables named $1, $2, and so on, representing the values of the captured groups from the matching regular expression. Overloads of Replace allow providing a MatchEvaluator instance instead of the replacement string, in which case the method referenced by the MatchEvaluator is called for each match, and its return value is used as the string replacement value.
Split	Splits a string in the places matched by the regular expression.

Many of the Regex methods receive as a parameter a RegexOptions value, which can affect the behavior of the regular expressions parser. Table 7-5 describes the members of the enumeration.

Table 7-5. *RegexOptions Enumeration Members*

RegexOptions Member	Description
Compiled	Creates a compiled regular expression. This increases execution time for all executions except the first time, which is slower.
CultureInvariant	Ignore cultural differences.
ECMAScript	Enables ECMAScript behavior of the parser.
ExplicitCapture	Specifies that all captures must be marked explicitly using the (?<name>) syntax. It is helpful when the expression contains many parentheses that don't need to be captured.
IgnoreCase	Performs a case-insensitive match.
IgnorePatternWhitespace	Instructs the parser to ignore spaces or tabs in the regular expression, except when they appear in a character class, such as [ ]. This is helpful when writing a pattern over multiple lines, to make it easier to read.
Multiline	In Multiline mode, the ^ and $ characters will match the beginning and end, respectively, of any line of text.
None	Doesn't alter the parser in any way.
RightToLeft	The matching will be done right-to-left.
Singleline	In Singleline mode, the dot metacharacter matches every character, including \n.

Two or more enumeration members can be combined using the bitwise OR operator, like this:

```
Regex regex = new Regex("^/(.*)-d([0-9]+)/.*-c([0-9]+)/?$");
                        RegexOptions.IgnoreCase | RegexOptions.Compiled);
```

The Keyword-Rich URL Factory

So now your project supports keyword-rich URLs, but doesn't use them effectively. Your site still generates old-fashioned, dynamic URLs. The fact that we support keyword-rich URLs doesn't bring any significant benefits. This leads us to a second exercise related to our URLs. It's time to update BalloonShop and make use of a few tricks to convert all your dynamic URLs to beautiful, keyword-rich URLs.

In the earlier chapters, we were wise enough to use a centralized class named Link that generates most of the site's links. This means that, now, updating all the links in our site is just a matter of updating that Link class.

Exercise: Generating Keyword-Rich URLs

1. Open `Link.cs` and add a reference to the `RegularExpressions` namespace:

    ```
    using System.Text.RegularExpressions;
    ```

2. Add two static members to the Link class, named `purifyUrlRegex` and `dashesRegex`:

    ```
    public class Link
    {
      // regular expression that removes characters that aren't a-z, 0-9, dash,
      // underscore or space
      private static Regex purifyUrlRegex = new Regex("[^-a-zA-Z0-9_ ]", ➥
    RegexOptions.Compiled);

      // regular expression that changes dashes, underscores and spaces to dashes
      private static Regex dashesRegex = new Regex("[-_ ]+",
    RegexOptions.Compiled);
    ```

3. Add the following method to the `Link` class. This method transforms a department, category or product name, such as `Balloons for Children`, to a URL-friendly string that can be used to build BalloonShop URLs, such as `Balloons-for-Children`.

    ```
    // prepares a string to be included in an URL
    private static string PrepareUrlText(string urlText)
    {
      // remove all characters that aren't a-z, 0-9, dash, underscore or space
      urlText = purifyUrlRegex.Replace(urlText, "");

      // remove all leading and trailing spaces
      urlText = urlText.Trim();

      // change all dashes, underscores and spaces to dashes
      urlText = dashesRegex.Replace(urlText, "-");

      // return the modified string
      return urlText;
    }
    ```

4. Modify the `ToDepartment` method in `Link` like this:

    ```
    public static string ToDepartment(string departmentId, string page)
    {
      // prepare department URL name
      DepartmentDetails d = CatalogAccess.GetDepartmentDetails(departmentId);
      string deptUrlName = PrepareUrlText(d.Name);
    ```

```
    // build department URL
    if (page == "1")
      return BuildAbsolute(String.Format("{0}-d{1}/", deptUrlName, ➥
departmentId));
    else
      return BuildAbsolute(String.Format("{0}-d{1}/Page={2}", deptUrlName, ➥
departmentId, page));
    }
```

5. Modify the ToCategory method in Link like this:

```
    public static string ToCategory(string departmentId, string categoryId, ➥
string page)
    {
      // prepare department and category URL names
      DepartmentDetails d = CatalogAccess.GetDepartmentDetails(departmentId);
      string deptUrlName = PrepareUrlText(d.Name);
      CategoryDetails c = CatalogAccess.GetCategoryDetails(categoryId);
      string catUrlName = PrepareUrlText(c.Name);

      // build category URL
      if (page == "1")
        return BuildAbsolute(String.Format("{0}-d{1}/{2}-c{3}/", ➥
deptUrlName, departmentId, catUrlName, categoryId));
      else
        return BuildAbsolute(String.Format("{0}-d{1}/{2}-c{3}/Page-{4}/", ➥
deptUrlName, departmentId, catUrlName, categoryId, page));
    }
```

Modify the ToProduct method in Link like this:

```
    public static string ToProduct(string productId)
    {
      // prepare product URL name
      ProductDetails p = CatalogAccess.GetProductDetails(productId.ToString());
      string prodUrlName = PrepareUrlText(p.Name);

      // build product URL
      return BuildAbsolute(String.Format("{0}-p{1}/", prodUrlName, productId));
    }
```

6. Load BalloonShop, and notice the new links. In Figure 7-4, the URL of the Love & Romance category, http://www.example.com/Anniversary-Balloons-d1/Love-Romance-c1/, is visible in Internet Explorer's status bar. Figure 7-5 shows the new URL of the I Love You (Simon Elvin) product.

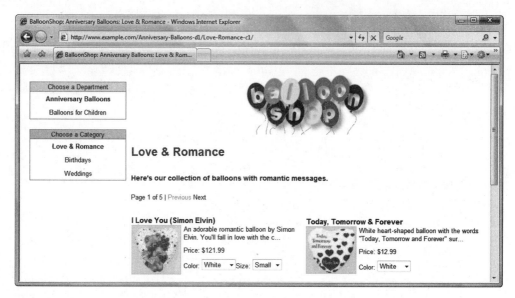

Figure 7-4. *Testing keyword-rich category URLs*

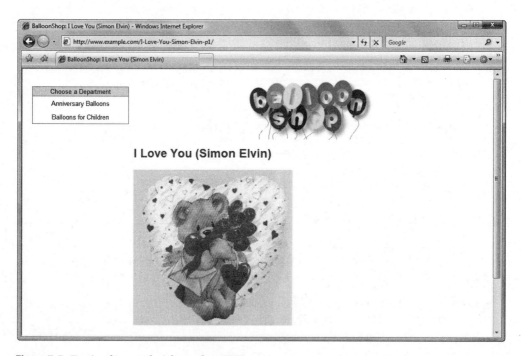

Figure 7-5. *Testing keyword-rich product URLs*

How it Works: Generating Keyword-Rich URLs

In this exercise, you modified the `ToDepartment`, `ToCategory`, and `ToProduct` methods of the `Link` class to build keyword-rich URLs instead of dynamic URLs. The heart of the changes lies in using regular expressions in the `PrepareUrlText` method, which receives as a parameter a string, such as a product or category name, and transforms it into a form that can be included in a URL. All characters except alphanumeric characters, dashes, underscores, and spaces are removed, and dashes are added as word separators.

The regular expressions used by PrepareUrlText are stored as static Regex members in the Link class: purifyUrlRegex and dashesRegex. These objects are used only by PrepareUrlText, but we're storing them as static members for performance reasons. If they were instance members, they would have to be recompiled by the regex engine on every use.

PrepareUrlText starts by using the first regular expression, purifyUrlRegex—[^-a-zA-Z0-9_]—to delete all characters that aren't alphanumeric, dash, space, or underscore, ensuring there are no characters left that could break our URL.

```
    // prepares a string to be included in an URL
    private static string PrepareUrlText(string urlText)
    {
      // remove all characters that aren't a-z, 0-9, dash, underscore or space
      urlText = purifyUrlRegex.Replace(urlText, "");
```

The Replace method of Regex is available as both a static method and an instance method. Here we used its instance version to replace the string portions matched by the regular expression with an empty string. In this case, the regular expression [^-a-zA-Z0-9_] matches all characters not (^) in the set of letters, numbers, dashes, underscores, or spaces. We indicate that the matching characters should be replaced with "", the empty string, effectively removing them.

Then we continue by removing the leading and trailing spaces from the string it receives as parameter, using the String.Trim function:

```
      // remove all leading and trailing spaces
      urlText = urlText.Trim();
```

Finally, we use the dashesRegex regular expression, [-_]+, to transform any groups of spaces, dashes, and underscores to dashes. For example, a string such as My___Balloon (note there are three underscores) would be replaced with My-Balloon. Then we return the transformed URL string:

```
      // change all dashes, underscores and spaces to dashes
      urlText = dashesRegex.Replace(urlText, "-");

      // return the modified string
      return urlText;
    }
```

PrepareUrlText is used by ToDepartment, ToCategory, and ToProduct to create product URLs. These methods also use the HttpUtility.UrlPathEncode function to ensure that no unaccepted characters appear in the final URLs. Using UrlPathEncode is a good programming practice when creating URLs.

Make sure all the links in your site are now search engine–friendly, and let's move on to the next task for this chapter.

Using the 301 and 302 HTTP Status Codes

With our current code, loading any of the following URLs in a web browser will get the same content—the product page of our "Welcome Back" balloon:

```
http://www.example.com/Welcome-Back-p33/
http://www.example.com/TYPO-p33/
http://www.example.com/Product.aspx?ProductID=33
```

This flexibility happens to have potentially adverse effects on your search engine rankings. If, for any reason, the search engines reach the same page using different links, they might think you have lots of different pages with identical content on your site and may incorrectly assume that you have a spam site or a site with low density of unique content. In such an extreme case, your site as a whole, or just parts of it, may be penalized and not get the best possible location in SERPs (Search Engine Result Pages).

Our goal for the next exercise is to ensure that the dynamic versions of our URLs, and even the misspelled versions of our product URLs, are redirected to their proper versions. To implement page redirection, you need to learn about the HTTP headers and the HTTP status codes.

Each time a web browser requests a URL from a web site, the server replies with a set of HTTP headers; the requested content follows after them. Most users never see this part of the communication, however, because web browsers do not normally display them.

As a web developer, you're probably familiar with the 200 status code, which indicates the request was successful, and with the 404 code, which indicates that the requested resource could not be found.

Among the HTTP status codes, there are a few that specifically address redirection issues. The most common of these redirection status codes are 301, which indicates that the requested resource has been *permanently* moved to a new location, and 302, which indicates that the relocation is only *temporary*.

When a web browser or a search engine makes a request whose response contains a redirection status code, they continue by browsing to the indicated location. The web browser will request the new URL and will update the address bar to reflect the new location. The process is described in Figure 7-6.

This theory is important for those times when you have one or more URLs that need to be changed, but you don't want to lose the search engine ranks they have achieved in time. This could happen, for example, when upgrading a website from dynamic URLs to keyword-rich URLs after the site has been indexed by search engines. In this scenario, the 301 redirect will be your best friend. Since 301 signals a permanent relocation, search engines will usually also transfer the link equity from the old URL to the new URL, usually maintaining your search engine rankings.

This means that if your original URL was ranking well for certain keywords (URL A in Figure 7-6), if 301 is used, then the new URL (URL B in Figure 7-6) will rank just like the old one, after search engines take note of the redirect. In practice, abusing of 301 isn't desirable, because there's no guarantee that the link equity will be completely transferred—and even if it does, it may take a while until you'll rank well again for the desired keywords.

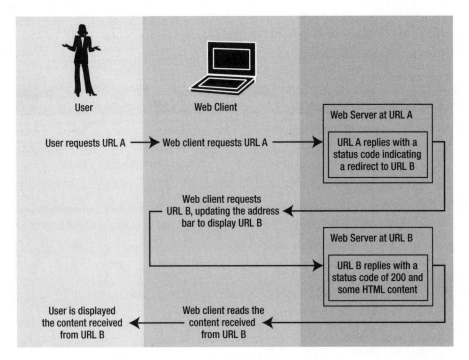

Figure 7-6. *URL redirection*

In ASP.NET, you can control the HTTP response headers through the System.Web. HttpResponse class. The following code snippet shows how you can 301 redirect requests to http://www.example.com/Product.aspx?ProductID=33 to http://www.example.com/ Welcome-Back-p33/.

```
if (context.Request.RawUrl == "/Product.aspx?ProductID=33")
{
 context.Response.Status = "301 Moved Permanently";
 context.Response.AddHeader("Location", "http://www.example.com/Welcome-Back-p33/");
}
```

Redirecting using UrlRewriter.NET is equally easy. You configure the redirection rules by adding <redirect> elements to the <rewriter> element in web.config. Under the covers, UrlRewriter.NET sets the 301 status code for you when the incoming request matches the redirection rule. A redirection rule looks like the following:

```
<redirect url="^?ProductID=33$" to="/Welcome-Back-p33/" permanent="true" />
```

As you can see, the syntax is pretty similar to the rewriting rules, except that you use <redirect> instead of <rewrite>. You use the attribute permanent="true" when you want UrlRewriter.NET to perform 301 redirects, and permanent="false" for 302 redirects.

In the exercise that follows we'll implement an automatic redirection system that redirects all versions of a product details page to its "proper" version. You may or may not want to do the same for other pages in your site—we'll leave this to you as an exercise because in practice you need to carefully consider the specifics of your project before deciding an automatic redirection policy.

Exercise: Implementing Automatic URL Correction

1. Modify the Link class in the Link.cs file by adding the following method:

```
// 301 redirects to correct product URL if not already there
public static void CheckProductUrl(string productId)
{
  // get requested URL
  HttpContext context = HttpContext.Current;
  string requestedUrl = context.Request.RawUrl;

  // get last part of proper URL
  string properUrl = Link.ToProduct(productId);
  string properUrlTrunc = properUrl.Substring(Math.Abs➥
(properUrl.Length - requestedUrl.Length));

  // 301 redirect to the proper URL if necessary
  if (requestedUrl != properUrlTrunc)
  {
    context.Response.Status = "301 Moved Permanently";
    context.Response.AddHeader("Location", properUrl);
  }
}
```

2. Modify the Page_Load function in Product.aspx.cs by adding a call to Link.CheckProductUrl:

```
protected void Page_Load(object sender, EventArgs e)
{
  // Retrieve ProductID from the query string
  string productId = Request.QueryString["ProductID"];
  ...
  // 301 redirect to the proper URL if necessary
  Link.CheckProductUrl(Request.QueryString["ProductID"]);
}
```

3. Load http://www.example.com/TYPO-p33/ and notice that page redirects to http://www.example.com/Welcome-Back-p33/. Using a tool such as the LiveHTTPHeaders Firefox extension (http://livehttpheaders.mozdev.org/), you can see the type of redirect used was 301 (see Figure 7-7).

■**Note** Other tools you can use to view the HTTP headers are the Web Development Helper for Internet Explorer, and Firebug or the Web Developer plug-in for Firefox.

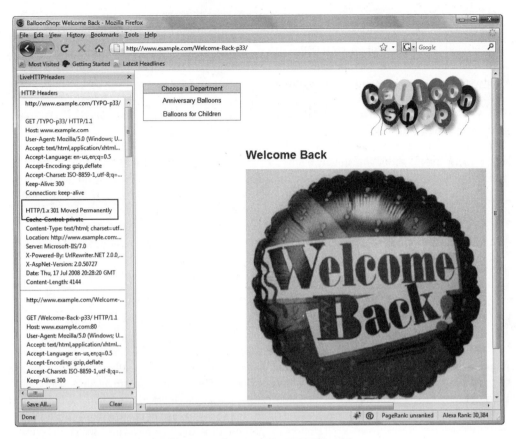

Figure 7-7. *Testing the response status code using LiveHTTPHeaders*

How It Works: Using 301 for Redirecting Content

The code follows some simple logic to get the job done. The `CheckProductUrl` method of the `Link` class verifies if a request should be redirected to another URL, and if so, it does a 301 redirection. The ASP.NET way of performing the redirection is by setting the HTTP header like this:

```
// 301 redirect to the proper URL if necessary
if (requestedUrl != properUrl)
{
  context.Response.Status = "301 Moved Permanently";
  context.Response.AddHeader("Location", properUrl);
}
```

Note that in case you extend the automatic URL correction functionality in your site, it would be appropriate to create a new class to deal with it, and move `CheckProductUrl` to that class.

Correctly Signaling 404 and 500 Errors

It is important to use the correct HTTP status code when something special happens to the visitor's request. You've already seen that, when performing redirects, knowledge of HTTP status codes can make an important difference to your SEO efforts. This time we will talk about 404 and 500.

The 404 status code is used to tell the visitor that he or she has requested a page that doesn't exist on the destination web site. Browsers and web servers have templates that users get when you make such a request—you know, you've seen them.

Hosting services let you specify a custom page to be displayed when such a 404 error occurs. This is obviously beneficial for your site, as you can provide some custom feedback to your visitor depending on what he or she was searching for. Sometimes, however, the 404 status code isn't automatically set for you, so you need to do it in your 404 script. If, for some reason, your site reacts to 404 errors by sending pages with the 200 OK status code, search engines will think that you have many different URLs hosting the same content, and your site may get penalized.

We'll be using the 404 status message in the following circumstances:

- When the visitor requests a page that does not exist in our web site

- When the visitor requests a product with an ID that does not exist in our database

The 500 status message is used to communicate that the web server or the application is having internal errors. Right now, when such an internal error occurs, BalloonShop serves Oops.aspx, but fails to correctly set the 500 status code. This is problematic because if Google indexes the site when the site faces technical errors, it will get a lot of identical pages marked as "good" with the 200 status code, replacing their previously indexed versions.

In the following exercise, we'll customize BalloonShop to use the 404 and 500 status codes correctly.

Exercise: Using the 500 HTTP Status Code

1. Add a new Web Form to your site, named NotFound.aspx. Don't use a code-behind file—instead use the BalloonShop.master Master Page, and alter the generated code as follows:

```
<%@ Page Language="C#" MasterPageFile="~/BalloonShop.master" ➥
Title="BalloonShop: What are you looking for?" %>

<script runat="server">
  protected void Page_Load(object sender, EventArgs e)
  {
    // set the 404 status code
    Response.StatusCode = 404;
  }
</script>
```

```
<asp:Content ID="Content1" ContentPlaceHolderID="head" Runat="Server">
</asp:Content>
<asp:Content ID="Content2" ContentPlaceHolderID="ContentPlaceHolder1" ➥
Runat="Server">
  <h1>Looking for balloons?</h1>
  <p>Unfortunately, the page that you asked for doesn't exist in our web site!
  </p>
  <p>Please visit our
    <asp:HyperLink runat="server" Target="~/" Text="catalog" />,
    or contact us at friendly_support@example.com!
  </p>
  <p>The <b>BalloonShop</b> team</p>
</asp:Content>
```

2. Alter `Oops.aspx` to correctly set the 500 status code:

```
<%@ Page Language="C#" %>
<!DOCTYPE html PUBLIC "-//W3C//DTD XHTML 1.0 Transitional//EN" ➥
"http://www.w3.org/TR/xhtml1/DTD/xhtml1-transitional.dtd">

<script runat="server">
  protected void Page_Load(object sender, EventArgs e)
  {
    // set the 500 status code
    Response.Status = "500 Internal Server Error";
  }
</script>
```

3. Modify `web.config`:

```
<customErrors mode="On" defaultRedirect="~/Oops.aspx">
  <error statusCode="404" redirect="~/NotFound.aspx" />
  <error statusCode="500" redirect="~/Oops.aspx" />
</customErrors>
```

4. Modify `Product.aspx.cs`:

```
protected void Page_Load(object sender, EventArgs e)
{
  // Retrieve ProductID from the query string
  string productId = Request.QueryString["ProductID"];
  // Retrieves product details
  ProductDetails pd = CatalogAccess.GetProductDetails(productId);
  // Does the product exist?
  if (pd.Name != null)
  {
    PopulateControls(pd);
  }
```

```
    else
    {
      Server.Transfer("~/NotFound.aspx");
    }
    // 301 redirect to the proper URL if necessary
    Link.CheckProductUrl(Request.QueryString["ProductID"]);
}
```

5. Finally, try to load a product with an ID that does not exist in our database, such as http://
www.example.com/Product.aspx?ProductID=555. You can admire the result in Figure 7-8.

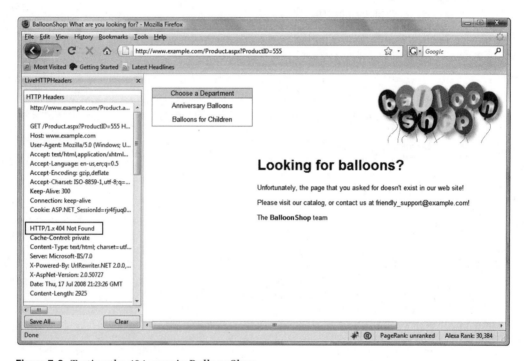

Figure 7-8. *Testing the 404 page in BalloonShop*

How It Works: Handling 404 and 500 Errors

Now if an application error happens, the visitor is shown a proper error page that comes along with a 500 status code. Not only will the human reader understand the site is having technical problems, but the search engines will as well. The same is true about the 404 error page. In addition, the 404 page is served not only to visitors trying to load invalid URLs, but also to visitors trying to load pages with syntactically correct URLs, but that refer to products that no longer exist in our database.

The Short UrlRewriter.NET Reference

Congratulations, you've completed the exercises for this chapter! Before we end, Table 7-6 gives a quick reference to UrlRewriter.NET's most important features. You'll find this table useful if you'll need to implement more complex rules yourself. You should also use the official documentation, which you can find at `http://urlrewriter.net/index.php/support/`.

Table 7-6. *UrlRewriter.NET Reference*

Element	Example	Description
Rewrite	`<rewrite url="^/P-([0-9]+).aspx$" to="/Product.aspx?ID=$1" processing="stop" />`	Rewrites the incoming request. The url attribute specifies the matching regular expression, and to specifies the rewritten URL. The value of the optional processing attribute specifies that if a match is found, the processing should continue (the default), stop, or restart.
Redirect	`<redirect url="^/P-(.+).html$" to="/Product.aspx?ID=$1" permanent="true" />`	Redirects the incoming request. If permanent is true (the default), a 301 redirect is performed; otherwise, a 302 redirect is used.
If	`<if address="192.168.0.1" /> <forbidden /> </if>`	Allows grouping one or more directives, which are parsed if the condition is true.
Unless	`<unless address="127.0.0.1" /> <set cookie="Visited" value="true" /> </if>`	Allows grouping one or more directives, which are parsed if the condition is false.
set status	`<set status="500" />`	Sets the status code to return to the client. If the status code is equal or greater than 300, the action is final; otherwise, the following directives are processed in sequence.
set property	`<if url="^/P-([0-9]+).aspx$"> <set property="ProductID" value="$1" /> </if>`	Sets a property in HttpContext.Current.Items using the last performed match. The example sets a property named Rewriter.ProductID.
set cookie	`<set cookie="Visited" value="true" />`	Adds a cookie to the collection of cookies sent to the client.
add header	`<add header="X-Powered-By" value="UrlRewriter.NET" />`	Adds a header value.
forbidden	`<forbidden />`	Returns a 403 Forbidden status code.
not-found	`<if url="^/old/.*$"> <not-found /> </if>`	Returns a 404 Not Found response to the client.
not-allowed	`<if method="DELETE"> <not-allowed /> </if>`	Returns a 405 Method Not Allowed response to the client.
gone	`<if url="^/old/.*$"> <gone /> </if>`	Returns a 410 Gone response to the client.
not-implemented	`<if header="User-Agent" match="MSIE" /> <not-implemented /> </if>`	Returns a 501 Not Implemented response to the client.

Summary

We're certain you've enjoyed this chapter! With only a few changes in its code, BalloonShop is now ready to face its online competition, with a solid search engine–optimized foundation. Of course, the SEO efforts don't end here.

When adding each new feature of the web site, we'll make sure to follow general SEO guidelines, so when we launch the web site, the search engines will be our friends, not our enemies.

In following chapters, we'll continue making small SEO improvements. For now, the foundations have been laid, and we're ready to continue implementing another exciting feature in BalloonShop: product searching!

CHAPTER 8

■ ■ ■

Searching the Catalog

"What are you looking for?" There is no place where you'll hear this question more frequently than in both brick-and-mortar and e-commerce stores. Like any other quality web store around, your BalloonShop will allow visitors to search through the product catalog. You'll see how easy it is to add new functionality to a working site by integrating the new components into the existing architecture.

In this chapter, you will

- Analyze the various ways in which the product catalog can be searched

- Implement a search engine that uses SQL Server's FULLTEXT engine

- Write the data tier and business tier code that interacts with the search stored procedure

- Create the user interface of the catalog search feature

Choosing How to Search the Catalog

As always, you need to think about a few things before starting to code. Always keep in mind that when designing a new feature, you must analyze that feature from the final user's perspective.

For the visual part, you'll use a text box in which the visitor can enter one or more words to search for. In BalloonShop, the words entered by the visitor will be searched for in the products' names and descriptions. The text entered by the visitor can be searched for in several ways:

- *Exact-match search*: If the visitor enters an entire phrase, this phrase is searched in the database as it is, without splitting the words and searching for them separately.

- *All-words search*: The phrase entered by the visitor is split into words, causing a search for products that contain every word entered by the visitor. This is like the exact-match search in that it still searches for all the entered words, but this time the order of the words is no longer important.

- *Any-words search*: Products must contain at least one of the entered words.

This simple classification isn't by any means complete. The search engine can be as complex as the one offered by modern search engines, which provides many options and features and shows a ranked list of results, or as simple as searching the database for the exact string provided by the visitor.

BalloonShop will support the any-words and all-words search modes. This decision leads to the visual design of the search feature (see Figure 8-1).

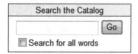

Figure 8-1. *The search box*

The text box is there, as expected, along with a check box that allows the visitor to choose between an all-words search and an any-words search.

Another decision you need to make here concerns how the matching products are displayed. The simplest solution to display the search results is to reuse the ProductsList.ascx web control you built in the previous chapter. A sample search page will look like Figure 8-2.

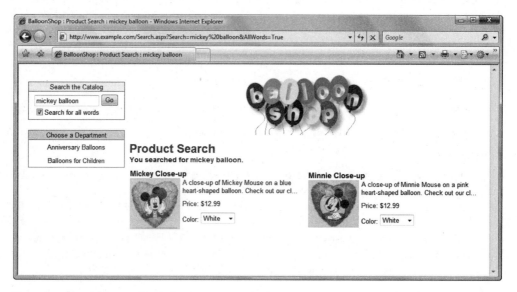

Figure 8-2. *A sample search results page*

The search results page employs paging, just as the other pages that contain product lists. If there are a lot of search results, you'll only present a fixed (but configurable) number of products per page and allow the visitor to browse through the pages using Previous and Next links.

Let's begin implementing the functionality by starting, as usual, with the data tier.

Teaching the Database to Search Itself

Within the database, there are two main ways to implement searching. You can implement database searching by using either of the following:

- *SQL Server's Full-Text Search feature*: This feature allows for advanced keyword searches, such as searching using the Boolean operators (AND, AND NOT, OR) and searching for inflected forms of words, such as plurals and various verb tenses, or words located in close proximity. Additionally, the Full-Text Search feature can also sort the results based on rank, placing the most likely matches at the top.

- *A custom search solution for which you need stored procedures, user-defined functions, and courage*: This solution was presented in the previous edition of this book, *Beginning ASP.NET 2.0 E-Commerce in C# 2005*, because at that time the Full-Text Search feature was not available for the free edition of SQL Server. If your environment has this limitation, you can download the chapter on product search (Chapter 5) of the previous edition for free from http://www.cristiandarie.ro/downloads/.

In this chapter, we'll analyze the Full-Text solution because it is available with all editions of SQL Server 2005 and 2008 (including the Express Edition).

This chapter will cover enough to get you started, and you can use the excellent MSDN resource, Full-Text Search Developer InfoCenter (http://msdn.microsoft.com/en-us/library/ms142519.aspx), for detailed information on how to use and customize SQL Server's Full-Text Search feature.

Installing SQL Server's Full-Text Feature

If you have installed SQL Server as instructed in Chapter 3, you should have it properly configured for creating full-text indexes and performing full-text searches. If this is the case, you can skip this section. Otherwise, read on to make sure you're prepared to add the product search feature to BalloonShop.

First, let's make sure you have installed the Full-Text Search feature on your system. The easiest way is to start the Services applet and look for SQL Server FullText Search (see Figure 8-3) or SQL Full-text Filter Daemon Launcher.

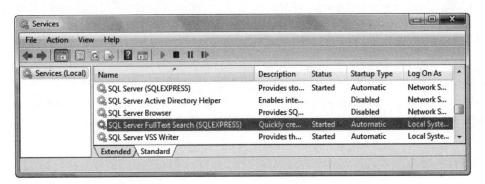

Figure 8-3. *Running the SQL Server FullText Search service*

You can also verify that the service is running and active by executing the following command using SQL Server Management Studio (see Figure 8-4). If the result of the query is 1, then you have Full-Text Search properly installed on your machine.

```
select fulltextserviceproperty('isfulltextinstalled')
```

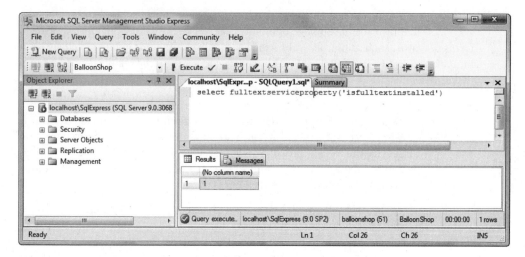

Figure 8-4. *Verifying that the SQL Server FullText Search service is installed*

If you don't have the FullText Search service installed, you have two options:

- Uninstall your current instance of SQL Server and reinstall it as explained in Chapter 3.

- Upgrade your current instance of SQL Server by adding support for full-text searching.

If you choose the second option, start by downloading SQL Server Express with Advanced Services from Microsoft, which comes in the form of an executable file named sqlexpr_adv.exe (at the time of writing this book, the download page is http://www.microsoft.com/express/ sql/download/default.aspx). Unfortunately, you can't use this executable to upgrade your SQL Server Express instance. Instead, you have to use Programs and Features (in Windows Vista) or Add/Remove Programs (in Windows XP), find the Microsoft SQL Server entry, and select Change. Then opt to update the database engine (not the workstation components), and select the Full-Text Search feature from the Database Services node (Figure 8-5).

The installer doesn't have access to the necessary setup files, so it will eventually ask for them. You get these files by unzipping (not executing) sqlexpr_adv.exe using a program such as WinZip or WinRAR, and extracting its contents to a folder on your disk. This folder contains a setup folder that you can then supply to the SQL Server setup program.

After the setup finishes, restart the SQL Server service and execute the query shown in Figure 8-4 to make sure you have correctly installed the Full-Text Search feature.

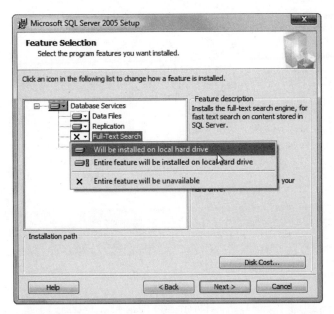

Figure 8-5. *Installing the SQL Server Full-Text Search feature*

Creating the FULLTEXT Catalog and Indexes

To be able to run FULLTEXT queries over your database, first you need to create a FULLTEXT catalog
in your database, which contains the FULLTEXT indexes, and then create FULLTEXT indexes for every
table on the columns that you want to make searchable.

Let's go through a step-by-step exercise to enable full-text searching of our database.

Exercise: Adding FULLTEXT Structures to BalloonShop

1. Start SQL Server Management Studio Express and log in using your balloonshop user, just like you did
   in the previous chapters. (You can also use Windows Authentication and log in using your Windows
   account, in which case you need to be sure to select the BalloonShop database before running SQL
   queries.)

2. Click the **New Query** button to open the query editor, and create the FULLTEXT catalog using the following command:

   ```
   CREATE FULLTEXT CATALOG BalloonShopFullText
   ```

   The command should execute quickly and give you a confirmation message like that shown in Figure 8-6.

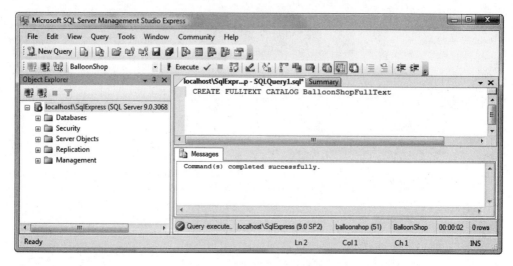

Figure 8-6. *Creating a FULLTEXT catalog in SQL Server Management Studio*

3. Now that the FULLTEXT catalog is set up, it's time to create the FULLTEXT indexes in our tables. Using SQL Server Management Studio, right-click the Product table and select **Design**.

4. From the Table Designer menu, choose **Full-text Index**. In the window that shows up, click **Add** to add a new FULLTEXT index. A new index template will be generated, as shown in Figure 8-7.

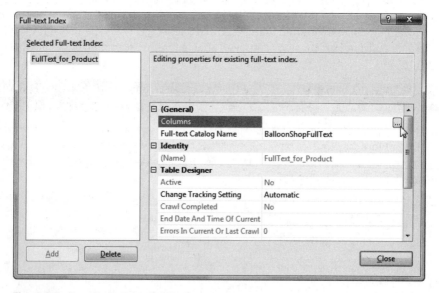

Figure 8-7. *Creating a FULLTEXT index*

5. You need to specify the columns of the Product table that you want indexed. Open the column selector window (by clicking the "..." button, as shown in Figure 8-7), and select the **Name** and **Description** columns, as shown in Figure 8-8.

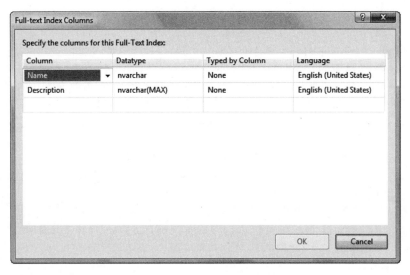

Figure 8-8. *Configuring the columns of the* FULLTEXT *index*

6. Finally, click **Close**, and then press **Ctrl+S** to save the changes to the table. Now open a new query window and execute the following query to ensure the index is working as expected:

```
SELECT ProductID, Name
FROM Product
WHERE Contains (Name, 'FORMSOF(INFLECTIONAL, Young)', LANGUAGE 'English')
```

7. The query asks for all the products that have the word "young," or an inflected form of it, in their name. The database tells us that we have a single product that matches this criterion (see Figure 8-9).

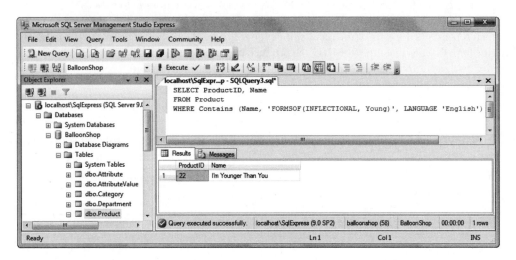

Figure 8-9. *Executing a query that uses the* FULLTEXT *index*

■**Note** FULLTEXT indexes, unlike regular indexes, may not always be in sync with the actual data in your tables. Because of the processing power they consume, FULLTEXT indexes are created and updated in the background by SQL Server so that normal database operations aren't affected by them. The index you've just created is set for automatic updates so that SQL Server will take care of managing it, but after you change the data in your tables, it may take a while until the FULLTEXT gets updated as well.

How it Works: The BalloonShop FULLTEXT Index

The Full-Text Search feature is really extraordinary, isn't it? It took just a few minutes (OK, maybe a little more) to enable such a powerful feature in your database. Now you have a whole world of new features at your fingertips—you just need to decide how it's best to use it.

If we're not interested in searching for inflected forms of a word, we can use a very simple form of the CONTAINS predicate, where its only parameters are the name of the column to be searched and the word you're searching for:

```
SELECT ProductID, Name
FROM Product
WHERE CONTAINS (Name, 'Young')
```

Instead of the name of the column (Name in this case) you can use *, which will extend the search to all the FULLTEXT indexed columns in the table.

Sorting by Relevance

The CONTAINS predicate doesn't allow sorting the results by relevance. To achieve this kind of sorting, we use a function named CONTAINSTABLE, which works similarly to the CONTAINS predicate, except it returns the search results in a table. This table contains a column named Rank, which represents the rank of the results (the higher the value, the better the match) and the ID of the item that has that rank (the ID of the product, in our case). Obviously, sorting in descending order by this column would generate a result set representing the search results sorted in descending order of relevance.

■**Note** SQL Server also supports a predicate named FREETEXT and a function named FREETEXTTABLE, which have functionality similar to CONTAINS and CONTAINSTABLE, but offer extended ease of use at the cost of flexibility. For example, FREETEXT doesn't allow using Boolean operators (AND, OR), which we need for implementing all-words searches.

For a simple test, execute the following query, which searches for products that contain "red" in their name or description:

```
SELECT ProductID, Name
FROM Product
WHERE Contains (*, 'baby')
```

Using our test data, this query returns two results:

```
ProductID   Name
----------- -------------------------------------------------------
10          I Can't Get Enough of You Baby
21          Baby Hi Little Angel
```

Now execute the following query, which uses CONTAINSTABLE instead of CONTAINS. Since CONTAINSTABLE returns a table, it needs to be in the FROM clause of a query:

```
SELECT *
FROM CONTAINSTABLE(Product, *, 'baby')
```

The results are as follows:

```
KEY         RANK
----------- -----------
10          96
21          112
```

Here, KEY represents the ID of the product and RANK represents the search result rank when searching for "baby." To transform this into something more human-friendly, we'll join this table with Product in order to obtain the name of the products. We're also ordering descending by rank to ensure the most relevant results are placed first:

```
SELECT ProductID, Name, Rank
FROM Product INNER JOIN
   CONTAINSTABLE(Product, *, 'baby') AS ProductResults
   ON Product.ProductID = ProductResults.[KEY]
ORDER BY Rank desc
```

```
ProductID   Name                                               Rank
----------- -------------------------------------------------- -----------
21          Baby Hi Little Angel                               112
10          I Can't Get Enough of You Baby                     96
```

When searching for more than one word, SQL Server allows placing individual ranking weights on each of the searched words. For BalloonShop, we're not interested in this feature, but it's good to know that it exists. Instead, for BalloonShop, we'd like to place more weight on the results that match the product's name than on matches on the product's description. With other words, products that contain the searched word in the title should be considered more relevant than products that contain that word in their description.

Let's start by testing the following query, which extracts the rank by searching in the Name column and the Description column.

```
SELECT ProductID, Name,
       NameResults.Rank as NameRank,
       DescriptionResults.Rank as DescriptionRank
FROM Product
LEFT OUTER JOIN
   CONTAINSTABLE(Product, Name, 'red') AS NameResults
   ON Product.ProductID = NameResults.[KEY]
LEFT OUTER JOIN
   CONTAINSTABLE(Product, Description, 'red') AS DescriptionResults
   ON Product.ProductID = DescriptionResults.[KEY]
```

To filter the nonmatching products and order by descending relevance, we also multiply the name rank by 3 to give these matches significantly more weight than description matches:

```
SELECT ProductID, Name,
       NameResults.Rank as NameRank,
       DescriptionResults.Rank as DescriptionRank
FROM Product
LEFT OUTER JOIN
   CONTAINSTABLE(Product, Name, 'red') AS NameResults
   ON Product.ProductID = NameResults.[KEY]
LEFT OUTER JOIN
   CONTAINSTABLE(Product, Description, 'red') AS DescriptionResults
   ON Product.ProductID = DescriptionResults.[KEY]
WHERE (NameResults.Rank IS NOT NULL) OR (DescriptionResults.Rank IS NOT NULL)
ORDER BY (ISNULL(NameResults.Rank, 0) * 3 +
          ISNULL(DescriptionResults.Rank, 0)) DESC
```

The results are as follows:

ProductID	Name	NameRank	DescriptionRank
5	Smiley Heart Red Balloon	80	48
59	Crystal Rose Red	80	48
16	I Love You Red Flourishes	80	24
7	Smiley Kiss Red Balloon	80	24
4	Today, Tomorrow & Forever	NULL	48
17	I Love You Script	NULL	48
18	Love Cascade Hearts	NULL	48

62	Crystal Etched Hearts	NULL	48
53	Smiley Face	NULL	48
20	Love Script	NULL	24
22	I'm Younger Than You	NULL	24
3	Funny Love	NULL	24
6	Love 24 Karat	NULL	24
11	Picture Perfect Love Swing	NULL	24
12	I Love You Roses	NULL	24
13	I Love You Script	NULL	24

Finally, to increase the chances we're finding the right product for our users, we'll make all searches on inflectional forms of words. Moreover, we'll use Boolean operators (AND, OR) to be able to perform both any-words searches and all-words searches. Here's the query we'll execute when a visitor makes an any-words search for "red balloon":

```
SELECT ProductID, Name,
       NameResults.Rank as NameRank,
       DescriptionResults.Rank as DescriptionRank
FROM Product
LEFT OUTER JOIN
   CONTAINSTABLE(Product, Name,
                'FORMSOF(INFLECTIONAL, red) OR FORMSOF(INFLECTIONAL, balloon)',
                LANGUAGE 'English') AS NameResults
   ON Product.ProductID = NameResults.[KEY]
LEFT OUTER JOIN
   CONTAINSTABLE(Product, Description,
                'FORMSOF(INFLECTIONAL, red) OR FORMSOF(INFLECTIONAL, balloon)',
                LANGUAGE 'English') AS DescriptionResults
   ON Product.ProductID = DescriptionResults.[KEY]
WHERE (NameResults.Rank IS NOT NULL) OR (DescriptionResults.Rank IS NOT NULL)
ORDER BY (ISNULL(NameResults.Rank, 0) * 3 +
          ISNULL(DescriptionResults.Rank, 0)) DESC
```

This returns 58 results. When performing an all-words search for the same words, we just need to use the AND Boolean operator instead of OR:

```
   CONTAINSTABLE(Product, Name,
                'FORMSOF(INFLECTIONAL, red) AND FORMSOF(INFLECTIONAL, balloon)',
                LANGUAGE 'English') AS NameResults
   ON Product.ProductID = NameResults.[KEY]
LEFT OUTER JOIN
   CONTAINSTABLE(Product, Description,
                'FORMSOF(INFLECTIONAL, red) AND FORMSOF(INFLECTIONAL, balloon)',
                LANGUAGE 'English') AS DescriptionResults
```

With this all-words search, the result set shrinks to just 16 results, which represent the products that contain both the words "red" and "balloon" in their name or description:

ProductID	Name	NameRank	DescriptionRank
5	Smiley Heart Red Balloon	64	16
7	Smiley Kiss Red Balloon	64	8
17	I Love You Script	NULL	16
18	Love Cascade Hearts	NULL	16
22	I'm Younger Than You	NULL	16
53	Smiley Face	NULL	16
62	Crystal Etched Hearts	NULL	16
59	Crystal Rose Red	NULL	8
20	Love Script	NULL	8
11	Picture Perfect Love Swing	NULL	8
12	I Love You Roses	NULL	8
13	I Love You Script	NULL	8
16	I Love You Red Flourishes	NULL	8
6	Love 24 Karat	NULL	8
3	Funny Love	NULL	8
4	Today, Tomorrow & Forever	NULL	8

Improving Relevance

The query just shown returns high-quality results, but it has two potential weaknesses. First, when doing an all-words search, the query requires all of the words to be found in the name or all of the words to be found in the description. If a product contains "balloon" in the title and "red" in the description, it will not be returned as a match on an all-words search. This might be what you want, but intuitively this behavior is not expected, because the product does contain all words—just not together in the same place.

The second weakness is that the query, even in any-words mode, doesn't assign greater rank to products that contain all of the words than those that contain only some of the words. A product name "red balloon" will have the same rank as a product simply named "red" or "balloon."

The all-improved version of our search query follows. Indeed, it has started looking scary, but it provides much improved results from the previous queries we've tested. Note that this time we're summing the rank for each word and ordering results in descending order of the sum, instead of summing up ranks for "name" and "description." (Also remember that you don't have to type the code by hand.)

```
DECLARE @Word1 NVARCHAR(15)
DECLARE @Word2 NVARCHAR(15)
DECLARE @NecessaryMatches INT

-- the words we're searching for
SET @Word1 = 'red'
SET @Word2 = 'balloon'
```

```
-- 1 for any-word matches, or the number of words for all-words matches
SET @NecessaryMatches = 1

/* Create the table variable that will contain the search results */
DECLARE @Matches TABLE
([Key] INT NOT NULL,
 Rank INT NOT NULL)

-- Save matches for the first word
IF @Word1 IS NOT NULL
  INSERT INTO @Matches
  SELECT COALESCE(NameResults.[KEY], DescriptionResults.[KEY]) AS [KEY],
         ISNULL(NameResults.Rank, 0) * 3 +
         ISNULL(DescriptionResults.Rank, 0) AS Rank
  FROM
    CONTAINSTABLE(Product, Name, @Word1,
                  LANGUAGE 'English') AS NameResults
    FULL OUTER JOIN
    CONTAINSTABLE(Product, Description, @Word1,
                  LANGUAGE 'English') AS DescriptionResults
    ON NameResults.[KEY] = DescriptionResults.[KEY]

-- Save the matches for the second word
IF @Word2 IS NOT NULL
  INSERT INTO @Matches
  SELECT COALESCE(NameResults.[KEY], DescriptionResults.[KEY]) AS [KEY],
         ISNULL(NameResults.Rank, 0) * 3 +
         ISNULL(DescriptionResults.Rank, 0) AS Rank
  FROM
    CONTAINSTABLE(Product, Name, @Word2,
                  LANGUAGE 'English') AS NameResults
    FULL OUTER JOIN
    CONTAINSTABLE(Product, Description, @Word2,
                  LANGUAGE 'English') AS DescriptionResults
    ON NameResults.[KEY] = DescriptionResults.[KEY]

-- Group results to get ranks and match counts
DECLARE @Results TABLE
([KEY] INT NOT NULL,
 Rank INT NOT NULL
 )

INSERT INTO @Results
SELECT M.[KEY], SUM(M.Rank) AS TotalRank
FROM @Matches M
GROUP BY M.[KEY]
HAVING COUNT(M.Rank) >= @NecessaryMatches
```

```
-- Return the matching products
SELECT Name, Rank FROM Product
JOIN @Results R
ON Product.ProductID = R.[KEY]
ORDER BY R.Rank DESC
```

The list of results is quite long, so we're not listing it here—but if you execute the query, you'll notice that although many records are returned, the first ones are those that contain both "red" and "balloon" in their title (the previous queries didn't do this).

To have this query perform an all-words search instead of an any-words search, you need to change the value of @NecessaryMatches to 2. This variable stores the number of necessary word matches for a product, in order to consider that product a valid search result. In all-words searches, all searched words must be found in the product name or description, so @NecessaryMatches must be equal to the number of searched words.

Performing the any-words search using this new query returns the same 16 results from a previous exercise, except that this time, again, the order in which they are presented is better, due to improved relevance calculation:

Name	Rank
Smiley Heart Red Balloon	496
Smiley Kiss Red Balloon	464
Crystal Rose Red	296
I Love You Red Flourishes	272
I Love You Script	64
Love Cascade Hearts	64
Crystal Etched Hearts	64
Smiley Face	64
Today, Tomorrow & Forever	56
I'm Younger Than You	40
Love Script	32
Funny Love	32
Love 24 Karat	32
Picture Perfect Love Swing	32
I Love You Roses	32
I Love You Script	32

We'll discuss the remaining details of the SQL code later, after creating necessary stored procedures in our database.

Creating the SearchCatalog Stored Procedure

You're probably eager to write some code! To eliminate some code redundancy, we'll compose not one, but two stored procedures in the data tier to support the search feature: SearchWord and SearchCatalog.

Exercise: Adding Search Functionality to the Data Tier

1. Let's first create the SearchWord procedure. Using SQL Server Management Studio, open a new query window and execute the following code, which creates the SearchWord stored procedure:

```
CREATE PROCEDURE SearchWord (@Word NVARCHAR(50))
AS


SET @Word = 'FORMSOF(INFLECTIONAL, "' + @Word + '")'

SELECT COALESCE(NameResults.[KEY], DescriptionResults.[KEY]) AS [KEY],
       ISNULL(NameResults.Rank, 0) * 3 +
       ISNULL(DescriptionResults.Rank, 0) AS Rank
FROM
  CONTAINSTABLE(Product, Name, @Word,
               LANGUAGE 'English') AS NameResults
  FULL OUTER JOIN
  CONTAINSTABLE(Product, Description, @Word,
               LANGUAGE 'English') AS DescriptionResults
  ON NameResults.[KEY] = DescriptionResults.[KEY]
```

2. Now create the SearchCatalog stored procedure. This stored procedure uses the SearchWord procedure to calculate the search results.

```
CREATE PROCEDURE SearchCatalog
(@DescriptionLength INT,
 @PageNumber TINYINT,
 @ProductsPerPage TINYINT,
 @HowManyResults INT OUTPUT,
 @AllWords BIT,
 @Word1 NVARCHAR(15) = NULL,
 @Word2 NVARCHAR(15) = NULL,
 @Word3 NVARCHAR(15) = NULL,
 @Word4 NVARCHAR(15) = NULL,
 @Word5 NVARCHAR(15) = NULL)
AS


/* @NecessaryMatches needs to be 1 for any-word searches and
   the number of words for all-words searches */
DECLARE @NecessaryMatches INT
SET @NecessaryMatches = 1
IF @AllWords = 1
  SET @NecessaryMatches =
    CASE WHEN @Word1 IS NULL THEN 0 ELSE 1 END +
    CASE WHEN @Word2 IS NULL THEN 0 ELSE 1 END +
    CASE WHEN @Word3 IS NULL THEN 0 ELSE 1 END +
    CASE WHEN @Word4 IS NULL THEN 0 ELSE 1 END +
    CASE WHEN @Word5 IS NULL THEN 0 ELSE 1 END;
```

```
/* Create the table variable that will contain the search results */
DECLARE @Matches TABLE
([Key] INT NOT NULL,
 Rank INT NOT NULL)

-- Save matches for the first word
IF @Word1 IS NOT NULL
  INSERT INTO @Matches
  EXEC SearchWord @Word1

-- Save the matches for the second word
IF @Word2 IS NOT NULL
  INSERT INTO @Matches
  EXEC SearchWord @Word2

-- Save the matches for the third word
IF @Word3 IS NOT NULL
  INSERT INTO @Matches
  EXEC SearchWord @Word3

-- Save the matches for the fourth word
IF @Word4 IS NOT NULL
  INSERT INTO @Matches
  EXEC SearchWord @Word4

-- Save the matches for the fifth word
IF @Word5 IS NOT NULL
  INSERT INTO @Matches
  EXEC SearchWord @Word5

-- Calculate the IDs of the matching products
DECLARE @Results TABLE
(RowNumber INT,
 [KEY] INT NOT NULL,
 Rank INT NOT NULL)

-- Obtain the matching products
INSERT INTO @Results
SELECT ROW_NUMBER() OVER (ORDER BY COUNT(M.Rank) DESC),
       M.[KEY], SUM(M.Rank) AS TotalRank
FROM @Matches M
GROUP BY M.[KEY]
HAVING COUNT(M.Rank) >= @NecessaryMatches

-- return the total number of results using an OUTPUT variable
SELECT @HowManyResults = COUNT(*) FROM @Results
```

```
-- populate the table variable with the complete list of products
SELECT Product.ProductID, Name,
        CASE WHEN LEN(Description) <= @DescriptionLength THEN Description
            ELSE SUBSTRING(Description, 1, @DescriptionLength) + '...' END
        AS Description, Price, Thumbnail, Image, PromoFront, PromoDept
FROM Product
INNER JOIN @Results R
ON Product.ProductID = R.[KEY]
WHERE R.RowNumber > (@PageNumber - 1) * @ProductsPerPage
  AND R.RowNumber <= @PageNumber * @ProductsPerPage
ORDER BY R.Rank DESC
```

3. Finally, you can test that the stored procedure works as expected by executing it from SQL Server Management Studio:

```
EXEC SearchCatalog @DescriptionLength=20, @PageNumber=1, ➥
@ProductsPerPage=10, @HowManyResults=null, @AllWords=0, @Word1='balloon'
```

How It Works: WordCount and SearchCatalog

In the first step of the exercise, you wrote the SearchWord stored procedure. This function returns all the products that contain the @Word string that the procedure receives as a parameter. The returned result set is formed from the product ID and the rank, which is calculated as three times the name rank plus the description rank. This way, we place more value on matches found on product names than on matches found on product descriptions.

SearchCatalog is a bit more complex. First of all, let's analyze its parameters:

- @DescriptionLength is the maximum length of the product description.

- @PageNumber specifies the page of results the visitor has requested.

- @ProductsPerPage specifies how many records to return. If @PageNumber is 3 and @ProductsPerPage is 5, the procedure will return the 11th to 15th records from the search results.

- @HowManyResults is an output parameter, which you'll set to the total number of search results. This will be read from the C# code to calculate the number of search results pages.

- @AllWords is a bit input parameter that specifies whether you should do an all-words or an any-words search.

- @Word1 to @Word5 are the words to be searched for. They all have a default value of NULL.

The stored procedure starts by declaring a new variable named @NecessaryMatches and calculating its value. When performing an any-words search, the value of @NecessaryMatches must be 1, and when performing an all-words search, the value must be equal to the number of words you're searching for:

```
/* @NecessaryMatches needs to be 1 for any-word searches and
   the number of words for all-words searches */
DECLARE @NecessaryMatches INT
SET @NecessaryMatches = 1
IF @AllWords = 1
  SET @NecessaryMatches =
    CASE WHEN @Word1 IS NULL THEN 1 ELSE 0 END +
    CASE WHEN @Word2 IS NULL THEN 1 ELSE 0 END +
    CASE WHEN @Word3 IS NULL THEN 1 ELSE 0 END +
```

```
      CASE WHEN @Word4 IS NULL THEN 1 ELSE 0 END +
      CASE WHEN @Word5 IS NULL THEN 1 ELSE 0 END;
```

The procedure continues by declaring a TABLE variable named @Matches, and populating it with the matching products for each word. The table has two rows: [KEY], which contains the product ID, and Rank, which contains the matching rank. If a product matches for more words, it will end up being listed multiple times in the @Matches table.

```
/* Create the table variable that will contain the search results */
DECLARE @Matches TABLE
([Key] INT NOT NULL,
 Rank INT NOT NULL)

-- Save matches for the first word
IF @Word1 IS NOT NULL
  INSERT INTO @Matches
  EXEC SearchWord @Word1

-- Save the matches for the second word
IF @Word2 IS NOT NULL
  INSERT INTO @Matches
  EXEC SearchWord @Word2
...
```

Finally, based on the values in @Matches, we find out the products that should be part of the search results, which are stored in a new table variable named @Results. When performing an any-words search, a product must match for a single word to be considered a valid search result. When performing all-words searches, a product must match for all words, so the number of times its [KEY] is found in @Matches must be equal to the number of words (which is stored, in that case, in @NecessaryMatches).

```
-- Calculate the IDs of the matching products
DECLARE @Results TABLE
(RowNumber INT,
 [KEY] INT NOT NULL,
 Rank INT NOT NULL)

-- Obtain the matching products
INSERT INTO @Results
SELECT ROW_NUMBER() OVER (ORDER BY COUNT(M.Rank) DESC),
       M.[KEY], SUM(M.Rank) AS TotalRank
FROM @Matches M
GROUP BY M.[KEY]
HAVING COUNT(M.Rank) >= @NecessaryMatches
```

Also note the @RowNumber variable in the Results table, which is then populated with—you guessed it—the row number in the table. This column will be used when selecting a subpage of products from this table.

Now that we have our search results in the @Results table variable, the typical code that returns the requested page of products follows. First, you set the value of the @HowManyResults output parameter (which will be read from the business tier) by counting the number of rows in @Results:

```
-- return the total number of results using an OUTPUT variable
SELECT @HowManyResults = COUNT(*) FROM @Results
```

Finally, there's our well-known query that returns a page of products using the data from the @Results table variable:

```
-- populate the table variable with the complete list of products
SELECT ROW_NUMBER() OVER (ORDER BY Product.ProductID),
       Product.ProductID, Name,
       CASE WHEN LEN(Description) <= @DescriptionLength THEN Description
            ELSE SUBSTRING(Description, 1, @DescriptionLength) + '...' END
       AS Description, Price, Thumbnail, Image, PromoFront, PromoDept
FROM Product
INNER JOIN @Results R
ON Product.ProductID = R.[KEY]
WHERE R.RowNumber > (@PageNumber - 1) * @ProductsPerPage
  AND R.RowNumber <= @PageNumber * @ProductsPerPage
ORDER BY R.Rank DESC
```

Implementing the Business Tier

The business tier consists of the SearchCatalog method, which calls the SearchCatalog stored procedure. This data feeds our older friend, the ProductsList.ascx Web User Control, which displays the search results.

Apart from a little bit of logic to handle splitting the search phrase into separate words (the presentation tier sends the whole phrase, but the data tier needs individual words), and to ensure we send a valid True/False value for the @AllWords parameter to the SearchCatalog stored procedure, there's nothing fantastic about this new method.

Like always, you set up the stored procedure parameters, execute the command, and return the results.

First, add a reference to System.Text.RegularExpressions to CatalogAccess.cs. We'll use this to split the input string into individual words.

```
using System.Text.RegularExpressions;
```

Then add the Search method to your CatalogAccess class:

```
// Search the product catalog
public static DataTable Search(string searchString, string allWords,
string pageNumber, out int howManyPages)
{
  // get a configured DbCommand object
  DbCommand comm = GenericDataAccess.CreateCommand();
  // set the stored procedure name
  comm.CommandText = "SearchCatalog";
```

```
// create a new parameter
DbParameter param = comm.CreateParameter();
param.ParameterName = "@DescriptionLength";
param.Value = BalloonShopConfiguration.ProductDescriptionLength;
param.DbType = DbType.Int32;
comm.Parameters.Add(param);
// create a new parameter
param = comm.CreateParameter();
param.ParameterName = "@AllWords";
param.Value = allWords.ToUpper() == "TRUE" ? "1" : "0";
param.DbType = DbType.Byte;
comm.Parameters.Add(param);
// create a new parameter
param = comm.CreateParameter();
param.ParameterName = "@PageNumber";
param.Value = pageNumber;
param.DbType = DbType.Int32;
comm.Parameters.Add(param);
// create a new parameter
param = comm.CreateParameter();
param.ParameterName = "@ProductsPerPage";
param.Value = BalloonShopConfiguration.ProductsPerPage;
param.DbType = DbType.Int32;
comm.Parameters.Add(param);
// create a new parameter
param = comm.CreateParameter();
param.ParameterName = "@HowManyResults";
param.Direction = ParameterDirection.Output;
param.DbType = DbType.Int32;
comm.Parameters.Add(param);

// define the maximum number of words
int howManyWords = 5;
// transform search string into array of words
string[] words = Regex.Split(searchString, "[^a-zA-Z0-9]+");

// add the words as stored procedure parameters
int index = 1;
for (int i = 0; i <= words.GetUpperBound(0) && index <= howManyWords; i++)
  // ignore short words
  if (words[i].Length > 2)
  {
    // create the @Word parameters
    param = comm.CreateParameter();
    param.ParameterName = "@Word" + index.ToString();
```

```
        param.Value = words[i];
        param.DbType = DbType.String;
        comm.Parameters.Add(param);
        index++;
    }

    // execute the stored procedure and save the results in a DataTable
    DataTable table = GenericDataAccess.ExecuteSelectCommand(comm);
    // calculate how many pages of products and set the out parameter
    int howManyProducts =
Int32.Parse(comm.Parameters["@HowManyResults"].Value.ToString());
    howManyPages = (int)Math.Ceiling((double)howManyProducts /
                  (double)BalloonShopConfiguration.ProductsPerPage);
    // return the page of products
    return table;
}
```

Because the code is pretty clear, it's not worth analyzing again in detail. However, note the following aspects:

- To guard against bogus values, we make sure to set the @AllWords parameter strictly to True or False, using the allWords.ToUpper() == "TRUE" ? "1" : "0" construct (the ternary operator).

- The words in the search phrase are split using the Regex.Split method, using as a separator a regular expression that matches all groups of characters that are not alphanumerical: [^a-zA-Z0-9]+. (Refer to Chapter 7 for a quick reference to regular expression metacharacters.)

- There's a for loop to add the @Word parameters. Short words (fewer than three letters long) are considered noise words and are not used for the search. Feel free to change this rule to suit your particular solution.

- The words searched for are returned through an out parameter, so the presentation tier is able to tell the visitor which words were actually used for searching.

- The number of pages is given by dividing the number of products by the number of products per page.

■**Note** The maximum number of allowed words and the list of characters used to split the search string are hard-coded. In case you think any of these could ever change, it's strongly recommended to save their values in web.config. Also note that increasing the maximum number of allowed words implies updating the SearchCatalog stored procedure as well.

Let's now create the presentation tier, where you'll use all the logic implemented so far.

Implementing the Presentation Tier

Let's see some colors now! The Search Catalog feature has two separate interface elements that you need to implement. The first one is the place where the visitor enters the search string, shown earlier in Figure 8-1.

This part of the UI will be implemented as a separate user control named SearchBox.ascx, which provides a text box and a check box for the visitor. The other part of the UI consists of the search results page (Search.aspx), which displays the products matching the search criteria (refer to Figure 8-2).

Creating the Search Box

The search box consists of a text box, a button, and a check box. Let's create them in the following exercise.

Exercise: Creating the SearchBox Web User Control

1. First, create a Web User Control named SearchBox.ascx in the UserControls folder, making sure you use a code-behind file.

2. You can create the control either by using the Design View window or by directly modifying the HTML. In this case, add the following code to the file:

```
<asp:Panel ID="searchPanel" runat="server" DefaultButton="goButton">
  <table class="SearchBox">
    <tr>
      <td class="SearchBoxHead">Search the Catalog</td>
    </tr>
    <tr>
      <td class="SearchBoxContent">
        <asp:TextBox ID="searchTextBox" Runat="server" Width="128px"
          MaxLength="100" />
        <asp:Button ID="goButton" Runat="server"
          Text="Go" Width="36px" onclick="goButton_Click" /><br />
        <asp:CheckBox ID="allWordsCheckBox" Runat="server"
          Text="Search for all words" />
      </td>
    </tr>
  </table>
</asp:Panel>
```

3. Switch to Design View. The control should look like Figure 8-10.

Figure 8-10. *SearchBox.ascx in Design View*

Note that the CssClass used for both controls will be applied at runtime and that the maximum size of 100 characters was set for the text box.

4. Add the following styles to BalloonShop.css:

```
.SearchBox {
  border-collapse:collapse;
  margin-top: 20px;
  width:200px;
}
.SearchBoxHead {
  border: #0468a4 1px solid;
  background-color: #FFFF99;
  text-align: center;
}
.SearchBoxContent {
  border: #0468a4 1px solid;
  padding: 5px 0px 5px 12px;
}
```

5. Add the following method to the Link class in Link.cs:

```
public static string ToSearch(string searchString, bool allWords, string page)
{
  if (page == "1")
    return BuildAbsolute(
      String.Format("/Search.aspx?Search={0}&AllWords={1}",
        searchString, allWords.ToString()));
  else
    return BuildAbsolute(
      String.Format("/Search.aspx?Search={0}&AllWords={1}&Page={2}",
        searchString, allWords.ToString(), page));
}
```

6. Switch to `SearchBox.ascx.cs` in Design View, double-click the **Go** button to generate its `Click` event handler, and complete it like this:

```
// Perform the product search
protected void goButton_Click(object sender, EventArgs e)
{
  ExecuteSearch();
}


// Redirect to the search results page
private void ExecuteSearch()
{
  string searchText = searchTextBox.Text;
  bool allWords = allWordsCheckBox.Checked;
  if (searchTextBox.Text.Trim() != "")
    Response.Redirect(Link.ToSearch(searchText, allWords, "1"));
}
```

7. Modify the code of `Page_Load` as follows. This ensures that the keywords typed in the search box and the state of the "all words" check box are retained when performing searches.

```
protected void Page_Load(object sender, EventArgs e)
{
  // don't repopulate control on postbacks
  if (!IsPostBack)
  {
    // load search box controls' values
    string allWords = Request.QueryString["AllWords"];
    string searchString = Request.QueryString["Search"];
    if (allWords != null)
      allWordsCheckBox.Checked = (allWords.ToUpper() == "TRUE");
    if (searchString != null)
      searchTextBox.Text = searchString;
  }
}
```

8. Add the newly created user control to `BalloonShop.master` by dragging it from Solution Explorer and dropping it above the `DepartmentsList` user control (see Figure 8-11).

9. Press **F5** to execute the project. The search box should rest nicely in its place. Trying to search for anything would generate an error, however, because the `Search.aspx` page doesn't exist yet.

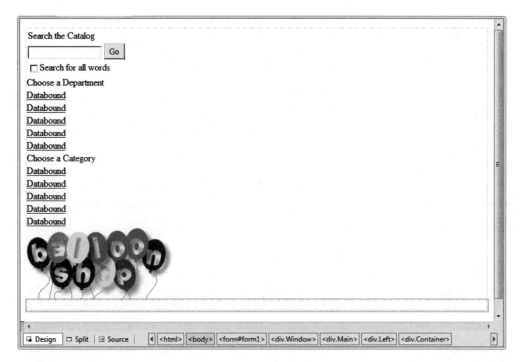

Figure 8-11. *Adding the search box to* `BalloonShop.master`

How It Works: The SearchBox Web User Control

The `SearchBox` user control isn't very complicated. When the visitor enters a new search string and presses Enter or clicks the Go button, the response is redirected to `Search.aspx`, which handles the search. `Search` recognizes the following query string parameters:

- `Search` specifies the search string entered by the visitor.

- `AllWords` specifies whether to do an all-words or an any-words search. You find its value by checking `allWordsCheckBox.Checked`, which returns `True` or `False`. A mighty hacker can, of course, play with the query string and change the value to something else, but our business tier contains code to guard against this kind of problem.

- `PageNumber` appears only in case the number of products is larger than the number of products per page (which you saved in `web.config`).

The `Page_Load` method checks the query string parameters and fills the search box contents accordingly. When the visitor performs a search, the page is reloaded (with a `Response.Redirect` to the `Search.aspx` page), so implicitly the search box contents are cleared. If you want to keep the values there (the string of the text box and the status of the check box), you must do this manually.

While we're here, note the check for the `IsPostBack` property of the page. After the visitor clicks the Go button to perform a search, the `SearchBox` control is loaded (`Page_Load` executes) and the `Click` event handler executes, which causes a page redirect (to `Search.aspx`). After the redirect happens, `SearchBox` is loaded once again in the new page (so `Page_Load` executes again). This suggests two problems:

- A performance problem because the `Page_Load` method is called twice.

- A functionality problem because you actually only want to set the check box and text box values when the control is reloaded in a new page. If their values are rewritten immediately after clicking the Go button, the user's input would be ignored (which is bad, of course).

To avoid these kinds of problems, ASP.NET offers the `Page.IsPostBack` property, which tells you if `Page_Load` is executed as a result of a postback, which is true when the method is executed in response to a user clicking the Go button or pressing Enter, and false when the method is executed when the control is loaded for the first time on a new page.

The first time `Page_Load` executes (after the button click), `IsPostBack` returns `true`. The second time `Page_Load` executes (the control is loaded in a fresh page), `IsPostBack` returns `false`. You don't want to fill the contents of the search box from the query string when the page is loaded from a postback event, because it will be automatically filled with data from the previous search by the ASP.NET postback mechanism. To test this, remove the `if` statement from `Page_Load` and try to do some consecutive different searches.

Because playing with postback is mostly used to improve performance, we'll cover it more seriously in the next chapter, where you'll use this technique in more pages of BalloonShop. However, you needed to use it here to make the search functionality, well, functional.

With this new theory in mind, the implementation of `Page_Load` in `SearchBox.ascx.cs` starts to make sense:

```
protected void Page_Load(object sender, EventArgs e)
{
  // don't repopulate control on postbacks
  if (!IsPostBack)
  {
    // load search box controls' values
    string allWords = Request.QueryString["AllWords"];
    string searchString = Request.QueryString["Search"];
    if (allWords != null)
      allWordsCheckBox.Checked = (allWords.ToUpper() == "TRUE");
    if (searchString != null)
      searchTextBox.Text = searchString;
  }
}
```

Displaying the Search Results

Now you'll create the Web Form that displays the search results. To simplify the work, you'll reuse the `ProductsList` user control to display the actual list of products. This control is currently listing products for the main page, for departments, and for categories. Of course, if you want to have the searched products displayed in another format, you need to create another user control.

In the following exercise, you'll create the `Search.aspx` Web Form and update `ProductsList`.

Exercise: Displaying Search Results

1. Let's create a new Web Form in the root of the BalloonShop folder. Right-click the www.example.com root entry in Solution Explorer and select **Add New Item.** In the dialog box, select the **Web Form** template, write **Search.aspx** for the name, make sure the two check boxes are selected and the language is Visual C#, and click **Add**.

2. In the dialog box that opens, select the **BalloonShop.master** Master Page and click **OK**.

3. Switch Search.aspx to Design View, add two Label controls, and then drag ProductsList.ascx from Solution Explorer to the Content area, as shown in Figure 8-12.

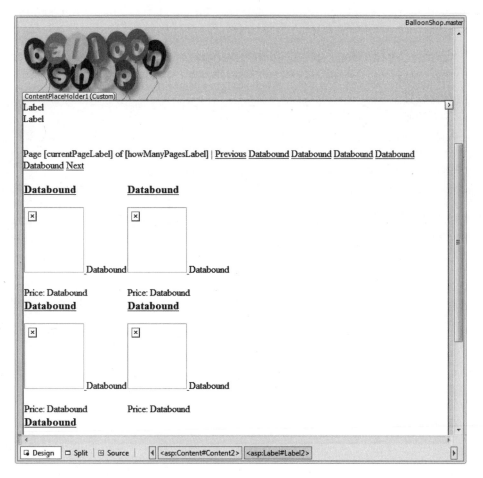

Figure 8-12. *Creating Search.aspx in Design View*

4. Clear the Text property of the Label controls. Set the name of the first label to titleLabel. The second label should be named descriptionLabel.

5. Set the CssClass property of the first Label control to CatalogTitle. Set the CssClass property of the second label to CatalogDescription.

The HTML code of the control should be like this, at this moment:

```
<%@ Page Language="C#" MasterPageFile="~/BalloonShop.master" AutoEventWir➥
eup="true" CodeFile="Search.aspx.cs" Inherits="Search" Title="" %>

<%@ Register src="UserControls/ProductsList.ascx" tagname="ProductsList" ➥
tagprefix="uc1" %>

<asp:Content ID="Content1" ContentPlaceHolderID="head" Runat="Server">
</asp:Content>
<asp:Content ID="Content2" ContentPlaceHolderID="ContentPlaceHolder1"➥
Runat="Server">
  <asp:Label CssClass="CatalogTitle" ID="titleLabel" runat="server">➥
  </asp:Label>
  <br />
  <asp:Label CssClass="CatalogDescription" ID="descriptionLabel" runat=➥
"server"></asp:Label>
  <br />
  <uc1:ProductsList ID="ProductsList1" runat="server" />
</asp:Content>
```

6. Go to the code file now and edit Page_Load like this:

```
public partial class Search : System.Web.UI.Page
{
  // Fill the form with data
  protected void Page_Load(object sender, EventArgs e)
  {
    // fill the table contents
    string searchString = Request.QueryString["Search"];
    titleLabel.Text = "Product Search";
    descriptionLabel.Text = "You searched for \"" + searchString + "\"";
    // set the title of the page
    this.Title = BalloonShopConfiguration.SiteName +
               " : Product Search : " + searchString;
  }
}
```

7. Finally, update the code-behind file of ProductsList.ascx to recognize the Search query string parameter and perform a product search in case the parameter is found:

```
private void PopulateControls()
{
  // Retrieve DepartmentID from the query string
  string departmentId = Request.QueryString["DepartmentID"];
  // Retrieve CategoryID from the query string
  string categoryId = Request.QueryString["CategoryID"];
  // Retrieve Page from the query string
  string page = Request.QueryString["Page"];
  if (page == null) page = "1";
  // Retrieve Search string from query string
  string searchString = Request.QueryString["Search"];
  // How many pages of products?
  int howManyPages = 1;
  // pager links format
  string firstPageUrl = "";
  string pagerFormat = "";

  // If performing a product search
  if (searchString != null)
  {
    // Retrieve AllWords from query string
    string allWords = Request.QueryString["AllWords"];
    // Perform search
    list.DataSource = CatalogAccess.Search(searchString, allWords,
page, out howManyPages);
    list.DataBind();
    // Display pager
    firstPageUrl = Link.ToSearch(searchString, allWords.ToUpper() == ➥
"TRUE", "1");
    pagerFormat = Link.ToSearch(searchString, allWords.ToUpper() == ➥
"TRUE", "{0}");
  }
  // If browsing a category...
  else if (categoryId != null)
  {
    ...
```

8. Press **F5** to execute the project. Type **love** in the search text box to get an output similar to Figure 8-13.

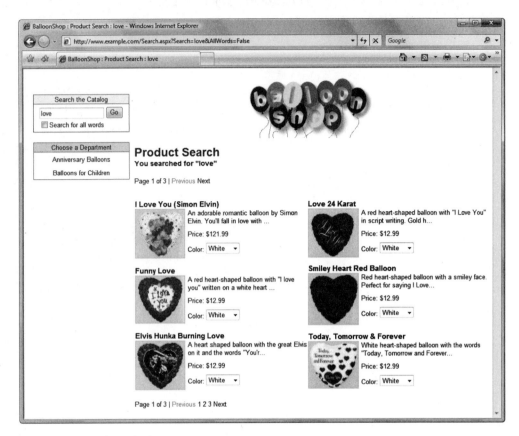

Figure 8-13. *Searching for love*

How It Works: Displaying Search Results

You've now finished implementing the search functionality of the catalog. Although you had quite a bit to write, the code wasn't that complicated, was it?

The single important detail of this exercise was calling the business tier `CatalogAccess.Search` method to get the search results and display them:

```
// If performing a product search
if (searchString != null)
{
    // Retrieve AllWords from query string
    string allWords = Request.QueryString["AllWords"];
    // Perform search
    list.DataSource = CatalogAccess.Search(searchString, allWords, ➡
page, out howManyPages);
    list.DataBind();
```

```
        // Display pager
        firstPageUrl = Link.ToSearch(searchString, allWords.ToUpper() == ➥
"TRUE", "1");
        pagerFormat = Link.ToSearch(searchString, allWords.ToUpper() == ➥
"TRUE", "{0}");
    }
```

Make sure to have a closer look at all the code that makes the product searching work. If you understand it correctly, you can easily update the code to make it work best for your particular solutions.

Summary

In this chapter, you implemented the search functionality of BalloonShop. You learned many useful tricks about SQL Server and C# programming—in particular, how to use SQL Server's Full-Text Search feature to perform complex product searches on your database.

In the business tier, you added the logic to process the string entered by the visitor and send the words to search for to the presentation tier. The presentation tier nicely displays the search results by reusing the ProductsList controls you wrote in Chapter 5.

CHAPTER 9

■ ■ ■

Improving Performance

Why walk when you can run? No, we won't talk about sports cars in this chapter. Instead, we'll analyze a few possibilities to improve the performance of the BalloonShop project.

For now, rest assured that you've already implemented good programming practices when building BalloonShop, such as

- Carefully designing the database; for example, having indexes on the columns used in table joins significantly improves query performance

- Writing efficient SQL code (starting from little tricks such as avoiding using the * wildcard to implementing efficient query logic) and storing that code within stored procedures (which are easier to maintain and run faster than ad hoc queries)

- Using smart data access techniques in the business tier

- Using fast ASP.NET objects and efficient techniques when building the presentation tier

However, you can gain even more performance by using a few new tricks. In this chapter, you'll briefly learn how to

- Avoid populating controls with data multiple times during postback events

- Disable `ViewState` to pass less data in client-server roundtrips

- Enable output page caching

■**Caution** This chapter is a very short introduction to just a few topics regarding ASP.NET performance. For serious coverage of these subjects, you should read an advanced ASP.NET book, such as *Pro ASP.NET 3.5 in C# 2008, Second Edition* (Apress, 2007).

Handling Postback

Postback is the mechanism by which the client (the web browser) informs the server about the events that happen to its server-side controls. When an event happens at the client side (such as a button click), the data about this event is *posted back* to the server, where it's handled using server-side code (the C# code from the code-behind files, in our case).

For example, if a visitor clicks your Button control, the data about this event is posted back on the server. At the server side, the button's Click event method executes, and the results are sent back to the client as HTML code.

Every time such an event happens, the ASP.NET page and all its controls (including user controls) get reloaded, and their Page_Load event executes. In our data-driven application, these Page_Load methods access the database to populate the page with information.

It may or may not be necessary to re-create the entire page after that button click. If clicking the button doesn't affect the data displayed on the page, then we don't need to reload all that data from the database and process it all over again because we can obtain it directly in its final form using the ASP.NET caching mechanism known as ViewState.

Thanks to this ViewState mechanism, the state of the controls in the page is not lost during postback events, even if you don't repopulate the controls in their Page_Load methods. As a result, most times it makes sense to load the page or control contents only when loading the page for the first time, and reload the page or control contents during postbacks only if those postback events affect the data that needs to be displayed by the page or control.

In the BalloonShop site, you've already seen an example of postback event handling in the SearchBox control, which avoided filling its controls in Page_Load during postbacks.

Also in SearchBox.ascx, it's easy to see a possible performance problem when looking at the ExecuteSearch method:

```
// Redirect to the search results page
private void ExecuteSearch()
{
  if (searchTextBox.Text.Trim() != "")
    Response.Redirect(Request.ApplicationPath +
              "/Search.aspx?Search=" + searchTextBox.Text +
              "&AllWords=" + allWordsCheckBox.Checked.ToString());
}
```

The code in this method redirects the visitor to the search results page. However, in the postback process, the original page that initiated the event (Default.aspx, Catalog.aspx, Product.aspx, or even Search.aspx) is reloaded once before being redirected (its Page_Load method is executed). That means all the composing controls—including DepartmentsList. ascx, CategoriesList.ascx, and ProductsList.ascx—and any other controls on the page are loaded twice: once in the original page, and then once again after the new page is loaded.

You can significantly improve performance by preventing Web User Controls or Web Forms from performing certain tasks (such as refreshing the DataList controls with information from the database) when they are being loaded as a result of a postback event. To do this, we use the IsPostBack property of the Page class. Let's see how it works by updating some BalloonShop classes in the following exercise.

Exercise: Speeding Up BalloonShop

1. Open the code-behind file of `DepartmentsList` and update its `Page_Load` method as shown here:

```
// Load department details into the DataList
protected void Page_Load(object sender, EventArgs e)
{
  // don't reload data during postbacks
  if (!IsPostBack)
  {
    // CatalogAccess.GetDepartments returns a DataTable object containing
    // department data, which is read in the ItemTemplate of the DataList
    list.DataSource = CatalogAccess.GetDepartments();
    // Needed to bind the data bound controls to the data source
    list.DataBind();
  }
}
```

2. Now, do the same in `CategoriesList.ascx.cs`:

```
protected void Page_Load(object sender, EventArgs e)
{
  // don't reload data during postbacks
  if (!IsPostBack)
  {
    // Obtain the ID of the selected department
    string departmentId = Request.QueryString["DepartmentID"];
    // Continue only if DepartmentID exists in the query string
    if (departmentId != null)
    {
      // Catalog.GetCategoriesInDepartment returns a DataTable
     // object containing category data, which is displayed by the DataList
      list.DataSource =
        CatalogAccess.GetCategoriesInDepartment(departmentId);
      // Needed to bind the data bound controls to the data source
      list.DataBind();
    }
  }
}
```

3. Apply the same change to `Catalog.aspx.cs`:

```
protected void Page_Load(object sender, EventArgs e)
{
  // don't reload data during postbacks
  if (!IsPostBack)
  {
    PopulateControls();
  }
}
```

4. Finally, open `Search.aspx.cs` and apply the following change:

```
// Fill the form with data
protected void Page_Load(object sender, EventArgs e)
{
  // don't reload data during postbacks
  if (!IsPostBack)
  {
    // fill the table contents
    string searchString = Request.QueryString["Search"];
    titleLabel.Text = "Product Search";
    descriptionLabel.Text = "You searched for \"" + searchString + "\"";
    // set the title of the page
    this.Title = BalloonShopConfiguration.SiteName +
             " : Product Search : " + searchString;
  }
}
```

How It Works: The IsPostBack Property

After completing the exercise, test your solution to see that everything works just like before. Apart from an increase in performance, nothing has really changed.

In `DepartmentsList.ascx.cs`, the list of departments is populated in `Page_Load`. However, during postback events, its state is maintained by ASP.NET using the `ViewState` mechanism (which we'll discuss next), and the response is redirected to another page anyway. Also, there are no postback events that should affect the way the departments list looks. For these reasons, it's more efficient to query the database for the list of departments only the first time a page is loaded, and never reload the list of departments during postback events.

The `Page.IsPostBack` function is your best friend in this instance. `IsPostBack` indicates whether the page is being loaded in response to a client postback or whether it's being loaded and accessed for the first time.

■**Tip** Performance tuning can be fun to play with, but *never* do experiments on a production system. Sometimes the results are unexpected, until you learn very well how the ASP.NET internals work.

Managing ViewState

HTTP (Hypertext Transfer Protocol) is a stateless protocol—the server doesn't retain any information about the previous client request. Without an additional mechanism over this protocol, the server can't retain the state of a simple HTML page between client requests (for example, which check boxes or radio buttons are selected).

ASP.NET has a built-in technique for dealing with this problem. When sending the HTML response to the client, by default ASP.NET encodes the current state of every control in a string called `ViewState`, in the form of a hidden form field called `__VIEWSTATE`.

ViewState is used to maintain the state of the web page during client postbacks. In other words, when the visitor performs any action that triggers a postback event, the page maintains its state after the event handler method executes at the server.

For this reason, in the previous exercise, you modified DepartmentsList.ascx.cs and the other controls and pages to first verify whether the control is being loaded as a result of a client postback. If it is, you don't need to query the database again to re-create the user interface, because its state is maintained by the ViewState mechanism.

The problem with ViewState is that it's transferred between the client and the server on every request. With pages that contain a large number of controls, the ViewState information can grow significantly, causing a lot of network traffic. The ViewState information can be disabled for an entire page, or just for specific controls on a page. However, when disabling ViewState for a control, you need to fill it with data even during postback events; otherwise, its contents will disappear.

■**Note** If you want to speed up a user control, you mainly have to choose between disabling its ViewState (causing less network traffic to happen) or letting ViewState be enabled but preventing further reprocessing of Page_Load during page postbacks (causing less database load when there are controls that work with the database). You can't apply both techniques, or else you'll get empty controls when postback events occur. Which technique is best for a particular control depends on the specifics of the control.

To see the encoded ViewState information for a page, you can do a simple test. Load BalloonShop in your web browser, right-click the page, and select View Source. Inside the HTML page code, you can see the ViewState information encoded as a hidden form element named __VIEWSTATE:

```
<input type="hidden" name="__VIEWSTATE"
value="dDwyMTAxNDE4MzM3O3Q8O2w8aTwxPjs+O2w8dDw7bDxpPDE+O2k8Mz47aTwxMT47PjtsPHQ8O2
w8aTwwPjs+O2w8dDxAMDxwPHA8bDxTZWxlY3RlZEluZGV4O0RhdGFTZXlzO............" />
```

■**Note** The value of the ViewState is not in human-readable form, but it isn't encrypted either. The information is stored as name-value pairs using the System.Web.UI.StateBag object. The simplest way to decipher the value stored in your ViewState is by going to a web page such as http://www.wilsondotnet.com/Demos/ViewState.aspx, which reveals what the ViewState string actually contains.

In the BalloonShop web site, you're mainly concerned about the ViewState for ProductsList.ascx, which can get quite large for a lot of products. The total page ViewState has close to 2KB if the page has six products, and less than 1KB if no products are displayed on the page.

The professional way to view how much space the ViewState occupies for every element on the page is to enable page tracing by opening a Web Form and modifying its Page directive. Update Default.aspx like this:

```
<%@ Page Trace="true" Language="C#" MasterPageFile="~/BalloonShop.master"
CompileWith="Default.aspx.cs" ClassName="Default_aspx" Title="Untitled Page" %>
```

After making this change, load Default.aspx and look at the tracing information appended at the bottom of the page. You can see a lot of info about your page, including the ViewState size for every control.

■**Note** This is obvious, but it has to be said: for performance and security reasons, always remember to turn off tracing and debug mode before releasing your pages to the Web.

By default, ViewState is enabled for all server controls. However, it can be disabled for a specific control or even for an entire page. For the pages and controls where we prevented reloading during postback events, we'll leave ViewState enabled.

You should disable ViewState for ProductsList.ascx because you need to populate it every time from the database anyway—all postback events that happen in your web site affect its contents, so using the cached version from the ViewState isn't an option. Moreover, the list of products causes a lot of ViewState data, so disabling its ViewState causes a significant network traffic improvement.

To disable ViewState for a control, change its EnableViewState property to False (by default it's True). Let's disable ViewState for the DataList control in ProductsList.ascx and for the entire SearchBox.ascx control in the following exercise.

Exercise: Disabling ViewState for Server-Side Controls

1. Open ProductsList.ascx in Design View, select the DataList, and open its Properties window by pressing **F4**.

2. Set the EnableViewState property to **False**, as shown in Figure 9-1.

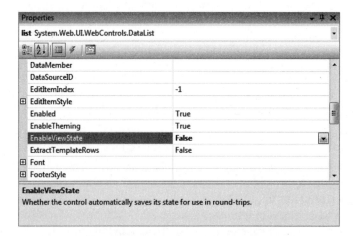

Figure 9-1. *Disabling ViewState for the DataList control*

How It Works: Disabling ViewState to Improve Performance

Now you have disabled `ViewState` for some of your controls. For your particular solutions, you'll decide which controls it's best to disable `ViewState` for.

So far, you've learned about letting ASP.NET manage the state of your controls, in which case you don't reload the controls with data from the database (by verifying the `IsPostBack` value) like you did with `DepartmentsList.ascx`. You also learned how to disable the `ViewState` information, in which case you rely on the control reading the database on every request.

Most of the time, you must not apply both techniques, because you risk ending up with "empty" controls when client postbacks occur, because the data isn't gathered from the database or the `ViewState`.

So far, your client's web site is an exception to that rule, however, because the only occasion (until now) in which a client postback occurs is in the `SearchBox` control, at which time the page is redirected (and so reloaded) anyway. Still, for a quick test, you can now disable `ViewState` for `DepartmentsList.ascx`, add a button somewhere in `Default.aspx`, and double-click it (in Design View) to create its `Click` event handler. Execute the page and click the button. The list of departments should disappear because its `ViewState` is not maintained, and it's not populated from the database, either.

Using Output Cache

Output page caching is an ASP.NET feature that increases the performance of your web application by caching the HTML content generated from dynamic pages or controls. In other words, a page or user control that has output caching enabled is only executed the first time it is requested. On subsequent requests, the page or control is served directly from the cache, instead of being executed again.

This can have an important effect on performance for BalloonShop, because most controls access the database to populate themselves with information. With output caching enabled, the controls only read the database the first time they are accessed. You can set the interval of time at which the cache expires, so the controls have the chance to execute again, and refresh them with current information.

The drawback with output caching is that if the information in the database changes in the meantime, your page will display outdated information (also called stale data). For controls whose data is susceptible to frequent updates, the duration of the cache should be shorter, or cache dependencies should be used.

Also, enabling output caching, although it saves server-processing power, consumes server memory and should be used with caution. This is especially true when storing multiple versions of the page.

You can enable output page caching for a Web Form or Web User Control using the `OutputCache` page directive, which has a number of optional parameters:

```
<%@ OutputCache
   Duration="#ofseconds"
   Location="Any | Client | Downstream | Server | None"
   Shared="True | False"
   VaryByControl="controlname"
   VaryByCustom="browser | customstring"
   VaryByHeader="headers"
   VaryByParam="parametername" %>
```

- `Duration`: Specifies the number of seconds the page is stored in cache. A page is stored in cache the first time it's generated, which happens the first time a visitor asks for it. All the subsequent requests for that page, during the period defined by `Duration`, are served directly from cache instead of being processed again. After the cache duration expires, the page is removed from the cache.

- `Location`: Specifies the place the actual data for the cache is stored. The default value (`Any`) caches the page on the client browser, on the web server, or on any proxy servers supporting HTTP 1.1 caching located between the client and the server.

- `Shared`: Applies only to user controls, and specifies whether the output of the user control should be cached once for all the pages that include the control, or whether multiple versions of the control should be cached for each page that contains it.

- `VaryByControl`: Used to vary the output cache depending on the values of server-side controls contained in the control or page being cached.

- `VaryByCustom`: Used to define custom caching requirements. Its most popular value is `"browser"`, which results in having different versions of the page cached at the server for each type of client-side browser. This feature is very useful if your dynamic web pages generate different HTML outputs depending on the client browser (this isn't the case for BalloonShop, however). If varying the output by browser type, the server retains different versions of the page that were generated for each kind and version of client browser.

- `VaryByHeader`: Used to vary the output cache by the value of different HTTP headers. When you set the value of `VaryByHeader` to a list of HTTP headers (separated by semicolons), multiple versions of the page are cached depending on the values of the mentioned headers. A typical value for `VaryByHeader` is `"Accept-Language"`, which instructs ASP.NET to cache multiple versions of the page for different languages.

- `VaryByParam`: Varies the output cache based on the values of the parameters passed to the server, which include the query string parameters. You'll see in the exercise how to vary the output page cache based on the query string parameters.

You can enable output caching for `DepartmentsList.ascx` by editing the file in HTML View and adding the following line at the beginning of the file:

```
<%@ OutputCache Duration="1000" VaryByParam="DepartmentIndex" %>
```

After adding this directive, ASP.NET retains the different output versions of `DepartmentsList.ascx`, depending on the value of the `DepartmentIndex` query string parameter.

Caution Implementing output caching can easily affect the behavior of your web site in unexpected ways. Also, the way output caching should be implemented depends on the exact stage of your web site. For now, you shouldn't use output caching, but only keep its possibilities in mind. You can start improving performance and tweaking your Web Forms or Web User Controls after you have a working web application.

For controls whose output also depends on the `CategoryIndex`, such as `CategoriesList.ascx` and `Catalog.ascx`, you can implement caching like this:

```
<%@ OutputCache Duration="1000" VaryByParam="DepartmentIndex;CategoryIndex" %>
```

Because `ProductsList.ascx` has many output versions (especially if you take searching into account), it's not recommended to implement caching for it. However, if you still want to do this, you need to make it vary on every possible query string parameter that could influence its output, with an `OutputCache` directive like this:

```
<%@ OutputCache Duration="1000"
VaryByParam="DepartmentIndex;CategoryIndex;Search;AllWords;PageNumber;
ProductsOnPage" %>
```

Alternatively, the * wildcard can be used to vary the output cache on any possible query string parameter:

```
<%@ OutputCache Duration="1000" VaryByParam="*" %>
```

Note You can test caching to make sure it actually works by either placing breakpoints in code (the code shouldn't execute at all when caching is enabled) or temporarily stopping SQL Server and then browsing through pages that were stored in cache (although for this to work, you'll need to implement caching on all the controls that perform data access).

Although implementing output page caching saves the database, it occupies web server memory. For this reason, it isn't feasible to implement output caching for controls such as `ProductsList`, which have a very large number of display possibilities. `ProductsList` has a different output for every department and category, not to mention the endless search possibilities.

Note For your own solutions, you'll need to carefully decide on which user controls to implement output page caching. You can start experimenting by playing with the different controls that you implemented for BalloonShop so far. One thing you should be aware of is that output page caching doesn't always behave as expected during client postbacks generated by other user controls in the page. For this reason, it's advisable to test your solution seriously every time you change output cache options.

Summary

This chapter was very short indeed, especially since it covered a topic that's very complex by its nature. Although ASP.NET performance tuning is out of the scope of this book, you took a quick look at the most useful features that allow you to improve a web site's performance.

In the next chapter, you'll learn how to accept payments for BalloonShop using PayPal.

CHAPTER 10

Receiving Payments Using PayPal

Let's collect some money! Your e-commerce web site needs a way to receive payments from customers. The preferred solution for established companies is to open a merchant account, but many small businesses choose to start with a solution that's simpler to implement, where they don't have to process credit card or payment information themselves.

A number of companies and web sites can help individuals or small businesses that don't have the resources to process credit card and wire transactions. These companies can be used to intermediate the payment between online businesses and their customers. Many of these payment-processing companies are relatively new, and the handling of any individual's financial details is very sensitive. Additionally, a quick search on the Internet will produce reports from both satisfied and unsatisfied customers for almost all of these companies. For these reasons, we are not recommending any specific third-party company.

Instead, this chapter lists some of the companies currently providing these services, and then demonstrates some of the functionality they provide with PayPal. You'll learn how to integrate PayPal with BalloonShop in the first two stages of development. In this chapter, you will

- Learn how to create a new PayPal Website Payments Standard account.

- Learn how to integrate PayPal in phase 1 of development, where you need a shopping cart and custom checkout mechanism.

Note This chapter is not a PayPal manual, but a quick guide to using PayPal. For any complex queries about the services provided, visit PayPal (`http://www.paypal.com`) or the Internet Payment Service Provider you decide to use. Also, you can buy components that make it easier to interact with these systems, such as the free ComponentOne PayPal eCommerce for ASP.NET by ComponentOne (`http://www.componentone.com`).

Considering Internet Payment Service Providers

Take a look at this list of Internet Payment Service Provider web sites. This is a diverse group, each having its advantages. Some of the providers transfer money person to person, and payments need to be verified manually; others offer sophisticated integration with your web site. Some providers work anywhere on the globe, whereas others work only for a single country.

The following list is not complete. You can find many other such companies by doing a Google search on "Internet Payment Service Providers."

- *2Checkout*: http://www.2checkout.com

- *AnyPay*: http://www.anypay.com

- *CCNow*: http://www.ccnow.com

- *Electronic Transfer*: http://www.electronictransfer.com

- *Moneybookers*: http://www.moneybookers.com

- *MultiCards*: http://www.multicards.com

- *Pay By Web*: http://www.paybyweb.com

- *Paymate*: http://www.paymate.com.au

- *PayPal*: http://www.paypal.com

- *ProPay*: http://www.propay.com

- *QuickPayPro*: http://www.quickpaypro.com

- *WorldPay*: http://worldpay.com

For the demonstration in this chapter, we chose to use PayPal. Apart from being quite popular, PayPal offers the services that fit very well into our web site for the first two stages of development. PayPal is available in a number of countries—the most up-to-date list can be found at http://www.paypal.com.

For the first phase of development (the current phase)—where you have only a searchable product catalog—with only a few lines of HTML code, PayPal enables you to add a shopping cart with checkout functionality. For the second phase of development, in which you will implement your own shopping cart, PayPal has a feature called Single Item Purchases that can be used to send the visitor directly to a payment page without the intermediate shopping cart. You'll use this feature of PayPal in Chapter 14.

For a summary of the features provided by PayPal, point your browser to http:// www.paypal.com and click the Merchant Services link. That page contains a few other useful links that will show you the main features available from PayPal.

Getting Started with PayPal

Probably the best description of this service is the one found on its web site: "PayPal is an account-based system that lets anyone with an email address securely send and receive online payments using their credit card or bank account."

Instead of paying the merchant directly, the visitor pays PayPal using a credit card or bank account. The merchant company then uses its PayPal account to get the money received from the customers. At the time of this writing, no cost is involved in creating a new PayPal account, and the service is free for the buyer. The fees involved when receiving money are shown at http://www.paypal.com/cgi-bin/webscr?cmd=_display-fees-outside.

Visit the PayPal web site to get updated and complete information, and, of course, visit its competitors before making a decision for your own e-commerce site. You'll also want to check which of the services are available in your country, what kind of credit cards and payment methods each company accepts, information about currency conversions, and so on.

PAYPAL LINKS AND RESOURCES

Check out these resources when you need more information than this short chapter provides:

- *Website Payments Standard Integration Guide*: This contains information previously contained in separate manuals, such as the Shopping Cart manual and the Instant Payments Notification manual. Get it at `https://www.paypal.com/en_US/pdf/PP_WebsitePaymentsStandard_IntegrationGuide.pdf`.

- *PayPal Developer Central*: This is the official resource for PayPal developers. Access it at `https://www.paypal.com/pdn`.

- *PayPalDev*: According to the site, this is an independent forum for PayPal developers. Access it at `http://www.paypaldev.org/`. You can also find numerous links to various other PayPal resources as well.

In the following exercise, you'll create a new PayPal account and then integrate it with BalloonShop. (These steps are also described in more detail in the PayPal manuals mentioned earlier.)

Exercise: Creating the PayPal Account

1. Browse to `http://www.paypal.com` using your favorite web browser.

2. Click the Sign Up link.

3. PayPal supports three account types: Personal, Premier, and Business. To receive credit card payments, you need to open a Premier or Business account. Choose your country from the combo box, and click **Continue**.

4. Complete all the requested information and you'll receive an email asking you to revisit the PayPal site to confirm the details you have entered.

How It Works: The PayPal Account

After the PayPal account is set up, the email address you provided will be your PayPal ID.

The PayPal service provides a lot of functionality, and because the site is easy to use and many of the functions are self-explanatory, we won't describe everything here. Remember that these sites are there for your business, so they're more than happy to assist with any of your queries.

Now let's see how you can actually use the new account for the web site.

Integrating the PayPal Shopping Cart and Checkout

In the first stage of development (the current stage), you need to integrate the shopping cart and checkout functionality from PayPal. In the second stage of development, after you create your own shopping cart, you'll only need to rely on PayPal's checkout mechanism.

To accept payments, you need to add two important elements to the user interface part of the site: Add to Cart buttons for each product and a View Cart button somewhere on the page. PayPal makes adding these buttons a piece of cake.

The functionality of these buttons is performed by secure links to the PayPal web site, which can be implemented as either forms or specially crafted URLs. Let's take a look at both methods. The following form represents the Add to Cart button for a product named "Welcome Back" that costs $12.99:

```
<form target="paypal" action="https://www.paypal.com/cgi-bin/webscr" method="post">
  <input type="hidden" name="cmd" value="_cart">
  <input type="hidden" name="business" value="balloon@example.com">
  <input type="hidden" name="item_name" value="Welcome Back">
  <input type="hidden" name="on0" value="Color" />
  <select name="os0">
    <option value="White">White</option>
    <option value="Black">Black</option>
    <option value="Red">Red</option>
    <option value="Orange">Orange</option>
    <option value="Yellow">Yellow</option>
    <option value="Green">Green</option>
    <option value="Blue">Blue</option>
    <option value="Indigo">Indigo</option>
    <option value="Purple">Purple</option>
  </select>

  <input type="hidden" name="amount" value="12.99">
  <input type="hidden" name="currency_code" value="USD">
  <input type="hidden" name="add" value="1">
  <input type="hidden" name="shopping_url"
   value="http://www.example.com/Welcome-Back-p33/>
  <input type="hidden" name="return" value="http://www.example.com" />
  <input type="hidden" name="cancel_return" value="http://www.example.com" />
  <input type="submit" name="submit" value="Add to Cart" />
</form>
```

The fields are predefined and their names are self-explanatory. The most important is business, which must be the email address you used when you registered the PayPal account (the email address that will receive the money). Consult PayPal's Website Payments Standard Integration Guide for more details.

The View Cart button can be generated using a similar structure. In your web,site, because ASP.NET works by default using a main form (and forms cannot be nested), you'll generate the buttons using links such as

```
https://www.paypal.com/cgi-bin/webscr?cmd=_cart&business=balloon@example.com➥
&item_name=Welcome+Back&amount=12.99&currency=USD&on0=Color&os0=White&add=1➥
&cancel_return=http://www.example.com&shopping_url=http://www.example.com/➥
Welcome-Back-p33/&return=http://www.example.com
```

■Note When using the URL query string to pass information to the server, you need to carefully encode the parameter values. For example, to pass the `Mistletoe T-Shirt` string as a URL parameter, you need to encode the space, which is not an allowed URL character. The space can be encoded as either %20 or +.

Loading this URL in your web browser will take you to a PayPal shopping cart page like the one shown in Figure 10-1.

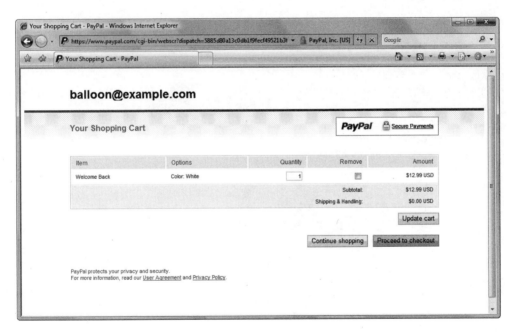

Figure 10-1. *The PayPal shopping cart*

■**Caution** Yes, it's just that simple to manufacture an Add to Cart link! The drawback of this simplicity is that it can be potentially used against you. After PayPal confirms the payment, you can ship the products to your customer. On each payment, you need to carefully check that the product prices correspond to the correct amounts, because it's very easy for anyone to add a fake product to the shopping cart, or an existing product with a modified price. This can be done simply by fabricating one of those PayPal Add to Cart links and navigating to it.

In BalloonShop, you need to add links such as the one shown previously (Add to Cart links) in the product details pages (`Product.aspx`) (see Figure 10-2), and you need to add the View Cart link on the main web page (so you'll update `BalloonShop.master` as well).

When using shopping cart URLs like PayPal's, you need to control the length of the product names and attributes, although it's unlikely that you'll end up with URLs so long that they can't be handled by web browsers. The page at `http://www.boutell.com/newfaq/misc/urllength.html` shows an interesting analysis of maximum URL lengths accepted by the most popular web browsers.

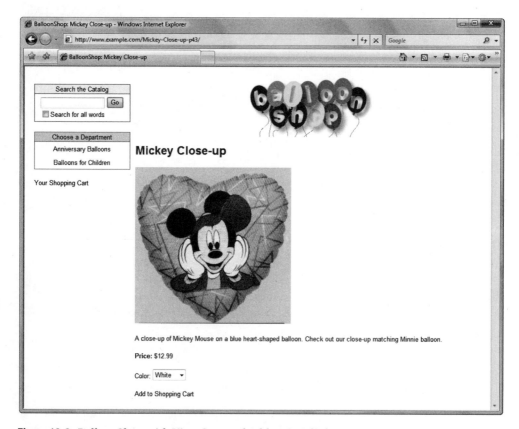

Figure 10-2. *BalloonShop with View Cart and Add to Cart links*

Now that you have a basic understanding of what you need to do, let's implement this code through an exercise.

Exercise: Integrating the PayPal Shopping Cart and Custom Checkout

1. Edit `web.config` by adding the following configuration items to the `<appSettings>` element:

```
<appSettings>
  <add key="PaypalUrl" value="https://www.paypal.com/cgi-bin/webscr?cmd=➥
_cart" />
  <add key="PaypalEmail" value="balloon@example.com" />
  <add key="PaypalCurrency" value="USD" />
  <add key="PaypalReturnUrl" value="http://www.example.com" />
  <add key="PaypalCancelUrl" value="http://www.example.com" />
  ...
</appSettings>
```

■**Note** Be sure to set the values of these elements correctly to reflect real URLs of your web site. Of special importance is the PayPal email address, which specifies the PayPal account that will receive your customer's money. You want to double-check that value to make sure it's correct.

2. Add the following property definitions to your `BalloonShopConfiguration` class:

```
// The PayPal shopping cart URL
public static string PaypalUrl
{
  get
  {
    return ConfigurationManager.AppSettings["PaypalUrl"];
  }
}

// The PayPal email account
public static string PaypalEmail
{
  get
  {
    return ConfigurationManager.AppSettings["PaypalEmail"];
  }
}
```

```
// Currency code (such as USD)
public static string PaypalCurrency
{
  get
  {
    return ConfigurationManager.AppSettings["PaypalCurrency"];
  }
}

// Return URL after a successful transaction
public static string PaypalReturnUrl
{
  get
  {
    return ConfigurationManager.AppSettings["PaypalReturnUrl"];
  }
}

// Return URL after a canceled transaction
public static string PaypalCancelUrl
{
  get
  {
    return ConfigurationManager.AppSettings["PaypalCancelUrl"];
  }
}
```

3. Open the `Link` class in `Link.cs` and add the following methods:

```
public static string ToPayPalViewCart()
{
  return HttpUtility.UrlPathEncode(
    String.Format("{0}&business={1}&return={2}&cancel_return={3}&display=1",
    BalloonShopConfiguration.PaypalUrl,
    BalloonShopConfiguration.PaypalEmail,
    BalloonShopConfiguration.PaypalReturnUrl,
    BalloonShopConfiguration.PaypalCancelUrl));
}

public static string ToPayPalAddItem(string productUrl, string productName➥
, decimal productPrice, string productOptions)
{
    return HttpUtility.UrlPathEncode(
        String.Format("{0}&business={1}&return={2}&cancel_return={3}&shopp➥
ing_url={4}&item_name={5}&amount={6:0.00}&currency={7}&on0=Options&os0={8}➥
&add=1",
            BalloonShopConfiguration.PaypalUrl,
            BalloonShopConfiguration.PaypalEmail,
            BalloonShopConfiguration.PaypalReturnUrl,
            BalloonShopConfiguration.PaypalCancelUrl,
            productUrl,
            productName,
```

```
        productPrice,
        BalloonShopConfiguration.PaypalCurrency,
        productOptions));
}
```

4. Open `BalloonShop.master` in Source View and add the View Cart link just below the `CategoriesList` control:

```
<div class="Container">
  <uc3:SearchBox ID="SearchBox1" runat="server" />
  <uc1:DepartmentsList ID="DepartmentsList1" runat="server" />
  <uc2:CategoriesList ID="CategoriesList1" runat="server" />
  <p>
    <asp:HyperLink ID="PayPalViewCart" runat="server" NavigateUrl=<%# ➥
Link.ToPayPalViewCart() %>>Your Shopping Cart</asp:HyperLink>
  </p>
</div>
```

5. Next, add the PayPal Add to Cart button in `Product.aspx`. Open `Product.aspx` and add a `HyperLink` control just below the product attributes:

```
  <p>
    <asp:PlaceHolder ID="attrPlaceHolder" runat="server"></asp:PlaceHolder>
  </p>
  <p>
    <asp:LinkButton ID="AddToCartButton" runat="server"
     onclick="AddToCartButton_Click">Add to Shopping Cart</asp:LinkButton>
  </p>
</asp:Content>
```

6. Your form should look like Figure 10-3 in Design View.

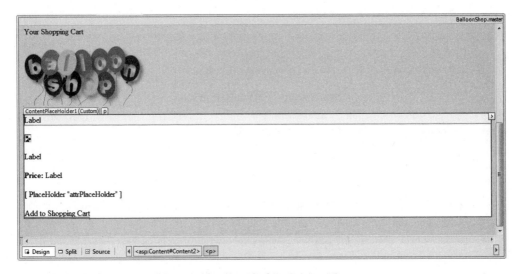

Figure 10-3. *Product.aspx with an Add to Cart link in Design View*

7. Switch to Design View, double-click the LinkButton to generate its Click event handler, and complete its code like this:

```
protected void AddToCartButton_Click(object sender, EventArgs e)
{
  // Retrieve ProductID from the query string
  string productId = Request.QueryString["ProductID"];
  // Retrieves product details
  ProductDetails pd = CatalogAccess.GetProductDetails(productId);

  // Retrieve the selected product options
  string options = "";
  foreach (Control cnt in attrPlaceHolder.Controls)
  {
    if (cnt is Label)
    {
      Label attrLabel = (Label)cnt;
      options += attrLabel.Text;
    }

    if (cnt is DropDownList)
    {
      DropDownList attrDropDown = (DropDownList)cnt;
      options += attrDropDown.Items[attrDropDown.SelectedIndex] + "; ";
    }
  }

  // The Add to Cart link
  string productUrl = Link.ToProduct(pd.ProductID.ToString());
  string destination = Link.ToPayPalAddItem(productUrl, pd.Name, pd.Price,
options);
  Response.Redirect(destination);
}
```

8. Press **F5** to execute the project. Experiment with the PayPal shopping cart to make sure that it works as advertised. Figure 10-4 shows the PayPal shopping cart in action.

How It Works: PayPal Integration

Yes, it was just that simple. Right now, all visitors became potential customers! They can click the Checkout button of the PayPal shopping cart, which allows them to buy the products!

After a customer makes a payment on the web site, an email notification is sent to the email address registered on PayPal and also to the customer. Your PayPal account reflects the payment, and you can view the transaction information in your account history or as a part of the history transaction log.

We touched on a few of the details of the PayPal shopping cart, but for a complete description of its functionality, you should read PayPal's Website Payments Standard Integration Guide. If you decide to use PayPal for your own web site, make sure you learn about all its features. For example, you can teach PayPal to automatically calculate shipping costs and tax for each order.

You also created a LinkButton control for the first time when you added the Add to Cart link in Product.aspx. This control functions like a Button control, except it looks like a normal link.

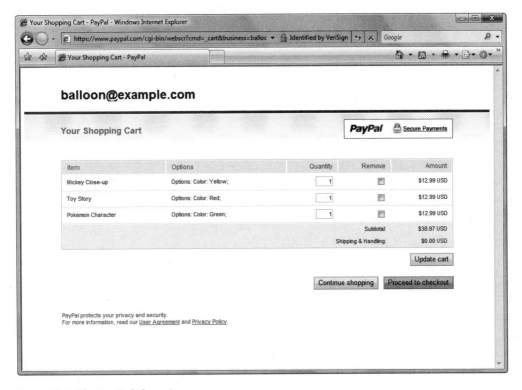

Figure 10-4. *The PayPal shopping cart*

Summary

In this chapter, you saw how to integrate PayPal into an e-commerce site—a simple payment solution that many small businesses choose so they don't have to process credit card or payment information themselves.

First we listed some of the alternatives to PayPal, before guiding you through the creation of a new PayPal account. We then covered how to integrate PayPal in stages 1 and 2 of development, discussing a shopping cart, a custom checkout mechanism, and how to direct the visitor straight to the payment page.

In the next chapter, we'll move on to look at a catalog administration page for BalloonShop.

CHAPTER 11

Catalog Administration: Departments and Categories

In the previous chapters, you worked with catalog information that already existed in the database. You have probably inserted some records yourself, or maybe you downloaded the department, category, and product information from this book's accompanying source code. Obviously, both ways are unacceptable for a real web site, so you need to write some code to allow easy management of your data. That said, the final detail to take care of before launching a web site is to create its administrative interface. Although visitors will never see this part, it's key to delivering a quality web site to your client.

In this chapter and the following one, you'll implement a catalog administration page. With this feature, you'll complete the first stage of your web site's development! Because this page can be implemented in many ways, a serious discussion with the client is required to get the specific list of required features.

In our case, we'll implement a control panel that allows managing the site's departments, categories, and products. In this chapter, we'll deal with administering departments and categories, leaving the rest for Chapter 12. More specifically in this chapter, we will create features that allow for

- Adding and removing departments

- Modifying existing departments' information (name and description)

- Viewing the list of categories that belong to a department

- Adding and removing categories

- Editing existing categories' information (name and description)

To secure the sensitive pages of your site, such as the administrative section, you'll also do the following:

- Implement a login form where the administrator needs to supply a username and password

Preparing to Create the Catalog Administration Page

Although the list of objectives might look intimidating at first, it will be easy to implement. We have already covered most of the theory in the previous chapters, but you'll still learn a few new bits of information in this chapter.

The first step toward creating the catalog administration page is to create a simple login mechanism for administrators. This mechanism will be extended in Chapter 16, where you'll add customer accounts. The user interface bit of the login functionality consists of a control named UserInfo that allows the administrator to authenticate himself or herself (see Figure 11-1).

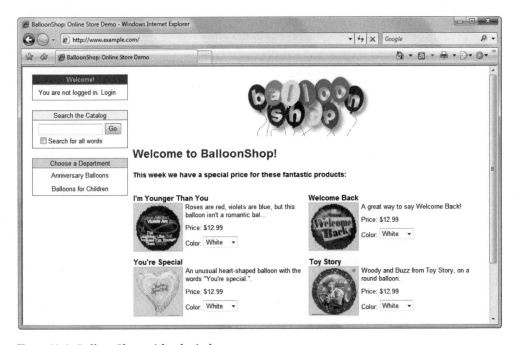

Figure 11-1. *BalloonShop with a login box*

After logging in as an administrator, the UserInfo box displays links to the administrative parts of the site. The first page of the catalog administration section that you'll build in this chapter will look like Figure 11-2 (note that it reuses the UserInfo control).

■**Tip** Although the list of departments looks like a DataList control, it's actually a GridView. You'll learn more about this control later, when you create the AdminDepartments Web Form. For now, it's important to know that it allows for easy integration of edit, select, and delete functionalities. When the Edit, Edit Categories (Select), or Delete buttons are clicked, events are generated that can be handled in code.

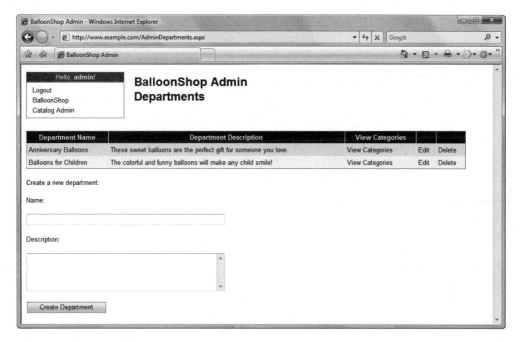

Figure 11-2. *Administering departments*

The functionality you'll implement for departments is much the same as you'll see for categories and products. More specifically, the administrator can

- Edit the department's name or description by clicking the Edit button

- Edit the categories for a specific department by clicking the Edit Categories button

- Completely remove a department from the database by clicking the Delete button (this works only if the department has no related categories; otherwise, the administrator is notified that the operation couldn't be completed)

When clicking the Edit button, the grid enters edit mode, and its fields become editable TextBox controls, as shown in Figure 11-3. Also, as you can see, instead of the Edit button, you get Update and Cancel buttons. Clicking Update updates the database with the changes, whereas clicking Cancel simply quits edit mode.

The administrator can add new departments by writing the new department's name and description in the TextBox controls below the grid, and clicking the Add button.

When the administrator clicks the Edit Categories button, the category administration page loads up. The user is presented with a similar page where he or she can edit the categories that belong to the selected department (see Figure 11-4).

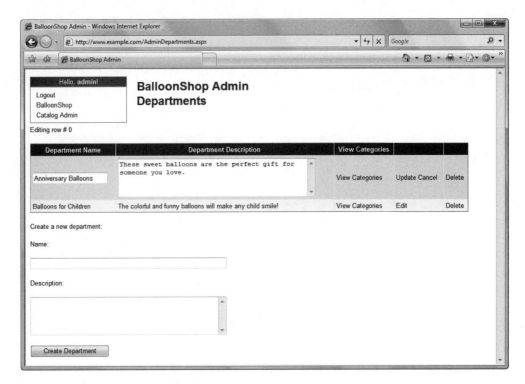

Figure 11-3. *Editing department information*

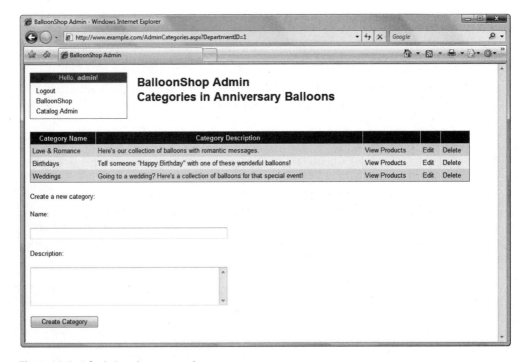

Figure 11-4. *Administering categories*

This page works similar to the one for editing departments, but there is an additional link that takes you back to the departments' page. When selecting a category, the page loads the list of products for that category (see Figure 11-5). You'll implement the products administration features in Chapter 12.

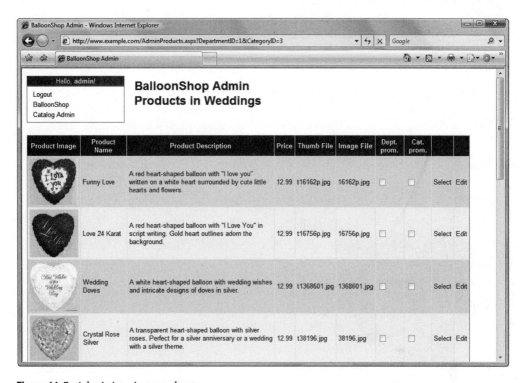

Figure 11-5. *Administering products*

Finally, the last page allows you to do additional product details management, such as changing the product's category, removing a product from a category or from the catalog, and so on (see Figure 11-6).

The navigation logic between the department, category, and product administration pages is done using query string parameters.

Figure 11-6. *Administering product details*

Authenticating Administrators

Before building any administrative pages, we need to put in place a security mechanism for restricting the access to these pages. Only authorized personnel should be able to modify the product catalog!

Security is obviously a large topic, and its complexity depends a lot on the value of the data you're protecting. While we don't have the resources to create such a secure environment as that implemented by banks, for example, when creating an online store, we still have a great responsibility to make sure our data and our customers' data is safe.

Our security implementation deals with these important concepts:

- *Authentication*: This is the process in which users are uniquely identified. The typical way to identify users, which we'll also implement in BalloonShop, is to ask for a username and a password.

- *Authorization*: This concept refers to the process of identifying the resources an authenticated user can access and restricting his or her access accordingly. For example, you can have administrators who can only edit product names and descriptions and administrators who can also view customers' personal data. The administrators of our little shop will have access to all the restricted areas, but as the site gets larger, you may want to delegate administrative tasks to more employees for both management and security reasons.

To ease the administrative work, modern authorization systems, including those supported by ASP.NET, support the notion of authorization roles (or groups). A role is a named set of permissions that can be assigned to users. In other words, a role contains permissions. Roles can be granted to or revoked from users; granting a role to a user has the same effect as granting the user all the permissions in that role. Roles are important because they allow the administrator to manage user privileges in a much more convenient way.

In this chapter, you'll create a new role named Administrators, which will have the privilege to access the web site administration pages. You'll add new roles in the following chapters.

In BalloonShop, we'll use an authentication method called **Forms authentication**, which allows you to control the login process through a Web Form. After the client is authenticated, ASP.NET automatically generates a cookie on the client, which is used to authenticate all subsequent requests. If the cookie is not found, the client is redirected to the login Web Form.

■Tip You should know that ASP.NET supports more authentication methods, which are presented in the MSDN article on ASP.NET authentication at `http://msdn.microsoft.com/en-us/library/aa291347.aspx`. Two other interesting and detailed articles on ASP.NET security are "Building Secure ASP.NET Applications: Authentication, Authorization, and Secure Communication" (`http://msdn.microsoft.com/en-us/library/aa302415.aspx`) and "Improving Web Application Security: Threats and Countermeasures" (`http://msdn.microsoft.com/en-us/library/ms994921.aspx`).

The username and password combinations can be saved in various formats and can be physically stored in different places. ASP.NET stores the passwords in **hashed form** by default.

HASHING

Hashing is a common method for storing passwords. The hash value of a password is calculated by applying a mathematical function (hash algorithm) to it. When the user tries to authenticate, the password is hashed, and the resulting hash value is compared to the hash value of the original (correct) password. If the two values are identical, then the entered password is correct. The essential property about the hash algorithm is that, theoretically, you cannot obtain the original password from its hash value (the algorithm is one way).

User passwords are stored in hashed form, so when the user tries to authenticate, the entered password is hashed, and the resulting hash value is compared to the hash value of the original (correct) password. If the two values are identical, then the entered password is the correct one.

ASP.NET has built-in support for storing user passwords directly in web.config, or in a special database structure that we'll conveniently call "the membership data structure." The name comes from ASP.NET's membership system, which refers to the ASP.NET system for user account management, login and user registration controls, and so on.

One part of this system is made up of the login controls offered by ASP.NET, which you can find on the Login tab of the Visual Web Developer toolbox. You'll learn how to use them to implement complete, working login/logout functionality and apply security restrictions to the admin pages without writing a single line of code! Everything is as simple as combining some login controls and applying templates to define the way they look and behave.

The controls you'll use in this chapter are as follows:

- Login is perhaps the most useful control of all. It displays a login box asking for the username and password, and a check box for the "remember me next time" feature. It has a number of color templates that you can apply, and if you don't like any of these templates, you can convert the whole control into a template (you'll see how to do this later in this chapter). This gives you access to all the individual controls that make up the Login control, so you can customize them separately.

- LoginView is capable of displaying various templates depending on the authentication state of the current user. The AnonymousTemplate is displayed if no user is logged in, and you'll generally want it to display the "You are not logged in" text and a link to the login page. If an administrator is logged in, your LoginView control displays links to the various administrative pages. In Chapter 16, when you'll allow your customers to create accounts on your site, your LoginView control will be updated to recognize the customers and display links to their personal pages.

- LoginName is a simple control that displays the name of the logged-in user. You'll use this control inside some templates of the LoginView control to display the "You're logged in as *username*" text.

- LoginStatus simply generates a Login link in case no user is logged in and a Logout link in case a user is logged in.

Let's add the security mechanism in the following exercise, where you'll

- Create a role named Administrators for your application, and then a user named admin that is associated with the role

- Add the UserInfo control to your application that displays data about the currently logged-in user (refer to Figure 11-1)

- Create a login page named Login.aspx

- Create a Master Page named Admin.master that you'll use when creating all administrative pages

- Create the first admin page for your site: AdminDepartments.aspx

- Make the AdminDepartments.aspx page accessible only by users of the Administrators role

Exercise: Implementing the Login Mechanism

1. The first step is to prepare the BalloonShop database for storing the ASP.NET membership data structures. The tool we use for this task is `aspnet_regsql.exe`; it can be executed at the Windows command prompt, where you can include various parameters to configure it instantly for your database. Alternatively, it can be run in Wizard mode, allowing you to set those options one at a time.

   Execute the tool from `C:\Windows\Microsoft.NET\Framework\v2.0.nnnnn\` with the following parameters. Note that the parameters are case sensitive and that we assume that your BalloonShop database has the balloonshop user with the ecommerce password. Make sure to replace *MACHINENAME* with the name of your local machine. (To find more about each parameter, simply execute `aspnet_regsql /?`.)

   ```
   aspnet_regsql -U balloonshop -P ecommerce -S MACHINENAME\SqlExpress ➡
   -A all -d BalloonShop
   ```

   The output should resemble this:

   ```
   C:\Windows\Microsoft.NET\Framework\v2.0.50727>aspnet_regsql -U balloonshop
   -P ecommerce -S THINKPADT61P\SqlExpress -A all -d BalloonShop

   Start adding the following features:
   Membership
   Profile
   RoleManager
   Personalization
   SqlWebEventProvider


   .......


   Finished.
   ```

2. Modify `web.config` to change the setting for the local SQL Server database, which is used to locate the membership data:

   ```
   <connectionStrings>
     <add name="BalloonShopConnection" connectionString="Server=(local)\Sql➡
   Express; Database=BalloonShop; User=balloonshop; Password=ecommerce" ➡
   providerName="System.Data.SqlClient" />
     <remove name="LocalSqlServer"/>
     <add name="LocalSqlServer" connectionString="Server=(local)\SqlExpress;➡
   Database=BalloonShop; User=balloonshop; Password=ecommerce" providerName=➡
   "System.Data.SqlClient" />
   </connectionStrings>
   ```

3. You can now use the ASP.NET Web Site Administration Tool, which can manage the membership data. Start the ASP.NET Web Site Administration Tool by clicking **WebSite ➤ ASP.NET Configuration**.

4. Click the **Security** tab. You should get a screen like the one shown in Figure 11-7.

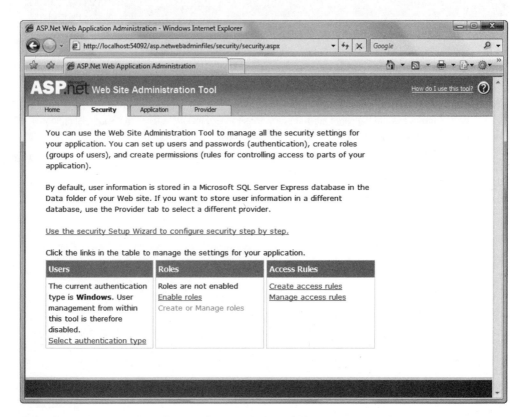

Figure 11-7. *The ASP.NET Web Site Administration Tool*

5. Click **Enable roles**.

6. Click **Create or Manage roles** and create a new role named **Administrators**. Click **Back**.

7. The default authentication type is "From a local network." Click **Select authentication type** and select the **From the Internet** option. Click **Done**.

8. Click **Create user** and add a new user that will be allowed to perform catalog administration tasks. We'll assume you'll add a new user named **admin** with the password **BalloonShop!**. Add some text of your choice for E-mail, Security Question, and Security Answer. Assign the user to the Administrators role by checking the check box, and click **Create User** (see Figure 11-8).

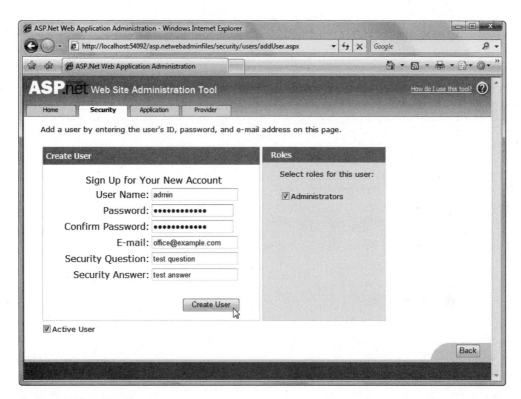

Figure 11-8. *Creating a new user*

■**Note** The default security settings require users to have strong passwords, so your password may be rejected if you try simpler passwords. This is because the ASP.NET membership system applies several rules to passwords, which are defined in `machine.config`. By default, passwords require a minimum length of seven characters, including at least one nonalphanumeric character (that is, a symbol character such as [, *, !, and so on). You can change these settings by editing the `machine.config` file, which is located in `<Windows Install Directory>\Microsoft.NET\Framework\<Version>\CONFIG\`. Look for the definition of the `AspNetSqlMembershipProvider` provider, which can include the `minRequiredPasswordLength` and `minRequiredNonalphanumericCharacters` attributes to define the length and complexity of the password (or you can do this in one go using the `passwordStrengthRegularExpression` parameter). However, be aware that changes you make in `machine.config` apply to *all* the web sites on your computer. An alternative is to override the definition of this provider in `web.config`—you'll learn more details about this in Chapter 16.

---

9. Click **Back** to get to the main Security page. Make sure that you have one role and one user, and then close the window.

10. Switch back to Visual Web Developer. You'll probably be asked to reload web.config, which was modified by an external program. Select **Yes**.

11. Next you'll create the UserInfo Web User Control, the Login Web Form, the Admin Master Page, and the AdminDepartments Web Form. First add the following styles to BalloonShop.css, which will be used in these pages:

```
.UserInfoHead {
  border: #cc6666 1px solid;
  background-color: #dc143c;
  color: #f5f5dc;
  text-align: center;
}
.UserInfoContent {
  border: #cc6666 1px solid;
  padding: 5px 0px 5px 12px;
  line-height: 20px;
}
.AdminTitle {
  font-size: 24px;
  font-weight: bold;
}
.Window .Main .Right .AdminHeader {
  margin: 5px 5px 5px 0px;
  width: 100%;
}
.AdminContents {
  margin: 5px 5px 5px 0px;
  width: 900px;
  float: left;
}
.AdminError {
  color: Red;
}
```

12. Now create a Web User Control named UserInfo.ascx in your UserControls folder.

13. In UserInfo, you'll use an ASP.NET control named LoginView, which can display different data (through templates) depending on the currently logged-in user. For users of the Administrators role, you'll display links to the administration pages, and if no users are logged in, you simply display a login link (using the LoginStatus control). You can edit the templates of the LoginView control by either using Design View or Source View. Either way, make sure your UserInfo Web User Control contains the following code:

```
<%@ Control Language="C#" AutoEventWireup="true" CodeFile="UserInfo.ascx.➥
cs" Inherits="UserControls_UserInfo" %>
<table cellspacing="0" border="0" width="200px" >
  <asp:LoginView ID="LoginView1" runat="server">
    <AnonymousTemplate>
      <tr>
        <td class="UserInfoHead">Welcome!</td>
      </tr>
      <tr>
        <td class="UserInfoContent">
          You are not logged in.
          <asp:LoginStatus ID="LoginStatus1" runat="server" />
        </td>
      </tr>
    </AnonymousTemplate>
    <RoleGroups>
      <asp:RoleGroup Roles="Administrators">
        <ContentTemplate>
          <tr>
            <td class="UserInfoHead">
              <asp:LoginName ID="LoginName2" runat="server" ➥
FormatString="Hello, <b>{0}</b>!" />
            </td>
          </tr>
          <tr>
            <td class="UserInfoContent">
              <asp:LoginStatus ID="LoginStatus2" runat="server" />
              <br />
              <a href="/">BalloonShop</a>
              <br />
              <a href="AdminDepartments.aspx">Catalog Admin</a>
            </td>
          </tr>
        </ContentTemplate>
      </asp:RoleGroup>
    </RoleGroups>
  </asp:LoginView>
</table>
```

14. Open `BalloonShop.master` and drag the `UserInfo` control from Solution Explorer just on top of the list of departments, as shown in Figure 11-9.

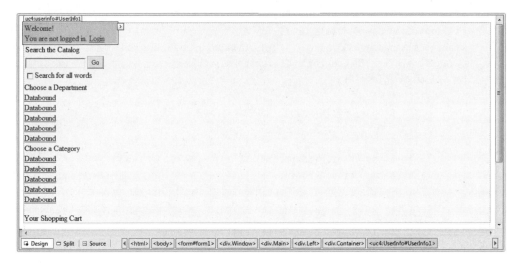

Figure 11-9. *Adding the UserInfo control to the Master Page*

15. Start your project and ensure that your UserInfo control looks good. The next step is to create the login page. Right-click the root entry in Solution Explorer, select **Add New Item**, choose the **Web Form** template, and name it Login.aspx. Make sure the two check boxes are checked and click **Add**.

16. In the dialog box that opens, select the **BalloonShop.master** entry and click **OK**.

17. Switch Login.aspx to Design View, add a Login control from the Login tab of the toolbox to the content placeholder, and then rename the control from Login1 to **loginControl**, as shown in Figure 11-10.

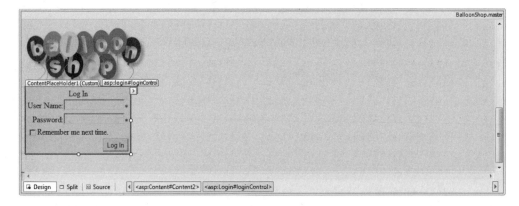

Figure 11-10. *The content area of Login.aspx in Design View*

18. Open web.config and change the <authentication> element under the <system.web> node, as shown next. This registers Login.aspx as the default login page, which visitors will be forwarded to if they click the Login link or when they try to access an unauthorized page.

```
<authentication mode="Forms">
  <forms name="BalloonShopLogin"
    loginUrl="Login.aspx" path="/" protection="All" timeout="60">
  </forms>
</authentication>
```

At this point, you have a working login and logout mechanism! Start your project to ensure the login and logout features are fully working (try to log in with the username **admin**, which should have as the password **BalloonShop!**, if you followed the instructions).

■**Note** After you type your username and password, it's not enough to just press the Enter key while the focus is on the Password text box or on the check box. You need to press the Tab key to give the Log In button the focus or click the Log In button with the mouse. You'll fix this problem in the next steps.

---

19. Continue by making a few cosmetic changes to your page. To make the Login control fully customizable by having access to its individual constituent controls, you need to convert it to a template. Click its **Smart Link** and choose **Convert to Template**, as shown in Figure 11-11.

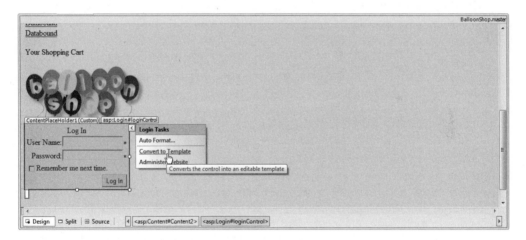

Figure 11-11. *Converting the Login control to a template*

20. Switch to Source View. After converting the control to a template, you'll see all of its constituent controls generated inside its <LayoutTemplate>. Modify the template as shown in the following code snippet:

```
<LayoutTemplate>
<table border="0" cellpadding="1">
<tr class="UserInfoText">
<td>
  <table border="0" cellpadding="0">
    <tr>
      <td class="CatalogTitle" align="left" colspan="2">
```

```
      Who Are You?<br /><br />
    </td>
  </tr>
  <tr>
.....
```

21. To make the Log In button the default when pressing the Enter key at login time, enclose the `<asp:Login>` element inside an `<asp:Panel>`, like this:

```
<asp:Panel ID="searchPanel" runat="server" ➡
DefaultButton="loginControl$LoginButton">
  <asp:Login ID="loginControl" runat="server">
  ...
  </asp:Login>
</asp:Panel>
```

22. Edit the code-behind file in `Login.aspx.cs`:

```
public partial class Login : System.Web.UI.Page
{
  protected void Page_Load(object sender, EventArgs e)
  {
    // get controls
    TextBox usernameTextBox = (TextBox)loginControl.FindControl("UserName");

    // set focus on the username text box when the page loads
    usernameTextBox.Focus();

    // set the page title
    this.Title = BalloonShopConfiguration.SiteName + ": Login";
  }
}
```

23. Now your login page not only that works well, but it also looks good and is very user-friendly. The next and final task for this exercise is to create the skeleton of your administrative part of the site. Start by creating a new Master Page to be used by all the admin pages you'll build for BalloonShop. Right-click the project name in Solution Explorer, choose **Add New Item**, select **Master Page**, and type **Admin.master** for the name. Choose **Visual C#** for the language, make sure **Place code in separate file** is checked, and click **Add**. (The **Select master page** check box must *not* be checked.)

24. While editing the page in Source View, modify the body like this:

```
<%@ Master Language="C#" AutoEventWireup="true" ➡
CodeFile="Admin.master.cs" Inherits="Admin" %>

<%@ Register src="UserControls/UserInfo.ascx" tagname="UserInfo" ➡
tagprefix ="uc1" %>
```

```
<!DOCTYPE html PUBLIC "-//W3C//DTD XHTML 1.0 Transitional//EN" ➥
"http://www.w3.org/TR/xhtml1/DTD/xhtml1-transitional.dtd">

<html xmlns="http://www.w3.org/1999/xhtml">
<head id="Head1" runat="server">
  <title>BalloonShop Admin</title>
</head>
<body>
  <form id="form1" runat="server">
  <div class="Window">
    <div class="Main">
      <div class="Left">
        <uc1:UserInfo ID="UserInfo1" runat="server" />
      </div>
      <div class="Right">
        <div class="AdminHeader">
          <asp:ContentPlaceHolder ID="titlePlaceHolder" runat="server">
          </asp:ContentPlaceHolder>
        </div>
      </div>
      <div class="AdminContents">
        <asp:ContentPlaceHolder ID="adminPlaceHolder" runat="server">
        </asp:ContentPlaceHolder>
      </div>
    </div>
  </div>
  </form>
</body>
</html>
```

25. Switch to Design View and verify that the form looks like Figure 11-12.

Figure 11-12. *Admin.master in Design View*

26. Add a new Web Form called **AdminDepartments.aspx** to the project. Make sure its language is **Visual C#** and that both check boxes (**Place code in separate file** and **Select master page**) are checked. Click **Add**, choose the **Admin.master** Master Page, and then click **OK**.

27. In `AdminDepartments.aspx`, write the following code:

```
<%@ Page Title="" Language="C#" MasterPageFile="~/Admin.master"
AutoEventWireup="true" CodeFile="AdminDepartments.aspx.cs"
Inherits="AdminDepartments" %

<asp:Content ID="Content2" ContentPlaceHolderID="titlePlaceHolder"
Runat="Server">
  <span class="AdminTitle">Catalog Admin</span>
</asp:Content>

<asp:Content ID="Content1" ContentPlaceHolderID="adminPlaceHolder"
Runat="Server">
  Some administration features here
</asp:Content>
```

28. Double-click `web.config` in Solution Explorer and add the following sections right after the `<connectionStrings>` element. We've included the code for all the admin sections you'll write in this chapter and the next, but feel free to add them as you need them.

```
<connectionStrings>
  ...
</connectionStrings>

<location path="AdminDepartments.aspx">
  <system.web>
    <authorization>
      <allow roles="Administrators" />
      <deny users="*" />
    </authorization>
  </system.web>
</location>

<location path="AdminCategories.aspx">
  <system.web>
    <authorization>
      <allow roles="Administrators" />
      <deny users="*" />
    </authorization>
  </system.web>
</location>

<location path="AdminProducts.aspx">
  <system.web>
    <authorization>
      <allow roles="Administrators" />
      <deny users="*" />
    </authorization>
```

```
      </system.web>
    </location>

    <location path="AdminProductDetails.aspx">
      <system.web>
        <authorization>
          <allow roles="Administrators" />
          <deny users="*" />
        </authorization>
      </system.web>
    </location>

    <system.web>
```

29. Load BalloonShop and try to access `AdminDepartments.aspx`. You'll be asked for your login information and you won't be allowed to access that page unless you're an administrator.

How It Works: The Security Mechanism

Congratulations for finishing this long exercise! First, test that your new features work as expected. Try also to access the `AdminDepartments.aspx` page without being logged in as admin, or try to log out when you're in the admin page. You should be forwarded to the login page.

In this exercise, you first added the Administrators role and the admin user to your site. You performed these tasks using the ASP.NET web application Administration page. Feel free to check out other options of that page as well. For instance, you can access and manage the options you saved to `web.config` (such as `SiteName`, and so on) by going to the Application tab, and then clicking "Create/Manage application settings."

After adding the admin user, you created the `UserInfo` Web User Control. There you used a number of the .NET login controls that were explained previously. You could have used the designer to build these controls and their templates—and you can still use the designer to edit them, which I encourage you to test—but in this exercise, it was easier to simply type the code. Let's see how these controls were used:

- `LoginView` is capable of displaying various templates depending on what user is logged in at the moment. The `AnonymousTemplate` is displayed if no user is logged in, and it generates the "You are not logged in" text and a link to the login page.

```
<AnonymousTemplate>
  <tr>
    <td class="UserInfoHead">Welcome!</td>
  </tr>
  <tr>
    <td class="UserInfoContent">
      You are not logged in.
      <asp:LoginStatus ID="LoginStatus1" runat="server" />
    </td>
  </tr>
</AnonymousTemplate>
```

- Under the RoleGroups template, you can find the HTML code that is displayed when an administrator is logged in.

- LoginName simply displays the "You are logged in as *username*" text. This text is defined in its FormatString property, where {0} is the username:

```
<asp:LoginName ID="LoginName2" runat="server" FormatString="Hello, ➡
<b>{0}</b>!" />
```

- LoginStatus displays a Login link that forwards you to the login page you configured in web.config, or a Log Out button that logs out the currently logged-in user and clears the current session information.

```
<asp:LoginStatus ID="LoginStatus1" runat="server" />
```

After writing the UserInfo control, you created Login.aspx. Creating this page was extremely simple, because its only role is to contain a Login control. That control does the login work by itself, without requiring you to write any code or configure any settings. The extra steps you took for creating Login.aspx were for customizing the look of the Login control and converting it into a template to have access to its inner controls. You customized it so that if the visitor presses Enter while any of the text boxes or the check box have focus, the Log In button will be automatically clicked (otherwise, the page would be refreshed without performing any login functionality).

Finally, Admin.Master was created to serve as a skeleton for all the administration pages, and you implemented the first administration page—AdminDepartments.aspx. You configured this page through web.config to be only accessible by users of the Administrators role:

```
<!-- Only administrators are allowed to access AdminDepartments.aspx -->
<location path="AdminDepartments.aspx">
  <system.web>
    <authorization>
      <allow roles="Administrators" />
      <deny users="*" />
    </authorization>
  </system.web>
</location>
```

Note that the authorization list is interpreted in sequential order. The following combination would reject all login attempts:

```
<deny users="*" />
<allow roles="Administrators" />
```

The * wildcard is used for "all identities." The other wildcard character, ?, means "anonymous users." If you wanted all anonymous users to be denied, you could have used the following:

```
<location path="AdminDepartments.aspx">
  <system.web>
    <authorization>
      <deny users="?" />
    </authorization>
  </system.web>
</location>
```

With this setting, any logged-in users (not only administrators) would be allowed access to the admin page.

■**Tip** By default, all visitors are allowed access to all pages, so you need to explicitly deny access to the sensitive pages.

Administering Departments

The department administration section will allow your client to add, remove, or change department information. To implement this functionality, you'll need to write the code for the presentation, business, and data layers. The page you're about to create is shown in Figure 11-13.

Figure 11-13 shows how the AdminDepartments Web Form will look.

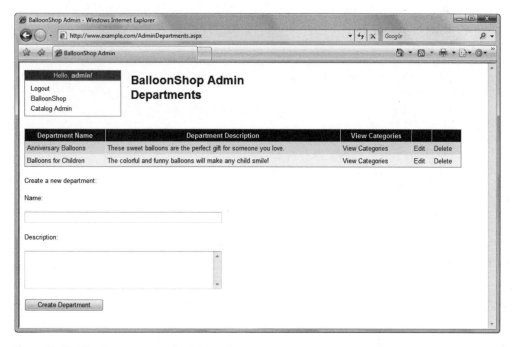

Figure 11-13. *The department administration page*

The form is formed from a list populated with the departments' information, and it also has four additional controls (a label, two text boxes, and a button) used to add new departments to the list.

The list control you see in Figure 11-13 is not a DataList, but a GridView control.

■**Tip** The GridView object is more powerful than the DataList, but its power comes at the expense of speed. For this reason, when the GridView's extra features are not used, you should stick with the DataList. ASP.NET also provides an even simpler and faster object, named Repeater. We don't use the Repeater object in this book, but you should take a look at its documentation for more information.

The GridView is more powerful than the DataList and has many more features; in this chapter, you'll only use part of the GridView's possibilities, particularly the ones that allow for easy integration of edit, select, and delete buttons, and database-bound column editing in Design View. You can see the mentioned controls in Figure 11-13, where the select button is called Edit Categories.

Everything you do here with the GridView is also possible with the DataList, but using the GridView eases your work considerably because of its rich set of built-in features. You don't have to worry about the performance penalty for using a more complex control, because the administration page won't be accessed frequently, compared to the main web site.

Exercise: Administering Departments

1. Start by creating the four stored procedures that perform the basic tasks for departments: retrieving departments, updating departments, deleting departments, and inserting departments. The procedure for retrieving departments already exists in the database, so you just need to add the other three: CatalogAddDepartment, CatalogUpdateDepartment, and CatalogDeleteDepartment.

```
USE BalloonShop

GO

CREATE PROCEDURE CatalogAddDepartment
(@DepartmentName nvarchar(50),
@DepartmentDescription nvarchar(1000))
AS
INSERT INTO Department (Name, Description)
VALUES (@DepartmentName, @DepartmentDescription)

GO

CREATE PROCEDURE CatalogUpdateDepartment
(@DepartmentID int,
@DepartmentName nvarchar(50),
@DepartmentDescription nvarchar(1000))
AS
UPDATE Department
SET Name = @DepartmentName, Description = @DepartmentDescription
WHERE DepartmentID = @DepartmentID
```

```
GO

CREATE PROCEDURE CatalogDeleteDepartment
(@DepartmentID int)
AS
DELETE FROM Department
WHERE DepartmentID = @DepartmentID
```

2. Let's now move to the middle tier. First let's add two new methods to the GenericDataAccess class, called ExecuteNonQuery and ExecuteScalar, which will wrap DbCommand's ExecuteNonQuery and ExecuteScalar methods in the same way ExecuteSelectCommand works with ExecuteReader. Start by adding these methods to the GenericDataAccess class:

```
// execute an update, delete, or insert command
// and return the number of affected rows
public static int ExecuteNonQuery(DbCommand command)
{
  // The number of affected rows
  int affectedRows = -1;
  // Execute the command making sure the connection gets closed in the end
  try
  {
    // Open the connection of the command
    command.Connection.Open();
    // Execute the command and get the number of affected rows
    affectedRows = command.ExecuteNonQuery();
  }
  catch (Exception ex)
  {
    // Log eventual errors and rethrow them
    Utilities.LogError(ex);
    throw;
  }
  finally
  {
    // Close the connection
    command.Connection.Close();
  }
  // return the number of affected rows
  return affectedRows;
}

// execute a select command and return a single result as a string
public static string ExecuteScalar(DbCommand command)
{
  // The value to be returned
  string value = "";
```

```
  // Execute the command making sure the connection gets closed in the end
  try
  {

    // Open the connection of the command
    command.Connection.Open();
    // Execute the command and get the number of affected rows
    value = command.ExecuteScalar().ToString();
  }
  catch (Exception ex)
  {
    // Log eventual errors and rethrow them
    Utilities.LogError(ex);
    throw;
  }
  finally
  {
    // Close the connection
    command.Connection.Close();
  }
  // return the result
  return value;
}
```

3. Now add three methods to the CatalogAccess class that you'll need to call from the AdminDepartments page (you'll also use the GetDepartments method that already exists): UpdateDepartment, DeleteDepartment, and AddDepartment. Add these methods to your CatalogAccess class, inside CatalogAccess.cs:

```
// Update department details
public static bool UpdateDepartment(string id, string name, string description)
{
  // get a configured DbCommand object
  DbCommand comm = GenericDataAccess.CreateCommand();
  // set the stored procedure name
  comm.CommandText = "CatalogUpdateDepartment";
  // create a new parameter
  DbParameter param = comm.CreateParameter();
  param.ParameterName = "@DepartmentId";
  param.Value = id;
  param.DbType = DbType.Int32;
  comm.Parameters.Add(param);
```

```
  // create a new parameter
  param = comm.CreateParameter();
  param.ParameterName = "@DepartmentName";
  param.Value = name;
  param.DbType = DbType.String;
  param.Size = 50;
  comm.Parameters.Add(param);

  // create a new parameter
  param = comm.CreateParameter();
  param.ParameterName = "@DepartmentDescription";
  param.Value = description;
  param.DbType = DbType.String;
  param.Size = 1000;
  comm.Parameters.Add(param);
  // result will represent the number of changed rows
  int result = -1;
  try
  {
    // execute the stored procedure
    result = GenericDataAccess.ExecuteNonQuery(comm);
  }
  catch
  {
    // any errors are logged in GenericDataAccess, we ignore them here
  }
  // result will be 1 in case of success
  return (result != -1);
}

// Delete department
public static bool DeleteDepartment(string id)
{
  // get a configured DbCommand object
  DbCommand comm = GenericDataAccess.CreateCommand();
  // set the stored procedure name
  comm.CommandText = "CatalogDeleteDepartment";
  // create a new parameter
  DbParameter param = comm.CreateParameter();
  param.ParameterName = "@DepartmentId";
  param.Value = id;
  param.DbType = DbType.Int32;
```

```
comm.Parameters.Add(param);
// execute the stored procedure; an error will be thrown by the
// database if the department has related categories, in which case
// it is not deleted
int result = -1;
try
{
  result = GenericDataAccess.ExecuteNonQuery(comm);
}
catch
{

  // any errors are logged in GenericDataAccess, we ignore them here
}
// result will be 1 in case of success
return (result != -1);
}

// Add a new department
public static bool AddDepartment(string name, string description)
{
  // get a configured DbCommand object
  DbCommand comm = GenericDataAccess.CreateCommand();
  // set the stored procedure name
  comm.CommandText = "CatalogAddDepartment";
  // create a new parameter
  DbParameter param = comm.CreateParameter();
  param.ParameterName = "@DepartmentName";
  param.Value = name;
  param.DbType = DbType.String;
  param.Size = 50;
  comm.Parameters.Add(param);
  // create a new parameter
  param = comm.CreateParameter();
  param.ParameterName = "@DepartmentDescription";
  param.Value = description;
  param.DbType = DbType.String;
  param.Size = 1000;
  comm.Parameters.Add(param);
  // result will represent the number of changed rows
  int result = -1;
```

```
   try
   {
     // execute the stored procedure
     result = GenericDataAccess.ExecuteNonQuery(comm);
   }
   catch
   {
     // any errors are logged in GenericDataAccess, we ignore them here
   }
   // result will be 1 in case of success
   return (result != -1);
 }
```

4. Now we continue by implementing AdminDepartments.aspx. Start by opening the file in Source View.

5. In the first placeholder, display the name of the page:

```
<asp:Content ID="Content1" ContentPlaceHolderID="titlePlaceHolder" ➡
runat="Server">
  <span class="AdminTitle">
    BalloonShop Admin
    <br />
    Departments
  </span>
</asp:Content>
```

6. Let's now deal with the second placeholder. Switch to Design View. From the toolbox, add one Label control and a GridView control, with the properties listed in Table 11-1, to the second placeholder.

Table 11-1. *Properties of Controls for Department Administration*

Control Type	ID Property	Text Property	CssClass Property
Label	statusLabel	(empty)	AdminError
GridView	grid		

7. Set the DataKeyNames property of the grid to **DepartmentID** and set its Width property to **100%**.

■Note Setting the DataKeyNames property allows you to find the DepartmentID of the selected departments.

---

8. Switch to Source View and add the controls that will allow new departments to be added, just after the grid:

```
<asp:Content ID="Content2" ContentPlaceHolderID="adminPlaceHolder" runat=➡
"Server">
  <p>
    <asp:Label ID="statusLabel" runat="server" Text=""></asp:Label>
  </p>
  <asp:GridView ID="grid" runat="server" DataKeyNames="DepartmentID" ➡
Width="100%">
  </asp:GridView>
  <p>Create a new department:</p>
  <p>Name:</p>
  <asp:TextBox ID="newName" runat="server" Width="400px" />
  <p>Description:</p>
  <asp:TextBox ID="newDescription" runat="server" Width="400px" Height➡
="70px" TextMode="MultiLine" />
  <p><asp:Button ID="createDepartment" Text="Create Department" runat➡
="server" /></p>
</asp:Content>
```

Now your page should look like Figure 11-14.

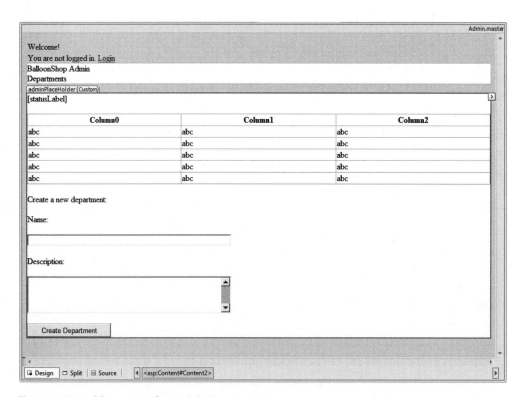

Figure 11-14. *Adding controls to* AdminDepartments.aspx

9. Click the GridView's **Smart Link** and choose **Add New Column**. Use this command to add two columns with the properties shown in Table 11-2.

Table 11-2. *Adding Bound Fields to Your Grid*

Field Type	Header Text	Data Field
BoundField	Department Name	Name
BoundField	Department Description	Description

Your Add Field window should look like Figure 11-15 when adding the Department Name bound field.

Figure 11-15. *Adding a bound column*

10. Add the **View Categories** column by adding a HyperLinkField with a text of **View Categories**. Set the data field to **DepartmentID** and the **URL format string** to **AdminCategories.aspx?DepartmentID={0}**, as shown in Figure 11-16.

11. Now add the functionality that allows the administrator to edit department details. Use the **Add New Column** command again to add a CommandField. Leave the header text empty, leave the button type set to **Link**, check the **Edit/Update** check box, and leave the **Show cancel button** check box checked. Click **OK**.

12. Finally, add the Delete button by clicking the **Smart Link** and choosing **Add New Column**. Choose the **ButtonField** field type, choose **Delete** for the command name, modify the text to **Delete**, and click **OK**.

13. Click GridView's **Smart Link** and choose **Edit Columns**. In the dialog box that opens, deselect **Auto-Generate Fields** (because you manually specified which columns to display). If you leave this check box checked, the GridView appends all columns retrieved from the data source to the manually created ones. At the end of this exercise, you might want to experiment with checking this check box, but for now, leave it unchecked. Click **OK**.

Okay, you've finished working on the columns, so your control should now look like Figure 11-17.

Figure 11-16. *Adding a HyperLinkField column*

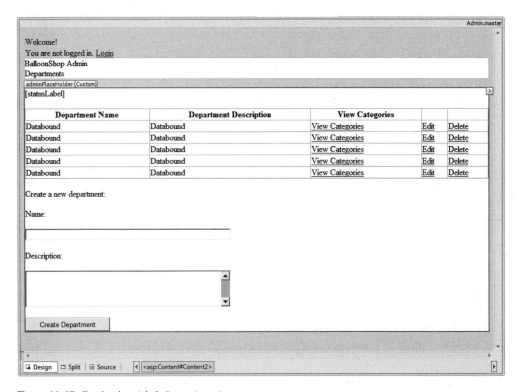

Figure 11-17. *Designing AdminDepartments.aspx*

14. To make the data grid functional, you need to populate it with data in the Page_Load method of
    AdminDepartments.aspx.cs:

```
protected void Page_Load(object sender, EventArgs e)
{
  // Load the grid only the first time the page is loaded
  if (!Page.IsPostBack)
  {
    // Load the departments grid
    BindGrid();
  }
}

// Populate the GridView with data
private void BindGrid()
{
  // Get a DataTable object containing the catalog departments
  grid.DataSource = CatalogAccess.GetDepartments();
  // Bind the data bound controls to the data source
  grid.DataBind();
}
```

15. Pause here to test whether what you've been working on so far works. Execute the project, log in as administrator, and go to the catalog admin page. The GridView control doesn't look like much at the moment, but you'll take care of its looks a bit later. If everything works as expected, you should be presented with a page that looks like Figure 11-18.

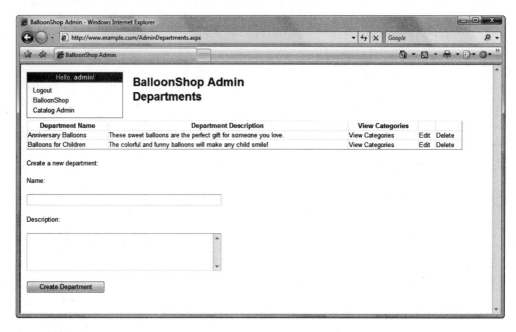

Figure 11-18. *Executing AdminDepartments.aspx*

16. To change the looks of the DataGrid, you'll use a skin, which will define the appearance of every GridView in the site. Open the **App_Themes** folder in Solution Explorer.

17. Right-click the **BalloonShopDefault** folder and choose **Add New Item**.

18. Select the **Skin File** template and change the name to **BalloonShop.skin**.

19. Add the following code, which represents the default skin for GridView controls, to BalloonShop.skin:

```
<asp:GridView runat="server" CssClass="Grid" CellPadding="4" AutoGenerate➥
Columns="False">
  <HeaderStyle CssClass="GridHeader" />
  <RowStyle CssClass="GridRow" />
  <AlternatingRowStyle CssClass="GridAlternateRow" />
  <SelectedRowStyle CssClass="GridSelectedRow"/>
</asp:GridView>
```

20. Add the following styles to `BalloonShop.css`:

```
.Grid {
  border-color: #E7E7FF;
  margin-top: 20px;
  width: 100%;
}
.GridHeader {
  color: White;
  background-color: Navy;
}
.GridRow
{
  color: Navy;
  background-color: #E7E7FF;
}
.GridSelectedRow
{
  color: #F7F7F7;
  background-color: #738A9C;
}
.GridEditingRow
{
  color: Navy;
}
.GridAlternateRow
{
  color: Navy;
  background-color: #F7F7F7;
}
```

21. Execute your project again to make sure your new skin and styles are in effect, as shown in Figure 11-19. Feel free to change your skin and styles files until the grid looks like you want it to.

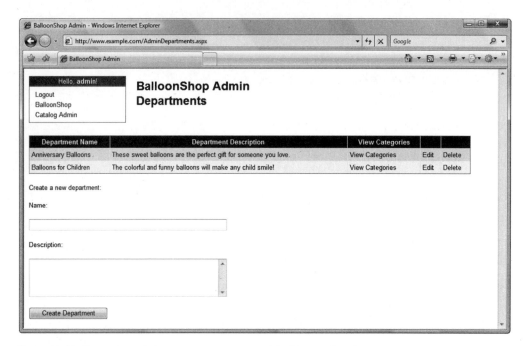

Figure 11-19. *Executing AdminDepartments.aspx with skins and styles*

22. Now that everything looks good, you can implement the functionality by writing the event handlers for the Edit, View Categories, and Delete buttons. You'll start with the row editing functionality. Open AdminDepartments.aspx in Design View and select the GridView control.

23. In the **Properties window**, double-click the **RowEditing** entry (as shown in Figure 11-20). Visual Web Developer generates the grid_RowEditing event handler for you in the code-behind file, This method is executed when the visitor clicks the Edit button in the grid, and it must enable edit mode for that row. Modify the code in grid_RowEditing like this:

```
// enter edit mode
protected void grid_RowEditing(object sender, GridViewEditEventArgs e)
{
  // Set the row for which to enable edit mode
  grid.EditIndex = e.NewEditIndex;
  // Set status message
  statusLabel.Text = "Editing row # " + e.NewEditIndex.ToString();
  // Reload the grid
  BindGrid();
}
```

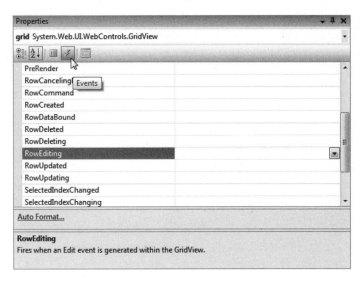

Figure 11-20. *Using Visual Web Developer to generate new event handlers*

24. While in edit mode, instead of placing the Edit button, the `GridView` places two buttons: Update and Cancel. To make editing functional, you need to supply code that reacts when these buttons are clicked. Let's start with the code that deals with the Cancel button. Follow the same procedure to generate `grid_RowCancelingEdit` and complete its code like this:

```
// Cancel edit mode
protected void grid_RowCancelingEdit(object sender,
GridViewCancelEditEventArgs e)
{
  // Cancel edit mode
  grid.EditIndex = -1;
  // Set status message
  statusLabel.Text = "Editing canceled";
  // Reload the grid
  BindGrid();
}
```

Now you have functional Edit and Cancel buttons. When the Edit button is clicked, the grid enters into edit mode, as shown in Figure 11-21.

Editing row # 0

Department Name	Department Description	View Categories		
Anniversary Balloons	These sweet balloons are	View Categories	Update Cancel	Delete
Balloons for Children	The colorful and funny balloons will make any child smile!	View Categories	Edit	Delete

Figure 11-21. *Editing department information*

■**Note** The problem with automatically generated editing controls is that they aren't configurable, unless transformed to **template columns**. You'll do this later in a separate exercise for the department description column, where the edit text box needs to be larger than the default size.

---

25. When the Update button is clicked, a `RowUpdating` event is raised. Generate its event handler like you did for the other two. Now add the following code for these two events:

```
// Update row
protected void grid_RowUpdating(object sender, GridViewUpdateEventArgs e)
{
  // Retrieve updated data
  string id = grid.DataKeys[e.RowIndex].Value.ToString();
  string name = ((TextBox)grid.Rows[e.RowIndex].Cells[0].Controls[0]).Text;
  string description = ((TextBox)grid.Rows[e.RowIndex].Cells[1].Controls➥
[0]).Text;
  // Execute the update command
  bool success = CatalogAccess.UpdateDepartment(id, name, description);
  // Cancel edit mode
  grid.EditIndex = -1;
  // Display status message
  statusLabel.Text = success ? "Update successful" : "Update failed";
  // Reload the grid
  BindGrid();
}
```

26. Finally, here's the code for the `DeleteCommand` event handler. Let Visual Web Developer generate its signature for you, and then add the following code:

```
// Delete a record
protected void grid_RowDeleting(object sender, GridViewDeleteEventArgs e)
{
  // Get the ID of the record to be deleted
  string id = grid.DataKeys[e.RowIndex].Value.ToString();
  // Execute the delete command
  bool success = CatalogAccess.DeleteDepartment(id);
  // Cancel edit mode
  grid.EditIndex = -1;
  // Display status message
  statusLabel.Text = success ? "Delete successful" : "Delete failed";
  // Reload the grid
  BindGrid();
}
```

27. The last bit of code to write in this exercise consists of adding the `addDepartmentButton_Click` event handler method. Generate its signature by double-clicking the **Add** button in the Design View window and complete the code like this:

```
  // Create a new department
  protected void createDepartment_Click(object sender, EventArgs e)
  {
    // Execute the insert command
    bool success = CatalogAccess.AddDepartment(newName.Text, newDescription➥
  .Text);
    // Display status message
    statusLabel.Text = success ? "Insert successful" : "Insert failed";
    // Reload the grid
    BindGrid();
  }
```

Tip The presentation tier should do input validation when possible—for example, you can check whether the department name and description are valid before trying to add them to the database. In the next chapter, you'll learn how to implement validation using the .NET validator controls.

How It Works: AdminDepartments.aspx

Be sure to test that the new features are functional. Try to add a new department, rename it, and then delete it.

This is the first exercise in which you worked with a GridView control, and it's important to understand how this complex control works. The GridView control is smart enough to be aware of the columns it reads from the data source and display them to the user. Moreover, as you saw when writing the code, you just tell the grid what row you want to enter edit mode, and it automatically transforms the labels into text boxes.

The GridView control supports a number of built-in column types: BoundField, CheckBoxField, HyperLinkField, ButtonField, CommandField, ImageField, and TemplateField. The last one, TemplateField, really lets you write your own HTML code for that column, whereas the others have predefined behavior. In this example, you met some of these column types, but you'll get to work with all of them by the end of this chapter!

BoundField is the most usual field type, simply reading the value from the database and displaying it in the grid. Each column type has a number of options you can set that affect its behavior. The most common options are shown in the Add New Column dialog box that you used to add your fields, but you can access more of their properties by clicking the GridView's Smart Link and choosing the Edit Columns entry.

To change the default look of the GridView, you have three main options: you can use the Auto Format feature of the grid (accessible by clicking the Smart Link), you can transform the columns into template columns and edit their format manually, or you can use skins. For this case, we chose to create a default skin for the GridView, because it offers the maximum efficiency with the least effort. Default skins apply to all controls of that kind in a web site, so your work will also be much easier when creating other grids later in this book. If you want to have more skins for a certain type of control, you need to create named skins by adding a SkinID property to their definition. However, here we preferred to build a default skin to format all the grids in BalloonShop in an identical way.

The simplest way to create a skin is to create a control instance using the designer, rip the unnecessary details, and copy what remains to the .skin file. For BalloonShop, we used styles from the CSS file in the skin, in an effort to keep all the site's colors in one place.

Your new C# code deals with the GridView control. For example, to enter a row into edit mode, you just need to set the GridView's EditItemIndex property to the index of the column you want to change in the EditCommand event handler method:

```
// Enter row into edit mode
protected void grid_RowEditing(object sender, GridViewEditEventArgs e)
{
  // Set the row for which to enable edit mode
  grid.EditIndex = e.NewEditIndex;
  // Set status message
  statusLabel.Text = "Editing row # " + e.NewEditIndex.ToString();
  // Reload the grid
  BindGrid();
}
```

The RowEditing event handler receives a GridViewEditEventArgs object named e, which contains, among other details, the index of the row on which the Edit button was clicked (e.NewItemIndex). You use this value to inform the GridView to enter into edit mode for that row. You take similar action in the CancelCommand event handler, where you cancel edit mode by setting the GridView's EditIndex to -1. The way these two event handlers work is fairly standard.

The methods that modify data (the event handlers for the Update and Delete buttons) need to read information from the data grid and the ID of the item on which the action happens. Because delete and update operations are based on departments' IDs, you need to obtain somehow the ID of the department to be updated or deleted. The problem is that you can't extract DepartmentID from the visible part of the GridView, because we chose not to display it for the user (it's a low-level detail, useless for the user).

So, how do you know the ID associated with a GridView row? Fortunately, the designers of the GridView control anticipated this problem and added a DataKeyNames property to the GridView, which can hold one or more keys for each row in the grid. When creating the grid, you set its DataKeyNames property to DepartmentID, causing the grid to retain the ID of each loaded department.

The code in grid_RowUpdating demonstrates how to get the ID of the row that is about to be updated:

```
// Update row
protected void grid_RowUpdating(object sender, GridViewUpdateEventArgs e)
{
  // Retrieve updated data
  string id = grid.DataKeys[e.RowIndex].Value.ToString();
```

The rest of the code shows how to retrieve data from the rows of the GridView. Each row in the grid is a collection of cells, and each cell is a collection of controls. Given that you know which control you are looking for, it becomes a fairly easy job to get the name or description of a department. You read the first cell of the row to obtain the name and the second cell to obtain the description. In both cases, you read the first control, which you cast to a TextBox to be able to read the Text property.

```
    // Retrieve updated data
    string id = grid.DataKeys[e.RowIndex].Value.ToString();
    string name = ((TextBox)grid.Rows[e.RowIndex].Cells[0].Controls[0]).Text;
    string description = ((TextBox)grid.Rows[e.RowIndex].Cells[1].
Controls[0]).Text;
```

To make this functionality even clearer, take a look at the following code block, which performs the same operation, but in a step-by-step fashion:

```
protected void grid_RowUpdating(object sender, GridViewUpdateEventArgs e)
{
    // Get the index of the row to be modified
    int rowIndex = e.RowIndex;
    // Get a reference to the row being updated
    GridViewRow gridViewRow = grid.Rows[rowIndex];
    // Get the first cell (one which contains the name)
    TableCell tableCell = gridViewRow.Cells[0];
    // Get the first control in the cell
    Control control = tableCell.Controls[0];
    // Access the control through a TextBox reference
    TextBox textBox = (TextBox)control;
    // Get the text from the TextBox
    string name = textBox.Text;
```

After the ID, new name, and new description of the department are known, the business tier is called to apply the changes. The CatalogAccess.UpdateDepartment method returns a Boolean value specifying whether the update was performed successfully, and then the status label is populated based on this value:

```
    // Execute the update command
    bool success = CatalogAccess.UpdateDepartment(id, name, description);
    // Cancel edit mode
    grid.EditIndex = -1;
    // Display status message
    statusLabel.Text = success ? "Update successful" : "Update failed";
    // Reload the grid
    BindGrid();
}
```

Styling the Department Administration Grid

In spite of the length of the exercise that you've just completed, you must admit that it was so easy to implement the editable GridView! You added columns to the GridView using Visual Web Developer's interface and set its layout and colors using a skin. Right now, the code of your grid in AdminDepartments.aspx looks like this:

```
<asp:GridView ID="grid" runat="server" DataKeyNames="DepartmentID" Width="100%"
    AutoGenerateColumns="False" onrowcancelingedit="grid_RowCancelingEdit"
    onrowdeleting="grid_RowDeleting" onrowediting="grid_RowEditing"
    onrowupdating="grid_RowUpdating">
    <Columns>
        <asp:BoundField DataField="Name" HeaderText="Department Name"
            SortExpression="Name" />
        <asp:BoundField DataField="Description" HeaderText="Department Description"
            SortExpression="Description" />
        <asp:HyperLinkField DataNavigateUrlFields="DepartmentID"
            DataNavigateUrlFormatString="AdminCategories.aspx?DepartmentID={0}"
            HeaderText="View Categories" Text="View Categories" />
        <asp:CommandField ShowEditButton="True" />
        <asp:ButtonField CommandName="Delete" Text="Delete" />
    </Columns>
</asp:GridView>
```

The interesting aspect is that you can't see any Label or TextBox controls, even though the GridView generates them when showing its data and when entering edit mode. The BoundField, HyperLinkField, CommandField, and ButtonField columns take care of rendering themselves without your intervention.

The problem with these automated controls is that you don't have much flexibility with how they show their data. Although you can use a number of techniques to format your GridView's styles, colors, or fonts (such as by using a skin), the only way to have complete access to the HTML code your grid generates for a certain column is to transform that column to a **template column**, instead of using predefined column types such as BoundField, HyperLinkField, and so on.

When using template columns, you need to manually supply the code for its templates. You'll do that in the following exercise, where you'll enlarge the description editing TextBox control.

Note When transforming an existing field to a template field, its different display templates (such as the editing template, EditItemTemplate, or the normal display template, ItemTemplate) are automatically generated for you so you won't lose any functionality.

Exercise: Implementing a Template Column

1. Open AdminDepartments.aspx in Design View, click the GridView's **Smart Link** and choose **Edit Columns**. Select the **Department Description** field and click **Convert this field into a TemplateField**.

2. You'll notice the panel on the right becomes empty, because now the GridView no longer takes care of your column's properties. Click **OK**.

3. Switch to Source View to see the generated code. The changes aren't so drastic, but now instead of a single line defining a `BoundField` entry, you can find a `TemplateField` entry containing the complete code for the `EditItemTemplate` and `ItemTemplate` templates. (Note that Visual Web Developer smartly generated bound `TextBox` and `Label` controls in the two templates, so if you now execute your project, you won't lose any functionality.)

```
<asp:TemplateField HeaderText="Department Description"
  SortExpression="Description">
  <EditItemTemplate>
    <asp:TextBox ID="TextBox1" runat="server" Text='<%# Bind("Description➡
") %>'></asp:TextBox>
  </EditItemTemplate>
  <ItemTemplate>
    <asp:Label ID="Label1" runat="server" Text='<%# Bind("Description") ➡
%>'></asp:Label>
  </ItemTemplate>
</asp:TemplateField>
```

4. While in Source View, change the name of the editing `TextBox`. Because you'll need its name to access its value from the code (when updating the departments' details), it's important to have a good name for it. Change the control's name from `TextBox1` to **descriptionTextBox**:

```
<asp:TextBox ID="descriptionTextBox" runat="server"
           Text='<%# Bind("Description") %>'></asp:TextBox>
```

5. After converting the description column to a `TemplateField`, you can edit its templates both in Source View and Design View. Switch to Design View, click the `GridView`'s **Smart Link**, and choose **Edit Templates**. Now, again using the **Smart Link**, you can choose which template to edit (see Figure 11-22).

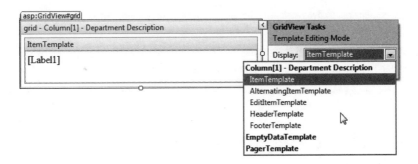

Figure 11-22. *Choosing a template to edit*

6. To modify the text box that appears when editing a department, choose **EditItemTemplate** from the list. Then select the `TextBox` control and modify it to suit your preferences by using the Properties window (see Figure 11-23). For this exercise, set its `TextMode` property to **MultiLine**, its `Width` to **400px**, and its `Height` to **70px**.

Figure 11-23. *Modifying the description editing text box*

7. The last step is to change the code-behind file for updating department data. Locate this line in the `grid_RowUpdating` method in `AdminDepartments.aspx.cs`:

```
string description = ((TextBox)grid.Rows[e.RowIndex].Cells[1].➥
Controls[0]).Text;
```

8. Change this line to

```
string description = ((TextBox)grid.Rows[e.RowIndex].FindControl("➥
descriptionTextBox")).Text;
```

How It Works: Using Template Columns in the GridView Control

Execute the project and test the updated functionality to make sure that it still works. Template columns are useful because they give you full control over how the column looks and behaves. In this exercise, you modified the `TextBox` control used for editing the department description, but now you can use the same technique to change any field in the table.

Because you can also change the names of the controls inside your template, you can now access them by name, instead of by location:

```
string description = ((TextBox)grid.Rows[e.RowIndex].FindControl("➥
descriptionTextBox")).Text;
```

This piece of code demonstrates how to obtain a reference of the `TextBox` control named `descriptionTextBox`, convert its `Control` reference to a `TextBox` reference, and extract its contents from there.

You'll see some other examples of template columns later in this chapter when you'll use `CheckBox` controls instead of `Label` and `TextBox` controls for displaying the value of `True/False` fields.

Administering Categories

The category administration bits are similar to what you did for departments, so we won't need to explain much this time. The main player in the whole categories administration part is the `AdminCategories.aspx` Web Form, but first you need to write the data tier and business tier code that will support its functionality.

Exercise: Administering Categories

1. First you'll create the stored procedures that you need to add to your BalloonShop database: `CatalogCreateCategory`, `CatalogUpdateCategory`, and `CatalogDeleteCategory`. The fourth stored procedure that you'll use, `CatalogGetCategories`, already exists in the database. Add these stored procedures to the BalloonShop database. These stored procedures will be covered in the following sections.

   `CatalogCreateCategory` adds a new category to the database. Apart from the name and description of the new category, you also need a `DepartmentID`, which specifies the department the category belongs to. Note that you don't need to specify a `CategoryID` (in fact, you can't) because `CategoryID` is an `IDENTITY` column in the `Category` table, and its value is automatically generated by the database when inserting a new record.

```
CREATE PROCEDURE CatalogCreateCategory
(@DepartmentID int,
@CategoryName nvarchar(50),
@CategoryDescription nvarchar(50))
AS
INSERT INTO Category (DepartmentID, Name, Description)
VALUES (@DepartmentID, @CategoryName, @CategoryDescription)
```

2. The `UpdateCategory` stored procedure updates the name and description of a category.

```
CREATE PROCEDURE CatalogUpdateCategory
(@CategoryID int,
@CategoryName nvarchar(50),
@CategoryDescription nvarchar(1000))
AS
UPDATE Category
SET Name = @CategoryName, Description = @CategoryDescription
WHERE CategoryID = @CategoryID
```

3. `CatalogDeleteCategory` deletes a certain category from the database. If the category has products that belong to it, the database raises an error because the deletion affects the database integrity—remember that you implemented the One-to-Many relationship between the `Category` and `Product` tables using a foreign-key relationship back in Chapter 5. In this case, the error is trapped in the business tier, which returns an error code to the presentation tier, which informs the user that an error has occurred.

```
CREATE PROCEDURE CatalogDeleteCategory
(@CategoryID int)
AS
DELETE FROM Category
WHERE CategoryID = @CategoryID
```

4. Now you'll write the methods of the CatalogAccess class that support the functionality required by the AdminCategories Web Form. These methods use the stored procedures mentioned earlier to perform their functionality: CatalogGetCategories, CatalogCreateCategory, CatalogUpdateCategory, and CatalogDeleteCategory. Add these methods to your CatalogAccess class in CatalogAccess.cs:

```
// Create a new Category
public static bool CreateCategory(string departmentId,
 string name, string description)
{
  // get a configured DbCommand object
  DbCommand comm = GenericDataAccess.CreateCommand();
  // set the stored procedure name
  comm.CommandText = "CatalogCreateCategory";
  // create a new parameter
  DbParameter param = comm.CreateParameter();
  param.ParameterName = "@DepartmentID";
  param.Value = departmentId;
  param.DbType = DbType.Int32;
  comm.Parameters.Add(param);
  // create a new parameter
  param = comm.CreateParameter();
  param.ParameterName = "@CategoryName";
  param.Value = name;
  param.DbType = DbType.String;
  param.Size = 50;
  comm.Parameters.Add(param);
  // create a new parameter
  param = comm.CreateParameter();
  param.ParameterName = "@CategoryDescription";
  param.Value = description;
  param.DbType = DbType.String;
  param.Size = 1000;
  comm.Parameters.Add(param);
  // result will represent the number of changed rows
  int result = -1;
  try
  {
    // execute the stored procedure
    result = GenericDataAccess.ExecuteNonQuery(comm);
  }
  catch
  {
    // any errors are logged in GenericDataAccess, we ignore them here
  }
```

```
  // result will be 1 in case of success
  return (result != -1);
}


// Update category details
public static bool UpdateCategory(string id, string name, string description)
{
  // get a configured DbCommand object
  DbCommand comm = GenericDataAccess.CreateCommand();
  // set the stored procedure name
  comm.CommandText = "CatalogUpdateCategory";
  // create a new parameter
  DbParameter param = comm.CreateParameter();
  param.ParameterName = "@CategoryId";
  param.Value = id;
  param.DbType = DbType.Int32;
  comm.Parameters.Add(param);
  // create a new parameter
  param = comm.CreateParameter();
  param.ParameterName = "@CategoryName";
  param.Value = name;
  param.DbType = DbType.String;
  param.Size = 50;
  comm.Parameters.Add(param);
  // create a new parameter
  param = comm.CreateParameter();
  param.ParameterName = "@CategoryDescription";
  param.Value = description;
  param.DbType = DbType.String;
  param.Size = 1000;
  comm.Parameters.Add(param);
  // result will represent the number of changed rows
  int result = -1;
  try
  {
    // execute the stored procedure
    result = GenericDataAccess.ExecuteNonQuery(comm);
  }
```

```
    catch
    {
      // any errors are logged in GenericDataAccess, we ignore them here
    }
    // result will be 1 in case of success
    return (result != -1);
  }


  // Delete Category
  public static bool DeleteCategory(string id)
  {
    // get a configured DbCommand object
    DbCommand comm = GenericDataAccess.CreateCommand();
    // set the stored procedure name
    comm.CommandText = "CatalogDeleteCategory";
    // create a new parameter
    DbParameter param = comm.CreateParameter();
    param.ParameterName = "@CategoryId";
    param.Value = id;
    param.DbType = DbType.Int32;
    comm.Parameters.Add(param);
    // execute the stored procedure; an error will be thrown by the
    // database if the Category has related categories, in which case
    // it is not deleted
    int result = -1;
    try
    {
      result = GenericDataAccess.ExecuteNonQuery(comm);
    }
    catch
    {
      // any errors are logged in GenericDataAccess, we ignore them here
    }
    // result will be 1 in case of success
    return (result != -1);
  }
```

5. Finally, you'll create the AdminCategories Web Form. This exercise is very similar to the one in which you created the AdminDepartments Web Form. The exercise mainly consists of preparing the GridView and the other constituent controls and then implementing the code-behind functionality. Because you already have a GridView skin, you won't need to bother with that detail again here.

Exercise: Implementing AdminCategories.aspx

1. Create a new Web Form named `AdminCategories.aspx` in the root folder of your project (make sure the **Place code in separate file** option is checked), based on the `Admin.master` template.

2. In the first placeholder, type the name of the page:

```
<asp:Content ID="Content1" ContentPlaceHolderID="titlePlaceHolder"
runat="Server">
  <span class="AdminTitle">
    BalloonShop Admin
    <br />
    Categories in
    <asp:HyperLink ID="deptLink" runat="server" />
  </span>
</asp:Content>
```

3. In the second placeholder, start by adding the status label and data grid controls:

```
<asp:Content ID="Content2" ContentPlaceHolderID="adminPlaceHolder"
Runat="Server">
  <p>
    <asp:Label ID="statusLabel" runat="server" Text=""></asp:Label>
  </p>
  <asp:GridView ID="grid" runat="server" DataKeyNames="CategoryID" Auto
GenerateColumns="false" Width="100%">
  </asp:GridView>
</asp:Content>
```

4. Continue by adding, also to the second placeholder, the controls for adding a new category manually:

```
  <p>Create a new category:</p>
  <p>Name:</p>
  <asp:TextBox ID="newName" runat="server" Width="400px" />
  <p>Description:</p>
  <asp:TextBox ID="newDescription" runat="server" Width="400px" Height=
"70px" TextMode="MultiLine" />
  <p><asp:Button ID="createCategory" Text="Create Category" runat
="server" /></p>
```

At this point, your control should look like Figure 11-24.

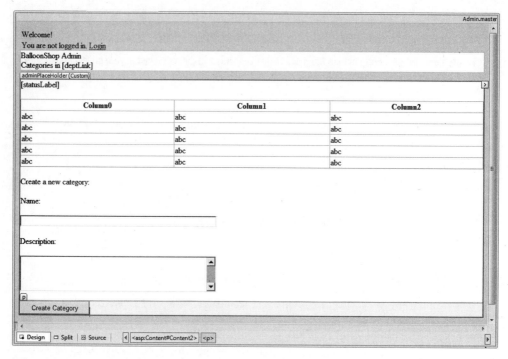

Figure 11-24. *AdminCategories.aspx in Design View*

5. Click the GridView's **Smart Link** and use its **Add New Column** command to add fields with the properties shown in Table 11-3 (leave the other properties to their defaults).

Table 11-3. *Setting the GridView's Field Properties*

Column Type	Header Text	Data Field	Other Properties
BoundField	Category Name	Name	
BoundField	Category Description	Description	
TemplateField			
CommandField			Select the **Edit/Update** and **Show cancel button** check boxes.
ButtonField			Set **Command Name** to **Delete** and set **Text** to **Delete**.

6. The template field from the list is the View Products link, which you're creating as a TemplateField because the HyperLinkField isn't flexible enough to generate the kind of link you need to create. Switch to Source View and modify the code of the template field like this:

```
<asp:TemplateField>
```

```
<ItemTemplate>
    <asp:HyperLink runat="server" ID="link" NavigateUrl='<%# "Admin➥
Products.aspx?DepartmentID=" + Request.QueryString["DepartmentID"] + ➥
"&amp;CategoryID=" + Eval("CategoryID")%>' Text="View Products">
    </asp:HyperLink>
  </ItemTemplate>
</asp:TemplateField>
```

7. Transform the `Category Description` field into a template column, just like you did for the description column in `AdminDepartments`. Then edit the column's **EditItemTemplate** like this:

```
<asp:TemplateField HeaderText="Category Description"
SortExpression="Description">
  <ItemTemplate>
    <asp:Label ID="Label1" runat="server" Text='<%# Bind("Description") %>'>
    </asp:Label>
  </ItemTemplate>
  <EditItemTemplate>
    <asp:TextBox ID="descriptionTextBox" runat="server" TextMode="MultiLine"
Text='<%# Bind("Description") %>' Height="70px" Width="400px" />
  </EditItemTemplate>
</asp:TemplateField>
```

Switch to Design View and verify that your control looks like Figure 11-25.

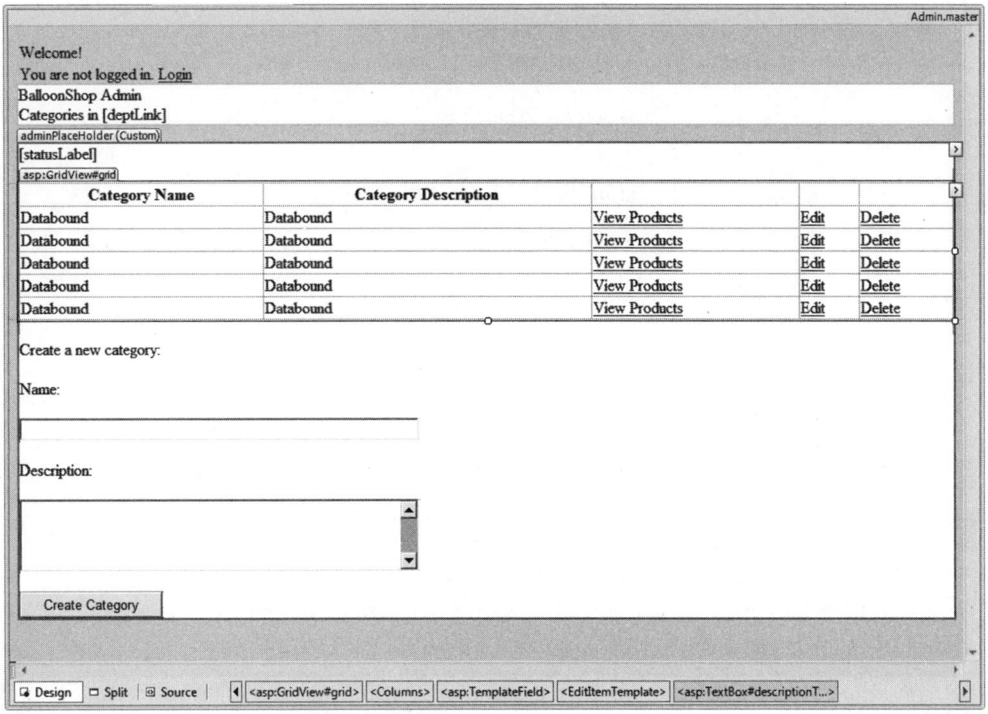

Figure 11-25. *AdminCategories.aspx in Design View*

8. Now you need to deal with the code-behind file. Use the techniques you already know to have Visual Web Developer generate the method signatures for you, and write the following code to AdminCategories. aspx.cs:

```
protected void Page_Load(object sender, EventArgs e)
{
  // Load the grid only the first time the page is loaded
  if (!Page.IsPostBack)
  {
    // Load the categories grid
    BindGrid();
    // Get DepartmentID from the query string
    string departmentId = Request.QueryString["DepartmentID"];
    // Obtain the department's name
    DepartmentDetails dd = CatalogAccess.GetDepartmentDetails(departmentId);
    string departmentName = dd.Name + "</b>";
    // Link to department
    deptLink.Text = departmentName;
    deptLink.NavigateUrl = "AdminDepartments.aspx";
  }
}


// Populate the GridView with data
private void BindGrid()
{
  // Get DepartmentID from the query string
  string departmentId = Request.QueryString["DepartmentID"];
  // Get a DataTable object containing the categories
  grid.DataSource = CatalogAccess.GetCategoriesInDepartment(departmentId);
  // Bind the data grid to the data source
  grid.DataBind();
}


// Enter row into edit mode
protected void grid_RowEditing(object sender, GridViewEditEventArgs e)
{
  // Set the row for which to enable edit mode
  grid.EditIndex = e.NewEditIndex;
  // Set status message
  statusLabel.Text = "Editing row # " + e.NewEditIndex.ToString();
  // Reload the grid
  BindGrid();
}
```

```csharp
// Cancel edit mode
protected void grid_RowCancelingEdit(object sender,
GridViewCancelEditEventArgs e)
{
  // Cancel edit mode
  grid.EditIndex = -1;
  // Set status message
  statusLabel.Text = "Editing canceled";
  // Reload the grid
  BindGrid();
}

// Update row
protected void grid_RowUpdating(object sender, GridViewUpdateEventArgs e)
{
  // Retrieve updated data
  string id = grid.DataKeys[e.RowIndex].Value.ToString();
  string name = ((TextBox)grid.Rows[e.RowIndex].Cells[0].Controls[0]).Text;
  string description = ((TextBox)grid.Rows[e.RowIndex].FindControl➥
("descriptionTextBox")).Text;
  // Execute the update command
  bool success = CatalogAccess.UpdateCategory(id, name, description);
  // Cancel edit mode
  grid.EditIndex = -1;
  // Display status message
  statusLabel.Text = success ? "Update successful" : "Update failed";
  // Reload the grid
  BindGrid();
}

// Delete a record
protected void grid_RowDeleting(object sender, GridViewDeleteEventArgs e)
{
  // Get the ID of the record to be deleted
  string id = grid.DataKeys[e.RowIndex].Value.ToString();
  // Execute the delete command
  bool success = CatalogAccess.DeleteCategory(id);
  // Cancel edit mode
  grid.EditIndex = -1;
  // Display status message
  statusLabel.Text = success ? "Delete successful" : "Delete failed";
  // Reload the grid
  BindGrid();
}
```

```
// Create a new category
protected void createCategory_Click(object sender, EventArgs e)
{
  // Get DepartmentID from the query string
  string departmentId = Request.QueryString["DepartmentID"];
  // Execute the insert command
  bool success = CatalogAccess.CreateCategory(departmentId, ➥
newName.Text, newDescription.Text);
  // Display results
  statusLabel.Text = success ? "Insert successful" : "Insert failed";
  // Reload the grid
  BindGrid();
}
```

How It Works: AdminCategories.aspx

Because this exercise was so similar to the exercise for administering departments, we won't go into many details here.

When creating the grid, the main difference was creating the View Products column as a `TemplateField` rather than as a `HyperLinkField`. This is because a more complex link had to be created, which needed to include both the `CategoryID` (from the data source) and the `DepartmentID` (from the query string).

```
<asp:HyperLink runat="server" ID="link" NavigateUrl='<%# "AdminProducts.➥
aspx?DepartmentID=" + Request.QueryString["DepartmentID"] + "&amp;➥
CategoryID=" + Eval("CategoryID")%>' Text="View Products">
</asp:HyperLink>
```

Note that we used the `Eval` function here, although the code automatically generated by Visual Web Developer uses `Bind`. As far as your code is concerned, these functions have similar functionality, but in other circumstances, `Bind` can be used to implement two-way data binding (we don't use this feature in this book).

As far as the code in the code-behind file is concerned, compared to the code for administering departments, sometimes you need to read the `DepartmentID` parameter from the query string, which represents the ID of the department for which you're editing the categories.

Summary

You've done a lot of coding in this chapter. You implemented one Master Page and two Web Forms based on it—AdminDepartments and AdminCategories—along with their middle-tier methods and stored procedures. You learned how to implement a simple authentication scheme so only administrators are allowed to access the catalog administration page.

You made contact with the GridView, which is probably the most powerful web control that comes packaged with the .NET Framework. You learned how to use the GridView's built-in features for editing, selecting, updating, and deleting records. You also learned how to use template columns to improve its functionality.

In the next chapter, we'll implement the remaining administrative features: the management of products.

CHAPTER 12

■ ■ ■

Catalog Administration: Products

Your administrators are now able to edit the departments and categories of your e-commerce web site. In this chapter, we add the missing features relating to managing products. More specifically, we will implement features in this chapter that will allow the site administrator to accomplish the following:

- Viewing the list of products in a specific category

- Editing product details, such as the product's name, description, price, or whether or not it is on promotion

- Assigning an existing product to an additional category (a product can belong to multiple categories) or moving it to another category

- Removing a product from a category

- Deleting a product from a catalog

- Allowing administrators to access the department, category, or product administration pages right from the catalog

There's quite a bit to go through, but not much more than what you've had to endure in the previous chapter. Feel free to look ahead at the figures to see the visual appearance of the new features. Let's start!

Chapter Roadmap

You're now ready for the next major part of the catalog administration page: the place where you edit the products that belong to the selected category. This one has a few more controls than the others, as shown in Figure 12-1.

When editing a product, the page will look similar to Figure 12-2.

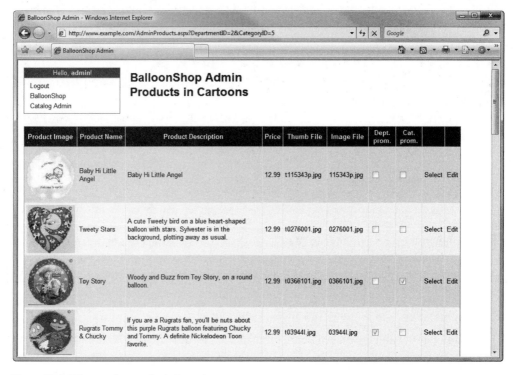

Figure 12-1. *The products administration page*

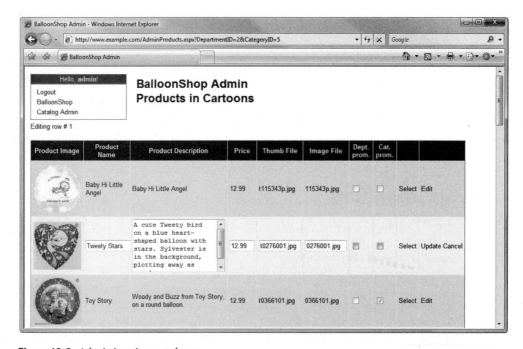

Figure 12-2. *Administering products*

Finally, the last page allows you to do additional product details management, such as changing the product's category, removing a product from a category or from the catalog, and so on (see Figure 12-3).

Figure 12-3. *Administering product details*

The interface is a bit more complex, but the theory isn't much more complicated than what you're already used to. You just need to display the products that belong to a selected category and allow the user to add new products to that category. The product-deleting feature is offered via a separate page, so you won't see a Delete link here.

Administering Products

You'll create the products administration interface in the next exercise. You'll start by creating the stored procedures that support the user interface functionality: CatalogGetAllProductsIncategory, CatalogCreateProduct, and CatalogUpdateProduct. Next you'll create the business tier methods that work with these procedures, and finally you'll implement AdminProducts.aspx, the Web Form that implements the features described in Figures 12-1 and 12-2.

Exercise: Administering Products

1. Start by creating the `CatalogGetAllProductsInCategory` stored procedure, which is your admin stored procedure that returns the list of products in a category and is a simplified version of `CatalogGetProductsInCategory`, which you created in Chapter 5. Add the stored procedure to your BalloonShop database:

```
CREATE PROCEDURE CatalogGetAllProductsInCategory
(@CategoryID INT)
AS
SELECT Product.ProductID, Name, Description, Price, Thumbnail,
       Image, PromoDept, PromoFront
FROM Product INNER JOIN ProductCategory
  ON Product.ProductID = ProductCategory.ProductID
WHERE ProductCategory.CategoryID = @CategoryID
```

2. The `CatalogCreateProduct` stored procedure is called to create a new product and assign it to a category. After adding the new product's record to the `Product` table, you read the `@@Identity` value to find out the generated ID, and then you assign this ID to the mentioned category. Add this stored procedure to your BalloonShop database:

```
CREATE PROCEDURE CatalogCreateProduct
(@CategoryID INT,
 @ProductName NVARCHAR(50),
 @ProductDescription NVARCHAR(MAX),
 @Price MONEY,
 @Thumbnail NVARCHAR(50),
 @Image NVARCHAR(50),
 @PromoFront BIT,
 @PromoDept BIT)
AS
-- Declare a variable to hold the generated product ID
DECLARE @ProductID int
-- Create the new product entry

INSERT INTO Product
    (Name,
     Description,
     Price,
     Thumbnail,
     Image,
     PromoFront,
     PromoDept)
VALUES
    (@ProductName,
     @ProductDescription,
     @Price,
```

```
    @Thumbnail,
    @Image,
    @PromoFront,
    @PromoDept)
-- Save the generated product ID to a variable
SELECT @ProductID = @@Identity
-- Associate the product with a category
INSERT INTO ProductCategory (ProductID, CategoryID)
VALUES (@ProductID, @CategoryID)
```

Note This line of code is of particular importance:

```
SELECT @ProductID = @@Identity
```

Identity columns are automatically generated by the database. If you've ever wondered how to determine which value has been generated for an identity column, here's the answer: the @@Identity system value. This needs to be saved into a variable immediately after the INSERT command because its value is reset after other SQL statements execute. After you determine which ID was generated for the new product, you can assign it to the category you received as a parameter:

```
INSERT INTO ProductCategory (ProductID, CategoryID)
VALUES (@ProductID, @CategoryID)
```

---

3. The CatalogUpdateProduct stored procedure updates the information of a product:

```
CREATE PROCEDURE CatalogUpdateProduct
(@ProductID INT,
 @ProductName VARCHAR(50),
 @ProductDescription VARCHAR(MAX),
 @Price MONEY,
 @Thumbnail VARCHAR(50),
 @Image VARCHAR(50),
 @PromoFront BIT,
 @PromoDept BIT)
AS
UPDATE Product
SET Name = @ProductName,
    Description = @ProductDescription,
    Price = @Price,
    Thumbnail = @Thumbnail,
    Image = @Image,
    PromoFront = @PromoFront,
    PromoDept = @PromoDept
WHERE ProductID = @ProductID
```

4. Let's now write the methods that work with your new stored procedures: GetAllProductsInCategory, CreateProduct, and UpdateProduct. What is important to note is the error-handling strategies implemented in these methods. In the Get... methods, all errors are important enough to be signaled to the user with an "oops" message, so we don't catch them in the business tier. Here, errors with update- and create-type methods are more likely due to bad input data, so we prefer to signal with a "friendlier" error message. In these cases, we catch any potential exceptions to prevent them from propagating, and we return the success value as a bool value. The presentation tier decides what to tell the visitor depending on this value.

Add the following code to your CatalogAccess class:

```
// retrieve the list of products in a category
public static DataTable GetAllProductsInCategory(string categoryId)
{
  // get a configured DbCommand object
  DbCommand comm = GenericDataAccess.CreateCommand();
  // set the stored procedure name
  comm.CommandText = "CatalogGetAllProductsInCategory";
  // create a new parameter
  DbParameter param = comm.CreateParameter();
  param.ParameterName = "@CategoryID";
  param.Value = categoryId;
  param.DbType = DbType.Int32;
  comm.Parameters.Add(param);
  // execute the stored procedure and save the results in a DataTable
  DataTable table = GenericDataAccess.ExecuteSelectCommand(comm);
  return table;
}

// Create a new product
public static bool CreateProduct(string categoryId, string name,➡
string description, string price, string Thumbnail, string ➡
Image, string PromoDept, string PromoFront)
{
  // get a configured DbCommand object
  DbCommand comm = GenericDataAccess.CreateCommand();
  // set the stored procedure name
  comm.CommandText = "CatalogCreateProduct";
  // create a new parameter
  DbParameter param = comm.CreateParameter();
  param.ParameterName = "@CategoryID";
  param.Value = categoryId;
  param.DbType = DbType.Int32;
  comm.Parameters.Add(param);
```

```
// create a new parameter
param = comm.CreateParameter();
param.ParameterName = "@ProductName";
param.Value = name;
param.DbType = DbType.String;
param.Size = 50;
comm.Parameters.Add(param);
// create a new parameter
param = comm.CreateParameter();
param.ParameterName = "@ProductDescription";
param.Value = description;
param.DbType = DbType.String;
comm.Parameters.Add(param);
// create a new parameter
param = comm.CreateParameter();
param.ParameterName = "@Price";
param.Value = price;
param.DbType = DbType.Decimal;
comm.Parameters.Add(param);
// create a new parameter
param = comm.CreateParameter();
param.ParameterName = "@Thumbnail";
param.Value = Thumbnail;
param.DbType = DbType.String;
comm.Parameters.Add(param);
// create a new parameter
param = comm.CreateParameter();
param.ParameterName = "@Image";
param.Value = Image;
param.DbType = DbType.String;
comm.Parameters.Add(param);
// create a new parameter
param = comm.CreateParameter();
param.ParameterName = "@PromoDept";
param.Value = PromoDept;
param.DbType = DbType.Boolean;
comm.Parameters.Add(param);
// create a new parameter
param = comm.CreateParameter();
param.ParameterName = "@PromoFront";
param.Value = PromoFront;
param.DbType = DbType.Boolean;
comm.Parameters.Add(param);
```

```csharp
  // result will represent the number of changed rows
  int result = -1;
  try
  {
    // execute the stored procedure
    result = GenericDataAccess.ExecuteNonQuery(comm);
  }
  catch
  {
    // any errors are logged in GenericDataAccess, we ignore them here
  }
  // result will be 1 in case of success
  return (result >= 1);
}

// Update an existing product
public static bool UpdateProduct(string productId, string name, string ➥
description, string price, string Thumbnail, string Image, string ➥
PromoDept, string PromoFront)
{
  // get a configured DbCommand object
  DbCommand comm = GenericDataAccess.CreateCommand();
  // set the stored procedure name
  comm.CommandText = "CatalogUpdateProduct";
  // create a new parameter
  DbParameter param = comm.CreateParameter();
  param.ParameterName = "@ProductID";
  param.Value = productId;
  param.DbType = DbType.Int32;
  comm.Parameters.Add(param);
  // create a new parameter
  param = comm.CreateParameter();
  param.ParameterName = "@ProductName";
  param.Value = name;
  param.DbType = DbType.String;
  param.Size = 50;
  comm.Parameters.Add(param);
  // create a new parameter
  param = comm.CreateParameter();
  param.ParameterName = "@ProductDescription";
  param.Value = description;
  param.DbType = DbType.String;
  comm.Parameters.Add(param);
  // create a new parameter
  param = comm.CreateParameter();
  param.ParameterName = "@Price";
  param.Value = price;
```

```
    param.DbType = DbType.Decimal;
    comm.Parameters.Add(param);
    // create a new parameter
    param = comm.CreateParameter();
    param.ParameterName = "@Thumbnail";
    param.Value = Thumbnail;
    param.DbType = DbType.String;
    param.Size = 50;
    comm.Parameters.Add(param);
    // create a new parameter
    param = comm.CreateParameter();
    param.ParameterName = "@Image";
    param.Value = Image;
    param.DbType = DbType.String;
    param.Size = 50;
    comm.Parameters.Add(param);
    // create a new parameter
    param = comm.CreateParameter();
    param.ParameterName = "@PromoDept";
    param.Value = PromoDept;
    param.DbType = DbType.Boolean;
    comm.Parameters.Add(param);
    // create a new parameter
    param = comm.CreateParameter();
    param.ParameterName = "@PromoFront";
    param.Value = PromoFront;
    param.DbType = DbType.Boolean;
    comm.Parameters.Add(param);
    // result will represent the number of changed rows
    int result = -1;
    try
    {
      // execute the stored procedure
      result = GenericDataAccess.ExecuteNonQuery(comm);
    }
    catch
    {
      // any errors are logged in GenericDataAccess, we ignore them here
    }
    // result will be 1 in case of success
    return (result != -1);
  }
```

5. It's time to create the presentation tier. Create a new Web Form named AdminProducts.aspx in the root folder of your project (make sure the **Place code in separate file** option is checked), based on the Admin.master template.

6. In the first placeholder, type the name of the page:

```
<asp:Content ID="Content1" ContentPlaceHolderID="titlePlaceHolder" runat=➥
"Server">
  <span class="AdminTitle">
    BalloonShop Admin
    <br />
    Products in
    <asp:HyperLink ID="catLink" runat="server" />
  </span>
</asp:Content>
```

7. In the second placeholder, start by adding the status label and data grid controls:

```
<asp:Content ID="Content2" ContentPlaceHolderID="adminPlaceHolder" Runat=➥
"Server">
  <p>
    <asp:Label ID="statusLabel" runat="server" Text=""></asp:Label>
  </p>
  <asp:GridView ID="grid" runat="server" DataKeyNames="ProductID" ➥
AutoGenerateColumns="false" Width="100%">
  </asp:GridView>
</asp:Content>
```

8. Switch to Design View and verify that your form looks like Figure 12-4.

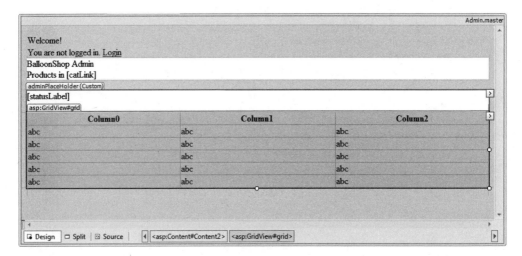

Figure 12-4. *AdminProducts.aspx in Design View*

9. Create the columns described in Table 12-1 by clicking the GridView's **Smart Link** and then clicking **Add New Column.**

Table 12-1. *GridView Field Properties*

Column Type	Header Text	Data Field	Other Properties
ImageField	Product Image	Thumbnail	Read-only; URL format string: ProductImages/{0}
BoundField	Product Name	Name	
BoundField	Product Description	Description	
BoundField	Price	Price	
BoundField	Thumb File	Thumbnail	
BoundField	Image File	Image	
CheckBoxField	Dept. prom.	PromoDept	
CheckBoxField	Cat. prom.	PromoFront	
TemplateField			
CommandField			Select **Edit/Update** and **Show Cancel Button** check boxes

---

■**Note** You didn't add a Delete button to the GridView because you'll implement this functionality later, in the product details page.

---

10. In the next few steps, you'll transform all editable columns into template columns to change the way they look when being edited (otherwise, they won't fit nicely on the screen). Moreover, you'll want to make other usability improvements such as enlarging the description text box to be multiline, or changing the format of product prices. Start with updating the **product name** by transforming the product name column into a template field (like you did in Chapter 11) and modifying its EditItemTemplate as shown:

```
<EditItemTemplate>
  <asp:TextBox ID="nameTextBox" runat="server" Width="97%"
             CssClass="GridEditingRow" Text='<%# Bind("Name") %>'>
  </asp:TextBox>
</EditItemTemplate>
```

11. Transform the **product description** field into a template field and then edit its EditItemTemplate in Source View:

```
<EditItemTemplate>
  <asp:TextBox ID="descriptionTextBox" runat="server"
     Text='<%# Bind("Description") %>' Height="100px" Width="97%"
     CssClass="GridEditingRow" TextMode="MultiLine" />
</EditItemTemplate>
```

12. Transform the **product price** field into a template field and edit its templates to format the price to be displayed with two decimal digits (as 19.99), instead of the default of four decimal digits (19.9900). In this case, you can also make its editing text box shorter to make better use of the space on the screen when entering edit mode:

```
<asp:TemplateField HeaderText="Price" SortExpression="Price">
  <ItemTemplate>
    <asp:Label ID="Label2" runat="server"
        Text='<%# String.Format("{0:0.00}", Eval("Price")) %>'>
    </asp:Label>
  </ItemTemplate>
  <EditItemTemplate>
    <asp:TextBox ID="priceTextBox" runat="server" Width="45px"
        Text='<%# String.Format("{0:0.00}", Eval("Price")) %>'>
    </asp:TextBox>
  </EditItemTemplate>
</asp:TemplateField>
```

13. Transform the **thumb** field into a template field to shrink its edit text box a little bit, as highlighted in the following code:

```
<EditItemTemplate>
  <asp:TextBox ID="thumbTextBox" Width="80px" runat="server"
        Text='<%# Bind("Thumbnail") %>'></asp:TextBox>
</EditItemTemplate>
```

14. Transform the **image** field into a template field and set its editing TextBox's width to **80px** and its name to **imageTextBox**, similar to what you did in the previous step.

```
<EditItemTemplate>
  <asp:TextBox ID="imageTextBox" Width="80px" runat="server"
        Text='<%# Bind("Image") %>'></asp:TextBox>
</EditItemTemplate>
```

15. Edit the template of the last `TemplateField` column to contain a link to the product details page:

```
<asp:TemplateField>
  <ItemTemplate>
    <asp:HyperLink
      Runat="server" Text="Select"
      NavigateUrl='<%# "AdminProductDetails.aspx?DepartmentID=" +
      Request.QueryString["DepartmentID"] + "&amp;CategoryID=" +
      Request.QueryString["CategoryID"] + "&amp;ProductID=" +
      Eval("ProductID") %>'
      ID="HyperLink1">
    </asp:HyperLink>
  </ItemTemplate>
</asp:TemplateField>
```

Now the `GridView` is ready, as shown in Figure 12-5.

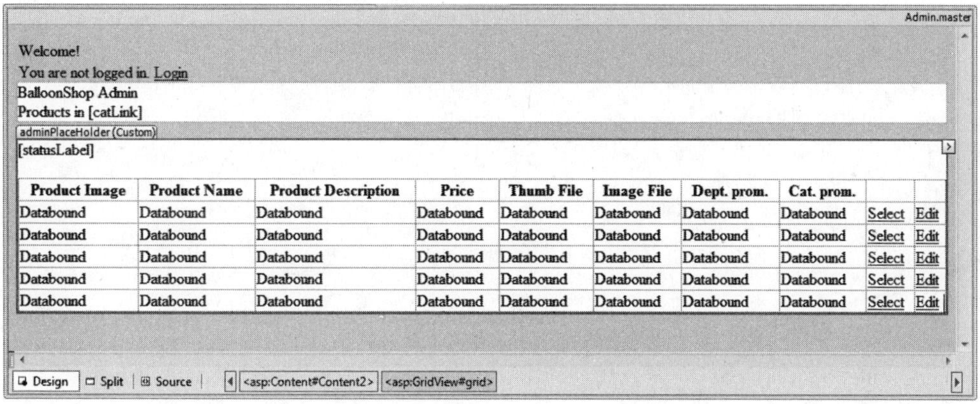

Figure 12-5. *The products grid in design view*

16. The final step for the user interface part is to create the controls for adding a new product. These controls need a new CSS definition, so add the following style to `BalloonShop.css`:

```
.WideLabel {
  display:-moz-inline-block;
  display:inline-block;
  width: 100px;
}
```

17. Add the following code, which represents the controls used to add new products, to the bottom of the page using Design View, or simply write the HTML code in Source View:

```
<p>Create a new product and assign it to this category:</p>
<p>
  <span class="WideLabel">Name:</span>
  <asp:TextBox ID="newName" runat="server" Width="400px" />
</p>
<p>
  <span class="WideLabel">Description:</span>
  <asp:TextBox ID="newDescription" runat="server" Width="400px"
              Height="70px" TextMode="MultiLine" />
</p>
<p>
  <span class="WideLabel">Price:</span>
  <asp:TextBox ID="newPrice" runat="server" Width="400px">0.00</asp:TextBox>
</p>
<p>
  <span class="WideLabel">Thumbnail file:</span>
  <asp:TextBox ID="newThumbnail" runat="server" Width="400px">Generic1.➥
png</asp:TextBox>
</p>
<p>
  <span class="WideLabel">Image file:</span>
  <asp:TextBox ID="newImage" runat="server" Width="400px">Generic2.➥
png</asp:TextBox>
</p>
<p>
  <span class="widelabel">Dept. promo:</span>
  <asp:CheckBox ID="newPromoDept" runat="server" />
</p>
<p>
  <span class="widelabel">Front promo:</span>
  <asp:CheckBox ID="newPromoFront" runat="server" />
</p>
<asp:Button ID="createProduct" runat="server" Text="Create Product" />
```

After all the changes, the user control should look like Figure 12-6 when viewed in Design View.

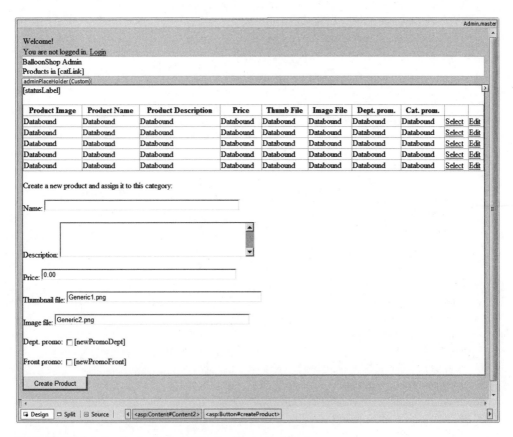

Figure 12-6. *AdminProducts.aspx in Design View, updated*

18. Now it's time to write the code. Remember to use Visual Web Developer to generate the event handler signatures for you and modify their code, as shown in the following code listing:

```
protected void Page_Load(object sender, EventArgs e)
{
  // Load the grid only the first time the page is loaded
  if (!Page.IsPostBack)
  {
    // Get CategoryID and DepartmentID from the query string
    string categoryId = Request.QueryString["CategoryID"];
    string departmentId = Request.QueryString["DepartmentID"];
    // Obtain the category name
    CategoryDetails cd = CatalogAccess.GetCategoryDetails(categoryId);
    string categoryName = cd.Name;
    // Link to department
    catLink.Text = categoryName;
    catLink.NavigateUrl = "AdminCategories.aspx?DepartmentID=" + departmentId;
```

```
      // Load the products grid
      BindGrid();
    }
}


// Populate the GridView with data
private void BindGrid()
{
  // Get CategoryID from the query string
  string categoryId = Request.QueryString["CategoryID"];
  // Get a DataTable object containing the products
  grid.DataSource = CatalogAccess.GetAllProductsInCategory(categoryId);
  // Needed to bind the data bound controls to the data source
  grid.DataBind();
}


// Enter row into edit mode
protected void grid_RowEditing(object sender, GridViewEditEventArgs e)
{
  // Set the row for which to enable edit mode
  grid.EditIndex = e.NewEditIndex;
  // Set status message
  statusLabel.Text = "Editing row # " + e.NewEditIndex.ToString();
  // Reload the grid
  BindGrid();
}


// Cancel edit mode
protected void grid_RowCancelingEdit(object sender,
GridViewCancelEditEventArgs e)
{
  // Cancel edit mode
  grid.EditIndex = -1;
  // Set status message
  statusLabel.Text = "Editing canceled";
  // Reload the grid
  BindGrid();
}
```

```
// Update a product
protected void grid_RowUpdating(object sender, GridViewUpdateEventArgs e)
{
  // Retrieve updated data
  try
  {
    string id = grid.DataKeys[e.RowIndex].Value.ToString();
    string name = ((TextBox)grid.Rows[e.RowIndex].➥
FindControl("nameTextBox")).Text;
    string description = ((TextBox)grid.Rows[e.RowIndex].FindControl➥
("descriptionTextBox")).Text;
    string price = ((TextBox)grid.Rows[e.RowIndex].FindControl➥
("priceTextBox")).Text;
    string thumbnail = ((TextBox)grid.Rows[e.RowIndex].FindControl➥
("thumbTextBox")).Text;
    string image = ((TextBox)grid.Rows[e.RowIndex].FindControl➥
("imageTextBox")).Text;
    string promoDept = ((CheckBox)grid.Rows[e.RowIndex].Cells[6].➥
Controls[0]).Checked.ToString();
    string promoFront = ((CheckBox)grid.Rows[e.RowIndex].Cells[7].➥
Controls[0]).Checked.ToString();
    // Execute the update command
    bool success = CatalogAccess.UpdateProduct(id, name, description, ➥
price, thumbnail, image, promoDept, promoFront);
    // Cancel edit mode
    grid.EditIndex = -1;
    // Display status message
    statusLabel.Text = success ? "Product update successful" : ➥
"Product update failed";
  }
  catch
  {
    // Display error
    statusLabel.Text = "Product update failed";
  }
  // Reload grid
  BindGrid();
}
```

```
// Create a new product
protected void createProduct_Click(object sender, EventArgs e)
{
    // Get CategoryID from the query string
    string categoryId = Request.QueryString["CategoryID"];
    // Execute the insert command
    bool success = CatalogAccess.CreateProduct(categoryId, newName.Text, ➥
newDescription.Text, newPrice.Text, newThumbnail.Text, newImage.Text, ➥
newPromoDept.Checked.ToString(), newPromoFront.Checked.ToString());
    // Display status message
    statusLabel.Text = success ? "Insert successful" : "Insert failed";
    // Reload the grid
    BindGrid();
}
```

How It Works: AdminProducts.aspx

Most methods are similar to those you wrote for the previous controls, except this time you did more work to customize their appearance, especially while in edit mode. Products can be updated or selected. The administrator can change the product's image using the product details admin page, which shows up when a product is selected in the list. You'll create the product details page next.

As usual, when selecting a product, you reload the form by adding its ID to the query string. AdminProductDetails allows you to assign the selected product to an additional category, move the product to another category, upload a picture for the product, remove the product from its category, or remove the product from the database.

Administering Product Details

The products list you built earlier is wonderful, but it lacks a few important features. The final page you're implementing will take care of these missing features. AdminProductDetails.aspx will allow you to

- View the product's pictures

- View which categories the product belongs to

- Remove the product from its category

- Remove the product from the database completely

- Assign the current product to an additional category

- Move the current product to another category

- Upload product pictures

Figure 12-7 shows how the control will look for the Mickey Close-up product.

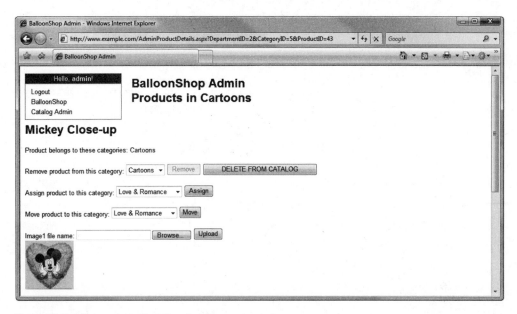

Figure 12-7. *The product details admin page in action*

When it comes to product removal, things aren't straightforward: You can either unassign the product from a category by removing the record from the ProductCategory table, or you can effectively remove the product from the Product table. Because products are accessed in the catalog by selecting a category, you must make sure there are no orphaned products (products that don't belong to any category), because they couldn't be accessed using the current administration interface.

So, if you added a Delete button to the data grid, what kind of deletion would that button have to do? Delete the product from the database? This would work, but it's a bit awkward if you have a product assigned to multiple categories and you only want to remove it from a single category. On the other hand, if the Delete button removes the product from the current category, you can create orphaned products because they exist in the Product table. You could fix that by allowing the site administrator to see the complete list of products without locating them by department and category.

The simple solution implemented in this chapter is like that. If the product belongs to more than one category, the Delete button unassigns the product from the current category. If the product belongs to only one category, the product is first unassigned from the current category and then also removed from the Product table.

Exercise: Administering Product Details

1. Start by adding the following stored procedures to the BalloonShop database:
   CatalogGetCategoriesWithProduct, CatalogGetCategoriesWithoutProduct,
   CatalogAssignProductToCategory, CatalogMoveProductToCategory,
   CatalogRemoveProductFromCategory, and CatalogDeleteProduct.

   The CatalogGetCategoriesWithProduct stored procedure returns a list of the categories that
   belong to the specified product. Only their IDs and names are returned because this is the only information we're interested in.

   ```
   CREATE PROCEDURE CatalogGetCategoriesWithProduct
   (@ProductID int)
   AS
   SELECT Category.CategoryID, Name
   FROM Category INNER JOIN ProductCategory
   ON Category.CategoryID = ProductCategory.CategoryID
   WHERE ProductCategory.ProductID = @ProductID
   ```

2. The CatalogGetCategoriesWithoutProduct stored procedure returns a list of the categories that
   don't contain a specified product. This is the list of categories that the product can be moved or assigned to.

   ```
   CREATE PROCEDURE CatalogGetCategoriesWithoutProduct
   (@ProductID int)
   AS
   SELECT CategoryID, Name
   FROM Category
   WHERE CategoryID NOT IN
      (SELECT Category.CategoryID
       FROM Category INNER JOIN ProductCategory
       ON Category.CategoryID = ProductCategory.CategoryID
       WHERE ProductCategory.ProductID = @ProductID)
   ```

3. The CatalogAssignProductToCategory stored procedure associates a product with a category by
   adding a ProductID, CategoryID value pair to the ProductCategory table:

   ```
   CREATE PROCEDURE CatalogAssignProductToCategory
   (@ProductID int, @CategoryID int)
   AS
   INSERT INTO ProductCategory (ProductID, CategoryID)
   VALUES (@ProductID, @CategoryID)
   ```

   Note that you don't do any verification here. If an error occurs (because the entered ProductID is not
   associated with any product, or the ProductID, CategoryID pair already exists in the ProductCategory
   table), it is trapped at the upper levels, and the administrator is notified. Still, since we talked about the
   error-handling techniques, it's worth noting that you can make the stored procedure smart enough to do
   some validation before attempting to add the ProductID, CategoryID pair to ProductCategory table.

■**Note** Following is a bulletproof version of the stored procedure that inserts the new record into ProductCategory only if the received ProductID and CategoryID values are valid and the pair doesn't already exist in the database:

```
CREATE PROCEDURE CatalogAssignProductToCategory
(@ProductID int, @CategoryID int)
AS
IF EXISTS
  (SELECT Name
   FROM Product
   WHERE ProductID = @ProductID)
  AND EXISTS
  (SELECT Name
   FROM Category
   WHERE CategoryID = @CategoryID)
  AND NOT EXISTS
  (SELECT *
   FROM ProductCategory
   WHERE CategoryID = @CategoryID AND ProductID = @ProductID)
INSERT INTO ProductCategory (ProductID, CategoryID)
VALUES (@ProductID, @CategoryID)
```

We won't use this version in practice because we prefer to be notified in case an illegal association is attempted.

---

4. CatalogMoveProductToCategory is the stored procedure that moves a product from one category to another:

```
CREATE PROCEDURE CatalogMoveProductToCategory
(@ProductID int, @OldCategoryID int, @NewCategoryID int)
AS
UPDATE ProductCategory
SET CategoryID = @NewCategoryID
WHERE CategoryID = @OldCategoryID
  AND ProductID = @ProductID
```

5. The CatalogRemoveProductFromCategory stored procedure verifies how many categories the product exists in. If the product exists in more than one category, the stored procedure just removes the product from the current category (ID received as a parameter). If the product is associated with a single category, it is first removed from the category and then effectively deleted from the database.

```
CREATE PROCEDURE CatalogRemoveProductFromCategory
(@ProductID int, @CategoryID int)
AS
DELETE FROM ProductCategory
WHERE CategoryID = @CategoryID AND ProductID = @ProductID
```

6. The `CatalogDeleteProduct` stored procedure verifies how many categories the product exists in. If the product exists in more than one category, the stored procedure just removes the product from the current category (ID received as a parameter). If the product is associated with a single category, it is first removed from the category and then effectively deleted from the database.

```
CREATE PROCEDURE CatalogDeleteProduct
(@ProductID INT)
AS
DELETE FROM ProductCategory WHERE ProductID=@ProductID
DELETE FROM Product where ProductID=@ProductID
```

2 IN 1

Don't add this new procedure to your database, but for your curiosity, here is a version of the previous two stored procedures that completely deletes a product from the catalog if it belongs to a single category, or simply removes it from the mentioned category if it belongs to more categories:

```
CREATE PROCEDURE CatalogDeleteProductFromCategoryOrFromCatalog
(@ProductID int, @CategoryID int)
AS
IF (SELECT COUNT(*) FROM ProductCategory WHERE ProductID=@ProductID)>1
  DELETE FROM ProductCategory
  WHERE CategoryID=@CategoryID AND ProductID=@ProductID
ELSE
 BEGIN
   DELETE FROM ProductCategory WHERE ProductID=@ProductID
   DELETE FROM Product where ProductID=@ProductID
 END
```

7. Add the following methods to the `CatalogAccess` class:

   `GetCategoriesWithProduct` gets the list of categories that are related to a specified product.

   `GetCategoriesWithoutProduct` returns the categories that do not contain the specified product.

   `AssignProductToCategory`, `MoveProductToCategory`, and `RemoveProductFromCategory` do what their names imply.

   `DeleteProduct` completely removes a product from the product catalog.

8. Add the following code to the `CatalogAccess` class:

```
// get categories that contain a specified product
public static DataTable GetCategoriesWithProduct(string productId)
{
  // get a configured DbCommand object
  DbCommand comm = GenericDataAccess.CreateCommand();
  // set the stored procedure name
  comm.CommandText = "CatalogGetCategoriesWithProduct";
```

```
  // create a new parameter
  DbParameter param = comm.CreateParameter();
  param.ParameterName = "@ProductID";
  param.Value = productId;
  param.DbType = DbType.Int32;
  comm.Parameters.Add(param);
  // execute the stored procedure
  return GenericDataAccess.ExecuteSelectCommand(comm);
}

// get categories that do not contain a specified product
public static DataTable GetCategoriesWithoutProduct(string productId)
{
  // get a configured DbCommand object
  DbCommand comm = GenericDataAccess.CreateCommand();
  // set the stored procedure name
  comm.CommandText = "CatalogGetCategoriesWithoutProduct";
  // create a new parameter
  DbParameter param = comm.CreateParameter();
  param.ParameterName = "@ProductID";
  param.Value = productId;
  param.DbType = DbType.Int32;
  comm.Parameters.Add(param);
  // execute the stored procedure
  return GenericDataAccess.ExecuteSelectCommand(comm);
}


// assign a product to a new category
public static bool AssignProductToCategory(string productId, string ➥
categoryId)
{
  // get a configured DbCommand object
  DbCommand comm = GenericDataAccess.CreateCommand();
  // set the stored procedure name
  comm.CommandText = "CatalogAssignProductToCategory";
  // create a new parameter
  DbParameter param = comm.CreateParameter();
  param.ParameterName = "@ProductID";
  param.Value = productId;
  param.DbType = DbType.Int32;
  comm.Parameters.Add(param);
  // create a new parameter
  param = comm.CreateParameter();
  param.ParameterName = "@CategoryID";
  param.Value = categoryId;
  param.DbType = DbType.Int32;
```

```
    comm.Parameters.Add(param);
    // result will represent the number of changed rows
    int result = -1;
    try
    {
      // execute the stored procedure
      result = GenericDataAccess.ExecuteNonQuery(comm);
    }
    catch
    {
      // any errors are logged in GenericDataAccess, we ignore them here
    }
    // result will be 1 in case of success
    return (result != -1);
}

// move product to a new category
public static bool MoveProductToCategory(string productId, string ➥
oldCategoryId,
 string newCategoryId)
{
  // get a configured DbCommand object
  DbCommand comm = GenericDataAccess.CreateCommand();
  // set the stored procedure name
  comm.CommandText = "CatalogMoveProductToCategory";
  // create a new parameter
  DbParameter param = comm.CreateParameter();
  param.ParameterName = "@ProductID";

  param.Value = productId;
  param.DbType = DbType.Int32;
  comm.Parameters.Add(param);
  // create a new parameter
  param = comm.CreateParameter();
  param.ParameterName = "@OldCategoryID";
  param.Value = oldCategoryId;
  param.DbType = DbType.Int32;
  comm.Parameters.Add(param);
  // create a new parameter
  param = comm.CreateParameter();
  param.ParameterName = "@NewCategoryID";
  param.Value = newCategoryId;
  param.DbType = DbType.Int32;
  comm.Parameters.Add(param);
  // result will represent the number of changed rows
  int result = -1;
```

```
  try
  {
    // execute the stored procedure
    result = GenericDataAccess.ExecuteNonQuery(comm);
  }
  catch
  {
    // any errors are logged in GenericDataAccess, we ignore them here
  }
  // result will be 1 in case of success
  return (result != -1);
}

// removes a product from a category
public static bool RemoveProductFromCategory(string productId, string ➥
categoryId)
{
  // get a configured DbCommand object
  DbCommand comm = GenericDataAccess.CreateCommand();
  // set the stored procedure name
  comm.CommandText = "CatalogRemoveProductFromCategory";
  // create a new parameter
  DbParameter param = comm.CreateParameter();
  param.ParameterName = "@ProductID";
  param.Value = productId;
  param.DbType = DbType.Int32;
  comm.Parameters.Add(param);
  // create a new parameter
  param = comm.CreateParameter();
  param.ParameterName = "@CategoryID";
  param.Value = categoryId;
  param.DbType = DbType.Int32;
  comm.Parameters.Add(param);
  // result will represent the number of changed rows
  int result = -1;
  try
  {
    // execute the stored procedure
    result = GenericDataAccess.ExecuteNonQuery(comm);
  }
  catch
  {
    // any errors are logged in GenericDataAccess, we ignore them here
  }
  // result will be 1 in case of success
  return (result != -1);
}
```

```
// deletes a product from the product catalog
public static bool DeleteProduct(string productId)
{
  // get a configured DbCommand object
  DbCommand comm = GenericDataAccess.CreateCommand();
  // set the stored procedure name
  comm.CommandText = "CatalogDeleteProduct";
  // create a new parameter
  DbParameter param = comm.CreateParameter();
  param.ParameterName = "@ProductID";
  param.Value = productId;
  param.DbType = DbType.Int32;
  comm.Parameters.Add(param);
  // result will represent the number of changed rows
  int result = -1;
  try
  {
    // execute the stored procedure
    result = GenericDataAccess.ExecuteNonQuery(comm);
  }
  catch
  {
    // any errors are logged in GenericDataAccess, we ignore them here
  }
  // result will be 1 in case of success
  return (result != -1);
}
```

9. We'll now implement the user interface component—AdminProductDetails.aspx. Create a new Web Form named AdminProductDetails.aspx in the root folder of your project (make sure the **Place code in separate file** option is checked), based on the Admin.master template.

10. In the first placeholder, type the name of the page:

```
<asp:Content ID="Content1" ContentPlaceHolderID="titlePlaceHolder" ➥
runat="Server">
  <span class="AdminTitle">
    BalloonShop Admin
    <br />
    Back to
    <asp:HyperLink ID="catLink" runat="server" />
  </span>
</asp:Content>
```

11. In the second placeholder, add controls to the form, as shown in Figure 12-8. Here you'll meet the FileUpload control for the first time.

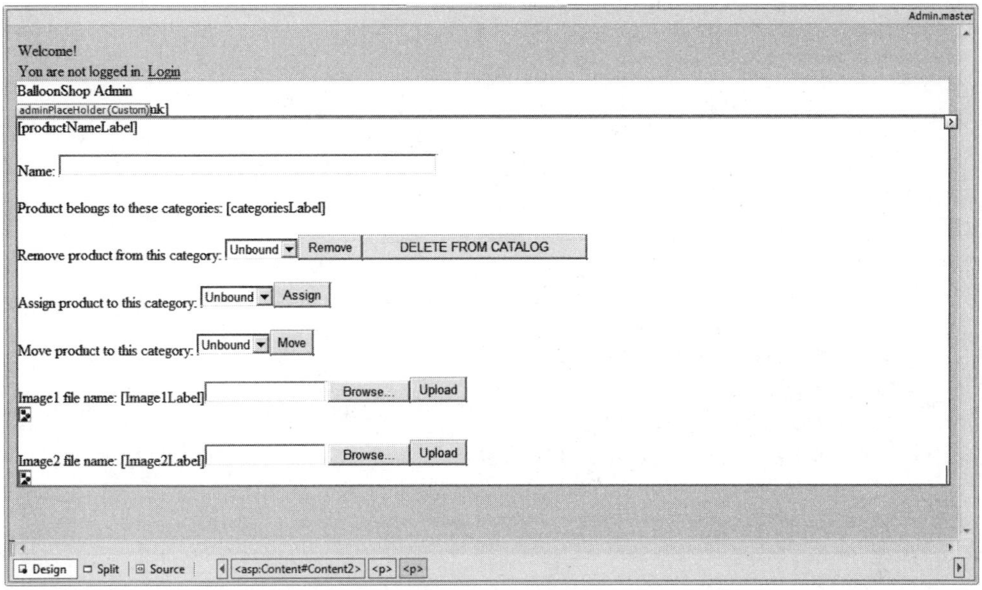

Figure 12-8. *The product details admin page*

The following is the associated source code:

```
<asp:Content ID="Content2" ContentPlaceHolderID="adminPlaceHolder" ➥
runat="Server">
  <asp:Label CssClass="AdminTitle" ID="productNameLabel" runat="server" />
  <p>
    <asp:Label ID="statusLabel" CssClass="AdminError" runat="server" />
  </p>
  <p>
    Product belongs to these categories:
    <asp:Label ID="categoriesLabel" runat="server" />
  </p>
  <p>
    Remove product from this category:
    <asp:DropDownList ID="categoriesListRemove" runat="server" />
    <asp:Button ID="removeButton" runat="server" Text="Remove" ➥
OnClick="removeButton_Click" />
    <asp:Button ID="deleteButton" runat="server" Text="DELETE ➥
FROM CATALOG" OnClick="deleteButton_Click" />
  </p>
  <p>
    Assign product to this category:
    <asp:DropDownList ID="categoriesListAssign" runat="server" />
    <asp:Button ID="assignButton" runat="server" Text="Assign" ➥
OnClick="assignButton_Click" />
  <p>
```

```
      Move product to this category:
      <asp:DropDownList ID="categoriesListMove" runat="server" />
      <asp:Button ID="moveButton" runat="server" Text="Move" ➥
OnClick="moveButton_Click" />
  </p>
  <p>
      Image1 file name:
      <asp:Label ID="Image1Label" runat="server" />
      <asp:FileUpload ID="image1FileUpload" runat="server" />
      <asp:Button ID="upload1Button" runat="server" Text="Upload" /><br />
      <asp:Image ID="image1" runat="server" />
  </p>
  <p>
      Image2 file name:
      <asp:Label ID="Image2Label" runat="server" />
      <asp:FileUpload ID="image2FileUpload" runat="server" />
      <asp:Button ID="upload2Button" runat="server" Text="Upload" /><br />
      <asp:Image ID="image2" runat="server" />
  </p>
</asp:Content>
```

12. Open the code-behind file and complete the AdminProductDetails class, as shown in the code snippet:

```
using System.Data;

public partial class AdminProductDetails : System.Web.UI.Page
{
  // store product, category, and department IDs as class members
  private string currentProductId, currentCategoryId, currentDepartmentId;

  protected void Page_Load(object sender, EventArgs e)
  {
    // Get DepartmentID, CategoryID, and ProductID from the query string
    // and save their values
    currentDepartmentId = Request.QueryString["DepartmentID"];
    currentCategoryId = Request.QueryString["CategoryID"];
    currentProductId = Request.QueryString["ProductID"];

    // Fill the controls with data only on the initial page load
    if (!IsPostBack)
    {
      // Fill controls with data
      PopulateControls();
    }
  }
```

```
  // Populate the controls
  private void PopulateControls()
  {
    // Retrieve product details and category details from database
    ProductDetails productDetails = CatalogAccess.GetProduct➥
Details(currentProductId);
    CategoryDetails categoryDetails = CatalogAccess.GetCategory➥
Details(currentCategoryId);
    // Set up labels and images
    productNameLabel.Text = productDetails.Name;
    image1.ImageUrl = Link.ToProductImage(productDetails.Thumbnail);
    image2.ImageUrl = Link.ToProductImage(productDetails.Image);

    // Link to department
    catLink.Text = categoryDetails.Name;
    catLink.NavigateUrl = "AdminCategories.aspx?DepartmentID=" ➥
+ currentDepartmentId;

    // Clear form
    categoriesLabel.Text = "";
    categoriesListAssign.Items.Clear();
    categoriesListMove.Items.Clear();
    categoriesListRemove.Items.Clear();

    // Fill categoriesLabel and categoriesListRemove with data
    string categoryId, categoryName;
    DataTable productCategories = CatalogAccess.GetCategories➥
WithProduct(currentProductId);
    for (int i = 0; i < productCategories.Rows.Count; i++)
    {
      // obtain category id and name
      categoryId = productCategories.Rows[i]["CategoryId"].ToString();
      categoryName = productCategories.Rows[i]["Name"].ToString();
      // add a link to the category admin page
      categoriesLabel.Text +=
        (categoriesLabel.Text == "" ? "" : ", ") +
        "<a href='AdminProducts.aspx?DepartmentID=" +
        CatalogAccess.GetCategoryDetails(currentCategoryId).DepartmentId +
        "&CategoryID=" + categoryId + "'>" +
        categoryName + "</a>";

      // populate the categoriesListRemove combo box
      categoriesListRemove.Items.Add(new ListItem(categoryName, ➥
categoryId));
    }
```

```
// Delete from catalog or remove from category?
if (productCategories.Rows.Count > 1)
{
  deleteButton.Visible = false;
  removeButton.Enabled = true;
}
else
{
  deleteButton.Visible = true;
  removeButton.Enabled = false;
}


// Fill categoriesListMove and categoriesListAssign with data
productCategories = CatalogAccess.GetCategoriesWithout➥
Product(currentProductId);
for (int i = 0; i < productCategories.Rows.Count; i++)
{
  // obtain category id and name
  categoryId = productCategories.Rows[i]["CategoryId"].ToString();
  categoryName = productCategories.Rows[i]["Name"].ToString();
  // populate the list boxes
  categoriesListAssign.Items.Add(new ListItem(categoryName, ➥
categoryId));
  categoriesListMove.Items.Add(new ListItem(categoryName, categoryId));
  }
 }
}
```

13. Open `AdminProductDetails.aspx` in Design View, double-click the first button (removeButton), and then complete its `Click` event handler method like this:

```
// Remove the product from a category
protected void removeButton_Click(object sender, EventArgs e)
{
  // Check if a category was selected
  if (categoriesListRemove.SelectedIndex != -1)
  {
    // Get the category ID that was selected in the DropDownList
    string categoryId = categoriesListRemove.SelectedItem.Value;
    // Remove the product from the category
    bool success = CatalogAccess.RemoveProductFromCategory(➥
currentProductId, categoryId);
```

```
      // Display status message
      statusLabel.Text = success ? "Product removed successfully"➥
   : "Product removal failed";
      // Refresh the page
      PopulateControls();
    }
    else
      statusLabel.Text = "You need to select a category";
  }
```

14. While in Design View, double-click the second button (deleteButton), and then complete its Click event handler method like this:

```
// delete a product from the catalog
protected void deleteButton_Click(object sender, EventArgs e)
{
  // Delete the product from the catalog
  CatalogAccess.DeleteProduct(currentProductId);
  // Need to go back to the categories page now
  Response.Redirect("AdminDepartments.aspx");
}
```

15. While in Design View, double-click the third button (assignButton), and then complete its Click event handler method like this:

```
// assign the product to a new category
protected void assignButton_Click(object sender, EventArgs e)
{
  // Check if a category was selected
  if (categoriesListAssign.SelectedIndex != -1)
  {
    // Get the category ID that was selected in the DropDownList
    string categoryId = categoriesListAssign.SelectedItem.Value;
    // Assign the product to the category
    bool success = CatalogAccess.AssignProductToCategory(➥
currentProductId, categoryId);
    // Display status message
    statusLabel.Text = success ? "Product assigned successfully"➥
   : "Product assignation failed";
    // Refresh the page
    PopulateControls();
  }
  else
    statusLabel.Text = "You need to select a category";
}
```

16. While in Design View, double-click the fourth button (moveButton), and then complete its Click event handler method like this:

```
// move the product to another category
protected void moveButton_Click(object sender, EventArgs e)
{
  // Check if a category was selected
  if (categoriesListMove.SelectedIndex != -1)
  {
    // Get the category ID that was selected in the DropDownList
    string newCategoryId = categoriesListMove.SelectedItem.Value;
    // Move the product to the category
    bool success = CatalogAccess.MoveProductToCategory(➥
currentProductId, currentCategoryId, newCategoryId);
    // If the operation was successful, reload the page,
    // so the new category will reflect in the query string
    if (!success)
      statusLabel.Text = "Couldn't move the product to the specified ➥
category";
    else
      Response.Redirect("AdminProductDetails.aspx" +
            "?DepartmentID=" + currentDepartmentId +
            "&CategoryID=" + newCategoryId +
            "&ProductID=" + currentProductId);
  }
  else
    statusLabel.Text = "You need to select a category";
}
```

17. While in Design View, double-click the two **Upload** buttons and complete their Click event handler code like this:

```
// upload product's first image
protected void upload1Button_Click(object sender, EventArgs e)
{
  // proceed with uploading only if the user selected a file
  if (image1FileUpload.HasFile)
  {
    try
    {
      string fileName = image1FileUpload.FileName;
      string location = Server.MapPath("./ProductImages/") + fileName;
      // save image to server
      image1FileUpload.SaveAs(location);
      // update database with new product details
      ProductDetails pd = CatalogAccess.GetProductDetails➥
(currentProductId);
      CatalogAccess.UpdateProduct(currentProductId, pd.Name, ➥
```

```
pd.Description, pd.Price.ToString(), fileName, pd.Image, ➡
pd.PromoDept.ToString(), pd.PromoFront.ToString());
      // reload the page
      Response.Redirect("AdminProductDetails.aspx" +
              "?DepartmentID=" + currentDepartmentId +
              "&CategoryID=" + currentCategoryId +
              "&ProductID=" + currentProductId);
    }
    catch
    {
      statusLabel.Text = "Uploading image 1 failed";
    }
  }
}

// upload product's second image
protected void upload2Button_Click(object sender, EventArgs e)
{
  // proceed with uploading only if the user selected a file
  if (image2FileUpload.HasFile)
  {
    try
    {
      string fileName = image2FileUpload.FileName;
      string location = Server.MapPath("./ProductImages/") + fileName;
      // save image to server
      image2FileUpload.SaveAs(location);
      // update database with new product details
      ProductDetails pd = CatalogAccess.GetProductDetails➡
(currentProductId);
      CatalogAccess.UpdateProduct(currentProductId, pd.Name, ➡
pd.Description, pd.Price.ToString(), pd.Thumbnail, fileName, ➡
pd.PromoDept.ToString(), pd.PromoFront.ToString());
      // reload the page
      Response.Redirect("AdminProductDetails.aspx" +
              "?DepartmentID=" + currentDepartmentId +
              "&CategoryID=" + currentCategoryId +
              "&ProductID=" + currentProductId);
    }
    catch
    {
      statusLabel.Text = "Uploading image 2 failed";
    }
  }
}
```

18. Test your new catalog admin page to see that everything works as expected.

How It Works: AdminProductDetails.aspx

It's worth taking a second look at the bits that are different from the previous exercises:

- The TieButton method tied the drop-down lists to their associated Go buttons.

- The FileUpload control uploaded product pictures to the server. The code is pretty clear, so take a closer look at the Click event handlers of the two Upload buttons to see how the FileUpload control is used in practice.

- Various tests are made in the buttons' Click event handlers to display accurate status messages to the visitor. A novelty in this control is checking whether a value of the drop-down lists has been selected before trying to read its value (this is useful especially in the situation when the list is empty).

- The DropDownList controls are populated in the PopulateControls method, and they are capable of storing a key for each of their entries, similar to what the DataKeyNames property does for the GridView. In our case, this key retains the IDs of the listed categories. You read this ID from the DropDownList controls when the user tries to move, assign, or remove the product from a selected category, by reading the SelectedItem.Value property of the list.

Summary

In this chapter, you implemented the administrative features for your products, including features for adding or editing product details, assigning products to categories, uploading product pictures, and so on. You also updated BalloonShop to include edit buttons in the catalog pages, so administrators can much more easily access the administration pages for updating the catalog information.

Now that the dry part of developing the administration end of our site is finished, we are finally ready to move on the really exciting features. In Chapter 13, you'll implement your own shopping cart in BalloonShop, replacing the PayPal shopping cart you've been using so far.

PART 2

■ ■ ■

Phase 2 of Development: Selling More and Increasing Profits

■ ■ ■

Creating Your Own Shopping Cart

Welcome to the second stage of development! During this stage, you'll start improving and adding new features to the already existing, fully functional e-commerce site.

So, what exactly can you improve? Well, the answer to this question isn't hard to find if you take a quick look at the popular e-commerce sites on the Web. They personalize the experience for the user, provide product recommendations, remember customers' preferences, and boast many other features that make the site easy to remember and hard to leave without first purchasing something.

In the first stage of development, you extensively relied on a third-party payment processor (PayPal) that supplied an integrated shopping cart, so you didn't record any shopping cart or order information in the database. Right now, your site isn't capable of displaying a list of "most wanted" products or any other information about the products that have been sold through the web site because, at this stage, you aren't tracking the products sold. Saving order information in the database is one of our priorities now because most of the features you want to implement next rely on having this information.

At the end of this chapter you'll have a functional shopping cart, but the visitor will not yet be able to order the products contained in it. You'll add this functionality in Chapter 14, when you implement a custom checkout system that integrates with your new shopping cart.

Specifically, in this chapter you'll learn how to

- Analyze the elements of a shopping cart

- Create the database structure that stores shopping cart records

- Implement the data tier, business tier, and presentation tier components of the shopping cart

- Update the PayPal Add to Cart buttons you created in Chapter 10 to work with the new shopping cart

- Create a shopping cart summary box to remind users of the products in their carts and of the total amounts

- Implement a shopping cart administration page that allows site administrators to delete shopping carts that weren't updated in a specified number of days

Designing the Shopping Cart

In this chapter, you'll build the shopping cart page (see Figure 13-1) and a shopping cart summary control that shows up in every catalog page except the shopping cart page (see Figure 13-2). You'll also create a shopping cart administration page (see Figure 13-3), which allows the administrator to delete old shopping cart records from the database to prevent the database from growing indefinitely.

You'll also appreciate the error-handling features in both the shopping cart and the shopping cart administration page. In the shopping cart, for example, serious errors cause the site to display the Oooops! message, whereas less-serious messages are simply logged (if the site is configured to log them in web.config), and the visitor is notified with a simple message. This happens, for example, if the user tries to update the shopping cart with bogus values, such as inserting a letter for the product quantity, and so on.

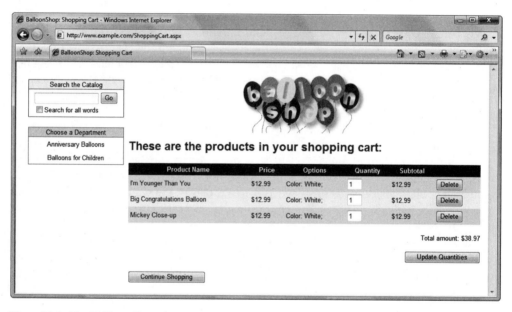

Figure 13-1. *The BalloonShop shopping cart*

Before starting to write the code for the shopping cart, let's take a closer look at what we're going to do.

First, note that you won't have any user personalization features at this stage of the site. It doesn't matter who buys your products at this point; you just want to know what products were sold and when. When you add user customization features in the later chapters, your task will be fairly simple: when the visitor authenticates, the visitor's temporary (anonymous) shopping cart will be associated with the visitor's account. Because you work with temporary shopping carts, even after implementing the customer account system, the visitor isn't required to supply additional information (log in) earlier than necessary.

Figure 13-2. *BalloonShop displays a shopping cart summary box.*

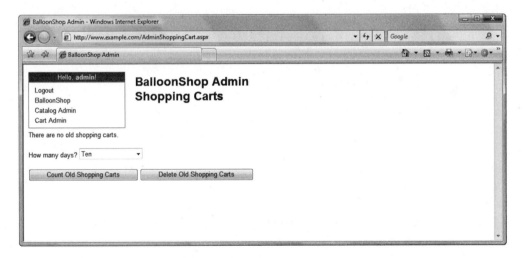

Figure 13-3. *The shopping cart administration page*

We use cookies to keep track of shopping carts. When the visitor clicks the Add to Cart button, the server first verifies whether a shopping cart cookie already exists on the visitor's computer. If it does, the specified product is added to the existing cart. Otherwise, the server generates a unique cart ID, saves it to the client's cookie, and then adds the product to the newly generated shopping cart.

Storing Shopping Cart Information

You'll store all shopping cart items in a single table, named ShoppingCart. You can create the new table by either following the steps in the next exercise or by simply executing the SQL script available from the Source Code page on the Apress web site (http://www.apress.com).

Remember that you can also create your table and implement the relationship using database diagrams, as shown in Chapter 5.

Follow the steps in the next exercise if you prefer to create your new table manually.

Exercise: Creating the ShoppingCart Table

1. In Database Explorer, expand your BalloonShop database, right-click **Tables**, and choose **Add New Table**.

2. Add new columns to your new table, as shown in Figure 13-4.

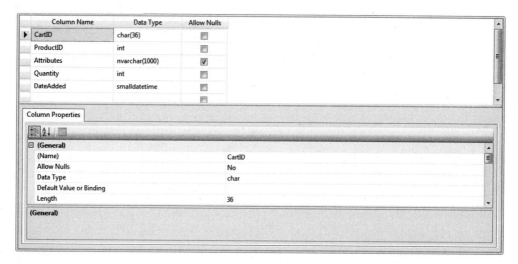

Figure 13-4. *Designing the ShoppingCart table*

■**Note** You can use either smalldatetime or datetime for the DateAdded column. smalldatetime stores the date with less precision than datetime (down to minutes), but occupies 4 bytes instead of 8.

---

3. Select both the CartID and ProductID fields and click the golden key symbol (or right-click and select **Set Primary Key**) to create a composite primary key formed of these two fields.

4. Press **Ctrl+S** to save the table. Choose **ShoppingCart** for the name and click **OK**.

5. Add a foreign key by right-clicking the table and selecting **Relationships**, or by going to **Table Designer ➤ Relationships**.

6. Click **Add** to create a new relationship entry.

7. Select the **Tables and Columns Specification** (see Figure 13-5) and then click the "**...**" button.

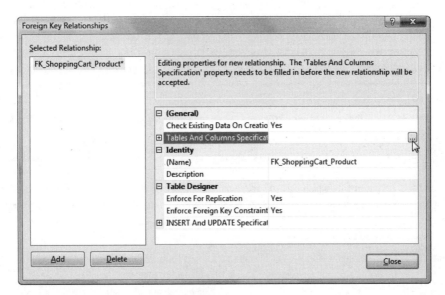

Figure 13-5. *Adding a new relationship*

8. Complete the form that appears, as shown in Figure 13-6.

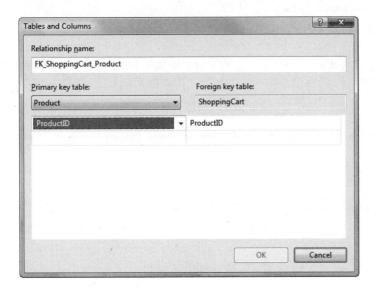

Figure 13-6. *Setting foreign key properties*

9. Click **OK** and then **Close**.

10. Save your table. Confirm the action when asked about applying changes to the Product and ShoppingCart tables.

How It Works: The ShoppingCart Table

CartID is the unique ID you'll generate for each shopping cart. Unlike the other unique identifiers you've seen so far, this is not an integer field; instead, it's a Char(36) field, which will be filled with a GUID string. A GUID (Globally Unique Identifier) is a value guaranteed to be unique across time and space. Two generated GUIDs will never be the same. The string representation of a GUID has 36 characters: The GUID itself is 32 bytes long, and its string representation also contains 4 separating dashes. An example of a GUID is ff8029a7-91e2-4ca2-b4e7-99a7588be751.

■Tip When you know the exact length of the strings you're storing in a table field, it's better to use the Char data type than VarChar.

The second field is ProductID, which, as expected, holds the ID of an existing product. To ensure that the cart doesn't hold any nonexistent products, you need to enforce the One-to-Many relationship between the ShoppingCart and Product tables through a FOREIGN KEY constraint. The relationship is tied between the ProductID columns in the ShoppingCart and Product tables.

The primary key is formed from both the CartID and ProductID fields (a **composite primary key**). This makes sense because a particular product can exist only once in a particular shopping cart, so a CartID, ProductID pair shouldn't appear more than once in the table. If the visitor adds a product more than once, you just increase the Quantity value.

Each record in ShoppingCart also has a DateAdded field, which is automatically populated with the current date when a new product is added to the cart, and is useful when deleting old records. We also have an Attributes column, which will store the product's attributes in the Color: White format.

■Tip Your implementation of the ShoppingCartAddItem procedure manually fills the DateAdded field using the GETDATE function. Alternatively, you can specify GETDATE as the default value for the DateAdded field.

Implementing the Data Tier

Because you have already created stored procedures in the previous chapters, we'll move a bit more quickly this time. You need to add the following stored procedures to the BalloonShop database:

- ShoppingCartAddItem adds a product to a shopping cart.
- ShoppingCartRemoveItem deletes a record from the ShoppingCart table.
- ShoppingCartUpdateItem modifies a shopping cart record.
- ShoppingCartGetItems gets the list of products in the specified shopping cart.
- ShoppingCartGetTotalAmount returns the total cost of the products in the specified product cart.

ShoppingCartAddItem

ShoppingCartAddItem is called when the visitor clicks the Add to Cart button for one of the products. If the selected product already exists in the shopping cart, its quantity is increased by one; if the product doesn't exist, a new record is added to the shopping cart.

Not surprisingly, the parameters ShoppingCartAddItem receives are CartID and ProductID. The stored procedure first searches to determine whether the ProductID, CartID pair exists in the ShoppingCart table. If it does, the stored procedure updates the current product quantity in the shopping cart by adding one unit. Otherwise, the procedure creates a new record for the product in ShoppingCart with a default quantity of 1, but not before checking whether the mentioned @ProductID is valid.

Add the following stored procedure to your BalloonShop database:

```
CREATE Procedure ShoppingCartAddItem
(@CartID char(36),
 @ProductID int,
 @Attributes nvarchar(1000))
AS
IF EXISTS
        (SELECT CartID
          FROM ShoppingCart
          WHERE ProductID = @ProductID AND CartID = @CartID)
    UPDATE ShoppingCart
    SET Quantity = Quantity + 1
    WHERE ProductID = @ProductID AND CartID = @CartID
ELSE
    IF EXISTS (SELECT Name FROM Product WHERE ProductID=@ProductID)
      INSERT INTO ShoppingCart (CartID, ProductID, Attributes, Quantity, DateAdded)
      VALUES (@CartID, @ProductID, @Attributes, 1, GETDATE())
```

You use the GETDATE system function to retrieve the current date and manually populate the DateAdded field, but you could set the GETDATE function as the default value of that field instead.

ShoppingCartRemoveItem

Following is the stored procedure that removes a product from the shopping cart. This happens when the visitor clicks the Remove button for one of the products in the shopping cart. Add the ShoppingCartRemoveItem stored procedure to your BalloonShop database:

```
CREATE PROCEDURE ShoppingCartRemoveItem
(@CartID char(36),
 @ProductID int)
AS
DELETE FROM ShoppingCart
WHERE CartID = @CartID and ProductID = @ProductID
```

ShoppingCartUpdateItem

ShoppingCartUpdateItem is used when you want to update the quantity of an existing shopping cart item. This stored procedure receives three values as parameters: @CartID, @ProductID, and @Quantity.

If @Quantity is 0 or less, ShoppingCartUpdateItem calls ShoppingCartRemoveItem to remove the mentioned product from the shopping cart. Otherwise, it updates the quantity of the product in the shopping cart and updates DateAdded to accurately reflect the time the record was last modified.

■**Tip** Updating the DateAdded field is important because the administrator can remove old shopping carts from the database, and you don't want to remove carts that were recently updated!

Add the ShoppingCartUpdateItem stored procedure to your BalloonShop database:

```
CREATE Procedure ShoppingCartUpdateItem
(@CartID char(36),
 @ProductID int,
 @Quantity int)
AS
IF @Quantity <= 0
  EXEC ShoppingCartRemoveItem @CartID, @ProductID
ELSE
  UPDATE ShoppingCart
  SET Quantity = @Quantity, DateAdded = GETDATE()
  WHERE ProductID = @ProductID AND CartID = @CartID
```

ShoppingCartGetItems

This stored procedure returns the ID, name, price, quantity, and subtotal for each product in the shopping cart. Because the ShoppingCart table only stores the ProductID for each product it stores, you need to join the ShoppingCart and Product tables to get the information you need. Add the ShoppingCartGetItems stored procedure to your BalloonShop database:

```
CREATE PROCEDURE ShoppingCartGetItems
(@CartID char(36))
AS
SELECT Product.ProductID, Product.Name, ShoppingCart.Attributes,
  Product.Price, ShoppingCart.Quantity,Product.Price * ➡
  ShoppingCart.Quantity AS Subtotal
FROM ShoppingCart INNER JOIN Product
ON ShoppingCart.ProductID = Product.ProductID
WHERE ShoppingCart.CartID = @CartID
```

> **Note** Subtotal is a computed column. It doesn't exist in any of the tables you joined, but it's generated using a formula, which in this case is the price of the product multiplied by its quantity. When sending back the results, Subtotal is regarded as a separate column.

ShoppingCartGetTotalAmount

ShoppingCartGetTotalAmount returns the total value of the products in the shopping cart. This is called when displaying the total amount for the shopping cart.

```
CREATE PROCEDURE ShoppingCartGetTotalAmount
(@CartID char(36))
AS
SELECT ISNULL(SUM(Product.Price * ShoppingCart.Quantity), 0)
FROM ShoppingCart INNER JOIN Product
ON ShoppingCart.ProductID = Product.ProductID
WHERE ShoppingCart.CartID = @CartID
```

> **Note** The ISNULL method is used to return 0 instead of a NULL total amount (this happens if the shopping cart is empty). You must do this because the business tier expects to receive a numerical value as the amount.

This stored procedure is different from the others in that it returns a single value instead of a result set. In the business tier, you'll retrieve this value using the ExecuteScalar method of the DbCommand object.

Implementing the Business Tier

You'll write the business layer methods for the shopping cart in a separate class named ShoppingCartAccess.

The ShoppingCartAccess class supports the functionality required for the presentation layer of the shopping cart and calls the stored procedures you wrote earlier. For example, when the visitor clicks the Add to Cart button, a method of the ShoppingCartAccess class named AddProduct is called.

None of the methods receives a CartID parameter, which might appear strange because all the stored procedures you've written so far require a CartID parameter. So, how does the AddItem method know which CartID to send to the ShoppingCartAddItem stored procedure?

Generating Shopping Cart IDs

Your site needs to know the cart ID of your visitor's shopping cart to perform its shopping cart functionality. You'll create a property named shoppingCartId in the ShoppingCartAccess class, which returns the cart ID of the current visitor. It's important to understand how this latter property works.

HTTP is, by its nature, a **stateless protocol**. Each individual client request is not associated with any previous requests from the same user. ASP.NET has a number of built-in features that overcome this problem, one of them being the session state that you've already met earlier in this book.

When it comes to identifying the visitor that browses your site and keeping track of the visitor's unique shopping cart, the first thing that comes to mind is **cookies**.

COOKIES

Cookies are client-side pieces of information that are managed by the visitor's browser; they are stored as name-value pairs. Cookies have the advantages of not consuming server resources (because they are managed at the client) and having configurable expiration. By saving data unique to your visitor in a cookie (such as the visitor's shopping cart ID), you can later find its ID by requesting the cookie from the client. Cookies are also useful because you can set them to expire when the browser session ends (so a new shopping cart is created every time the visitor comes back to the site), or you can set them to exist indefinitely on the client computer, effectively allowing you to control how long the shopping cart is remembered by your application.

If you store the cart ID in the visitor's cookie, you'll have access to it when the visitor returns after a period of time. If the shopping cart cookie doesn't exist, it can mean that the visitor used your shopping cart for the first time, so you generate a new GUID and save it to the cookie. If the cookie exists, you take the GUID from there and use the shopping cart associated with it.

What about customers that have disabled (or whose browsers don't support) cookies? Well, the backup strategy is to also use the visitor's **session**. ASP.NET's session relies, by default, on using cookies, but by changing a simple setting, you can enable cookieless session support. An alternative option to support cookieless browsers is to append the session ID to the query string, as many popular e-commerce web sites do. Both solutions have the same effect and allow the customers to use your shopping cart even if their browsers don't support cookies (however, in this case, their shopping carts are lost if they close their browser session and return after a while, unlike when using cookies).

SESSION

Session handling is a great ASP.NET feature that allows you to keep track of variables specific to a certain visitor accessing the web site. While your visitor browses various pages of the web site, its session variables are persisted by the web server, and the web application can keep track of certain visitor data by uniquely identifying the visitor (you can track, for example, data such as the visitor ID or the visitor's favorite background color, name, email address, and so on). The visitor's session object stores pairs of values (variable name, variable value) that are accessible for the visitor's entire visit on your web site.

In ASP.NET, you can access the session data through the `Session` object. You can use this object to preserve data between client requests. This data is stored on the server side and is not passed back and forth during requests—only a session identifier is passed. This means that storing large quantities of data in the visitor's session occupies the server's memory, but doesn't increase network traffic. In this chapter, you'll only use the session to store the ID of your visitor's shopping cart.

So, shoppingCartId is a read-only property that returns the CartID of the visitor for whom the call has been made. In this property, you'll use a cookie named BalloonShop_CartID and a session variable with the same name to keep track of your visitor's shopping cart records.

Let's create the ShoppingCartAccess class and add its shoppingCartId property in the following exercise.

Exercise: Preparing the ShoppingCartAccess Class

1. We prefer to store the number of days for the cookie expiration in the config file rather than in code, so open web.config and add this configuration setting:

```
<appSettings>
  <add key="CartPersistDays" value="10" />
...
```

■Note Setting the expiration time to 0 generates nonpersistent cookies (they are automatically deleted when the visitor's session ends).

2. Add the following public property to return the configuration value:

```
// Returns the number of days for shopping cart expiration
public static int CartPersistDays
{
  get
  {
    return int.Parse(ConfigurationManager.AppSettings["CartPersistDays"]);
  }
}
```

3. Now for the real code that deals with the visitor's shopping cart. Right-click the App_Code folder in Solution Explorer and select **Add New Item**.

4. Select **Class** from the Templates window and name it ShoppingCartAccess.cs.

5. After the file is in place, add a reference to the System.Data.Common assembly and write the shoppingCartId property as shown here:

```
using System;
using System.Web;
using System.Data.Common;

/// <summary>
/// Supports Shopping Cart functionality
/// </summary>
public class ShoppingCartAccess
{
```

```csharp
public ShoppingCartAccess()
{
  //
  // TODO: Add constructor logic here
  //
}

// returns the shopping cart ID for the current user
private static string shoppingCartId
{
  get
  {
    // get the current HttpContext
    HttpContext context = HttpContext.Current;
    // try to retrieve the cart ID from the user cookie
    string cartId = context.Request.Cookies["BalloonShop_CartID"].Value;
    // if the cart ID isn't in the cookie...
    {
      // check if the cart ID exists as a cookie
      if (context.Request.Cookies["BalloonShop_CartID"] != null)
      {
        // return the id
        return cartId;
      }
      else
      // if the cart ID doesn't exist in the cookie as well, generate
      // a new ID
      {
        // generate a new GUID
        cartId = Guid.NewGuid().ToString();
        // create the cookie object and set its value
        HttpCookie cookie = new HttpCookie("BalloonShop_CartID", cartId);
        // set the cookie's expiration date
        int howManyDays = BalloonShopConfiguration.CartPersistDays;
        DateTime currentDate = DateTime.Now;
        TimeSpan timeSpan = new TimeSpan(howManyDays, 0, 0, 0);
        DateTime expirationDate = currentDate.Add(timeSpan);
        cookie.Expires = expirationDate;
        // set the cookie on the client's browser
        context.Response.Cookies.Add(cookie);
        // return the CartID
        return cartId.ToString();
      }
    }
  }
}
```

How It Works: ShoppingCartAccess and Cart IDs

The strategy of the shoppingCartID property is something like this:

1. Check whether the CartID is stored in the user cookie. If the cookie is found, use its value and also save the value to the session so next time it will be found from the first attempt, without needing to read the cookie from the client again.

2. If the CartID doesn't exist in the session or a cookie, generate a new GUID and save it to both the session and the cookie, effectively creating a new shopping cart.

When you set an expiration time for the cookie, it becomes a persistent cookie and is saved as a file by the computer's browser. We set our cookie to expire in ten days, so the visitor's shopping cart exists for ten days from the time it is created. If an expiration date is not specified, the cookie is stored only for the current browser session.

What If the Visitor Doesn't Like Cookies?

Using the session as a backup strategy "against" cookies isn't enough to support cookieless browsers because, by default, ASP.NET uses cookies to track session information.

To configure your web site to work with browsers that have cookies disabled, you need to configure ASP.NET's session to work without cookies. To do that, you need to open web.config and make this change:

```
<sessionState
    mode="InProc"
    stateConnectionString="tcpip=127.0.0.1:42424"
    sqlConnectionString="data source=127.0.0.1;Trusted_Connection=yes"
    cookieless="true"
    timeout="20" />
```

In cookieless mode, an ID for the session state is automatically saved by ASP.NET in the query string:

```
http://localhost/BalloonShop/(vcmq0tz22y2okxzdq1bo2w45)/default.aspx
```

Unfortunately, this looks a bit ugly, but works without using cookies. Now it's just a matter of taste and knowledge of your customers to enable or disable this feature. We won't use this feature in BalloonShop.

Implementing the Shopping Cart Access Functionality

Here we create five methods in the business tier that correspond to the five stored procedures you wrote earlier. Add the methods presented in the following sections to the ShoppingCartAccess class.

AddItem

AddItem calls the ShoppingCartAddItem stored procedure. If the product already exists in the shopping cart, its quantity is increased by one. Otherwise, the product is added with a default quantity of one:

```csharp
// Add a new shopping cart item
public static bool AddItem(string productId, string attributes)
{
  // get a configured DbCommand object
  DbCommand comm = GenericDataAccess.CreateCommand();
  // set the stored procedure name
  comm.CommandText = "ShoppingCartAddItem";
  // create a new parameter
  DbParameter param = comm.CreateParameter();
  param.ParameterName = "@CartID";
  param.Value = shoppingCartId;
  param.DbType = DbType.String;
  param.Size = 36;
  comm.Parameters.Add(param);
  // create a new parameter
  param = comm.CreateParameter();
  param.ParameterName = "@ProductID";
  param.Value = productId;
  param.DbType = DbType.Int32;
  comm.Parameters.Add(param);
  // create a new parameter
  param = comm.CreateParameter();
  param.ParameterName = "@Attributes";
  param.Value = attributes;
  param.DbType = DbType.String;
  comm.Parameters.Add(param);
  // returns true in case of success and false in case of an error
  try
  {
    // execute the stored procedure and return true if it executes
    // successfully, and false otherwise
    return (GenericDataAccess.ExecuteNonQuery(comm) != -1);
  }
  catch
  {
    // prevent the exception from propagating, but return false to
    // signal the error
    return false;
  }
}
```

UpdateItem

UpdateItem calls the ShoppingCartUpdateItem stored procedure to change the quantity of a product that already exists in the shopping cart:

```
// Update the quantity of a shopping cart item
public static bool UpdateItem(string productId, int quantity)
{
  // get a configured DbCommand object
  DbCommand comm = GenericDataAccess.CreateCommand();
  // set the stored procedure name
  comm.CommandText = "ShoppingCartUpdateItem";
  // create a new parameter
  DbParameter param = comm.CreateParameter();
  param.ParameterName = "@CartID";
  param.Value = shoppingCartId;
  param.DbType = DbType.String;
  param.Size = 36;
  comm.Parameters.Add(param);
  // create a new parameter
  param = comm.CreateParameter();
  param.ParameterName = "@ProductID";
  param.Value = productId;
  param.DbType = DbType.Int32;
  comm.Parameters.Add(param);
  // create a new parameter
  param = comm.CreateParameter();
  param.ParameterName = "@Quantity";
  param.Value = quantity;
  param.DbType = DbType.Int32;
  comm.Parameters.Add(param);
  // returns true in case of success and false in case of an error
  try
  {
    // execute the stored procedure and return true if it executes
    // successfully, and false otherwise
    return (GenericDataAccess.ExecuteNonQuery(comm) != -1);
  }
  catch
  {
    // prevent the exception from propagating, but return false to
    // signal the error
    return false;
  }
}
```

RemoveItem

Now add the RemoveItem method, which causes the removal of one product from the customer's shopping cart:

```csharp
// Remove a shopping cart item
public static bool RemoveItem(string productId)
{
  // get a configured DbCommand object
  DbCommand comm = GenericDataAccess.CreateCommand();
  // set the stored procedure name
  comm.CommandText = "ShoppingCartRemoveItem";
  // create a new parameter
  DbParameter param = comm.CreateParameter();
  param.ParameterName = "@CartID";
  param.Value = shoppingCartId;
  param.DbType = DbType.String;
  param.Size = 36;
  comm.Parameters.Add(param);
  // create a new parameter
  param = comm.CreateParameter();
  param.ParameterName = "@ProductID";
  param.Value = productId;
  param.DbType = DbType.Int32;
  comm.Parameters.Add(param);
  // returns true in case of success and false in case of an error
  try
  {

    // execute the stored procedure and return true if it executes
    // successfully, and false otherwise
    return (GenericDataAccess.ExecuteNonQuery(comm) != -1);
  }
  catch
  {
    // prevent the exception from propagating, but return false to
    // signal the error
    return false;
  }
}
```

GetItems

GetItems retrieves all the products in the customer's shopping cart. This is called from the presentation tier when the visitor wants to view the cart:

```csharp
// Retrieve shopping cart items
public static DataTable GetItems()
{
  // get a configured DbCommand object
  DbCommand comm = GenericDataAccess.CreateCommand();
  // set the stored procedure name
  comm.CommandText = "ShoppingCartGetItems";
```

```
  // create a new parameter
  DbParameter param = comm.CreateParameter();
  param.ParameterName = "@CartID";
  param.Value = shoppingCartId;
  param.DbType = DbType.String;
  param.Size = 36;
  comm.Parameters.Add(param);
  // return the result table
  DataTable table = GenericDataAccess.ExecuteSelectCommand(comm);
  return table;
}
```

GetTotalAmount

GetTotalAmount does exactly what its name suggests, and it's a bit more interesting than the others because it uses SqlCommand's ExecuteScalar method, which we haven't used so far. Add it to the ShoppingCart class, and we'll discuss the details:

```
// Retrieve shopping cart items
public static decimal GetTotalAmount()
{
  // get a configured DbCommand object
  DbCommand comm = GenericDataAccess.CreateCommand();
  // set the stored procedure name
  comm.CommandText = "ShoppingCartGetTotalAmount";
  // create a new parameter
  DbParameter param = comm.CreateParameter();
  param.ParameterName = "@CartID";
  param.Value = shoppingCartId;
  param.DbType = DbType.String;
  param.Size = 36;
  comm.Parameters.Add(param);
  // return the result table
  return Decimal.Parse(GenericDataAccess.ExecuteScalar(comm));
}
```

Implementing the Presentation Tier

Okay, now that the foundation functionality is in place, you can add the presentation tier bits. Building the user interface for the shopping cart functionality involves the following major steps:

- Creating Add to Cart buttons (refer to Figure 13-2)

- Showing shopping cart summary information in catalog pages (refer to Figure 13-2)

- Creating the actual shopping cart page (refer to Figure 13-1)

- Allowing the visitor to update product quantities in the shopping cart

    Let's deal with these tasks one by one.

Updating the Add to Cart Buttons

Right now your Add to Cart buttons in Product.aspx redirect your visitor to the PayPal shopping cart. To change them to work with your new shopping cart, open Products.aspx.cs and edit the last part of AddToCartButton_Click like this:

```
protected void AddToCartButton_Click(object sender, EventArgs e)
{
  // Retrieve ProductID from the query string
  string productId = Request.QueryString["ProductID"];

  // Retrieve the selected product options
  string options = "";
  foreach (Control cnt in attrPlaceHolder.Controls)
  {
    if (cnt is Label)
    {
      Label attrLabel = (Label)cnt;
      options += attrLabel.Text;
    }

    if (cnt is DropDownList)
    {
      DropDownList attrDropDown = (DropDownList)cnt;
      options += attrDropDown.Items[attrDropDown.SelectedIndex] + "; ";
    }
  }

  // Add the product to the shopping cart
  ShoppingCartAccess.AddItem(productId, options);
}
```

After making this change, build the project (Ctrl+Shift+B) and then load the site to make sure the buttons appear okay. Now click the Add to Cart button on one of the products on the site. If you don't get any errors, the product was probably successfully added to the shopping cart; right now, you can't see this in the web site, because you still need to implement functionality for viewing the shopping cart.

Showing the Shopping Cart Summary

The shopping cart summary is implemented as a Web User Control named CartSummary.ascx. You'll use this control in the BalloonShop.master Master Page, so it shows up in every page that implements it. However, you'll write a bit of code in your control to make sure it doesn't also appear in the shopping cart page, because you don't want to show both the cart and its summary on the same page.

Exercise: Showing the Shopping Cart Summary

1. Let's start with the simple details. Add the following style to `BalloonShop.css`:

```
.CartSummary {
  border: #0468a4 2px solid;
  background-color: snow;
  padding: 3px 2px 5px;
}
```

2. Add a new Web User Control to your `UserControls` folder, named `CartSummary.ascx`. Make sure the language is Visual C# and that the **Place code in separate file** check box is checked.

3. Add the following code to `CartSummary.ascx`:

```
<table class="CartSummary" border="0" cellpadding="0" cellspacing="1" ➥
width="200">
  <tr>
    <td>
      <b>
        <asp:Label ID="cartSummaryLabel" runat="server" /></b>
        <asp:HyperLink ID="viewCartLink" runat="server" NavigateUrl=➥
"../ShoppingCart.aspx"
          CssClass="CartLink" Text="(view details)" />
        <asp:DataList ID="list" runat="server">
          <ItemTemplate>
            <%# Eval("Quantity") %>
            x
            <%# Eval("Name") %>
          </ItemTemplate>
        </asp:DataList>
        <img src="Images/line.gif" border="0" width="99%" height="1" />
        Total: <span class="ProductPrice">
          <asp:Label ID="totalAmountLabel" runat="server" />
        </span>
    </td>
  </tr>
</table>
```

4. Go to the control's code-behind file (`CartSummary.ascx.cs`) and add the `Page_Prerender` function, along with its `PopulateControls` helper function, like this:

```
// fill cart summary contents in the PreRender stage
protected void Page_PreRender(object sender, EventArgs e)
{
  PopulateControls();
}

// fill the controls with data
```

```
private void PopulateControls()
{
  // get the items in the shopping cart
  System.Data.DataTable dt = ShoppingCartAccess.GetItems();
  // if the shopping cart is empty...
  if (dt.Rows.Count == 0)
  {
    cartSummaryLabel.Text = "Your shopping cart is empty.";
    totalAmountLabel.Text = String.Format("{0:c}", 0);
    viewCartLink.Visible = false;
    list.Visible = false;
  }
  else
  // if the shopping cart is not empty...
  {
    // populate the list with the shopping cart contents
    list.Visible = true;
    list.DataSource = dt;
    list.DataBind();
    // set up controls
    cartSummaryLabel.Text = "Cart summary ";
    viewCartLink.Visible = true;
    // display the total amount
    decimal amount = ShoppingCartAccess.GetTotalAmount();
    totalAmountLabel.Text = String.Format("{0:c}", amount);
  }
}
```

5. Because you'll include the shopping cart summary control in the Master Page, normally it will show up in every page of your web site. If you don't want your shopping cart summary to show up when the visitor is viewing the shopping cart page, add the following code to the CartSummary class in CartSummary.ascx.cs:

```
// we don't want to display the cart summary in the shopping cart page
protected void Page_Init(object sender, EventArgs e)
{
  // get the current page
  string page = Request.AppRelativeCurrentExecutionFilePath;
  // if we're in the shopping cart, don't display the cart summary
  if (String.Compare(page, "~/ShoppingCart.aspx", true) == 0)
    this.Visible = false;
  else
    this.Visible = true;
}
```

6. The tough part's over now. Build the project to ensure everything compiles okay.

7. Open BallonShop.master in Design View and then drag CartSummary.ascx from Solution Explorer to BalloonShop.master, as shown in Figure 13-7.

8. Execute the project to ensure the shopping cart summary shows up as expected. Just don't expect the view details link to work, because you haven't implemented the ShoppingCart.aspx file yet.

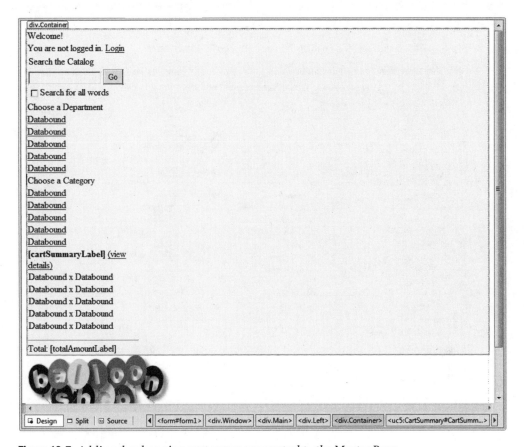

Figure 13-7. *Adding the shopping cart summary control to the Master Page*

How It Works: The Shopping Cart Summary

The important bit to understand here is the way we used the Page_PreRender method to populate the control with data.

We used Page_PreRender instead of the Load event, because Load fires *before* the Click event of the Add to Cart buttons, so the summary is updated before—not after—the cart is updated. PreRender, on the other hand, fires later in the control life cycle, so we used it to ensure that the cart summary is properly updated.

To learn more about the life cycle of ASP.NET controls, see an advanced ASP.NET book.

Displaying the Shopping Cart

Finally, you've arrived at the shopping cart, your primary goal for this chapter. The shopping cart is a Web Form named ShoppingCart.aspx, based on the BalloonShop.master Master Page. Follow the steps in the next exercise to build your shopping cart page.

Exercise: Implementing the Shopping Cart

1. Right-click the project name in Solution Explorer and click **Add New Item**.

2. Select the **Web Form** template, write **ShoppingCart.aspx** for its name, make sure the language is Visual C#, and select the two check boxes (**Place code in separate file** and **Select master page**), as shown in Figure 13-8. Click **Add**.

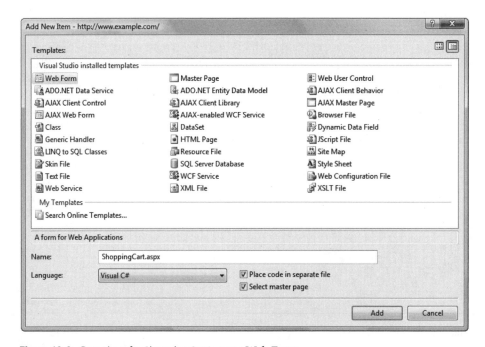

Figure 13-8. *Creating the ShoppingCart.aspx Web Form*

3. Choose the BalloonShop.master file in the dialog box that opens and click **OK**.

4. If you prefer to work in Design View, create a form as shown in Figure 13-9, and set the controls' properties as shown in Table 13-1.

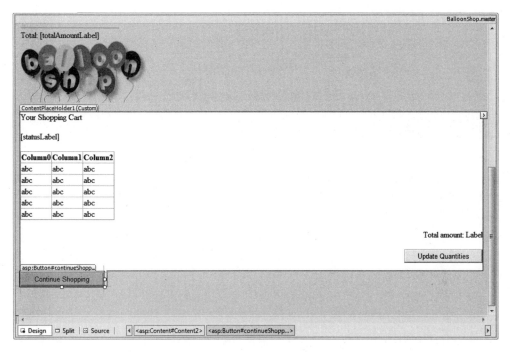

Figure 13-9. *ShoppingCart.aspx in Design View*

Table 13-1. *Control Properties in ShoppingCart.ascx*

Control Type	ID Property	Text Property
Label	titleLabel	Your Shopping Cart
Label	statusLabel	(empty)
GridView	grid	
Label	totalAmountLabel	
Button	updateButton	Update Quantities

5. Feel free to play with the control's look to customize it according to your preferences. The source code of your page should look something like this:

```
<%@ Page Title="BalloonShop: Shopping Cart" Language="C#" MasterPageFile=➥
"~/BalloonShop.master"
   AutoEventWireup="true" CodeFile="ShoppingCart.aspx.cs" Inherits=➥
"ShoppingCart" %>

<asp:Content ID="Content1" ContentPlaceHolderID="head" runat="Server">
</asp:Content>
<asp:Content ID="Content2" ContentPlaceHolderID="ContentPlaceHolder1" ➥
runat="Server">
```

```
<p>
  <asp:Label ID="titleLabel" runat="server" Text="Your Shopping Cart" ➡
CssClass="CatalogTitle" />
</p>
<p>
  <asp:Label ID="statusLabel" runat="server" />
</p>
<asp:GridView ID="grid" runat="server">
</asp:GridView>
<p align="right">
  <span>Total amount: </span>
  <asp:Label ID="totalAmountLabel" runat="server" Text="Label" />
</p>
<p align="right">
  <asp:Button ID="updateButton" runat="server" Text="Update Quantities" />
</p>
</asp:Content>
```

6. Now it's time to deal with the GridView control. Set its AutoGenerateColumns property to **false**, DataKeyNames to **ProductID**, Width to **100%**, and BorderWidth to **0px**.

7. In Design View, select the **GridView**, click the **Smart Link**, and choose **Add New Column** to add the grid columns listed in Table 13-2.

Table 13-2. *Setting the Properties of the GridView Control*

Column Type	Header Text	Data Field	Other Properties
BoundField	Product Name	Name	Read-only
BoundField	Price	Price	Read-only
BoundField	Attributes	Attributes	Read-only
TemplateField	Quantity		
BoundField	Subtotal	Subtotal	Read-only
ButtonField			Command name: DeleteText; DeleteButton type: Button

■**Note** The Product Name, Price, and Subtotal columns are marked as read-only. If you transform them to template fields, Visual Web Developer won't generate their EditItemTemplate but only their ItemTemplate. Also, they won't be editable if the GridView enters edit mode (we don't use this feature here, however, but you know the functionality from Chapter 11).

8. Click the GridView's **Smart Link** and choose **Edit Columns**. From the Selected Fields list, select **Price** and set its DataFormatString property to **{0:c}**.

9. Do the same for the Subtotal field (set the DataFormatString to **{0:c}**).

10. The Quantity field is a template field, so you need to fill its contents manually. Switch to Source View and add the following TextBox to the ItemTemplate:

```
<asp:TemplateField HeaderText="Quantity">
<ItemTemplate>
<asp:TextBox ID="editQuantity" runat="server" CssClass="GridEditingRow"
        Width="24px" MaxLength="2" Text='<%#Eval("Quantity")%>' />
</ItemTemplate>
</asp:TemplateField>
```

11. Verify that the content area of your Web Form looks like Figure 13-10.

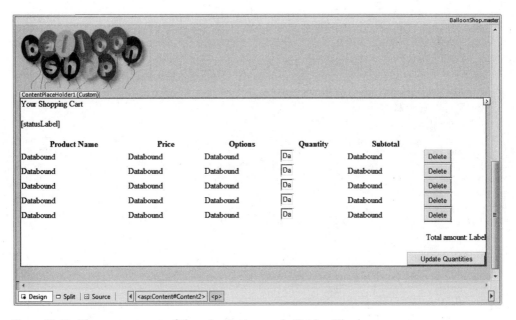

Figure 13-10. *The content area of ShoppingCart.aspx in Design View*

The grid code is as follows:

```
<asp:GridView ID="grid" runat="server" AutoGenerateColumns="False" ➡
DataKeyNames="ProductID"
   Width="100%" BorderWidth="0px" OnRowDeleting="grid_RowDeleting">
   <Columns>
```

```
<asp:BoundField DataField="Name" HeaderText="Product Name" ➥
      ReadOnly="True" SortExpression="Name">
            <ControlStyle Width="100%" />
        </asp:BoundField>
        <asp:BoundField DataField="Price" DataFormatString="{0:c}" ➥
    HeaderText="Price" ReadOnly="True"
           SortExpression="Price" />
        <asp:BoundField DataField="Attributes" HeaderText="Options" ➥
    ReadOnly="True"/>
        <asp:TemplateField HeaderText="Quantity">
          <ItemTemplate>
            <asp:TextBox ID="editQuantity" runat="server"➥
    CssClass="GridEditingRow" Width="24px"
              MaxLength="2" Text='<%#Eval("Quantity")%>' />
          </ItemTemplate>
        </asp:TemplateField>
        <asp:BoundField DataField="Subtotal" DataFormatString="{0:c}" ➥
    HeaderText="Subtotal"
          ReadOnly="True" SortExpression="Subtotal" />
        <asp:ButtonField ButtonType="Button" CommandName="Delete" ➥
    Text="Delete"></asp:ButtonField>
     </Columns>
   </asp:GridView>
```

12. The visual part is ready. Open the code-behind file now (ShoppingCart.aspx.cs) and complete its
    Page_Load method to populate the controls, as shown in the following code listing:

```
using System;
using System.Data;
using System.Collections.Generic;
using System.Linq;
using System.Web;
using System.Web.UI;
using System.Web.UI.WebControls;

public partial class ShoppingCart: System.Web.UI.Page
{
    protected void Page_Load(object sender, EventArgs e)
    {
      // populate the control only on the initial page load
      if (!IsPostBack)
        PopulateControls();
    }
```

```csharp
// fill shopping cart controls with data
private void PopulateControls()
{
  // get the items in the shopping cart
  DataTable dt = ShoppingCartAccess.GetItems();
  // if the shopping cart is empty...
  if (dt.Rows.Count == 0)
  {
    titleLabel.Text = "Your shopping cart is empty!";
    grid.Visible = false;
    updateButton.Enabled = false;
    totalAmountLabel.Text = String.Format("{0:c}", 0);
  }
  else
  // if the shopping cart is not empty...
  {
    // populate the list with the shopping cart contents
    grid.DataSource = dt;
    grid.DataBind();
    // set up controls
    titleLabel.Text = "These are the products in your shopping cart:";
    grid.Visible = true;
    updateButton.Enabled = true;
    // display the total amount
    decimal amount = ShoppingCartAccess.GetTotalAmount();
    totalAmountLabel.Text = String.Format("{0:c}", amount);
  }
}
```

How It Works: The Shopping Cart Page

The steps in this exercise are probably familiar to you by now. You created a new Web Form and then added a number of controls to it, including a GridView control, to which you added and formatted columns afterward.

Feel free to execute the project, add a few products to the cart, and then click the view details link in the cart summary. Your shopping cart should display your products nicely. It takes a couple of more exercises to make the Update Quantities button functional.

Editing Product Quantities

You learned how to work with editable GridView controls in Chapter 11. However, this time you won't use the GridView's editing functionality, because you want to allow the visitor to update several product quantities at once, not only record by record. Of course, if you prefer, you can always implement the editing functionality just like you learned in Chapter 11, but in this chapter, you'll learn a new way of doing things.

Exercise: Editing Product Quantities

1. Open ShoppingCart.aspx in Design View, select the GridView, and use Visual Web Developer to generate the RowDeleting event handler.

2. Complete the code as shown in the following code listing:

```
// remove a product from the cart
protected void grid_RowDeleting(object sender, GridViewDeleteEventArgs e)
{
  // Index of the row being deleted
  int rowIndex = e.RowIndex;
  // The ID of the product being deleted
  string productId = grid.DataKeys[rowIndex].Value.ToString();
  // Remove the product from the shopping cart
  bool success = ShoppingCartAccess.RemoveItem(productId);
  // Display status
  statusLabel.Text = success ? "Product successfully removed!" :
              "There was an error removing the product! ";
  // Repopulate the control
  PopulateControls();
}
```

3. In ShoppingCart.aspx, double-click the **Update Quantities** button and complete the automatically generated code like this:

```
// update shopping cart product quantities
protected void updateButton_Click(object sender, EventArgs e)
{
  // Number of rows in the GridView
  int rowsCount = grid.Rows.Count;
  // Will store a row of the GridView
  GridViewRow gridRow;
  // Will reference a quantity TextBox in the GridView
  TextBox quantityTextBox;
  // Variables to store product ID and quantity
  string productId;
  int quantity;
  // Was the update successful?
  bool success = true;
  // Go through the rows of the GridView
  for (int i = 0; i < rowsCount; i++)
  {
    // Get a row
    gridRow = grid.Rows[i];
    // The ID of the product being deleted
    productId = grid.DataKeys[i].Value.ToString();
    // Get the quantity TextBox in the Row
```

```
quantityTextBox = (TextBox)gridRow.FindControl("editQuantity");
// Get the quantity, guarding against bogus values
if (Int32.TryParse(quantityTextBox.Text, out quantity))
{
  // Update product quantity
  success = success && ShoppingCartAccess.UpdateItem(productId, quantity);
}
else
{
  // if TryParse didn't succeed
  success = false;
}

// Display status message
statusLabel.Text = success ?
"Your shopping cart was successfully updated!" :
"Some quantity updates failed! Please verify your cart!";
}
// Repopulate the control
PopulateControls();
}
```

How It Works: Editing Product Quantities

Yep, this was interesting all right. Allowing the visitor to edit multiple GridView entries at once is certainly very useful. Take a close look at the code and make sure you understand how the GridView is parsed, how the proper TextBox control is found, and how its value is read. Then, the ShoppingCartAccess class is simply used to update the product quantities.

When reading the values from the TextBox controls and converting them to integers, you use a .NET 2.0 method called TryParse. This static method of the Int32 class (you can find it in other similar classes, too) is similar to Parse, but doesn't throw an exception if the conversion cannot be done—which can easily happen if the visitor enters a letter instead of a number in the quantity box, for example.

TryParse returns a bool value representing the success of the operation and returns the converted value as an out parameter:

```
// Get the quantity, guarding against bogus values
if (Int32.TryParse(quantityTextBox.Text, out quantity))
```

The ShoppingCartAccess.UpdateItem method also returns a bool value specifying whether the update completed successfully or not. Should either this method or TryParse return false, you set the value of the success variable to false. If after processing all rows, the value of success is false, you inform the visitor that at least one of the rows couldn't be updated.

If ShoppingCartAccess.UpdateItem generates a database error for some reason, the error is logged using the log mechanism that you implemented in Chapter 4—if you enabled the error-handling routine, that is—because it can be disabled by changing an option in web.config.

Administering the Shopping Cart

Now that you've finished writing the shopping cart, you need to take two more things into account, and both are related to administration issues:

- How to delete from the product catalog a product that exists in shopping carts.

- How to remove old shopping cart elements by building a simple shopping cart administration page. This is important, because without this feature, the ShoppingCart table keeps growing.

Deleting Products that Exist in Shopping Carts

The catalog administration pages offer the possibility to completely delete products from the catalog. Before removing a product from the Product table, however, you need to remove related records from the related tables first (otherwise, the Foreign Key constraints in the database won't allow the action).

For example, look at the CatalogDeleteProduct stored procedure that first deletes all related records from ProductCategory before deleting the Product record:

```
DELETE FROM ProductCategory WHERE ProductID=@ProductID
DELETE FROM Product where ProductID=@ProductID
```

Now the problem reappears with the ShoppingCart table: the Product and ShoppingCart tables are tied through a FOREIGN KEY constraint on their ProductID fields. The database doesn't allow deleting products from Product that have related ShoppingCart records.

The solution is to update the CatalogDeleteProduct stored procedure to also remove all the references to the product from the ShoppingCart table before attempting to delete it from the database.

Update the CatalogDeleteProduct stored procedure by executing this command (you can use the same screen as the one where you create new procedures, or you can use SQL Server Express Manager):

```
ALTER PROCEDURE CatalogDeleteProduct
(@ProductID int)
AS
DELETE FROM ShoppingCart WHERE ProductID=@ProductID
DELETE FROM ProductCategory WHERE ProductID=@ProductID
DELETE FROM Product where ProductID=@ProductID
```

This way, the site administrators can (once again) remove products from the database.

Removing Old Shopping Carts

The second problem with the shopping cart is that at this moment no mechanism exists to delete the old records from the ShoppingCart table. On a high activity web site with many users and many shopping carts, the ShoppingCart table can grow very large.

With the default setting in web.config, shopping cart IDs are stored at the client browser for ten days. As a result, you can assume that any shopping carts that haven't been updated in the last ten days are invalid and can be safely removed.

In the following exercise, you'll quickly implement a simple shopping cart administration page, where the administrator can see how many old shopping cart entries exist and can delete them if necessary.

The most interesting aspect you need to understand is the logic behind the database stored procedure that calculates the records that need to be deleted. The goal is to delete all shopping carts that haven't been updated in a certain amount of time.

This isn't as simple as it sounds—at first sight, you might think all you have to do is delete all the records in ShoppingCart whose DateAdded value is older than a specified date. However, this strategy doesn't work with shopping carts that are modified over time (say, the visitor has been adding items to the cart each week in the past three months). If the last change to the shopping cart is recent, none of its elements should be deleted, even if some are very old. In other words, you should either remove all elements in a shopping cart or none of them. The age of a shopping cart is given by the age of its most recently modified or added product.

■**Tip** If you look at the ShoppingCartUpdateItem stored procedure, you'll notice it also updates the DateAdded field of a product each time the quantity changes.

For the shopping cart admin page, you'll build two stored procedures (ShoppingCartRemoveOldCarts and ShoppingCartCountOldCarts), but they both work using the same logic to calculate the shopping cart elements that are old and should be removed. First, you should learn a little bit about the SQL logic that retrieves the old shopping cart elements.

Take a look at the following query, which returns how many days have passed since the day the last cart item was added or modified for each cart ID:

```
SELECT CartID,
       MIN(DATEDIFF(dd,DateAdded,GETDATE())) as DaysFromMostRecentRecord
FROM ShoppingCart
GROUP BY CartID
```

The DATEDIFF function returns the difference, in days (because of the dd parameter), between the date specified by DateAdded and the current date (specified by GETDATE). GROUP BY groups the results by CartID, and for each CartID, the MIN aggregate function calculates the most recent record.

To select all the elements from the carts that haven't been modified in the past ten days, you need a query like this:

```
SELECT CartID
FROM ShoppingCart
GROUP BY CartID
HAVING MIN(DATEDIFF(dd,DateAdded,GETDATE())) >= 10
```

You'll implement the shopping cart administration page in the next exercise. You'll implement everything, starting from the stored procedures and finishing with the presentation tier, in a single exercise.

Exercise: Implementing the Cart Admin Page

1. Add the `ShoppingCartRemoveOldCarts` stored procedure to the database. It receives as a parameter the maximum number of days for a shopping cart age. All shopping carts older than that are deleted.

```
CREATE PROCEDURE ShoppingCartDeleteOldCarts
(@Days smallint)
AS
DELETE FROM ShoppingCart
WHERE CartID IN
(SELECT CartID
FROM ShoppingCart
GROUP BY CartID
HAVING MIN(DATEDIFF(dd,DateAdded,GETDATE())) >= @Days)
```

2. Add `ShoppingCartCountOldCarts`, which returns the number of shopping cart elements that would be deleted by a `ShoppingCartCountOldCarts` call:

```
CREATE PROCEDURE ShoppingCartCountOldCarts
(@Days smallint)
AS
SELECT COUNT(CartID)
FROM ShoppingCart
WHERE CartID IN
(SELECT CartID
FROM ShoppingCart
GROUP BY CartID
HAVING MIN(DATEDIFF(dd,DateAdded,GETDATE())) >= @Days)
```

3. Add these methods to the `ShoppingCartAccess` class (located in `ShoppingCartAccess.cs`). They are used to interact with the two stored procedures you wrote earlier.

```
// Counts old shopping carts
public static int CountOldCarts(byte days)
{
  // get a configured DbCommand object
  DbCommand comm = GenericDataAccess.CreateCommand();
  // set the stored procedure name
  comm.CommandText = "ShoppingCartCountOldCarts";
  // create a new parameter
  DbParameter param = comm.CreateParameter();
  param.ParameterName = "@Days";
  param.Value = days;
  param.DbType = DbType.Byte;
  comm.Parameters.Add(param);
```

```
    // execute the procedure and return number of old shopping carts
    try
    {
      return Byte.Parse(GenericDataAccess.ExecuteScalar(comm));
    }
    catch
    {
      return -1;
    }
  }

  // Deletes old shopping carts
  public static bool DeleteOldCarts(byte days)
  {
    // get a configured DbCommand object
    DbCommand comm = GenericDataAccess.CreateCommand();
    // set the stored procedure name
    comm.CommandText = "ShoppingCartDeleteOldCarts";
    // create a new parameter
    DbParameter param = comm.CreateParameter();
    param.ParameterName = "@Days";
    param.Value = days;
    param.DbType = DbType.Byte;
    comm.Parameters.Add(param);
    // execute the procedure and return true if no problem occurs
    try
    {
      GenericDataAccess.ExecuteNonQuery(comm);
      return true;
    }
    catch
    {
      return false;
    }
  }
}
```

4. Create a new Web Form at the root of the `BalloonShop` project, named `AdminShoppingCart.aspx`, based on the `Admin.master` Master Page.

5. While in Source View, add this code to the first placeholder:

```
<asp:Content ID="Content1" ContentPlaceHolderID="titlePlaceHolder" ➥
runat="Server">
  <span class="AdminTitle">
    BalloonShop Admin
    <br />
    Shopping Carts
  </span>
</asp:Content>
```

6. Add the following content to the second placeholder:

```
<asp:Content ID="Content2" ContentPlaceHolderID="adminPlaceHolder" ➥
runat="Server">
  <p>
    <asp:Label ID="countLabel" runat="server">Hello!
    </asp:Label></p>
  <p>
    <span>How many days?</span>
    <asp:DropDownList ID="daysList" runat="server">
      <asp:ListItem Value="0">All shopping carts</asp:ListItem>
      <asp:ListItem Value="1">One</asp:ListItem>
      <asp:ListItem Value="10" Selected="True">Ten</asp:ListItem>
      <asp:ListItem Value="20">Twenty</asp:ListItem>
      <asp:ListItem Value="30">Thirty</asp:ListItem>
      <asp:ListItem Value="90">Ninety</asp:ListItem>
    </asp:DropDownList>
  </p>
  <p>
    <asp:Button ID="countButton" runat="server" Text="Count Old Shopping ➥
Carts" />
    <asp:Button ID="deleteButton" runat="server" Text="Delete Old ➥
Shopping Carts" />
  </p>
</asp:Content>
```

Now if you switch to Design View, you should see a form like the one shown in Figure 13-11.

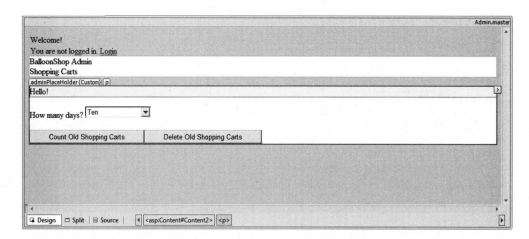

Figure 13-11. *AdminShoppingCart.aspx in Design View*

Double-click the **Delete Old Shopping Carts** button, and complete its `Click` event handler with the following code:

```
// deletes old shopping carts
protected void deleteButton_Click(object sender, EventArgs e)
{
  byte days = byte.Parse(daysList.SelectedItem.Value);
  ShoppingCartAccess.DeleteOldCarts(days);
  countLabel.Text = "The old shopping carts were removed from the database";
}
```

7. Double-click the **Count Old Shopping Carts** button and complete its `Click` event handler with the following code:

```
// counts old shopping carts
protected void countButton_Click(object sender, EventArgs e)
{
  byte days = byte.Parse(daysList.SelectedItem.Value);
  int oldItems = ShoppingCartAccess.CountOldCarts(days);
  if (oldItems == -1)
    countLabel.Text = "Could not count the old shopping carts!";
  else if (oldItems == 0)
    countLabel.Text = "There are no old shopping carts.";
  else
    countLabel.Text = "There are " + oldItems.ToString() +
                      " old shopping carts.";
}
```

8. To restrict this page to administrator-only access, open `web.config` and add the following block, after the one that deals with `CatalogAdmin.aspx`:

```
<!-- Only administrators are allowed to access AdminShoppingCart.aspx -->
<location path="AdminShoppingCart.aspx">
  <system.web>
    <authorization>
      <allow roles="Administrators" />
      <deny users="*" />
    </authorization>
  </system.web>
</location>
```

9. Finally, add a link to this new page. Open `UserInfo.ascx` in Source View and add a link to the shopping cart admin page for the Administrators role group, just after the link to the catalog admin page:

```
<td class="UserInfoContent">
  <asp:LoginStatus ID="LoginStatus2" runat="server" />
  <br />
  <a href="/">BalloonShop</a>
  <br />
  <a href="AdminDepartments.aspx">Catalog Admin</a>
  <br />
  <a href="AdminShoppingCart.aspx">Cart Admin</a>
</td>
```

How It Works: The Shopping Cart Admin Page

Congratulations, you're done! Your new shopping cart admin page should work as expected.

Summary

In this chapter, you learned how to store the shopping cart information in the database, and you learned a few things in the process as well. Probably the most interesting was the way you can store the shopping cart ID as a cookie on the client, because you haven't done anything similar so far in this book.

When writing the code for the user interface, you learned how to allow the visitor to update multiple `GridView` records with a single click. At the end, you updated the administrative part of the web site to deal with the new challenges implied by your custom-created shopping cart.

You'll complete the functionality offered by the custom shopping cart in the next chapter with a custom checkout system. You'll add a Place Order button to the shopping cart, which allows you to save the shopping cart information as a separate order in the database.

See you in the next chapter!

CHAPTER 14

■■■

Accepting and Processing Customer Orders

Your new shopping cart works well, except that it doesn't yet allow your visitors to actually place orders, which is rather troubling since that is the point of all this! We'll deal with that issue in this chapter in two separate stages:

1. First we'll implement the visitor side of the order placement mechanism. More precisely, we'll add a Place Order button to the shopping cart page that creates a PayPal order containing the products in the shopping cart (remember, at this stage, we still don't handle financial transactions ourselves).

2. Next we'll implement a simple orders administration page, so the site administrator can view and handle pending orders.

The code for each part of the site will be presented in the usual way, starting with the database tier, continuing with the business tier, and finishing with the presentation tier (user interface).

Implementing an Order-Placing System

The entire order-placing system is related to the Proceed to Checkout button that you're about to add to your shopping cart. Figure 14-1 shows how this button will look after you update the `ShoppingCart.aspx` page.

Looking at the figure, the button looks boring for something that is the center of this chapter's universe. Still, a lot of logic is hidden behind it, so let's consider what you want to happen when the customer clicks that button. Remember that at this stage, it doesn't matter who places the order, but it's important to store information in the database about the products that were ordered.

Basically, two things need to happen when the customer clicks the Proceed to Checkout button:

1. First, the order must be stored somewhere in the database. You'll create a couple of new tables (Orders and OrderDetail) and write the code that saves the ordered products to these tables.

2. Secondly, the customer must be redirected to a PayPal payment page where the customer pays the necessary amount for the order.

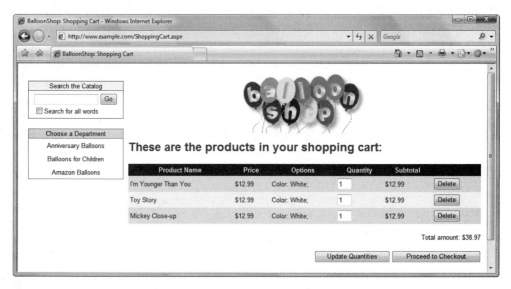

Figure 14-1. *The shopping cart with a Proceed to Checkout button*

■**Note** Since we're in development phase 2, you still don't do the credit card transactions yourself, but use a third-party payment processor instead. You no longer need the PayPal shopping cart because you implemented your own in the previous chapter. Instead, as you'll see, you'll use the Single Item Purchases option of PayPal, which redirects the visitor directly to a payment page.

A problem that arises when using a third-party payment processor is that the customer can change her mind and cancel the order while at the checkout page. This can result in orders that are saved to the database (the order is saved *before* the page is redirected to the payment page), but for which payment wasn't completed. This makes it obvious that a payment confirmation system is necessary, along with a database structure able to store status information about each order.

The confirmation system that you'll implement is simple. Every payment processor, including PayPal, can be instructed to send a confirmation message after a payment has been processed. The site administrator can manually check, in the administration page, which orders have been paid for. The orders for which the payment has been confirmed are known as *verified orders*. You'll see later in this chapter how to manage them in the order management part of the site.

■**Note** PayPal and its competitors offer automated systems that notify your web site when a payment has been completed or canceled. However, in this book, we don't aim at visiting the intimate details of any of these payment systems—you'll need to do your homework and study the documentation of the company you choose. The PayPal Instant Payment Notification documentation is included in the Order Management Integration Guide, which at the time of this writing can be downloaded at `https://www.paypal.com/en_US/pdf/PP_OrderManagement_IntegrationGuide.pdf`.

Now that you have an idea of what the Proceed to Checkout button will do, the next major concerns are *what* product order information to store in the database and *how* to store it. As you saw in the previous chapters, deciding how to store information gives you a better idea of how the whole system works.

Storing Orders in the Database

As pointed out earlier, we start implementing the new feature by creating the necessary data structures. This should not surprise you at this point. You know that deciding what information to use and how to store it helps a great deal when analyzing a new feature and represents the technical foundation of that feature's implementation.

There are two types of information that we want to store when an order is placed:

- *Details about the order as a whole*: What date was the order created? Have the products been shipped, and if so, when? And what's the order's status now? We'll store this data in a table named `Orders`, where each record represents an order.

- *Product details for the order*: What products were ordered in which order? We'll store this data in a table named `OrderDetail`, where each record represents an ordered product. Many records of this table will be associated with one record in the `Orders` table, forming a One-to-Many relationship between the tables (you might want to revisit Chapter 5, where the table relationships are explained).

■**Tip** So far, we have been consistent about naming our tables in singular form (`ShoppingCart`, `Department`, and so on). However, here, we make an exception for the `Orders` table, because `ORDER` is an SQL keyword. For the purposes of this book, we prefer to break the naming convention to avoid any confusion while writing the SQL code, and generally speaking, it isn't good practice to use SQL keywords as object names.

These tables have a One-to-Many relationship, enforced through a FOREIGN KEY constraint on their OrderID fields. One-to-Many is the usual relationship implemented between an Orders table and an OrderDetail table. The OrderDetail table contains *many* records that belong to *one* order. You might want to revisit Chapter 5, where the table relationships are explained in more detail.

You'll create these tables in the following exercise. This time we don't explain each step in great detail, as you've been through these processes before in this book. Feel free to refer to previous chapters if anything is unclear.

Exercise: Adding the Orders and the OrderDetail Tables to the Database

1. First add the Orders table to the database with the columns described in Table 14-1.

Table 14-1. *The Orders Table*

Column Name	Data Type	Allow Nulls	Other Properties
OrderID	int	No	Primary key, identity
DateCreated	smalldatetime	No	Default: GETDATE()
DateShipped	smalldatetime	Yes	
Verified	bit	No	Default value or binding: 0
Completed	bit	No	Default value or binding: 0
Canceled	bit	No	Default value or binding: 0
Comments	nvarchar(1000)	Yes	
CustomerName	nvarchar(50)	Yes	
CustomerEmail	nvarchar(50)	Yes	
ShippingAddress	nvarchar(500)	Yes	

■**Caution** Don't forget to set the default of GETDATE() to the DateCreated column. Don't forget to set OrderID as a primary key and an identity column. Leave Identity Seed and Identity Increment at their default values of 1. Remember that making a column an identity column tells the database to automatically generate values for it when new records are added to the table—you can't supply your own values for that field when adding new records. The generated ID value can be found by reading the @@Identity system variable. You'll use this when creating the CreateOrder stored procedure a bit later.

2. Add the OrderDetail table (see Table 14-2).

Table 14-2. *The OrderDetail Table*

Column Name	Data Type	Allow Nulls	Other Properties
OrderID	int	No	Primary key
ProductID	int	No	Primary key
ProductName	nvarchar(50)	No	
Quantity	int	No	
UnitCost	money	No	
Subtotal		No	Computed Column Specification Formula: Quantity × UnitCost Is persisted: No

■**Caution** Don't forget to set the composite primary key formed of OrderID and ProductID.

3. Enforce the One-to-Many relationship between Orders and OrderDetail by adding a FOREIGN KEY constraint on the OrderID column in OrderDetail to reference the OrderID column in Orders. Do this by either using database diagrams or opening the table in Database Explorer and clicking **Table Designer ➤ Relationships** (as you learned in Chapter 5).

■**Note** Although ProductID is part of the primary key in OrderDetail, you don't place a FOREIGN KEY constraint on it (referencing the Product table), because products can change in time or can even be removed, while the existing orders should remain unchanged. ProductID is simply used to form the primary key of OrderDetail because at any given time, each product has a unique ProductID. However, the ProductID in OrderDetail is not required to point to an existing, real product.

How It Works: The Orders Table

The Orders table basically contains two categories of information: data about the order (the first seven fields), and data about the customer that made the order (last three fields).

The professional way to store customer data is to use a separate table, named Customer, and reference that table from the Orders table. We chose not to take that approach in this chapter because at this stage of development storing customer data is optional and it may not justify the implementation costs. Right now, we don't need to know who bought our products, because the third-party payment processor deals with these details. You'll create the Customer table in Chapter 16, where you add customer accounts functionality to BalloonShop.

Third-party payment processors, such as PayPal, store and manage the complete customer information, so it doesn't need to be stored in your database as well. The `CustomerName`, `ShippingAddress`, and `CustomerEmail` fields have been added as optional fields that can be filled by the administrator if it's easier to have this information at hand for certain (or all) orders. These are convenience fields that will be removed in Chapter 16 when you implement a scheme for storing complete customer details.

Now take a look at the other fields. `OrderID` is the primary key of the table, and is an identity column so you won't need to bother to find new IDs when adding new orders. `DateCreated` also has a pretty obvious role—you need to know the date when each order was created. This column has a default value of `GETDATE()`, which means that it will be automatically filled with the current date when adding new records if a specific value is not specified. `DateShipped` is populated with the date an order has been shipped.

Three bit fields show the status of the order: `Verified`, `Completed`, and `Canceled`. These fields store 0 for No and 1 for Yes. If your business grows, you'll need to extend this system to a professional order pipeline, which you'll learn how to do in Chapter 17. For now, these three bit fields will do the job.

The `Verified` field is set to 1 after the payment has been confirmed by the payment processor. The site administrator marks the order as verified upon receipt of the payment confirmation mail. After the payment is confirmed, the products are shipped, so the `DateShipped` field is populated and the `Completed` bit is also set to 1.

The administrator might want to mark an order as canceled (by setting the `Canceled` bit to 1) if it hasn't been verified in a certain amount of time or for other various reasons. The `Comments` field is used to record whatever special information might show up about the order.

How It Works: The OrderDetail Table

Let's see now what information the `OrderDetail` table contains. Figure 14-2 shows what some typical `OrderDetail` records look like.

	OrderID	ProductID	ProductName	Quantity	UnitCost	Subtotal
4	4	22	I'm Younger Than You	1	12.99	12.99
5	5	26	You're Special	1	12.99	12.99
6	6	26	You're Special	1	12.99	12.99
7	7	22	I'm Younger Than You	1	12.99	12.99
8	8	26	You're Special	1	12.99	12.99
9	9	39	Toy Story	1	12.99	12.99

Figure 14-2. *Sample data in `OrderDetail`*

Each record in `OrderDetail` represents an ordered product that belongs to the order specified by `OrderID`. The primary key is formed by both `OrderID` and `ProductID` because a particular product can be ordered only once in one order. A `Quantity` field contains the number of ordered items, so it wouldn't make any sense to have one `ProductID` recorded more than once for one order.

You might be wondering why apart from the product ID you also store the price and product name in the `OrderDetail` table. The question is valid because if you have the product ID, you can get all the product's details from the `Product` table without having any duplicated information.

The reason is this: the actual order detail data is stored in the `ProductName`, `Quantity`, and `UnitCost` fields. You can't rely on `ProductID` to store order data, because product IDs, names, and prices can change in time. `ProductID` is simply used to form the primary key (in this role, it saves you from needing to create another primary key field), and it's also useful because it's the only programmatic way to link back to the original product (if the product still exists).

The last and most interesting column in OrderDetail is Subtotal, which represents the quantity multiplied by the unit price. Because it isn't persisted, this column doesn't occupy any disk space, and most importantly, it is always in sync with the other fields.

Creating Orders in the Database

Here you'll write the CreateOrder stored procedure, which takes the products from a shopping cart and creates an order with them. This procedure gets called when the customer decides that he wants to buy the products in the shopping cart and clicks the Proceed to Checkout button.

Creating a new order implies adding a new record to the Orders table and a number of records (one record for each product) to the OrderDetail table.

Add the CreateOrder stored procedure to the BalloonShop database, and then we'll talk a bit more about it:

```
CREATE PROCEDURE CreateOrder
(@CartID char(36))
AS
/* Insert a new record into Orders */
DECLARE @OrderID int
INSERT INTO Orders DEFAULT VALUES
/* Save the new Order ID */
SET @OrderID = @@IDENTITY
/* Add the order details to OrderDetail */
INSERT INTO OrderDetail
     (OrderID, ProductID, ProductName, Quantity, UnitCost)
SELECT
     @OrderID, Product.ProductID, Product.Name,
     ShoppingCart.Quantity, Product.Price
FROM Product JOIN ShoppingCart
ON Product.ProductID = ShoppingCart.ProductID
WHERE ShoppingCart.CartID = @CartID
/* Clear the shopping cart */
DELETE FROM ShoppingCart
WHERE CartID = @CartID
/* Return the Order ID */
SELECT @OrderID
```

The procedure starts by creating the new record in the Orders table. As you can see, when adding a new record, you don't specify any column values, as some of them allow NULLs, while the others have default values specified.

After adding the new record, you need to read the @@Identity system variable (which represents the order ID that was just generated) to a local variable named @OrderID:

```
/* Insert a new record into Orders*/
DECLARE @OrderID int
INSERT INTO Orders DEFAULT VALUES
/* Obtain the new Order ID */
SET @OrderID = @@IDENTITY
```

This is the standard mechanism of extracting the newly generated ID. You must save the value of @@IDENTITY immediately after the INSERT statement, because its value is lost afterward.

Using the @OrderID variable, you add the OrderDetail records by gathering information from the Product and ShoppingCart tables. From ShoppingCart, you need the list of the products and their quantities, and from Product, you get their names and prices.

After creating the order, the visitor's shopping cart is emptied. The last step for the CreateOrder stored procedure is to return the OrderID to the calling function. This is required when providing the order number to the customer.

Updating the Business Layer

Luckily, at this stage, you only need a single method named CreateOrder. Add this method to your ShoppingCartAccess class:

```
// Create a new order from the shopping cart
public static string CreateOrder()
{
  // get a configured DbCommand object
  DbCommand comm = GenericDataAccess.CreateCommand();
  // set the stored procedure name
  comm.CommandText = "CreateOrder";
  // create a new parameter
  DbParameter param = comm.CreateParameter();
  param.ParameterName = "@CartID";
  param.Value = shoppingCartId;
  param.DbType = DbType.String;
  param.Size = 36;
  comm.Parameters.Add(param);
  // return the result table
  return GenericDataAccess.ExecuteScalar(comm);
}
```

The method calls the CreateOrder stored procedure in the usual way. It returns the OrderID of the newly created order. ExecuteScalar is the DbCommand method used to execute stored procedures that return a single value.

Note that we don't catch the error here. If an exception occurs while trying to create the order, we prefer to let it propagate and have the "Oops" message displayed to the visitor (and logged as such), because we consider this to be a critical error.

Adding the Checkout Button

This button is the only addition on the visitor side for the custom checkout. You'll place the button in the ShoppingCart Web Form and then implement the functionality by handling its Click event.

Let's do all this in the following exercise.

Exercise: Adding Proceed-to-Checkout Functionality

1. Open ShoppingCart.aspx and add the following button next to the Update Quantities button:

```
<p align="right">
  <asp:Button ID="updateButton" runat="server" Text="Update Quantities"
    onclick="updateButton_Click" />
  <asp:Button ID="checkoutButton" runat="server"
    Text="Proceed to Checkout" />
</p>
```

In Design View, the content area of the form should look like Figure 14-3 now.

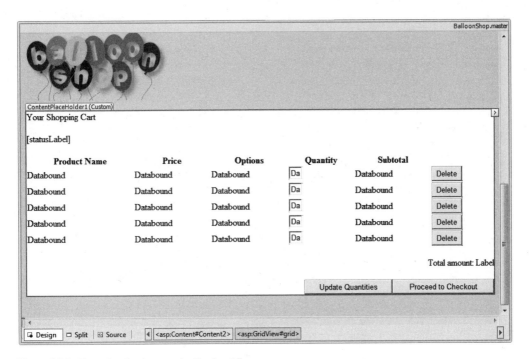

Figure 14-3. *ShoppingCart.aspx in Design View*

2. Cool, now you have a checkout button in the shopping cart. This button should be enabled only when the shopping cart is not empty. Take care of this issue by modifying `PopulateControls` in `ShoppingCart.aspx.cs`:

```
// fill shopping cart controls with data
private void PopulateControls()
{
  // get the items in the shopping cart
  DataTable dt = ShoppingCartAccess.GetItems();
  // if the shopping cart is empty...
  if (dt.Rows.Count == 0)
  {
    titleLabel.Text = "Your shopping cart is empty!";
    grid.Visible = false;
    updateButton.Enabled = false;
    checkoutButton.Enabled = false;
    totalAmountLabel.Text = String.Format("{0:c}", 0);
  }
  else
  // if the shopping cart is not empty...
  {
    // populate the list with the shopping cart contents
    grid.DataSource = dt;
    grid.DataBind();
    // setup controls
    titleLabel.Text = "These are the products in your shopping cart:";
    grid.Visible = true;
    updateButton.Enabled = true;
    checkoutButton.Enabled = true;
    // display the total amount
    decimal amount = ShoppingCartAccess.GetTotalAmount();
    totalAmountLabel.Text = String.Format("{0:c}", amount);
  }
}
```

3. Now it's time to implement the checkout button's functionality. Because this functionality depends on the company that processes your payments, you might need to suit it for the payment-processing company you're working with. If you use PayPal, double-click `checkoutButton` and complete its `Click` event handler like this:

```
// create a new order and redirect to a payment page
protected void checkoutButton_Click(object sender, EventArgs e)
{
  // Get the total amount
  decimal amount = ShoppingCartAccess.GetTotalAmount();
  // Create the order and store the order ID
  string orderId = ShoppingCartAccess.CreateOrder();
  string ordername = BalloonShopConfiguration.SiteName + " Order " + orderId;
```

```
  // Go to PayPal checkout
  string destination = Link.ToPayPalCheckout(ordername, amount);
  Response.Redirect(destination);
}
```

4. Add the following method to the Link class:

```
public static string ToPayPalCheckout(string orderName, decimal ➥
orderAmount)
{
  return HttpUtility.UrlPathEncode(  return HttpUtility.UrlPathEncode(
      String.Format("{0}/business={1}&item_name={2}&amount➥
={3:0.00}&currency ={4}&return={5}&cancel_return={6}",
          BalloonShopConfiguration.PaypalUrl,
          BalloonShopConfiguration.PaypalEmail,
          orderName,
          orderAmount,
          BalloonShopConfiguration.PaypalCurrency,
          BalloonShopConfiguration.PaypalReturnUrl,
          BalloonShopConfiguration.PaypalCancelUrl));
}
```

5. Modify the web.config setting for PaypalUrl:

```
<add key="PaypalUrl" value="https://www.paypal.com/xclick" />
```

How It Works: Placing a New Order

First of all, if you use a company other than PayPal to process your payments, you'll need to modify the code in checkoutButton_Click accordingly.

When the visitor clicks the Proceed to Checkout button, three important actions happen. First, the shopping cart's total amount is saved to a temporary variable. Second, the order is created in the database by calling ShoppingCart. CreateOrder. At this point the shopping cart is emptied, which is the reason you needed to save the total amount first.

Third, the link to the PayPal payment page is created. Note that the values of the business, return, and cancel addresses are stored in web.config. Optionally, you could also call the Utilities.SendMail method to email the administrator when an order is made, or you can rely on the messages that PayPal sends when a payment is processed.

Administering Orders

So your visitor just made an order. Now what?

After giving visitors the option to pay for your products, you need to make sure they actually get what they paid for. BalloonShop needs a carefully designed orders administration page, where an administrator can quickly see the status of pending orders.

■**Note** This chapter doesn't intend to help you create a perfect orders administration system, but rather something simple and functional enough to get you on the right track.

The orders administration part of the site will consist of two Web Forms, named AdminOrders.aspx and AdminOrderDetails.aspx. When first loaded, the admin page will offer you various ways to select orders, as shown in Figure 14-4.

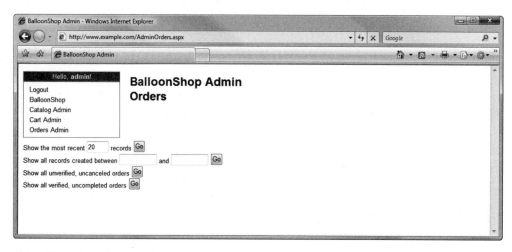

Figure 14-4. *The orders admin page*

After clicking one of the Go buttons, the matching orders show up in a data grid, as shown in Figure 14-5.

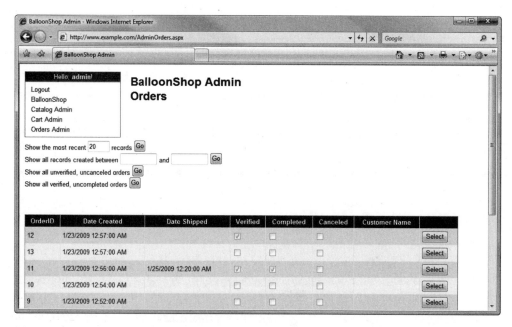

Figure 14-5. *The orders admin page showing a list of orders*

When you click the Select button for an order, you're sent to a page where you can view and update order information (see Figure 14-6).

A Web Form named `AdminOrders.aspx` handles the functionality shown in Figures 14-4 and 14-5. When selecting an order, its details are displayed by a separate control you'll write later in this chapter, named `AdminOrderDetails.aspx`.

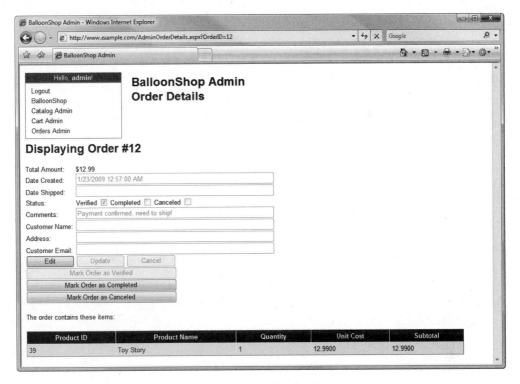

Figure 14-6. *The form that allows administering order details*

Client-Side Validation and Using the ASP.NET Validator Controls

It's time to write the user interface. This time you'll learn how to use the new ASP.NET **validator controls**, which represent the standard way for ASP.NET applications to implement **client-side validation**.

Whereas server-side validation occurs on the server and you program it with C# code, client-side validation occurs in your user's browser and is implemented with JavaScript. Server-side validation is more powerful because on the server you have access to the databases and to more powerful languages and libraries; however, client-side validation is still very important and widely used because it's *fast* from the user's point of view. Although for server code to execute you need a round trip to the server, client-side code executes right away inside the browser.

As a result, using client-side validation for simple tasks such as reminding the user that he forgot to enter his phone number or credit card expiration date is beneficial and improves the overall user experience with your web site.

Then comes ASP.NET, which is a web technology that theoretically lets you do anything without writing client-side code. Although ASP.NET generates a lot of JavaScript code for you, it doesn't require you to understand it, unless you need to manually implement some fancy features—such as our `TieButton` method.

To let you have client-side validation without knowing JavaScript and to make things easier for you even if you do know JavaScript, ASP.NET contains a number of controls called validator controls. They place various conditions on the input controls of your form (such as text boxes) and don't allow the page to be submitted if the rules aren't obeyed.

■**Note** In some circumstances, if the client has JavaScript disabled, these controls don't work as expected (they won't prevent the page from being submitted), but you still can (and should) check at the server side if the page is valid. In other words, in the vast majority of cases, the simple presence of the validator controls will prevent the page from being submitted with invalid values, but this is not guaranteed, so you need to do a server-side check as well as a backup strategy.

In our case, our validator controls won't allow submitting the page (such as when clicking the Go buttons) if the dates entered by the user aren't valid (see Figure 14-7).

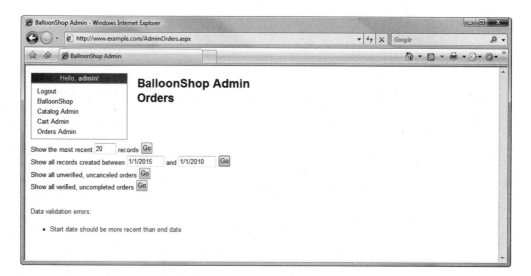

Figure 14-7. *Validator controls at work*

The .NET Framework provides more validator controls, each specialized in a certain type of validation: `RequiredFieldValidator`, `RangeValidator`, `RegularExpressionValidator`, `CompareValidator`, and `CustomValidator`. Also, the `ValidationSummary` control can display a list of all errors retrieved by all validator controls in the page.

We'll only briefly analyze the way `CompareValidator` and `RangeValidator` work, because they are used for BalloonShop. Still, the way all the validation controls work is similar, with the exception of `CustomValidator`, which is more powerful, and its validation logic can be programmed manually. You'll also work with the ValidationSummary control, which gathers all the error messages from the validation controls in the page and presents them in a separate list (the error message in Figure 14-7 is generated by this control).

You'll use two RangeValidator controls to test whether the data typed in the two date text boxes is correct and whether their values are in a specified range. When adding a new RangeValidator control, you usually set these properties:

- ControlToValidate: Set this property to the control that you want to validate (in this case, one of the text boxes).

- Display: If you don't use a ValidationSummary control, you can leave this set to Dynamic or Static, which results in the error message being displayed right in the place where the validator is placed. But because you'll use the ValidationSummary control to do the displaying work, set Display to None so that the error messages aren't displayed twice.

- ErrorMessage: This property contains the message to be displayed if the control is not validated.

- Type: This property specifies the data type that should exist in the control being validated. You'll set this property to Date for the two text boxes.

- MinimumValue, MaximumValue: These specify the minimum and maximum values that should exist in the control being validated.

You'll also use a CompareValidator to ensure that the end date is more recent than the start date. You'll specify these properties:

- ControlToCompare, ControlToValidate: These properties specify the two controls that need to be compared. The one specified by ControlToValidate is the reference control.

- Operator: This specifies what kind of comparison should be done between the values of the two controls. Possible values are Equal, NotEqual, GreaterThan, GreaterThanEqual, LessThan, LessThanEqual, and DataTypeCheck. When DataTypeCheck is selected, only the data type of ControlToValidate is verified, and the control specified by ControlToCompare is ignored.

For the ValidationSummary control, you only set the CssClass property to a proper style for displaying errors. You also set the HeaderText property, which represents the header to be displayed before the list of errors. Other than that, there are no special properties that you'll set. Note that you can change the layout of the generated error message by setting the DisplayMode property. You also can set it up to raise a dialog box by setting the ShowMessageBox property to True.

Validation is, by default, enabled through the controls' EnableValidation property, whose default value is True. You'll set this property to False for the buttons for which you don't want validation enabled.

The controls that need valid values to operate, such as the Go button associated with the dates, need to check the value of Page.IsValid to ensure the values are valid. This is important because in some cases (for example, if JavaScript is not enabled on the client), the page may submit even if the page doesn't contain valid values.

Displaying Existing Orders

In the next few pages, you'll implement AdminOrders.aspx, a form that allows the administrator to view the orders that have been placed on the web site. Because the list of orders will become very long in time, it is important to have a few well-chosen filtering options.

The administrator will be able to select the orders using the following criteria:

- Show the most recent orders.

- Show orders that took place in a certain period of time.

- Show pending orders. This shows the recent orders that have not been canceled and for which payment confirmation from PayPal is still pending. The administrator needs to mark these orders as verified when the financial transaction is confirmed. Otherwise, if the payment is not confirmed in a reasonable amount of time, the administrator probably will want to cancel the order (marking it as canceled), in which case the order will not appear in this list on future requests.

- Show orders that need to be shipped (they are verified but not yet completed). These are the orders that have been paid for, but for which the products haven't yet shipped. After the products are shipped, the administrator will mark the order as completed.

We'll create these features in the following exercise.

Exercise: Creating the Orders Administration Page

1. We'll now continue by creating the stored procedures needed for catalog administration: OrdersGetByRecent, OrdersGetByDate, OrdersGetUnverifiedUncanceled, and OrdersGetVerifiedUncompleted.

In the OrdersGetByRecent stored procedure, the SET ROWCOUNT statement is used to limit the number of rows returned by the SELECT statement. The parameter, @Count, specifies the number of records. The SELECT command simply returns the necessary rows, in descending order of the date they were created. Create OrdersGetByRecent by executing this SQL code:

```
CREATE PROCEDURE OrdersGetByRecent
(@Count smallint)
AS
-- Set the number of rows to be returned
SET ROWCOUNT @Count
-- Get list of orders
SELECT OrderID, DateCreated, DateShipped,
       Verified, Completed, Canceled, CustomerName
FROM Orders
ORDER BY DateCreated DESC
-- Reset rowcount value
SET ROWCOUNT 0
```

At the end, you set ROWCOUNT to 0, which tells SQL Server to stop limiting the number of returned rows.

ORDER BY is used to sort the returned results from the SELECT statement. The default sorting mode is ascending, but adding DESC sets the descending sorting mode (so the most recent orders will be listed first).

2. OrdersGetByDate simply returns all the records in which the current date is between the start and end dates that are supplied as parameters. The results are sorted descending by date.

```
CREATE PROCEDURE OrdersGetByDate
(@StartDate smalldatetime,
 @EndDate smalldatetime)
AS
SELECT OrderID, DateCreated, DateShipped,
       Verified, Completed, Canceled, CustomerName
FROM Orders
WHERE DateCreated BETWEEN @StartDate AND @EndDate
ORDER BY DateCreated DESC
```

3. OrdersGetUnverifiedUncanceled returns the orders that have not been verified yet but have not been canceled, either. In other words, you'll see the orders that need to be either verified (and then completed when the shipment is done) or canceled (if the payment isn't confirmed in a reasonable amount of time). The code is fairly straightforward:

```
CREATE PROCEDURE OrdersGetUnverifiedUncanceled
AS
SELECT OrderID, DateCreated, DateShipped,
       Verified, Completed, Canceled, CustomerName
FROM Orders
WHERE Verified=0 AND Canceled=0
ORDER BY DateCreated DESC
```

4. OrdersGetVerifiedUncompleted returns all the orders that have been verified but not yet completed. The administrator will want to see these orders when a shipment has been done and the order needs to be marked as Completed. (When an order is marked as completed, the DateShipped field is populated.)

```
CREATE PROCEDURE OrdersGetVerifiedUncompleted
AS
SELECT OrderID, DateCreated, DateShipped,
       Verified, Completed, Canceled, CustomerName
FROM Orders
WHERE Verified=1 AND Completed=0
ORDER BY DateCreated DESC
```

5. It's time for the data access methods. Create a new class named OrdersAccess in your application's App_Code folder. Then add a reference to the System.Data and System.Data.Common namespaces, like this:

```csharp
using System;
using System.Collections.Generic;
using System.Linq;
using System.Web;
using System.Data;
using System.Data.Common;

/// <summary>
/// Summary description for OrdersAccess
/// </summary>
public class OrdersAccess
{
  public OrdersAccess()
  {
    //
    // TODO: Add constructor logic here
    //
  }
}
```

6. Now you can start adding your business tier methods to the OrdersAccess class. The GetByRecent method calls the OrdersGetByRecent stored procedure and returns a list of the most recent orders to the calling function.

```csharp
// Retrieve the recent orders
public static DataTable GetByRecent(int count)
{
  // get a configured DbCommand object
  DbCommand comm = GenericDataAccess.CreateCommand();
  // set the stored procedure name
  comm.CommandText = "OrdersGetByRecent";
  // create a new parameter
  DbParameter param = comm.CreateParameter();
  param.ParameterName = "@Count";
  param.Value = count;
  param.DbType = DbType.Int32;
  comm.Parameters.Add(param);
  // return the result table
  DataTable table = GenericDataAccess.ExecuteSelectCommand(comm);
  return table;
}
```

7. The GetByDate method returns all the orders that have been placed in a certain period of time, specified by a start date and an end date.

```
// Retrieve orders that have been placed in a specified period of time
public static DataTable GetByDate(string startDate, string endDate)
{
  // get a configured DbCommand object
  DbCommand comm = GenericDataAccess.CreateCommand();

  // set the stored procedure name
  comm.CommandText = "OrdersGetByDate";
  // create a new parameter
  DbParameter param = comm.CreateParameter();
  param.ParameterName = "@StartDate";
  param.Value = startDate;
  param.DbType = DbType.Date;
  comm.Parameters.Add(param);
  // create a new parameter
  param = comm.CreateParameter();
  param.ParameterName = "@EndDate";
  param.Value = endDate;
  param.DbType = DbType.Date;
  comm.Parameters.Add(param);
  // return the result table
  DataTable table = GenericDataAccess.ExecuteSelectCommand(comm);
  return table;
}
```

8. The GetUnverifiedUncanceled method returns a list of orders that have not been verified yet, but were not canceled, either. These are the records that need to be either verified (and then set to completed when the shipment is done) or canceled (most probable if the payment isn't confirmed in a reasonable amount of time).

```
// Retrieve orders that need to be verified or canceled
public static DataTable GetUnverifiedUncanceled()
{
  // get a configured DbCommand object
  DbCommand comm = GenericDataAccess.CreateCommand();
  // set the stored procedure name
  comm.CommandText = "OrdersGetUnverifiedUncanceled";
  // return the result table
  DataTable table = GenericDataAccess.ExecuteSelectCommand(comm);
  return table;
}
```

9. The `GetVerifiedUncompleted` method returns all the orders that have been verified but not yet completed. The administrator will want to see these orders when a shipment has been done to mark the order as completed.

```
// Retrieve orders that need to be shipped/completed
public static DataTable GetVerifiedUncompleted()
{
  // get a configured DbCommand object
  DbCommand comm = GenericDataAccess.CreateCommand();

  // set the stored procedure name
  comm.CommandText = "OrdersGetVerifiedUncompleted";
  // return the result table
  DataTable table = GenericDataAccess.ExecuteSelectCommand(comm);
  return table;
}
```

10. Create a new Web Form at the root of the BalloonShop project, named `AdminOrders.aspx`, based on the `Admin.master` master page.

11. While in Source View, change the code of the first placeholder like this:

```
<asp:Content ID="Content1" ContentPlaceHolderID="titlePlaceHolder" ➥
runat="Server">
  <span class="AdminTitle">
    BalloonShop Admin
    <br />
    Orders
  </span>
</asp:Content>
```

12. Extend the security mechanism for the page you created. Modify `web.config` by adding the following lines just after the ones for `CatalogAdmin.aspx` and `ShoppingCartAdmin.aspx`:

```
<!-- Only administrators are allowed to access AdminOrders.aspx -->
<location path="AdminOrders.aspx">
  <system.web>
    <authorization>
      <allow roles="Administrators" />
      <deny users="*" />
    </authorization>
  </system.web>
</location>
```

```
<!-- Only administrators are allowed to access AdminOrders.aspx -->
<location path="AdminOrderDetails.aspx">
  <system.web>
    <authorization>
      <allow roles="Administrators" />
      <deny users="*" />
    </authorization>
  </system.web>
</location>
```

13. Open UserInfo.ascx in Source View and add a link to the orders administration page to be displayed when an administrator logs in:

```
<td class="UserInfoContent">
  <asp:LoginStatus ID="LoginStatus2" runat="server" />
  <br />
  <a href="/">BalloonShop</a>
  <br />
  <a href="AdminDepartments.aspx">Catalog Admin</a>
  <br />
  <a href="AdminShoppingCart.aspx">Cart Admin</a>
  <br />
  <a href="AdminOrders.aspx">Orders Admin</a>
</td>
```

14. Build the web site, execute the project, log in as admin, and go to your orders administration page, which should look like Figure 14-8.

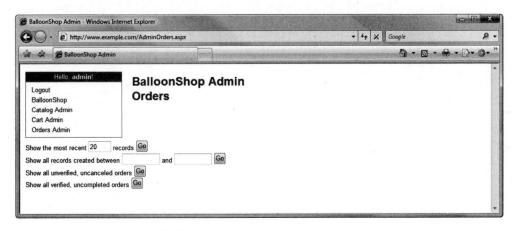

Figure 14-8. *The form that will allow administering orders*

15. Let's now write the code for the second placeholder in `AdminOrders.aspx`. Add `Label` controls, `Button` controls, a `GridView`, and a `PlaceHolder` control to the second placeholder in `AdminOrders.aspx`, as shown in Figure 14-9.

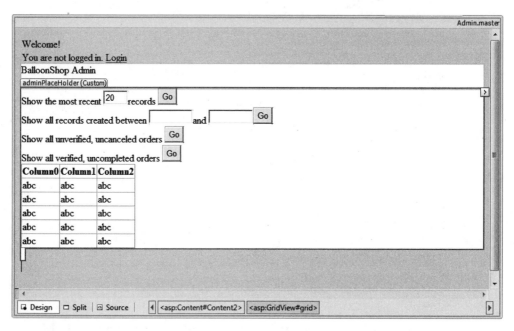

Figure 14-9. *Adding controls to AdminOrders.aspx*

The code that generates these controls is as follows:

```
<asp:Content ID="Content2" ContentPlaceHolderID="adminPlaceHolder" runat=
"Server">
  Show the most recent
  <asp:TextBox ID="recentCountTextBox" runat="server" MaxLength="4" ➥
Width="40px" Text="20" />
  records
  <asp:Button ID="byRecentGo" runat="server" Text="Go" /><br />
  Show all records created between
  <asp:TextBox ID="startDateTextBox" runat="server" Width="72px" />
  and
  <asp:TextBox ID="endDateTextBox" runat="server" Width="72px" />
  <asp:Button ID="byDateGo" runat="server" Text="Go" />
  <br />
  Show all unverified, uncanceled orders
  <asp:Button ID="unverfiedGo" runat="server" Text="Go" />
  <br />
```

```
Show all verified, uncompleted orders
<asp:Button ID="uncompletedGo" runat="server" Text="Go" />
<br />
<asp:GridView ID="grid" runat="server">
</asp:GridView>
<br />
</asp:Content>
```

16. Now edit the `GridView` control. First set its ID to **grid**, its `AutoGenerateColumns` property to **False**, and its `DataKeyNames` property to **OrderID**.

17. Add columns (see Table 14-3) to the `GridView` by clicking its **Smart Link** and choosing **Add New Column**.

Table 14-3. *Setting the Fields of the GridView Control*

Column Type	Header Text	Data Field	Other Properties
BoundField	Order ID	OrderID	Read-only
BoundField	Date Created	DateCreated	Read-only
BoundField	Date Shipped	DateShipped	Read-only
CheckBoxField	Verified	Verified	Read-only
CheckBoxField	Completed	Completed	Read-only
CheckBoxField	Canceled	Canceled	Read-only
BoundField	Customer Name	CustomerName	Read-only
ButtonField			Set **Command Name** to **Select**, **Text** to **Select**, and **Button Type** to **Button**.

■**Note** This is the first time in BalloonShop when you change the button type to `Button`. If you think it looks better this way, feel free to make this change in the other grid as well. Just select the grids you want to change, click their Smart Link, select Edit Columns, select the `ButtonField` column you want to change, and change its `ButtonType` property to `Button`.

18. Okay, your grid is ready. Now add the validator controls. You can find the range validators on the Validation tab of the toolbox. The validator controls provide a quick and easy way to validate the input values at the presentation tier level. In this form, you'll test whether the values entered into the date text boxes are valid before querying the business tier with them. Just above the data grid, add a `Label` control (which is *not* related to the validation controls but is used for notifying the administrator about the status), two `RangeValidator` controls, a `CompareValidator` control, and a `ValidationSummary` control, as shown in Figure 14-10.

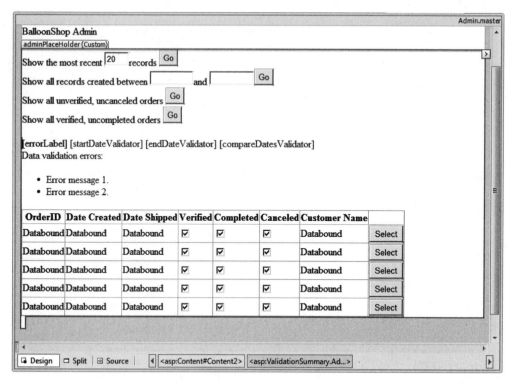

Figure 14-10. *Adding the validation controls*

19. Now set the properties for each of the newly added controls as noted in Table 14-4.

Table 14-4. *Setting the New Control's Properties in* AdminOrders.aspx

Control	Property Name	Property Value
Label	(ID)	errorLabel
	Text	(empty)
	CssClass	AdminError
	EnableViewState	False
RangeValidator	(ID)	startDateValidator
	ControlToValidate	startDateTextBox
	Display	None
	ErrorMessage	Invalid start date
	MaximumValue	1/1/2015
	MinimumValue	1/1/1999
	Type	Date
RangeValidator	(ID)	endDateValidator

Table 14-4. *Setting the New Control's Properties in* AdminOrders.aspx *(Continued)*

Control	Property Name	Property Value
	ControlToValidate	endDateTextBox
	Display	None
	ErrorMessage	Invalid end date
	MaximumValue	1/1/2015
	MinimumValue	1/1/1999
	Type	Date
CompareValidator	(ID)	compareDatesValidator
	ControlToCompare	endDateTextBox
	ControlToValidate	startDateTextBox
	Display	None
	ErrorMessage	Start date should be more recent than end date
	Operator	LessThan
	Type	Date
ValidationSummary	(ID)	validationSummary
	CssClass	AdminError
	HeaderText	Data validation errors:

20. Execute the project and browse to the orders admin page (you may need to login as admin first). Enter invalid dates and try clicking any of the admin buttons. You'll get a page like the one shown earlier in Figure 14-7.

21. A problem occurs if wrong dates are written, because *none* of the Go buttons can be used. We actually want the restrictions to apply only to the Go button associated with the dates. Change the CausesValidation property of the first, third, and fourth Go buttons to False (the default is True).

22. It's time to write the code. While in Design View, double-click the **Go** buttons to have their Click event handlers generated for you, and complete their code as shown:

```
// list the most recent orders
protected void byRecentGo_Click(object sender, EventArgs e)
{
  // how many orders to list?
  int recordCount;

  // load the new data into the grid
  if (int.TryParse(recentCountTextBox.Text, out recordCount))
    grid.DataSource = OrdersAccess.GetByRecent(recordCount);
```

```
    else
      errorLabel.Text = "Please enter a valid number!";
    // refresh the data grid
    grid.DataBind();
  }


  // get unverified, uncanceled orders
  protected void unverfiedGo_Click(object sender, EventArgs e)
  {
    // load the grid with the requested data
    grid.DataSource = OrdersAccess.GetUnverifiedUncanceled();
    // refresh the data grid
    grid.DataBind();
  }


  // list the orders that happened between specified dates
  protected void byDateGo_Click(object sender, EventArgs e)
  {
    // check if the page is valid (we have date validator controls)
    if ((Page.IsValid) && (startDateTextBox.Text+endDateTextBox.Text != ""))
    {
      // get the dates
      string startDate = startDateTextBox.Text;
      string endDate = endDateTextBox.Text;
      // load the grid with the requested data
      grid.DataSource = OrdersAccess.GetByDate(startDate, endDate);
    }
    else
      errorLabel.Text = "Please enter valid dates!";
    // refresh the data grid
    grid.DataBind();
  }


  // get verified but uncompleted orders
  protected void uncompletedGo_Click(object sender, EventArgs e)
  {
    // load the grid with the requested data
    grid.DataSource = OrdersAccess.GetVerifiedUncompleted();
    // refresh the data grid
    grid.DataBind();
  }
```

23. Switch again to Design View, use Visual Web Developer to generate the `SelectedIndexChanged` event handler for the first `GridView` control (the one in `OrdersAdmin`, not the one in `AdminOrderDetails`), and then complete its code like this:

```
// Load the details of the selected order
protected void grid_SelectedIndexChanged(object sender, EventArgs e)
{
  string destination = String.Format("AdminOrderDetails.aspx?OrderID={0}",
    grid.DataKeys[grid.SelectedIndex].Value.ToString());
  Response.Redirect(destination);
}
```

24. Feel free to play with your new administration page. Try to break it by writing bad data to the record count or to the date text boxes. Except for the Select buttons of the `GridView`, whose functionality hasn't been implemented yet, everything should work as expected.

How It Works: Listing Customer Orders

The detail to be aware of for this form is the way the validator controls work.

This form uses both server-side and client-side validation. The value for the most recent records count is verified at server side to be a valid integer. If it isn't, an error message is displayed to the visitor:

```
// load the new data into the grid
if (int.TryParse(recentCountTextBox.Text, out recordCount))
  grid.DataSource = OrdersAccess.GetByRecent(recordCount);
else
  errorLabel.Text = "Please enter a valid number!";
// refresh the data grid
```

The date text boxes are validated using validation controls, which try to operate at client side while also having a server-side mechanism in case the client doesn't support JavaScript.

```
// check if the page is valid (we have date validator controls)
if (Page.IsValid)
{
  ...
```

The validator controls you wrote apply the following requirements for the entered dates:

- The values in `startDateTextBox` and `endDateTextBox` must be correctly formatted dates between 1/1/1999 and 1/1/2015.

- The start date needs to be more recent than the end date.

The first requirement is implemented using `RangeValidator` controls, and the second using a `CompareValidator`. The `ValidationSummary` control gets the errors from the validator controls and displays them in a single, easy-to-read list.

When creating the control, you also added a `Label` control named `errorLabel`, which you used to display other errors than those generated by the validator controls. You set its `EnableViewState` property to `False`, so its value will be cleared after a successful Go command executes.

Administering Order Details

The AdminOrderDetails form allows the administrator to edit the details of a particular order. The most common tasks are marking an unverified order as either verified or canceled (it can't be directly marked as completed if it isn't verified yet), and marking a verified order as completed when the shipment is dispatched. Refer to Figure 14-6 as a reminder of how this form will look.

Here you're providing the administrator with three very useful buttons: Mark this Order as Verified, Mark this Order as Completed, and Mark this Order as Canceled. These buttons are enabled or disabled depending on the status of the order.

The Edit, Update, and Cancel buttons allow the administrator to manually edit any of the details of an order. When the Edit button is clicked, all the check boxes and text boxes (except for the one holding the order ID) become editable.

Now you have an idea about what you'll be doing with this control. You'll implement it in the usual style starting with the data tier.

Exercise: Creating the Order Details Administration Page

1. We start again with the stored procedures. OrderGetInfo returns the data needed to populate the text boxes of the form with general order information, such as the total amount, date created, date shipped, and so on.

```
CREATE PROCEDURE OrderGetInfo
(@OrderID int)
AS
SELECT OrderID,
       (SELECT SUM(Subtotal) FROM OrderDetail WHERE OrderID = @OrderID)
       AS TotalAmount,
       DateCreated,
       DateShipped,
       Verified,
       Completed,
       Canceled,
       Comments,
       CustomerName,
       ShippingAddress,
       CustomerEmail
FROM Orders
WHERE OrderID = @OrderID
```

Note that a subquery is used to generate the TotalAmount field. All the other data you need is read from the Orders table, but to get the total amount of an order, you need to look at the OrderDetail table as well.

The subquery that returns the total amount of a particular order uses the SUM function to add up the subtotal of each product in the order (remember Subtotal is a calculated column), as follows:

SELECT SUM(Subtotal) FROM OrderDetail WHERE OrderID = @OrderID

This subquery gets executed for each row of the outer query, and its result is saved as a calculated column named TotalAmount.

2. OrderGetDetails returns the list of products that belong to a specific order. This will be used to populate the data grid containing the order details, situated at the bottom of the control.

```
CREATE PROCEDURE OrderGetDetails
(@OrderID int)
AS
SELECT Orders.OrderID,
       ProductID,
       ProductName,
       Quantity,
       UnitCost,
       Subtotal
FROM OrderDetail JOIN Orders
ON Orders.OrderID = OrderDetail.OrderID
WHERE Orders.OrderID = @OrderID
```

3. The OrderUpdate procedure is called when the user is updating the order.

```
CREATE PROCEDURE OrderUpdate
(@OrderID int,
 @DateCreated smalldatetime,
 @DateShipped smalldatetime = NULL,
 @Verified bit,
 @Completed bit,
 @Canceled bit,
 @Comments NVARCHAR(200),
 @CustomerName NVARCHAR(50),
 @ShippingAddress NVARCHAR(200),
 @CustomerEmail NVARCHAR(50))
AS
UPDATE Orders
SET DateCreated=@DateCreated,
    DateShipped=@DateShipped,
    Verified=@Verified,
    Completed=@Completed,
    Canceled=@Canceled,
    Comments=@Comments,
    CustomerName=@CustomerName,
    ShippingAddress=@ShippingAddress,
    CustomerEmail=@CustomerEmail
WHERE OrderID = @OrderID
```

4. OrderMarkVerified is called when the administrator clicks the Mark this Order as Verified button. It sets the Verified bit of the selected order to 1.

```
CREATE PROCEDURE OrderMarkVerified
(@OrderID int)
AS
UPDATE Orders
SET Verified = 1
WHERE OrderID = @OrderID
```

5. OrderMarkCompleted is called when the administrator clicks the Mark this Order as Completed button. It not only sets the Completed bit to 1 but also updates the DateShipped field because an order is completed just after the shipment has been done.

```
CREATE PROCEDURE OrderMarkCompleted
(@OrderID int)
AS
UPDATE Orders
SET Completed = 1,
    DateShipped = GETDATE()
WHERE OrderID = @OrderID
```

6. OrderMarkCanceled is called when the administrator clicks the Mark this Order as Canceled button.

```
CREATE PROCEDURE OrderMarkCanceled
(@OrderID int)
AS
UPDATE Orders
SET Canceled = 1
WHERE OrderID = @OrderID
```

7. We now start implementing the business tier. Apart from the usual methods that pass data back and forth between the user interface and the database stored procedures, we create a struct named OrderInfo. Instances of this struct store information about one order and are used to pass order information from the business tier methods to the presentation tier.

Although you can add this struct to any of the existing files in the App_Code folder (or even create a new file for it if you prefer), for consistency and clarity you should add the OrderInfo struct at the beginning of the OrdersAccess.cs file, after the using statements and before the OrdersAccess class.

```
/// <summary>
/// Wraps order data
/// </summary>
public struct OrderInfo
{
  public int OrderID;
  public decimal TotalAmount;
  public string DateCreated;
  public string DateShipped;
  public bool Verified;
  public bool Completed;
```

```
    public bool Canceled;
    public string Comments;
    public string CustomerName;
    public string ShippingAddress;
    public string CustomerEmail;
}
```

8. We'll now add the data access methods to the OrdersAccess class: GetInfo, GetDetails, Update, MarkVerified, MarkCompleted, and MarkCanceled.

   GetInfo gets information related to a particular order from the database and saves the data into an OrderInfo object, which is then returned. Add the methods to the OrdersAccess class:

```
// Retrieve order information
public static OrderInfo GetInfo(string orderID)
{
  // get a configured DbCommand object
  DbCommand comm = GenericDataAccess.CreateCommand();
  // set the stored procedure name
  comm.CommandText = "OrderGetInfo";
  // create a new parameter
  DbParameter param = comm.CreateParameter();
  param.ParameterName = "@OrderID";
  param.Value = orderID;
  param.DbType = DbType.Int32;
  comm.Parameters.Add(param);

  // obtain the results
  DataTable table = GenericDataAccess.ExecuteSelectCommand(comm);
  DataRow orderRow = table.Rows[0];
  // save the results into an OrderInfo object
  OrderInfo orderInfo;
  orderInfo.OrderID = Int32.Parse(orderRow["OrderID"].ToString());
  orderInfo.TotalAmount=Decimal.Parse(orderRow["TotalAmount"].ToString());
  orderInfo.DateCreated = orderRow["DateCreated"].ToString();
  orderInfo.DateShipped = orderRow["DateShipped"].ToString();
  orderInfo.Verified = bool.Parse(orderRow["Verified"].ToString());
  orderInfo.Completed = bool.Parse(orderRow["Completed"].ToString());
  orderInfo.Canceled = bool.Parse(orderRow["Canceled"].ToString());
  orderInfo.Comments = orderRow["Comments"].ToString();
  orderInfo.CustomerName = orderRow["CustomerName"].ToString();
  orderInfo.ShippingAddress = orderRow["ShippingAddress"].ToString();
  orderInfo.CustomerEmail = orderRow["CustomerEmail"].ToString();
  // return the OrderInfo object
  return orderInfo;
}
```

9. `GetDetails` returns the order details of the specified order.

```
// Retrieve the order details (the products that are part of that order)
public static DataTable GetDetails(string orderID)
{
  // get a configured DbCommand object
  DbCommand comm = GenericDataAccess.CreateCommand();
  // set the stored procedure name
  comm.CommandText = "OrderGetDetails";
  // create a new parameter
  DbParameter param = comm.CreateParameter();
  param.ParameterName = "@OrderID";
  param.Value = orderID;
  param.DbType = DbType.Int32;
  comm.Parameters.Add(param);
  // return the results
  DataTable table = GenericDataAccess.ExecuteSelectCommand(comm);
  return table;
}
```

10. This stored procedure updates an order and is called when the Update button in `AdminOrderDetails` is clicked. It receives the order details as an `OrderInfo` parameter and saves them to the database.

```
// Update an order
public static void Update(OrderInfo orderInfo)
{
  // get a configured DbCommand object
  DbCommand comm = GenericDataAccess.CreateCommand();
  // set the stored procedure name
  comm.CommandText = "OrderUpdate";
  // create a new parameter
  DbParameter param = comm.CreateParameter();
  param.ParameterName = "@OrderID";
  param.Value = orderInfo.OrderID;
  param.DbType = DbType.Int32;
  comm.Parameters.Add(param);
  // create a new parameter
  param = comm.CreateParameter();
  param.ParameterName = "@DateCreated";
  param.Value = orderInfo.DateCreated;
  param.DbType = DbType.DateTime;
  comm.Parameters.Add(param);
  // The DateShipped parameter is sent only if data is available
  if (orderInfo.DateShipped.Trim() != "")
  {
    param = comm.CreateParameter();
    param.ParameterName = "@DateShipped";
    param.Value = orderInfo.DateShipped;
    param.DbType = DbType.DateTime;
    comm.Parameters.Add(param);
```

```
  }
  // create a new parameter
  param = comm.CreateParameter();
  param.ParameterName = "@Verified";
  param.Value = orderInfo.Verified;
  param.DbType = DbType.Byte;
  comm.Parameters.Add(param);
  // create a new parameter
  param = comm.CreateParameter();
  param.ParameterName = "@Completed";
  param.Value = orderInfo.Completed;
  param.DbType = DbType.Byte;
  comm.Parameters.Add(param);
  // create a new parameter
  param = comm.CreateParameter();
  param.ParameterName = "@Canceled";
  param.Value = orderInfo.Canceled;
  param.DbType = DbType.Byte;
  comm.Parameters.Add(param);

  // create a new parameter
  param = comm.CreateParameter();
  param.ParameterName = "@Comments";
  param.Value = orderInfo.Comments;
  param.DbType = DbType.String;
  comm.Parameters.Add(param);
  // create a new parameter
  param = comm.CreateParameter();
  param.ParameterName = "@CustomerName";
  param.Value = orderInfo.CustomerName;
  param.DbType = DbType.String;
  comm.Parameters.Add(param);
  // create a new parameter
  param = comm.CreateParameter();
  param.ParameterName = "@ShippingAddress";
  param.Value = orderInfo.ShippingAddress;
  param.DbType = DbType.String;
  comm.Parameters.Add(param);
  // create a new parameter
  param = comm.CreateParameter();
  param.ParameterName = "@CustomerEmail";
  param.Value = orderInfo.CustomerEmail;
  param.DbType = DbType.String;
  comm.Parameters.Add(param);
  // return the results
  GenericDataAccess.ExecuteNonQuery(comm);
}
```

11. The `MarkVerified` method is called when the Mark this Order as Verified button is clicked, and sets the `Verified` bit of the specified order in the database to 1.

```
// Mark an order as verified
public static void MarkVerified(string orderId)
{
  // get a configured DbCommand object
  DbCommand comm = GenericDataAccess.CreateCommand();
  // set the stored procedure name
  comm.CommandText = "OrderMarkVerified";
  // create a new parameter
  DbParameter param = comm.CreateParameter();
  param.ParameterName = "@OrderID";
  param.Value = orderId;
  param.DbType = DbType.Int32;
  comm.Parameters.Add(param);
  // return the results
  GenericDataAccess.ExecuteNonQuery(comm);
}
```

12. The `MarkCompleted` method is called when the Mark this Order as Completed button is clicked, and sets the `Completed` bit of the specified order to 1.

```
// Mark an order as completed
public static void MarkCompleted(string orderId)
{
  // get a configured DbCommand object
  DbCommand comm = GenericDataAccess.CreateCommand();
  // set the stored procedure name
  comm.CommandText = "OrderMarkCompleted";
  // create a new parameter
  DbParameter param = comm.CreateParameter();
  param.ParameterName = "@OrderID";
  param.Value = orderId;
  param.DbType = DbType.Int32;
  comm.Parameters.Add(param);
  // return the results
  GenericDataAccess.ExecuteNonQuery(comm);
}
```

13. The `MarkCanceled` method is called when the Mark this Order as Canceled button is clicked, and sets the `Canceled` bit of the specified order to 1.

```
// Mark an order as canceled
public static void MarkCanceled(string orderId)
{
  // get a configured DbCommand object
  DbCommand comm = GenericDataAccess.CreateCommand();
  // set the stored procedure name
  comm.CommandText = "OrderMarkCanceled";
  // create a new parameter
  DbParameter param = comm.CreateParameter();
  param.ParameterName = "@OrderID";
  param.Value = orderId;
  param.DbType = DbType.Int32;
  comm.Parameters.Add(param);
  // return the results
  GenericDataAccess.ExecuteNonQuery(comm);
}
```

14. Finally, we're going to implement the user interface. Start by creating the `AdminOrderDetails.aspx` Web Form, just like you created the other admin forms.

15. Edit the first content placeholder like this:

```
<asp:Content ID="Content1" ContentPlaceHolderID="titlePlaceHolder" ➥
runat="Server">
  <span class="AdminTitle">BalloonShop Admin
    <br />
    Order Details </span>
</asp:Content>
```

16. Open the control in Design View and populate it as shown in Figure 14-11. The properties for each constituent control are shown in Table 14-5, and the `GridView` columns are listed in Table 14-6. For the `GridView` control, you also need to set its `AutoGenerateColumns` property to `False`.

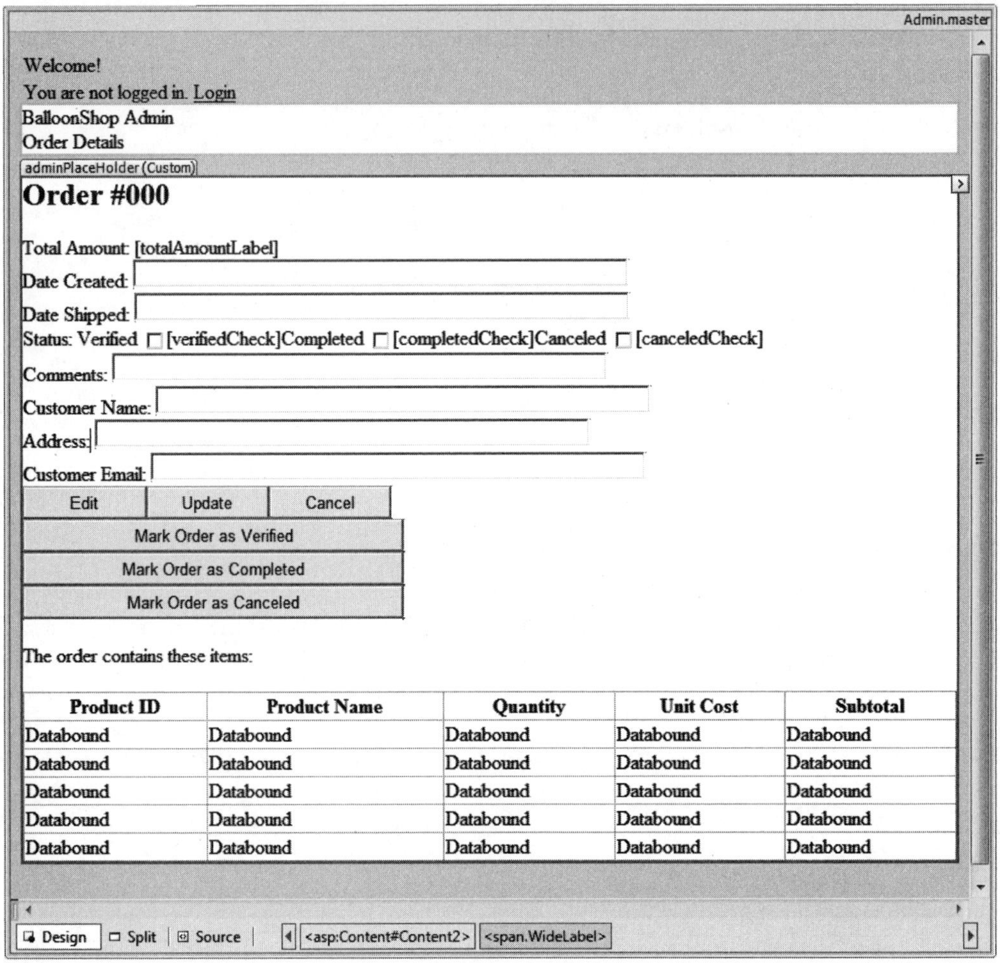

Figure 14-11. *AdminOrderDetails.aspx in Design View*

■**Tip** When setting controls' properties, remember that Visual Studio .NET allows you to set properties on more than one control at a time—you can select, for example, the TextBox controls on the right and set their Width to 400px, and so on.

Table 14-5. *Setting Controls' Properties in AdminOrderDetails.aspx*

Control Type	ID	Text	CssClass	Width
Label	orderIdLabel	Order #000	AdminTitle	
Label	totalAmountLabel	(empty)		
TextBox	dateCreatedTextBox			400px

Table 14-5. *Setting Controls' Properties in* `AdminOrderDetails.aspx` *(Continued)*

Control Type	ID	Text	CssClass	Width
TextBox	dateShippedTextBox			400px
CheckBox	verifiedCheck			400px
CheckBox	completedCheck			400px
CheckBox	canceledCheck			400px
TextBox	commentsTextBox			400px
TextBox	customerNameTextBox			400px
TextBox	shippingAddressTextBox			400px
TextBox	customerEmailTextBox			400px
Button	editButton	Edit		100px
Button	updateButton	Update		100px
Button	cancelButton	Cancel		100px
Button	markVerifiedButton	Mark Order as Verified		305px
Button	markCompletedButton	Mark Order as Completed		305px
Button	markCanceledButton	Mark Order as Canceled		305px
Label	(doesn't matter)	The order contains these items:		
GridView	grid			100%

Table 14-6. *Setting the Fields of the GridView Control*

Column Type	Header Text	Data Field	Other Properties
BoundField	Product ID	ProductID	Read-only
BoundField	Product Name	ProductName	Read-only
BoundField	Quantity	Quantity	Read-only
BoundField	Unit Cost	UnitCost	Read-only
ButtonField	Subtotal	Subtotal	Read-only

To make sure we're on the same page, here's the source code of the control:

```
<asp:Content ID="Content2" ContentPlaceHolderID="adminPlaceHolder" ➥
runat="Server">
  <h2>
    <asp:Label ID="orderIdLabel" runat="server" CssClass="AdminTitle" ➥
Text="Order #000" />
  </h2>
```

```
  <span class="WideLabel">Total Amount:</span>
  <asp:Label ID="totalAmountLabel" runat="server" CssClass=➥
"ProductPrice" />
  <br />
  <span class="WideLabel">Date Created:</span>
  <asp:TextBox ID="dateCreatedTextBox" runat="server" Width="400px" />
  <br />
  <span class="WideLabel">Date Shipped:</span>
  <asp:TextBox ID="dateShippedTextBox" runat="server" Width="400px" />
  <br />
  <span class="WideLabel">Status:</span>
  Verified
  <asp:CheckBox ID="verifiedCheck" runat="server" />
  Completed
  <asp:CheckBox ID="completedCheck" runat="server" />
  Canceled
  <asp:CheckBox ID="canceledCheck" runat="server" />
  <br />
  <span class="WideLabel">Comments:</span>
  <asp:TextBox ID="commentsTextBox" runat="server" Width="400px" />
  <br />
  <span class="WideLabel">Customer Name:</span>
  <asp:TextBox ID="customerNameTextBox" runat="server" Width="400px" />
  <br />
  <span class="WideLabel">Address:</span>
  <asp:TextBox ID="shippingAddressTextBox" runat="server" Width="400px" />
  <br />
  <span class="WideLabel">Customer Email:</span>
  <asp:TextBox ID="customerEmailTextBox" runat="server" Width="400px" />
  <br />
  <asp:Button ID="editButton" runat="server" Text="Edit" Width="100px" />
  <asp:Button ID="updateButton" runat="server" Text="Update" Width=➥
"100px" />
  <asp:Button ID="cancelButton" runat="server" Text="Cancel" Width=➥
"100px" /><br />
  <asp:Button ID="markVerifiedButton" runat="server" Text="Mark Order as ➥
Verified" Width="310px" /><br />
  <asp:Button ID="markCompletedButton" runat="server" Text="Mark Order ➥
as Completed" Width="310px" /><br />
  <asp:Button ID="markCanceledButton" runat="server" Text="Mark Order as ➥
Canceled" Width="310px" /><br />
  <p>
    The order contains these items:
  </p>
  <asp:GridView ID="grid" runat="server" AutoGenerateColumns="False" ➥
BackColor="White" Width="100%">
    <Columns>
```

```
        <asp:BoundField DataField="ProductID" HeaderText="Product ID" ➥
    ReadOnly="True" SortExpression="ProductID" />
        <asp:BoundField DataField="ProductName" HeaderText="Product Name" ➥
    ReadOnly="True" SortExpression="ProductName" />
        <asp:BoundField DataField="Quantity" HeaderText="Quantity" ➥
    ReadOnly="True" SortExpression="Quantity" />
        <asp:BoundField DataField="UnitCost" HeaderText="Unit Cost" ➥
    ReadOnly="True" SortExpression="UnitCost" />
        <asp:BoundField DataField="Subtotal" HeaderText="Subtotal" ➥
    ReadOnly="True" SortExpression="Subtotal" />
      </Columns>
    </asp:GridView>
</asp:Content>
```

17. Start writing the code-behind logic of AdminOrderDetails.aspx by adding some code to Page_Load:

```
public partial class AdminOrderDetails : System.Web.UI.Page
{
  // set up the form
protected void Page_Load(object sender, EventArgs e)
{
  // check if we must display order details
  if (!Page.IsPostBack && Request.QueryString["OrderID"] != null)
  {
    string orderId = Request.QueryString["OrderID"];
    // fill constituent controls with data
    PopulateControls(orderId);
    // set edit mode
    SetEditMode(false);
  }
}
}
```

18. Add PopulateControls just after Page_Load. This method gets the order information into an OrderInfo object, which was especially created for this purpose, by calling the GetInfo method of the OrdersAccess class. Using the information from that object, the method fills the constituent controls with data. At the end, you call OrdersAccess.GetDetails, which returns the products in the specified order.

```
// populate the form with data
private void PopulateControls(string orderId)
{
  // obtain order info
  OrderInfo orderInfo = OrdersAccess.GetInfo(orderId);
  // populate labels and text boxes with order info
  orderIdLabel.Text = "Displaying Order #" + orderId;
  totalAmountLabel.Text = String.Format("{0:c}", orderInfo.TotalAmount);
  dateCreatedTextBox.Text = orderInfo.DateCreated;
  dateShippedTextBox.Text = orderInfo.DateShipped;
  verifiedCheck.Checked = orderInfo.Verified;
```

```
    completedCheck.Checked = orderInfo.Completed;
    canceledCheck.Checked = orderInfo.Canceled;
    commentsTextBox.Text = orderInfo.Comments;
    customerNameTextBox.Text = orderInfo.CustomerName;
    shippingAddressTextBox.Text = orderInfo.ShippingAddress;
    customerEmailTextBox.Text = orderInfo.CustomerEmail;
    // by default the Edit button is enabled, and the
    // Update and Cancel buttons are disabled
    editButton.Enabled = true;
    updateButton.Enabled = false;
    cancelButton.Enabled = false;
    // Decide which one of the other three buttons
    // should be enabled and which should be disabled
    if (canceledCheck.Checked || completedCheck.Checked)
    {
      // if the order was canceled or completed ...
      markVerifiedButton.Enabled = false;
      markCompletedButton.Enabled = false;
      markCanceledButton.Enabled = false;
    }
    else if (verifiedCheck.Checked)
    {
      // if the order was not canceled but is verified ...
      markVerifiedButton.Enabled = false;
      markCompletedButton.Enabled = true;
      markCanceledButton.Enabled = true;
    }
    else
    {
      // if the order was not canceled and is not verified ...
      markVerifiedButton.Enabled = true;
      markCompletedButton.Enabled = false;
      markCanceledButton.Enabled = true;
    }

    // fill the data grid with order details
    grid.DataSource = OrdersAccess.GetDetails(orderId);
    grid.DataBind();
  }
```

19. Write the SetEditMode method now, which enables or disables edit mode for the information text boxes.

```
    // enable or disable edit mode
    private void SetEditMode(bool enable)
    {
      dateCreatedTextBox.Enabled = enable;
      dateShippedTextBox.Enabled = enable;
      verifiedCheck.Enabled = enable;
```

```
        completedCheck.Enabled = enable;
        canceledCheck.Enabled = enable;
        commentsTextBox.Enabled = enable;
        customerNameTextBox.Enabled = enable;
        shippingAddressTextBox.Enabled = enable;
        customerEmailTextBox.Enabled = enable;
        editButton.Enabled = !enable;
        updateButton.Enabled = enable;
        cancelButton.Enabled = enable;
    }
```

This method receives a `bool` parameter that specifies whether you enter or exit edit mode. When entering edit mode, all text boxes and the Update and Cancel buttons become enabled, while the Edit button is disabled. The reverse happens when exiting edit mode (this happens when either the Cancel or Update button is clicked).

20. Now start implementing the code that allows the administrator to edit order information. To make your life easier, first double-click each of the buttons (Edit, Cancel, and Update) in Design View to let Visual Studio generate the signatures of the event handlers. Here's the code:

```
// enter edit mode
protected void editButton_Click(object sender, EventArgs e)
{
    string orderId = Request.QueryString["OrderID"];
    PopulateControls(orderId);
    SetEditMode(true);
}


// cancel edit mode
protected void cancelButton_Click(object sender, EventArgs e)
{
    string orderId = Request.QueryString["OrderID"];
    PopulateControls(orderId);
}


// update order information
protected void updateButton_Click(object sender, EventArgs e)
{
  // Store the new order details in an OrderInfo object
  OrderInfo orderInfo = new OrderInfo();
  string orderId = Request.QueryString["OrderID"];
  orderInfo.OrderID = Int32.Parse(orderId);
  orderInfo.DateCreated = dateCreatedTextBox.Text;
  orderInfo.DateShipped = dateShippedTextBox.Text;
  orderInfo.Verified = verifiedCheck.Checked;
  orderInfo.Completed = completedCheck.Checked;
  orderInfo.Canceled = canceledCheck.Checked;
  orderInfo.Comments = commentsTextBox.Text;
  orderInfo.CustomerName = customerNameTextBox.Text;
```

```
      orderInfo.ShippingAddress = shippingAddressTextBox.Text;
      orderInfo.CustomerEmail = customerEmailTextBox.Text;
      // try to update the order
      try
      {
        // Update the order
        OrdersAccess.Update(orderInfo);
      }
      catch (Exception ex)
      {
        // In case of an error, we simply ignore it
      }
      // Exit edit mode
      SetEditMode(false);
      // Update the form
      PopulateControls(orderId);
    }
```

■**Note** Here we didn't implement a mechanism to let the administrator know whether the update was successful or failed—if something happens, we just ignore the error. You've learned various error-handling techniques in this and previous chapters, and you can choose to implement whichever technique you think is best for your application.

---

21. Do the same for the last three buttons:

```
// mark order as verified
protected void markVerifiedButton_Click(object sender, EventArgs e)
{
  // obtain the order ID from the query string
  string orderId = Request.QueryString["OrderID"];
  // mark order as verified
  OrdersAccess.MarkVerified(orderId);
  // update the form
  PopulateControls(orderId);
}

// mark order as completed
protected void markCompletedButton_Click(object sender, EventArgs e)
{
  // obtain the order ID from the query string
  string orderId = Request.QueryString["OrderID"];
  // mark the order as completed
  OrdersAccess.MarkCompleted(orderId);
  // update the form
```

```
    PopulateControls(orderId);
}

// mark order as canceled
protected void markCanceledButton_Click(object sender, EventArgs e)
{
  // obtain the order ID from the query string
  string orderId = Request.QueryString["OrderID"];
  // mark the order as canceled
  OrdersAccess.MarkCanceled(orderId);
  // update the form
  PopulateControls(orderId);
}
```

22. Switch AdminOrderDetails.aspx to Source View and disable the ViewState of the page.

```
<%@ Page Title="" Language="C#" MasterPageFile="~/Admin.master" ➥
AutoEventWireup="true"
   CodeFile="AdminOrderDetails.aspx.cs" Inherits="AdminOrderDetails" ➥
EnableViewState="false" %>
```

How It Works: AdminOrderDetails.aspx

Whew, you've written a lot of code for this control. The code itself isn't complicated, but you had to deal with a lot of user interface elements.

Because we talked about each method while writing the code, it should be pretty clear how the page works. Run it now and play with the buttons to make sure everything works as it should.

Summary

We covered a lot of ground in this chapter. You implemented a system by which you can both take orders and manually administer them.

You accomplished this in two separate stages. You added a Proceed to Checkout button onto the shopping cart control to allow the visitor to order the products in the shopping cart. You implemented a simple orders administration page where the site administrator can view and handle pending orders.

In addition, you looked at the use of validation controls and also, importantly, set the scene for entirely automating the order system.

Because order data is now stored in the database, you can create various statistics and run calculations based on the items sold. In the next chapter, you'll learn how to implement a "Visitors who bought this also bought . . ." feature, which wouldn't have been possible without the order data stored in the database.

■ ■ ■

CHAPTER 15

Product Recommendations

One of the most important advantages of an Internet store, compared to a brick-and-mortar location, is the capability to customize the web site for each visitor based on his or her preferences, or on preferences based on data gathered from similar visitors. If your web site knows how to suggest additional products to your visitors in a clever way, they might end up buying more than initially planned. You have undoubtedly already seen this strategy in action on many successful ecommerce sites, and there is a reason for that—it increases profits.

In this chapter, you'll implement a simple but efficient product recommendation system in your BalloonShop web store. You will

- Add product recommendations to the product details pages. These recommendations will promote additional products that were ordered together with a particular product.

- Add product recommendations to the shopping cart pages. These recommendations will promote products that were ordered together with the products in the shopping cart.

Implementing these features isn't particularly difficult, but finding the perfect recommendations mechanism is always an interesting task.

Increasing Sales with Dynamic Recommendations

You can implement a product recommendations system in several ways, depending on your kind of store. Here are a few popular ones:

- *Up-selling*: Up-selling is the strategy of offering consumers the opportunity to purchase an upgrade or a little something extra based on their requested purchase. Perhaps the most famous example of up-selling—"Would you like to super-size that?"—is mentioned to customers when they order a meal at McDonald's. This seemingly innocent question greatly increases the company's profit margin.

- *Cross-selling*: Cross-selling is the practice of offering customers complementary products. Continuing with the McDonald's analogy, when someone orders a hamburger, you'll always hear the phrase, "Would you like fries with that?" Because it's widely acknowledged that fries go with burgers, and the consumer is ordering a burger, it's likely that the consumer also likes french fries—the mere mention of french fries is likely to generate a new sale.

- *Featured products on the home page*: BalloonShop already permits the site administrator to choose the products featured on the main page and on the department pages.

In this chapter, you'll implement a dynamic recommendations system with both up-selling and cross-selling strategies. Because at this point BalloonShop retains which products were sold, you will implement the "customers who bought this product also bought . . ." feature in this chapter. This system has the advantage of needing no manual maintenance. Our site will automatically help us to increase our profits without any further intervention!

As mentioned earlier, we'll implement the dynamic recommendations system in the visitor's shopping cart and in the product details page. After adding the new bits to your shop, the product details page will contain the product recommendations list at the bottom of the page, as shown in Figure 15-1.

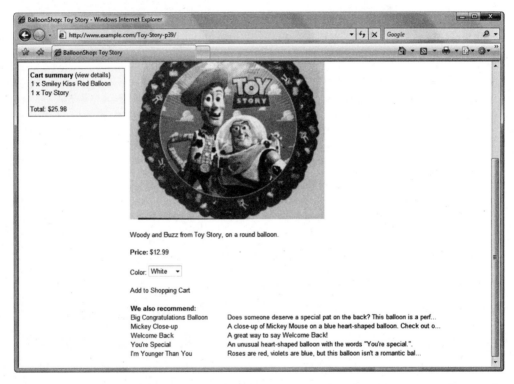

Figure 15-1. *The product details page with the dynamic recommendations system implemented*

The shopping cart page gets a similar addition, as shown in Figure 15-2.

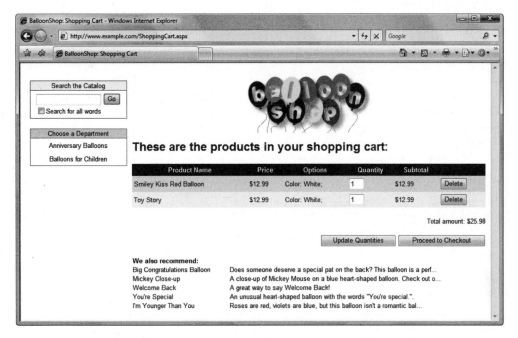

Figure 15-2. *The product details page with the dynamic recommendations system implemented*

Implementing the Data Tier

Before writing any code, you first need to understand the logic you'll implement for making product recommendations. We'll focus here on the logic of recommending products that were ordered together with another specific product. Afterward, the recommendations for the shopping cart page will function in a similar way, but will take more products into consideration.

So you need to find out what other products were bought by customers who also bought the product for which you're calculating the recommendations (in other words, determine "customers who bought this product also bought . . ." information). Let's develop the SQL logic to achieve the list of product recommendations step by step.

■**Tip** Because SQL is very powerful, you can actually implement the exact same functionality in several ways. We'll cover here one of the options, but when implementing the actual stored procedures, you'll be shown other options as well.

To find what other products were ordered together with a specific product, you need to join two instances of the OrderDetail table on their OrderID fields. Feel free to review the "Joining Data Tables" section in Chapter 5 for a quick refresher about table joins. Joining multiple instances of a single table is just like joining different data tables that contain the same data.

You join two instances of OrderDetail—called od1 and od2—on their OrderID fields, while filtering the ProductID value in od1 for the ID of the product you're looking for. This way, in the od2 side of the relationship you'll get all the products that were ordered in the orders that contain the product you're looking for.

The SQL code that gets all the products that were ordered together with the product identified by a ProductID of 4 is

```
SELECT od2.ProductID
FROM OrderDetail od1 JOIN OrderDetail od2 ON od1.OrderID = od2.OrderID
WHERE od1.ProductID = 4
```

This code returns a long list of products, which includes the product with the ProductID of 4, such as this one:

```
ProductID
-----------
1
4
7
10
14
18
22
26
30
1
4
7
10
14
18
4
14
18
22
26
30
```

Starting from this list of results, you need to get the products that are most frequently bought along with this product. The first problem with this list of products is that it includes the product with the ProductID of 4. To eliminate it from the list (because, of course, you can't put it in the recommendations list), you simply add one more rule to the WHERE clause:

```
SELECT od2.ProductID
FROM OrderDetail od1
JOIN OrderDetail od2 ON od1.OrderID = od2.OrderID
WHERE od1.ProductID = 4 and od2.ProductID != 4
```

Not surprisingly, you get a list of products that is similar to the previous one, except it doesn't contain the product with a ProductID of 4 anymore:

```
ProductID
-----------
1
7
10
14
18
22
26
30
1
7
10
14
18
14
18
22
26
30
```

Now the list of returned products is shorter, but it contains multiple entries for the products that were ordered more than once in the orders that contain the product identifier 4. To get the most relevant recommendations, you need to see which products appear more frequently in this list. You do this by grouping the results of the previous query by ProductID and sorting in descending order by how many times each product appears in the list (this number is given by the Rank-calculated column in the following code snippet):

```
SELECT od2.ProductID, COUNT(od2.ProductID) AS Rank
FROM OrderDetail od1
JOIN OrderDetail od2 ON od1.OrderID = od2.OrderID
WHERE od1.ProductID = 4 AND od2.ProductID != 4
GROUP BY od2.ProductID
ORDER BY Rank DESC
```

This query now returns a list such as the following:

```
ProductID   rank
----------- -----------
14          3
18          3
22          2
26          2
30          2
1           2
7           2
10          2
```

If you don't need the rank to be returned, you can rewrite this query by using the COUNT aggregate function directly in the ORDER BY clause. You can also use the TOP keyword to specify how many records you're interested in. If you want the top five products of the list, this query does the trick:

```
SELECT TOP 5 od2.ProductID
FROM OrderDetail od1
JOIN OrderDetail od2 ON od1.OrderID = od2.OrderID
WHERE od1.ProductID = 4 AND od2.ProductID != 4
GROUP BY od2.ProductID
ORDER BY COUNT(od2.ProductID) DESC
```

The results of this query are

```
ProductID
-----------
18
14
22
10
7
```

Because this list of numbers doesn't make much sense to a human eye, you'll also want to know the name and the description of the recommended products. The following query does exactly this by querying the Product table for the IDs returned by the previous query (the description isn't requested because of space reasons):

```
SELECT ProductID, Name
FROM Product
WHERE ProductID IN
    (
    SELECT TOP 5 od2.ProductID
    FROM OrderDetail od1
    JOIN OrderDetail od2 ON od1.OrderID = od2.OrderID
    WHERE od1.ProductID = 4 AND od2.ProductID != 4
    GROUP BY od2.ProductID
    ORDER BY COUNT(od2.ProductID) DESC
    )
```

Based on the data from the previous fictional results, this query returns something like this:

```
ProductID   Name
----------- ----------------------------------------------------
18          Love Cascade Hearts
14          Love Rose
22          I'm Younger Than You
10          I Can't Get Enough of You
7           Smiley Kiss Red Balloon
```

Alternatively, you might want to calculate the product recommendations only using data from the orders that happened in the last *n* days. For this, you need an additional join with the Orders table, which contains the date_created field. The following code calculates product recommendations based on orders placed in the past 30 days:

```
DECLARE @current_date DATETIME
SET @current_date = GETDATE()

SELECT ProductID, Name
FROM Product
WHERE ProductID IN
    (
    SELECT TOP 5 od2.ProductID
    FROM OrderDetail od1
    JOIN OrderDetail od2 ON od1.OrderID = od2.OrderID
    JOIN Orders ON od1.OrderID = Orders.OrderID
    WHERE od1.ProductID = 4 AND od2.ProductID != 4
      AND DATEDIFF(dd, Orders.DateCreated, @current_date) < 30
    GROUP BY od2.ProductID
    ORDER BY COUNT(od2.ProductID) DESC
    )
```

Note that we've used a temporary variable (@current_date) to store the current date for performance reasons. It's okay to use the GETDATE() function directly in your query, but in that case, the function is executed multiple times—once for every row the query returns.

We won't use this trick in BalloonShop, but it's worth keeping in mind as a possibility.

Adding Product Recommendations

Make sure you understand the data tier logic explained earlier, as you'll implement it in the CatalogGetProductRecommendations stored procedure. The only significant difference from the queries shown earlier is that you'll also ask for the product description, which will be truncated at a specified number of characters.

The CatalogGetProductRecommendations stored procedure is called when displaying Product.aspx to show what products were ordered together with the selected product. Add this stored procedure to the BalloonShop database:

```
CREATE PROCEDURE CatalogGetProductRecommendations
(@ProductID INT,
 @DescriptionLength INT)
AS
SELECT ProductID,
       Name,
       CASE WHEN LEN(Description) <= @DescriptionLength THEN Description
            ELSE SUBSTRING(Description, 1, @DescriptionLength) + '...' END
       AS Description
FROM Product
WHERE ProductID IN
    (
    SELECT TOP 5 od2.ProductID
    FROM OrderDetail od1
    JOIN OrderDetail od2 ON od1.OrderID = od2.OrderID
    WHERE od1.ProductID = @ProductID AND od2.ProductID != @ProductID
    GROUP BY od2.ProductID
    ORDER BY COUNT(od2.ProductID) DESC
    )
```

An Alternate Solution Using Subqueries

Because SQL is so versatile, CatalogGetProductRecommendations can be written in a variety of
ways. In our case, one popular alternative to using table joins is using subqueries. Here's a
version of CatalogGetProductRecommendations that uses subqueries instead of joins. The
commented code is self- explanatory:

```
CREATE PROCEDURE CatalogGetProductRecommendations2
(@ProductID INT,
 @DescriptionLength INT)
AS
--- Returns the product recommendations
SELECT ProductID,
       Name,
       CASE WHEN LEN(Description) <= @DescriptionLength THEN Description
            ELSE SUBSTRING(Description, 1, @DescriptionLength) + '...' END
       AS Description
FROM Product
WHERE ProductID IN
    (
    -- Returns the products that were ordered together with @ProductID
    SELECT TOP 5 ProductID
    FROM OrderDetail
    WHERE OrderID IN
        (
        -- Returns the orders that contain @ProductID
        SELECT DISTINCT OrderID
        FROM OrderDetail
        WHERE ProductID = @ProductID
        )
```

```
-- Must not include products that already exist in the visitor's cart
AND ProductID <> @ProductID
-- Group the ProductID so we can calculate the rank
GROUP BY ProductID
-- Order descending by rank
ORDER BY COUNT(ProductID) DESC
)
```

Adding Shopping Cart Recommendations

The logic for showing shopping cart recommendations is very similar to what you did earlier, except now you need to take into account all products that exist in the shopping cart, instead of a single product. Add the following procedure to your BalloonShop database:

```
CREATE PROCEDURE CatalogGetCartRecommendations
(@CartID CHAR(36),
 @DescriptionLength INT)
AS
--- Returns the product recommendations
SELECT ProductID,
       Name,
       CASE WHEN LEN(Description) <= @DescriptionLength THEN Description
            ELSE SUBSTRING(Description, 1, @DescriptionLength) + '...' END
       AS Description
FROM Product
WHERE ProductID IN
   (
   -- Returns the products that exist in a list of orders
   SELECT TOP 5 od1.ProductID AS Rank
   FROM OrderDetail od1
     JOIN OrderDetail od2
       ON od1.OrderID=od2.OrderID
     JOIN ShoppingCart sp
       ON od2.ProductID = sp.ProductID
   WHERE sp.CartID = @CartID
       -- Must not include products that already exist in the visitor's cart
     AND od1.ProductID NOT IN
     (
     -- Returns the products in the specified shopping cart
     SELECT ProductID
     FROM ShoppingCart
     WHERE CartID = @CartID
     )
   -- Group the ProductID so we can calculate the rank
   GROUP BY od1.ProductID
   -- Order descending by rank
   ORDER BY COUNT(od1.ProductID) DESC
   )
```

The alternate version of this procedure, which uses subqueries instead of table joins, looks like this:

```
CREATE PROCEDURE CatalogGetCartRecommendations2
(@CartID CHAR(36),
 @DescriptionLength INT)
AS


--- Returns the product recommendations
SELECT ProductID,
       Name,
       CASE WHEN LEN(Description) <= @DescriptionLength THEN Description
            ELSE SUBSTRING(Description, 1, @DescriptionLength) + '...' END
       AS Description
FROM Product
WHERE ProductID IN
    (
    -- Returns the products that exist in a list of orders
    SELECT TOP 5 ProductID
    FROM OrderDetail
    WHERE OrderID IN
        (
        -- Returns the orders that contain certain products
        SELECT DISTINCT OrderID
        FROM OrderDetail
        WHERE ProductID IN
            (
            -- Returns the products in the specified shopping cart
            SELECT ProductID
            FROM ShoppingCart
            WHERE CartID = @CartID
            )
        )
    -- Must not include products that already exist in the visitor's cart
    AND ProductID NOT IN
        (
        -- Returns the products in the specified shopping cart
        SELECT ProductID
        FROM ShoppingCart
        WHERE CartID = @CartID
        )
    -- Group the ProductID so we can calculate the rank
    GROUP BY ProductID
    -- Order descending by rank
    ORDER BY COUNT(ProductID) DESC
    )
```

Implementing the Business Tier

The business tier of the product recommendations system consists of two methods named GetRecommendations. One of them is located in the CatalogAccess class and retrieves recommendations for a product details page, and the other one is located in the ShoppingCartAccess class and retrieves recommendations to be displayed in the visitor's shopping cart.

Add this GetRecommendations method to your CatalogAccess class:

```
// gets product recommendations
public static DataTable GetRecommendations(string productId)
{
  // get a configured DbCommand object
  DbCommand comm = GenericDataAccess.CreateCommand();
  // set the stored procedure name
  comm.CommandText = "CatalogGetProductRecommendations";
  // create a new parameter
  DbParameter param = comm.CreateParameter();
  param.ParameterName = "@ProductID";
  param.Value = productId;
  param.DbType = DbType.Int32;
  comm.Parameters.Add(param);
  // create a new parameter
  param = comm.CreateParameter();
  param.ParameterName = "@DescriptionLength";
  param.Value = BalloonShopConfiguration.ProductDescriptionLength;
  param.DbType = DbType.Int32;
  comm.Parameters.Add(param);
  // execute the stored procedure
  return GenericDataAccess.ExecuteSelectCommand(comm);
}
```

Add this version of the GetRecommendations method to your ShoppingCartAccess class:

```
// gets product recommendations for the shopping cart
public static DataTable GetRecommendations()
{
  // get a configured DbCommand object
  DbCommand comm = GenericDataAccess.CreateCommand();
  // set the stored procedure name
  comm.CommandText = "CatalogGetCartRecommendations";
  // create a new parameter
  DbParameter param = comm.CreateParameter();
  param.ParameterName = "@CartID";
  param.Value = shoppingCartId;
  param.DbType = DbType.String;
  param.Size = 36;
  comm.Parameters.Add(param);
```

```
// create a new parameter
param = comm.CreateParameter();
param.ParameterName = "@DescriptionLength";
param.Value = BalloonShopConfiguration.ProductDescriptionLength;
param.DbType = DbType.Int32;
comm.Parameters.Add(param);
// execute the stored procedure
return GenericDataAccess.ExecuteSelectCommand(comm);
}
```

Implementing the Presentation Tier

Creating the user interface for product recommendations implies three major steps:

- Creating a new Web User Control that displays the product recommendations. This new control will be named ProductRecommendations.ascx.

- Adding ProductRecommendations.ascx to Product.aspx, where it must display the "customers who bought this product also bought..." list.

- Adding ProductRecommendations.ascx to ShoppingCart.aspx, where it displays the "customers who bought these products also bought..." list.

Let's do these steps in the following exercise.

Exercise: Creating the User Interface

1. Add the following styles to BalloonShop.css:

```
.RecommendationsHead {
  font-weight: bold;
}

.RecommendationLabel {
  display:-moz-inline-block;
  display:inline-block;
  width: 200px;
}
```

2. Add a new Web User Control named ProductRecommendations.ascx to your UserControls folder.

3. Write this code in the Source View window of the control, representing a DataList showing the product recommendations list:

```
<%@ Control Language="C#" AutoEventWireup="true" CodeFile="ProductRecomm➡
endations.ascx.cs" Inherits="UserControls_ProductRecommendations" %>
<asp:DataList ID="list" runat="server" ShowHeader="false">
  <HeaderStyle CssClass=" RecommendationsHead " />
  <HeaderTemplate>
```

```
    We also recommend:
  </HeaderTemplate>
  <ItemTemplate>
    <a class="RecommendationLabel" href='<%# Link.ToProduct(Eval("Product➥
ID").ToString())%>'>
      <%# Eval("Name") %>
    </a>
    <%# Eval("Description") %>
  </ItemTemplate>
</asp:DataList>
```

4. Switch to the code-behind file and add two methods, LoadProductRecommendations and
   LoadCartRecommendations:

```csharp
using System;
using System.Data;

public partial class UserControls_ProductRecommendations : System.Web.UI.➥
UserControl
{
  public void LoadProductRecommendations(string productId)
  {
    // display product recommendations
    DataTable table = CatalogAccess.GetRecommendations(productId);
    if (table.Rows.Count > 0)
    {
      list.ShowHeader = true;
      list.DataSource = table;
      list.DataBind();
    }
  }

  public void LoadCartRecommendations()
  {
    // display product recommendations
    DataTable table = ShoppingCartAccess.GetRecommendations();
    if (table.Rows.Count > 0)
    {
      list.ShowHeader = true;
      list.DataSource = table;
      list.DataBind();
    }
  }
}
```

5. Open Product.aspx in Design View, drag ProductRecommendations.ascx from Solution Explorer
   to the bottom of the form, and change its ID to **recommendations**. Your new form will look like Figure 15-3.

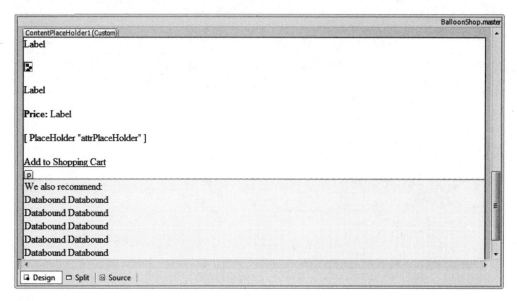

Figure 15-3. *Product.aspx in Design View*

6. In `Product.aspx.cs`, update `PopulateControls` by adding the code that generates the product recommendations right at the beginning of the method:

```
// Fill the control with data
private void PopulateControls(ProductDetails pd)
{
  // Display product recommendations
  string productId = pd.ProductID.ToString();
  recommendations.LoadProductRecommendations(productId);
```

7. Now do the same for `ShoppingCart.aspx`. Open `ShoppingCart.aspx` in Design View, drag `ProductRecommendations.ascx` from Solution Explorer to the bottom of the form, and change its ID to **recommendations**, as shown in Figure 15-4.

8. Modify `PopulateControls` in `ShoppingCartAccess` to load shopping cart recommendations:

```
// fill shopping cart controls with data
private void PopulateControls()
{
  // Display product recommendations
  recommendations.LoadCartRecommendations();
```

9. Test your web site now to ensure that the new functionality works as expected. The results should resemble the screenshots presented at the beginning of this chapter.

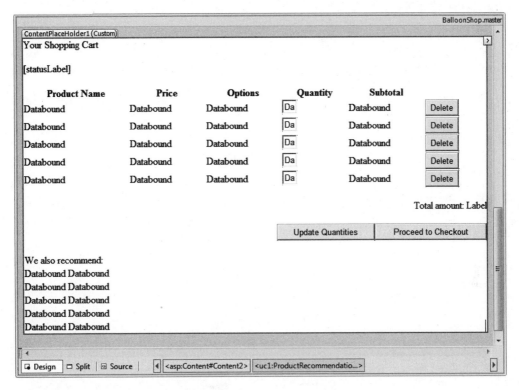

Figure 15-4. *ShoppingCart.aspx in Design View*

How It Works: Displaying Product Recommendations

The most complex part of this new functionality is creating the database stored procedures. In this exercise, you just needed to display the calculated products inside the `Product.aspx` and `ShoppingCart.aspx` Web Forms.

Summary

In this short chapter, you added a new and interesting functionality to the BalloonShop web site. With product recommendations, you have more chances to convince visitors to buy products from the BalloonShop web site.

In the next chapter, you'll enter the third stage of development by adding customer accounts functionality.

Phase 3 of Development: Advanced E-Commerce

CHAPTER 16

■ ■ ■

Creating Customer Accounts

So far in this book, you've built a basic (but functional) site and hooked it into PayPal for taking payments and confirming orders. In this last section of the book, you'll take things a little further. By cutting out PayPal from the ordering process, you can gain better control and reduce overhead. This isn't as complicated as you might think, but you must be careful to do things right.

This chapter lays the groundwork for this task by implementing a customer account system.

To make e-commerce sites more user-friendly, details such as credit card numbers are stored in a database so that visitors don't have to retype this information each time they place an order. The customer account system you'll implement will do this and will include all the web pages required for entering such details.

As well as implementing these web pages, you'll need to take several other factors into account. First, simply placing credit card numbers, expiry dates, and so on into a database in plain text isn't ideal. This method might expose this data to unscrupulous people with access to the database. This could occur remotely or be perpetrated by individuals within your client's organization. Rather than enforcing a prohibitively restrictive access policy to such data, it's much easier to encrypt sensitive information and retrieve it programmatically when required. You'll create a security library to make this easier.

Secondly, secure communications are important because you'll be capturing sensitive information such as credit card details via the Web. You can't just put a form up for people to access via HTTP and allow them to send it to you because the data could be intercepted. You'll learn how to use SSL over HTTPS connections to solve this problem.

You'll be taking the BalloonShop application to the point where you can move on and implement your own backend order pipeline in the next chapters.

In this chapter, you'll learn how to

- Store customer accounts

- Implement the security classes

- Add customer account functionality to BalloonShop

- Create the checkout page

Storing Customer Accounts

You can handle customer account functionality in web sites in many ways. In general, however, they share the following features:

- Customers log in via a login page or dialog box to get access to secured areas of the web site.

- Once logged in, the web application remembers the customer until the customer logs out (either manually via a Log Out button or automatically if the session times out or a server error occurs).

- All secure pages in a web application need to check whether a customer is logged in before allowing access.

First, let's look at the general implementation details for the BalloonShop e-commerce site.

Creating a BalloonShop Customer Account Scheme

Actually, you've already done a lot of the work here—back in Chapters 11 and 12, you implemented a system whereby site administrators can log in and, among other things, edit products in the catalog. You did this using forms authentication, and you created a login page, `Login.aspx`, to allow users in an Administrators role to log in. The current login status—that is, whether a user is logged in—is shown using a user control you created: `Login.ascx`.

In this chapter, you'll take things a little further by extending the system for use with customers. You must make several changes to enable this, but the starting point is to include a new role, in addition to Administrators, which we'll call (surprisingly enough) Customers. Customers will then log in using the same login page as administrators, but because they are in a different role, the similarity ends there. They will not, for example, have access to the administration tools that administrators can use. They will, however, have access to a **customer details page**, where they can view and edit address, contact, and credit card details prior to placing an order. Another major addition is that of a **registration page**, where new customers can sign up on the site.

As you can see, the amount of user data you need to store has increased now that you're catering to customers, with address data and so on needing somewhere to live. Luckily, ASP.NET introduces the concept of **user profiles**, flexible storage systems that fit this need perfectly, with minimal effort. Later in the chapter, you'll see how user profiles can be quickly configured using the `web.config` file, and how you can hook into this information from your code.

Of course, there are alternatives to using the forms authentication system. You could use Microsoft Passport authentication—although many people prefer not to because it ties accounts into a proprietary system and can be time consuming and tricky to set up correctly. You could also use Windows Authentication, where user accounts are associated with Windows accounts stored on the hosting server or in the domain of the hosting server. This solution is great for intranet sites, where users already have domain accounts, but is difficult to set up and maintain for Internet sites, and is usually avoided in such cases. Alternatively, you could implement your own custom system, which gives you the most flexibility at the cost of increased development time.

One important thing you'd have to do in a custom system, as mentioned in Chapter 11, is secure user passwords. It isn't a good idea to store user passwords in your database in plain text, because this information is a potential target for attack. Instead, you should store what is known as the **hash** of the password. A hash is a unique string that represents the password, but cannot be converted back into the password itself. To validate the password entered by the user, you simply need to generate a hash for the password entered and compare it with the hash stored in your database. If the hashes match, the passwords entered match as well, so you can be sure that the supplied password is correct. The ASP.NET forms authentication system you'll use in this chapter handles this side of things for you, and ensures that user passwords are stored securely (and in a case-sensitive way, providing enhanced security). However, it's still worth looking at as a general technique, and so the security library you'll create shortly includes hashing capabilities.

Hashing is a one-way system, but to store credit card details securely, you'll need to use a more advanced, bidirectional form of encryption. This enables you to store credit card details securely, but get access to them when you need to; that is, when the customer pays for an order.

The specifics of implementing this scheme in your application include the following tasks:

- Adding a user profile schema to the application

- Modifying the site to allow customer accounts, including registration and detail editing pages

- Modifying ShoppingCart.ascx, which will now redirect the user to a checkout page called Checkout.aspx

The SecurityLib Classes

The two areas you've seen so far where security functionality is required are

- Password hashing

- Credit card encryption

Both tasks can be carried out by classes in the SecurityLib directory, which you'll add as a subdirectory of App_Code. The reason for separating this functionality from the main code of the web site in this case is purely logical. Of course, at some point, you may want to access this code in another application. Having all the relevant files in one place makes it easy to copy elsewhere or even to extract it and put it into a shared class library. To facilitate all this, the classes in the SecurityLib directory are all placed in a separate namespace—also called SecurityLib. Note that to share the code in a class library requires Visual C# Express or the full version of Visual Studio, because Visual Web Developer Express doesn't allow you to create class libraries. The SecurityLib directory contains the following files:

- `PasswordHasher.cs`: Contains the `PasswordHasher` class, which contains the shared method `Hash` that returns a hash for the password supplied.

- `SecureCard.cs`: Contains the `SecureCard` class, which represents a credit card. This class can be initialized with credit card information, which is then accessible in encrypted format. Alternatively, it can be initialized with encrypted credit card data and provide access to the decrypted information contained within.

- `SecureCardException.cs`: Should there be any problems during encryption or decryption, the exception contained in this file, `SecureCardException`, is thrown by `SecureCard`.

- `StringEncryptor.cs`: The class contained in this file, `StringEncryptor`, is used by `SecureCard` to encrypt and decrypt data. This means that if you want to change the encryption method, you only need to modify the code here, leaving the `SecureCard` class untouched.

- `StringEncryptorException.cs`: Contains the `StringEncryptorException` exception, thrown by `StringEncryptor` if an error occurs.

We'll look at the code for hashing first, followed by encryption.

Hashing

Hashing, as has already been noted, is a means by which a unique value can be obtained that represents an object. In practice, this means doing the following:

1. Serializing the object being hashed into a byte array

2. Hashing the byte array, obtaining a new hashed byte array

3. Converting the hashed byte array into the format required for storage

For passwords, this is simple because converting a string (which is an array of characters) into a byte array is no problem. Converting the resultant hashed byte array into a string for database storage and quick comparison is also simple.

The actual method used to convert the source byte array into a hashed byte array can vary. The `System.Security.Cryptography` namespace in .NET contains several classes for hashing and allows you to provide your own if necessary, although we won't go into details of this here. The two main hashing algorithms found in the .NET Framework are SHA1 (Secure Hash Algorithm) and MD5 (Message Digest, another name for the hash code generated). SHA1 generates a 160-bit hash (regardless of the size of the input data), whereas MD5 generates a 128-bit hash; therefore, SHA1 is generally considered more secure (although slower) than MD5. The Framework also contains other versions of the SHA1 hash algorithm that generate longer hashes, up to 512 bits, as well as hash algorithms that work using a key (shared secret) and the data to be hashed.

In the `SecurityLib` implementation, you'll use SHA1, although it's easy to change this if you require stronger security. You'll see the code that achieves this in the `PasswordHasher` class in the following exercise.

Exercise: Implementing the PasswordHasher Class

1. Create a new subdirectory in the App_Code directory of BalloonShop called SecurityLib.

2. Add a new class file to SecurityLib called PasswordHasher.cs with code as follows:

```csharp
using System;
using System.Collections.Generic;
using System.Text;
using System.Security.Cryptography;

namespace SecurityLib
{
  public static class PasswordHasher
  {
    private static SHA1Managed hasher = new SHA1Managed();

    public static string Hash(string password)
    {
      // convert password to byte array
      byte[] passwordBytes =
        System.Text.ASCIIEncoding.ASCII.GetBytes(password);

      // generate hash from byte array of password
      byte[] passwordHash = hasher.ComputeHash(passwordBytes);

      // convert hash to string
      return Convert.ToBase64String(passwordHash, 0, passwordHash.Length);
    }
  }
}
```

3. Add a new web page to the root of the BalloonShop web site called SecurityLibTester.aspx, using the usual options for having code in an external file and selecting the default BalloonShop Master Page.

4. Add the following code to SecurityLibTester.aspx:

```
<%@ Page Title="SecurityLib Test Page" Language="C#" MasterPageFile=➥
"~/BalloonShop.master" AutoEventWireup="true" CodeFile="SecurityLibTester➥
.aspx.cs" Inherits="SecurityLibTester" %>

<asp:Content ID="Content1" ContentPlaceHolderID="head" runat="Server">
</asp:Content>
<asp:Content ID="Content2" ContentPlaceHolderID="ContentPlace➥
```

```
Holder1" runat="Server">
  Enter your password:<br />
  <asp:TextBox ID="pwdBox1" runat="server" />
  <br />
  Enter your password again:
  <br />
  <asp:TextBox ID="pwdBox2" runat="server" />
  <br />
  <asp:Button ID="processButton" runat="server" Text="Process" ➥
OnClick="processButton_Click" />
  <br />
  <asp:Label ID="result" runat="server" />
</asp:Content>
```

5. Modify SecurityLibTester.aspx.cs as follows:

```csharp
using System;
using System.Text;
using SecurityLib;

public partial class SecurityLibTester : System.Web.UI.Page
{
  protected void processButton_Click(object sender, EventArgs e)
  {
    string hash1 = PasswordHasher.Hash(pwdBox1.Text);
    string hash2 = PasswordHasher.Hash(pwdBox2.Text);
    StringBuilder sb = new StringBuilder();
    sb.Append("The hash of the first password is: ");
    sb.Append(hash1);
    sb.Append("<br />The hash of the second password is: ");
    sb.Append(hash2);
    if (hash1 == hash2)
    {
      sb.Append("<br />The passwords match! Welcome!");
    }
    else
    {
      sb.Append("<br />Password invalid. "
        + "Armed guards are on their way.");
    }
    result.Text = sb.ToString();
  }
}
```

6. Load SecurityLibTester.aspx, enter two passwords, and click **Process**. The result is shown in Figure 16-1.

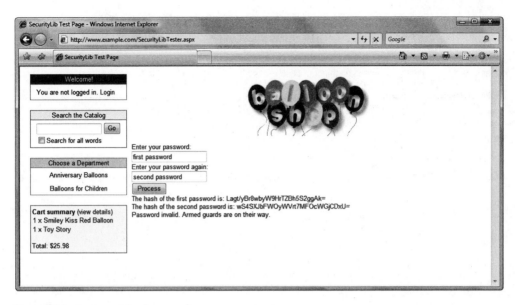

Figure 16-1. *Password hasher result*

How It Works: Implementing the PasswordHasher Class

The code in the PasswordHasher class follows the steps that were discussed earlier. First, you use the utility method System.Text.ASCIIEncoding.ASCII.GetBytes to convert the password string into a byte array:

```
// convert password to byte array
byte[] passwordBytes =
  System.Text.ASCIIEncoding.ASCII.GetBytes(password);
```

Next you use the private shared member hasher, an instance of SHA1Managed, to generate a hash byte array:

```
// generate hash from byte array of password
byte[] passwordHash = hasher.ComputeHash(passwordBytes);
```

Finally, you convert the hash back into a string using the utility function Convert.ToBase64String, and return the result:

```
// convert hash to string
return Convert.ToBase64String(passwordHash, 0, passwordHash.Length);
```

All the hash algorithm classes in the .NET Framework use this ComputeHash method to get a hash from an input array of bytes. To increase the size of the hash, you can replace the hasher with another one of these, for example:

```
public static class PasswordHasher
{
  private static SHA512Managed hasher = new SHA512Managed();
  ...
}
```

This change would result in a 512-bit hash, which is probably a bit excessive in this sort of application!

The client page, `SecurityLibTest.aspx`, hashes two passwords and compares the result. The code is basic enough to ignore for now, but it's important to note that the generated hashes vary a great deal for even simple changes to the input data, even just changes of case—one of the defining features of good hash generation.

Encryption

Encryption comes in many shapes and sizes and continues to be a hot topic. No definitive solution to encrypting data exists, although plenty of advice can be given. In general, there are two forms of encryption:

- *Symmetric encryption*: A single key is used both to encrypt and decrypt data.

- *Asymmetric encryption*: Separate keys are used to encrypt and decrypt data. The encryption key is commonly known as the **public key**, and anyone can use it to encrypt information. The decryption key is known as the **private key**, because it can only be used to decrypt data that has been encrypted using the public key. The encryption key (public key) and the decryption key (private key) are mathematically related and are always generated in pairs. The public key and private key can't be obtained one from another. If you have a public key/private key pair, you can send the public key to parties that need to encrypt information for you. You will be the only one who knows the private key associated with that public key and thus the only one able to decrypt the information.

Note In some situations, such as digital signing, the private key is used for encryption, and the public key is used for decryption. However, this doesn't apply to the techniques in this chapter.

Although asymmetric encryption is more secure, it also requires much more processing power. Symmetric encryption is faster but can be less secure because both the encryptor and the decryptor have knowledge of a single key. With symmetric encryption, the encryptor needs to send the key to the decryptor. With Internet communications, there is often no way of ensuring that this key remains a secret from third parties when it is sent to the encryptor.

Asymmetric encryption gets around this by using key pairs. There is never a need for the decryption key to be divulged, so it's much more difficult for a third party to break the encryption. Because it requires a lot more processing power, however, the practical method of operation is to use asymmetric encryption to exchange a symmetric key over the Internet, which is then used for symmetric encryption. Users can then be safe in the knowledge that this key has not been exposed to third parties.

In the `BalloonShop` application, things are much simpler than with Internet communications—you just need to encrypt data for storage in the database and decrypt it again when required—so you can use a symmetric algorithm.

■**Note** Behind the scenes, asymmetric encryption is going on, however, because that is the method used to encrypt the credit card details that are sent over the Internet. You don't need to do much to enable this, as you'll see in the "Secure Connections" section later in this chapter.

As with hashing, several algorithms can be used for both symmetric and asymmetric encryption. The .NET Framework contains implementations of several of these in the System. Security.Cryptography namespace.

The two available asymmetric algorithms are DSA (Digital Signature Algorithm) and RSA (Rivest-Shamir-Adleman, from the names of its inventors: Ronald Rivest, Adi Shamir, and Leonard Adleman). Of these, DSA can only be used to "sign" data so that its authenticity can be verified, whereas RSA is more versatile (although slower than DSA when used to generate digital signatures). DSA is the current standard for digital authentication used by the U.S. government.

The symmetric algorithms found in the .NET Framework are DES (Data Encryption Standard), Triple DES (3DES), RC2 ("Ron's Code," or "Rivest's Cipher" depending on who you ask, also from Ronald Rivest), and Rijndael (from the names of its inventors, John Daemen and Vincent Rijman).

DES AND RIJNDAEL

DES has been the standard for some time now, although this is gradually changing. It uses a 64-bit key; however, in practice only 56 of these bits are used (8 bits are parity bits), which is not strong enough to avoid being broken using today's computers.

Both Triple DES and RC2 are variations of DES. Triple DES effectively encrypts data using three separate DES encryptions with three keys totaling 168 bits when parity bits are subtracted. The RC2 variant can have key lengths up to 128 bits (longer keys are also possible using RC3, RC4, and so on), so it can be made weaker or stronger than DES depending on the key size.

Rijndael is a completely separate encryption method and is the current Advanced Encryption Standard (AES) standard; several competing algorithms were considered before Rijndael was chosen. This standard is intended to replace DES and is gradually becoming the most used (and secure) symmetric encryption algorithm.

The tasks that must be carried out when encrypting and decrypting data are a little more involved than hashing. The classes in the .NET Framework are optimized to work with data streams so you have a bit more work to do with data conversion. You also have to define both a key and an initialization vector (IV) to perform encryption and decryption. The IV is required due to the nature of encryption: Calculating the encrypted values for one sequence of bits involves using the encrypted values of the immediately preceding sequence of bits. Because no such values exist at the start of encryption, an IV is used instead. In practice, both the IV and the key can be represented as a byte array, which in the case of DES encryption is 64 bits (8 bytes) long.

■**Note** At http://en.wikipedia.org/wiki/Block_cipher_modes_of_operation, you can learn more about the various modes of encryption.

The steps required for encrypting a string into an encrypted string are as follows:

1. Convert the source string into a byte array.

2. Initialize an encryption algorithm class.

3. Use the encryption algorithm class to generate an encryptor object, supporting the ICryptoTransform interface. This requires key and IV values.

4. Use the encryptor object to initialize a cryptographic stream (CryptoStream object). This stream also needs to know that you are encrypting data and needs a target stream to write encrypted data to.

5. Use the cryptographic stream to write encrypted data to a target memory stream using the source byte array created previously.

6. Extract the byte data stored in the stream.

7. Convert the byte data into a string.

Decryption follows a similar scheme:

1. Convert the source string into a byte array.

2. Fill a memory stream with the contents of the byte array.

3. Initialize an encryption algorithm class.

4. Use the encryption algorithm class to generate a decryptor object, supporting the ICryptoTransform interface. This requires key and IV values.

5. Use the decryptor object to initialize a cryptographic stream (CryptoStream object). This stream also needs to know that you are decrypting data and needs a source stream to read encrypted data from.

6. Use the cryptographic stream to read decrypted data (can use the StreamReader.ReadToEnd method to get the result as a string).

In the BalloonShop code, you'll use DES, but the code in the StringEncryptor class could be replaced with code to use any of the algorithms specified previously.

Exercise: Implementing the StringEncryptor Class

1. Add a new class to the SecurityLib directory called StringEncryptorException with code as follows:

```
using System;
using System.Collections.Generic;
using System.Text;
```

```csharp
namespace SecurityLib
{
  public class StringEncryptorException : Exception
  {
    public StringEncryptorException(string message)
      : base(message)
    {
    }
  }
}
```

2. Add another new class to the SecurityLib directory called StringEncryptor with code as follows:

```csharp
using System;
using System.Collections.Generic;
using System.Text;
using System.Security.Cryptography;
using System.IO;

namespace SecurityLib
{
  public static class StringEncryptor
  {
    public static string Encrypt(string sourceData)
    {
      // set key and initialization vector values
      byte[] key = new byte[] { 1, 2, 3, 4, 5, 6, 7, 8 };
      byte[] iv = new byte[] { 1, 2, 3, 4, 5, 6, 7, 8 };
      try
      {
        // convert data to byte array
        byte[] sourceDataBytes =
          System.Text.ASCIIEncoding.ASCII.GetBytes(sourceData);

        // get target memory stream
        MemoryStream tempStream = new MemoryStream();

        // get encryptor and encryption stream
        DESCryptoServiceProvider encryptor =
          new DESCryptoServiceProvider();
        CryptoStream encryptionStream =
          new CryptoStream(tempStream,
            encryptor.CreateEncryptor(key, iv),
            CryptoStreamMode.Write);
```

```
      // encrypt data
      encryptionStream.Write(sourceDataBytes, 0,
        sourceDataBytes.Length);
      encryptionStream.FlushFinalBlock();

      // put data into byte array
      byte[] encryptedDataBytes = tempStream.GetBuffer();

      // convert encrypted data into string
      return Convert.ToBase64String(encryptedDataBytes, 0,
        (int)tempStream.Length);
    }
    catch
    {
      throw new StringEncryptorException(
        "Unable to encrypt data.");
    }
  }

  public static string Decrypt(string sourceData)
  {
    // set key and initialization vector values
    byte[] key = new byte[] { 1, 2, 3, 4, 5, 6, 7, 8 };
    byte[] iv = new byte[] { 1, 2, 3, 4, 5, 6, 7, 8 };
    try
    {
      // convert data to byte array
      byte[] encryptedDataBytes =
        Convert.FromBase64String(sourceData);

      // get source memory stream and fill it
      MemoryStream tempStream =
        new MemoryStream(encryptedDataBytes, 0,
          encryptedDataBytes.Length);


      // get decryptor and decryption stream
      DESCryptoServiceProvider decryptor =
        new DESCryptoServiceProvider();
      CryptoStream decryptionStream =
        new CryptoStream(tempStream,
          decryptor.CreateDecryptor(key, iv),
          CryptoStreamMode.Read);
```

```
      // decrypt data
      StreamReader allDataReader =
        new StreamReader(decryptionStream);
      return allDataReader.ReadToEnd();
    }
    catch
    {
      throw new StringEncryptorException(
        "Unable to decrypt data.");
    }
  }
 }
}
```

3. Add a new web page to the root of BalloonShop called `SecurityLibTester2.aspx` with the usual options and code as follows:

```
<%@ Page Title="SecurityLib Test Page 2" Language="C#" MasterPageFile=➡
"~/BalloonShop.master" AutoEventWireup="true"
  CodeFile="SecurityLibTester2.aspx.cs" Inherits="SecurityLibTester2" %>

<asp:Content ID="Content1" ContentPlaceHolderID="head" runat="Server">
</asp:Content>
<asp:Content ID="Content2" ContentPlaceHolderID="ContentPlace➡
Holder1" runat="Server">
  Enter data to encrypt:
  <br />
  <asp:TextBox ID="encryptBox" runat="server" />
  <br />
  Enter data to decrypt:
  <br />
  <asp:TextBox ID="decryptBox" runat="server" />
  <br />
  <asp:Button ID="processButton" runat="server" Text="Process" ➡
OnClick="processButton_Click" />
  <br />
  <asp:Label ID="result" runat="server" />
</asp:Content>
```

4. Modify the code in `SecurityLibTester2.aspx.cs` in `SecurityLibTester` as follows:

```
using System;
using System.Text;
using SecurityLib;
```

```csharp
public partial class SecurityLibTester2 : System.Web.UI.Page
{
  protected void processButton_Click(object sender, EventArgs e)
  {
    string stringToEncrypt = encryptBox.Text;
    string stringToDecrypt = decryptBox.Text;
    string encryptedString =
    StringEncryptor.Encrypt(stringToEncrypt);
    if (stringToDecrypt == "")
    {
      stringToDecrypt = encryptedString;
    }
    string decryptedString =
    StringEncryptor.Decrypt(stringToDecrypt);

    StringBuilder sb = new StringBuilder();
    sb.Append("Encrypted data: ");
    sb.Append(encryptedString);
    sb.Append("<br />Decrypted data: ");
    sb.Append(decryptedString);
    result.Text = sb.ToString();
  }
}
```

5. Load `SecurityLibTester2.aspx`, enter a string to encrypt in the first text box (leave the second text box blank unless you have a ready-encoded string to decrypt), and click **Process**. The result is shown in Figure 16-2.

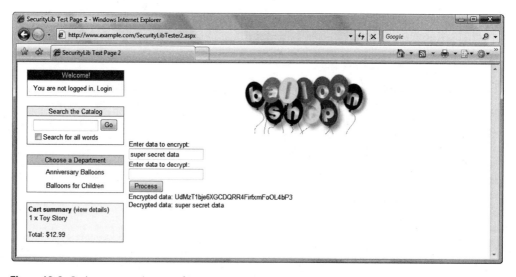

Figure 16-2. *String encryption result*

How It Works: Implementing the StringEncryptor Class

The StringEncryptor class has two shared methods, Encrypt and Decrypt, which encrypt and decrypt data. We'll look at each of these in turn.

Encrypt starts by defining two hard-coded byte arrays for the key and IV used in encryption:

```
public static string Encrypt(string sourceData)
{
   // set key and initialization vector values
   byte[] key = new byte[] { 1, 2, 3, 4, 5, 6, 7, 8 };
   byte[] iv = new byte[] { 1, 2, 3, 4, 5, 6, 7, 8 };
```

Both these arrays are set to temporary values here. They could just as easily take any other values, depending on the key you want to use. Alternatively, they could be loaded from disk, although having the values compiled into your code in this way could stop people from discovering the values used quite effectively. This method isn't foolproof—the data could be extracted if anyone gets access to your DLLs (Dynamic Link Libraries), but it's secure enough for our purposes. Note that you initialize these values each time the method is called rather than using constant values. One reason for this is that the iv array is modified as part of the encryption process, so the values would be different if you didn't re-initialize it. In effect, this would mean that the first few bytes of the decrypted data would be garbled. Therefore, you should use your own values, not the temporary ones used in the previous code snippet. You can use the classes and methods in the System.Security.Cryptography namespace to generate such values automatically, or you can just insert random numbers.

The encryption code is contained in a try...catch block in case an error occurs. The code follows the steps laid out earlier, starting with the conversion of the source string into a byte array:

```
try
{
   // convert data to byte array
   byte[] sourceDataBytes =
      System.Text.ASCIIEncoding.ASCII.GetBytes(sourceData);
```

Next, a MemoryStream object is initialized, which is used to store encrypted data:

```
   // get target memory stream
   MemoryStream tempStream = new MemoryStream();
```

Now you get the encryptor object—in this case, an instance of the DESCryptoServiceProvider class—and use it with the key and IV created earlier to generate a CryptoStream object (specifying an encryption operation via the CreateEncryptor method and CryptoStreamMode.Write mode):

```
   // get target memory stream
   MemoryStream tempStream = new MemoryStream();

   // get encryptor and encryption stream
   DESCryptoServiceProvider encryptor =
      new DESCryptoServiceProvider();
   CryptoStream encryptionStream =
      new CryptoStream(tempStream,
         encryptor.CreateEncryptor(key, iv),
         CryptoStreamMode.Write);
```

If you wanted to substitute a different encryption algorithm, this is where you would change the code (although you might also have to change the amount of data contained in the key and IV arrays).

■**Note** Note that the suffix of this class is `CryptoServiceProvider`. This indicates an unmanaged implementation of the DES encryption algorithm. There is no managed implementation of this algorithm in the .NET Framework, although there is a managed implementation of the Rijndael algorithm. In practice, however, this makes little (if any) difference to application performance.

The next section of code performs the actual encryption, writing the resultant byte array to the `MemoryStream` created earlier:

```
// encrypt data
encryptionStream.Write(sourceDataBytes, 0,
  sourceDataBytes.Length);
encryptionStream.FlushFinalBlock();
```

The `FlushFinalBlock` call here is essential. Without this call, unwritten data might be left in the buffer of the `CryptoStream`. This call forces the stream writing to complete so that all the data you require is contained in the `MemoryStream` object.

Next you grab the data from the `MemoryStream` and place it into a byte array:

```
// put data into byte array
byte[] encryptedDataBytes = tempStream.GetBuffer();
```

Finally, you convert the resultant byte array into a string and return it:

```
// convert encrypted data into string
return Convert.ToBase64String(encryptedDataBytes, 0,
  (int)tempStream.Length);
```

If anything goes wrong during this process, a `StringEncryptorException` exception is thrown:

```
catch
{
  throw new StringEncryptorException(
    "Unable to encrypt data.");
}
}
```

Note that this exception class doesn't do very much, and you might think that just throwing a standard `Exception` would be good enough. However, by creating your own type, it's possible for Structured Exception Handling (SEH) code that uses this class to test for the specific type of this new exception, filtering out `StringEncryptorException` exceptions from others that might occur.

The Decrypt method is very similar to Encrypt. You start in the same way by initializing the key and IV before moving into a try...catch block and converting the source string into a byte array:

```
public static string Decrypt(string sourceData)
{
  // set key and initialization vector values
  byte[] key = new byte[] { 1, 2, 3, 4, 5, 6, 7, 8 };
  byte[] iv = new byte[] { 1, 2, 3, 4, 5, 6, 7, 8 };
  try
  {
    // convert data to byte array
    byte[] encryptedDataBytes =
      Convert.FromBase64String(sourceData);
```

This time, however, you need a stream that is filled with this source byte array because the CryptoStream will be reading from a stream rather than writing to one:

```
    // get source memory stream and fill it
    MemoryStream tempStream =
      new MemoryStream(encryptedDataBytes, 0,
        encryptedDataBytes.Length);
```

The next code snippet is similar, although you use the CreateDecryptor method and CryptoStreamMode.Read mode to specify decryption:

```
    // get decryptor and decryption stream
    DESCryptoServiceProvider decryptor =
      new DESCryptoServiceProvider();
    CryptoStream decryptionStream =
      new CryptoStream(tempStream,
        decryptor.CreateDecryptor(key, iv),
        CryptoStreamMode.Read);
```

Finally, you get the decrypted data out of the CryptoStream using a StreamReader object, which handily allows you to grab the data and put it straight into a string for returning. As with Encrypt, the last step is to add the code that throws a StringEncryptorException exception if anything goes wrong:

```
    // decrypt data
    StreamReader allDataReader =
      new StreamReader(decryptionStream);
    return allDataReader.ReadToEnd();
  }
  catch
  {
    throw new StringEncryptorException(
      "Unable to decrypt data.");
  }
}
```

The client code for this class simply encrypts and decrypts data, demonstrating that things are working properly. The code for this is very simple, so it's not detailed here.

Now that you have the `StringEncryptor` class code, the last step in creating the `SecureLib` library is to add the `SecureCard` class.

Exercise: Implementing the SecureCard Class

1. Add a new class to the `SecurityLib` directory called `SecureCardException.cs` with code as follows:

```
using System;

namespace SecurityLib
{
  public class SecureCardException : Exception
  {
    public SecureCardException(string message)
      : base(message)
    {
    }
  }
}
```

2. Add another new file to the `SecurityLib` directory called `SecureCard.cs` with code as follows:

```
using System;
using System.Collections.Generic;
using System.Text;
using System.Xml;

namespace SecurityLib
{
  public class SecureCard
  {
    private bool isDecrypted = false;
    private bool isEncrypted = false;
    private string cardHolder;
    private string cardNumber;
    private string issueDate;
    private string expiryDate;
    private string issueNumber;
    private string cardType;
    private string encryptedData;
    private XmlDocument xmlCardData;
```

```csharp
public SecureCard(string newEncryptedData)
{
  // constructor for use with encrypted data
  encryptedData = newEncryptedData;
  DecryptData();
}

public SecureCard(string newCardHolder,
  string newCardNumber, string newIssueDate,
  string newExpiryDate, string newIssueNumber,
  string newCardType)
{
  // constructor for use with decrypted data
  cardHolder = newCardHolder;
  cardNumber = newCardNumber;
  issueDate = newIssueDate;
  expiryDate = newExpiryDate;
  issueNumber = newIssueNumber;
  cardType = newCardType;
  EncryptData();
}

private void CreateXml()
{
  // encode card details as XML document
  xmlCardData = new XmlDocument();
  XmlElement documentRoot =
    xmlCardData.CreateElement("CardDetails");
  XmlElement child;

  child = xmlCardData.CreateElement("CardHolder");
  child.InnerXml = cardHolder;
  documentRoot.AppendChild(child);

  child = xmlCardData.CreateElement("CardNumber");
  child.InnerXml = cardNumber;
  documentRoot.AppendChild(child);

  child = xmlCardData.CreateElement("IssueDate");
  child.InnerXml = issueDate;
  documentRoot.AppendChild(child);

  child = xmlCardData.CreateElement("ExpiryDate");
  child.InnerXml = expiryDate;
  documentRoot.AppendChild(child);
```

```
    child = xmlCardData.CreateElement("IssueNumber");
    child.InnerXml = issueNumber;
    documentRoot.AppendChild(child);

    child = xmlCardData.CreateElement("CardType");
    child.InnerXml = cardType;
    documentRoot.AppendChild(child);
    xmlCardData.AppendChild(documentRoot);
}

private void ExtractXml()
{
    // get card details out of XML document
    cardHolder =
      xmlCardData.GetElementsByTagName(
        "CardHolder").Item(0).InnerXml;
    cardNumber =
      xmlCardData.GetElementsByTagName(
        "CardNumber").Item(0).InnerXml;
    issueDate =
      xmlCardData.GetElementsByTagName(
        "IssueDate").Item(0).InnerXml;
    expiryDate =
      xmlCardData.GetElementsByTagName(
        "ExpiryDate").Item(0).InnerXml;
    issueNumber =
      xmlCardData.GetElementsByTagName(
        "IssueNumber").Item(0).InnerXml;
    cardType =
      xmlCardData.GetElementsByTagName(
        "CardType").Item(0).InnerXml;
}

private void EncryptData()
{
    try
    {
        // put data into XML doc
        CreateXml();
        // encrypt data
        encryptedData =
          StringEncryptor.Encrypt(xmlCardData.OuterXml);
        // set encrypted flag
        isEncrypted = true;
    }
```

```
  catch
  {
   throw new SecureCardException("Unable to encrypt data.");
  }
}

private void DecryptData()
{
  try
  {
    // decrypt data
    xmlCardData = new XmlDocument();
    xmlCardData.InnerXml =
      StringEncryptor.Decrypt(encryptedData);
    // extract data from XML
    ExtractXml();
    // set decrypted flag
    isDecrypted = true;
  }
  catch
  {
   throw new SecureCardException("Unable to decrypt data.");
  }
}

public string CardHolder
{
  get
  {
    if (isDecrypted)
    {
      return cardHolder;
    }
    else
    {
      throw new SecureCardException("Data not decrypted.");
    }
  }
}

public string CardNumber
{
  get
  {
    if (isDecrypted)
    {
      return cardNumber;
    }
```

```csharp
      else
      {
        throw new SecureCardException("Data not decrypted.");
      }
    }
  }
}

public string CardNumberX
{
  get
  {
    if (isDecrypted)
    {
      return "XXXX-XXXX-XXXX-"
          + cardNumber.Substring(cardNumber.Length - 4, 4);
    }
    else
    {
      throw new SecureCardException("Data not decrypted.");
    }
  }
}

public string IssueDate
{
  get
  {
    if (isDecrypted)
    {
      return issueDate;
    }
    else
    {
      throw new SecureCardException("Data not decrypted.");
    }
  }
}

public string ExpiryDate
{
  get
  {
    if (isDecrypted)
    {
      return expiryDate;
    }
```

```csharp
      else
      {
        throw new SecureCardException("Data not decrypted.");
      }
    }
  }
}

public string IssueNumber
{
  get
  {
    if (isDecrypted)
    {
      return issueNumber;
    }
    else
    {
      throw new SecureCardException("Data not decrypted.");
    }
  }
}

public string CardType
{
  get
  {
    if (isDecrypted)
    {
      return cardType;
    }
    else
    {
      throw new SecureCardException("Data not decrypted.");
    }
  }
}

public string EncryptedData
{
  get
  {
    if (isEncrypted)
    {
      return encryptedData;
    }
```

```
        else
        {
          throw new SecureCardException("Data not decrypted.");
        }
      }
    }
  }
}
```

3. Add a new web page to the root of BalloonShop called SecurityLibTester3.aspx, with the usual options and code as follows:

```
<%@ Page Title="SecurityLib Test Page 3" Language="C#" MasterPageFile=➥
"~/BalloonShop.master" AutoEventWireup="true" CodeFile="SecurityLib➥
Tester3.aspx.cs" Inherits="SecurityLibTester3" %>

<asp:Content ID="Content1" ContentPlaceHolderID="head" runat="Server">
</asp:Content>
<asp:Content ID="Content2" ContentPlaceHolderID="ContentPlaceHolder1" ➥
runat="Server">
  Card holder:<br />
  <asp:TextBox ID="cardHolderBox" runat="server" />
  <br />
  Card number:<br />
  <asp:TextBox ID="cardNumberBox" runat="server" />
  <br />
  Issue date:<br />
  <asp:TextBox ID="issueDateBox" runat="server" />
  <br />
  Expiry date:<br />
  <asp:TextBox ID="expiryDateBox" runat="server" />
  <br />
  Issue number:<br />
  <asp:TextBox ID="issueNumberBox" runat="server" />
  <br />
```

```
  Card type:<br />
  <asp:TextBox ID="cardTypeBox" runat="server" />
  <br />
  <asp:Button ID="processButton" runat="server" Text="Process" ➥
OnClick="processButton_Click" />
  <br />
  <asp:Label ID="result" runat="server" />
</asp:Content>
```

4. Modify the code in SecurityLibTester3.aspx.cs as follows:

```
using System;
using System.Text;
using SecurityLib;

public partial class SecurityLibTester3 : System.Web.UI.Page
{
  protected void processButton_Click(object sender, EventArgs e)
  {
    SecureCard encryptedCard =
    new SecureCard(cardHolderBox.Text, cardNumberBox.Text,
      issueDateBox.Text, expiryDateBox.Text,issueNumberBox.Text,
      cardTypeBox.Text);
    string encryptedData = encryptedCard.EncryptedData;
    SecureCard decryptedCard = new SecureCard(encryptedData);
    string decryptedData = string.Format(
      "{0}, {1}, {2}, {3}, {4}, {5}",
      decryptedCard.CardHolder, decryptedCard.CardNumber,
      decryptedCard.IssueDate, decryptedCard.ExpiryDate,
      decryptedCard.IssueNumber, decryptedCard.CardType);
    StringBuilder sb = new StringBuilder();
    sb.Append("Encrypted data:<br />");
    sb.Append("<textarea style=\"width:400px;height:150px;\">");
    sb.Append(encryptedData);
    sb.Append("</textarea><br />Decrypted data:");
    sb.Append(decryptedData);
    result.Text = sb.ToString();
  }
}
```

5. Browse to SecurityLibTester3.aspx, enter card details to encrypt, and click **Process**. The result is shown in Figure 16-3.

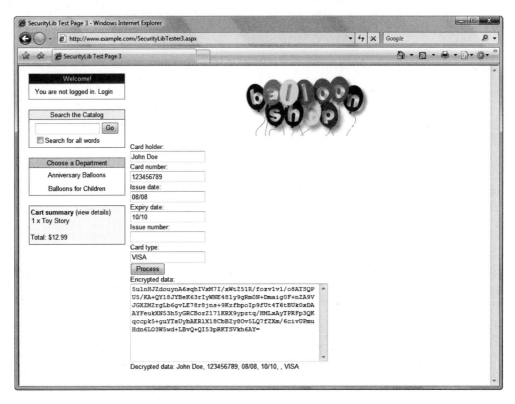

Figure 16-3. *Credit card encryption result*

How It Works: Implementing the SecureCard Class

There is a bit more code here than in previous examples, but it's all quite simple. First, you have the private member variables to hold the card details as individual strings, as an encrypted string, and in an intermediate XML document. You also have Boolean flags indicating whether the data has been successfully encrypted or decrypted:

```
using System;
using System.Collections.Generic;
using System.Text;
using System.Xml;


namespace SecurityLib
{
  public class SecureCard
  {
    private bool isDecrypted = false;
    private bool isEncrypted = false;
    private string cardHolder;
```

```
private string cardNumber;
private string issueDate;
private string expiryDate;
private string issueNumber;
private string cardType;
private string encryptedData;
private XmlDocument xmlCardData;
```

Next there are two constructors, for encrypting or decrypting credit card data:

```
public SecureCard(string newEncryptedData)
{
  // constructor for use with encrypted data
  encryptedData = newEncryptedData;
  DecryptData();
}


public SecureCard(string newCardHolder,
  string newCardNumber, string newIssueDate,
  string newExpiryDate, string newIssueNumber,
  string newCardType)
{
  // constructor for use with decrypted data
  cardHolder = newCardHolder;
  cardNumber = newCardNumber;
  issueDate = newIssueDate;
  expiryDate = newExpiryDate;
  issueNumber = newIssueNumber;
  cardType = newCardType;
  EncryptData();
}
```

The main work is carried out in the private EncryptData and DecryptData methods, which we'll come to shortly. First, you have two utility methods for packaging and unpackaging data in XML format (which makes it easier to get at the bits you want when exchanging data with the encrypted format):

```
private void CreateXml()
{
  // encode card details as XML document
  xmlCardData = new XmlDocument();
  XmlElement documentRoot =
    xmlCardData.CreateElement("CardDetails");
  XmlElement child;

  child = xmlCardData.CreateElement("CardHolder");
  child.InnerXml = cardHolder;
  documentRoot.AppendChild(child);
```

```
      child = xmlCardData.CreateElement("CardNumber");
      child.InnerXml = cardNumber;
      documentRoot.AppendChild(child);

      child = xmlCardData.CreateElement("IssueDate");
      child.InnerXml = issueDate;
      documentRoot.AppendChild(child);

      child = xmlCardData.CreateElement("ExpiryDate");
      child.InnerXml = expiryDate;
      documentRoot.AppendChild(child);

      child = xmlCardData.CreateElement("IssueNumber");
      child.InnerXml = issueNumber;
      documentRoot.AppendChild(child);

      child = xmlCardData.CreateElement("CardType");
      child.InnerXml = cardType;
      documentRoot.AppendChild(child);
      xmlCardData.AppendChild(documentRoot);
   }

   private void ExtractXml()
   {
     // get card details out of XML document
     cardHolder =
       xmlCardData.GetElementsByTagName(
         "CardHolder").Item(0).InnerXml;
     cardNumber =
       xmlCardData.GetElementsByTagName(
         "CardNumber").Item(0).InnerXml;
     issueDate =
       xmlCardData.GetElementsByTagName(
         "IssueDate").Item(0).InnerXml;

     expiryDate =
       xmlCardData.GetElementsByTagName(
         "ExpiryDate").Item(0).InnerXml;
     issueNumber =
       xmlCardData.GetElementsByTagName(
         "IssueNumber").Item(0).InnerXml;
     cardType =
       xmlCardData.GetElementsByTagName(
         "CardType").Item(0).InnerXml;
   }
```

These methods use simple XML syntax to address data elements.

The EncryptData method starts by using the previous CreateXml method to package the details supplied in the SecureCard constructor into XML format:

```
private void EncryptData()
{
  try
  {
    // put data into XML doc
    CreateXml();
```

Next, the XML string contained in the resultant XML document is encrypted into a single string and stored in the _encryptedData member:

```
    // encrypt data
    encryptedData =
      StringEncryptor.Encrypt(xmlCardData.OuterXml);
```

Finally, the isEncrypted flag is set to true to indicate success—or it throws a SecureCardException exception if anything goes wrong:

```
    // set encrypted flag
    isEncrypted = true;
  }
  catch
  {
    throw new SecureCardException("Unable to encrypt data.");
  }
}
```

The DecryptData method gets the XML from its encrypted form and uses it to populate a new XML document:

```
private void DecryptData()
{
  try
  {
    // decrypt data
    xmlCardData = new XmlDocument();
    xmlCardData.InnerXml =
      StringEncryptor.Decrypt(encryptedData);
```

The method then gets the data in the XML document into the private member variables for card details using ExtractXml and either sets the isDecrypted flag to True or throws an exception, depending on whether the code succeeds:

```
        // extract data from XML
        ExtractXml();

        // set decrypted flag
        isDecrypted = true;
    }
    catch
    {
        throw new SecureCardException("Unable to decrypt data.");
    }
}
```

Next you come to the publicly accessible properties of the class. There are quite a few of these, so we won't show them all. Several are for reading card detail data, such as CardHolder:

```
public string CardHolder
{
    get
    {
        if (isDecrypted)
        {
            return cardHolder;
        }
        else
        {
            throw new SecureCardException("Data not decrypted.");
        }
    }
}
```

Note that the data is only accessible when isDecrypted is true, so if an exception has been thrown during decryption, then no data is available here (an exception is thrown instead). Also, note that the data isn't accessible after encryption—the data used to initialize a SecureCard object is only accessible in encrypted form. This is more a use-case decision than anything else, because this class is only really intended for encryption and decryption, not for persistently representing credit card details. After a SecureCard instance has been used to encrypt card details, you shouldn't subsequently need access to the unencrypted data, only the encrypted string.

One interesting property here is CardNumberX, which displays only a portion of the number on a credit card. This is handy when showing a user existing details and is becoming standard practice because it lets the customer know what card they have stored without exposing the details to prying eyes:

```
public string CardNumberX
{
    get
    {
        if (isDecrypted)
        {
            return "XXXX-XXXX-XXXX-"
                + cardNumber.Substring(cardNumber.Length - 4, 4);
        }
```

```
        else
        {
          throw new SecureCardException("Data not decrypted.");
        }
      }
    }
```

The last property worth looking at is `EncryptedData`, which is used when extracting the encrypted credit card details for database storage:

```
public string EncryptedData
{
  get
  {
    if (isEncrypted)
    {
      return encryptedData;
    }
    else
    {
      throw new SecureCardException("Data not decrypted.");
    }
  }
}
```

The structure here is much like the other properties, although this time the `isEncrypted` flag restricts access rather than the `isDecrypted` flag.

Before moving on to the client code, it's important to explain and justify one design consideration that you have probably already noticed. At no point are any of the card details validated. In fact, this class will work perfectly well with empty strings for any properties. This is so the class can remain as versatile as possible. It's more likely that credit card details will be validated as part of the user interface used to enter them or even not at all. This isn't at all dangerous—if invalid details are used, then the credit card transaction simply fails, and you handle that using very similar logic to that required to deal with lack of funds (that is, you notify the customer of failure and request another card). Of course, there are also simple data-formatting issues (dates are usually MM/YY, for example), but as noted, these can be dealt with externally to the `SecureCard` class.

The client code for this class allows you to see how an encrypted card looks. As you can see, a lot of data is generated, hence the rather large column size in the Customer database. You can also see that both encryption and decryption are working perfectly, so you can now move on to the customer account section of this chapter.

Customer Logins

As mentioned earlier in this chapter, allowing customers to log in to the site simply means using the same login system that administrators use, but defining a Customers role to use rather than an Administrators role. You can do this now using the ASP.NET Web Site Administration Tool as before. This is shown in Figure 16-4.

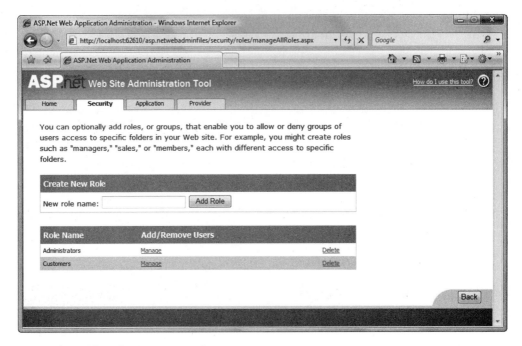

Figure 16-4. *Adding the Customers role*

Next you need to make it possible for customers to create their own accounts. ASP.NET is very helpful here by providing the extremely useful CreateUserWizard control, which (as is becoming a common theme) does most of the hard work for us.

Simply adding a CreateUserWizard control to a page results in the interface shown in Figure 16-5.

Figure 16-5. *Default CreateUserWizard interface*

Just having this control on a site is enough to enable users to add themselves to the membership database. For BalloonShop, however, you'll need to tweak the control a little. Specifically, you'll do the following:

- Format the display of the control.

- Place the control in a `LoginView` control so that only users who aren't logged in can see it.

- Provide a link to the page containing the control so that users who aren't logged in can register.

- Add code behind so that new users are automatically added to the Customers role.

- Add a redirect to the customer details page for after the user has registered.

- Make the control send a welcome email to the new user.

To keep things simple for now, we'll have the contact details and credit card information for the user editable on a separate page, which we'll look at later in the chapter.

So, let's go ahead and add the new page. At this point, you'll create a fully functioning user registration page and update `UserInfo.ascx` accordingly, but you'll leave the emailing and customer details page unfinished for now.

Exercise: Enabling Customer Registration

1. If you haven't already done so, add the Customers role using the Security tab of the ASP.NET Web Site Administration Tool, as shown previously in Figure 16-4.

2. Add a new Web Form to the BalloonShop web site called `Register.aspx` by using the usual `BalloonShop.master` Master Page and the code-behind model.

3. In Design View, drag a `LoginView` control into the page content region.

4. Select the `LoggedInTemplate` of the `LoginView` control and add the text **You are already registered.**, as shown in Figure 16-6.

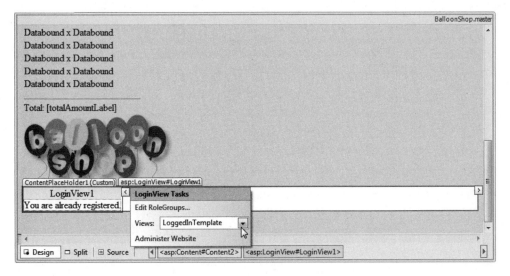

Figure 16-6. *Creating a LoginView template*

5. Select the AnonymousTemplate in the LoginView control and drag a CreateUserWizard control to the template.

6. Autoformat the CreateUserWizard control with the Professional style.

7. Change the CreateUserButtonText property of the CreateUserWizard control to Sign Up.

8. Set the CancelDestinationPageUrl and ContinueDestinationPageUrl properties of the CreateUserWizard control to ~/.

9. Add an event handler for the CreatedUser event of the CreateUserWizard control as follows (and, while you're looking at the code behind, add the Title attribute configuration code as shown):

```
using System;
using System.Web.UI.WebControls;
using System.Web.Security;

public partial class Register : System.Web.UI.Page
{
  protected void Page_Load(object sender, EventArgs e)
  {
    // Set the title of the page
    this.Title = BalloonShopConfiguration.SiteName +
              " : Register";
  }

  protected void CreateUserWizard1_CreatedUser(object sender,
  EventArgs e)
  {
    Roles.AddUserToRole((sender as CreateUserWizard).UserName,
    "Customers");
  }
}
```

10. In UserInfo.ascx, modify the AnonymousTemplate to include a link to the registration page as follows:

```
<AnonymousTemplate>
  <tr>
    <td class="UserInfoHead">Welcome!</td>
  </tr>
  <tr>
    <td class="UserInfoContent">
      You are not logged in.
      <br />
      <asp:LoginStatus ID="LoginStatus1" runat="server" />
```

```
        or
        <asp:HyperLink runat="server" ID="registerLink"
          NavigateUrl="~/Register.aspx" Text="Register"
          ToolTip="Go to the registration page"/>
      </td>
    </tr>
  </AnonymousTemplate>
```

11. Also in `UserInfo.ascx`, add a new `RoleGroup` template to the `RoleGroups` section for users in the Customers role:

```
<RoleGroups>
...
  <asp:RoleGroup Roles="Customers">
    <ContentTemplate>
      <tr>
        <td class="UserInfoHead">
          <asp:LoginName ID="LoginName2" runat="server"
FormatString="Hello, <b>{0}</b>!" />
        </td>
      </tr>
      <tr>
        <td class="UserInfoContent">
          <asp:LoginStatus ID="LoginStatus1" runat="server" />
          <br />
          <asp:HyperLink runat="server" ID="detailsLink"
            NavigateUrl="~/CustomerDetails.aspx"
            Text="Edit Details"
            ToolTip="Edit your personal details" />
        </td>
      </tr>
    </ContentTemplate>
  </asp:RoleGroup>
...
</RoleGroups>
```

■**Note** This code includes a link to `CustomerDetails.aspx`, the page you'll add shortly to edit address and credit card details for users. Rather than add this later, it's included here to save some typing later on.

---

12. Open the BalloonShop application in a browser, click the **Register** link in the top left, and enter details for a new customer, as shown in Figure 16-7.

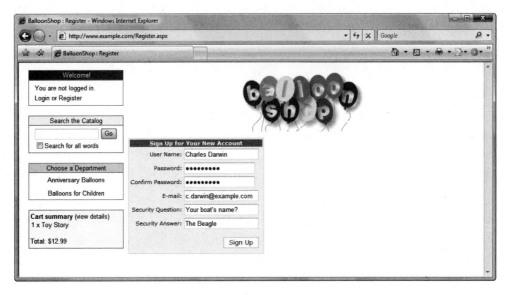

Figure 16-7. *Registering a new user*

13. Click **Sign Up**.

■**Note** You may have your password rejected when you click Sign Up because the ASP.NET membership system applies several rules to passwords, as defined in `machine.config`. By default, passwords require a minimum length of seven characters, including at least one nonalphanumeric character (that is, a symbol character such as [, *, or !). We'll look at how you can change this setting (and provide a more helpful error message) shortly.

---

14. Click **Continue** and verify that the `UserInfo.ascx` display is updated as shown in Figure 16-8.

Figure 16-8. *User info display*

How It Works: Enabling Customer Registration

The ASP.NET controls for adding membership functionality to a web site are truly a joy to use. This is the sort of thing that has often taken quite some time to implement and even longer to implement well. Now you can add this functionality in minutes.

Further customization is also possible. You can add any number of wizard pages to the `CreateUserWizard` control and make things work exactly as you want. For most purposes, however, the default functionality is all you need.

One thing you'll probably want to change, as noted in the exercise, is the set of rules that are applied to password complexity. This is defined by the `AspNetSqlMembershipProvider` provider contained in `machine.config` (which you can find in `<Windows Install Directory>\Microsoft.NET\Framework\<Version>\CONFIG\`). The code for this provider definition is as follows:

```
<membership>
  <providers>
    <add name="AspNetSqlMembershipProvider"
      type="System.Web.Security.SqlMembershipProvider, System.Web,
        Version=2.0.0.0, Culture=neutral,
        PublicKeyToken=b03f5f7f11d50a3a"
      connectionStringName="LocalSqlServer"
      enablePasswordRetrieval="false" enablePasswordReset="true"
      requiresQuestionAndAnswer="true" applicationName="/"
      requiresUniqueEmail="false" passwordFormat="Hashed"
      maxInvalidPasswordAttempts="5" passwordAttemptWindow="10"
      passwordStrengthRegularExpression="" />
  </providers>
</membership>
```

This definition can include two additional attributes, `minRequiredPasswordLength` and `minRequired`➡ `NonalphanumericCharacters`, to define the length and complexity of the password, or you can do this in one go using the `passwordStrengthRegularExpression` parameter. The first two of these attributes aren't included in the default definition, but you can add them yourself. However, be aware that changes you make in `machine.config` will apply to *all* the web sites on your computer. An alternative is to override the definition of this provider in `web.config` as follows:

```
<system.web>
  ...
  <membership>
    <providers>
      <remove name="AspNetSqlMembershipProvider" />
      <add name="AspNetSqlMembershipProvider"
        type="System.Web.Security.SqlMembershipProvider,
          System.Web,
          Version=2.0.0.0, Culture=neutral,
          PublicKeyToken=b03f5f7f11d50a3a"
        connectionStringName="LocalSqlServer"
        enablePasswordRetrieval="false" enablePasswordReset="true"
        requiresQuestionAndAnswer="true" applicationName="/"
        requiresUniqueEmail="false" passwordFormat="Hashed"
        maxInvalidPasswordAttempts="5" passwordAttemptWindow="10"
        minRequiredPasswordLength="6"
        minRequiredNonalphanumericCharacters="0"
        passwordStrengthRegularExpression="" />
    </providers>
  </membership>
  ...
</system.web>
```

The passwords used on the BalloonShop site have been restricted to a minimum of six characters, but with no requirement for nonalphanumeric characters. To do this, you have to remove the definition taken from `machine.config` using a `<remove>` entry and then add it again using `<add>`.

■**Note** In the preceding code, the text string for the `type` attribute is split over multiple lines. If you use this code, remember to place the whole string on a single line to avoid errors.

Whatever complexity you use, it is worthwhile to replace the default password error message for `CreateUserWizard`, which displays simply "Please enter a different password." You can do this using the `PasswordRegular`➡ `ExpressionErrorMessage` property of the `CreateUserWizard` control. For the preceding complexity, you can use "Your password must be at least 6 characters long," for example.

The `CreateUserWizard` control also has a `PasswordRegularExpression` parameter that you can use to restrict the password. However, any expression you use here applies only to this control—and the restrictions from the membership provider will still be applied (assuming you use the membership provider included with ASP.NET, which we are using here).

One final point to note in the preceding exercise before we move on is the code behind:

```
protected void CreateUserWizard1_CreatedUser(object sender,
  EventArgs e)
{
  Roles.AddUserToRole((sender as CreateUserWizard).UserName,
    "Customers");
}
```

This uses one of the utility classes provided as part of the ASP.NET membership system, `Roles`, to perform what might otherwise be a much more complicated task—adding a user to a role. The `Roles` class includes several other useful methods that you might be interested in. The membership system also includes other utility classes for you to use, including `Membership` and `MemberhipUser`, as well as `Profile`, which you'll see in action in the next section.

Customer Details

The next thing to look at is how you store customer details, as well as enable users to edit those details. This is a feature that is common to a huge number of web sites, including a huge proportion of e-commerce sites. In fact, web developers want to implement this feature so often that ASP.NET includes a system—**user profiles**—for doing so with very little effort. We'll look at the user profiles feature in some depth shortly.

After you've implemented a customer details scheme you'll also have to implement a Web Form where users can edit their details. This involves some of the code from earlier in the chapter, because credit card details must be encrypted. When you implement this form, you'll also be exposing customer profile details via the `ObjectDataSource` control. This isn't difficult and is well worth it because you can bind to customer profile data using the handy `FormView` control. This control includes edit capabilities, so a little work at the beginning will result in a great payoff.

Before you get to this editing page, however, let's take a look at user profiles so you can build your own.

User Profiles in ASP.NET

The user profile system enables you to define any number of custom data fields that can be stored, along with user login details, in the ASPNETDB database that we're currently using for membership and security information. To tap into this resource, you just declare the fields you want to define for users (along with the data type of those fields) in the web.config file for your application. Behind the scenes, the ASP.NET Framework uses this information to dynamically create classes that you can use to access user details. Functionally, this behavior is exhibited in much the same way that Web Form classes allow you access to controls on a page without ever having to declare them in code-behind files; that is to say, it "just happens" and you can use it.

To declare fields to use in user profiles, you use the <profile> element in the <system.web> section of your web.config file, like so:

```
<profile>
  <properties>
    <add name="param1" type"System.String" />
    <add name="param2" type"System.Int32" />
    <group name="paramGroup1">
      <add name="param3" type"System.String" />
      <add name="param4" type"System.String" />
    </group>
  </properties>
</profile>
```

This information is used to create an object that exposes these properties to the code behind for a Web Form, with the name Profile. This object, an instance of a dynamically generated class called ProfileCommon, can then be accessed in code behind as follows:

```
Profile.param1 = "New value for param1";
Profile.paramGroup1.param3 = "New value for param3";
```

If a user is logged in, then the preceding code results in these values being stored in the membership database. You can retrieve values from the database in much the same way. And that's pretty much all there is to it. Each user has unique profile values stored in the database, and the preceding code is pretty much all you need to gain access to this information.

Admittedly, we've skimmed over things a little here; for example, data types—you can define whatever data types you want for profile properties as long as they are serializable. Also, in the preceding code, you may note that two properties, param3 and param4, are defined as part of a property group to make things easier. The code to achieve this is so simple that it hardly seemed worth noting.

As with other functionality in the ASP.NET Framework, the preceding behavior is completely customizable. You can, if you want to, create a profile provider to replace this one, adding as much complexity as you need. For the purposes of the BalloonShop application, however, this provides everything you need.

User Profiles in BalloonShop

For the BalloonShop application, you'll use the following profile definition in web.config:

```
<system.web>
  <profile>
    <properties>
      <add name="CreditCard" type="System.String" />
      <add name="Address1" type="System.String" />
      <add name="Address2" type="System.String" />
      <add name="City" type="System.String" />
      <add name="Region" type="System.String" />
      <add name="PostalCode" type="System.String" />
      <add name="Country" type="System.String" />
      <add name="ShippingRegion" type="System.String" />
      <add name="DayPhone" type="System.String" />
      <add name="EvePhone" type="System.String" />
      <add name="MobPhone" type="System.String" />
    </properties>
  </profile>
```

To keep things simple, all this data is stored in string format. The CreditCard information stored here is an encrypted string that is created using SecurityLib. The ShippingRegion information is actually the ID or a record in the ShippingRegion table, which you'll add as part of the example.

In the next exercise, you'll implement this system, including the custom data-binding scheme. This involves a lot of work and gives us plenty to discuss afterward, but it's well worth the effort!

Exercise: Implementing User Profiles for BalloonShop

1. Add the profile information (shown just before this exercise) to web.config.

2. Add a new table to the **BalloonShop** database called ShippingRegion, with columns as shown in Table 16-1.

Table 16-1. *The ShippingRegion Table*

Column Name	Column Type	Description
ShippingRegionID	int	The ID of the shipping region; primary key and identity
ShippingRegion	nvarchar(100)	The description of the shipping region

3. Add the values Please Select, US / Canada, Europe, and Rest of World to the ShippingRegion column in the new table. With auto-numbering of the identity column, Please Select should have a ShippingRegionID value of 1—this is important!

4. Add a new class to the App_Code directory of the project called ProfileWrapper, with code as follows:

```csharp
using System;
using System.Web;
using System.Web.Security;
using SecurityLib;


/// <summary>
/// A wrapper around profile information, including
/// credit card encryption functionality.
/// </summary>
public class ProfileWrapper
{
  private string address1;
  private string address2;
  private string city;
  private string region;
  private string postalCode;
  private string country;
  private string shippingRegion;
  private string dayPhone;
  private string evePhone;
  private string mobPhone;
  private string email;
  private string creditCard;
  private string creditCardHolder;
  private string creditCardNumber;
  private string creditCardIssueDate;
  private string creditCardIssueNumber;
  private string creditCardExpiryDate;
  private string creditCardType;

  public ProfileWrapper()
  {
    ProfileCommon profile =
    HttpContext.Current.Profile as ProfileCommon;
    address1 = profile.Address1;
    address2 = profile.Address2;
    city = profile.City;
    region = profile.Region;
    postalCode = profile.PostalCode;
    country = profile.Country;
    shippingRegion =
      (profile.ShippingRegion == null
      || profile.ShippingRegion == ""
      ? "1" : profile.ShippingRegion);
```

```csharp
  dayPhone = profile.DayPhone;
  evePhone = profile.EvePhone;
  mobPhone = profile.MobPhone;
  email = Membership.GetUser(profile.UserName).Email;

  try
  {
    SecureCard secureCard = new SecureCard(profile.CreditCard);
    creditCard = secureCard.CardNumberX;
    creditCardHolder = secureCard.CardHolder;
    creditCardNumber = secureCard.CardNumber;
    creditCardIssueDate = secureCard.IssueDate;
    creditCardIssueNumber = secureCard.IssueNumber;
    creditCardExpiryDate = secureCard.ExpiryDate;
    creditCardType = secureCard.CardType;
  }
  catch
  {
    creditCard = "Not entered.";
  }
}

public void UpdateProfile()
{
  ProfileCommon profile =
   HttpContext.Current.Profile as ProfileCommon;
  profile.Address1 = address1;
  profile.Address2 = address2;
  profile.City = city;
  profile.Region = region;
  profile.PostalCode = postalCode;
  profile.Country = country;
  profile.ShippingRegion = shippingRegion;
  profile.DayPhone = dayPhone;
  profile.EvePhone = evePhone;
  profile.MobPhone = mobPhone;
  profile.CreditCard = creditCard;
  MembershipUser user = Membership.GetUser(profile.UserName);
  user.Email = email;
  Membership.UpdateUser(user); try
  {
    SecureCard secureCard = new SecureCard(
        creditCardHolder, creditCardNumber,
        creditCardIssueDate, creditCardExpiryDate,
        creditCardIssueNumber, creditCardType);
    profile.CreditCard = secureCard.EncryptedData;
  }
```

```
      catch
      {
        creditCard = "";
      }
    }
  }
```

5. For each of the 17 private fields of ProfileWrapper, add a corresponding public property. For example, for address1, add the following property:

```
public string Address1
{
  get
  {
    return address1;
  }
  set
  {
    address1 = value;
  }
}
```

6. Add a class to App_Code called ProfileDataSource, with code as follows:

```
using System;
using System.Collections.Generic;

/// <summary>
/// A further wrapper around ProfileWrapper, exposing data
/// in a form usable by ObjectDataSource.
/// </summary>
public class ProfileDataSource
{
  public ProfileDataSource()
  {
  }

  public List<ProfileWrapper> GetData()
  {
    List<ProfileWrapper> data = new List<ProfileWrapper>();
    data.Add(new ProfileWrapper());
    return data;
  }

  public void UpdateData(ProfileWrapper newData)
  {
    newData.UpdateProfile();
  }
}
```

7. Add a new user control to the `UserControls` directory called `CustomerDetailsEdit.ascx`.

8. In the Design View for `CustomerDetailsEdit.ascx`, drag an `ObjectDataSource` control onto the page.

9. Right-click the `ObjectDataView` control and select **Configure Data Source**.

10. Select **ProfileDataSource** from the drop-down selection, as shown in Figure 16-9.

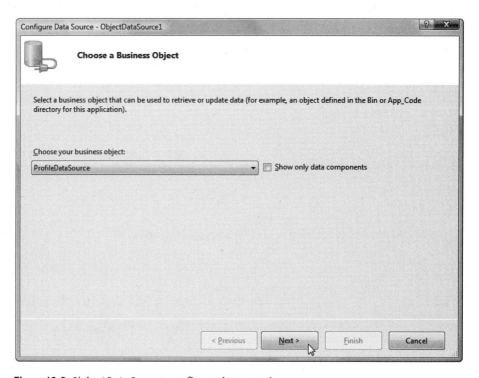

Figure 16-9. *ObjectDataSource configuration, step 1*

11. On the next step of the wizard, select **GetData(), returns List<ProfileWrapper>** for the `SELECT` method and **UpdateDate(ProfileWrapper newData)** for the `UPDATE` method. Leave the `INSERT` and `DELETE` methods blank—users can't add or delete profile information. Click **Finish**.

■**Tip** You may need to recompile your project before Visual Web Developer can read your `ProfileDataSource` class.

---

12. Drag a `SqlDataSource` control onto the page and configure it to use the `BalloonShopConnection` connection string and to get the `ShippingRegionID` and `ShippingRegion` fields from the `ShippingRegion` table. The code for the completed data source control should look as follows in Source View:

```
<asp:SqlDataSource ID="SqlDataSource1" runat="server"
ConnectionString="<%$ ConnectionStrings:BalloonShopConnection%>"
SelectCommand="SELECT [ShippingRegionID], [ShippingRegion] FROM
[ShippingRegion]" />
```

13. In Design View, drag a FormView control onto CustomerDetailsEdit.ascx and choose ObjectDataSource1 as its data source (the DataSourceID property). The templates are auto-generated from the fields of ProfileWrapper, as shown in Figure 16-10.

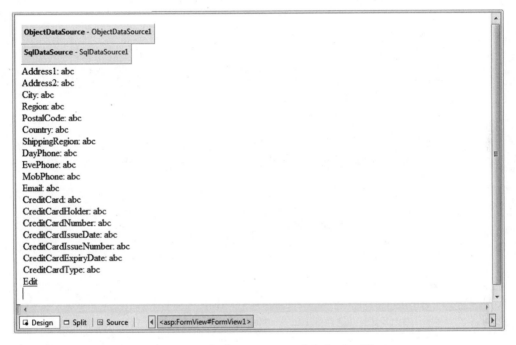

Figure 16-10. *Automatic generation of the* FormView *template for* ProfileWrapper

14. In the Source View for CustomerDetailsEdit.ascx, delete the whole of the <InsertItemTemplate> template, which should be on lines 84 to 157, or thereabouts.

15. Replace the <ItemTemplate> with the following code:

```
<ItemTemplate>
<table class="UserDetailsTable">
  <tr><td>Address line 1: </td><td width="350px">
    <asp:Label ID="Address1Label" runat="server"
      Text='<%# Bind("Address1") %>' />
  </td></tr>
  <tr><td>Address line 2: </td><td>
    <asp:Label ID="Address2Label" runat="server"
      Text='<%# Bind("Address2") %>' />
  </td></tr>
```

```
<tr><td>City: </td><td>
  <asp:Label ID="CityLabel" runat="server"
    Text='<%# Bind("City") %>' />
</td></tr>
<tr><td>Region: </td><td>
  <asp:Label ID="RegionLabel" runat="server"
    Text='<%# Bind("Region") %>' />
</td></tr>
<tr><td>Zip / Postal Code: </td><td>
  <asp:Label ID="PostalCodeLabel" runat="server"
    Text='<%# Bind("PostalCode") %>'>
  </asp:Label>
</td></tr>
<tr><td>Country: </td><td>
  <asp:Label ID="CountryLabel" runat="server"
    Text='<%# Bind("Country") %>' />
</td></tr>
<tr><td>Shipping Region: </td><td>
  <asp:DropDownList Width="350px" ID="ShippingRegionDropDown"
    runat="server"
    SelectedValue='<%# Bind("ShippingRegion") %>'
    DataSourceID="SqlDataSource1"
    DataTextField="ShippingRegion"
    DataValueField="ShippingRegionID"
    enabled="false">
  </asp:DropDownList>
</td></tr>
<tr><td>Daytime Phone no: </td><td>
  <asp:Label ID="DayPhoneLabel" runat="server"
    Text='<%# Bind("DayPhone") %>' />
</td></tr>
<tr><td>Evening Phone no: </td><td>
  <asp:Label ID="EvePhoneLabel" runat="server"
    Text='<%# Bind("EvePhone") %>' />
</td></tr>
<tr><td>Mobile Phone no: </td><td>
  <asp:Label ID="MobPhoneLabel" runat="server"
    Text='<%# Bind("MobPhone") %>' />
</td></tr>
<tr><td>Email: </td><td>
  <asp:Label ID="EmailLabel" runat="server"
    Text='<%# Bind("Email") %>' />
</td></tr>
<tr><td>Credit Card: </td><td>
  <asp:Label ID="CreditCardLabel" runat="server"
    Text='<%# Bind("CreditCard") %>' />
</td></tr>
```

```
    <tr><td>
      <asp:Button ID="EditButton" runat="server"
        CausesValidation="False" CommandName="Edit"
        Text="Edit" />
    </td></tr>
  </table>
</ItemTemplate>
```

16. Replace the `<EditItemTemplate>` with the following code:

```
<EditItemTemplate>
<table class="UserDetailsTable">
  <tr><td>Address line 1: </td><td width="350px">
    <asp:TextBox Width="340px" ID="Address1TextBox" runat="server"
      Text='<%# Bind("Address1") %>' />
  </td></tr>
  <tr><td>Address line 2: </td><td>
    <asp:TextBox Width="340px" ID="Address2TextBox" runat="server"
      Text='<%# Bind("Address2") %>' />
  </td></tr>
  <tr><td>City: </td><td>
    <asp:TextBox Width="340px" ID="CityTextBox" runat="server"
      Text='<%# Bind("City") %>' />
  </td></tr>
  <tr><td>Region: </td><td>
    <asp:TextBox Width="340px" ID="RegionTextBox" runat="server"
      Text='<%# Bind("Region") %>' />
  </td></tr>
  <tr><td>Zip / Postal Code: </td><td>
    <asp:TextBox Width="340px" ID="PostalCodeTextBox"
      runat="server" Text='<%# Bind("PostalCode") %>' />
  </td></tr>
  <tr><td>Country: </td><td>
    <asp:TextBox Width="340px" ID="CountryTextBox" runat="server"
      Text='<%# Bind("Country") %>' />
  </td></tr>
  <tr><td>Shipping Region: </td><td>
    <asp:DropDownList Width="350px" ID="ShippingRegionDropDown"
      runat="server"
      SelectedValue='<%# Bind("ShippingRegion") %>'
      DataSourceID="SqlDataSource1"
      DataTextField="ShippingRegion"
      DataValueField="ShippingRegionID">
    </asp:DropDownList>
  </td></tr>
  <tr><td>Daytime Phone no: </td><td>
    <asp:TextBox Width="340px" ID="DayPhoneTextBox" runat="server"
      Text='<%# Bind("DayPhone") %>' />
```

```
        </td></tr>
        <tr><td>Evening Phone no: </td><td>
          <asp:TextBox Width="340px" ID="EvePhoneTextBox" runat="server"
            Text='<%# Bind("EvePhone") %>' />
        </td></tr>
        <tr><td>Mobile Phone no: </td><td>
          <asp:TextBox Width="340px" ID="MobPhoneTextBox" runat="server"
            Text='<%# Bind("MobPhone") %>' />
        </td></tr>
        <tr><td>Email: </td><td>
          <asp:TextBox Width="340px" ID="EmailBox" runat="server"
            Text='<%# Bind("Email") %>' />
        </td></tr>
        <tr><td valign="top">Credit Card: </td><td>
          <table cellpadding="0" cellspacing="0" border="0">
            <tr><td width="140px">Cardholder name: </td>
              <td width="200px">
              <asp:TextBox Width="200px" ID="CreditCardHolderLabel"
                runat="server" Text='<%# Bind("CreditCardHolder") %>' />
            </td></tr>
            <tr><td>Card type: </td><td>
              <asp:TextBox Width="200px" ID="CreditCardTypeLabel"
                runat="server" Text='<%# Bind("CreditCardType") %>' />
            </td></tr>
            <tr><td>Card number: </td><td>
              <asp:TextBox Width="200px" ID="CreditCardNumberLabel"
                runat="server" Text='<%# Bind("CreditCardNumber") %>' />
            </td></tr>
            <tr><td>Issue date: </td><td>
              <asp:TextBox Width="200px" ID="CreditCardIssueDateLabel"
                runat="server"
                Text='<%# Bind("CreditCardIssueDate") %>' />
            </td></tr>
            <tr><td>Expiry date: </td><td>
              <asp:TextBox Width="200px" ID="CreditCardExpiryDateLabel"
                runat="server"
                Text='<%# Bind("CreditCardExpiryDate") %>' />
            </td></tr>
            <tr><td>Issue number: </td><td>
              <asp:TextBox Width="200px" ID="CreditCardIssueNumberLabel"
                runat="server"
                Text='<%# Bind("CreditCardIssueNumber") %>' />
            </td></tr>
          </table>
        </td></tr>
```

```
  <tr><td>
    <asp:Button ID="UpdateButton" runat="server"
      CausesValidation="True" CommandName="Update"
      Text="Update" /> <asp:Button ID="UpdateCancelButton"
      runat="server" CausesValidation="False" CommandName="Cancel"
      Text="Cancel" />
  </td></tr>
</table>
</EditItemTemplate>
```

17. Add the following class definitions to `BalloonShop.css`:

```
.UserDetailsTable {
  width: 100%;
  background-color: #ccccff;
  border: Solid 1px Navy;
  line-height: 20px;
}
```

18. Add the following code to `CustomerDetailsEdit.ascx.cs`:

```
using System;
using System.Web.UI.WebControls;

public partial class UserControls_CustomerDetailsEdit :➡
System.Web.UI.UserControl
{
  public bool Editable
  {
    get
    {
      if (ViewState["editable"] != null)
      {
        return (bool)ViewState["editable"];
      }
      else
      {
        return true;
      }
    }
    set
    {
      ViewState["editable"] = value;
    }
  }
```

```csharp
    protected override void OnPreRender(EventArgs e)
    {
      // Find and set edit button visibility
      Button EditButton =
       FormView1.FindControl("EditButton") as Button;
      if (EditButton != null)
      {
        EditButton.Visible = Editable;
      }
    }
  }
}
```

19. Add a new Web Form to the root of BalloonShop called `CustomerDetails.aspx`, with code as follows:

```aspx
<%@ Page Title="BalloonShop : Customer Details" Language="C#"
MasterPageFile="~/BalloonShop.master" AutoEventWireup="true"
CodeFile="CustomerDetails.aspx.cs" Inherits="CustomerDetails" %>

<%@ Register TagPrefix="uc1" TagName="CustomerDetailsEdit"
Src="UserControls/CustomerDetailsEdit.ascx" %>

<asp:Content ID="Content1" ContentPlaceHolderID="head" runat=➡
"Server"></asp:Content>
<asp:Content ID="Content2" ContentPlaceHolderID="ContentPlace➡
Holder1" runat="Server">
  <h1>
    <span class="CatalogTitle">Edit Your Details</span>
  </h1>
  <uc1:CustomerDetailsEdit ID="CustomerDetailsEdit1" runat="server" />
</asp:Content>
```

20. Modify the `Page_Load` handler in `CustomerDetails.aspx.cs` to set the page title:

```csharp
protected void Page_Load(object sender, EventArgs e)
{
  // Set the title of the page
  this.Title = BalloonShopConfiguration.SiteName +
            " : Customer Details";
}
```

21. Add the following location security to `web.config`:

```xml
<!-- Only existing customers can access CustomerDetails.aspx -->
<location path="CustomerDetails.aspx">
  <system.web>
    <authorization>
      <allow roles="Customers" />
      <deny users="*" />
    </authorization>
  </system.web>
</location>
```

22. In `Register.aspx`, change the `ContinueDestinationPageUrl` property of the `CreateFormWizard` control to `CustomerDetails.aspx`.

23. Have a cup of coffee—you've earned it.

24. Fire up a browser and either log in as an existing user and click **Edit Details**, or register a new user. Either way, you'll be greeted with the page shown in Figure 16-11.

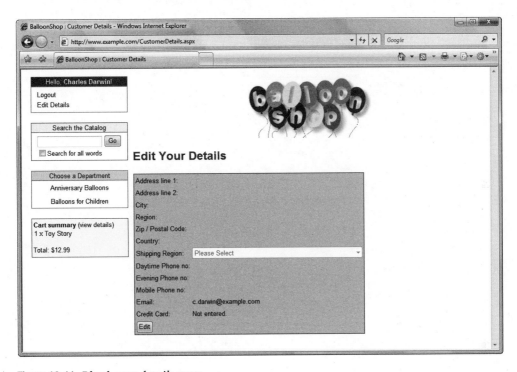

Figure 16-11. *Blank user details page*

25. Click **Edit** and enter some details, as shown in Figure 16-12.

26. Click **Update** and note how the credit card number is displayed as XXXX-XXXX-XXXX-1234.

27. Log out (you should be redirected to the log in page), and then log back in again as a different user. When you look at the user details for this user, you should see that the details are blank—they are unique to users.

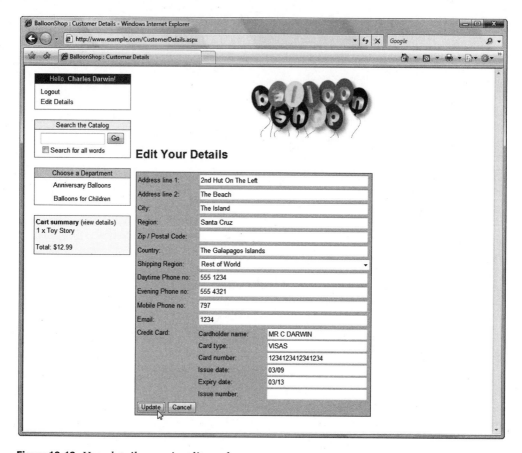

Figure 16-12. *User details page in edit mode*

How It Works: Implementing User Profiles for BalloonShop

That was a long exercise! Still, at no point have you seen any particularly complicated code. In fact, most of it was to make the user details edit form look good. Still, there's plenty to analyze, starting with the way that user profile data is exposed to the FormView control via an ObjectDataSource control.

Sadly, there is no direct way to bind user profile data to controls. Many methods are available for doing this (for example, a fellow author and friend, Dave Sussman, created a generic way to do this—see http://blogs.ipona.com/davids/archive/2004/10/29/414.aspx). You could even take the simple option—ignore data binding and build a form yourself, setting Text properties of TextBox or Label controls to appropriate values in the code behind. Because you have encrypted credit card details available, you needed to take a slightly oblique approach to keep the data in the database secure; going with the data bound approach is also a good test for your ASP.NET development muscles.

To start with, let's look at ProfileWrapper. The code for this class starts with a reference to the SecurityLib library and a bunch of private fields. These fields cover all the fields defined in web.config, along with credit card fields obtained from the SecureCard class in the SecurityLib namespace:

```
using System;
using System.Web;
using System.Web.Security;
using SecurityLib;

/// <summary>
/// A wrapper around profile information, including
/// credit card encryption functionality.
/// </summary>
public class ProfileWrapper
{
  private string address1;
  private string address2;
  private string city;
  private string region;
  private string postalCode;
  private string country;
  private string shippingRegion;
  private string dayPhone;
  private string evePhone;
  private string mobPhone;
  private string email;
  private string creditCard;
  private string creditCardHolder;
  private string creditCardNumber;
  private string creditCardIssueDate;
  private string creditCardIssueNumber;
  private string creditCardExpiryDate;
  private string creditCardType;
```

These fields all have associated public properties, which weren't all listed to save space.

Next, the constructor for the ProfileWrapper class obtains the profile information for the currently logged-in user and populates the preceding fields. Because this class isn't the code behind for a Web Form, you can't use the Page.Profile property to access this information, so instead you used the static HttpContext.Current property to obtain the current context. From this, you get the ProfileCommon instance that you're interested in:

```
public ProfileWrapper()
{
  ProfileCommon profile =
    HttpContext.Current.Profile as ProfileCommon;
```

From this object, you extract all the data you want. Most of this is simply a case of examining properties of the ProfileCommon instance, but in some cases more code is required. For instance, for shippingRegion, we wanted to use a drop-down list rather than a text box (because limited options are available), so we initialized the field accordingly—if profile.ShippingRegion is empty, you instead use the text 1, which matches the ShippingRegionID for Please Select in the ShippingRegion table. You could do this for some of the other properties, notably Country, but for brevity we've kept things simple.

You also extracted the email address of the user by obtaining a `MembershipUser` object via `Membership.GetUser` and passing the username obtained from the profile as a parameter. You then used the `Email` property of this object to obtain the email address. Strictly speaking, the user's email address isn't part of the user's profile, but it makes sense to expose it here for easy editing.

`creditCard` also needs more work. You needed to decrypt any information stored and use the decrypted data to fill the appropriate fields: `creditCardHolder`, `creditCardNumber`, and so on. Because a decryption failure results in an exception, this decryption is performed in a `try...catch` block.

```
      address1 = profile.Address1;
      address2 = profile.Address2;
      city = profile.City;
      region = profile.Region;
      postalCode = profile.PostalCode;
      country = profile.Country;
      shippingRegion =
        (profile.ShippingRegion == null
        || profile.ShippingRegion == ""
        ? "1" : profile.ShippingRegion);
      dayPhone = profile.DayPhone;
      evePhone = profile.EvePhone;
      mobPhone = profile.MobPhone;
      email = Membership.GetUser(profile.UserName).Email;
      try
      {
        SecureCard secureCard = new SecureCard(profile.CreditCard);
        creditCard = secureCard.CardNumberX;
        creditCardHolder = secureCard.CardHolder;
        creditCardNumber = secureCard.CardNumber;
        creditCardIssueDate = secureCard.IssueDate;
        creditCardIssueNumber = secureCard.IssueNumber;
        creditCardExpiryDate = secureCard.ExpiryDate;
        creditCardType = secureCard.CardType;
      }
      catch
      {
        creditCard = "Not entered.";
      }
    }
```

Next the `UpdateProfile` method sets profile data, email data, and credit card details from the data contained in the object instance from which it is called. Again, the code here is simple, with only some minor trickery required to obtain the encrypted form of the credit card data. There's nothing here you haven't seen elsewhere, so there's no need to repeat the code here.

To use object data with the `ObjectDataSource` control, you needed to pass an object supporting `IEnumerable` as the return result of a `SELECT` method. This is because `ObjectDataSource` is designed to work with data lists as well as single data items. `ProfileDataSource` acts as an interface between `ObjectDataSource` and `ProfileWrapper`, simply using the `IEnumerable` that is supporting generic list class `List<T>` to pass data to

ObjectDataSource. The code instantiates an instance of List<ProfileWrapper> and adds a single item, the user's profile data, to this list and then returns it.

```
public List<ProfileWrapper> GetData()
{
  List<ProfileWrapper> data = new List<ProfileWrapper>();
  data.Add(new ProfileWrapper());
  return data;
}
```

Because List<T> actually supports IEnumerable<T>, this is a strongly typed binding, meaning that the UPDATE method is passed an argument of type T when ObjectDataSource calls it. In this case, T is ProfileWrapper, so to update the profile information, you just called the UpdateProfile method:

```
public void UpdateData(ProfileWrapper newData)
{
  newData.UpdateProfile();
}
```

Next you used these classes to populate a FormView control via the aforementioned ObjectDataSource control. The templates created needed a bit of modification, because we didn't want to display all the credit card fields on the initial item view. We also wanted to use a drop-down list for the shippingRegion property, and we bound that drop-down list to the ShippingRegion table using simple data-binding syntax.

This customization required a lot of code, but most of this was for general display purposes, so there's no real need to go through it in any depth here. Suffice to say that the credit card details get fully displayed for the editing template.

■**Note** We haven't done it here, but it would be relatively easy to modify this code to enable customers to store multiple credit cards, with one selected as a default to use for purchases. You could, for example, store an array of strings for credit card details, each containing one encrypted card, along with a default card property. Alternatively, you could extend SecureCard to provide a single encrypted string for multiple cards. The only reason this hasn't been done here is to keep things moving—there's no reason to get bogged down in lengthy, uninteresting code at this point. Another feature that's lacking here is the inclusion of validation controls to ensure that required fields are filled in. Again, this is easy to add, but would have filled up another page or so if included here.

You used a user control to store the customer details editing form, CustomerDetailsEdit.ascx. There's a good reason for this—later you'll want to display the same information to customers when they place their orders, giving them a last chance to modify details. To facilitate this reuse, CustomerDetails.ascx.cs includes two public properties, Editable and Title, which can be used to hide the EditButton button and set the title for the FormView control, respectively. This customization happens in the OnPreRender event handler for the control, to cater for the fact that these properties may be set later on in the life cycle of the control, and we still want them to work if this happens. For the Edit Details page, you use the default values for these properties; later you'll supply nondefault values for them.

The page displaying the CustomerDetailsEdit.ascx user control (CustomerDetails.aspx) needed to have its access limited to users in the Customers role, so you added the required security code to web.config. Note that the code in web.config prevents users in the Administrators role from editing profiles. This isn't a problem, however, because administrators don't need to store this information.

Finally, you tested things out by entering some details for a customer and verified that the information added applied only to that customer.

Now that you have this information available, you can move on to the next step—providing a new checkout page.

The Checkout Page

The new checkout page will display an order summary and customer details, which can be reviewed before the customer places an order. This page appears when a customer clicks the Proceed to Checkout button after viewing his shopping cart.

In the next exercise, you'll implement and secure this page.

Exercise: Implementing a New Checkout Page

1. Add a new page to the BalloonShop application called Checkout.aspx and modify the code as follows:

```
<%@ Page Title="" Language="C#" MasterPageFile="~/BalloonShop.master" ➥
AutoEventWireup="true" CodeFile="Checkout.aspx.cs" Inherits="Checkout" %>

<%@ Register TagPrefix="uc1" TagName="CustomerDetailsEdit"
Src="UserControls/CustomerDetailsEdit.ascx" %>

<asp:Content ID="Content1" ContentPlaceHolderID="head" runat="Server">
</asp:Content>
<asp:Content ID="Content2" ContentPlaceHolderID="ContentPlaceHolder1" ➥
runat="Server">
  <asp:Label ID="titleLabel" runat="server"
    CssClass="CatalogTitle" Text="Confirm Your Order" />
  <br /><br />
  <asp:GridView ID="grid" runat="server" Width="100%"
    AutoGenerateColumns="False" DataKeyNames="ProductID"
    BorderWidth="1px" >
    <Columns>
      <asp:BoundField DataField="Name" HeaderText="Product Name"
        ReadOnly="True" SortExpression="Name" />
      <asp:BoundField DataField="Price" DataFormatString="{0:c}"
        HeaderText="Price" ReadOnly="True"
        SortExpression="Price" />
      <asp:BoundField DataField="Quantity" HeaderText="Quantity"
        ReadOnly="True" SortExpression="Quantity" />
```

```
          <asp:BoundField DataField="Subtotal" ReadOnly="True"
            DataFormatString="{0:c}" HeaderText="Subtotal"
            SortExpression="Subtotal" />
        </Columns>
      </asp:GridView>
      <asp:Label ID="Label2" runat="server" Text="Total amount: "
        CssClass="ProductDescription" />
      <asp:Label ID="totalAmountLabel" runat="server" Text="Label"
        CssClass="ProductPrice" />
      <br /><br />
      <uc1:CustomerDetailsEdit ID="CustomerDetailsEdit1"
        runat="server" Editable="false" Title="User Details" />
      <br />
      <asp:Label ID="InfoLabel" runat="server" />
      <br /><br />
      <asp:Button ID="placeOrderButton" runat="server"
        Text="Place order" OnClick="placeOrderButton_Click" />
    </asp:Content>
```

2. Modify Checkout.aspx.cs as follows:

```csharp
using System;
using System.Data;

public partial class Checkout : System.Web.UI.Page
{
  protected void Page_Load(object sender, EventArgs e)
  {
    if (!IsPostBack)
      PopulateControls();
  }

  // fill controls with data
  private void PopulateControls()
  {
    // get the items in the shopping cart
    DataTable dt = ShoppingCartAccess.GetItems();
    // populate the list with the shopping cart contents
    grid.DataSource = dt;
    grid.DataBind();
    grid.Visible = true;
    // display the total amount
    decimal amount = ShoppingCartAccess.GetTotalAmount();
    totalAmountLabel.Text = String.Format("{0:c}", amount);
```

```csharp
// check customer details
bool addressOK = true;
bool cardOK = true;
if (Profile.Address1 + Profile.Address2 == ""
    || Profile.ShippingRegion == ""
    || Profile.ShippingRegion == "Please Select"
    || Profile.Country == "")
{
  addressOK = false;
}
if (Profile.CreditCard == "")
{
  cardOK = false;
}

// report/hide place order button
if (!addressOK)
{
  if (!cardOK)
  {
    InfoLabel.Text =
      "You must provide a valid address and credit card "
      + "before placing your order.";
  }
  else
  {
    InfoLabel.Text =
      "You must provide a valid address before placing your "
      + "order.";
  }
}
else if (!cardOK)
{
  InfoLabel.Text = "You must provide a credit card before "
    + "placing your order.";
}
else
{
  InfoLabel.Text =
    "Please confirm that the above details are "
    + "correct before proceeding.";
}
placeOrderButton.Visible = addressOK && cardOK;
}
```

```
    protected void placeOrderButton_Click(object sender,
      EventArgs e)
    {

      // Get the total amount
      decimal amount = ShoppingCartAccess.GetTotalAmount();
      // Create the order and store the order ID
      string orderId = ShoppingCartAccess.CreateOrder();
      string ordername = BalloonShopConfiguration.SiteName +
        " Order " + orderId;
      // Go to PayPal Checkout
      string destination = Link.ToPayPalCheckout(ordername,
        amount);
      Response.Redirect(destination);
    }
}
```

3. Modify web.config as follows:

```
<!-- Only existing customers can access Checkout.aspx -->
<location path="Checkout.aspx">
  <system.web>
    <authorization>
      <allow roles="Customers" />
      <deny users="*" />
    </authorization>
  </system.web>
</location>
```

4. Modify ShoppingCart.aspx.cs as follows:

```
// Redirect to the checkout page
protected void checkoutButton_Click(object sender, EventArgs e)
{
  // Redirect to the checkout page
  Response.Redirect("Checkout.aspx");
}
```

5. Log in, edit your customer details, and place an order via the shopping cart page. If your details are correct, you should be able to click **Proceed to Checkout**; otherwise, you'll have to add valid customer details before proceeding. Your checkout page should look like Figure 6-13.

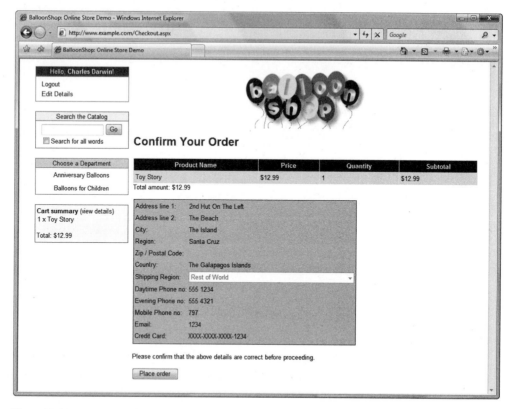

Figure 16-13. *Your new checkout page*

How It Works: Implementing a New Checkout Page

We haven't really done much that is particularly difficult here—most of the work was already done. All we've really done is reorganize existing code to prepare for a new order backend.

The new checkout page, Checkout.aspx, now appears when customers click Proceed to Checkout from the shopping cart view. It displays the current shopping cart using code very similar to—but not identical to—code in ShoppingCart.aspx. The code is different in that editing is no longer possible—quantities and order items are fixed. Checkout.aspx also includes a noneditable version of the CustomerUserDetails.ascx control, customized using the Editable and Title properties you added earlier.

As with ShoppingCart.aspx, you use a code-behind method called PopulateControls to get and bind to data. The major differences here are that you don't need to check for existing shopping cart items (we know there will be some at this stage), and that you also check for valid address and credit card details before allowing the user to proceed:

```
// check customer details
bool addressOK = true;
bool cardOK = true;
if (Profile.Address1 + Profile.Address2 == ""
   || Profile.ShippingRegion == ""
   || Profile.ShippingRegion == "1"
   || Profile.Country == "")
```

```
{
  addressOK = false;
}
if (Profile.CreditCard == "")
{
  cardOK = false;
}
```

This code, which checks the validity of the address and credit card, merits a little extra discussion. First, notice the validation of the address. The address is validated by checking a few of the fields for data (Address1 and Address2 combined *must* contain data for a valid order, and a country and shipping region must be set). This may look overly simple, but it's fine here—if address problems occur further down the line, you can deal with problems as they arise. The shipping region is also interesting because you check for a value of 1, which corresponds to Please Select in the database—hence the importance of this record having an ID field value of 1, as noted earlier. As far as credit card details go, you just check that some data is stored, not what that data is. Again, problems here can be dealt with later.

Assuming that the data is okay, the placeOrder button allows users to actually place an order. Notice that the code here is the same code you used in the earlier incarnation of the ShoppingCart.aspx page. In fact, none of the extra details are used. This isn't a problem because you now have everything you need to hook into a proper, fleshed-out order pipeline, as you'll see in subsequent chapters.

A final note—the web.config file has again been modified so that users must log in before the checkout page is visible. Using this setting, clicking on Proceed to Checkout takes users straight to the login page if they aren't logged in.

Setting Up Secure Connections

Customers can now register on your site, log in, and change details. However, the current system involves sending potentially sensitive information over HTTP. This protocol isn't secure, and the information could be intercepted and stolen. To avoid this, you need to set up the application to work with SSL (Secure Socket Layer) connections using HTTPS (HyperText Transport Protocol [Secure]).

To do this, you have a bit of groundwork to get through first. Unless you've already been using an SSL connection on your web server, you are unlikely to have the correct configuration to do so. This configuration involves obtaining a security certificate for your server and installing it via IIS management.

Security certificates are basically public/private key pairs similar to those discussed earlier in the chapter relating to asymmetric encryption. You can generate these yourself if your domain controller is configured as a certification authority, but this method has its problems. Digital signing of SSL certificates is such that browsers using the certificate will not be able to verify the identity of your certification authority, and may therefore doubt your security. This isn't disastrous, but may affect consumer confidence, because users are presented with a warning message when they attempt to establish a secure connection.

The alternative is to obtain SSL certificates from a known and respected organization that specializes in web security, such as VeriSign. Web browsers such as Internet Explorer have built-in root certificates from organizations such as this and are able to authenticate the digital signature of SSL certificates supplied by them. This means that no warning message will appear and an SSL secured connection will be available with a minimum of fuss.

This section assumes that you take this latter option, although if you want to create your own certificates, that won't affect the end result.

Obtaining an SSL Certificate from VeriSign

Obtaining a certificate from VeriSign is a relatively painless experience, and full instructions are available on the VeriSign web site (`http://www.verisign.com/`). You also can get test certificates from VeriSign, which are free to use for a trial period. The basic steps are as follows:

1. Sign up for a trial certificate on the VeriSign web site.

2. Generate a Certificate Signing Request (CSR) via IIS management on your web server. This involves filling out various personal information, including the name of your web site, and so on.

3. Copy the contents of the generated CSR into the VeriSign request system.

4. Shortly afterward, you'll receive a certificate from VeriSign that you copy into IIS management to install the certificate.

There is a little more to it than that, but as noted, detailed instructions are available on the VeriSign web site, and you shouldn't run into any difficulties.

Enforcing SSL Connections

After the certificate is installed, you can access any web pages on your web server using an SSL connection by replacing the `http://` part of the URL used to access the page with `https://` (assuming that your firewall is set up to allow an SSL connection, which by default uses port 443, if you use a firewall—this doesn't apply to local connections). Obviously, you don't need SSL connections for all areas of the site, and shouldn't enforce it in all places because it can reduce performance. However, you do want to make sure that the checkout, login, and customer detail modification pages are accessible only via SSL. While you're at it, you can also secure the admin pages. This isn't so important at this stage, but later, when you have full order and user admin controls, it doesn't hurt to make things secure here.

There are several ways to achieve this restriction. One way is to configure individual pages via IIS management. IIS can be configured in such a way that attempts to access the `Login.aspx` page using HTTP will be rejected. However, this isn't quite the route you want to go down for BalloonShop, because it makes certain things—namely redirections between URLs that start with `http://` and URLs that start with `https://`—slightly difficult to manage. Rather than giving an error message when users attempt to access `Login.aspx` without SSL, it's better to detect unsecure connections in code and redirect accordingly. This means that users trying to access `Login.aspx` without SSL are automatically redirected to the same page, but with SSL. Similarly, we want users attempting to use SSL to access a page such as `Default.aspx`—which doesn't need to be secured—to be redirected to a non-SSL connection to the same page. This results in a seamless experience for users.

We'll look at this in more detail in a moment. First, however, it's worth mentioning an attribute that ASP.NET supplies for use with the `<forms>` definition in `web.config`. You can set the attribute `requireSSL` to `true` for this element, which will prevent user login cookies from being exchanged over a non-SSL connection. However, this enforces the requirement that, once logged in, users can only be authenticated for pages viewed over SSL. This setting *does not* prevent users from looking at pages such as `Default.aspx` over a standard HTTP connection. However, user-aware controls (such as `UserInfo.ascx` in BalloonShop) will not have access to user information unless SSL is used. This attribute is for use only when you are happy to enforce SSL connections site-wide. Because SSL connections introduce a performance hit due to the encryption and decryption required, this isn't recommended for most web sites.

Including Redirections to Enforce Required SSL Connections

One way to enforce SSL connections is to use absolute URLs everywhere a link is used on the site, using for example `https://<server>/CustomerDetails.aspx` for the Edit Details link in `UserInfo.ascx` and the `http://` protocol for most other links. If you did this in combination with SSL enforcement in IIS, you could prevent users from accessing secured pages quite effectively. If they tried rewriting the URL by hand, they would likely end up with an error message because IIS prevents secured pages from being transmitted via HTTP. However, this involves a lot of work to modify and maintain links, and we have a far more elegant technique at our disposal.

The core concept behind the technique presented here is that every page—bar none—uses a Master Page. This Master Page is either `BalloonShop.master` or `Admin.master`. We want to force pages using `Admin.master` to *always* use SSL, and force pages using `BalloonShop.master` to *sometimes* use SSL, where the "sometimes" translates as "where specified by the page."

The simplest of these, `Admin.master`, requires the following code in `Admin.master.cs`:

```
protected override void OnInit(EventArgs e)
{
  if (!Request.IsSecureConnection)
  {
    Response.Redirect(Request.Url.AbsoluteUri.ToLower().Replace(
      "http://", "https://"), true);
  }
  base.OnInit(e);
}
```

Here you detect whether an SSL connection is in use with `Request.IsSecureConnection`, and if it isn't, redirect to a page with the same URL as the current page, but starting with `https` rather than `http`. You do this at the `OnInit` stage of the page life cycle; that is, before the page has had a chance to do much processing that would be wasted.

Similarly, in `BalloonShop.master.cs`, you redirect to an SSL connection if required or to a standard HTTP connection if SSL isn't required. This prevents other nonsecured pages in the site from being accessed via SSL when not required. To control this redirection, you include a property that pages using `BalloonShop.master` can set, saying whether they require SSL or not. This property, `EnforceSSL`, is defined as follows:

```
public bool EnforceSSL
{
  get
  {
    if (ViewState["enforceSSL"] != null)
    {
      return (bool)ViewState["enforceSSL"];
    }
    else
    {
      return false;
    }
  }
  set
  {
    ViewState["enforceSSL"] = value;
  }
}
```

We use ViewState here to streamline things, but other than that, this is a simple Boolean property.

Now, because this property may be set fairly late in the life cycle of the Master Page, you can't act on it in OnInit. Instead, you check the value of this property in OnPreRender and redirect then (if necessary):

```
protected override void OnPreRender(EventArgs e)
{
  if (EnforceSSL)
  {
    if (!Request.IsSecureConnection)
    {
      Response.Redirect(
        Request.Url.AbsoluteUri.ToLower().Replace(
        "http://", "https://"), true);
    }
  }
  else if (Request.IsSecureConnection)
  {
    Response.Redirect(Request.Url.AbsoluteUri.ToLower().Replace(
      "https://", "http://"), true);
  }
}
```

With this scheme, the user is only aware that something is going on when logging in. At this point the user is redirected from a secure to a nonsecure connection. From that point on, the user is redirected from secure to nonsecure connections transparently—secure when needed, nonsecure when not. Users will, of course, always be able to tell what type of connection they have, because the standard "padlock" symbol is displayed as per usual. The URL will also be there to reassure them.

The code behind required for SSL secured pages is

```
protected override void OnInit(EventArgs e)
{
  (Master as BalloonShop).EnforceSSL = true;
  base.OnInit(e);
}
```

This code needs to be added to Login.aspx.cs, Register.aspx.cs, CustomerDetails.aspx.cs, and Checkout.aspx.cs. Note that the call to base.OnInit(e) is required for proper theme functionality. Without this call, the ASP.NET theme doesn't get applied, and the CSS styles and so on won't be loaded.

Summary

In this chapter, you've implemented a customer account system that customers can use to store their details for use during order processing. You've looked at many aspects of the customer account system, including encrypting sensitive data and securing web connections for obtaining it.

You started by creating a set of classes in a new namespace called SecurityLib for hashing and encrypting strings, and a secure credit card representation that makes it easy to exchange credit card details between the encrypted and decrypted format.

After this, you implemented a customer login scheme using a new user role called Customers. This required some, but not many modifications to the existing Forms Authentication scheme, as well as the addition of a registration page. You also added customer details functionality using the ASP.NET Membership controls and the SecurityLib namespace and classes. After all this was implemented, you prepared the way for a new order process with a new checkout page.

Finally, we looked at how to secure data passing over the Internet using secure SSL connections. This involved obtaining and installing a certificate from a known certification authority (VeriSign, for example), restricting access to SSL where appropriate, and modifying the redirection code slightly to use SSL connections.

In the next chapter, we'll look at how to create the framework for the order-processing pipeline, enabling you to automate even more of the supply process.

■ ■ ■

CHAPTER 17

Storing Customer Orders

The BalloonShop e-commerce application is shaping up nicely. We've added customer account management capabilities, and we're keeping track of customer addresses and credit card information, which is stored in a secure way. However, we're not currently using this information in our order tracking system, which was created in phase 2 of development. We currently don't associate an order with the account of the customer who placed that order.

In this chapter, we'll make the modifications required for customers to place orders that are associated with their user profiles. This feature will allow us to track in our database the orders placed by a particular customer and lay the foundation for implementing the order pipeline and credit card transactions in the following chapters.

Also in this chapter, we'll take a look at dealing with tax and shipping charges. Many options are available for implementing functionality to cope with these, but we'll just examine a simple way of doing things and lay the groundwork for your own further development.

This chapter is divided into three parts as follows:

- Enabling customers to place orders through their accounts

- Modifying the orders administration section to integrate the new features

- Adding tax and shipping charges

In the next chapter, we'll start to implement a more sophisticated order system, and the code we'll write in this chapter will facilitate that. Therefore, we'll be making some modifications that won't seem necessary at this stage, but they'll make your life easier later on.

Adding Orders to Customer Accounts

To enable customers to place orders, we need to make several modifications to our current order-placing mechanism. Right now, the orders we store in our database aren't associated with our existing customers. In this section, we'll update BalloonShop to enable our customers to place orders through their accounts (which they can now create).

This section is divided into two parts as follows:

- *Placing customer orders*: In this section, you'll enable customers to place orders.

- *Accessing customer orders*: In this section, you'll enable the order-processing system in later chapters to access customer orders.

Placing Customer Orders

To enable customers to place orders using ASP.NET membership, you need to make several modifications. You'll modify the database and business tier to enable customer orders to be placed and provide new code in the presentation tier to expose this functionality.

We won't use many step-by-step exercises in this chapter, but we'll make the changes in the usual order, starting with the database.

Updating the Orders Table

Currently the Orders table doesn't allow for as much information as you'll need to implement customer orders. There are also some modifications that you'll need in later chapters, so you need to add the new columns shown in Table 17-1 to the Orders table.

Table 17-1. *The Orders Table*

Column Name	Column Type	Description
CustomerID	uniqueidentifier	The ID of the customer that placed the order
Status	int	The current status of the order, which you'll use in later chapters to determine what stage of order processing has been reached; default value 0
AuthCode	varchar(50)	The authentication code used to complete the customer credit card transaction
Reference	varchar(50)	The unique reference code of the customer credit card transaction

All except the first of these columns are related to advanced order processing, including credit card transactions, and you'll look at these columns in more detail later. You might also wonder why the CustomerID column is of type uniqueidentifier, which is quite reasonable. The reason is simply because this is how users are identified in the ASP.NET membership system. Effectively, this column provides a link to the aspnet_Users membership table, in the ASPNETDB database.

Note that you won't be using some of the columns that already exist in the Orders table, such as Verified and Completed. This is because this information is now encapsulated in the Status column. You also won't need the old fields relating to customer identification, such as CustomerName, because now this information is stored elsewhere. Don't delete these deprecated columns, however, or you'll lose backward compatibility with code earlier in this book.

■**Note** To enable this database to be used with both the code in this section of the book and the code in the earlier part of this book, it's necessary to make the new columns nullable, because earlier data won't supply values for them.

Modify your Orders table using this piece of SQL code:

```
-- Adding the three new fields: customer_id, auth_code and reference.
ALTER TABLE Orders ADD CustomerID UNIQUEIDENTIFIER;
ALTER TABLE Orders ADD Status    INT DEFAULT 0;
ALTER TABLE Orders ADD AuthCode   VARCHAR(50);
ALTER TABLE Orders ADD Reference  VARCHAR(50);
```

Updating the CreateCustomerOrder Stored Procedure

Currently, the CreateOrder stored procedure is used to add orders to the database:

```
CREATE PROCEDURE CreateOrder
(@CartID char(36))
AS
/* Insert a new record into Orders */
DECLARE @OrderID int
INSERT INTO Orders DEFAULT VALUES
/* Save the new Order ID */
SET @OrderID = @@IDENTITY
/* Add the order details to OrderDetail */
INSERT INTO OrderDetail
     (OrderID, ProductID, ProductName, Quantity, UnitCost)
SELECT
     @OrderID, Product.ProductID, Product.Name,
     ShoppingCart.Quantity, Product.Price
FROM Product JOIN ShoppingCart
ON Product.ProductID = ShoppingCart.ProductID
WHERE ShoppingCart.CartID = @CartID
/* Clear the shopping cart */
DELETE FROM ShoppingCart
WHERE CartID = @CartID
/* Return the Order ID */
SELECT @OrderID
```

Now, when an order is created in the new system, more data needs to be added to the database, so we create a different (although very similar) stored procedure, CreateCustomerOrder (the differences are shown in bold):

```
CREATE PROCEDURE CreateCustomerOrder
(@CartID char(36),
 @CustomerID uniqueidentifier)
AS
/* Insert a new record into Orders */
DECLARE @OrderID int
INSERT INTO Orders (CustomerID) VALUES (@CustomerID)
/* Save the new Order ID */
SET @OrderID = @@IDENTITY
```

```
/* Add the order details to OrderDetail */
INSERT INTO OrderDetail
     (OrderID, ProductID, ProductName, Quantity, UnitCost)
SELECT
     @OrderID, Product.ProductID, Product.Name,
     ShoppingCart.Quantity, Product.Price
FROM Product JOIN ShoppingCart
ON Product.ProductID = ShoppingCart.ProductID
WHERE ShoppingCart.CartID = @CartID
/* Clear the shopping cart */
DELETE FROM ShoppingCart
WHERE CartID = @CartID
/* Return the Order ID */
SELECT @OrderID
```

The new data here is the inclusion of a `CustomerID` value with the order.

Business Tier Modifications

To use your new stored procedure, you need to modify the `ShoppingCartAccess` class. Rather than removing the old `CreateOrder` method, however, add the following method:

```
// Create a new order with customer ID
public static string CreateCommerceLibOrder()
{
  // get a configured DbCommand object
  DbCommand comm = GenericDataAccess.CreateCommand();
  // set the stored procedure name
  comm.CommandText = "CreateCustomerOrder";
  // create parameters
  DbParameter param = comm.CreateParameter();
  param.ParameterName = "@CartID";
  param.Value = shoppingCartId;
  param.DbType = DbType.String;
  param.Size = 36;
  comm.Parameters.Add(param);
  // create a new parameter
  param = comm.CreateParameter();
  param.ParameterName = "@CustomerId";
  param.Value =
     Membership.GetUser(
     HttpContext.Current.User.Identity.Name)
     .ProviderUserKey;
  param.DbType = DbType.Guid;
  param.Size = 16;
  comm.Parameters.Add(param);
  // return the result table
  return GenericDataAccess.ExecuteScalar(comm);
}
```

In case you don't have it already, you also need to add a reference to System.Web.Security at the beginning of the file.

This new method, CreateCommerceLibOrder, is more or less the same as the old order-placing code, but there is a new parameter to use: @CustomerID. The GUID to use for this customer identification is obtained using the ASP.NET membership classes. You obtain a MembershipUser class using Membership.GetUser by passing the name of the current user obtained from the current context. Next, you use the ProviderUserKey property of the MembershipUser object you receive to obtain the unique GUID that identifies the current user.

Note the naming of this new method, which includes the name CommerceLib. In later chapters, this name helps identify the new code that is associated with the new, advanced order-processing scheme.

Presentation Tier Modifications

You'll use the preceding method in the checkout page you added in the last chapter. You'll do this in the following exercise, as well as add an order confirmation page that users will be redirected to after placing an order.

Exercise: Adding Customer Orders to BalloonShop

1. Modify the placeOrderButton_Click method in Checkout.aspx.cs as follows:

```
protected void placeOrderButton_Click(object sender, EventArgs e)
{
  // Store the total amount
  decimal amount = ShoppingCartAccess.GetTotalAmount();
  // Create the order and store the order ID
  string orderId = ShoppingCartAccess.CreateCommerceLibOrder();
  // Redirect to the confirmation page
  Response.Redirect("OrderPlaced.aspx");
}
```

2. Add a new Web Form to the project called OrderPlaced.aspx by using the BalloonShop.master Master Page:

```
<%@ Page Title="" Language="C#" MasterPageFile="~/BalloonShop.master" ➥
AutoEventWireup="true" CodeFile="OrderPlaced.aspx.cs" Inherits="Order➥
Placed" %>

<asp:Content ID="Content1" ContentPlaceHolderID="head" Runat="Server">
</asp:Content>
<asp:Content ID="Content2" ContentPlaceHolderID="ContentPlaceHolder1" ➥
Runat="Server">
  Thank you for your order, please come again!
</asp:Content>
```

3. Add the following title-setting code and method override to the code-behind file for this form, `OrderPlaced.aspx.cs`:

```
protected override void OnInit(EventArgs e)
{
  // Uncomment to enforce SSL (as explained in Chapter 16)
  // (Master as BalloonShop).EnforceSSL = true;
  base.OnInit(e);
}

protected void Page_Load(object sender, EventArgs e)
{
  // Set the title of the page
  this.Title = BalloonShopConfiguration.SiteName +
             " : Order Placed";
}
```

4. Modify `web.config` as follows:

```
<!-- Only existing customers can access OrderPlaced.aspx -->
<location path="OrderPlaced.aspx">
  <system.web>
    <authorization>
      <allow roles="Customers" />
      <deny users="*" />
    </authorization>
  </system.web>
</location>
```

5. Place an order or two using the new system to check that the code works. You'll need to log on to do this and supply enough details to get past the validation on the checkout page.

How It Works: Adding Customer Orders to BalloonShop

The code added in this exercise is very simple and hardly merits much discussion. Still, you may want to modify the text displayed on `OrderPlaced.aspx` to include additional information that customers might require after placing an order. Also, note that this new page is secured via SSL and the `Customer` role. Customers who aren't logged in won't need to see this page.

After you've implemented more of the new ordering code, you'll be able to provide more information to customers, such as sending them confirmation emails and enabling them to check on order statuses, past and present. For now, however, this is as far as we can take things.

Accessing Customer Orders

After orders have been placed, you'll need to access them. This involves various modifications to the database business tier to provide new data structures and access code. Although essential in the next chapter and beyond, for now, you'll implement a simple (admin only) test form to access customer order data.

Database Modifications

You only need to make one modification here: Add a stored procedure to get access to the new information in the modified Orders table. Add the following stored procedure to the BalloonShop database:

```
CREATE PROCEDURE CommerceLibOrderGetInfo
(@OrderID int)
AS
SELECT OrderID,
       DateCreated,
       DateShipped,
       Comments,
       Status,
       CustomerID,
       AuthCode,
       Reference
FROM Orders
WHERE OrderID = @OrderID
```

This is very similar to the existing OrderGetInfo stored procedure, but rewritten to take into account the new columns.

Business Layer Modifications

The current order access code—stored in App_Code/OrdersAccess.cs—and the data for an order can be wrapped in a struct called OrderInfo. This struct is then used by various methods to manipulate order details.

The OrderInfo struct doesn't give you access to the new data stored in the Orders table, and it doesn't allow you to access order details or customer and credit card information. In short, you need something a little more advanced.

To achieve this, add a new class called CommerceLibAccess to the App_Code directory. You'll actually store two other classes in the same file, as per code in previous chapters (excepting the fact that in previous chapters only structs have shared files with a main class). Having a single file makes it easy to group classes that are functionally linked. All the classes in this file will facilitate data access, and you'll start by looking with a class to wrap rows in the OrderDetail table. Before doing this, however, add the following namespace references to the CommerceLibAccess.cs file:

```
using System.Data.Common;
using System.Data;
using System.Text;
using System.Collections.Generic;
using System.Web.Profile;
using System.Web.Security.
using SecurityLib;
```

These namespaces provide the class required for us to access and process order and customer information.

The CommerceLibOrderDetailInfo Class

Add the following class to `CommerceLibAccess.cs`:

```
/// <summary>
/// Wraps order detail data
/// </summary>
public class CommerceLibOrderDetailInfo
{
  public int OrderID;
  public int ProductID;
  public string ProductName;
  public int Quantity;
  public double UnitCost;
  public string ItemAsString;

  public double Subtotal
  {
    get
    {
      return Quantity * UnitCost;
    }
  }

  public CommerceLibOrderDetailInfo(DataRow orderDetailRow)
  {
    OrderID = Int32.Parse(orderDetailRow["OrderID"].ToString());
    ProductID = Int32.Parse(orderDetailRow["ProductId"].ToString());
    ProductName = orderDetailRow["ProductName"].ToString();
    Quantity = Int32.Parse(orderDetailRow["Quantity"].ToString());
    UnitCost = Double.Parse(orderDetailRow["UnitCost"].ToString());
    // set info property
    Refresh();
  }

  public void Refresh()
  {
    ItemAsString = Quantity.ToString() + " " + ProductName + ", $" +
UnitCost.ToString() + " each, total cost $" + Subtotal.ToString();
  }
}
```

This class wraps a row from the `OrderDetail` table. Note that we aren't using a struct for this functionality. This is because structs can't have constructors, and to make initialization easier, this class uses a constructor that takes a `DataRow` object to initialize itself. This constructor simply parses the OrderID, ProductID, ProductName, Quantity, and UnitCost columns and associates them with public fields. We could hide these fields by making them private, and expose them via properties, but for our purposes this access scheme is fine—and is a lot quicker to type in!

The constructor finishes with a call to a publicly accessible Refresh method, which sets a utility field called ItemAsString. This field, as you'll see later, makes it easier to quickly extract a descriptive piece of text concerning the data contained in a CommerceLibOrderDetailInfo instance.

Subtotal is another piece of information exposed by this class. Like ItemAsString, this is really just for convenience and simply returns the number of items multiplied by the cost of a single item.

The GetOrderDetails Method

The first method to add to the CommerceLibAccess class is one that obtains the OrderDetail rows associated with an order. Add the following method to the class:

```
public class CommerceLibAccess
{
  public static List<CommerceLibOrderDetailInfo> GetOrderDetails(string orderId)
  {
    // use existing method for DataTable
    DataTable orderDetailsData = OrdersAccess.GetDetails(orderId);
    // create List<>
    List<CommerceLibOrderDetailInfo> orderDetails =
      new List<CommerceLibOrderDetailInfo>(
      orderDetailsData.Rows.Count);
    foreach (DataRow orderDetail in orderDetailsData.Rows)
    {
      orderDetails.Add(
        new CommerceLibOrderDetailInfo(orderDetail));
    }
    return orderDetails;
  }
}
```

There are several things to note here. First, this class returns a generic list of CommerceLibOrderDetailInfo objects. The (in my view, quite fabulous) generic list classes make it easy to perform complex list operations on data without writing any of the code, and they are great timesavers.

We already have a similar method to this one in the OrdersAccess class, so we start by using that method to get a DataTable containing the data we are interested in. Next we take each row in that table, create an instance of the CommerceLibOrderDetailInfo class from it, and add it to the generic list of objects.

The CommerceLibOrderInfo Class

Add the following class to CommerceLibAccess.cs:

```
/// <summary>
/// Wraps order data
/// </summary>
public class CommerceLibOrderInfo
{
  public int OrderID;
  public string DateCreated;
  public string DateShipped;
  public string Comments;
  public int Status;
  public string AuthCode;
  public string Reference;
  public MembershipUser Customer;
  public ProfileCommon CustomerProfile;
  public SecureCard CreditCard;
  public double TotalCost;
  public string OrderAsString;
  public string CustomerAddressAsString;

  public List<CommerceLibOrderDetailInfo> OrderDetails;

  public CommerceLibOrderInfo(DataRow orderRow)
  {
    OrderID = Int32.Parse(orderRow["OrderID"].ToString());
    DateCreated = orderRow["DateCreated"].ToString();
    DateShipped = orderRow["DateShipped"].ToString();
    Comments = orderRow["Comments"].ToString();
    Status = Int32.Parse(orderRow["Status"].ToString());
    AuthCode = orderRow["AuthCode"].ToString();
    Reference = orderRow["Reference"].ToString();
    Customer = Membership.GetUser(
      new Guid(orderRow["CustomerID"].ToString()));
    CustomerProfile =
      (HttpContext.Current.Profile as ProfileCommon)
        .GetProfile(Customer.UserName);
    CreditCard = new SecureCard(CustomerProfile.CreditCard);
    OrderDetails =
      CommerceLibAccess.GetOrderDetails(
      orderRow["OrderID"].ToString());
    // set info properties
    Refresh();
  }
```

```
  public void Refresh()
  {
    // calculate total cost and set data
    StringBuilder sb = new StringBuilder();
    TotalCost = 0.0;
    foreach (CommerceLibOrderDetailInfo item in OrderDetails)
    {
      sb.AppendLine(item.ItemAsString);
      TotalCost += item.Subtotal;
    }
    sb.AppendLine();
    sb.Append("Total order cost: $");
    sb.Append(TotalCost.ToString());
    OrderAsString = sb.ToString();

    // get customer address string
    sb = new StringBuilder();
    sb.AppendLine(Customer.UserName);
    sb.AppendLine(CustomerProfile.Address1);
    if (CustomerProfile.Address2 != "")
    {
      sb.AppendLine(CustomerProfile.Address2);
    }
    sb.AppendLine(CustomerProfile.City);
    sb.AppendLine(CustomerProfile.Region);
    sb.AppendLine(CustomerProfile.PostalCode);
    sb.AppendLine(CustomerProfile.Country);
    CustomerAddressAsString = sb.ToString();
  }
}
```

This class wraps a row from the Orders table and is a little more complicated than the CommerceLibOrderDetailInfo class. Again, a constructor is used that takes a DataRow object to initialize the class, but this time you need to create user and credit card data using the data extracted.

To obtain this additional information, the code starts by getting an instance of the user references by the order using the GUID stored in CustomerID. The ASP.NET membership system makes this easy—you simply pass the GUID to Membership.GetUser and receive a MembershipUser object. From this object, you can find out the name of the user and pass that to the GetProfile method of the ProfileCommon object currently in use. Strangely, this method isn't a static method, so you need to access the current instance from the current context to do this.

After you've obtained a ProfileCommon instance for the customer, you simply store it in a publicly accessible field, just like the other order information. This will make it easy for you later, because you'll be able to access customer profile information with very simple syntax. From the information stored in the ProfileCommon instance, you also initialize an instance of SecureCard, giving you speedy access to customer credit card details when you need them.

Next, the constructor uses the GetOrderDetails method described previously to obtain the details of the order using the OrderId obtained from the DataRow. Again, this is to enable you to access these order details directly through the CommerceLibOrderInfo class, which is another time-saving operation.

Finally, a Refresh method similar to the one in CommerceLibOrderDetailInfo is used to initialize some utility fields: TotalCost, OrderAsString, and CustomerAddressAsString. You'll use all of these for speedier access to order details later.

The GetOrder Method

The second method to add to the CommerceLibAccess class is a method to obtain an order, in the form of a CommerceLibOrderInfo object. To do this, you use the new CommerceLibOrderGetInfo stored procedure. Add the following method to CommerceLibAccess:

```
public static CommerceLibOrderInfo GetOrder(string orderID)
{
  // get a configured DbCommand object
  DbCommand comm = GenericDataAccess.CreateCommand();
  // set the stored procedure name
  comm.CommandText = "CommerceLibOrderGetInfo";
  // create a new parameter
  DbParameter param = comm.CreateParameter();
  param.ParameterName = "@OrderID";
  param.Value = orderID;
  param.DbType = DbType.Int32;
  comm.Parameters.Add(param);
  // obtain the results
  DataTable table = GenericDataAccess.ExecuteSelectCommand(comm);
  DataRow orderRow = table.Rows[0];
  // save the results into an CommerceLibOrderInfo object
  CommerceLibOrderInfo orderInfo =
    new CommerceLibOrderInfo(orderRow);
  return orderInfo;
}
```

Because we've made the data structures nice and simple, there's not really much to shout about here. You get a command in the standard way, using GenericDataAccess.CreateCommand, configure it for your new stored procedure, use it to get a DataTable, and use the first row in the resulting table to initialize a CommerceLibOrderInfo instance. You've already done all the hard work here, in the constructor for CommerceLibOrderInfo.

Presentation Tier Modifications

You haven't added anything to require any data tier modifications yet, but you have implemented a lot of code that is used behind the scenes. To test this code, you'll implement a simple test form that enables administrators to view order information. You're not going to implement massive changes to the order administration code at this stage, because you'll just end up modifying it later after you've finished the new order-processing system.

Exercise: Viewing Customer Orders on a Test Form

1. Add a new Web Form to the BalloonShop application called OrderTest.aspx by using the Admin.master Master Page:

```
<%@ Page Title="" Language="C#" MasterPageFile="~/Admin.master" ➥

AutoEventWireup="true" CodeFile="OrderTest.aspx.cs" Inherits="OrderTest"%>

<asp:Content ID="Content1" ContentPlaceHolderID="titlePlaceHolder" ➥
runat="Server">
  <span class="AdminTitle">BalloonShop Customer Order Access Test</span>
</asp:Content>
<asp:Content ID="Content2" ContentPlaceHolderID="adminPlaceHolder" ➥
runat="Server">
  Order number:
  <asp:TextBox runat="server" ID="orderIDBox" />
  <br />
  <asp:Button runat="server" ID="goButton" Text="Go" />
  <br /><br />
  <asp:Label runat="server" ID="resultLabel" />
  <br /><br />
  <strong>Customer address:</strong>
  <br />
  <asp:Label runat="server" ID="addressLabel" />
  <br /><br />
  <strong>Customer credit card:</strong>
  <br />
  <asp:Label runat="server" ID="creditCardLabel" />
  <br /><br />
  <strong>Order details:</strong>
  <br />
  <asp:Label runat="server" ID="orderLabel" />
</asp:Content>
```

2. Switch to Design View and double-click the **Go** button to add an event handler.

3. Modify the code for the event handler as follows:

```
using System;

public partial class OrderTest : System.Web.UI.Page
{
  protected void goButton_Click(object sender, EventArgs e)
  {
```

```
        try
        {
          CommerceLibOrderInfo orderInfo = CommerceLibAccess.GetOrder(
            orderIDBox.Text);
          resultLabel.Text = "Order found.";
          addressLabel.Text = orderInfo.CustomerAddressAsString.Replace(
            "\n", "<br />");
          creditCardLabel.Text = orderInfo.CreditCard.CardNumberX;
          orderLabel.Text =
            orderInfo.OrderAsString.Replace("\n", "<br />");
        }
        catch
        {
          resultLabel.Text = "No order found, or order is in old format.";
          addressLabel.Text = "";
          creditCardLabel.Text = "";
          orderLabel.Text = "";
        }
      }
    }
```

4. Modify web.config as follows:

```
<!-- Only administrators are allowed to access OrderTest.aspx -->
<location path="OrderTest.aspx">
  <system.web>
    <authorization>
      <allow roles="Administrators" />
      <deny users="*" />
    </authorization>
  </system.web>
</location>
```

5. Log in to the BalloonShop web application as an administrator and navigate to the OrderTest.aspx page (by typing in the URL, as no page links to this test form).

6. Using Database Explorer in Visual Web Developer Express or any other tool capable of examining data in SQL Server tables, determine the OrderId of an order in the Orders table that contains a value for CustomerID (that is, an order placed since making the modifications earlier in this chapter). Note that the Status field in the database for the order must be 0 or you'll receive an error. It should be 0 already, if you set the default value for the Status column to 0 earlier in this chapter.

7. Enter the OrderID value in the text box on OrderTest.aspx and click **Go**. A typical result is shown in Figure 17-1.

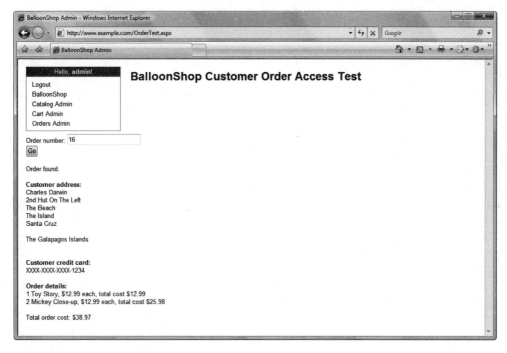

Figure 17-1. *Retrieved order details*

How It Works: Viewing Customer Orders on a Test Form

The simple code in this exercise uses the data tier classes defined earlier to access a customer order. The code is notable for its simplicity. The order information is obtained in a single line of code in the event handler for the Go button:

```
CommerceLibOrderInfo orderInfo =
    CommerceLibAccess.GetOrder(orderIDBox.Text);
```

After an instance of CommerceLibOrderInfo has been obtained, the event handler simply populates some Label controls on the page using some of the utility members you created earlier. Note that both CustomerAddressAsString and OrderAsString return a plain text string, so to view it in HTML format, you replace the end-of-line characters with line break elements, for example:

```
addressLabel.Text = orderInfo.CustomerAddressAsString.Replace(
    "\n", "<br />");
```

The event handler code also checks for exceptions when obtaining order information, which may occur for nonexistent orders or orders placed before the implementation of customer orders.

Handling Tax and Shipping Charges

One feature that is common to many e-commerce web sites is adding charges for tax and/or shipping. Obviously this isn't always the case—digital download sites have no need to charge for shipping, for example, because no physical shipment is involved. However, the chances are fairly high that you'll want to include additional charges of one kind or another in your orders.

In fact, this can be very simple, although not always. It really depends on how complicated you want to make things. In this chapter, we'll keep things simple and provide basic but extensible functionality for both tax and shipping charges. First, let's discuss the issues.

Tax Issues

The subject of tax and e-commerce web sites has a complicated history. To begin with, you could usually get away with anything. Taxing was poorly enforced, and many sites simply ignored tax completely. This was especially true for international orders, where it was often possible for customers to avoid paying tax much of the time—unless orders were intercepted by customs officers!

Then more people started to become aware of e-commerce web sites, and taxation bodies such as the IRS realized that they were losing a lot of money—or at least not getting all that they could. A flurry of activity ensued as various organizations worldwide attempted to hook into this revenue stream. A range of solutions were proposed, and some solutions were even implemented with varied complexity and mixed results. Now things are becoming a little more settled.

The key concept to be aware of when thinking about tax is a **nexus**. A nexus is a sufficient presence in the taxing jurisdiction to justify the collection of tax. Effectively, this means that when shipping internationally, you may not be responsible for what happens unless your company has a significant presence in the destination country. When shipping internally to a country (or within, say, the European Union), you probably will be responsible. The legislation is a little unclear, and we certainly haven't examined the laws for every country in the world, but this general rule tends to hold true.

The other key issues can be summed up by the following:

- Taxation depends on where you are shipping from and where you are shipping to.

- National rules apply.

- The type of product you are selling is important.

Some countries have it easier than others. Within the United Kingdom, for example, you can charge the current VAT rate on all purchases where it applies (some types of product are exempt or charged at a reduced rate) and be relatively happy that you've done all you can. If you want to take things one step further, you can consider an offshore business to ship your goods (Amazon does it, so why shouldn't you?). Other countries, notably the United States, have a much more complex system to deal with. Within the United States, sales tax varies not just from state to state, but often within states as well. In fact, pretty much the only time you'll know exactly what to do is when you are shipping goods to a customer in the same tax area as your business. At other times, well, to be perfectly honest, your guess is as good as ours.

In this book, the taxation scheme you add is as simple as possible. A database table will include information concerning various tax rates that can be applied, and the choice of these will for now depend on the shipping region of the customer. All products are considered to be taxable at the same rate. This does leave a lot to be desired, but at least tax will be calculated and applied. You can replace it with your own system later.

Shipping Issues

Shipping is somewhat simpler to deal with than tax, although again you can make things as complicated as you want. Because sending out orders from a company that trades via an e-commerce frontend is much the same as sending out orders from, say, a mail order company, the practices are very much in place and relatively easy to come to grips with. There may be new ways of doing things at your disposal, but the general principles are well known.

You may well have an existing relationship with a postal service from pre-online trading times, in which case, it's probably easiest to keep things as close to the "old" way of doing things as possible. However, if you're just starting out, or revising the way you do things, you have plenty of options to consider.

The simplest option is not to worry about shipping costs at all, which makes sense if there are no costs, for example, in the case of digital downloads. Alternatively, you could simply include the cost of shipping in the cost of your products. Or you could impose a flat fee regardless of the items ordered or the destination. However, some of these options could involve customers either overpaying or underpaying, which isn't ideal.

The other extreme involved is accounting for the weight and dimensions of all the products ordered and calculating the exact cost yourself. This can be simplified slightly, because some shipping companies (including FedEx, and so on) provide useful APIs to help you. In some cases, you can use a dynamic system to calculate the shipping options available (overnight, three to four days, and so on) based on a number of factors, including package weight and delivery location. The exact methods for doing this, however, can vary a great deal between shipping companies, and we'll leave it to you to implement such a solution if you require it.

In this book, we'll again take a simple line. For each shipping region in the database, you'll provide a number of shipping options for the user to choose from, each of which will have an associated cost. This cost is simply added to the cost of the order. This is the reason why, in Chapter 12, you included a ShippingRegion table—its use will soon become apparent.

Implementing Tax and Shipping Charges

As expected, you need to make several modifications to BalloonShop to enable the tax and shipping schemes outlined previously. You have two more database tables to add, Tax and Shipping, as well as modifications to make to the Orders table. You'll need to add new stored procedures and make some modifications to existing ones. Some of the business tier classes need modifications to account for these changes, and the presentation tier must include a method for users to select a shipping method (the taxing scheme is selected automatically). So, without further ado, let's get started.

Database Modifications

In this section, you'll add the new tables, Tax and Shipping, and modify the Orders table and stored procedures.

The Tax Table

The Tax table simply provides a number of tax options that are available, each of which has a name and a percentage tax rate. Table 17-2 shows the table structure that you'll need to add.

Table 17-2. *The Tax Table*

Column Name	Column Type	Description
TaxID	int	The ID of the tax option. This column is the primary key.
TaxType	varchar(100)	A text description of the tax option.
TaxPercentage	float	The percentage tax rate for this option.

These columns are not nullable. Figure 17-2 shows the data to add to this table.

	TaxID	TaxType	TaxPercentage
1	1	Sales Tax at 8.5%	8.5
2	2	No Tax	0

Figure 17-2. *Data for the Tax table*

If you prefer SQL, here's the code:

```
CREATE TABLE Tax (
  TaxID INT NOT NULL PRIMARY KEY,
  TaxType VARCHAR(100) NOT NULL,
  TaxPercentage FLOAT NOT NULL
)


GO


INSERT INTO TAX (TaxID, TaxType, TaxPercentage)
VALUES (1, 'Sales Tax at 8.5%', 8.5),
       (2, 'No Tax', 0)
```

The Shipping Table

The Shipping table is also very simple. It provides a number of shipping options, each of which has a name, a cost, and an associated shipping region. Table 17-3 shows the table structure that you'll need to add.

These columns are not nullable. Figure 17-3 shows the data to add to this table.

Table 17-3. *The Shipping Table*

Column Name	Column Type	Description
ShippingID	int	The ID of the shipping option. This column is the primary key and identity.
ShippingType	varchar(100)	A text description of the shipping option.
ShippingCost	money	The cost (to the customer) of the shipping option.
ShippingRegionID	int	The ID of the shipping region that this option applies to.

ShippingID	Shipping Type	ShippingCost	ShippingRegionID
1	Next Day Delivery ($20)	20.00	2
2	3-4 Days ($10)	10.00	2
3	7 Days ($5)	5.00	2
4	By Air (7 Days, $25)	25.00	3
5	By Sea (28 days, $10)	10.00	3
6	By Air (10 days, $35)	35.00	4
7	By Sea (38 days, $30)	30.00	4

Figure 17-3. *Data for the Shipping table*

The code that creates and populates this table is

```
CREATE TABLE Shipping (
  ShippingID INT NOT NULL PRIMARY KEY,
  ShippingType VARCHAR(100) NOT NULL,
  ShippingCost MONEY NOT NULL,
  ShippingRegionID INT
)

GO

INSERT INTO Shipping (ShippingID, ShippingType, ShippingCost, ShippingRegionID)
VALUES (1, 'Next Day Delivery ($20)', 20, 2),
       (2, '3-4 Days ($10)', 10, 2),
       (3, '7 Days ($5)', 5, 2),
       (4, 'By Air (7 Days, $25)', 25, 3),
       (5, 'By Sea (28 days, $10)', 10, 3),
       (6, 'By Air (10 days, $35)', 35, 4),
       (7, 'By Sea (38 days, $30), 30, 4)
```

Orders Table Modifications

The modifications to the Orders table are to associate an order with one entry each from the Tax and Shipping tables, as shown in Table 17-4.

You can add these columns to the Orders table and their respective foreign keys using this SQL code:

Table 17-4. *Orders Table Modifications*

Column Name	Column Type	Description
TaxID	int	The ID of the tax option to use for the order
ShippingID	int	The ID of the shipping option to use for the order

```
ALTER TABLE Orders ADD TaxID INT;
ALTER TABLE Orders ADD ShippingID INT;

ALTER TABLE Orders ADD CONSTRAINT FK_Orders_Tax
FOREIGN KEY(TaxID) REFERENCES Tax (TaxID)

ALTER TABLE Orders ADD CONSTRAINT FK_Orders_Shipping
FOREIGN KEY(ShippingID) REFERENCES Shipping (ShippingID)
```

CommerceLibOrderGetInfo Modifications

The existing CommerceLibOrderGetInfo stored procedure now needs to include the tax and shipping data for an order. The new stored procedure is as follows:

```
ALTER PROCEDURE CommerceLibOrderGetInfo
(@OrderID int)
AS
SELECT OrderID,
       DateCreated,
       DateShipped,
       Comments,
       Status,
       CustomerID,
       AuthCode,
       Reference,
       Orders.ShippingID,
       ShippingType,
       ShippingCost,
       Orders.TaxID,
       TaxType,
       TaxPercentage
FROM Orders
LEFT OUTER JOIN Tax ON Tax.TaxID = Orders.TaxID
LEFT OUTER JOIN Shipping ON Shipping.ShippingID = Orders.ShippingID
WHERE OrderID = @OrderID
```

Here there are two joins to the Tax and Shipping tables, both of which are LEFT OUTER joins so that data will be retrieved from the Orders table regardless of the value of TaxID and ShippingID (to enable backward compatibility among other issues).

CreateCustomerOrder Modifications

You also need to modify `CreateCustomerOrder` so that a tax and a shipping option are added when an order is added. The modifications are as follows:

```
ALTER PROCEDURE CreateCustomerOrder
(@CartID char(36),
 @CustomerID uniqueidentifier,
 @ShippingID int,
 @TaxID int)
AS
/* Insert a new record into Orders */
DECLARE @OrderID int
INSERT INTO Orders (CustomerID, ShippingID, TaxID)
VALUES (@CustomerID, @ShippingID, @TaxID)
/* Save the new Order ID */
SET @OrderID = @@IDENTITY
/* Add the order details to OrderDetail */
INSERT INTO OrderDetail
    (OrderID, ProductID, ProductName, Quantity, UnitCost)

SELECT
    @OrderID, Product.ProductID, Product.Name,
    ShoppingCart.Quantity, Product.Price
FROM Product JOIN ShoppingCart
ON Product.ProductID = ShoppingCart.ProductID
WHERE ShoppingCart.CartID = @CartID
/* Clear the shopping cart */
DELETE FROM ShoppingCart
WHERE CartID = @CartID
/* Return the Order ID */
SELECT @OrderID
```

The two new parameters to deal with are `@ShippingID` and `@TaxID`.

The CommerceLibShippingGetInfo Stored Procedure

You need to add a new stored procedure so that a list of shipping options associated with a shipping region can be obtained. The `CommerceLibShippingGetInfo` stored procedure achieves this:

```
CREATE PROCEDURE CommerceLibShippingGetInfo
(@ShippingRegionID int)
AS
SELECT ShippingID,
    ShippingType,
    ShippingCost
FROM Shipping
WHERE ShippingRegionID = @ShippingRegionID
```

Business Layer Modifications

To work with the new database tables and stored procedures, you need to make several changes to CommerceLibAccess.cs. You need to add two structs to represent tax and shipping options, TaxInfo and ShippingInfo. You also need to give access to shipping info based on shipping regions and modify CommerceLibOrderInfo to use the tax and shipping structs. You must modify CreateCommerceLibOrder in ShoppingCartAccess to configure tax and shipping for new orders as well.

The TaxInfo and ShippingInfo Structs

These structs use very simple code, which you can add to the top of CommerceLibAccess.cs:

```
/// <summary>
/// Wraps tax data
/// </summary>
public struct TaxInfo
{
  public int TaxID;
  public string TaxType;
  public double TaxPercentage;
}

/// <summary>
/// Wraps shipping data
/// </summary>
public struct ShippingInfo
{
  public int ShippingID;
  public string ShippingType;
  public double ShippingCost;
  public int ShippingRegionId;
}
```

There's not much to comment on here. The fields in the struct simply match up to the columns in the associated tables.

The GetShippingInfo Method

This method obtains a List<ShippingInfo> object containing shipping information for a shipping region. If it's not there already, this code requires a reference to the System.Collections. Generic namespace in the file. Add this method to the CommerceLibAccess class:

```
public static List<ShippingInfo> GetShippingInfo(
  int shippingRegionId)
{
  // get a configured DbCommand object
  DbCommand comm = GenericDataAccess.CreateCommand();
  // set the stored procedure name
  comm.CommandText = "CommerceLibShippingGetInfo";
```

```
  // create a new parameter
  DbParameter param = comm.CreateParameter();
  param.ParameterName = "@ShippingRegionId";
  param.Value = shippingRegionId;
  param.DbType = DbType.Int32;
  comm.Parameters.Add(param);
  // obtain the results
  DataTable table = GenericDataAccess.ExecuteSelectCommand(comm);
  List<ShippingInfo> result = new List<ShippingInfo>();
  foreach (DataRow row in table.Rows)
  {
    ShippingInfo rowData = new ShippingInfo();
    rowData.ShippingID = int.Parse(row["ShippingId"].ToString());
    rowData.ShippingType = row["ShippingType"].ToString();
    rowData.ShippingCost =
      double.Parse(row["ShippingCost"].ToString());
    rowData.ShippingRegionId = shippingRegionId;
    result.Add(rowData);
  }
  return result;
}
```

Here the ID of a shipping region is accepted as a parameter and used to access the CommerceLibShippingGetInfo stored procedure added earlier. The collection is assembled from row data.

CreateCommerceLibOrder Modifications

This method, in ShoppingCartAccess.cs, needs modifying as follows (again, a reference to System.Collections.Generic may be necessary):

```
public static string CreateCommerceLibOrder(int shippingId, int taxId)
{
  // get a configured DbCommand object
  DbCommand comm = GenericDataAccess.CreateCommand();
  // set the stored procedure name
  comm.CommandText = "CreateCustomerOrder";
  // create parameters
  DbParameter param = comm.CreateParameter();
  param.ParameterName = "@CartID";
  param.Value = shoppingCartId;
  param.DbType = DbType.String;
  param.Size = 36;
  comm.Parameters.Add(param);
  // create a new parameter
  param = comm.CreateParameter();
  param.ParameterName = "@CustomerId";
  param.Value =
```

```
    Membership.GetUser(
    HttpContext.Current.User.Identity.Name)
    .ProviderUserKey;
  param.DbType = DbType.Guid;
  param.Size = 16;
  comm.Parameters.Add(param);
  // create a new parameter
  param = comm.CreateParameter();
  param.ParameterName = "@ShippingId";
  param.Value = shippingId;
  param.DbType = DbType.Int32;
  comm.Parameters.Add(param);
  // create a new parameter
  param = comm.CreateParameter();
  param.ParameterName = "@TaxId";
  param.Value = taxId;
  param.DbType = DbType.Int32;
  comm.Parameters.Add(param);
  // return the result table
  return GenericDataAccess.ExecuteScalar(comm);
}
```

Here, two more parameters have been added to match up with the revised stored procedure
CreateCustomerOrder.

CommerceLibOrderInfo Modifications

This class requires several modifications. First you need to add two new fields for tax and
shipping info:

```
public class CommerceLibOrderInfo
{
  ...
  public ShippingInfo Shipping;
  public TaxInfo Tax;
```

Next, the constructor needs to be modified to extract this new data from the row returned
by the CommerceLibOrderGetInfo stored procedure:

```
public CommerceLibOrderInfo(DataRow orderRow)
{
  ...
  CreditCard = new SecureCard(CustomerProfile.CreditCard);
  OrderDetails =
    CommerceLibAccess.GetOrderDetails(
    orderRow["OrderID"].ToString());
  // Get Shipping Data
  if (orderRow["ShippingID"] != DBNull.Value
    && orderRow["ShippingType"] != DBNull.Value
    && orderRow["ShippingCost"] != DBNull.Value)
```

```
{
  Shipping.ShippingID =
      Int32.Parse(orderRow["ShippingID"].ToString());
  Shipping.ShippingType = orderRow["ShippingType"].ToString();
  Shipping.ShippingCost =
      double.Parse(orderRow["ShippingCost"].ToString());
}
else
{
  Shipping.ShippingID = -1;
}
// Get Tax Data
if (orderRow["TaxID"] != DBNull.Value
  && orderRow["TaxType"] != DBNull.Value
  && orderRow["TaxPercentage"] != DBNull.Value)

{
  Tax.TaxID = Int32.Parse(orderRow["TaxID"].ToString());
  Tax.TaxType = orderRow["TaxType"].ToString();
  Tax.TaxPercentage =
    double.Parse(orderRow["TaxPercentage"].ToString());
}
else
{
  Tax.TaxID = -1;
}
// set info properties
Refresh();
}
```

Note here that checks are made for null values for tax and shipping information. If data isn't found for tax information, TaxID will be set to -1. Similarly, no shipping data will result in ShippingID being -1. If all is well, these situations shouldn't occur, but just in case they do (especially if you end up modifying the tax and shipping schemes), this will prevent an error from occurring.

Finally, the Refresh method needs to include tax and shipping costs in its calculation of total cost and in its creation of the OrderAsString field:

```
public void Refresh()
{
  // calculate total cost and set data
  StringBuilder sb = new StringBuilder();
  TotalCost = 0.0;
  foreach (CommerceLibOrderDetailInfo item in OrderDetails)
  {
    sb.AppendLine(item.ItemAsString);
    TotalCost += item.Subtotal;
  }
```

```
   // Add shipping cost
   if (Shipping.ShippingID != -1)
   {
     sb.AppendLine("Shipping: " + Shipping.ShippingType);
     TotalCost += Shipping.ShippingCost;
   }

   // Add tax
   if (Tax.TaxID != -1 && Tax.TaxPercentage != 0.0)
   {
     double taxAmount = Math.Round(TotalCost * Tax.TaxPercentage,
       MidpointRounding.AwayFromZero) / 100.0;
     sb.AppendLine("Tax: " + Tax.TaxType + ", $"
       + taxAmount.ToString());
     TotalCost += taxAmount;
   }
   sb.AppendLine();
   sb.Append("Total order cost: $");
   sb.Append(TotalCost.ToString());
   OrderAsString = sb.ToString();
   ...
 }
```

The calculation of the tax amount involves some mathematical functionality from the System.Math class, but otherwise it's all simple stuff.

Presentation Layer Modifications

Finally we come to the presentation layer. In fact, due to the changes we've made, the only changes to make here are to the checkout page.

Checkout.aspx Modifications

The .aspx page simply needs a means of selecting a shipping type prior to placing an order. This can be achieved using a drop-down list:

```
<asp:Label ID="InfoLabel" runat="server" />
<br /><br />
Shipping type:
<asp:DropDownList ID="shippingSelection" runat="server" />
<br /><br />
<asp:Button ID="placeOrderButton" runat="server"
  Text="Place order" OnClick="placeOrderButton_Click" />
</asp:Content>
```

Now you need to populate this list and/or hide it in the code behind.

Checkout.aspx.cs Modifications

The code behind for this page already checks to see whether an order can be placed in
PopulateControls, based on whether a valid address and credit card have been entered. You
can use this information to set the visibility of the new list control (shippingSelection) and
populate the shipping option list accordingly. The code to modify is as follows:

```
private void PopulateControls()
{
  ...
  placeOrderButton.Visible = addressOK && cardOK;
  shippingSelection.Visible = addressOK && cardOK;

  // Populate shipping selection
  if (addressOK && cardOK)
  {
    int shippingRegionId = int.Parse(Profile.ShippingRegion);
    List<ShippingInfo> shippingInfoData =
      CommerceLibAccess.GetShippingInfo(shippingRegionId);
    foreach (ShippingInfo shippingInfo in shippingInfoData)
    {
      shippingSelection.Items.Add(
        new ListItem(shippingInfo.ShippingType,
          shippingInfo.ShippingID.ToString()));
    }
    shippingSelection.SelectedIndex = 0;
  }
}
```

This code uses the CommerceLibAccess.GetShippingInfo method added earlier, and creates
ListItem controls dynamically for adding to the drop-down list. Note also that a valid selection
in the list is ensured by setting the initially selected item in the drop-down list to the item with
an index of 0—that is, the first entry in the list.

Next, you need to modify the placeOrderButton_Click event handler to create an order
with tax and shipping option references. For the shipping option, you use the selected item in
the drop-down list; for the tax option, you make an arbitrary selection based on the shipping
region of the customer and the items you added earlier to the Tax table.

```
protected void placeOrderButton_Click(object sender, EventArgs e)
{
  // Store the total amount
  decimal amount = ShoppingCartAccess.GetTotalAmount();
  // Get shipping ID or default to 0
  int shippingId = 0;
  int.TryParse(shippingSelection.SelectedValue, out shippingId);
```

```
  // Get tax ID or default to "No tax"
  string shippingRegion =
    (HttpContext.Current.Profile as ProfileCommon).ShippingRegion;
  int taxId;
  switch (shippingRegion)
  {
    case "2":
      taxId = 1;
      break;
    default:
      taxId = 2;
      break;
  }

  // Create the order and store the order ID
  string orderId =
    ShoppingCartAccess.CreateCommerceLibOrder(shippingId, taxId);
  // Redirect to the conformation page
  Response.Redirect("OrderPlaced.aspx");
}
```

Note that this is one of the most crucial pieces of code in this chapter. Here you'll most likely make any modifications to the tax and shipping systems if you decide to add your own system, because choices are made on this page. The database and business layer changes are far more generic—although that's not to say that modifications wouldn't be necessary.

Exercise: Testing Tax and Shipping Charges

1. Before testing that the new system is working for tax and shipping charges, use the OrderTest.aspx page to check that old orders are unaffected. The information retrieved for an old order should be unaffected because the data is unchanged.

2. Place a new order, preferably with a customer in the United States/Canada shipping region (as this is currently the only region where tax is applied). Notice that on the checkout page you must select a shipping option, as shown in Figure 17-4.

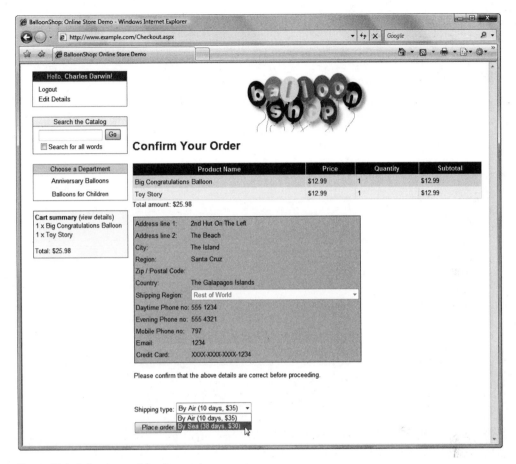

Figure 17-4. *Selecting a shipping region*

3. After placing the order, check the OrderID of the order in the database and then retrieve the order using OrderTest.aspx. The result is shown in Figure 17-5.

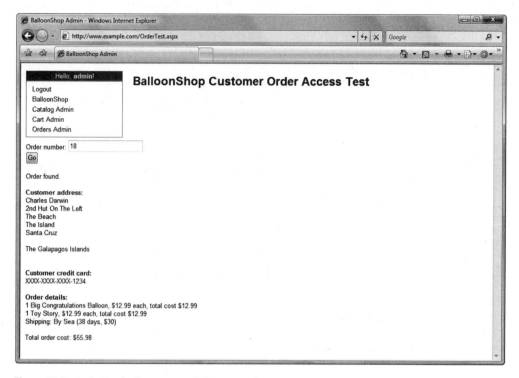

Figure 17-5. *Order including tax and shipping charges*

How It Works: Testing Tax and Shipping Charges

In this chapter leading up to this example, you've pretty much examined how the tax and shipping charges operate, but let's recap.

First, the customer is required to select a shipping region for their address. Without this shipping region being selected, visitors cannot place orders, because they cannot select a shipping option. When a visitor places an order, the shipping region selected is attached to the order in the Orders table. The tax requirement for the order is also attached, although this requires no user input (and is currently selected using a very simple algorithm, although this wouldn't be difficult to change).

Next, when you use the CommerceLibOrderInfo class, the tax and shipping is automatically taken into account in both the total cost and text representation of the order.

Further Development

There are several ways to proceed from here. Perhaps the first might be to add an administration system for tax and shipping options. This hasn't been implemented here partly because it would be trivial given the experience you've had so far in this book, and partly because the techniques laid out here are more of a template for development then a fully developed way of doing things. There are so many options to choose from for both tax and shipping calculations that only the basics are discussed here.

Hooking into online services for tax and shipping cost calculations is an attractive option; for shipping services, this is very much a possibility. In fact, the services offered by shipping companies such as FedEx use a similar way of going about things as the credit card gateway companies we'll look at later in this book. Much of the code you'd have to write to access these services will be very similar to that for credit card processing, although of course you'll have to adapt it to get the specifics right. Sadly, there may be more major changes required, such as adding weights and dimensions to products, but that very much depends on what products you are selling. For items in the BalloonShop catalog, many products are lighter than air, so shipping could be very cheap.

Summary

In this chapter, you've extended the BalloonShop site to enable customers to place orders using all the new data and techniques introduced in Chapter 12. Much of the modification made in this chapter lays the groundwork for the order pipeline to be used in the rest of this book. You've also included a quick way to examine customer orders, although this is by no means a fully fleshed-out administration tool—that will come later.

You also implemented a simple system for adding tax and shipping charges to orders. This system is far from being a universal solution, but it works and it's simple. More importantly, the techniques can easily be built on to introduce more complex algorithms and user interaction to select tax and shipping options and price the order accordingly.

From the next chapter onward, you'll be expanding on the customer ordering system even more by starting to develop a professional order pipeline for order processing.

■ ■ ■

CHAPTER 18

Implementing the
Order Pipeline, Part 1

Implementing the order pipeline is the first step we're making for creating a professional order management system. In this and the next chapter, we'll build our own order-processing pipeline that deals with credit card authorization, stock checking, shipping, e-mail notification, and so on. We'll leave the credit card–processing specifics for Chapter 20, but in this chapter, we'll show you where this process fits into the picture.

Order pipeline functionality is an extremely useful capability for an e-commerce site. Order pipeline functions let us keep track of orders at every stage in the process and provide auditing information that we can refer to later or if something goes wrong during the order processing. We can do all this without relying on a third-party accounting system, which can also reduce costs.

The bulk of this chapter deals with what a pipeline system is and constructing this system, which also involves a small amount of modification to the way things currently work and some additions to the database we've been using. However, the code in this chapter isn't much more complicated than the code we've already been using. The real challenges are in designing the system. After designing the order pipeline, the features you'll add to it in this chapter are

- Updating the status of an order

- Setting credit card authentication details

- Setting the order shipment date

- Sending e-mails to customers and suppliers

- Retrieving order details and the customer address

By the end of the next chapter, customers will be able to place orders into our pipeline, and we'll be able to follow the progress of these orders as they pass through various stages. Although no real credit card processing will take place yet, we'll end up with a fairly complete system, including a new administration web page that can be used by suppliers to confirm that they have items in stock and that orders have been shipped. To start with, however, we need a bit more background about what we're actually trying to achieve.

What Is an Order Pipeline?

Any commercial transaction, whether in a shop on the street, over the Internet, or anywhere else, has several related tasks that must be carried out before it can be considered complete. For example, you can't simply remove an item of clothing from a fashion boutique without paying for it and say that you have bought it—remuneration is (unfortunately!) an integral part of any purchase. In addition, a transaction can only complete successfully if each of the tasks carried out completes successfully. If a customer's credit card is rejected, for example, then no funds can be taken from it, so a purchase can't be made.

The sequence of tasks carried out as part of a transaction is often thought of in terms of a pipeline. In this analogy, orders start at one end of the pipe and come out of the other end when they are completed. Along the way, they must pass through several pipeline sections, each of which is responsible for a particular task or a related group of tasks. If any pipeline section fails to complete, then the order "gets stuck" and might require outside interaction before it can move further along the pipeline, or it might be canceled completely.

For example, the simple pipeline shown in Figure 18-1 applies to transactions in a street shop.

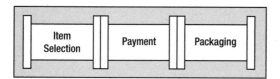

Figure 18-1. *Transactions for a street shop*

Here the last section might be optional, and might involve additional tasks such as gift-wrapping. The payment stage might also take one of several methods of operation, because the customer could pay using cash, credit card, gift certificates, and so on.

As you'll see in the next section, the e-commerce purchasing pipeline becomes longer, but isn't really any more complicated.

Understanding the BalloonShop Order Pipeline

In BalloonShop, the pipeline will look like the one in Figure 18-2.

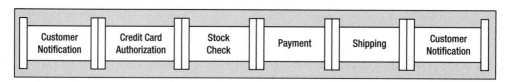

Figure 18-2. *The BalloonShop order pipeline*

The tasks carried out in these pipeline sections are, in order:

- *Customer Notification*: An email is sent notifying the customer that order processing has started, and confirming the items to be sent and the address that goods will be sent to.

- *Credit Card Authorization*: The credit card used for purchasing is checked, and the total order amount is set aside (although no payment is taken at this stage).

- *Stock Check*: An email is sent to the supplier with a list of the items that have been ordered. Processing continues when the supplier confirms that the goods are available.

- *Payment*: The credit card transaction is completed using the funds set aside earlier.

- *Shipping*: An email is sent to the supplier confirming that payment for the items ordered has been taken. Processing continues when the supplier confirms that the goods have been shipped.

- *Customer Notification*: An email is sent notifying the customer that the order has been shipped, and thanking them for using the BalloonShop web site.

Note In terms of implementation, as you'll see shortly, there are actually more stages than this, because the stock check and shipping stages consist of two pipeline sections: one for sending the email and one that waits for confirmation.

As orders flow through this pipeline, entries are added to a new database table called Audit. These entries can be examined to see what has happened to an order and are an excellent way of identifying problems if they occur. Each entry in the Orders table also will be flagged with a status, identifying which point in the pipeline it has reached.

To process the pipeline, you'll create classes representing each stage. These classes carry out the required processing and then modify the status of the order in the Orders database to advance the order. You'll also need a coordinating class (or processor), which can be called for any order and will execute the appropriate pipeline stage class. This processor will be called once when the order is placed, and in normal operation, will be called twice more: once for stock confirmation and once for shipping confirmation.

To make life easier, you'll also define a common interface supported by each pipeline stage class to enable the order processor class to access each stage in a standard way. You'll also define several utility functions and expose several common properties in the order processor class, which will be used as and when necessary by the pipeline stages. For example, the ID of the order should be accessible to all pipeline stages, so to save code duplication, you'll put that information in the order processor class.

Now, let's get on to the specifics. You'll build a series of classes that we'll refer to collectively as the CommerceLib classes. These classes could be contained in a separate assembly, but for simplicity, we'll include them in the BalloonShop code. This also simplifies access to customer information because you'll have access to the user profile classes defined by ASP.NET, as used in the last chapter. To differentiate the code from the existing code, however, you'll place all the CommerceLib files in a subdirectory of the App_Code directory and in a CommerceLib namespace. The CommerceLib directory will contain the following classes:

- OrderProcessor: The main class for processing orders

- OrderProcessorException: The custom exception class for use in the order processor and pipeline sections

- IPipelineSection: The interface definition for pipeline sections

- Customer, OrderDetails, *and* OrderDetail: The classes used to store data extracted from the database, for ease of access

- PSInitialNotification, PSCheckFunds, PSCheckStock, PSStockOK, PSTakePayment, PSShipGoods, PSShipOK, *and* PSFinalNotification: The pipeline section classes

The progress of an order through the pipeline as mediated by the order processor relates to the pipeline shown earlier (see Figure 18-3).

The process shown in Figure 18-3 is divided into three sections as follows:

- Customer places order

- Supplier confirms stock

- Supplier confirms shipping

The first stage is as follows:

1. When the customer confirms an order, Checkout.aspx creates the order in the database and calls OrderProcessor to begin order processing.

2. OrderProcessor detects that the order is new and calls PSInitialNotification.

3. PSInitialNotification sends an email to the customer confirming the order and advances the order stage. It also instructs OrderProcessor to continue processing.

4. OrderProcessor detects the new order status and calls PSCheckFunds.

5. PSCheckFunds checks that funds are available on the customer's credit card and stores the details required to complete the transaction if funds are available. If this is successful, then the order stage is advanced and OrderProcessor is told to continue.

6. OrderProcessor detects the new order status and calls PSCheckStock.

7. PSCheckStock sends an email to the supplier with a list of the items ordered, instructs the supplier to confirm via OrderAdmin.aspx, and advances the order status.

8. OrderProcessor terminates.

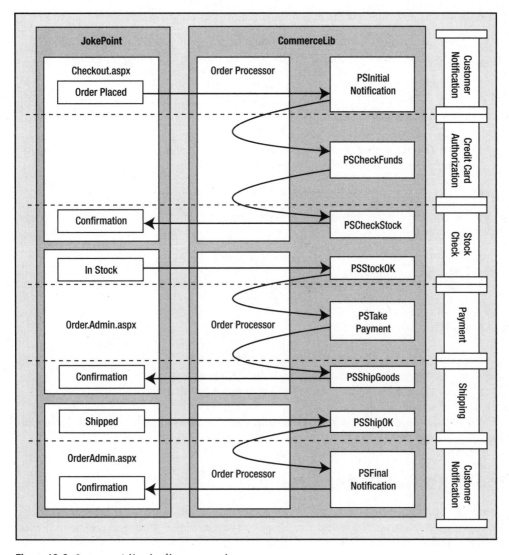

Figure 18-3. *CommerceLib pipeline processing*

The second stage is as follows:

1. When the supplier confirms that stock is available, OrderAdmin.aspx calls OrderProcessor to continue order processing.

2. OrderProcessor detects the new order status and calls PSStockOK.

3. PSStockOK advances the order status and tells OrderProcessor to continue.

4. OrderProcessor detects the new order status and calls PSTakePayment.

5. PSTakePayment uses the transaction details stored earlier by PSCheckFunds to complete the transaction, advances the order status, and tells OrderProcessor to continue.

6. `OrderProcessor` detects the new order status and calls `PSShipGoods`.

7. `PSShipGoods` sends an email to the supplier with a confirmation of the items ordered, instructs the supplier to ship these goods to the customer, and advances the order status.

8. `OrderProcessor` terminates.

The third stage is as follows:

1. When the supplier confirms that the goods have been shipped, `OrderAdmin.aspx` calls `OrderProcessor` to continue order processing.

2. `OrderProcessor` detects the new order status and calls `PSShipOK`.

3. `PSShipOK` enters the shipment date in the database, advances the order status, and tells `OrderProcessor` to continue.

4. `OrderProcessor` detects the new order status and calls `PSFinalNotification`.

5. `PSFinalNotification` sends an email to the customer confirming that the order has been shipped and advances the order stage.

6. `OrderProcessor` terminates.

If anything goes wrong at any point in the pipeline processing, such as a credit card being declined, an email will be sent to an administrator. This administrator then has all the information necessary to check what has happened, get in contact with the customer involved, and cancel or replace the order if necessary.

No point in this process is particularly complicated; it's just that a lot of code is required to put this into action!

Building the Order Pipeline

Building this pipeline involves adding a lot of code, so to simplify things, this process is broken down into stages. First, you'll add the basic framework and include a "dummy" pipeline section to check that things are working. Next, you'll add additional functionality that will be required by the "real" pipeline sections. Then, in the next chapter you'll add these pipeline sections, before integrating credit card functionality in Chapter 20.

The Basic Order Pipeline

To start with, then, let's add the basics.

Database Modifications

There isn't much to change in the database at this point, but you do need to add a new table, `Audit`, and associated stored procedures.

The Audit Table

During order processing, one of the most important functions of the pipeline is to maintain an up-to-date audit trail. The implementation of this involves adding records to a new database table called Audit. You need to create this table with the fields shown in Table 18-1.

Table 18-1. *The Audit Table*

Column Name	Column Type	Description
AuditID	int	Primary key, also set as table identity
OrderID	int	The ID of the order that the audit entry applies to
DateStamp	datetime	The date and time that the audit entry was created; default value is GETDATE()
Message	varchar(512)	The text of the audit entry
MessageNumber	int	An identifying number for the audit entry type

Alternatively, you can create this table and link it to Orders using this piece of SQL code:

```
CREATE TABLE Audit (
  AuditID INT NOT NULL PRIMARY KEY IDENTITY(1,1),
  OrderID INT NOT NULL,
  DateStamp DATETIME NOT NULL DEFAULT GETDATE(),
  Message NVARCHAR(512),
  MessageNumber INT
)

GO

ALTER TABLE Audit ADD CONSTRAINT FK_Audit_Orders
FOREIGN KEY(OrderID) REFERENCES Orders (OrderID)
```

Entries will be added by OrderProcessor and by individual pipeline stages to indicate successes and failures. These can then be examined to see what has happened to an order, an important function when it comes to error checking.

The MessageNumber column is interesting because it allows you to associate specific messages with an identifying number. It would be possible to have another database table allowing you to match these message numbers with descriptions, although this isn't really necessary, because the scheme used for numbering (as you'll see later in the chapter) is descriptive. In addition, the Message column already provides human-readable information.

The CreateAudit Stored Procedure

Now that you have the new Audit table, you need a way to add entries. You'll do this with the following stored procedure:

```
CREATE PROCEDURE CreateAudit
(@OrderID int,
 @Message nvarchar(512),
 @MessageNumber int)
AS

INSERT INTO Audit (OrderID, Message, MessageNumber)
VALUES (@OrderID, @Message, @MessageNumber)
```

Business Tier Modifications

There are several new classes to consider here, as well as a new method to add to the CommerceLibAccess class you created earlier. The new classes we'll look at in this section are

- CommerceLibException: Standard exception to be used by the order processor

- OrderProcessorMailer: Utility class allowing the order processor to send emails with simple syntax

- IPipelineSection: Standard interface for pipeline sections

- OrderProcessor: Controlling class for order processing

- PSDummy: Test pipeline section

You'll also need to modify the BalloonShopConfiguration class to include additional order processor configuration properties.

The CreateAudit Method

This method is a wrapper around the CreateAudit stored procedure added earlier and uses standard code. Add the following code to the CommerceLibAccess class:

```
public static void CreateAudit(int orderID, string message,
  int messageNumber)
{
  // get a configured DbCommand object
  DbCommand comm = GenericDataAccess.CreateCommand();
  // set the stored procedure name
  comm.CommandText = "CreateAudit";
  // create a new parameter
  DbParameter param = comm.CreateParameter();
  param.ParameterName = "@OrderID";
  param.Value = orderID;
  param.DbType = DbType.Int32;
  comm.Parameters.Add(param);
  // create a new parameter
  param = comm.CreateParameter();
  param.ParameterName = "@Message";
  param.Value = message;
  param.DbType = DbType.String;
```

```
    param.Size = 512;
    comm.Parameters.Add(param);
    // create a new parameter
    param = comm.CreateParameter();
    param.ParameterName = "@MessageNumber";
    param.Value = messageNumber;
    param.DbType = DbType.Int32;
    comm.Parameters.Add(param);
    // execute the stored procedure
    GenericDataAccess.ExecuteNonQuery(comm);
  }
```

You'll see more details about the messageNumber parameter used for auditing later in the chapter, when we analyze the order processor functionality in an exercise.

The OrderProcessorException Class

This is the first new class that you'll add to the CommerceLib library. Add a subdirectory called CommerceLib to the BalloonShop App_Code directory. Add a new class to this directory called CommerceLibException with the following code:

```
using System;

namespace CommerceLib
{
  /// <summary>
  /// Standard exception for order processor
  /// </summary>
  public class OrderProcessorException : ApplicationException
  {
    private int sourceStage;

    public OrderProcessorException(string message, int exceptionSourceStage) : ➥
base(message)
    {
      sourceStage = exceptionSourceStage;
    }

    public int SourceStage
    {
      get
      {
        return sourceStage;
      }
    }
  }
}
```

This code extends the base exception class ApplicationException, adding an integer property called SourceStage. This property allows you to identify the pipeline section (if any) that is responsible for throwing the exception.

Note that we use ApplicationException instead of Exception as the base class for this new exception class. This is recommended because the base Exception class is the base class for all exceptions; that is, both application and runtime exceptions. ApplicationException derives directly from Exception and should be used for exceptions thrown from application code. Another class, SystemException, which also derives directly from Exception, is used by runtime code. This distinction gives you a simple way to see roughly what code is generating exceptions even before examining any exceptions thrown. The Microsoft recommendation is to neither catch nor throw SystemException-derived classes in your code. In practice, however, we often do, because often try...catch blocks have a default catch block to catch all exceptions.

BalloonShop Configuration Modifications

The BalloonShopConfiguration class already includes a number of configuration properties for the site, or, to be more specific, allows access to properties stored in web.config. The OrderProcessor class (which you'll add shortly) needs various additional pieces of information in order to function. The new code to add to this class is as follows:

```
public static class BalloonShopConfiguration
{
  ...

  // Returns the email address for customers to contact the site
  public static string CustomerServiceEmail
  {
    get
    {
      return
        ConfigurationManager.AppSettings["CustomerServiceEmail"];
    }
  }

  // The "from" address for auto-generated order processor emails
  public static string OrderProcessorEmail
  {
    get
    {
      return
        ConfigurationManager.AppSettings["OrderProcessorEmail"];
    }
  }
}
```

```
// The email address to use to contact the supplier
public static string SupplierEmail
{
  get
  {
    return ConfigurationManager.AppSettings["SupplierEmail"];
  }
}
}
```

The new settings exposed by this class are as follows:

- CustomerServiceEmail: The email address that customers can use to send in queries about orders

- OrderProcessorEmail: An email address used as the "from" address for emails sent from the order processor to the administrator

- SupplierEmail: The email address of the product supplier, so that the order processor can send order notifications when the products are ready for picking/shipping

For testing purposes, you can set all of these settings to your email address. Later you will probably want to change some or all of these appropriately.

■**Note** Depending on the size of your enterprise, you may have multiple suppliers, in which case you'll probably want to store supplier information in the BalloonShop database and associate each product or product range with a different supplier. To keep things simple, however, the code in this book assumes that you only have one supplier—which may well use the same email address as the site administrator.

You also need to add the relevant properties to the <appSettings> section of web.config:

```
<appSettings>
  ...
  <add key="CustomerServiceEmail" value="customersupport@example.com" />
  <add key="OrderProcessorEmail" value="orderprocessor@example.com" />
  <add key="SupplierEmail" value="supplier@example.com" />
</appSettings>
```

The OrderProcessorMailer Class

This class enables code to send emails during order processing. Add a new class named OrderProcessorMailer to the App_Code/CommerceLib directory with code as follows:

```
namespace CommerceLib
{
  /// <summary>
  /// Mailing utilities for OrderProcessor
  /// </summary>
  public static class OrderProcessorMailer
  {
    public static void MailAdmin(int orderID, string subject,
      string message, int sourceStage)
    {
      // Send mail to administrator
      string to = BalloonShopConfiguration.ErrorLogEmail;
      string from = BalloonShopConfiguration.OrderProcessorEmail;
      string body = "Message: " + message
          + "\nSource: " + sourceStage.ToString()
          + "\nOrder ID: " + orderID.ToString();
      Utilities.SendMail(from, to, subject, body);
    }
  }
}
```

The only method of this class, `MailAdmin`, uses the `Utilities.SendMail` method to send an email to the site administrator by using settings from `BalloonShopConfiguration`. Later, when we need to send mails to customers and suppliers, we'll add more code to this class.

The IPipelineSection Interface

This `IPipelineSection` interface is implemented by all pipeline section classes so that `OrderProcessor` can use them in a standard way. Add the following interface definition in a file called `IPipelineSection.cs` in the `App_Code/CommerceLib` directory:

```
namespace CommerceLib
{
  /// <summary>
  /// Standard interface for pipeline sections
  /// </summary>
  public interface IPipelineSection
  {
    void Process(OrderProcessor processor);
  }
}
```

This interface exposes a single method, `Process`, that `OrderProcessor` will use to process an order through the pipeline stage in question. This method includes a reference to the calling class, so that pipeline sections will have access to order information and utility methods exposed by the `OrderProcessor` class.

The OrderProcessor Class

As is probably apparent now, the OrderProcessor class (which is the class responsible for moving an order through the pipeline) is a little more complicated than the classes you've seen so far in this chapter. However, you can start simply and build up additional functionality as needed. To start with, you'll create a version of the OrderProcessor class with the following functionality:

- Dynamically selects a pipeline section supporting IPipelineSection

- Adds basic auditing data

- Gives access to the current order and customer details

- Gives access to administrator mailing

- Mails the administrator in case of error

The code for this class, which you should also add to the App_Code/CommerceLib directory in a new file named OrderProcessor.cs, is as follows:

```
namespace CommerceLib
{
  /// <summary>
  /// Main class, used to obtain order information,
  /// run pipeline sections, audit orders, etc.
  /// </summary>
  public class OrderProcessor
  {
    internal IPipelineSection CurrentPipelineSection;
    internal bool ContinueNow;
    internal CommerceLibOrderInfo Order;

    public OrderProcessor(string orderID)
    {
      // get order
      Order = CommerceLibAccess.GetOrder(orderID);
    }

    public OrderProcessor(CommerceLibOrderInfo orderToProcess)
    {
      // get order
      Order = orderToProcess;
    }

    public void Process()
    {
```

```
      // configure processor
      ContinueNow = true;

      // log start of execution
      CreateAudit("Order Processor started.", 10000);

      // process pipeline section
      try
      {
        while (ContinueNow)
        {
          ContinueNow = false;
          GetCurrentPipelineSection();
          CurrentPipelineSection.Process(this);
        }
      }
      catch (OrderProcessorException ex)
      {
        MailAdmin("Order Processing error occurred.",
          ex.Message, ex.SourceStage);
        CreateAudit("Order Processing error occurred.", 10002);
        throw new OrderProcessorException(
          "Error occurred, order aborted. "
          + "Details mailed to administrator.", 100);
      }
      catch (Exception ex)
      {
        MailAdmin("Order Processing error occurred.", ex.Message,
          100);
        CreateAudit("Order Processing error occurred.", 10002);
        throw new OrderProcessorException(
          "Unknown error, order aborted. "
          + "Details mailed to administrator.", 100);
      }
      finally
      {
        CommerceLibAccess.CreateAudit(Order.OrderID,
          "Order Processor finished.", 10001);
      }
    }

    public void CreateAudit(string message, int messageNumber)
    {
      CommerceLibAccess.CreateAudit(Order.OrderID, message,
        messageNumber);
    }
```

```
  public void MailAdmin(string subject, string message,
    int sourceStage)
  {
    OrderProcessorMailer.MailAdmin(Order.OrderID, subject,
      message, sourceStage);
  }

  private void GetCurrentPipelineSection()
  {
    // select pipeline section to execute based on order status
    // for now just provide a dummy
    CurrentPipelineSection = new PSDummy();
  }
 }
}
```

This class includes two constructors, which are used to initialize the order processor with order information by either using the ID of an order or by simply using a CommerceLibOrderInfo instance. The class also includes its own versions of the CommerceLibAccess.CreateAudit and OrderProcessorMailer.MailAdmin methods, both of which are time savers that enable you to call these methods with the order ID parameter filled in automatically.

We'll walk through the rest of the code here shortly. Suffice to say for now that the only pipeline section used is PSDummy, which you'll add next.

The PSDummy Class

The PSDummy class is a dummy pipeline section that you'll use in your basic pipeline implementation to check that things are working correctly. Add this class to the App_Code/CommerceLib directory, to a new file named PSDummy.cs:

```
namespace CommerceLib
{
  /// <summary>
  /// Summary description for PSDummy
  /// </summary>
  public class PSDummy : IPipelineSection
  {
    public void Process(OrderProcessor processor)
    {
      processor.CreateAudit("PSDoNothing started.", 99999);
      processor.CreateAudit("Customer: "
        + processor.Order.Customer.UserName, 99999);
      processor.CreateAudit("First item in order: "
        + processor.Order.OrderDetails[0].ItemAsString, 99999);
      processor.MailAdmin("Test.", "Test mail from PSDummy.", 99999);
      processor.CreateAudit("PSDoNothing finished.", 99999);
    }
  }
}
```

The code here uses the AddAudit and MailAdmin methods of OrderProcessor to show that the code has executed correctly. Again, we'll look at this code in more detail shortly.

Presentation Tier Modifications

All you need to do now for the order processor to process an order is to add some very simple code to the checkout page.

Checkout Page Modifications

Add the following bold code to placeOrderButton_Click in Checkout.aspx.cs:

```
using CommerceLib;

...

  protected void placeOrderButton_Click(object sender, EventArgs e)
  {
    ...
    // Create the order and store the order ID
    string orderId = ShoppingCartAccess.CreateCommerceLibOrder(shippingId, ➥
taxId);
    // Process order
    OrderProcessor processor = new OrderProcessor(orderId);
    processor.Process();
    // Redirect to the conformation page
    Response.Redirect("OrderPlaced.aspx");
  }
```

Let's now test the skeleton of our order-processing system by following a few simple steps.

Exercise: Basic Order Processing

1. Open the BalloonShop web application in a browser.

2. Log in as a customer you've previously created, add some products to your cart, and place an order.

3. Check your inbox for new mail. You should receive a message that looks similar to Figure 18-4.

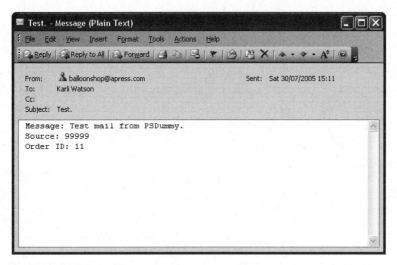

Figure 18-4. *Email from PSDummy*

4. Examine the Audit table in the database to see the new entries. An example is shown in Figure 18-5 (note that the dates are in dd/mm/yyyy format in this figure).

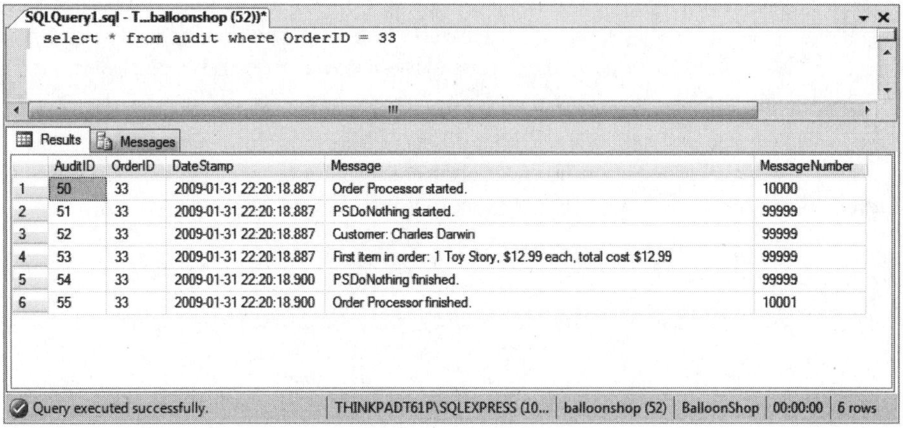

Figure 18-5. *Audit table entries from PSDummy*

How It Works: Basic Order Processing

The main body of the OrderProcessor class is the Process method, which is called by Checkout.aspx (and will be called later by the order admin pages) to process an order. The order to be processed is set by the constructor of OrderProcessor as noted earlier, and is indicated either by an ID or a CommerceLibOrderInfo object.

The first thing that Process does is set ContinueNow to true and log the start of its execution in the Audit table:

```
public void Process()
{
  // configure processor
  ContinueNow = true;

  // log start of execution
  CreateAudit("Order Processor started.", 10000);
```

■**Note** 10000 is the message number to store for the audit entry—we'll look at these codes in more detail in a little while.

Next we come to the order processing itself. The model used here checks the Boolean ContinueNow field before processing a pipeline section. This allows sections to specify either that processing should continue when they're finished with the current task (by setting ContinueNow to true) or that processing should pause (by setting ContinueNow to false). This is necessary because you need to wait for external input at certain points along the pipeline, such as checking whether stock is available.

The pipeline section to process is selected by the private GetCurrentPipelineSection method, which eventually selects a section based on the status of the order, but currently just has the job of setting the CurrentPipelineSection field to an instance of PSDummy:

```
private void GetCurrentPipelineSection()
{
  // select pipeline section to execute based on order status
  // for now just provide a dummy
  CurrentPipelineSection = new PSDummy();
}
```

Back to Process, you see this method being called in a try block:

```
// process pipeline section
try
{
  while (ContinueNow)
  {
    ContinueNow = false;
    GetCurrentPipelineSection();
```

Note that ContinueNow is set to false in the while loop—the default behavior is to stop after each pipeline section.

After you have a pipeline section, you need to process it. All sections support the simple IPipelineSection interface, defined as follows:

```
public interface IPipelineSection
{
   void Process(OrderProcessor processor);
}
```

All pipeline sections use a Process method to perform their work, and this method requires an OrderProcessor reference because the pipeline sections need access to the order and customer details exposed by the order processor.

The last part of the while loop (and try block) in OrderProcessor calls this method:

```
      CurrentPipelineSection.Process(this);
    }
  }
```

This calls the Process method in PSDummy, which we'll come back to shortly.

The last part of the Process method in OrderProcessor involves catching exceptions, which might be OrderProcessorException instances or other exception types. In either case, you send an email to the administrator using the MailAdmin method (we'll cover this in a little while), add an audit entry, and throw a new OrderProcessorException that can be caught by users of the OrderProcessor class:

```
        catch (OrderProcessorException ex)
        {
          MailAdmin("Order Processing error occurred.",
            ex.Message, ex.SourceStage);
          CreateAudit("Order Processing error occurred.", 10002);
          throw new OrderProcessorException(
            "Error occurred, order aborted. "
            + "Details mailed to administrator.", 100);
        }
        catch (Exception ex)
        {
          MailAdmin("Order Processing error occurred.", ex.Message,
            100);
          CreateAudit("Order Processing error occurred.", 10002);
          throw new OrderProcessorException(
            "Unknown error, order aborted. "
            + "Details mailed to administrator.", 100);
        }
```

Regardless of whether processing is successful, you add a final audit entry saying that the processing has completed:

```
        finally
        {
          CommerceLibAccess.CreateAudit(Order.OrderID,
            "Order Processor finished.", 10001);
        }
      }
    }
```

At this point, it's worth examining the message number scheme chosen for order-processing audits. In all cases, the audit message number is a five-digit number. The first digit of this number is either 1 if an audit is being added by OrderProcessor, or 2 if the audit is added by a pipeline section. The next two digits are used for the pipeline stage that added the audit (which maps directly to the status of the order when the audit was added). The final two digits uniquely identify the message within this scope. For example, so far you've seen the following message numbers:

- 10000: Order processor started.

- 10001: Order processor finished.

- 10002: Order processor error occurred.

Later you'll see a lot of these that start with 2, as you get on to pipeline sections, and include the necessary information for identifying the pipeline section, as noted previously. We hope you'll agree that this scheme allows for plenty of flexibility, although you can, of course, use whatever numbers you see fit. As a final note, numbers ending in 00 and 01 are used for starting and finishing messages for both the order processor and pipeline stages, whereas 02 and above are for other messages. There is no real reason for this apart from consistency between the components.

The PSDummy class that is used in this skeleton processor performs some basic functions to check that things are working correctly:

```
public class PSDummy : IPipelineSection
{
  public void Process(OrderProcessor processor)
  {
    processor.CreateAudit("PSDoNothing started.", 99999);
    processor.CreateAudit("Customer: "
      + processor.Order.Customer.UserName, 99999);
    processor.CreateAudit("First item in order: "
      + processor.Order.OrderDetails[0].ItemAsString, 99999);
    processor.MailAdmin("Test.", "Test mail from PSDummy.",
      99999);
    processor.CreateAudit("PSDoNothing finished.", 99999);
  }
}
```

The code here uses the AddAudit and .MailAdmin methods of OrderProcessor to generate something to show that the code has executed correctly. Note that the numbering schemes outlined previously aren't used there, as this isn't a real pipeline section.

That was a lot of code to get through, but it did have the effect of making the client code very simple:

```
// Process order
OrderProcessor processor = new OrderProcessor(orderId);
processor.Process();
```

Short of setting all the configuration details in web.config, there is very little to do because OrderProcessor does a lot of work for you. It's worth noting that the code you have at this point is for the most part a consequence of the design choices made earlier. This is an excellent example of how a strong design can lead straight to powerful and robust code.

Adding More Functionality to OrderProcessor

You need to add a few more bits and pieces to the OrderProcessor class to make it fully functional for use with the pipeline sections that you'll add in the next chapter.

You need to look at

- Updating the status of an order

- Setting and getting credit card authentication details

- Setting the order shipment date

Database Modifications

All the modifications in this section are stored procedures.

The CommerceLibOrderUpdateStatus Stored Procedure

Each pipeline section needs the capability to change the status of an order, advancing it to the next pipeline section. Rather than simply incrementing the status, this functionality is kept flexible, just in case you end up with a more complicated branched pipeline. This requires a new stored procedure, CommerceLibOrderUpdateStatus:

```
CREATE PROCEDURE CommerceLibOrderUpdateStatus
(@OrderID int,
 @Status int)
AS

UPDATE Orders
SET Status = @Status
WHERE OrderID = @OrderID
```

The CommerceLibOrderSetAuthCode Stored Procedure

In Chapter 20, when we deal with credit card usage, you'll need to set data in the AuthCode and Reference fields in the Orders table.

This requires a new stored procedure, CommerceLibOrderSetAuthCode:

```
CREATE PROCEDURE CommerceLibOrderSetAuthCode
(@OrderID int,
 @AuthCode nvarchar(50),
 @Reference nvarchar(50))
AS

UPDATE Orders
SET AuthCode = @AuthCode, Reference = @Reference
WHERE OrderID = @OrderID
```

The CommerceLibOrderSetDateShipped Stored Procedure

When an order is shipped, you should update the shipment date in the database, which can simply be the current date. The new stored procedure to do this, CommerceLibOrderSetDateShipped, is as follows:

```
CREATE PROCEDURE CommerceLibOrderSetDateShipped
(@OrderID int)
AS

UPDATE Orders
SET DateShipped = GetDate()
WHERE OrderID = @OrderID
```

Business Tier Modifications

Next you need to modify CommerceLibAccess to use the new stored procedures. All the methods in this section act in much the same way as some of the other methods of CommerceLibAccess that you've seen already.

The UpdateOrderStatus Method

This method calls the CommerceLibOrderUpdateStatus stored procedure. Add the following code to your CommerceLibAccess class:

```csharp
  public static void UpdateOrderStatus(int orderID, int status)
  {
    // get a configured DbCommand object
    DbCommand comm = GenericDataAccess.CreateCommand();
    // set the stored procedure name
    comm.CommandText = "CommerceLibOrderUpdateStatus";
    // create a new parameter
    DbParameter param = comm.CreateParameter();
    param.ParameterName = "@OrderID";
    param.Value = orderID;
    param.DbType = DbType.Int32;
    comm.Parameters.Add(param);
    // create a new parameter
    param = comm.CreateParameter();
    param.ParameterName = "@Status";
    param.Value = status;
    param.DbType = DbType.Int32;
    comm.Parameters.Add(param);
    // execute the stored procedure
    GenericDataAccess.ExecuteNonQuery(comm);
  }
```

The SetOrderAuthCodeAndReference Method

This method uses the CommerceLibOrderSetAuthCode stored procedure to set the AuthCode and Reference fields in Orders. Add it to your CommerceLibAccess class:

```
public static void SetOrderAuthCodeAndReference(int orderID,
  string authCode, string reference)
{
  // get a configured DbCommand object
  DbCommand comm = GenericDataAccess.CreateCommand();
  // set the stored procedure name
  comm.CommandText = "CommerceLibOrderSetAuthCode";
  // create a new parameter
  DbParameter param = comm.CreateParameter();
  param.ParameterName = "@OrderID";
  param.Value = orderID;
  param.DbType = DbType.Int32;
  comm.Parameters.Add(param);
  // create a new parameter
  param = comm.CreateParameter();
  param.ParameterName = "@AuthCode";
  param.Value = authCode;
  param.DbType = DbType.String;
  param.Size = 50;
  comm.Parameters.Add(param);
  // create a new parameter
  param = comm.CreateParameter();
  param.ParameterName = "@Reference";
  param.Value = reference;
  param.DbType = DbType.String;
  param.Size = 50;
  comm.Parameters.Add(param);
  // execute the stored procedure
  GenericDataAccess.ExecuteNonQuery(comm);
}
```

The SetOrderDateShipped Method

The last method to add to CommerceLibAccess, SetOrderDateShipped, is as follows:

```
public static void SetOrderDateShipped(int orderID)
{
  // get a configured DbCommand object
  DbCommand comm = GenericDataAccess.CreateCommand();
  // set the stored procedure name
  comm.CommandText = "CommerceLibOrderSetDateShipped";
```

```
    // create a new parameter
    DbParameter param = comm.CreateParameter();
    param.ParameterName = "@OrderID";
    param.Value = orderID;
    param.DbType = DbType.Int32;
    comm.Parameters.Add(param);
    // execute the stored procedure
    GenericDataAccess.ExecuteNonQuery(comm);
}
```

CommerceLibOrderInfo Modifications

Finally, for convenience, you can allow the preceding methods to be called via the
CommerceLibOrderInfo class. This enables you to skip the orderID parameter because
CommerceLibOrderInfo instances know what their IDs are. You can also update local fields while
you make the changes. This requires the following new methods on the CommerceLibOrderInfo
class (you should find it in CommerceLibAccess.cs):

```
public void UpdateStatus(int status)
{
  // call static method
  CommerceLibAccess.UpdateOrderStatus(OrderID, status);
  // update field
  Status = status;
}


public void SetAuthCodeAndReference(string authCode,
  string reference)
{
  // call static method
  CommerceLibAccess.SetOrderAuthCodeAndReference(OrderID,
    authCode, reference);
  // update fields
  AuthCode = authCode;
  Reference = reference;
}

public void SetDateShipped()
{
  // call static method
  CommerceLibAccess.SetOrderDateShipped(OrderID);
  // update field
  DateShipped = DateTime.Now.ToString();
}
```

Summary

You've started to build the backbone of the application and prepared it for the lion's share of the order pipeline–processing functionality, which you'll implement in Chapter 19.

Specifically, we've covered the following:

- The basic framework for your order pipeline

- The database additions for auditing data and storing additional required data in the Orders table

- How to put orders into the pipeline when they are placed in BalloonShop

In the next chapter, you'll go on to implement the order pipeline.

CHAPTER 19

■ ■ ■

Implementing the Order Pipeline, Part 2

In the previous chapter, you completed the basic functionality of the `OrderProcessor` component, which is responsible for moving orders through the pipeline stages. You saw a quick demonstration of this using a dummy pipeline section, but we haven't yet implemented the pipeline discussed at the beginning of the previous chapter.

In this chapter, we'll add the required pipeline sections so that we can process orders from start to finish, although we won't be adding full credit card transaction functionality until the next chapter.

We'll also look at the web administration of orders by modifying the order administration pages added earlier in the book to take into account the new order-processing system.

Implementing the Pipeline Sections

The `OrderProcessor` code is complete, except for one important section—the pipeline stage selection. Rather than forcing the processor to use `PSDummy`, you actually want to select one of the pipeline stages outlined in Chapter 18, depending on the status of the order. Before you do this, let's run through the code for each of the pipeline sections in turn, and some new utility code, which will take you to the point where the order pipeline is complete apart from actual credit card authorization.

Business Tier Modifications

The first thing we'll look at in this section is some modifications to the `OrderProcessorMailer` class that are required for pipeline sections to send mail to customers and suppliers. After that, we'll move on to the pipeline sections; each section requires a new class in the `App_Code/CommerceLib` folder. (Remember that this code is available in the Source Code area of the Apress web site, at `http://www.apress.com`). By the time you get to the next Exercise section, you should have eight new classes with the following names (they all start with PS, short for Pipeline Section):

- `PSInitialNotification`
- `PSCheckFunds`
- `PSCheckStock`

- PSStockOK

- PSTakePayment

- PSShipGoods

- PSShipOK

- PSFinalNotification

We'll discuss the classes you are creating as you go.

OrderProcessorMailer Modifications

The OrderProcessorMailer class needs two new methods, MailCustomer and MailSupplier. The new methods to add to OrderProcessorMailer are as follows:

```
public static void MailCustomer(MembershipUser customer,
  string subject, string body)
{
  // Send mail to customer
  string to = customer.Email;
  string from = BalloonShopConfiguration.CustomerServiceEmail;
  Utilities.SendMail(from, to, subject, body);
}

public static void MailSupplier(string subject, string body)
{
  // Send mail to supplier
  string to = BalloonShopConfiguration.SupplierEmail;
  string from = BalloonShopConfiguration.OrderProcessorEmail;
  Utilities.SendMail(from, to, subject, body);
}
```

You will also need to reference the System.Web.Security namespace. These methods use properties from BalloonShopConfiguration and the Utilities.SendMail method to send mail to customers and suppliers.

OrderProcessor Modifications

As with MailAdmin, we'll provide some new methods in OrderProcessor for mailing so that pipeline sections don't use OrderProcessorMailer directly. The code for this is simply two new methods, as follows. Add these new methods to your OrderProcessor class:

```
public void MailCustomer(string subject, string message)
{
  OrderProcessorMailer.MailCustomer(Order.Customer, subject, message);
}
```

```
public void MailSupplier(string subject, string message)
{
  OrderProcessorMailer.MailSupplier(subject, message);
}
```

Doing this is really according to personal taste. It wouldn't really matter if order pipeline sections used OrderProcessorMailer methods, although in the case of MailCustomer it does simplify the syntax slightly.

The PSInitialNotification Class

PSInitialNotification is the first pipeline stage and is responsible for sending an email to the customer confirming that the order has been placed. The code for this class starts off in what will soon become a very familiar fashion. Add a new class file named PSInitialNotification.cs to your CommerceLib folder, and add this code to it:

```
namespace CommerceLib
{
  /// <summary>
  /// 1st pipeline stage - used to send a notification email to
  /// the customer, confirming that the order has been received
  /// </summary>
  public class PSInitialNotification : IPipelineSection
  {
    private OrderProcessor orderProcessor;

    public void Process(OrderProcessor processor)
    {
      // set processor reference
      orderProcessor = processor;
      // audit
      orderProcessor.CreateAudit("PSInitialNotification started.", 20000);

      try
      {
        // send mail to customer
        orderProcessor.MailCustomer("BalloonShop order received.", GetMailBody());
        // audit
        orderProcessor.CreateAudit(
          "Notification e-mail sent to customer.", 20002);
        // update order status
        orderProcessor.Order.UpdateStatus(1);
        // continue processing
        orderProcessor.ContinueNow = true;
      }
```

```
      catch
      {
        // mail sending failure
        throw new OrderProcessorException(
          "Unable to send e-mail to customer.", 0);
      }
      // audit
      processor.CreateAudit("PSInitialNotification finished.", 20001);
    }
  }
}
```

The class implements the IPipelineSection interface; it contains a private field for storing a reference to the order processor, and the IPipelineSection.Process method implementation. This method starts by storing the reference to OrderProcessor, which all the pipeline sections will do because using the members it exposes (either in the Process method or in other methods) is essential. An audit entry is also added using the numbering scheme introduced earlier (the initial 2 signifies that it's coming from a pipeline section, the next 00 means that it's the first pipeline section, and the final 00 shows that it's the start message for the pipeline section).

The remainder of the Process method sends the email, using the MailCustomer method of OrderProcessor. A private method, GetMailBody, is used to build a message body, which we'll look at shortly. After the mail is sent, you add an audit message to change the status of the order and tell the order processor that it's okay to move straight on to the next pipeline section.

If all goes according to plan, the Process method finishes by adding a final audit entry.

Now add the GetMailBody method to the class, which is used to build up an email body to send to the customer using a StringBuilder object. The text uses customer and order data, but follows a generally accepted e-commerce email format:

```
private string GetMailBody()
{
  // construct message body
  string mail;
  mail = "Thank you for your order! The products you have "
       + "ordered are as follows:\n\n"
       + orderProcessor.Order.OrderAsString
       + "\n\nYour order will be shipped to:\n\n"
       + orderProcessor.Order.CustomerAddressAsString
       + "\n\nOrder reference number:\n\n"
       + orderProcessor.Order.OrderID.ToString()
       + "\n\nYou will receive a confirmation e-mail when this "
       + "order has been dispatched. Thank you for shopping "
       + "at BalloonShop!";
  return mail;
}
```

When this pipeline stage finishes, processing moves straight on to PSCheckFunds.

The PSCheckFunds Class

The PSCheckFunds pipeline stage is responsible for making sure that the customer has the required funds available on a credit card. For now, you'll provide a dummy implementation of this, and just assume that these funds are available. Let's create this class in your CommerceLib folder.

The code starts in the same way as PSInitialNotification, the System.Text namespace:

```
namespace CommerceLib
{
  /// <summary>
  /// 2nd pipeline stage - used to check that the customer
  /// has the required funds available for purchase
  /// </summary>
  public class PSCheckFunds : IPipelineSection
  {
    private OrderProcessor orderProcessor;

    public void Process(OrderProcessor processor)
    {
      // set processor reference
      orderProcessor = processor;
      // audit
      orderProcessor.CreateAudit("PSCheckFunds started.", 20100);
```

Even though you aren't actually performing a check, you set the authorization and reference codes for the transaction to make sure that the code in OrderProcessor works properly:

```
      try
      {
        // check customer funds
        // assume they exist for now
        // set order authorization code and reference
        orderProcessor.Order.SetAuthCodeAndReference("AuthCode",
          "Reference");
```

You finish up with some auditing, the code required for continuation, and error checking:

```
        // audit
        orderProcessor.CreateAudit("Funds available for purchase.",
          20102);
        // update order status
        orderProcessor.Order.UpdateStatus(2);
        // continue processing
        orderProcessor.ContinueNow = true;
      }
```

```
      catch
      {
        // fund checking failure
        throw new OrderProcessorException(
          "Error occured while checking funds.", 1);
      }
      // audit
      processor.CreateAudit("PSCheckFunds finished.", 20101);
    }
  }
}
```

When this pipeline stage finishes, processing moves straight on to PSCheckStock.

The PSCheckStock Class

The PSCheckStock pipeline stage sends an email instructing the supplier to check stock availability. Create it together with your other order pipeline classes, in the CommerceLib folder:

```
namespace CommerceLib
{
  /// <summary>
  /// 3rd pipeline stage - used to send a notification email to
  /// the supplier, asking whether goods are available
  /// </summary>
  public class PSCheckStock : IPipelineSection
  {
    private OrderProcessor orderProcessor;

    public void Process(OrderProcessor processor)
    {
      // set processor reference
      orderProcessor = processor;
      // audit
      orderProcessor.CreateAudit("PSCheckStock started.", 20200);
```

Mail is sent in a similar way to PSInitialNotification, using a private method to build up the body. This time, however, we use MailSupplier:

```
      try
      {
        // send mail to supplier
        orderProcessor.MailSupplier("BalloonShop stock check.",
          GetMailBody());
```

As before, you finish by auditing and updating the status, although this time you don't tell the order processor to continue straight away:

```
    // audit
    orderProcessor.CreateAudit(
      "Notification e-mail sent to supplier.", 20202);
    // update order status
    orderProcessor.Order.UpdateStatus(3);
  }
  catch
  {
    // mail sending failure
    throw new OrderProcessorException(
      "Unable to send e-mail to supplier.", 2);
  }
  // audit
  processor.CreateAudit("PSCheckStock finished.", 20201);
}
```

The code for building the message body is simple; it just lists the items in the order and tells the supplier to confirm via the BalloonShop web site (using the order administration page AdminOrders.aspx, which you'll modify later):

```
private string GetMailBody()
{
  // construct message body
  string mail =
    "The following goods have been ordered:\n\n"
    + orderProcessor.Order.OrderAsString
    + "\n\nPlease check availability and confirm via "
    + "http://www.example.com/AdminOrders.aspx"
    + "\n\nOrder reference number:\n\n"
    + orderProcessor.Order.OrderID.ToString();
  return mail;
  }
 }
}
```

Note that the URL used here isn't a real one—you should replace it with a URL of your own. When this pipeline stage finishes, processing pauses. Later, when the supplier confirms that stock is available, processing moves on to PSStockOK.

The PSStockOK Class

The PSStockOK pipeline section doesn't do much at all. It just confirms that the supplier has the product in stock and moves on. Its real purpose is to look for orders that have a status corresponding to this pipeline section and know that they are currently awaiting stock confirmation.

```
namespace CommerceLib
{
  /// <summary>
  /// Summary description for PSStockOK
  /// </summary>
  public class PSStockOK : IPipelineSection
  {
    private OrderProcessor orderProcessor;

    public void Process(OrderProcessor processor)
    {
      // set processor reference
      orderProcessor = processor;
      // audit
      orderProcessor.CreateAudit("PSStockOK started.", 20300);
      // the method is called when the supplier confirms that stock is
      // available, so we don't have to do anything here except audit
      orderProcessor.CreateAudit("Stock confirmed by supplier.",
        20302);
      // update order status
      orderProcessor.Order.UpdateStatus(4);
      // continue processing
      orderProcessor.ContinueNow = true;
      // audit
      processor.CreateAudit("PSStockOK finished.", 20301);
    }
  }
}
```

When this pipeline stage finishes, processing moves straight on to PSTakePayment.

The PSTakePayment Class

The PSTakePayment pipeline section completes the transaction started by PSCheckFunds. As with that section, you only provide a dummy implementation here.

```
namespace CommerceLib
{
  /// <summary>
  /// 5th pipeline stage - takes funds from customer
  /// </summary>
  public class PSTakePayment : IPipelineSection
  {
    private OrderProcessor orderProcessor;


    public void Process(OrderProcessor processor)
    {
```

```
      // set processor reference
      orderProcessor = processor;
      // audit
      orderProcessor.CreateAudit("PSTakePayment started.", 20400);
      try
      {
        // take customer funds
        // assume success for now
        // audit
        orderProcessor.CreateAudit(
          "Funds deducted from customer credit card account.", 20402);
        // update order status
        orderProcessor.Order.UpdateStatus(5);
        // continue processing
        orderProcessor.ContinueNow = true;
      }
      catch
      {
        // fund checking failure
        throw new OrderProcessorException(
          "Error occured while taking payment.", 4);
      }
      // audit
      processor.CreateAudit("PSTakePayment finished.", 20401);
    }
  }
}
```

When this pipeline stage finishes, processing moves straight on to PSShipGoods.

The PSShipGoods Class

The PSShipGoods pipeline section is remarkably similar to PSCheckStock, because it sends an email to the supplier and stops the pipeline until the supplier has confirmed that stock has shipped. This operation should not be combined with PSCheckStock because after you've checked that the goods are in stock, you need to take payment before shipping the goods.

```
namespace CommerceLib
{
  /// <summary>
  /// 6th pipeline stage - used to send a notification email to
  /// the supplier, stating that goods can be shipped
  /// </summary>

  public class PSShipGoods : IPipelineSection
  {
    private OrderProcessor orderProcessor;
```

```
public void Process(OrderProcessor processor)
{
  // set processor reference
  orderProcessor = processor;
  // audit
  orderProcessor.CreateAudit("PSShipGoods started.", 20500);
  try
  {
    // send mail to supplier
    orderProcessor.MailSupplier("BalloonShop ship goods.",
      GetMailBody());
    // audit
    orderProcessor.CreateAudit(
      "Ship goods e-mail sent to supplier.", 20502);
    // update order status
    orderProcessor.Order.UpdateStatus(6);
  }
  catch
  {
    // mail sending failure
    throw new OrderProcessorException(
      "Unable to send e-mail to supplier.", 5);
  }
  // audit
  processor.CreateAudit("PSShipGoods finished.", 20501);
}
```

As before, a private method called GetMailBody is used to build the message body for the
email sent to the supplier:

```
private string GetMailBody()
{
  // construct message body
  string mail =
    "Payment has been received for the following goods:\n\n"
    + orderProcessor.Order.OrderAsString
    + "\n\nPlease ship to:\n\n"
    + orderProcessor.Order.CustomerAddressAsString
    + "\n\nWhen goods have been shipped, please confirm via "
    + "http://www.example.com/AdminOrders.aspx"
    + "\n\nOrder reference number:\n\n"
    + orderProcessor.Order.OrderID.ToString();
  return mail;
  }
 }
}
```

Again, the URL used here isn't a real one. When this pipeline stage finishes, processing pauses. Later, when the supplier confirms that the order has been shipped, processing moves on to PSShipOK.

The PSShipOK Class

The PSShipOK pipeline section is very similar to PSStockOK, although it has slightly more to do. Because you know that items have shipped, a shipment date value can be added to the Orders table. Technically, this isn't really necessary, because all audit entries are dated. However, this method ensures that all the information is easily accessible in one database table.

```
namespace CommerceLib
{
  /// <summary>
  /// 7th pipeline stage - after confirmation that supplier has
  /// shipped goods
  /// </summary>
  public class PSShipOK : IPipelineSection
  {
    private OrderProcessor orderProcessor;

    public void Process(OrderProcessor processor)
    {
      // set processor reference
      orderProcessor = processor;
      // audit
      orderProcessor.CreateAudit("PSShipOK started.", 20600);
      // set order shipment date
      orderProcessor.Order.SetDateShipped();
      // audit
      orderProcessor.CreateAudit("Order dispatched by supplier.", 20602);
      // update order status
      orderProcessor.Order.UpdateStatus(7);
      // continue processing
      orderProcessor.ContinueNow = true;
      // audit
      processor.CreateAudit("PSShipOK finished.", 20601);
    }
  }
}
```

When this pipeline stage finishes, processing moves straight on to PSFinalNotification.

The PSFinalNotification Class

The last pipeline section—PSFinalNotification—is very similar to the first, in that it sends email to the customer. This section confirms that the order has shipped:

```
namespace CommerceLib
{
  /// <summary>
  /// 8th pipeline stage - used to send a notification email to
  /// the customer, confirming that the order has been shipped
  /// </summary>
  public class PSFinalNotification : IPipelineSection
  {
    private OrderProcessor orderProcessor;

    public void Process(OrderProcessor processor)
    {
      // set processor reference
      orderProcessor = processor;
      // audit
      orderProcessor.CreateAudit("PSFinalNotification started.",
        20700);
      try
      {
        // send mail to customer
        orderProcessor.MailCustomer("BalloonShop order dispatched.",
          GetMailBody());
        // audit
        orderProcessor.CreateAudit(
          "Dispatch e-mail sent to customer.", 20702);
        // update order status
        orderProcessor.Order.UpdateStatus(8);
      }
      catch
      {
        // mail sending failure
        throw new OrderProcessorException(
          "Unable to send e-mail to customer.", 7);
      }
      // audit
      processor.CreateAudit("PSFinalNotification finished.", 20701);
    }
```

It uses a familiar-looking GetMailBody method to build the body of the email:

```
private string GetMailBody()
{
  // construct message body
  string mail =
      "Your order has now been dispatched! The following "
    + "products have been shipped:\n\n"
    + orderProcessor.Order.OrderAsString
    + "\n\nYour order has been shipped to:\n\n"
```

```
          + orderProcessor.Order.CustomerAddressAsString
          + "\n\nOrder reference number:\n\n"
          + orderProcessor.Order.OrderID.ToString()
          + "\n\nThank you for shopping at BalloonShop!";
      return mail;
    }
  }
}
```

When this pipeline section finishes, the order status is changed to 8, which represents a completed order. Further attempts to process the order using OrderProcessor result in an exception being thrown.

The GetCurrentPipelineSection Method

There's one more thing to add to OrderProcessor now that you have the proper pipeline section classes—a full implementation of GetCurrentPipelineSection. Modify your GetCurrentPipelineSection method in OrderProcessor like this:

```
private void GetCurrentPipelineSection()
{
  // select pipeline section to execute based on order status
  switch (Order.Status)
  {
    case 0:
      CurrentPipelineSection = new PSInitialNotification();
      break;
    case 1:
      CurrentPipelineSection = new PSCheckFunds();
      break;
    case 2:
      CurrentPipelineSection = new PSCheckStock();
      break;
    case 3:
      CurrentPipelineSection = new PSStockOK();
      break;
    case 4:
      CurrentPipelineSection = new PSTakePayment();
      break;

    case 5:
      CurrentPipelineSection = new PSShipGoods();
      break;
    case 6:
      CurrentPipelineSection = new PSShipOK();
      break;
```

```
      case 7:
        CurrentPipelineSection = new PSFinalNotification();
        break;
      case 8:
        throw new OrderProcessorException(
          "Order has already been completed.", 100);
      default:
        throw new OrderProcessorException(
          "Unknown pipeline section requested.", 100);
    }
  }
```

This method simply consists of a large `switch` statement that selects a pipeline section to execute based on the status of the order being processed.

Presentation Tier Modifications

In a little while, you'll be implementing a new order admin system, allowing suppliers to mark orders as "in stock" or "shipped." Before that, however, you can check that things are working okay by providing a new test page. In fact, you can simply modify the `OrderTest.aspx` page you used earlier in the book. You'll do this in the following exercise and then we'll analyze the results.

Exercise: Testing the Order Pipeline

1. Modify the code in `OrderTest.aspx` to add new user interface items by adding the highlighted code:

```
...
<strong>Order details:</strong>
<br />
<asp:Label runat="server" ID="orderLabel" />
<asp:Label runat="server" ID="orderLabel" />
<br /><br />
<strong>Process order:</strong>
<br />
<asp:Button ID="processButton" runat="server" Text="Go"
  Enabled="False" OnClick="processButton_Click" />
<br />
<asp:Label ID="processResultLabel" runat="server" />
</asp:Content>
```

2. Modify the code for `goButton_Click` in `OrderTest.aspx.cs` as follows:

```
using CommerceLib;

...
```

```csharp
protected void goButton_Click(object sender, EventArgs e)
{
  try
  {
    CommerceLibOrderInfo orderInfo =
      CommerceLibAccess.GetOrder(orderIDBox.Text);
    resultLabel.Text = "Order found.";
    addressLabel.Text =
      orderInfo.CustomerAddressAsString.Replace("\n", "<br />");
    creditCardLabel.Text = orderInfo.CreditCard.CardNumberX;
    orderLabel.Text = orderInfo.OrderAsString.Replace("\n", "<br />");
    processButton.Enabled = true;
    processResultLabel.Text = "";
  }
  catch
  {
    resultLabel.Text = "No order found, or order is in old format.";
    addressLabel.Text = "";
    creditCardLabel.Text = "";
    orderLabel.Text = "";
    processButton.Enabled = false;
  }
}
```

3. Add a new click handler for the processButton button in OrderTest.aspx.cs as follows:

```csharp
protected void processButton_Click(object sender, EventArgs e)
{
  try
  {
    OrderProcessor processor = new OrderProcessor(orderIDBox.Text);
    processor.Process();
    CommerceLibOrderInfo orderInfo =
      CommerceLibAccess.GetOrder(orderIDBox.Text);
    processResultLabel.Text = "Order processed, status now: "
      + orderInfo.Status.ToString();
  }

  catch
  {
    CommerceLibOrderInfo orderInfo =
      CommerceLibAccess.GetOrder(orderIDBox.Text);
    processResultLabel.Text =
      "Order processing error, status now: "
      + orderInfo.Status.ToString();
  }
}
```

4. Save the new files, log in, browse to the OrderTest.aspx page, select an existing order by its ID, and then click the button to process the first phase of the order.

5. Check your (customer account) mail for the customer notification email. An example is shown here:

```
Payment has been received for the following goods:

1 Toy Story, $12.99 each, total cost $12.99
1 Mickey Close-up, $12.99 each, total cost $12.99
Shipping: By Air (10 days, $35)

Total order cost: $60.98

Please ship to:

Charles Darwin
2nd Hut On The Left
The Beach
The Island
Santa Cruz

The Galapagos Islands

When goods have been shipped, please confirm via
http://www.example.com/AdminOrders.aspx

Order reference number:

34
```

6. Check your (administrator) mail for the stock check email (as shown next).

```
The following goods have been ordered:

1 Toy Story, $12.99 each, total cost $12.99
1 Mickey Close-up, $12.99 each, total cost $12.99
Shipping: By Air (10 days, $35)

Total order cost: $60.98

Please check availability and confirm via
http://www.example.com/AdminOrders.aspx

Order reference number:

34
```

7. Continue processing on the OrderTest.aspx page by clicking the button again, calling OrderProcessor. Process for the second time.

8. Check your mail for the ship goods email:

Payment has been received for the following goods:

1 Toy Story, $12.99 each, total cost $12.99
1 Mickey Close-up, $12.99 each, total cost $12.99
Shipping: By Air (10 days, $35)

Total order cost: $60.98

Please ship to:

Charles Darwin
2nd Hut On The Left
The Beach
The Island
Santa Cruz

The Galapagos Islands

When goods have been shipped, please confirm via
http://www.example.com/AdminOrders.aspx

Order reference number:

34

9. Continue processing on the `OrderTest.aspx` page by clicking the button again, calling `OrderProcessor.`
`Process` for the third time.

10. Check your mail for the shipping confirmation email:

Your order has now been dispatched! The following products have been shipped:

1 Toy Story, $12.99 each, total cost $12.99
1 Mickey Close-up, $12.99 each, total cost $12.99
Shipping: By Air (10 days, $35)

Total order cost: $60.98

Your order has been shipped to:

Charles Darwin
2nd Hut On The Left
The Beach
The Island
Santa Cruz

The Galapagos Islands

Order reference number:

34

Thank you for shopping at BalloonShop!

11. Examine the new audit entries for the order (see Figure 19-1).

	AuditID	OrderID	DateStamp	Message	MessageNumber
1	91	34	2009-01-31 23:15:28.960	Order Processor started.	10000
2	92	34	2009-01-31 23:15:28.960	PSInitialNotification started.	20000
3	93	34	2009-01-31 23:15:32.780	Notification e-mail sent to customer.	20002
4	94	34	2009-01-31 23:15:32.780	PSInitialNotification finished.	20001
5	95	34	2009-01-31 23:15:32.780	PSCheckFunds started.	20100
6	96	34	2009-01-31 23:15:32.780	Funds available for purchase.	20102
7	97	34	2009-01-31 23:15:32.780	PSCheckFunds finished.	20101
8	98	34	2009-01-31 23:15:32.840	PSCheckStock started.	20200
9	99	34	2009-01-31 23:15:35.510	Notification e-mail sent to supplier.	20202
10	100	34	2009-01-31 23:15:35.510	PSCheckStock finished.	20201
11	101	34	2009-01-31 23:15:35.510	Order Processor finished.	10001
12	102	34	2009-01-31 23:16:19.330	Order Processor started.	10000
13	103	34	2009-01-31 23:16:19.330	PSStockOK started.	20300
14	104	34	2009-01-31 23:16:19.330	Stock confirmed by supplier.	20302
15	105	34	2009-01-31 23:16:19.330	PSStockOK finished.	20301
16	106	34	2009-01-31 23:16:19.347	PSTakePayment started.	20400
17	107	34	2009-01-31 23:16:19.347	Funds deducted from customer credit card account.	20402
18	108	34	2009-01-31 23:16:19.347	PSTakePayment finished.	20401
19	109	34	2009-01-31 23:16:19.347	PSShipGoods started.	20500
20	110	34	2009-01-31 23:16:36.247	Ship goods e-mail sent to supplier.	20502
21	111	34	2009-01-31 23:16:36.263	PSShipGoods finished.	20501
22	112	34	2009-01-31 23:16:36.263	Order Processor finished.	10001
23	113	34	2009-01-31 23:17:07.093	Order Processor started.	10000
24	114	34	2009-01-31 23:17:07.093	PSShipOK started.	20600
25	115	34	2009-01-31 23:17:07.093	Order dispatched by supplier.	20602
26	116	34	2009-01-31 23:17:07.093	PSShipOK finished.	20601
27	117	34	2009-01-31 23:17:07.093	PSFinalNotification started.	20700
28	118	34	2009-01-31 23:17:39.230	Dispatch e-mail sent to customer.	20702
29	119	34	2009-01-31 23:17:39.230	PSFinalNotification finished.	20701
30	120	34	2009-01-31 23:17:39.230	Order Processor finished.	10001

Figure 19-1. *Audit entries for the completed order*

How It Works: Testing the Order Pipeline

The example code tested your order pipeline by causing a single order to be processed by each pipeline section in turn, and providing the expected results. The modifications to the OrderTest.aspx page and code behind provided a button that simply called the OrderProcessor.Process method on the order being viewed. The other modifications to the code were to enable or disable the processing button depending on whether an order is being viewed.

One interesting point to note is what happens if you continue to try to process an order after it has been completed. The result of clicking the processing button again is shown in Figure 19-2.

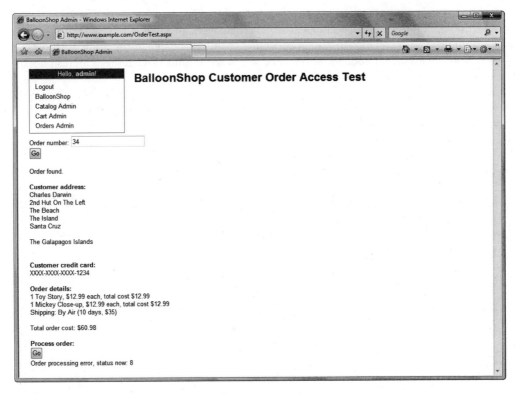

Figure 19-2. *Order completed error*

If you check your mail, you'll see the details:

```
Message: Order has already been completed.
Source: 100
Order ID: 34
```

The error message mailed to the administrator should be enough to get started in detective work, finding out what has happened.

Administering BalloonShop Orders

The current order administration page, implemented in `AdminOrders.aspx` and `AdminUserControls\AdminOrderDetails.aspx`, is no longer applicable to your order system. Now you have new data to handle, new functionality required for suppliers, and an audit trail to display.

This means you need to make several modifications. You'll start, as usual, with the database modifications, which require several new stored procedures. Moving on to the business tier, you'll need to update several methods and add several more to give access to the new stored procedures and allow the presentation tier to obtain and update data. Finally, in the presentation tier, you'll need to update the files responsible for order administration.

Note that your new data structures mean that customer-related information, including the customer name, email address, and postal address, are no longer editable by administrators. It would be possible to do this, but because customers can edit that information themselves, we won't implement it here. In fact, at some point, it might be nice to add a customer administration page, usable by administrators, to check on customer activity and edit customer accounts. We'll leave this task to you because by the end of this book, you'll be familiar with all the necessary techniques.

Database Modifications

As noted, the required additions here are all stored procedures. In addition, they all start with the string CommerceLib to distinguish them from earlier additions. This is especially necessary as many of these stored procedures (and the business tier methods that use them) will replace or upgrade existing functionality.

The CommerceLibOrderGetAuditTrail Stored Procedure

This stored procedure gets the Audit table entries that are associated with a given order:

```
CREATE PROCEDURE CommerceLibOrderGetAuditTrail
(@OrderID int)
AS
SELECT OrderID,
       AuditID,
       DateStamp,
       Message,
       MessageNumber
FROM Audit
WHERE OrderID = @OrderID
```

The CommerceLibOrdersGetByCustomer Stored Procedure

This stored procedure gets the orders that have been made by a specific customer by using the GUID that identifies a customer:

```
CREATE PROCEDURE CommerceLibOrdersGetByCustomer
(@CustomerID uniqueidentifier)
AS
SELECT OrderID,
       DateCreated,
       DateShipped,
       Comments,
       Status,
       CustomerID,
       AuthCode,
       Reference,
       Orders.ShippingID,
```

```
            ShippingType,
            ShippingCost,
            Orders.TaxID,
            TaxType,
            TaxPercentage
FROM Orders
LEFT OUTER JOIN Tax ON Tax.TaxID = Orders.TaxID
LEFT OUTER JOIN Shipping ON Shipping.ShippingID = Orders.ShippingID
WHERE CustomerID = @CustomerID
```

The CommerceLibOrdersGetByDate Stored Procedure

This stored procedure mirrors the OrdersGetByDate stored procedure used earlier in the book. As with that stored procedure, this one gets the orders that were placed between two dates. The difference here is that different data is returned:

```
CREATE PROCEDURE CommerceLibOrdersGetByDate
(@StartDate smalldatetime,
 @EndDate smalldatetime)
AS

SELECT OrderID,
        DateCreated,
        DateShipped,
        Comments,
        Status,
        CustomerID,
        AuthCode,
        Reference,
        Orders.ShippingID,
        ShippingType,
        ShippingCost,
        Orders.TaxID,
        TaxType,
        TaxPercentage

FROM Orders
LEFT OUTER JOIN Tax ON Tax.TaxID = Orders.TaxID
LEFT OUTER JOIN Shipping ON Shipping.ShippingID = Orders.ShippingID
WHERE DateCreated BETWEEN @StartDate AND @EndDate
ORDER BY DateCreated DESC
```

The CommerceLibOrdersGetByRecent Stored Procedure

This stored procedure replaces the OrdersGetByRecent stored procedure. It obtains the most recent orders that have been placed, where the number of orders to return is selected by a parameter:

```
CREATE PROCEDURE CommerceLibOrdersGetByRecent
(@Count smallint)
AS

SET ROWCOUNT @Count

SELECT OrderID,
       DateCreated,
       DateShipped,
       Comments,
       Status,
       CustomerID,
       AuthCode,
       Reference,
       Orders.ShippingID,
       ShippingType,
       ShippingCost,
       Orders.TaxID,
       TaxType,
       TaxPercentage
FROM Orders
LEFT OUTER JOIN Tax ON Tax.TaxID = Orders.TaxID
LEFT OUTER JOIN Shipping ON Shipping.ShippingID = Orders.ShippingID
ORDER BY DateCreated DESC

SET ROWCOUNT 0
```

The CommerceLibOrdersGetByStatus Stored Procedure

Again, this stored procedure is a replacement. However, this time the new stored procedure replaces two earlier ones: OrdersGetUnverifiedUncanceled and OrdersGetVerifiedUncompleted. Because this information is now represented by a single status field, you can provide a single, more versatile stored procedure:

```
CREATE PROCEDURE CommerceLibOrdersGetByStatus
(@Status int)
AS
SELECT OrderID,
       DateCreated,
       DateShipped,
       Comments,
       Status,
       CustomerID,
       AuthCode,
       Reference,
       Orders.ShippingID,
       ShippingType,
       ShippingCost,
```

```
        Orders.TaxID,
        TaxType,
        TaxPercentage
FROM Orders
LEFT OUTER JOIN Tax ON Tax.TaxID = Orders.TaxID
LEFT OUTER JOIN Shipping ON Shipping.ShippingID = Orders.ShippingID
WHERE Status = @Status
```

The CommerceLibOrderUpdate Stored Procedure

Finally, this stored procedure replaces the OrderUpdate stored procedure used earlier, making use of your new data:

```
CREATE PROCEDURE CommerceLibOrderUpdate
(@OrderID int,
 @DateCreated smalldatetime,
 @DateShipped smalldatetime = NULL,
 @Status int,
 @Comments varchar(200),
 @AuthCode varchar(50),
 @Reference varchar(50))
AS
UPDATE Orders
SET DateCreated=@DateCreated,
    DateShipped=@DateShipped,
    Status=@Status,
    Comments=@Comments,
    AuthCode=@AuthCode,
    Reference=@Reference
WHERE OrderID = @OrderID
```

Business Tier Modifications

The modifications in this section apply mainly to the CommerceLibAccess and CommerceLibOrderInfo classes. However, to give easy access to audit trail info, you also need to add a new class, called (surprisingly enough) CommerceLibAuditInfo.

Apart from allowing access to your new data, you have one more thing to add, which you'll do first. You need to provide a human-readable version of order statuses, which you'll use later to display information in the order admin page.

Adding Human-Readable Status Information

You can store order status strings in any number of places. One option is to store them in the database, perhaps in a table called Status. You could then link to the Orders table by matching the existing Orders.Status field to, say, Status.StatusID.

However, it's reasonable to regard status information as static. Although the Orders table is capable of containing any integer for an order status, the CommerceLib code uses order status information in a more formal way. The statuses that exist, in fact, are a consequence of the pipeline structure we've chosen, which is independent of the database. For this reason, you should include status information in your code.

You could store human-readable status strings in web.config, in an external resource file (useful for multilingual sites), or anywhere else you choose. In this chapter, you'll put this information in a static read-only string array in the CommerceLibAccess class, where you can access it from wherever you choose. The indexes of the entries in the array match the status values that are used in your order pipeline. Add the following member to the CommerceLibAccess class, in CommerceLibAccess.cs:

```
public class CommerceLibAccess
{
  public static readonly string[] OrderStatuses =
    {"Order placed, notifying customer", // 0
    "Awaiting confirmation of funds",    // 1
    "Notifying supplier-stock check",    // 2
    "Awaiting stock confirmation",       // 3
    "Awaiting credit card payment",      // 4
    "Notifying supplier-shipping",       // 5
    "Awaiting shipment confirmation",    // 6
    "Sending final notification",        // 7
    "Order completed",                   // 8
    "Order canceled"};                   // 9
...
```

Note the one new status here—Order canceled, with a value of 9—for when you want to cancel a customer order.

For the purposes of data binding to the CommerceLibOrderInfo class, you also provide a new public property to expose order statuses as strings. Add the following members to CommerceLibOrderInfo:

```
public string StatusAsString
{
  get
  {
    try
    {
      return CommerceLibAccess.OrderStatuses[Status];
    }
    catch
    {
      return "Status unknown";
    }
  }
}
public string CustomerName
{
```

```
  get
  {
    return Customer.UserName;
  }
}
```

The CommerceLibAuditInfo Class

You'll expose audit trail data via this new class, which is very similar to (although simpler than) the CommerceLibOrderInfo and CommerceLibOrderDetailInfo classes added earlier. As with these classes, you can add CommerceLibAuditInfo to the CommerceLibAccess.cs file:

```
/// <summary>
/// Wraps audit trail data
/// </summary>
public class CommerceLibAuditInfo
{
  public int AuditID { get; private set; }
  public int OrderID { get; private set; }
  public DateTime DateStamp { get; private set; }
  public string Message { get; private set; }
  public int MessageNumber { get; private set; }

  public CommerceLibAuditInfo(DataRow auditRow)
  {
    AuditID = (int)auditRow["AuditID"];
    OrderID = (int)auditRow["OrderID"];
    DateStamp = (DateTime)auditRow["DateStamp"];
    Message = auditRow["Message"] as string;
    MessageNumber = (int)auditRow["messageNumber"];
  }
}
```

■**Note** In this piece of code, we've used a new feature in C# 2008 named **automatic properties**, which allow writing property definitions using just a few lines of code.

The constructor of this class uses a DataRow object to initialize the class, so next you need a method to get the audit trail for an order.

The GetOrderAuditTrail Method

To get the audit trail for an order, you'll add a new method to CommerceLibAccess called GetOrderAuditTrail, which uses the ID of an order to get audit entries via the CommerceLibOrderGetAuditTrail stored procedure. Here you can use generic collections by returning audit information in the form of a List<CommerceLibAuditInfo> class.

Add the following method to CommerceLibAccess:

```
public static List<CommerceLibAuditInfo> GetOrderAuditTrail(
  string orderID)
{
  // get a configured DbCommand object
  DbCommand comm = GenericDataAccess.CreateCommand();
  // set the stored procedure name
  comm.CommandText = "CommerceLibOrderGetAuditTrail";
  // create a new parameter
  DbParameter param = comm.CreateParameter();
  param.ParameterName = "@OrderID";
  param.Value = orderID;
  param.DbType = DbType.Int32;
  comm.Parameters.Add(param);
  // obtain the results
  DataTable orderAuditTrailData =
    GenericDataAccess.ExecuteSelectCommand(comm);
  // create List<>
  List<CommerceLibAuditInfo> orderAuditTrail =
    new List<CommerceLibAuditInfo>(
    orderAuditTrailData.Rows.Count);
  foreach (DataRow orderAudit in orderAuditTrailData.Rows)
  {
    orderAuditTrail.Add(new CommerceLibAuditInfo(orderAudit));
  }
  return orderAuditTrail;
}
```

CommerceLibOrderInfo Modifications

To bind to a CommerceLibOrderInfo, you need to do one more thing. Unfortunately, data-bindable objects such as DataGrid don't work with public fields, only properties. This means that every one of the public fields in CommerceLibOrderInfo—for example OrderID—needs to be exposed via a property. For example

```
public int OrderID;
```

needs to be replaced with

```
private int orderID;
```

```
public int OrderID
{
  get
  {
    return orderID;
  }
```

```
  set
  {
    orderID = value;
  }
}
```

Or, using the C# 2008 syntax, this can also be written as

```
public int OrderID{get; set;}
```

Make this change to all the public fields in CommerceLibOrderInfo. Fortunately, the automatic properties feature in C# 2008 makes things easy:

```
public class CommerceLibOrderInfo
{
  public int OrderID { get; set; }
  public string DateCreated { get; set; }
  public string DateShipped { get; set; }
  public string Comments { get; set; }
  public int Status { get; set; }
  public string AuthCode { get; set; }
  public string Reference { get; set; }
  public MembershipUser Customer { get; set; }
  public ProfileCommon CustomerProfile { get; set; }
  public SecureCard CreditCard { get; set; }
  public double TotalCost { get; set; }
  public string OrderAsString { get; set; }
  public string CustomerAddressAsString { get; set; }
  public ShippingInfo Shipping { get; set; }
  public TaxInfo Tax { get; set; }
```

To make use of your new properties, you also need to transform ShippingInfo and Tax to a classes like this:

```
public class ShippingInfo
{
  public int ShippingID;
  public string ShippingType;
  public double ShippingCost;
  public int ShippingRegionId;
}

public class TaxInfo
{
  public int TaxID;
  public string TaxType;
  public double TaxPercentage;
}
```

Finally, modify the constructor of CommerceLibOrderInfo to create new instances of your ShippingInfo and Tax members:

```
public CommerceLibOrderInfo(DataRow orderRow)
{
  Shipping = new ShippingInfo();
  Tax = new TaxInfo();
```

CommerceLibOrderDetailInfo Modifications

As with CommerceLibOrderInfo, fields need to be upgraded to properties here:

```
public class CommerceLibOrderDetailInfo
{
  public int OrderID { get; set; }
  public int ProductID { get; set; }
  public string ProductName { get; set; }
  public int Quantity { get; set; }
  public double UnitCost { get; set; }
  public string ItemAsString { get; set; }
```

Exposing an Audit Trail via CommerceLibOrderInfo

The CommerceLibOrderInfo class is already versatile, as it exposes customer and order detail information on the fly. You can extend this class even further by allowing access to audit trail information directly. First, you need to add a new private field to CommerceLibOrderInfo to hold this data:

```
private List<CommerceLibAuditInfo> auditTrail;
```

Next, you need to give access to this field via a property. Here you can use a "lazy initialization" scheme and only load the audit trail when it's requested. When this happens, you use the new CommerceLibAccess.GetOrderAuditTrail method to obtain the audit trail data:

```
public List<CommerceLibAuditInfo> AuditTrail
{
  get
  {
    if (auditTrail == null)
    {
      auditTrail = CommerceLibAccess.GetOrderAuditTrail(
        OrderID.ToString());
    }
    return auditTrail;
  }
}
```

The ConvertDataTableToOrders Method

Next, you need to add several methods to CommerceLibAccess to let the order admin page obtain lists of CommerceLibOrderInfo objects by using various filters. In all cases, you can return this information in the form of a List<CommerceLibOrderInfo> generic collection. Because the generic GenericDataAccess.ExecuteSelectCommand method you use to get data returns a DataTable, it makes sense to provide a standard way to convert between these list types. Along the way, you can discard invalid or old data (such as existing orders from the code in the first part of this book).

Add the following method to CommerceLibAccess:

```
public static List<CommerceLibOrderInfo>
  ConvertDataTableToOrders(DataTable table)
{
  List<CommerceLibOrderInfo> orders =
    new List<CommerceLibOrderInfo>(table.Rows.Count);
  foreach (DataRow orderRow in table.Rows)
  {
    try
    {
      // try to add order
      orders.Add(new CommerceLibOrderInfo(orderRow));
    }
    catch
    {
      // can't add this order
    }
  }
  return orders;
}
```

The GetOrdersByCustomer Method

This is the first of the new CommerceLibAccess methods that will use the ConvertDataTableToOrders method added in the last section. In this case, the method passes the GUID ID of a customer to the CommerceLibOrdersGetByCustomer stored procedure and returns the resultant orders in the form of a List<CommerceLibOrderInfo> collection.

Add the following method to CommerceLibAccess:

```
public static List<CommerceLibOrderInfo> GetOrdersByCustomer(
  string customerID)
{
  // get a configured DbCommand object
  DbCommand comm = GenericDataAccess.CreateCommand();
  // set the stored procedure name
  comm.CommandText = "CommerceLibOrdersGetByCustomer";
```

```
    // create a new parameter
    DbParameter param = comm.CreateParameter();
    param.ParameterName = "@CustomerID";
    param.Value = new Guid(customerID);
    param.DbType = DbType.Guid;
    comm.Parameters.Add(param);
    // obtain the results
    return ConvertDataTableToOrders(
      GenericDataAccess.ExecuteSelectCommand(comm));
  }
```

The GetOrdersByDate Method

Similarly, this method uses the CommerceLibOrdersGetByDate stored procedure to get the orders between two dates.

Add the following method to CommerceLibAccess:

```
public static List<CommerceLibOrderInfo> GetOrdersByDate(
  string startDate, string endDate)
{
  // get a configured DbCommand object
  DbCommand comm = GenericDataAccess.CreateCommand();
  // set the stored procedure name
  comm.CommandText = "CommerceLibOrdersGetByDate";
  // create a new parameter
  DbParameter param = comm.CreateParameter();
  param.ParameterName = "@StartDate";
  param.Value = startDate;
  param.DbType = DbType.Date;
  comm.Parameters.Add(param);
  // create a new parameter
  param = comm.CreateParameter();
  param.ParameterName = "@EndDate";
  param.Value = endDate;
  param.DbType = DbType.Date;
  comm.Parameters.Add(param);
  // obtain the results
  return ConvertDataTableToOrders(
    GenericDataAccess.ExecuteSelectCommand(comm));
}
```

The GetOrdersByRecent Method

This method uses the CommerceLibOrdersGetByRecent stored procedure to get the most recently placed orders. The number of orders to return is determined by the count parameter.

Add the following method to CommerceLibAccess:

```
public static List<CommerceLibOrderInfo> GetOrdersByRecent(
  int count)
{
  // get a configured DbCommand object
  DbCommand comm = GenericDataAccess.CreateCommand();

  // set the stored procedure name
  comm.CommandText = "CommerceLibOrdersGetByRecent";
  // create a new parameter
  DbParameter param = comm.CreateParameter();
  param.ParameterName = "@Count";
  param.Value = count;
  param.DbType = DbType.Int32;
  comm.Parameters.Add(param);
  // obtain the results
  return ConvertDataTableToOrders(
    GenericDataAccess.ExecuteSelectCommand(comm));
}
```

The GetOrdersByStatus Method

The last order-obtaining stored procedure to use is CommerceLibOrdersGetByStatus.
    Add the following method to CommerceLibAccess:

```
public static List<CommerceLibOrderInfo> GetOrdersByStatus(
  int status)
{
  // get a configured DbCommand object
  DbCommand comm = GenericDataAccess.CreateCommand();
  // set the stored procedure name
  comm.CommandText = "CommerceLibOrdersGetByStatus";
  // create a new parameter
  DbParameter param = comm.CreateParameter();
  param.ParameterName = "@Status";
  param.Value = status;
  param.DbType = DbType.Int32;
  comm.Parameters.Add(param);
  // obtain the results
  return ConvertDataTableToOrders(
    GenericDataAccess.ExecuteSelectCommand(comm));
}
```

The UpdateOrder Method

The last business tier addition to make is a method for updating orders. Previously you've
achieved this using the OrderAccess.Update method, which used an OrderInfo struct parameter to
specify the data to update. Now you have a more "active" representation of order data, namely

CommerceLibOrderInfo, so this is no longer a suitable option. Instead, you'll simply have a parameter for each field you want to update.

Add the following method to CommerceLibAccess:

```
public static void UpdateOrder(int orderID,
  string newDateCreated, string newDateShipped,
  int newStatus, string newAuthCode, string newReference,
  string newComments)
{
  // get a configured DbCommand object
  DbCommand comm = GenericDataAccess.CreateCommand();
  // set the stored procedure name
  comm.CommandText = "CommerceLibOrderUpdate";
  // create a new parameter
  DbParameter param = comm.CreateParameter();
  param.ParameterName = "@OrderID";
  param.Value = orderID;
  param.DbType = DbType.Int32;
  comm.Parameters.Add(param);
  // create a new parameter
  param = comm.CreateParameter();
  param.ParameterName = "@DateCreated";
  param.Value = DateTime.Parse(newDateCreated);
  param.DbType = DbType.DateTime;
  comm.Parameters.Add(param);
  // The DateShipped parameter is sent only if data is available
  if (newDateShipped != null && newDateShipped != "")
  {
    param = comm.CreateParameter();
    param.ParameterName = "@DateShipped";
    param.Value = DateTime.Parse(newDateShipped);
    param.DbType = DbType.DateTime;
    comm.Parameters.Add(param);
  }
  // create a new parameter
  param = comm.CreateParameter();
  param.ParameterName = "@Status";
  param.Value = newStatus;
  param.DbType = DbType.Int32;
  comm.Parameters.Add(param);
  // create a new parameter
  param = comm.CreateParameter();
  param.ParameterName = "@AuthCode";
  param.Value = newAuthCode;
  param.DbType = DbType.String;
  comm.Parameters.Add(param);
  // create a new parameter
  param = comm.CreateParameter();
```

```
param.ParameterName = "@Reference";
param.Value = newReference;
param.DbType = DbType.String;
comm.Parameters.Add(param);
// create a new parameter
param = comm.CreateParameter();
param.ParameterName = "@Comments";
param.Value = newComments;
param.DbType = DbType.String;
comm.Parameters.Add(param);
// update the order
GenericDataAccess.ExecuteNonQuery(comm);
}
```

One point to note here concerns the newDateShipped parameter, which is an instance of a string, but might be null. Here you can use the HasValue property to see if a value has been supplied and must also use the Value parameter to pass a value to the SQL parameter, because this expects a plain DateTime value.

Presentation Tier Modifications

As noted earlier, to tie in to the new order information, you need to modify both AdminOrders. aspx and AdminOrderDetails.aspx. The modifications vary between fairly major and quite subtle, because you'll be using roughly the same look and feel.

Modifying the AdminOrders.aspx Page

This page could be modified in all manner of ways to achieve the new functionality you want. In some setups, it might be better not to use this page at all, but rather implement this functionality as a Windows Forms application. This may be appropriate, for example, if your suppliers are in-house and on the same network. Alternatively, it might be better to combine this Windows Forms approach with web services.

Whichever method you choose, the basic functionality is the same: Suppliers and administrators should be able to view a list of orders that need attention and edit them or advance them in the pipeline manually. This is simply a case of calling the OrderProcess.Process method as described earlier.

To simplify things in this section, you'll use the same page for both administrators and suppliers. This might not be ideal in all situations, because you might not want to expose all order details and audit information to external suppliers. However, for demonstration purposes, this reduces the amount of code you have to get through. In a more advanced setup, you could provide a new Suppliers role in the existing security setup and restrict the functionality of this page accordingly.

As a starting point, you'll take the existing AdminOrders.aspx code and rewrite it to provide the functionality required. In fact, you can simplify the code slightly to achieve this, because you won't need to update order data as completely as you did before.

The first thing to change is the list of filters that can be used to obtain orders. Specifically, you'll add two new ones for obtaining orders by customer or by ID, and replace the filters for "unverified, uncanceled" and "verified, uncompleted" orders. The two replacements will be for supplier use—to display orders awaiting stock or shipment.

The most interesting new addition here is the filter for orders by customer. You'll simplify things here by providing a drop-down selection of customer names, which you can obtain (along with IDs) from your user database. You can set up a connection to this database by dragging a SqlDataSource control (call it CustomerNameDS) onto the existing AdminOrders.aspx form and following the wizard steps. The exact process for doing this varies depending on your configuration, but the important thing is to use the following SQL query when requested:

```
SELECT vw_aspnet_Users.UserName, vw_aspnet_Users.UserId
  FROM vw_aspnet_Users
  INNER JOIN aspnet_UsersInRoles
  ON vw_aspnet_Users.UserId = aspnet_UsersInRoles.UserId
  INNER JOIN aspnet_Roles
  ON aspnet_UsersInRoles.RoleId = aspnet_Roles.RoleId
  WHERE (aspnet_Roles.RoleName = 'Customers')
```

You'll likely be prompted to save the connection string along the way, which is a sensible thing to do in case you want to use this database again in the future. You'll end up with code similar to the following:

```
<asp:SqlDataSource ID="CustomerNameDS" runat="server"
  ConnectionString=
  "<%$ ConnectionStrings:BalloonShopConnection %>"
  SelectCommand="SELECT vw_aspnet_Users.UserName,
    vw_aspnet_Users.UserId FROM vw_aspnet_Users INNER JOIN
    aspnet_UsersInRoles ON vw_aspnet_Users.UserId =
    aspnet_UsersInRoles.UserId INNER JOIN aspnet_Roles ON
    aspnet_UsersInRoles.RoleId = aspnet_Roles.RoleId WHERE
    (aspnet_Roles.RoleName = 'Customers')" />
```

Next, replace the code in AdminOrders.aspx for the existing filters with the following:

```
Show orders by customer
<asp:DropDownList ID="userDropDown" runat="server"
  DataSourceID="CustomerNameDS" DataTextField="UserName"
  DataValueField="UserId" />
<asp:Button ID="byCustomerGo" runat="server"
  Text="Go" OnClick="byCustomerGo_Click" />
<br />
Get order by ID
<asp:TextBox ID="orderIDBox" runat="server" Width="77px" />
<asp:Button ID="byIDGo" runat="server" Text="Go" OnClick="byIDGo_Click" />
<br />
Show the most recent
<asp:TextBox ID="recentCountTextBox" runat="server" MaxLength="4"
  Width="40px">20</asp:TextBox>
```

```
orders
<asp:Button ID="byRecentGo" runat="server"
  Text="Go" OnClick="byRecentGo_Click" />
<br />
Show all orders created between
<asp:TextBox ID="startDateTextBox" runat="server" Width="72px" />
and
<asp:TextBox ID="endDateTextBox" runat="server" Width="72px" />
<asp:Button ID="byDateGo" runat="server"
  Text="Go" OnClick="byDateGo_Click" />
<br />
Show all orders awaiting stock check
<asp:Button ID="awaitingStockGo" runat="server"
  Text="Go" OnClick="awaitingStockGo_Click" />
<br />
Show all orders awaiting shipment
<asp:Button ID="awaitingShippingGo" runat="server"
  Text="Go" OnClick="awaitingShippingGo_Click" />
<br />
...
```

The next line after this code (indicated by the ellipsis) should be the errorLabel label. You can leave this label, and the validation controls that follow, as they are.

Note that the userDropDown control includes the UserId field as its DataValueField. The data for each item is therefore the GUID value that identifies a user, making data retrieval in the code behind very easy, as you'll see shortly.

Next, you need to change the columns in the grid control, the GridView that displays order information. You'll leave the styling unchanged, however. The modified set of columns is as follows:

```
<Columns>
  <asp:BoundField DataField="OrderID" HeaderText="Order ID"
    ReadOnly="True" SortExpression="OrderID" />
  <asp:BoundField DataField="DateCreated"
    HeaderText="Date Created" ReadOnly="True"
    SortExpression="DateCreated" />
  <asp:BoundField DataField="DateShipped"
    HeaderText="Date Shipped" ReadOnly="True"
    SortExpression="DateShipped" />
  <asp:BoundField DataField="StatusAsString" HeaderText="Status"
    ReadOnly="True" SortExpression="StatusAsString" />
  <asp:BoundField DataField="CustomerName"
    HeaderText="Customer Name" ReadOnly="True"
    SortExpression="CustomerName" />
  <asp:ButtonField CommandName="Select" Text="Select" />
</Columns>
```

Now we can move on to AdminOrders.aspx.cs. In fact, you can delete all the existing code apart from the grid_SelectedIndexChanged method. Then you need to supply one method for each Go button. You'll do this in the order they appear in the user interface, starting with the customer filter:

```
// Display orders by customer
protected void byCustomerGo_Click(object sender, EventArgs e)
{
  try
  {
    List<CommerceLibOrderInfo> orders =
      CommerceLibAccess.GetOrdersByCustomer(
      userDropDown.SelectedValue);
    grid.DataSource = orders;
    if (orders.Count == 0)
    {
      errorLabel.Text =
        "Selected customer has made no orders.";
    }
    grid.DataBind();
  }
  catch
  {
    errorLabel.Text = "Couldn't get the requested orders!";
  }
}
```

Here you get the necessary data with a single line of code. You simply call CommerceLibAccess. GetOrdersByCustomer, passing in the selected value from the userDropDown control added previously. Now you can see the benefit of storing the GUID that identifies users in the drop-down list control.

After you have a list of orders in the form of a List<CommerceLibOrderInfo> collection, you can simply bind that collection to grid. The generic collection classes are ideal for this sort of use.

There's also an additional piece of error-checking code here—a check to see if any orders have been returned. If any orders have been returned, you bind the data to the grid as usual (it won't be visible, so this is fine), but report the error via the errorLabel control. The errorLabel control is also used if an error occurs.

Next, we have the filter for a single order. This is necessary for suppliers who, as you may recall, receive an email including the order ID. This means that they can quickly jump to the order that requires their attention. The code is as follows:

```
// Display single order only
protected void byIDGo_Click(object sender, EventArgs e)
{
  string destination = String.Format("AdminOrderDetails.aspx?OrderID={0}",
    orderIDBox.Text);
  Response.Redirect(destination);
}
```

Note that a generic list is still used to bind to grid here. The only difference is that it will only ever contain a single item.

As a shortcut, the code in this method also stores the retrieved order information automatically. You may recall from earlier chapters that the AdminOrderDetails.aspx control uses a value stored in session state to bind to an order, so you simply set this value and make the control visible.

If an error occurs, you report it via errorLabel in the standard way.

The remainder of the new button click handler methods operate in much the same way. Each one calls one of the new methods of the CommerceLibAccess class to obtain a list of orders, and then binds that list to the grid control or displays an error. Next up is the method for obtaining recent orders:

```
// Display the most recent orders
protected void byRecentGo_Click(object sender, EventArgs e)
{
  try
  {
    int recordCount = Int32.Parse(recentCountTextBox.Text);
    List<CommerceLibOrderInfo> orders =
      CommerceLibAccess.GetOrdersByRecent(recordCount);
    grid.DataSource = orders;
    if (orders.Count == 0)
    {
      errorLabel.Text = "No orders to get.";
    }
    grid.DataBind();
  }
  catch
  {
    errorLabel.Text = "Couldn't get the requested orders!";
  }
}
```

Then we have the method for getting orders between two dates:

```
// Display orders that happened in a specified period of time
protected void byDateGo_Click(object sender, EventArgs e)
{
  try
  {
    string startDate = startDateTextBox.Text;
    string endDate = endDateTextBox.Text;
    List<CommerceLibOrderInfo> orders =
      CommerceLibAccess.GetOrdersByDate(startDate, endDate);
    grid.DataSource = orders;
```

```
      if (orders.Count == 0)
      {
        errorLabel.Text =
          "No orders between selected dates.";
      }
      grid.DataBind();
    }
    catch
    {
      errorLabel.Text = "Couldn't get the requested orders!";
    }
  }
```

And finally, we have two methods for getting orders that are either awaiting a stock check or shipment, both of which use CommerceLibAccess.GetOrdersByStatus:

```
// Display orders awaiting stock
protected void awaitingStockGo_Click(object sender, EventArgs e)
{
  try
  {
    List<CommerceLibOrderInfo> orders =
      CommerceLibAccess.GetOrdersByStatus(3);
    grid.DataSource = orders;
    if (orders.Count == 0)
    {
      errorLabel.Text = "No orders awaiting stock check.";
    }
    grid.DataBind();
  }
  catch
  {
    errorLabel.Text = "Couldn't get the requested orders!";
  }
}

// Display orders awaiting shipping
protected void awaitingShippingGo_Click(object sender, EventArgs e)
{
  try
  {
    List<CommerceLibOrderInfo> orders =
      CommerceLibAccess.GetOrdersByStatus(6);
    grid.DataSource = orders;
```

```
    if (orders.Count == 0)
    {
      errorLabel.Text = "No orders awaiting shipment.";
    }
    grid.DataBind();
  }
  catch
  {
    errorLabel.Text = "Couldn't get the requested orders!";
  }
}
```

The only differences between these two methods are the status code passed and the error messages possible.

Modifying the AdminOrderDetails Form

The other page to modify is AdminOrderDetails.aspx, which shows the details of an order. Earlier in the book, this control also included the capability to modify order data, but we're removing most of this functionality here, as mentioned earlier. We're also providing the capability for orders to be pushed along the pipeline when they are stuck at the Awaiting Confirmation of Stock and Awaiting Confirmation of Shipment stages. Finally, you'll add a second DataGrid control where audit trail data will be displayed.

Let's start by enabling the page ViewState, which will be necessary in the new code. You should remove the EnableViewState="false" bit from AdminOrderDetails.aspx:

```
<%@ Page Title="" Language="C#" MasterPageFile="~/Admin.master"
AutoEventWireup="true" CodeFile="AdminOrderDetails.aspx.cs"
Inherits="AdminOrderDetails" %>
```

Next, we modify the order information display table. This table needs to be modified as follows:

```
<asp:Content ID="Content2" ContentPlaceHolderID="adminPlaceHolder" runat="Server">
  <h2>
    <asp:Label ID="orderIdLabel" runat="server" CssClass="AdminTitle"
    Text="Order #000" />
  </h2>
  <span class="WideLabel">Total Amount:</span>
  <asp:Label ID="totalAmountLabel" runat="server" />
  <br />
  <span class="WideLabel">Date Created:</span>
  <asp:TextBox ID="dateCreatedTextBox" runat="server" Width="400px"
    enabled="false" />
  <br />
```

```
<span class="WideLabel">Date Shipped:</span>
<asp:TextBox ID="dateShippedTextBox" runat="server" Width="400px" />
<br />
<span class="WideLabel">Status:</span>
<asp:DropDownList ID="statusDropDown" runat="server" />
<br />
<span class="WideLabel">Auth Code:</span>
<asp:TextBox ID="authCodeTextBox" runat="server" Width="400px" />
<br />
<span class="WideLabel">Reference No:</span>
<asp:TextBox ID="referenceTextBox" runat="server" Width="400px" />
<br />
<span class="WideLabel">Comments:</span>
<asp:TextBox ID="commentsTextBox" runat="server" Width="400px" />
<br />
<span class="WideLabel">Customer Name:</span>
<asp:TextBox ID="customerNameTextBox" runat="server" Width="400px"
  enabled="false"  />
<br />
<span class="WideLabel">Shipping Address:</span>
<asp:TextBox ID="shippingAddressTextBox" runat="server" Width="400px"
  Height="200px" TextMode="MultiLine" enabled="false"  />
<br />
<span class="WideLabel">Shipping Type:</span>
<asp:TextBox ID="shippingTypeTextBox" runat="server" Width="400px"
  enabled="false" />
<br />
<span class="WideLabel">Customer Email:</span>
<asp:TextBox ID="customerEmailTextBox" runat="server" Width="400px"
  enabled="false"  />
```

Apart from the fields removed and the additional fields added, note that the order status is displayed in a DropDownList, and that the customer data fields have their enabled attribute set to false. This is because editing of this data is no longer allowed.

Next, the buttons beneath this table need replacing as follows:

```
<asp:Button ID="editButton" runat="server"
  Text="Edit" Width="100px" OnClick="editButton_Click" />
<asp:Button ID="updateButton" runat="server"
  Text="Update" Width="100px" OnClick="updateButton_Click" />
<asp:Button ID="cancelButton" runat="server"
  Text="Cancel" Width="100px" OnClick="cancelButton_Click" />
<br />
<asp:Button ID="processOrderButton" runat="server"
  Text="Process Order" Width="310px"
  OnClick="processOrderButton_Click" />
<br />
```

```
<asp:Button ID="cancelOrderButton" runat="server"
  Text="Cancel Order" Width="310px"
  OnClick="cancelOrderButton_Click" />
```

The buttons for marking the order as verified or completed are replaced with a single button for processing the order. You'll change the text on this button as appropriate, because you can also use it when suppliers are checking stock or shipping orders. The cancel order button has also changed slightly, in keeping with the new scheme.

Finally, you need to add a new GridView for the audit trail, using the same style as the GridView for order details:

```
<asp:Label ID="Label1" runat="server" CssClass="AdminPageText"
  Text="Order audit trail:" />
<br />
<asp:GridView ID="auditGrid" runat="server"
  AutoGenerateColumns="False" BackColor="White"
  BorderColor="#E7E7FF" BorderStyle="None" BorderWidth="1px"
  CellPadding="3" GridLines="Horizontal" Width="100%">
  <FooterStyle BackColor="#B5C7DE" ForeColor="#4A3C8C" />
  <RowStyle BackColor="#E7E7FF" ForeColor="#4A3C8C" />
  <Columns>
    <asp:BoundField DataField="AuditID" HeaderText="Audit ID"
      ReadOnly="True" SortExpression="AuditID" />
    <asp:BoundField DataField="DateStamp" HeaderText="Date Stamp"
      ReadOnly="True" SortExpression="DateStamp" />
    <asp:BoundField DataField="MessageNumber"
      HeaderText="Message Number" ReadOnly="True"
      SortExpression="MessageNumber" />
    <asp:BoundField DataField="Message" HeaderText="Message"
      ReadOnly="True" SortExpression="Message" />
  </Columns>
  <PagerStyle BackColor="#E7E7FF" ForeColor="#4A3C8C"
    HorizontalAlign="Right" />
  <SelectedRowStyle BackColor="#738A9C" Font-Bold="True"
    ForeColor="#F7F7F7" />
  <HeaderStyle BackColor="#4A3C8C" Font-Bold="True"
    ForeColor="#F7F7F7" />
  <AlternatingRowStyle BackColor="#F7F7F7" />
</asp:GridView>
```

Next, you come to the code behind AdminOrderDetails.aspx. The first modifications here are to remove the button handlers you no longer need (markVerifiedButton_Click, markCompletedButton_Click, and markCanceledButton_Click) and add a reference to CommerceLib. Next, you need to populate the list items in the statusDropDown control. You do this in PopulateControls:

```
// populate the form with data
private void PopulateControls(string orderId)
{
...

    // show status items
    statusDropDown.Items.Clear();
    for (int i = 0; i < CommerceLibAccess.OrderStatuses.Length; i++)
    {
      statusDropDown.Items.Add(
        new ListItem(CommerceLibAccess.OrderStatuses[i], i.ToString()));
    }
    statusDropDown.SelectedIndex = orderInfo.Status;
}
```

This code uses the static string array added to CommerceLibAccess earlier. The next modification is to PopulateControls, because the data we are populating is different. The new version of this method starts as follows:

```
// populate the form with data
private void PopulateControls()
{
    // obtain order info
    CommerceLibOrderInfo orderInfo =
      CommerceLibAccess.GetOrder(orderId);
    // populate labels and text boxes with order info
    orderIdLabel.Text = "Displaying Order #" + orderId;
    totalAmountLabel.Text = String.Format("{0:c} ", orderInfo.TotalCost);
    dateCreatedTextBox.Text = orderInfo.DateCreated.ToString();
    dateShippedTextBox.Text = orderInfo.DateShipped.ToString();
    statusDropDown.SelectedIndex = orderInfo.Status;
    authCodeTextBox.Text = orderInfo.AuthCode;
    referenceTextBox.Text = orderInfo.Reference;
    commentsTextBox.Text = orderInfo.Comments;
    customerNameTextBox.Text = orderInfo.CustomerName;
    shippingAddressTextBox.Text = orderInfo.CustomerAddressAsString;
    shippingTypeTextBox.Text = orderInfo.Shipping.ShippingType;
    customerEmailTextBox.Text = orderInfo.Customer.Email;
```

This is very similar to the original code, but uses a CommerceLibOrderInfo object to populate the (slightly different) fields. Because you've changed the buttons too, you need to decide which of them to enable and what text to display on the order-processing button.

```
// Decide which one of the buttons should
// be enabled and which should be disabled
switch (orderInfo.Status)
{
  case 8:
  case 9:
    // if the order was canceled or completed...
    processOrderButton.Text = "Process Order";
    processOrderButton.Enabled = false;
    cancelOrderButton.Enabled = false;
    break;
  case 3:
    // if the order is awaiting a stock check...
    processOrderButton.Text = "Confirm Stock for Order";
    processOrderButton.Enabled = true;
    cancelOrderButton.Enabled = true;
    break;
  case 6:
    // if the order is awaiting shipment...
    processOrderButton.Text = "Confirm Order Shipment";
    processOrderButton.Enabled = true;
    cancelOrderButton.Enabled = true;
    break;
  default:
    // otherwise...
    processOrderButton.Text = "Process Order";
    processOrderButton.Enabled = true;
    cancelOrderButton.Enabled = true;
    break;
}
```

A switch statement is used here to enable or disable buttons according to the current status. The rest of the code in PopulateControls binds order info and audit trail data and is as follows:

```
// fill the data grid with order details
grid.DataSource = orderInfo.OrderDetails;
grid.DataBind();

// fill the audit data grid with audit trail
auditGrid.DataSource = orderInfo.AuditTrail;
auditGrid.DataBind();
}
```

The SetEditMode method is also slightly different because the controls to enable or disable have changed:

```
// enable or disable edit mode
private void SetEditMode(bool enable)
{
  dateShippedTextBox.Enabled = enable;
  statusDropDown.Enabled = enable;
  authCodeTextBox.Enabled = enable;
  referenceTextBox.Enabled = enable;
  commentsTextBox.Enabled = enable;
  editButton.Enabled = !enable;
  updateButton.Enabled = enable;
  cancelButton.Enabled = enable;
}
```

The code for the Edit and Cancel buttons remains unchanged, but Update needs rewriting to use the new business tier method. The code is as follows:

```
// update order information
protected void updateButton_Click(object sender, EventArgs e)
{
  int orderId = int.Parse(Request.QueryString["OrderID"]);
  try
  {
    // Get new order data
    string dateCreated = dateCreatedTextBox.Text;
    string dateShipped = dateShippedTextBox.Text;
    int status = int.Parse(statusDropDown.SelectedValue);
    string authCode = authCodeTextBox.Text;
    string reference = referenceTextBox.Text;
    string comments = commentsTextBox.Text;
    // Update the order
    CommerceLibAccess.UpdateOrder(orderId, dateCreated,
      dateShipped, status, authCode, reference, comments);
  }
  catch
  {
    // In case of an error, we simply ignore it
  }
  // Exit edit mode and populate the form again
  SetEditMode(false);
  PopulateControls(orderId.ToString());
}
```

Again, the code is only slightly different. You extract the data in a similar way, but use several local variables rather than a single OrderInfo instance. These variables are passed to CommerceLibAccess.UpdateOrder to update the order.

The code for the order-processing button is, thanks to the order processor class, very simple:

```
// continue order processing
protected void processOrderButton_Click(object sender, EventArgs e)
{
  string orderId = Request.QueryString["OrderID"];
  OrderProcessor processor = new OrderProcessor(orderId);
  processor.Process();
  PopulateControls(orderId);
}
```

You instantiate an OrderProcessor instance for the selected order (found from the string in the session state) and call Process. This same call works for suppliers and administrators. Whatever stage the order has reached, this call attempts to push it forward. After order processing (which may involve a lot of work, but should be quick if all goes well), you repopulate the order data to update it.

Finally, you have the code required to cancel an order, which just means setting the status to 9. The code is already in place to do this, and you call it as follows:

```
// cancel order
protected void cancelOrderButton_Click(object sender, EventArgs e)
{
  string orderId = Request.QueryString["OrderID"];
  CommerceLibAccess.UpdateOrderStatus(int.Parse(orderId), 9);
  PopulateControls(orderId);
}
```

Don't take this for the other Cancel button, which only has the roles of resetting the form to its initial data and disabling editing mode:

```
// cancel order
protected void cancelButton_Click(object sender, EventArgs e)
{
  string orderId = Request.QueryString["OrderID"];
  PopulateControls(orderId);
  SetEditMode(false);
}
```

Testing the Order Administration Page

All that remains now is to check that everything is working properly. To do this, use the web interface to place an order and then examine it via the AdminOrders.aspx page. You should see that the order is awaiting confirmation of stock, as shown in Figure 19-3.

Click Select and scroll down until the button for confirming stock appears, as shown in Figure 19-4.

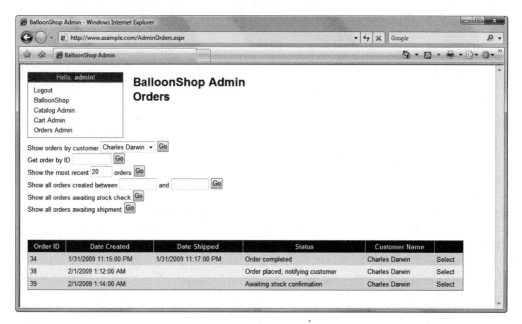

Figure 19-3. *Order awaiting stock confirmation*

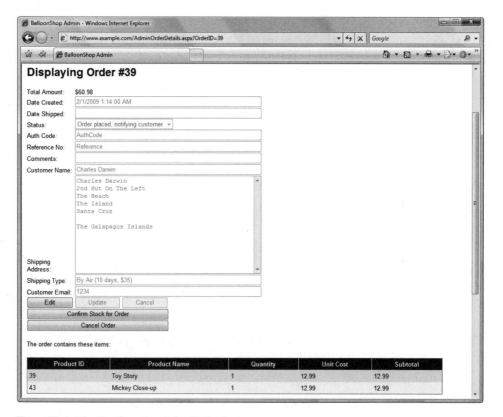

Figure 19-4. *The Confirm Stock for Order button*

Click the Confirm Stock for Order button, and the order will be processed. Because this happens very quickly, you will soon be presented with the next stage, a prompt to confirm shipment. Click the Confirm Order Shipment button, and the order will be completed.

If you scroll down further, you can see all audit trail messages that have been stored in the database concerning this order, as shown in Figure 19-5.

Audit ID	Date Stamp	Message Number	Message
141	2/1/2009 1:14:17 AM	10000	Order Processor started.
142	2/1/2009 1:14:17 AM	20000	PSInitialNotification started.
143	2/1/2009 1:14:17 AM	20002	Notification e-mail sent to customer.
144	2/1/2009 1:14:17 AM	20001	PSInitialNotification finished.
145	2/1/2009 1:14:17 AM	20100	PSCheckFunds started.
146	2/1/2009 1:14:17 AM	20102	Funds available for purchase.
147	2/1/2009 1:14:17 AM	20101	PSCheckFunds finished.
148	2/1/2009 1:14:17 AM	20200	PSCheckStock started.
149	2/1/2009 1:14:22 AM	20202	Notification e-mail sent to supplier.
150	2/1/2009 1:14:22 AM	20201	PSCheckStock finished.
151	2/1/2009 1:14:22 AM	10001	Order Processor finished.
152	2/1/2009 1:19:47 AM	10000	Order Processor started.
153	2/1/2009 1:19:47 AM	20300	PSStockOK started.
154	2/1/2009 1:19:47 AM	20302	Stock confirmed by supplier.
155	2/1/2009 1:19:47 AM	20301	PSStockOK finished.
156	2/1/2009 1:19:47 AM	20400	PSTakePayment started.
157	2/1/2009 1:19:47 AM	20402	Funds deducted from customer credit card account.
158	2/1/2009 1:19:47 AM	20401	PSTakePayment finished.
159	2/1/2009 1:19:47 AM	20500	PSShipGoods started.
160	2/1/2009 1:19:47 AM	20502	Ship goods e-mail sent to supplier.
161	2/1/2009 1:19:47 AM	20501	PSShipGoods finished.
162	2/1/2009 1:19:47 AM	10001	Order Processor finished.
163	2/1/2009 1:19:51 AM	10000	Order Processor started.
164	2/1/2009 1:19:51 AM	20600	PSShipOK started.
165	2/1/2009 1:19:51 AM	20602	Order dispatched by supplier.
166	2/1/2009 1:19:51 AM	20601	PSShipOK finished.
167	2/1/2009 1:19:51 AM	20700	PSFinalNotification started.
168	2/1/2009 1:19:51 AM	20702	Dispatch e-mail sent to customer.
169	2/1/2009 1:19:51 AM	20701	PSFinalNotification finished.
170	2/1/2009 1:19:51 AM	10001	Order Processor finished.

Figure 19-5. *Audit trail messages for this order*

Summary

You've taken giant strides toward completing your e-commerce application in this chapter. Now you have a fully audited, secure backbone for the application.

Specifically, we've covered the following:

- Modifications to the BalloonShop application to enable your own pipeline processing

- The basic framework for the order pipeline

- The database additions for auditing data and storing additional required data in the `Orders` table

- The implementation of most of the order pipeline, apart from those sections that deal with credit cards

- A simple implementation of an order administration web page

The only thing missing that needs to be added before you can deliver this application to the outside world is credit card–processing functionality, which we'll look at in the next chapter.

CHAPTER 20

■ ■ ■

Credit Card Transactions

The last thing we need to do before launching the e-commerce site is enable credit card processing. In this chapter, we examine how we can build this into the pipeline we created in the previous chapter.

We'll start by looking at the theory behind credit card transactions, the sort of organizations that help achieve credit card processing, and the sort of transactions that are possible. Moving on, we'll take one example organization, DataCash, and discuss the specifics of their transaction application program interfaces (APIs), the means by which we use their credit card transaction features. After that, we'll build a new class library that helps use one of these transaction APIs via some simple test code.

Finally, we'll integrate the API with the BalloonShop e-commerce application and order-processing pipeline.

Credit Card Transaction Fundamentals

For transactions, banks and other financial institutions use secure networks based on the X.25 protocol rather than Transmission Control Protocol/Internet Protocol (TCP/IP), the primary means by which data is transmitted across the Internet. You don't need to know much about X.25 apart from the fact that it's a different networking protocol that isn't compatible with TCP/IP. As such, X.25 networks are completely separate from the Internet, and although it's possible to get direct access to them, this isn't likely to be a reasonable option. To do so, we might have to enter into some serious negotiation with the owners of the network we want to use. The owners will want to be completely sure that we are reliable customers who are capable of enforcing the necessary safeguards to prevent an attack on *their* system. Accordingly, the network owner won't be handing out these licenses to just anyone—most people can't afford the security measures required (which include locking your servers in a cage, sending daily backup tapes down a secure chute, having three individuals with separate keys to access these tapes, and so on).

The alternative is to access these networks via a gateway provider. This enables us to perform our side of the credit card transaction protocol over the Internet (using a secure protocol) while relying on a chosen gateway to communicate with X.25 networks. Although there is likely to be a cost involved with this, the provider should have a deal with financial institutions to help keep costs low and pass the savings on to us (after the gateway takes its share), so it's likely to be much cheaper than having your own X.25 connection. This method is also likely to be cheaper than using a third-party payment processor, because we only need the minimum functionality since we are handling our own order pipeline. There is no need, for example, to use all the order-auditing functionality offered by a company such as PayPal, because we already have all this functionality in our implementation.

Working with Credit Card Payment Gateways

To work with a gateway organization, we first need to open a merchant bank account. This can be done at most banks; the bank will provide you a merchant ID that you can use when signing up with the gateway. The next step is to find a suitable gateway. This can be a lot of hard work!

Although it isn't hard to find a gateway, the challenge lies in finding a competent one that offers services at an acceptable price and quality. Literally hundreds of companies are eager to take a cut of your sales. A quick search on the Internet for "credit card gateway" will produce a long list. The web sites of these companies are for the most part pure brochureware—you'll find yourself reading through pages of text about how they are the best and most secure at what they do, only to end up with a form to fill in so that a customer service representative can call you to "discuss your needs." In the long run, you can rest assured that at least you will probably only have to go through the procedure once.

You'll probably find that most of the organizations offering this service are offering similar packages. However, some key points to look for include the banks they do business with (your merchant bank account will have to be at one of these), the currencies they deal in, and, of course, the costs.

Table 20-1 shows some of the gateway services available. In this chapter, we'll look at one organization that is easy to deal with—DataCash.

Table 20-1. *Gateway Services*

United States Gateways	URL	United Kingdom Gateways	URL
Authorize.Net	http://www.authorize.net	Arcot	http://www.arcot.com
Cardservice	http://cardservice.com	DataCash	http://www.datacash.com
First Data	http://www.firstdata.com	WorldPay	http://www.worldpay.com
ICVerify	http://www.icverify.com		

In this chapter, we'll demonstrate implementing credit card transactions with DataCash. DataCash is a credit card gateway organization based in the United Kingdom. You'll need a UK merchant bank account if you want to use it in the final application. However, you don't have to worry about this for now: it's very easy to get access to a rather useful test account—you don't even need a merchant bank account.

As you'll see later in this chapter, DataCash lets us perform test transactions using so-called "magic" credit card numbers, which will accept or decline transactions without performing any actual financial transactions. This is fantastic for development purposes, because we certainly don't want to use our own credit cards for testing!

Understanding Credit Card Transactions

Whichever gateway you use, the basic principles of credit card transactions are the same. First, the sort of transactions we'll be dealing with in an e-commerce web site are known as Card Not Present (CNP) transactions, which means we don't have the credit card in front of us and we can't verify the customer signature. This isn't a problem; after all, you've probably been performing CNP transactions for some time now online, over the phone, by mail, and so on. It's just something to be aware of should you see the CNP acronym.

Several advanced services are offered by various gateways, including cardholder address verification, security code checking, fraud screening, and so on. Each of these adds an additional layer of complexity to your credit card processing, and we're not covering those details here. Rather, this chapter provides a starting point from which you can add these services if required. Whether or not you choose these optional extra services depends on how much money is passing through your system and the trade-off between the costs of implementing the services and the potential costs, which could be prevented by these extra services if something goes wrong. If you are interested in these services, that customer service representative mentioned previously will be happy to explain things.

As it stands now, we can perform several types of transactions:

- *Authorization*: Check a card for adequate funds and perform a deduction.

- *Preauthorization*: Check a card for funds and allocate them if available; this doesn't deduct funds immediately.

- *Fulfillment*: Complete a preauthorized transaction, deducting the funds already allocated.

- *Refund*: Refund a completed transaction or simply put money on a credit card.

Again, the specifics vary, but these are the basic types.

In this chapter, we'll use the preauthorization/fulfillment model, which means we don't take payment until just before we instruct our supplier to ship goods. This structure was hinted at by the structure of the pipeline we created in the previous chapter.

Working with DataCash

Now that we've covered the basics, let's consider how we'll get things working in the Balloon-Shop application using the DataCash system. The first thing to do is to get a test account with DataCash by following these steps:

1. Go to http://www.datacash.com.

2. Head to the Developers Area ➤ Get a Test Account section of the web site.

3. Enter your details and submit the form.

4. From the e-mail you receive, make a note of your account username and password, as well as the additional information required for accessing the DataCash reporting system.

■**Note** After you obtain your test account, be sure to download the DataCash Developer's Guide at `https://testserver.datacash.com/software/DevelopersGuide.pdf`. This is the official document you can rely on to have accurate and recent information about any DataCash services.

We'll be doing a lot of XML manipulation when communicating with DataCash, because we'll need to create XML documents to send to DataCash and to extract data from XML responses. In the following few pages, we'll take a quick look at the XML required for the operations we'll be performing and the responses we can expect. We'll discuss the communication protocol, which implies discussing the XML files that reflect the following stages of a transaction:

- Preauthentication request

- Response to the preauthentication request

- Fulfillment request

- Fulfillment response

We'll implement these stages into the BalloonShop order pipeline. While reading this chapter, always remember to use the official documentation, which contains the most current and relevant updates, at `https://testserver.datacash.com/software/DevelopersGuide.pdf`.

Preauthentication Request

When you send a preauthentication request to DataCash, you need to include the following information:

- DataCash username (known as the DataCash client)

- DataCash password

- A unique transaction reference number (explained later in this section)

- The amount of money to be debited

- The currency used for the transaction (USD, EUR, GBP, and so on)

- The type of the transaction (the code `pre` for preauthentication and the code `fulfill` for fulfillment)

- The credit card number

- The credit card expiry date

- The credit card issue date (if applicable to the type of credit card being used)

- The credit card issue number (if applicable to the type of credit card being used)

The unique transaction reference number must be a number between 6 and 12 digits long, which we choose to uniquely identify the transaction with an order. Because we can't use a short number, we can't just use the order ID values we've been using up until now for orders. We can, however, use this order ID as the starting point for creating a reference number by simply adding a high number to it, such as 1,000,000. We can't duplicate the reference number in any future transactions; we must be sure that after a transaction is completed, it won't execute again, which could result in charging the customer twice. This process implies, however, that if a credit card is rejected, we might need to create a whole new order for the customer to generate a new and unique reference number to send to the gateway, but that shouldn't be a problem.

The XML request is formatted in the following way, with the values detailed previously shown in bold:

```xml
<?xml version="1.0" encoding="UTF-8"?>
<Request>
  <Authentication>
    <password>DataCash password</password>
    <client>DataCash client</client>
  </Authentication>
  <Transaction>
    <TxnDetails>
      <merchantreference>Unique reference number</merchantreference>
      <amount currency='Currency Type'>Cash amount</amount>
    </TxnDetails>
    <CardTxn>
      <method>pre</method>
      <Card>
        <pan>Credit card number</pan>
        <expirydate>Credit card expiry date</expirydate>
      </Card>
    </CardTxn>
  </Transaction>
</Request>
```

Response to Preauthentication Request

The response to a preauthentication request includes the following information:

- The status code number, which indicates what happened. The code will be 1 if the transaction is successful or another of several other codes if something else happens. For a complete list of return codes for a DataCash server, see https://testserver.datacash.com/software/returncodes.shtml.

- The reason for the status, which is basically a string explaining the status in English. For a status of 1, this string is ACCEPTED.

- An authentication code and a reference number, which are provided for use in completing the transaction in the fulfillment request stage (discussed next).

- The time that the transaction was processed.

- The mode of the transaction, which is TEST when using the test account.

- Confirmation of the type of credit card used.

- Confirmation of the country that the credit card was issued in.

- The authorization code used by the bank (for reference only).

The XML for this is formatted as follows:

```
<?xml version="1.0" encoding="utf-8"?>
<Response>
  <status>Status code</status>
  <reason>Reason</reason>
  <merchantreference>Authentication code</merchantreference>
  <datacash_reference>Reference number</datacash_reference>
  <time>Time</time>
  <mode>TEST</mode>
  <CardTxn>
    <card_scheme>Card Type</card_scheme>
    <country>Country</country>
    <issuer>Card issuing bank</issuer>
    <authcode>Bank authorization code</authcode>
  </CardTxn>
</Response>
```

Fulfillment Request

For a fulfillment request, we need to send the following information:

- DataCash username (the DataCash client)

- DataCash password

- The type of the transaction (for fulfillment, the code fulfill)

- The authentication code received earlier

- The reference number received earlier

We can, optionally, include additional information, such as a confirmation of the amount to be debited from the credit card, although this isn't really necessary.

The fulfillment request XML message is formatted as follows:

```
<?xml version="1.0" encoding="UTF-8"?>
<Request>
  <Authentication>
    <password>DataCash password</password>
    <client>DataCash client</client>
  </Authentication>
```

```
    <Transaction>
      <HistoricTxn>
        <reference>Reference Number</reference>
        <authcode>Authentication code</authcode>
        <method>fulfill</method>
      </HistoricTxn>
    </Transaction>
</Request>
```

Fulfillment Response

The response to a fulfillment request includes the following information:

- The status code number, which indicates what happened. The code will be 1 if the transaction is successful or another of several other codes if something else happens. Again, for a complete list of codes, see `https://testserver.datacash.com/software/returncodes.shtml`.

- The reason for the status, which is basically a string explaining the status in English. For a status of 1, this string is `FULFILLED OK`.

- Two copies of the reference code.

- The time that the transaction was processed.

- The mode of the transaction, which is `TEST` when using the test account.

    The XML message for the fulfillment response is formatted as follows:

```
<?xml version="1.0" encoding="utf-8"?>
<Response>
  <status>Status code</status>
  <reason>Reason</reason>
  <merchantreference>Reference Code</merchantreference>
  <datacash_reference>Reference Code</datacash_reference>
  <time>Time</time>
  <mode>TEST</mode>
</Response>
```

Exchanging XML Data with DataCash

You could build up the XML documents shown previously piece by piece, but the .NET Framework allows you to do things in a much better way. The solution presented here involves XML serialization. It's possible to configure any .NET class so that it can be serialized as an XML document, and that XML document also can be used to instantiate classes. This involves converting all public fields and properties into XML data, and is the basis for the web services functionality in .NET.

    The default behavior for this is to create XML documents with elements named the same as the public fields and properties that you are serializing. For example, you might have the following class and member:

```
public class TestClass
{
  public string TestMember;
}
```

This is serialized as follows:

```
<?xml version="1.0" encoding="utf-8"?>
<TestClass>
  <TestMember>Value</TestMember>
</TestClass>
```

You can override this behavior using XML serialization attributes. You can force pieces of data to be formatted in elements with custom names, as attributes, as plain text, and so on.

For example, you could force the previous class to serialize as an attribute as follows:

```
public class TestClass
{
  [XmlAttribute("TestAttribute")]
  public string TestMember;
}
```

The [XmlAttribute()] part means that the member that follows should be serialized as an attribute, and the string parameter names the attribute. This class now serializes as follows:

```
<?xml version="1.0" encoding="utf-8"?>
<TestClass TestAttribute="Value" />
```

You can use several of these attributes, and you'll see some of them in the example that follows. This example demonstrates how you can create classes that represent DataCash requests and responses, which are capable of serializing to and deserializing from an XML representation. This makes it easy to send data to DataCash and allows you to use the full power of .NET classes to provide an intelligent way of accessing data.

In the example that follows, you'll create the classes necessary to exchange data with DataCash and try out these classes using some simple client code. Note that several classes are used to build up the XML because the structure involves several nested elements rather than a flat structure.

Exercise: Communicating with DataCash

1. Create a new subdirectory in the App_Code directory of BalloonShop, called DataCashLib.

2. Add the AmountClass class to the DataCashLib folder:

```
using System.Xml.Serialization;

namespace DataCashLib
{
```

```
  public class AmountClass
  {
    [XmlAttribute("currency")]
    public string Currency;

    [XmlText()]
    public string Amount;
  }
}
```

3. Add the following class, AuthenticationClass:

```
using System.Xml.Serialization;

namespace DataCashLib
{
  public class AuthenticationClass
  {
    [XmlElement("password")]
    public string Password;

    [XmlElement("client")]
    public string Client;
  }
}
```

4. Add the following class, CardClass:

```
using System.Xml.Serialization;

namespace DataCashLib
{
  public class CardClass
  {
    [XmlElement("pan")]
    public string CardNumber;

    [XmlElement("expirydate")]
    public string ExpiryDate;

    [XmlElement("startdate")]
    public string StartDate;

    [XmlElement("issuenumber")]
    public string IssueNumber;
  }
}
```

5. Add the following class, CardTxnRequestClass:

```
using System.Xml.Serialization;

namespace DataCashLib
{
  public class CardTxnRequestClass
  {
    [XmlElement("method")]
    public string Method;

    [XmlElement("Card")]
    public CardClass Card = new CardClass();
  }
}
```

6. Add the following class, CardTxnResponseClass:

```
using System.Xml.Serialization;

namespace DataCashLib
{
  public class CardTxnResponseClass
  {
    [XmlElement("card_scheme")]
    public string CardScheme;

    [XmlElement("country")]
    public string Country;

    [XmlElement("issuer")]
    public string Issuer;

    [XmlElement("authcode")]
    public string AuthCode;
  }
}
```

7. Add the following class, HistoricTxnClass:

```
using System.Xml.Serialization;

namespace DataCashLib
{
  public class HistoricTxnClass
  {
    [XmlElement("reference")]
    public string Reference;
```

```
    [XmlElement("authcode")]
    public string AuthCode;

    [XmlElement("method")]
    public string Method;

    [XmlElement("tran_code")]
    public string TranCode;

    [XmlElement("duedate")]
    public string DueDate;
  }
}
```

8. Add the following class, TxnDetailsClass:

```
using System.Xml.Serialization;

namespace DataCashLib
{
  public class TxnDetailsClass
  {
    [XmlElement("merchantreference")]
    public string MerchantReference;

    [XmlElement("amount")]
    public AmountClass Amount = new AmountClass();
  }
}
```

9. Add the following class, TransactionClass:

```
using System.Xml.Serialization;

namespace DataCashLib
{
  public class TransactionClass
  {
    [XmlElement("TxnDetails")]
    public TxnDetailsClass TxnDetails = new TxnDetailsClass();
    private CardTxnRequestClass cardTxn;

    private HistoricTxnClass historicTxn;


    [XmlElement("CardTxn")]
    public CardTxnRequestClass CardTxn
    {
```

```csharp
    get
    {
      if (historicTxn == null)
      {
        if (cardTxn == null)
        {
          cardTxn = new CardTxnRequestClass();
        }
        return cardTxn;
      }
      else
      {
        return null;
      }
    }
    set
    {
      cardTxn = value;
    }
}

[XmlElement("HistoricTxn")]
public HistoricTxnClass HistoricTxn
{
  get
  {
    if (cardTxn == null)
    {
      if (historicTxn == null)
      {
        historicTxn = new HistoricTxnClass();
      }
      return historicTxn;
    }
    else
    {
      return null;
    }
  }
  set
  {
    historicTxn = value;
  }
    }
  }
}
```

10. Add the following class, DataCashRequest (this class also requires using references to System.Net, System.Text, and System.IO):

```csharp
using System.Xml.Serialization;
using System.IO;
using System.Net;
using System.Text;

namespace DataCashLib
{
  [XmlRoot("Request")]
  public class DataCashRequest
  {
    [XmlElement("Authentication")]
    public AuthenticationClass Authentication =
    new AuthenticationClass();

    [XmlElement("Transaction")]
    public TransactionClass Transaction = new TransactionClass();

    public DataCashResponse GetResponse(string url)
    {
      // Configure HTTP Request
      HttpWebRequest httpRequest = WebRequest.Create(url)
      as HttpWebRequest;
      httpRequest.Method = "POST";

      // Prepare correct encoding for XML serialization
      UTF8Encoding encoding = new UTF8Encoding();

      // Use Xml property to obtain serialized XML data
      // Convert into bytes using encoding specified above and
      // get length
      byte[] bodyBytes = encoding.GetBytes(Xml);
      httpRequest.ContentLength = bodyBytes.Length;

      // Get HTTP Request stream for putting XML data into
      Stream httpRequestBodyStream =
      httpRequest.GetRequestStream();

      // Fill stream with serialized XML data
      httpRequestBodyStream.Write(bodyBytes, 0, bodyBytes.Length);
      httpRequestBodyStream.Close();

      // Get HTTP Response
      HttpWebResponse httpResponse = httpRequest.GetResponse()
      as HttpWebResponse;
      StreamReader httpResponseStream =
```

```
        new StreamReader(httpResponse.GetResponseStream(),
        System.Text.Encoding.ASCII);

        // Extract XML from response
        string httpResponseBody = httpResponseStream.ReadToEnd();
        httpResponseStream.Close();


        // Ignore everything that isn't XML by removing headers
        httpResponseBody = httpResponseBody.Substring(
        httpResponseBody.IndexOf("<?xml"));

        // Deserialize XML into DataCashResponse
        XmlSerializer serializer =
        new XmlSerializer(typeof(DataCashResponse));
        StringReader responseReader =
        new StringReader(httpResponseBody);

        // Return DataCashResponse result
        return serializer.Deserialize(responseReader)
        as DataCashResponse;
    }

    [XmlIgnore()]
    public string Xml
    {
      get
      {
        // Prepare XML serializer
        XmlSerializer serializer =
          new XmlSerializer(typeof(DataCashRequest));

        // Serialize into StringBuilder
        StringBuilder sb = new StringBuilder();
        StringWriter sw = new StringWriter(sb);
        serializer.Serialize(sw, this);
        sw.Flush();

        // Replace UTF-16 encoding with UTF-8 encoding
        string xml = sb.ToString();
        xml = xml.Replace("utf-16", "utf-8");
        return xml;
      }
    }
  }
}
```

11. Add the following class, DataCashResponse (which needs additional using references to System. Text and System.IO):

```csharp
using System.Xml.Serialization;
using System.IO;
using System.Text;

namespace DataCashLib
{
  [XmlRoot("Response")]
  public class DataCashResponse
  {
    [XmlElement("status")]
    public string Status;


    [XmlElement("reason")]
    public string Reason;

    [XmlElement("information")]
    public string information;

    [XmlElement("merchantreference")]
    public string MerchantReference;

    [XmlElement("datacash_reference")]
    public string DatacashReference;

    [XmlElement("time")]
    public string Time;

    [XmlElement("mode")]
    public string Mode;

    [XmlElement("CardTxn")]
    public CardTxnResponseClass CardTxn;

    [XmlIgnore()]
    public string Xml
    {
      get
      {
        // Prepare XML serializer
        XmlSerializer serializer =
          new XmlSerializer(typeof(DataCashResponse));
```

```
            // Serialize into StringBuilder
            StringBuilder sb = new StringBuilder();
            StringWriter sw = new StringWriter(sb);
            serializer.Serialize(sw, this);
            sw.Flush();

            // Replace UTF-16 encoding with UTF-8 encoding
            string xml = sb.ToString();
            xml = xml.Replace("utf-16", "utf-8");
            return xml;
        }
    }
  }
}
```

12. Now you've finished adding the classes, so add a new Web Form to the root of BalloonShop called `DataCashLibTest.aspx`, for testing (use the standard BalloonShop Master Page for now).

13. Add a single multiline `TextBox` control to the page called `OutputBox` and make it big enough to see plenty of text, such as in the highlighted code:

```
<%@ Page Title="" Language="C#" MasterPageFile="~/BalloonShop.master"
AutoEventWireup="true" CodeFile="DataCashLibTest.aspx.cs" Inherits=➥
"DataCashLibTest" %>

<asp:Content ID="Content1" ContentPlaceHolderID="head" Runat="Server">
</asp:Content>
<asp:Content ID="Content2" ContentPlaceHolderID="ContentPlaceHolder1" ➥
Runat="Server">
  <asp:TextBox ID="OutputBox" runat="server" Height="400px"
               TextMode="MultiLine" Width="700px"></asp:TextBox>
</asp:Content>
```

14. Add `using` references to `DataCashLib` and `System.Text` to the top of `DataCashLibTest.aspx.cs`.

15. Modify the code in `DataCashLibTest.aspx.cs` as follows, replacing the values for `dataCashClient` and `dataCashPassword` with your own values (obtained when you signed up with DataCash). You'll also have to change the Merchant Reference number to be a different value, or else you'll get a duplicate reference response returned to you:

```
using System;
using DataCashLib;
using System.Text;
using System.IO;
using System.Xml.Serialization;
```

```csharp
public partial class DataCashLibTest : System.Web.UI.Page
{
  protected void Page_Load(object sender, EventArgs e)
  {
    // Prepare StringBuilder for output
    StringBuilder sb = new StringBuilder();

    // Initialize variables
    DataCashRequest request;
    XmlSerializer requestSerializer =
        new XmlSerializer(typeof(DataCashRequest));
    DataCashResponse response;
    XmlSerializer responseSerializer =
        new XmlSerializer(typeof(DataCashResponse));
    StringBuilder xmlBuilder;
    StringWriter xmlWriter;
    string dataCashUrl =
        "https://testserver.datacash.com/Transaction";
    string dataCashClient = "99341800";
    string dataCashPassword = "bbdNsX7p";

    // Construct pre request
    request = new DataCashRequest();
    request.Authentication.Client = dataCashClient;
    request.Authentication.Password = dataCashPassword;
    request.Transaction.TxnDetails.MerchantReference = "9999999";
    request.Transaction.TxnDetails.Amount.Amount = "49.99";
    request.Transaction.TxnDetails.Amount.Currency = "GBP";
    request.Transaction.CardTxn.Method = "pre";
    request.Transaction.CardTxn.Card.CardNumber =
        "4444333322221111";
    request.Transaction.CardTxn.Card.ExpiryDate = "10/11";

    // Display pre request
    sb.AppendLine("Pre Request:");
    xmlBuilder = new StringBuilder();
    xmlWriter = new StringWriter(xmlBuilder);
    requestSerializer.Serialize(xmlWriter, request);
    sb.AppendLine(xmlBuilder.ToString());
    sb.AppendLine();

    // Get pre response
    response = request.GetResponse(dataCashUrl);
```

```
        // Display pre response
        sb.AppendLine("Pre Response:");
        xmlBuilder = new StringBuilder();
        xmlWriter = new StringWriter(xmlBuilder);
        responseSerializer.Serialize(xmlWriter, response);
        sb.AppendLine(xmlBuilder.ToString());
        sb.AppendLine();

        // Construct fulfil request
        request = new DataCashRequest();
        request.Authentication.Client = dataCashClient;
        request.Authentication.Password = dataCashPassword;
        request.Transaction.HistoricTxn.Method = "fulfill";
        request.Transaction.HistoricTxn.AuthCode =
            response.MerchantReference;
        request.Transaction.HistoricTxn.Reference =
            response.DatacashReference;

        // Display fulfil request
        sb.AppendLine("Fulfil Request:");
        xmlBuilder = new StringBuilder();
        xmlWriter = new StringWriter(xmlBuilder);
        requestSerializer.Serialize(xmlWriter, request);
        sb.AppendLine(xmlBuilder.ToString());
        sb.AppendLine();

        // Get fulfil response
        response = request.GetResponse(dataCashUrl);

        // Display fulfil response
        sb.AppendLine("Fulfil Response:");
        xmlBuilder = new StringBuilder();
        xmlWriter = new StringWriter(xmlBuilder);
        responseSerializer.Serialize(xmlWriter, response);
        sb.AppendLine(xmlBuilder.ToString());

        // Output result
        OutputBox.Text = sb.ToString();
    }
}
```

16. Now build and run the solution. You should get a response similar to that shown in Figure 20-1.

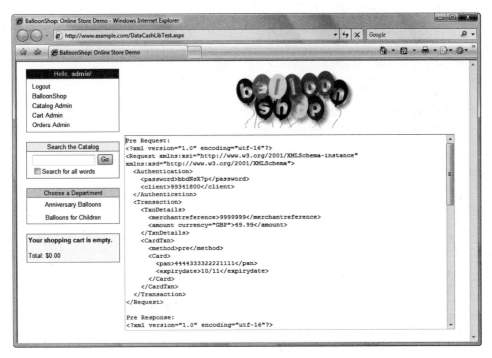

Figure 20-1. *Testing the DataCash library*

The complete text displayed in the OutputBox text box is as follows:

```
Pre Request:
<?xml version="1.0" encoding="utf-16"?>
<Request xmlns:xsi="http://www.w3.org/2001/XMLSchema-instance" ➥
xmlns:xsd="http://www.w3.org/2001/XMLSchema">
  <Authentication>
    <password>bbdNsX7p</password>
    <client>99341800</client>
  </Authentication>
  <Transaction>
    <TxnDetails>
      <merchantreference>9999999</merchantreference>
      <amount currency="GBP">49.99</amount>
    </TxnDetails>
    <CardTxn>
      <method>pre</method>
      <Card>
        <pan>4444333322221111</pan>
        <expirydate>10/11</expirydate>
      </Card>
    </CardTxn>
  </Transaction>
</Request>
```

```
Pre Response:
<?xml version="1.0" encoding="utf-16"?>
<Response xmlns:xsi="http://www.w3.org/2001/XMLSchema-instance" ➥
xmlns:xsd="http://www.w3.org/2001/XMLSchema">
  <status>1</status>
  <reason>ACCEPTED</reason>
  <merchantreference>9999999</merchantreference>
  <datacash_reference>4100200060169590</datacash_reference>
  <time>1233501175</time>
  <mode>TEST</mode>
  <CardTxn>
    <card_scheme>VISA</card_scheme>
    <authcode>955537</authcode>
  </CardTxn>
</Response>

Fulfil Request:
<?xml version="1.0" encoding="utf-16"?>
<Request xmlns:xsi="http://www.w3.org/2001/XMLSchema-instance" ➥
xmlns:xsd="http://www.w3.org/2001/XMLSchema">
  <Authentication>
    <password>bbdNsX7p</password>
    <client>99341800</client>
  </Authentication>
  <Transaction>
    <TxnDetails>
      <amount />
    </TxnDetails>
    <HistoricTxn>
      <reference>4100200060169590</reference>
      <authcode>9999999</authcode>
      <method>fulfill</method>
    </HistoricTxn>
  </Transaction>
</Request>

Fulfil Response:
<?xml version="1.0" encoding="utf-16"?>
<Response xmlns:xsi="http://www.w3.org/2001/XMLSchema-instance" ➥
xmlns:xsd="http://www.w3.org/2001/XMLSchema">
  <status>1</status>
  <reason>FULFILLED OK</reason>
  <merchantreference>4100200060169590</merchantreference>
  <datacash_reference>4100200060169590</datacash_reference>
  <time>1233501176</time>
  <mode>TEST</mode>
</Response>
```

17. Log on to `https://testserver.datacash.com/reporting2` to see the transaction log for your Data-Cash account (note that this view takes a while to update, so you might not see the transaction right away).

How It Works: Communicating with DataCash

You've created code to represent the XML documents that you're exchanging. Two root classes—DataCashRequest and DataCashResponse—encapsulate XML requests and responses. These classes contain instances of the other classes defined, which contain instances of other classes, and so on, relating to the structure of the XML documents described earlier.

Each of the members of these classes has an associated XML serialization attribute, matching the data with the way it will be formatted when the request or response classes are serialized. For example, many of the string members appear as follows:

```
[XmlElement("status")]
public string Status;
```

The Status field will be formatted as follows:

```
<status>Status data</status>
```

The correct capitalization is included while at the same time allowing you to set the status data using standard PascalCasing format.

■**Note** PascalCasing is where variable names start with a capital letter, and each subsequent word in the name also has a capital letter, such as `ThisIsAVariable`. One alternative scheme is camelCasing, where the first word isn't capitalized—for example, `thisIsAVariable`. The capitalization in the names of these casing schemes serves as a reminder of their usage.

One of the classes used, `TransactionClass`, is slightly more complicated than the others, because the `<Transaction>` element contains one of either `<CardTxn>` or `<HistoricTxn>`, depending on whether the request is a `pre` request or a `fulfil` request. Instead of using fields, this class uses properties that ensure that only one of these two elements is used.

The `DataCashRequest` class also has a method called `GetResponse` that sends the request and packages the returned response as a `DataCashResponse` class. In the code to do this, you start by creating an `HttpWebRequest` instance for the URL supplied as a parameter:

```
public DataCashResponse GetResponse(string url)
{
  HttpWebRequest httpRequest = WebRequest.Create(url)
    as HttpWebRequest;
```

This request is then defined as a POST request with the appropriate encoding:

```
httpRequest.Method = "POST";
UTF8Encoding encoding = new UTF8Encoding();
```

■Note HTTP requests can be sent in a number of formats, the most common being GET and POST. The difference here is that GET requests have just a URL and header information; POST requests have all this plus a message body. Think of an HTTP POST request as if it were an email, with the HTTP response being the email reply. In both cases, header information is like the address and subject of the email, and body information is like the message body of an email.

Next, you need to supply the body of the POST request, which is the XML document you want to send. To do this, you get the serialized version of the data contained in the object via the Xml property (which simply serializes the DataCashRequest instance into XML, by using the XML serialization attributes):

```
byte[] bodyBytes = encoding.GetBytes(Xml);
```

You also need to specify the length of the data contained in the HTTP header for the request:

```
httpRequest.ContentLength = bodyBytes.Length;
```

Next, you take the XML data and place it into the request via standard stream manipulation code:

```
Stream httpRequestBodyStream =
    httpRequest.GetRequestStream();
httpRequestBodyStream.Write(bodyBytes, 0, bodyBytes.Length);
httpRequestBodyStream.Close();
```

After you have the request class, you can obtain the response, also via stream manipulation:

```
HttpWebResponse httpResponse = httpRequest.GetResponse()
    as HttpWebResponse;
StreamReader httpResponseStream =
    new StreamReader(httpResponse.GetResponseStream(),
        System.Text.Encoding.ASCII);
string httpResponseBody = httpResponseStream.ReadToEnd();
httpResponseStream.Close();
```

You only need the XML data contained in this stream, so clip off the headers at the beginning of the data returned before deserializing it. You do this using the String.Substring method to obtain the section of the string that starts with "<?xml", the location of which is found using the String.IndexOf method.

```
httpResponseBody =
    httpResponseBody.Substring(
        httpResponseBody.IndexOf("<?xml"));
XmlSerializer serializer =
    new XmlSerializer(typeof(DataCashResponse));
StringReader responseReader =
    new StringReader(httpResponseBody);
```

Finally, you cast the deserialized object into a DataCashResponse object for further manipulation:

```
        return serializer.Deserialize(responseReader)
           as DataCashResponse;
    }
```

After the transaction has completed, you can check that everything has worked properly via the DataCash reporting web interface.

Integrating DataCash with BalloonShop

Now you have a new set of classes that you can use to perform credit card transactions. However, you need to modify a few things to integrate it with your existing e-commerce application and pipeline.

Business Tier Modifications

In fact, *all* the modifications you'll make to BalloonShop occur at the business tier because we've slipped in the data and presentation tier modifications already. We also have AuthCode and Reference fields ready to use for the database. In the presentation tier, we have the user interface elements in place to check on these values. All you have to do is make the PSCheckFunds and PSTakePayment pipeline sections work.

Modifying the BalloonShopConfiguration Class

Before modifying the pipeline itself, you have to modify the order processor configuration, because you now have three new pieces of information that CommerceLib requires to operate:

- DataCash client

- DataCash password

- DataCash URL

You can give access to this information via the BalloonShopConfiguration class as with the other similar information required for order processing. Add the following three properties to BalloonShopConfiguration:

```
// DataCash client code
public static string DataCashClient
{
  get
  {
    return ConfigurationManager.AppSettings["DataCashClient"];
  }
}
```

```
// DataCash password
public static string DataCashPassword
{
  get
  {
    return ConfigurationManager.AppSettings["DataCashPassword"];
  }
}

// DataCash currency
public static string DataCashCurrency
{
  get
  {
    return ConfigurationManager.AppSettings["DataCashCurrency"];
  }
}

// DataCash server URL
public static string DataCashUrl
{
  get
  {
    return ConfigurationManager.AppSettings["DataCashUrl"];
  }
}
```

This uses information in the web.config file of BalloonShop. Modify web.config as follows, supplying your own client and password data as before:

```
<appSettings>
  ...
  <add key="DataCashClient" value="99341800" />
  <add key="DataCashPassword" value="bbdNsX7p" />
  <add key="DataCashCurrency" value="GBP" />
  <add key="DataCashUrl"
    value="https://testserver.datacash.com/Transaction" />
</appSettings>
```

Modifying the PSCheckFunds Pipeline Section Class

The final changes involve modifying the pipeline section classes that deal with credit card transactions. The infrastructure for storing and retrieving authentication code and reference information has already been included, via the OrderProcessor.SetOrderAuthCodeAndReference method and the AuthCode and Reference properties.

The modifications to PSCheckFunds are as follows:

```csharp
using DataCashLib;

namespace CommerceLib
{
  /// <summary>
  /// 2nd pipeline stage - used to check that the customer
  /// has the required funds available for purchase
  /// </summary>
  public class PSCheckFunds : IPipelineSection
  {
    private OrderProcessor orderProcessor;

    public void Process(OrderProcessor processor)
    {
      // set processor reference
      orderProcessor = processor;
      // audit
      orderProcessor.CreateAudit("PSCheckFunds started.", 20100);
      try
      {
        // check customer funds via DataCash gateway
        // configure DataCash XML request
        DataCashRequest request = new DataCashRequest();
        request.Authentication.Client =
            BalloonShopConfiguration.DataCashClient;
        request.Authentication.Password =
            BalloonShopConfiguration.DataCashPassword;

        request.Transaction.TxnDetails.MerchantReference =
          orderProcessor.Order.OrderID.ToString()
          .PadLeft(6, '0').PadLeft(7, '5');
        request.Transaction.TxnDetails.Amount.Amount =
          orderProcessor.Order.TotalCost.ToString();
        request.Transaction.TxnDetails.Amount.Currency =
          BalloonShopConfiguration.DataCashCurrency;
        request.Transaction.CardTxn.Method = "pre";
        request.Transaction.CardTxn.Card.CardNumber =
          orderProcessor.Order.CreditCard.CardNumber;
        request.Transaction.CardTxn.Card.ExpiryDate =
          orderProcessor.Order.CreditCard.ExpiryDate;
        if (orderProcessor.Order.CreditCard.IssueDate != "")
        {
          request.Transaction.CardTxn.Card.StartDate =
            orderProcessor.Order.CreditCard.IssueDate;
        }
```

```
        if (orderProcessor.Order.CreditCard.IssueNumber != "")
        {
          request.Transaction.CardTxn.Card.IssueNumber =
            orderProcessor.Order.CreditCard.IssueNumber;
        }
        // get DataCash response
        DataCashResponse response =
          request.GetResponse(
          BalloonShopConfiguration.DataCashUrl);
        if (response.Status == "1")
        {
          // update order authorization code and reference
          orderProcessor.Order.SetAuthCodeAndReference(
            response.MerchantReference,
            response.DatacashReference);
          // audit
          orderProcessor.CreateAudit(
            "Funds available for purchase.", 20102);
          // update order status
          orderProcessor.Order.UpdateStatus(2);
          // continue processing
          orderProcessor.ContinueNow = true;
        }
        else
        {
          // audit
          orderProcessor.CreateAudit(
            "Funds not available for purchase.", 20103);
          // mail admin

          orderProcessor.MailAdmin("Credit card declined.",
            "XML data exchanged:\n" + request.Xml + "\n\n"
            + response.Xml, 1);
        }
      }
      catch
      {
        // fund checking failure
        throw new OrderProcessorException(
          "Error occured while checking funds.", 1);
      }
      // audit
      processor.CreateAudit("PSCheckFunds finished.", 20101);
    }
  }
}
```

Modifying the PSTakePayment Pipeline Section Class

The modifications to PSTakePayment are as follows:

```
using DataCashLib;

namespace CommerceLib
{
  /// <summary>
  /// 5th pipeline stage - takes funds from customer
  /// </summary>
  public class PSTakePayment : IPipelineSection
  {
    private OrderProcessor orderProcessor;

    public void Process(OrderProcessor processor)
    {
      // set processor reference
      orderProcessor = processor;
      // audit
      orderProcessor.CreateAudit("PSTakePayment started.", 20400);
      try
      {
        // take customer funds via DataCash gateway
        // configure DataCash XML request
        DataCashRequest request = new DataCashRequest();
        request.Authentication.Client =
          BalloonShopConfiguration.DataCashClient;

        request.Authentication.Password =
          BalloonShopConfiguration.DataCashPassword;
        request.Transaction.HistoricTxn.Method =
          "fulfill";
        request.Transaction.HistoricTxn.AuthCode =
          orderProcessor.Order.AuthCode;
        request.Transaction.HistoricTxn.Reference =
          orderProcessor.Order.Reference;
        // get DataCash response
        DataCashResponse response =
          request.GetResponse(
          BalloonShopConfiguration.DataCashUrl);
        if (response.Status == "1")
        {
          // audit
          orderProcessor.CreateAudit(
            "Funds deducted from customer credit card account.",
            20402);
```

```
            // update order status
            orderProcessor.Order.UpdateStatus(5);
            // continue processing
            orderProcessor.ContinueNow = true;
        }
        else
        {
            // audit
            orderProcessor.CreateAudit(
             "Error taking funds from customer credit card account.",
             20403);
            // mail admin
            orderProcessor.MailAdmin(
               "Credit card fulfillment declined.",
               "XML data exchanged:\n" + request.Xml + "\n\n" +
               response.Xml, 1);
        }
    }
    catch
    {
        // fund checking failure
        throw new OrderProcessorException(
           "Error occured while taking payment.", 4);
    }
    // audit
    processor.CreateAudit("PSTakePayment finished.", 20401);
    }
  }
}
```

Testing the Pipeline

Now that you have all this in place, it's important to test with a few orders. You can do this easily by making sure you create a customer with "magic" credit card details. As mentioned earlier in the chapter, these are numbers that DataCash supplies for testing purposes and can be used to obtain specific responses from DataCash. A sample of these numbers is shown in Table 20-2; a full list is available on the DataCash web site.

Table 20-2. *DataCash Credit Card Test Numbers*

Card Type	Card Number	Return Code	Description	Sample Message
Switch	4936000000000000001	1	Authorizes with a random authorization code	AUTH CODE ??????
	4936000000000000019	7	Declines the transaction	DECLINED
	6333000000000005	1	Authorizes with a random authorization code	AUTH CODE ??????

Table 20-2. *DataCash Credit Card Test Numbers (Continued)*

Card Type	Card Number	Return Code	Description	Sample Message
	6333000000000013	7	Declines the transaction	`DECLINED`
	6333000000123450	1	Authorizes with a random authorization code	`AUTH CODE ??????`
Visa	4242424242424242	7	Declines the transaction	`DECLINED`
	4444333322221111	1	Authorizes with a random authorization code	`AUTH CODE ??????`
	4546389010000131	1	Authorizes with a random authorization code	`AUTH CODE ??????`

If you use one of the cards whose transactions get authorized, you'll be able to finish test transactions successfully, and the audit trail will look like Figure 20-2.

Audit ID	Date Stamp	Message Number	Message
224	2/1/2009 6:08:23 PM	10000	Order Processor started.
225	2/1/2009 6:08:23 PM	20000	PSInitialNotification started.
226	2/1/2009 6:08:23 PM	20002	Notification e-mail sent to customer.
227	2/1/2009 6:08:23 PM	20001	PSInitialNotification finished.
228	2/1/2009 6:08:23 PM	20100	PSCheckFunds started.
229	2/1/2009 6:08:25 PM	20102	Funds available for purchase.
230	2/1/2009 6:08:25 PM	20101	PSCheckFunds finished.
231	2/1/2009 6:08:25 PM	20200	PSCheckStock started.
232	2/1/2009 6:08:25 PM	20202	Notification e-mail sent to supplier.
233	2/1/2009 6:08:25 PM	20201	PSCheckStock finished.
234	2/1/2009 6:08:25 PM	10001	Order Processor finished.
235	2/1/2009 6:09:00 PM	10000	Order Processor started.
236	2/1/2009 6:09:00 PM	20300	PSStockOK started.
237	2/1/2009 6:09:00 PM	20302	Stock confirmed by supplier.
238	2/1/2009 6:09:00 PM	20301	PSStockOK finished.
239	2/1/2009 6:09:00 PM	20400	PSTakePayment started.
240	2/1/2009 6:09:01 PM	20402	Funds deducted from customer credit card account.
241	2/1/2009 6:09:01 PM	20401	PSTakePayment finished.
242	2/1/2009 6:09:01 PM	20500	PSShipGoods started.
243	2/1/2009 6:09:01 PM	20502	Ship goods e-mail sent to supplier.
244	2/1/2009 6:09:01 PM	20501	PSShipGoods finished.
245	2/1/2009 6:09:01 PM	10001	Order Processor finished.
246	2/1/2009 6:09:10 PM	10000	Order Processor started.
247	2/1/2009 6:09:10 PM	20600	PSShipOK started.
248	2/1/2009 6:09:10 PM	20602	Order dispatched by supplier.
249	2/1/2009 6:09:10 PM	20601	PSShipOK finished.
250	2/1/2009 6:09:10 PM	20700	PSFinalNotification started.
251	2/1/2009 6:09:10 PM	20702	Dispatch e-mail sent to customer.
252	2/1/2009 6:09:10 PM	20701	PSFinalNotification finished.
253	2/1/2009 6:09:10 PM	10001	Order Processor finished.

Figure 20-2. *Audit trail for successful transaction*

Going Live

Moving from the test account to the live one is now simply a matter of replacing the DataCash information in `web.config`. After you have set up a merchant bank account, you can use these details to set up a new DataCash account, obtaining new client and password data along the way. You also need to change the URL that you send data to—it needs to be the live server. Other than removing the test user accounts from the database, this is all you need to do before exposing your newly completed e-commerce application to customers.

Summary

In this chapter, we have completed our e-commerce application by integrating it with credit card authorization. Once you've put your own products in the database, hooked it up with your suppliers, obtained a merchant bank account, and put it on the Web, you're ready to go! Okay, so that's still quite a lot of work, but none of it is particularly difficult. The hard work is behind you now!

Specifically in this chapter, we have looked at the theory behind credit card transactions on the Web and at one full implementation—DataCash. We created a library that can be used to access DataCash and integrated it with our application.

CHAPTER 21

■ ■ ■

Product Reviews

At this point, we have a complete and functional e-commerce web site. However, this doesn't stop us from adding even more features to make it more useful and pleasant for visitors.

By adding a product reviews system to your web site, you can increase the chances that visitors will return to your site, either to write a review for a product they bought or to see what other people think about that product.

A review system can also help you learn your customers' tastes, which enables you to improve the product recommendations and even make changes in the web site or the structure of the product catalog based on customer feedback.

To make things easy for both the customer and us, we'll add the list of product reviews and the form to add a new product review to the product details pages. The form to add a new product will show up for only registered users, because we decided not to allow anonymous reviews (however, you can easily change this if you like). We'll create the code for this new feature in the usual way, starting from the database and finishing with the user interface (UI).

Planning the Product Reviews Feature

The product reviews feature is simple enough. It is governed by two simple design decisions:

- The list of reviews and the interface elements necessary for adding new reviews should be displayed below the list of product recommendations on the product details pages, as shown in Figure 21-1.

- Only registered users can write product reviews. If the user is not logged in, we should invite the reader to log in and write a review, as shown in Figure 21-2.

We store the product reviews in a database table named review, which is manipulated by two stored procedures—CatalogGetProductReviews and CatalogAddProductReview—whose names are self-describing. The other code we'll write will only package this functionality in a form that is accessible to your visitors.

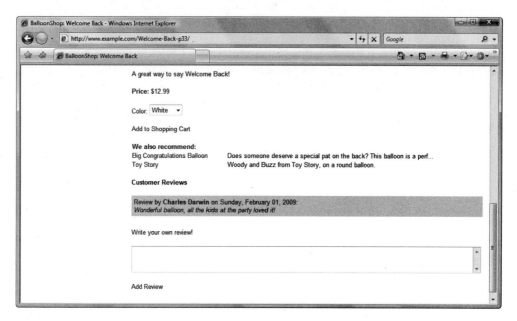

Figure 21-1. *The product details page containing product reviews*

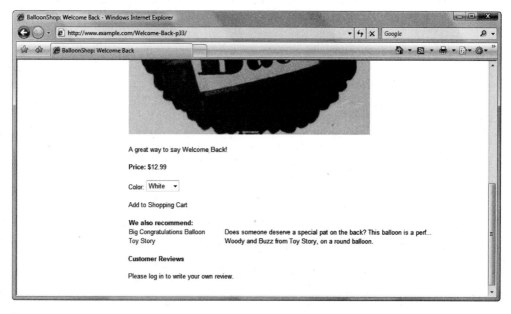

Figure 21-2. *Log in and write a review!*

Implementing Product Reviews

Follow the steps of this exercise to create the database table, stored procedures, business tier, and presentation tier functionality required for the product reviews feature.

Exercise: Implementing Product Reviews

1. Start SQL Server Management Studio, load the BalloonShop database, and open a new SQL query page. Then execute this code, which adds the Review table in your BalloonShop database:

```
-- Create review table
CREATE TABLE Review (
   ReviewID INT NOT NULL  PRIMARY KEY IDENTITY(1,1),
   CustomerID UNIQUEIDENTIFIER NOT NULL,
   ProductID INT NOT NULL,
   Review NVARCHAR(MAX) NOT NULL,
   DateCreated DATETIME NOT NULL)
```

2. Execute the following code, which creates the CatalogGetProductReviews stored procedure in the BalloonShop database. The CatalogGetProductReviews stored procedure retrieves the reviews for the product identified by the inProductId parameter. We also need the name of the reviewer, so we made an INNER JOIN with the customer table.

```
-- Create CatalogGetProductReviews stored procedure
CREATE PROCEDURE CatalogGetProductReviews(@ProductID INT)
AS
SELECT u.UserName as CustomerName,
       r.Review as ProductReview,
       r.DateCreated as ReviewDate
FROM Review r
INNER JOIN aspnet_Users u ON u.UserID = r.CustomerID
WHERE r.ProductID = @ProductID
ORDER BY r.DateCreated DESC
```

3. Execute the following code, which adds the CatalogAddProductReview stored procedure in the BalloonShop database. When a registered visitor adds a product review, the CatalogAddProductReview stored procedure is called.

```
-- Create CatalogAddProductReview stored procedure
CREATE PROCEDURE CatalogAddProductReview
(@CustomerId UNIQUEIDENTIFIER, @ProductId INT, @Review NVARCHAR(MAX))
AS
INSERT INTO Review (CustomerID, ProductID, Review, DateCreated)
   VALUES (@CustomerId, @ProductId, @Review, GETDATE())
```

4. Add the corresponding business tier methods to the Catalog class in App_Code/CatalogAccess.cs:

```
// Gets the reviews for a specific product
public static DataTable GetProductReviews(string productId)
{
  // get a configured DbCommand object
  DbCommand comm = GenericDataAccess.CreateCommand();
  // set the stored procedure name
  comm.CommandText = "CatalogGetProductReviews";
  // create a new parameter
  DbParameter param = comm.CreateParameter();
  param.ParameterName = "@ProductID";
  param.Value = productId;
  param.DbType = DbType.Int32;
  comm.Parameters.Add(param);
  // execute the stored procedure
  return GenericDataAccess.ExecuteSelectCommand(comm);
}

// Add a new shopping cart item
public static bool AddReview(string customerId, string productId, string review)
{
  // get a configured DbCommand object
  DbCommand comm = GenericDataAccess.CreateCommand();
  // set the stored procedure name
  comm.CommandText = "CatalogAddProductReview ";
  // create a new parameter
  DbParameter param = comm.CreateParameter();
  param.ParameterName = "@CustomerID";
  param.Value = customerId;
  param.DbType = DbType.String;
  comm.Parameters.Add(param);
  // create a new parameter
  param = comm.CreateParameter();
  param.ParameterName = "@ProductID";
  param.Value = productId;
  param.DbType = DbType.Int32;
  comm.Parameters.Add(param);
  // create a new parameter
  param = comm.CreateParameter();
  param.ParameterName = "@Review";
  param.Value = review;
  param.DbType = DbType.String;
  comm.Parameters.Add(param);
  // returns true in case of success or false in case of an error
  try
  {
```

```
    // execute the stored procedure and return true if it executes
    // successfully, or false otherwise
    return (GenericDataAccess.ExecuteNonQuery(comm) != -1);
  }
  catch
  {
    // prevent the exception from propagating, but return false to
    // signal the error
    return false;
  }
}
```

5. The UI consists of the `ProductReviews.ascx` Web User Control that will be placed on the product details page. Start by creating `ProductReviews.ascx` in the `UserControls` folder (using a code-behind file) and editing it like this:

```
<%@ Control Language="C#" AutoEventWireup="true"
CodeFile="ProductReviews.ascx.cs" Inherits="UserControls_ProductReviews"%>

<p class="ReviewHead">Customer Reviews</p>

<asp:DataList ID="list" runat="server" ShowFooter="true"
CssClass="ReviewTable">
  <ItemStyle CssClass="ReviewTable" />
  <ItemTemplate>
    <p>
      Review by <strong>
        <%# Eval("CustomerName") %></strong> on
      <%# String.Format("{0:D}", Eval("ReviewDate")) %>:
      <br />
      <i>
        <%# Eval("ProductReview") %></i>
    </p>
  </ItemTemplate>
  <FooterTemplate>
  </FooterTemplate>
</asp:DataList>

<asp:Panel ID="addReviewPanel" runat="server">
  <p>
    Write your own review!</p>
  <p>
    <asp:TextBox runat="server" ID="reviewTextBox" Rows="3"
      Columns="88" TextMode="MultiLine" />
  </p>
  <asp:LinkButton ID="addReviewButton" runat="server"
    OnClick="addReviewButton_Click">Add Review</asp:LinkButton>
</asp:Panel>
```

```
<asp:LoginView ID="LoginView1" runat="server">
  <AnonymousTemplate>
    <p>
      Please log in to write your own review.</p>
  </AnonymousTemplate>
</asp:LoginView>
```

6. Open the code-behind file and complete the event handlers like this:

```
using System;
using System.Web;
using System.Data;
using System.Web.Security;

public partial class UserControls_ProductReviews : System.Web.UI.↵
UserControl
{
  protected void Page_Load(object sender, EventArgs e)
  {
    // Retrieve ProductID from the query string
    string productId = Request.QueryString["ProductID"];
    // display product recommendations
    DataTable table = CatalogAccess.GetProductReviews(productId);
    if (table.Rows.Count > 0)
    {
      list.ShowHeader = true;
      list.DataSource = table;
      list.DataBind();
    }
    // show or hide the review panel
    addReviewPanel.Visible =
      (HttpContext.Current.User != null
        && HttpContext.Current.User.Identity.IsAuthenticated);
  }

  protected void addReviewButton_Click(object sender, EventArgs e)
  {
    string customerId = Membership.GetUser(
      HttpContext.Current.User.Identity.Name)
      .ProviderUserKey.ToString();
    string productId = Request.QueryString["ProductID"];
    CatalogAccess.AddReview(customerId, productId, reviewTextBox.Text);
    Response.Redirect(HttpContext.Current.Request.RawUrl);
  }
}
```

7. Add the following styles at the end BalloonShop.css:

```
.ReviewHead {
  font-weight: bold;
}

.ReviewTable {
  background: #ccddff;
  border-bottom: #fff solid 3px;
  display: block;
  padding: 5px;
  width: 100%;
}
```

8. Drag ProductReviews.ascx from Solution Explorer to the bottom of the placeholder in Product.aspx.

9. Load BalloonShop in your browser and click a product to view its product details page. If you're not logged in and the product has no reviews, you'll see the output shown in Figure 21-2. A sample output for a product that has one review was presented in Figure 21-1.

How It Works: The Reviews Componentized Template

The ProductReviews.ascx control is made up of three important controls:

- A DataList control that displays the existing product reviews.

- A Panel control that contains the controls necessary to create a new customer review.

- A LoginView control that displays the following message to unauthenticated users: "Please log in to write your own review."

The code that makes things work is pretty straightforward and reuses the concepts you've already met earlier in this book.

Summary

Yep, it was that simple. Although you might want to add improvements for your own solution (for example, allow the visitors to edit their reviews, or forbid them from adding more reviews), the base is there, and it works as expected.

You're now all set to proceed to the final chapter of this book, where you'll learn how to sell items to your customer from an outside source (we've chosen Amazon.com) by using XML Web Services.

CHAPTER 22

Integrating Amazon Web Services

So far in this book, you've learned how to integrate external functionality provided PayPal and DataCash to process payments from your customers. In this chapter, you'll learn new possibilities for integrating features from external sources through web services. Knowing how to interact with third-party web services can offer you an important advantage over your competitors. More specifically, in this chapter you will

- Learn what web services are

- Learn how to connect to the Amazon E-Commerce Service

- Use the Amazon E-Commerce Service to sell Amazon balloons through BalloonShop

Introducing Web Services

A *web service* is a piece of functionality that is exposed through a web interface using standard Internet protocols such as HTTP. The messages exchanged by the client and the server are encoded using an XML-based protocol named Simple Object Access Protocol (SOAP), or using Representational State Transfer (REST), and are sent to the server over the HTTP protocol.

REST uses carefully crafted URLs with specific name-value pairs to call specific methods on the servers. REST is considered to be the easiest way to communicate with the web services that expose this interface. When using REST to access a web service, you simply make an HTTP GET request, and you'll receive the response in XML format.

SOAP is an XML-based standard for encoding the information transferred in a web service request or response. SOAP is fostered by a number of organizations, including powerful companies such as Microsoft, IBM, and Sun.

The beauty of using web services is that the client and the server can use any technology, any language, and any platform. As long as they exchange information with a standard protocol such as SOAP over HTTP, there is no problem if the client is a cell phone and the server is a Java application running on Solaris, for example.

The possibilities are exciting, and we recommend you purchase a book that specializes in web services to discover more about their world. Refer to the list of public web services at http://www.xmethods.net to get an idea of the kinds of external functionality you can integrate into your application.

In this chapter, you'll learn how to integrate Amazon Web Services (AWS) to interact with Amazon and sell Amazon.com products through your BalloonShop web site.

You already have an e-commerce web site that sells balloons to its customers. You can go further and make some more money from their passion for balloons by incorporating related gifts from Amazon.com into your site. Do you do this for free? Oh no, you'll display Amazon.com's details on your site, but the final checkout will be processed by Amazon.com, and Amazon.com will deliver, in your bank account, a small commission for purchases made from your web site. Sounds like easy money, doesn't it?

In this chapter, you'll learn how to use AWS to add a special department called "Amazon Balloons" to your web store, which you can see in Figure 22-1. This will be a special department in that it will be handled differently than the others—for example, payment is handled directly by Amazon when the visitor wants to buy a product. This chapter explores just a small subset of AWS's full power, so if you really want to make a fortune out of this service, you should dig deeper to find more substance.

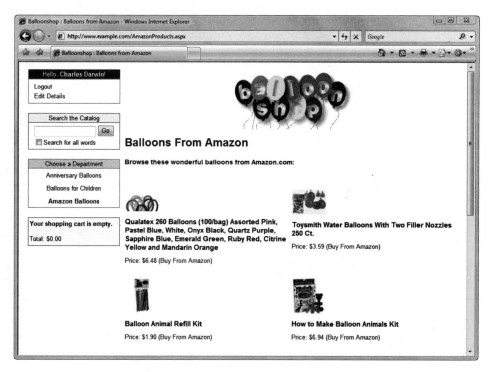

Figure 22-1. *Integrating the "Balloons from Amazon" department into BalloonShop*

The rest of the chapter is divided into two parts. In the first part, you'll learn how to access AWS; in the second part, you'll integrate AWS into the BalloonShop web site.

■**Tip** The code in this chapter is independent of the rest of the site, so all you need to get started integrating Amazon.com functionality is the code from the first four chapters (so you have a working product catalog). Of course, with minor adjustments you can also adapt this code to your own personal solutions.

Creating Your Amazon.com Web Services Account

The official AWS web site is located at `http://aws.amazon.com`. You can find the latest version of the documentation at `http://developer.amazonwebservices.com/connect`—be sure to bookmark this URL because you'll find it very useful.

Before moving on, you need to create your account with AWS. To access AWS, you need an **access key ID**, which identifies your account in the AWS system. The access key ID is a 20-character alphanumeric string.

If you don't already have one, apply now at `http://www.amazon.com/gp/aws/registration/registration-form.html`.

The access key ID gives you access to more Amazon web services and Alexa web services (Alexa is a service owned by Amazon.com), as you can see in Figure 22-2. The access key isn't public information (you're not supposed to share it with anyone), but it's free for anyone to get one.

For the paid web services, or for the services that need to be accessed in a secure way, Amazon.com uses another key called a *secret access key*, which you also get upon registration. We will not be using the secret access key in this chapter, however. To access AWS, you need only the access key.

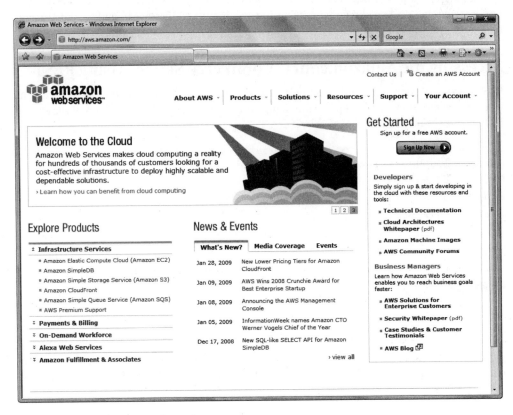

Figure 22-2. *Amazon.com web services*

Obtaining an Amazon.com Associate ID

The access key ID you created earlier is your key to retrieving data through the Amazon AWS. This data allows you to compose the "Balloons from Amazon" department you saw in Figure 22-1.

If you want to earn commissions for Amazon.com products you sell via your site, you will also need an **associate ID**. The associate ID is used in the Buy From Amazon links you'll display in your special Amazon.com department, and it's the key that Amazon.com uses to identify you as the origin of that sale. So before moving further, if you want to make any money out of your Amazon balloons department, go get your associate ID from http://associates.amazon.com/gp/associates/apply/main.html.

Note that the associate ID and the access key ID are two independent keys you have with Amazon.com, each of them with its own purpose. The associate ID is an ID that you can include in the Amazon.com links in your web site so that Amazon.com knows that the visitors who click those links came from you. The associate ID is not secret, because anyone browsing your web site can see the ID in the Amazon.com links in your site. All you need to sell Amazon.com products through your web site is an associate ID. You don't need an access key ID, which is required only when connecting to Amazon.com web services.

In BalloonShop, we connect to Amazon.com web services (and use the access key ID) to perform searches on Amazon.com's catalog and obtain the products we include in the Amazon balloons department.

Accessing the Amazon.com E-Commerce Service Using REST

REST web services are accessed by requesting a properly formed URL. Try the following link in your browser (don't forget to replace the string [Your Access Key ID] with your real access key ID that you obtained earlier):

```
http://webservices.amazon.com/onca/xml?Service=AWSECommerceService
&AWSAccessKeyId=[Your Access Key ID]
&Operation=ItemLookup
&IdType=ASIN
&ItemId=1590598644
```

■**Tip** Make sure you type the entire URL on a single line; we've broken it down here to individual elements to make it easier to read.

Your browser will display an XML structure with information about the book you are reading now. Figure 22-3 shows this XML. (We'll discuss displaying the products, visually, in BalloonShop later. For now we are interested in seeing the data that is returned from the request.)

Figure 22-3. *The XML response of an Amazon.com web service request*

Pretty cool, huh? You have just seen REST in action. Every product in the Amazon.com database has a unique identifier called an **Amazon.com standard item number** (ASIN). For books, the ASIN is the book's ISBN (this book has the ASIN 1590598644).

The web service request you just made tells AWS the following: I have an access key ID (AWSAccessKeyId=*[Your Access Key ID]*), and I want to make an item lookup operation (&Operation=ItemLookup) to learn more about the product with the 1590598644 ASIN (&IdType=ASIN&ItemId=1590598644).

You didn't get much information about this book in this example—no price or availability information and no links to the cover picture or customer reviews. You can fine-tune the data you want to receive using response groups (a *response group* is a set of information about the product).

■**Note** At the time of writing, AWS lists more than 35 possible response groups. In this book, we'll explain the purpose of only those response groups we're using for BalloonShop; for the complete list, see the AWS documentation.

So, let's ask for some more data by using response groups. At the end of the link you composed earlier, add the following string to get more specific information about the book: &ResponseGroup=Request,SalesRank,Small,Images,VariationSummary. The complete link should look like this:

```
http://webservices.amazon.com/onca/xml?Service=AWSECommerceService
&AWSAccessKeyId=[Your Access Key ID]
&Operation=ItemLookup
&IdType=ASIN
&ItemId=1590598644
&ResponseGroup=Request,SalesRank,Small,Images,VariationSummary
```

The new XML response from Amazon.com includes more details about the Amazon.com item, as shown in Figure 22-4.

Figure 22-4. *More response groups*

■**Caution** Always remember to replace [Your Subscription ID] with your own Subscription ID. The figures display the Subscription ID the authors used when writing the book, but obviously, you should use your own.

We've just mixed five response groups: SalesRank, Request, Small, Images, and OfferSummary. To learn more about the response groups, go to http://docs.amazonwebservices.com/ AWSECommerceService/latest/DG/, click the HTML link for the latest version of the documentation, click the Response Groups link, expand the API Reference entry, and click Response Groups. Here's the description for the five response groups used in the previous example:

- The request response group is a default response group in every kind of operation, and it returns the list of name-value pairs you used to make the request.

- The SalesRank response group returns data about the current Amazon.com sales rank of the product.

- The Small response group returns general item data (ASIN, item name, URL, and so on) about items included in the response. This is a default response group for an ItemLookup operation (like we have in this example).

- The Images response group gives you the addresses for the three pictures (small, medium, and large) for each item in the response.

- The OfferSummary response group returns price information for each item in the response.

To populate the future "Amazon Balloons" department, you'll search the Amazon.com Toys department for the "balloons" keyword. The REST URL looks like this:

```
http://webservices.amazon.com/onca/xml?Service=AWSECommerceService
&SubscriptionId=[Your Subscription ID]
&Operation=ItemSearch
&SearchKeywords=balloons
&SearchIndex=Toys
&ResponseGroup=Request,Medium
```

Accessing the Amazon.com E-Commerce Service Using SOAP

Using SOAP, you use a very complex API to access the needed Amazon.com functionality. The following code, which performs the same search operation for balloons that you did earlier with REST, is using the AWSECommerceService, ItemSearch, ItemSearchRequest, and ItemSearchResponse objects from the Amazon API to perform the operation:

```
// Create Amazon objects
AWSECommerceService amazonService = new AWSECommerceService();
ItemSearch itemSearch = new ItemSearch();
ItemSearchRequest itemSearchRequest = new ItemSearchRequest();
ItemSearchResponse itemSearchResponse;
// Set up Amazon objects
itemSearch.SubscriptionId = "your Subscription ID";
itemSearchRequest.Keywords = "balloons";
itemSearchRequest.SearchIndex = "Toys";
itemSearchRequest.ResponseGroup = new string[] {"Request", "Medium"};
itemSearch.Request = new AmazonEcs.ItemSearchRequest[1] { itemSearchRequest };
// Perform the search
itemSearchResponse = amazonService.ItemSearch(itemSearch)
```

Integrating AWS with BalloonShop

The goal is to allow your customers to buy some Amazon.com balloons through your web store. For this, you'll add a special department named "Amazon Balloons," with no categories, to your departments list. When this department is clicked, your products list will be populated with some Amazon.com products (as shown earlier in Figure 22-1), each of them having a Buy from Amazon link attached to it instead of the usual Add to Cart link.

Writing the Amazon Access Code

Follow the steps in the exercise to build the code that accesses the Amazon ECS system using both SOAP and REST.

Exercise: Accessing Amazon ECS

1. Let's begin by adding a web reference to the Amazon AWS. This is only required if you plan to access AWS through SOAP. Right-click the project entry Solution Explorer and choose **Add Web Reference**.

2. In the dialog box that appears, enter the address of the AWS e-commerce service:

   ```
   http://webservices.amazon.com/AWSECommerceService/AWSECommerceService.wsdl
   ```

3. Click **Go**.

4. Change the web reference name to something easier to type, such as **AmazonEcs**, and click **Add Reference** (see Figure 22-5). A new folder in your project named App_WebReferences will contain your new reference to the Amazon ECS.

5. Open web.config and add the following configuration parameters:

   ```
   <appSettings>
     ...
     <add key="AmazonRestUrl"
   value="http://webservices.amazon.com/onca/xml?Service=AWSECommerceService"/>
     <add key="AmazonSubscriptionID" value="1R4EF7NSY0ATN521WQR2"/>
     <add key="AmazonAssociateID" value="cristiand-20"/>
     <add key="AmazonSearchKeywords" value="balloons"/>
     <add key="AmazonSearchIndex" value="Toys"/>
     <add key="AmazonResponseGroups" value="Request,Medium"/>
     <add key="AmazonEcs.AWSECommerceService"
   value="http://soap.amazon.com/onca/soap?Service=AWSECommerceService"/>
   </appSettings>
   ```

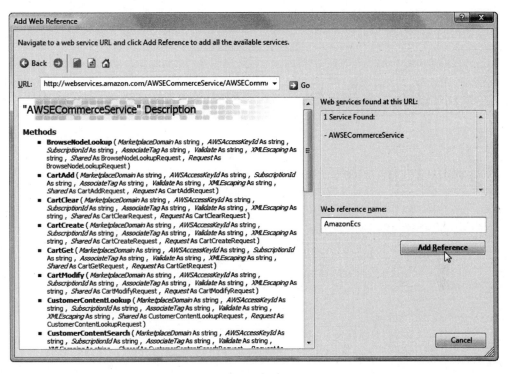

Figure 22-5. *Adding a new web reference to your project*

6. Add the following properties to the `BalloonShopConfiguration` class to allow for easier retrieval of the data you saved to `web.config`:

```csharp
// Amazon ECS REST URL
public static string AmazonRestUrl
{
  get
  {
    return ConfigurationManager.AppSettings["AmazonRestUrl"];
  }
}

// Subscription ID to access ECS
public static string SubscriptionId
{
  get
  {
    return ConfigurationManager.AppSettings["AmazonSubscriptionID"];
  }
}
```

```csharp
// the Amazon.com associate ID
public static string AssociateId
{
  get
  {
    return ConfigurationManager.AppSettings["AmazonAssociateID"];
  }
}

// keywords used to do the Amazon search
public static string SearchKeywords
{

  get
  {
    return ConfigurationManager.AppSettings["AmazonSearchKeywords"];
  }
}

// search location
public static string SearchIndex
{
  get
  {
    return ConfigurationManager.AppSettings["AmazonSearchIndex"];
  }
}

// the Amazon response groups
public static string ResponseGroups
{
  get
  {
    return ConfigurationManager.AppSettings["AmazonResponseGroups"];
  }
}
```

7. Add a new class named `AmazonAccess` to your `App_Code` folder.

8. Start coding your new class by adding references to the `System.Xml`, `System.Data`, and `AmazonEcs` namespaces:

```csharp
using System.Xml;
using System.Data;
using AmazonEcs;
```

9. Continue by adding the `GetResponseTable` method, which returns a configured `DataTable` object to be filled with the Amazon search results. This `DataTable` will ultimately be returned to the presentation tier, which will display the product data to the visitors.

```
public class AmazonAccess
{
  public AmazonAccess()
  {
    //
    // TODO: Add constructor logic here
    //
  }

  // returns a configured DataTable object that can be read by the UI
  private static DataTable GetResponseTable()
  {
    DataTable dt = new DataTable();
    dt.Columns.Add(new DataColumn("ASIN", Type.GetType("System.String")));
    dt.Columns.Add(new DataColumn("ProductName", ➥
Type.GetType("System.String")));
    dt.Columns.Add(new DataColumn("ProductPrice",
    Type.GetType("System.String")));
    dt.Columns.Add("ProductImageUrl", typeof(string));
    return dt;
  }
}
```

10. Add the `GetAmazonDataWithSoap` method, which does pretty much what it says.

```
// perform the Amazon search with SOAP and return results as a DataTable
public static DataTable GetAmazonDataWithSoap()
{
  // Create Amazon objects
  AWSECommerceService amazonService = new AWSECommerceService();
  ItemSearch itemSearch = new ItemSearch();
  ItemSearchRequest itemSearchRequest = new ItemSearchRequest();
  ItemSearchResponse itemSearchResponse;
  // Set up Amazon objects
  itemSearch.SubscriptionId = BalloonShopConfiguration.SubscriptionId;
  itemSearchRequest.Keywords = BalloonShopConfiguration.SearchKeywords;
  itemSearchRequest.SearchIndex = BalloonShopConfiguration.SearchIndex;
  itemSearchRequest.ResponseGroup =
  BalloonShopConfiguration.ResponseGroups.Split(',');
  itemSearch.Request = new AmazonEcs.ItemSearchRequest[1] ➥
{ itemSearchRequest };

  // Will store search results
  DataTable responseTable = GetResponseTable();
  // If any problems occur, we prefer to send back empty result set
  // instead of throwing exception
```

```
    try
    {
      itemSearchResponse = amazonService.ItemSearch(itemSearch);
      Item[] results = itemSearchResponse.Items[0].Item;
      // Browse the results
      foreach (AmazonEcs.Item item in results)
      {
        // product with incomplete information will be ignored
        try
        {

          //create a datarow, populate it, and add it to the table
          DataRow dataRow = responseTable.NewRow();
          dataRow["ASIN"] = item.ASIN;
          dataRow["ProductName"] = item.ItemAttributes.Title;
          dataRow["ProductImageUrl"] = item.SmallImage.URL;
          dataRow["ProductPrice"] = item.OfferSummary.LowestNewPrice.
        FormattedPrice;
          responseTable.Rows.Add(dataRow);
        }
        catch
        {
          // Ignore products with incomplete information
        }
      }
    }
    catch (Exception e)
    {
      // ignore the error
    }
    // return the results
    return responseTable;
}
```

11. Finally, add the GetAmazonDataWithRest method:

```
// perform the Amazon search with REST and return results as a DataTable
public static DataTable GetAmazonDataWithRest()
{
  // The response data table
  DataTable responseTable = GetResponseTable();
  // Compose the Amazon REST request URL
  string amazonRequest = string.Format("{0}&SubscriptionId={1}➡
&Operation=ItemSearch&Keywords={2}&SearchIndex={3}&ResponseGroup={4}", ➡
BalloonShopConfiguration.AmazonRestUrl, ➡
BalloonShopConfiguration.SubscriptionId, ➡
BalloonShopConfiguration.SearchKeywords, ➡
```

```
BalloonShopConfiguration.SearchIndex, ➥
BalloonShopConfiguration.ResponseGroups);
  // If any problems occur, we prefer to send back empty result set
  // instead of throwing exception
  try
  {
    // Load the Amazon response
    XmlDocument responseXmlDoc = new XmlDocument();
    responseXmlDoc.Load(amazonRequest);
    // Prepare XML document for searching
    XmlNamespaceManager xnm = new XmlNamespaceManager(
      responseXmlDoc.NameTable);
    xnm.AddNamespace("amz", ➥
"http://webservices.amazon.com/AWSECommerceService/2005-10-05");
    // Get the list of Item nodes
    XmlNodeList itemNodes = responseXmlDoc.SelectNodes➥
"/amz:ItemSearchResponse/amz:Items/amz:Item", xnm);
    // Copy node data to the DataTable
    foreach (XmlNode itemNode in itemNodes)
    {
      try
      {
        // Create a new datarow and populate it with data
        DataRow dataRow = responseTable.NewRow();
        dataRow["ASIN"] = itemNode["ASIN"].InnerText;
        dataRow["ProductName"] = itemNode["ItemAttributes"]["Title"]➥
.InnerText;
        dataRow["ProductImageUrl"] = itemNode["SmallImage"]["URL"]➥
.InnerText;
        dataRow["ProductPrice"] = itemNode["OfferSummary"]
      ["LowestNewPrice"]["FormattedPrice"].InnerText;
        // Add the row to the results table
        responseTable.Rows.Add(dataRow);
      }
      catch
      {
        // Ignore products with incomplete information
      }
    }
  }
  catch
  {
    // Ignore all possible errors
  }
  return responseTable;
}
```

How It Works: Working with Amazon ECS

The important points you need to understand from this exercise follow:

- The search parameter commands were saved to `web.config`, so you can change the behavior of the "Amazon Balloons" pages without modifying any C# code.

- To enable accessing ECS, you added a web reference to its WDSL file. Visual Studio was kind enough to do the rest for you, giving you direct access to the classes exposed by Amazon. To make your life even easier, you wrote a reference to the `AmazonEcs` namespace at the beginning of your file.

- The heart of the `AmazonAccess` class is composed of the two `GetAmazon...` methods, which offer identical functionality to the presentation tier, but using different access technologies: one uses SOAP; the other uses REST.

To understand these two methods, we suggest starting with the REST one. After composing the REST URL, the request is submitted to Amazon, and the results are saved to an XML document (which will look something like what you saw in Figures 22-1 and 22-2).

```
// Load the Amazon response
XmlDocument responseXmlDoc = new XmlDocument();
responseXmlDoc.Load(amazonRequest);
```

The logic that follows is extremely simple. On the retrieved XML document we make an XPath query to filter the `Item` nodes, because these contain the data we're interested in. By analyzing the response hierarchy, you will know what nodes to ask for to get your data. We also catch and ignore the eventual exceptions that can happen in case one of the nodes we're trying to query doesn't exist.

Although the logic is simple enough, its implementation details can look a bit confusing if you're not used to parsing and working with XML documents. We strongly recommend that you grab some additional documentation on that topic, as its importance to everyday development projects has increased dramatically in the past few years.

`GetAmazonDataWithSoap` performs the exact same actions, but this time by using the Amazon ECS API and the classes provided by it, instead of manually parsing an XML response file.

Implementing the Presentation Tier

Let's have another look at what we want to achieve in Figure 22-1.

Exercise: Displaying Amazon.com Products in BalloonShop

1. Open `DepartmentsList.ascx` in Source View and add the `FooterTemplate` element, like this:

```
<FooterTemplate>
  <a runat="server" href="~/AmazonProducts.aspx"
     class='<%# Request.AppRelativeCurrentExecutionFilePath ==
     "~/AmazonProducts.aspx" ? "DepartmentSelected" : ➡
"DepartmentUnselected" %>' >
  Amazon Balloons
  </a>
</FooterTemplate>
```

2. Add a new Web Form to your solution named `AmazonProducts.aspx` based on the `BalloonShop.master` Master Page.

3. Open `AmazonProducts.aspx` in Source View and modify it like this:

```
<%@ Page Title="Balloonshop : Balloons from Amazon" Language="C#"
MasterPageFile="~/BalloonShop.master" AutoEventWireup="true"
CodeFile="AmazonProducts.aspx.cs" Inherits="AmazonProducts" %>

<asp:Content ID="Content1" ContentPlaceHolderID="head" runat="Server">
</asp:Content>
<asp:Content ID="Content2" ContentPlaceHolderID="ContentPlaceHolder1" ➥
runat="Server">
  <h1 class="CatalogTitle">
    Balloons From Amazon
  </h1>
  <h2 class="CatalogDescription">
    Browse these wonderful balloons from Amazon.com:
  </h2>
  <asp:DataList ID="list" runat="server" RepeatColumns="2">
    <ItemTemplate>
      <img src='<%# Eval("ProductImageUrl") %>' border="0" />
      <h3 class="ProductTitle">
        <%# Eval("ProductName") %>
      </h3>
      <p class="DetailSection">
        Price: </span><span class="ProductPrice">
          <%# Eval("ProductPrice") %>
          (<a target="_blank" href="http://www.amazon.com/exec/obidos/➥
ASIN/
<%# Eval("ASIN") %>/ref=nosim/<%# BalloonShopConfiguration.Associ➥
ateId %>">Buy From Amazon</a>)
      </p>
      <br />
    </ItemTemplate>
  </asp:DataList>
</asp:Content>
```

4. Switch `AmazonProducts.aspx` to Design View and drag the `AmazonProductsList.ascx` control from Solution Explorer to the bottom of the page, as shown in Figure 22-6.

5. Load `AmazonProducts.aspx` to ensure your page looks like Figure 22-1.

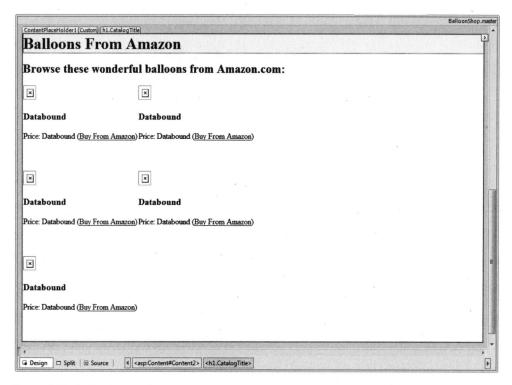

Figure 22-6. *Designing the Amazon page*

How It Works: Displaying Amazon.com Products in BalloonShop

In this exercise, you simply updated BalloonShop to display Amazon.com products by employing the techniques you studied in the first part of the chapter. The new functionality isn't especially complex, but the possibilities are exciting. When the Buy from Amazon links are clicked, Amazon.com associates that customer and what she purchases to your associate ID (which is mentioned in the links).

The code-behind file `AmazonProductsList.ascx.cs` calls `AmazonAccess.GetAmazonDataWithRest` to get the data to populate the list of products. This data is read to build the Amazon links to the retrieved products:

```
<a target="_blank" href="http://www.amazon.com/exec/obidos/ASIN/
<%# Eval("ASIN") %>/ref=nosim/<%# BalloonShopConfiguration.AssociateId %>">
```

However, you must know that Amazon offers many ways in which you can allow your visitors to buy their products. If you log in to the Associates page, you'll see a number of link types you can build and integrate into your web site.

Perhaps the most interesting and powerful is the possibility to create and manage Amazon shopping carts from your C# code, by using the Amazon API. If you're really into integrating Amazon.com into your web site, you should study the ECS documentation carefully and make the most of it.

Summary

In this chapter, you learned how to access AWS using REST and SOAP. You can use the same techniques when accessing any kind of external functionality exposed through these protocols.

Congratulations, you have just finished your journey into learning about building e-commerce web sites with *Beginning ASP.NET E-Commerce in C# 2008: From Novice to Professional*! You have the knowledge to build customized solutions that are even more interesting and powerful than what we showed you in this book. We really hope you've enjoyed reading this book, and we wish you good luck with your own personal development projects!

Index

■Special Characters

$ metacharacter, 206–207

& (ampersand) character, 207

* metacharacter, 206

* wildcard, 74

^ metacharacter, 206–207

{m,n} metacharacter, 206

+ metacharacter, 206

( ) metacharacter, 206

/? expression, 207

. metacharacter, 206

\ metacharacter, 206

? metacharacter, 206

■Numerics

301 HTTP status code, 216–219

302 HTTP status code, 216–219

404 HTTP status code, 220

500 HTTP status code, 220–222

■A

access codes, 83–85, 682–688

access key ID, 677

accounts, AWS, 677. *See also* customer accounts

add header element, 223

Add to Cart button, 270

Add to Cart link, 682

Add Web Reference option, 682

Add Web Site dialog, 34

AddAudit method, 578, 582

AddDepartment stored procedure, 300

AddItem method, 380

AdminDepartments.aspx page, 297

Administrative Tools section, 34

Administrators role, 466, 495

Admin.master master page, 422, 527, 543

AdminOrderDetails form, 430

AdminOrderDetails.aspx Web Form, 414, 437–438, 627, 633

AdminOrders.aspx page, 621, 627, 633

AdminOrders.aspx Web Form, 414–415, 422–424, 622–624

AdminProductDetailsAdmin.aspx page, 364

Adobe Flash, 22

ADO.NET, 79

aliases, 136

Allow Nulls column, 67

all-words search, 225

ALTER PROCEDURE syntax, 77

Amazon Web Services (AWS)

accessing, 678–681

accounts, creating, 677

associate ID, 678

integrating with BalloonShop, 682–690

overview, 675–676

AmazonAccess class, 688, 690

Amazon.com standard item number (ASIN), 679

AmazonEcs namespace, 684, 688

AmazonProducts.aspx file, 689

AmazonProductsList.ascx.cs file, 690

AmazonProductsList.aspx control, 689

AmountClass class, 644

ampersand (&) character, 207

AnonymousTemplate template, 498

any-words search, 225

App_Code, 589

App_Code directory
  CommerceLib directory, 566, 573, 575
  CommerceLibAccess class, 537
  communicating with DataCash, 644
  DepartmentDetails class, 150
  order details administration page, 432
  orders administration page, 419
  user profiles, 505
App_WebReferences folder, 682
application errors, 222
ApplicationException class, 572
<appSettings> element, 89, 273, 573
architecture
  three-tier, 15–20, 24
  two-tier, 19
AS keyword, 133
ASIN (Amazon.com standard item
    number), 679
ASP.NET
  debugging, 38
  overview, 20–24
  validator controls, 415–417
aspnet_regsql.exe tool, 287
aspnet_Users membership table, 532
AspNetSqlMembershipProvider
    provider, 501
.aspx extension, 23
associate ID, AWS, 678
asymmetric encryption, 472
Attribute data table, 182–183
AttributeName field, 187
AttributeValue data table, 182, 184–185
AttributeValue field, 187
AttributeValueID field, 187
attrTable DataTable object, 194
Audit database table, 565, 569, 608
AuditID column, 569
AuthCode column, 532
AuthCode field, 583, 659
AuthCode property, 660

authentication, defined, 285
AuthenticationClass class, 645
authorization, defined, 285
AutoGenerateColumns property, 425, 437
automatic properties, 613
automatic URL correction, 218–219
AutoNumber column, 67
AWS. See Amazon Web Services
AWSECommerceService object, 681

■B
backups, 8
BalloonShop project
  credit card transactions
    business tier modifications, 659–664
    live account, 666
    testing pipeline, 664–665
  development environment, 29–34
  downloading code, 53
  integrating AWS with, 682–690
  order administration
    business tier modifications, 611–621
    database modifications, 608–611
    overview, 607–608
    testing order administration page,
      633–635
  overview, 29
  search engine optimization, 197–204
  site skeleton, implementing, 45–53
  SQL Server database, creating, 39–44
  user profiles, 504–520
  Web application, creating, 35–38
BalloonShopConfiguration class, 79, 89, 570,
    572–573, 659–660, 683
BalloonShopConnection connection
    string, 508
BalloonShop.master Master Page, 527,
    535, 689
Binary data type, 66
business field, 270

business tier (middle tier)

    custom shopping cart, 380–383

    overview, 15

    pipeline implementation, 589–602

    product attributes, 188–189

    product catalog, 89–97, 147–158, 243–245

    product recommendations, 457–458

Buy From Amazon link, 678

■C

C#, 24, 146

caching, 263–265

CancelDestinationPageUrl property, 498

Canceled bit, 437

Capture class, 209

CaptureCollection class, 209

CardClass class, 645

CardNumberX property, 494

<CardTxn> element, 657

CardTxnRequestClass class, 646

CardTxnResponseClass class, 646

Cart Admin page, 402

Cascading Style Sheets (CSS) files, 98

CASE keyword, 134

Cassini web server, 32

catalog. *See* product catalog

catalog administration

    categories, 320–324

    departments, 299–317

    products

        details of, 348–364

        overview, 333–348

Catalog class, 670

catalog_get_ProductAttributeValues stored procedure, 183

CatalogAccess class, 79, 89, 150, 152–153, 188, 243, 457

CatalogAccess.cs file, 149

CatalogAddProductReview stored procedure, 667, 669

Catalog.aspx Web Form, 163, 204, 207

CatalogGetAllProductsInCategory stored procedure, 334

CatalogGetCategoriesInDepartment procedure, 141, 154

CatalogGetCategoriesWithoutProduct stored procedure, 350

CatalogGetCategoriesWithProduct stored procedure, 350

CatalogGetCategoryDetails stored procedure, 140

CatalogGetDepartmentDetails stored procedure, 140, 151

CatalogGetProductAttributeValues stored procedure, 185, 187–189, 194

CatalogGetProductDetails stored procedure, 141

CatalogGetProductRecommendations stored procedure, 453

CatalogGetProductReviews stored procedure, 667–669

CatalogGetProductsInCategory stored procedure, 142–143

CatalogGetProductsOnCatalogPromotion stored procedure, 141–142

CatalogGetProductsOnDepartmentPromotion stored procedure, 143–145

CatalogMoveProductToCategory stored procedure, 351

catch block, 87, 572

CategoriesList.ascx control, 159

Category table, 121

Category URL, 200

CategoryDetails struct, 151

CategoryID field, 119, 121

CategoryID parameter, 159

CategoryIndex class, 265

CausesValidation property, 427

Certificate Signing Request (CSR), 526

Char data type, 66

checkout, PayPal, 270–277

Checkout button, 411–413

checkout page, 520–521, 523–525

Checkout.aspx.cs file, 557–558, 560

CheckProductUrl method, 219

Click event method, 258

clients, knowing, 9–10

client-server architecture, 19, 22

client-side validation, 415–417

code-behind model, 22

coding standards, 26–27

Color attribute, 196

columns, 64–68

comm object, 145

command object, 82

CommandText property, 81

Comments field, 408

CommerceLib class, 535, 566, 571, 608, 611

CommerceLibAccess class, 537, 539, 542,
    552, 557, 570, 584–585, 611–612,
    616–617, 624–625, 632

CommerceLibAccess.cs file, 537

CommerceLibAuditInfo class, 613

CommerceLibException class, 570–571

CommerceLibOrderDetailInfo class,
    538–539, 542, 613, 616

CommerceLibOrderGetAuditTrail stored
    procedure, 608, 613

CommerceLibOrderGetInfo stored
    procedure, 550

CommerceLibOrderInfo class, 540–542,
    554–556, 560, 577, 580, 586, 611–614,
    616–617, 630

CommerceLibOrderSetAuthCode stored
    procedure, 583–585

CommerceLibOrderSetDateShipped stored
    procedure, 584

CommerceLibOrdersGetByCustomer stored
    procedure, 608–609, 617

CommerceLibOrdersGetByDate stored
    procedure, 609, 618

CommerceLibOrdersGetByRecent stored
    procedure, 609–610, 618

CommerceLibOrdersGetByStatus stored
    procedure, 610–611, 619

CommerceLibOrderUpdate stored
    procedure, 611

CommerceLibOrderUpdateStatus stored
    procedure, 583

CommerceLibShippingGetInfo stored
    procedure, 551–553

CompareValidator control, 417, 429

Compiled member, 211

Completed bit, 436

ComputeHash method, 471

<configSections> element, 201

<configuration> element, 201

Configure Data Source control, 508

Connections tab, 34

ConnectionString property, 80

ContentPageFolder object, 48

ContentPlaceHolder element, 48, 53

ContinueDestinationPageUrl property,
    498, 515

ContinueNow field, 580

ControlToCompare property, 417

ControlToValidate property, 417

conversion rate, 10–11

ConvertDataTableToOrders method, 617

Convert.ToBase64String utility function, 471

cookies, 376

COUNT aggregate function, 452

count parameter, 618

CreateAudit method, 570–571, 577

CreateAudit stored procedure, 569–570

CreateCategory stored procedure, 321

CreateCommand method, 84, 96, 149, 542

CreateCommerceLibOrder method, 535, 553–554

CreateConnection method, 84

CreateCustomerOrder stored procedure, 533–534, 551

CreateDecryptor method, 481

CreateOrder stored procedure, 409–410

CreateParameter method, 145

CreateProduct stored procedure, 335

CreateUserButtonText property, 498

CreateUserWizard control, 496–498

CreateXml method, 493

credit card transactions, 637–639, 659–666

cross joins, 186, 187

cross-selling, 447

cryptographic stream, 474

CSR (Certificate Signing Request), 526

CSS (Cascading Style Sheets) files, 98

CssClass property, 98, 107, 417

CultureInvariant member, 211

CurrentPipelineSection field, 580

customer accounts
    checkout page, 520–521, 523–525
    customer details
        overview, 502–503
        user profiles in ASP.NET, 503
        user profiles in BalloonShop, 504–520
    customer logins, 495–502
    overview, 465–467
    SecurityLib class
        encryption, 472–495
        hashing, 468–470, 472
        overview, 467–468
    setting up secure connections
        enforcing SSL connections, 526–529
        obtaining SSL certificates, 526
        overview, 525–526
    storing, 466

Customer class, 566

customer details page, 466

customer orders. *See also* tax and shipping charges
    accessing, 536–545
    administering
        business tier, 611–621
        database modifications, 608–611
        overview, 607–608
        presentation tier, 621–633
        testing order administration page, 633–635
    displaying existing orders, 417–418
    implementing order-placing system, 403–413
    order details, 430–445
    overview, 413–415
    placing, 532–536
    processing, 7, 11–12
    reducing costs of, 6–7
    validation, 415–417

customer satisfaction, 10–11

Customer table, 407

CustomerAddressAsString field, 545

CustomerID column, 532

customers
    acquiring information about, 12
    bringing back, 7
    getting, 5
    making spend more, 6
    servicing, 7

Customers role, 495

CustomerServiceEmail class, 573

CustomValidator control, 416

■D

dashesRegex regular expression, 212, 215

Data Encryption Standard (DES), 473

data tables
    columns, 64–68
    data types, 65–67
    default values, 67
    indexes, 69
    overview, 61–62
    primary keys, 62–64
data tier
    custom shopping cart, 372–375
    overview, 15
    paging at, 137
    product attributes, 182–188
    product recommendations, 449–456
data types, 65–67
databases, communicating with
    overview, 72
    SQL, 73–76
    stored procedures, 76–77
Databases node, 41
DataCash system
    exchanging XML data, 643–659
    fulfillment request and response, 642–643
    integrating with BalloonShop, 659–664
    overview, 639–640
    preauthentication request and response,
        640–642
dataCashClient, 652
DataCashLibTest.aspx Web Form, 652
DataCashLibTest.aspx.cs file, 652
dataCashPassword class, 652
DataCashRequest class, 649, 657
DataCashResponse class, 651, 657–658
DataGrid control, 627
DataKeyNames property, 425
DataList control, 98, 104, 159, 167, 189, 194
DataRow object, 541
DataRowView item, 194
DataTable class, 83, 684
date_created field, 453

DateShipped field, 408, 432
DateStamp column, 569
DateTime data type, 65
DbCommand object, 145, 149
DbParameter object, 145–146
DbProviderFactory class, 84
debugging, 37
declarative security, 286
Decrypt method, 479, 481
DecryptData method, 491, 493
decryptor object, 474
Default.aspx file, 23, 37, 39, 50, 53
Default.aspx.cs file, 39
DELETE statement, 75–76
DeleteCategory stored procedure, 321
DeleteDepartment stored procedure, 301
Department data table, 61–62, 65–66, 69
Department URL, 200
Department-Category relation, 118
DepartmentDetails object, 150–151
DepartmentID field, 119, 121
DepartmentID parameter, 159
DepartmentIndex query string
    parameter, 264
DepartmentsList control, 98, 104
DepartmentsList.ascx Web User Control, 60,
    98, 688
DES (Data Encryption Standard), 473
Description field name, 121, 127
development environment, 29–34
Digital Signature Algorithm (DSA), 473
Display property, 417
DisplayMode property, 417
DISTINCT clause, 144
Download Now! link, 30
DropDownList control, 195, 628
DSA (Digital Signature Algorithm), 473
Duration parameter, 264
dynamic product recommendations, 447–448
dynamic URLs, 199

■ E

ECMAScript member, 211

EditButton button, 519

<EditItemTemplate> template, 511

emailing error reports, 88

EnableValidation property, 417

EnableViewState property, 429

Encrypt method, 479

EncryptData method, 491–493

_encryptedData member, 493

encryption

    overview, 472–474

    SecureCard class, 482–495

    StringEncryptor class, 474–482

encryptor object, 474

Enforce password policy check box, 42

errorLabel control, 623–624

ErrorMessage property, 417

exact-match search, 225

Exception class, 88

exceptions, catching and handling, 86–87

EXEC command, 188

Execute method, 82

ExecuteNonQuery method, 82

ExecuteReader method, 82

ExecuteScalar method, 82, 410

ExecuteSearch method, 258

ExecuteSelectCommand method, 96, 617

ExplicitCapture member, 211

■ F

featured products, 447

fields, 62

finally block, 87

FindControl control, 194

Flash, 22

flexible architecture, 14

FooterTemplate element, 688

for loop, 245

forbidden element, 223

FOREIGN KEY constraint, 120–121, 407

foreign keys, 120

<forms> definition, 527

FormView control, 502, 519

FROM keyword, 76

Front page URL, 200

Full Text Search feature, 30–32

FULLTEXT catalog and indexes, 229–232

Full-Text Search Developer InfoCenter, 227

full-text search feature, 227–232

■ G

generic data access code, 83–85

GenericDataAccess class, 79, 89, 149, 542, 617

GET request, 675

GetAmazonDataWithRest method, 686, 690

GetAmazonDataWithSoap class, 685, 688

GetByDate method, 421

GetByRecent method, 420

GetCategoryDetails method, 151–152

GetCurrentPipelineSection method, 580, 601–602

GETDATE( ) function, 408, 453

GetDepartmentDetails method, 149–150

GetDepartments stored procedure, 60, 76

GetDetails method, 434

GetInfo method, 433, 441

GetItems method, 383

GetMailBody( ) method, 592, 598

GetOrder method, 542

GetOrderAuditTrail method, 613–614, 616

GetOrderDetails method, 539, 542

GetOrdersByCustomer method, 617–618, 624

GetOrdersByDate method, 618

GetOrdersByRecent method, 618–619

GetOrdersByStatus method, 619

GetProductAttributeValues stored procedure, 182

GetProductDetails method, 152–154

GetProductsInCategory method, 143, 157–158

GetProductsOnDeptPromo method, 156–157

GetProductsOnFrontPromo method, 154–155

GetRecommendations method, 457

GetResponseTable method, 684

GetShippingInfo method, 552–553, 557

GetTotalAmount method, 383

GetUnverifiedUncanceled method, 421

GetVerifiedUncompleted method, 422

goButton_Click, 602

gone element, 223

GridView control, 300, 425, 429, 439

Group class, 209

GroupCollection class, 209

Groups collection, 210

growth, designing for, 14–15

GUID value, 623

■H

hashing, 285, 467–472

HasValue property, 621

Header Web User Control, 46

headers, 104

HeaderText property, 417

<HistoricTxn> element, 657

HistoricTxnClass, 646

Hosting services, 220

hosts file, 33

howManyPages parameter, 154

HTML Server Controls, 23–24

HTTP (Hypertext Transfer Protocol)

    headers, 216

    overview, 260

    status codes, 216–222

HttpContext.Current property, 517

HTTPS (HyperText Transport Protocol [Secure]), 525

HttpUtility class, 208, 215

HttpWebRequest, 657

Hypertext Transfer Protocol. *See* HTTP

HyperText Transport Protocol (Secure) (HTTPS), 525

■I

ID parameter, 577

IDENTITY column, 184

identity columns, 67–68

If element, 223

IgnoreCase member, 211

IgnorePatternWhitespace member, 211

IIS (Internet Information Services), 29, 32–33

IIS Frontpage Extensions node, 33

IIS Manager tool, 34

Image field name, 127

Image variable data type, 66

Images folder, 49

Images response group, 681

indexes, 69

IndexOf method, 658

initialization vector (IV), 473

inProductId parameter, 669

input parameters, 145

INSERT INTO command, 139, 186

INSERT statement, 74–75, 185, 410

<InsertItemTemplate> template, 509

Int data type, 65

Intelligencia.UrlRewriter assembly, 200

Internet Information Services (IIS), 29, 32–33

Internet payment service providers, 267–268

IPipelineSection class, 566, 570, 574, 581, 592

IPipelineSection.cs file, 574

ISAPI filter, 199

ISAPI_Rewrite product, 199

isDecrypted flag, 493

isEncrypted flag, 493

IsMatch method, 210

IsPostBack property, 258

IsSecureConnection method, 527

ItemAsString utility field, 539

ItemDataBound event, 189, 194

ItemLookup operation, 681

ItemSearch object, 681

ItemSearchRequest object, 681

ItemSearchResponse object, 681

ItemTemplate control, 194

<ItemTemplate> template, 509

IV (initialization vector), 473

■J

JavaScript, 22

JOIN clause, 135

joining data tables, 134–136

junction tables, 119

■K

keyword-rich URLs

   for BalloonShop, 200–204

   generating, 211–215

   ISAPI_Rewrite, 199

   overview, 198–199

   UrlRewriter.NET, 199

■L

Label control, 98

LEFT function, 133

Link class, 211–212, 214, 218–219

link factory, 102

Link.cs file, 218

list_ItemDataBound method, 190, 194

List<CommerceLibAuditInfo> class, 613

List<CommerceLibOrderInfo> collection, 617, 624

List<ShippingInfo> object, 552

Location combo box, 36

Location parameter, 264

logic, adding to site

   business tier code, 89

   commands, 81–83

   connecting to SQL server, 79–81

   exceptions, 86–87

   generic data access code, 83–85

   sending emails, 88

   stored procedures, 81–83

logins, customer, 495–502

Logins node, 42

LoginView control, 497

■M

MailAdmin method, 577, 578, 581–582

MailCustomer method, 590, 592

MailMessage class, 88

MailSupplier method, 590

Management Tools—Basic option, 32

many-to-many relationships, 117–120

MarkCanceled method, 437

MarkCompleted method, 436

MarkVerified method, 436

Master Pages, 23, 45–53, 527

Match class, 209–210

MatchCollection class, 209

Matches method, 210

MatchEvaluator class, 209

MembershipUser class, 518, 535, 541

MemoryStream object, 480

Message column, 569

MessageNumber column, 569

messageNumber parameter, 571

metacharacters, 206–207

Microsoft Passport authentication, 466

middle tier. See business tier

MinimumValue property, 417

Money data type, 65

MoveProductToCategory stored procedure, 351

MSDN Express Library, 30

Multiline member, 211

■N

Name field name, 121, 127

NChar data type, 66

.NET regular expressions, 208–211

newDateShipped parameter, 621

nexus, 546

None member, 211

nonsecure connection, 528

not-allowed element, 223

not-found element, 223

NotFound.aspx file, 220

not-implemented element, 223

NText data type, 66

n-Tier Architecture, 19–20

NULL value, 67

nullable columns, 67

NVarChar data type, 66

nvarchar(max) data type, 128

■O

ObjectDataSource control, 502, 508, 518

od1 instance, 450

od2 instance, 450

OfferSummary response group, 681

OnDepartmentPromotion field name, 127

one-to-many relationships, 117–118

OnInit property, 528

OnPreRender event handler, 519

Operator property, 417

OR operator, 211

Order Administration page, 633–635

ORDER BY clause, 452

OrderAsString field, 545, 555

OrderDetail class, 566

OrderDetail table, 407–409, 430, 450, 537

OrderDetails class, 566

OrderDetailsAdmin.ascx control, 625, 629–630

OrderGetDetails stored procedure, 431

OrderGetInfo stored procedure, 430–431, 537

OrderID column, 569

OrderID field, 406

OrderID primary key, 408

OrderInfo object, 432–434, 441, 537, 619, 632

OrderMarkCanceled stored procedure, 432

OrderMarkCompleted stored procedure, 432

OrderMarkVerified stored procedure, 432

OrderProcess class, 621

OrderProcessor class, 566, 569–572, 575–577, 583–586, 589–591, 604, 633, 660

OrderProcessor.cs file, 575

OrderProcessorEmail class, 573

OrderProcessorException class, 566, 571–572, 581

OrderProcessorMailer class, 570, 573–574, 577, 589–590

orders. *See* customer orders

Orders database, 565

Orders table, 406–409, 532, 549–550, 611

OrdersAccess class, 419, 433, 441, 539

OrdersAccess.cs file, 432

OrdersAdmin.ascx properties, 426

OrdersGetByDate stored procedure, 419

OrdersGetByRecent stored procedure, 418–420

OrdersGetUnverifiedUncanceled stored procedure, 419

OrdersGetVerifiedUncompleted stored procedure, 419

OrderUpdate stored procedure, 431

Out parameter, 146

output cache, 263–265

output parameters, 146

OutputBox text box, 655

OutputCache page directive, 263, 265

■P

Page_Load function, 218, 258, 514, 629

pageNumber parameter, 154

Pager Web user control, 167, 170

paging, implementing, 138

param3 property, 503

param4 property, 503

parameters, 140, 145–146

PasswordHasher class, 469

PasswordHasher.cs file, 468

PasswordRegularExpression parameter, 502

passwordStrengthRegularExpression parameter, 501

PayPal

cost of, 11

overview, 10–11, 267–268

setting up, 268–269

shopping cart and checkout, 270–277

performance improvement, 257–265

pipeline implementation

administering orders

business tier, 611–621

database modifications, 608–611

overview, 607–608

presentation tier, 621–633

testing order administration page, 633–635

business tier, 570–578, 589–602

database modifications, 568–570

OrderProcessor class, 583–586

overview, 563–568, 589

presentation tier, 578–582, 602–607

Place code in a separate file check box, 47, 51

PlaceHolder control, 194

placeOrderButton_Click method, 535, 557

PopulateControls( ) function, 412, 441, 524, 557, 630–631

postback mode, 258, 629

PrepareUrlText method, 214

presentation tier

integrating AWS with BalloonShop, 688–690

overview, 15

paging at, 137

pipeline implementation, 578–582, 602–607

product attributes, 189–196

product catalog, 159–179, 246–255

product recommendations, 458–461

shopping cart, 383–395

Price field name, 127

PRIMARY KEY constraint, 64, 67, 120

primary keys, 62–64

Process( ) method, 580–581, 592, 604, 621, 633

processButton button, 603

processing parameter, 204

processing="stop" attribute, 208

product attributes

business tier, 188–189

data tier, 182–188

overview, 181–182

presentation tier, 189–196

Product Attributes Presentation, implementing, 189

product catalog

administering

categories, 320–324

departments, 299–317

products, 333–364

business tier, 147–158

communicating with database, 72–77

custom error page, 110

data storage, 116

data tables, 61–68

displaying list of departments, 97–101, 104

link factory, 102

logic, adding, 79–97

overview, 55–56

parameterized stored procedures, 145–146

presentation tier, 159–179

previewing, 56–59

querying new data, 133–139

storing new data, 115–127

writing stored procedures, 139–145

product recommendations

business tier, 457–458

data tier, 449–456

dynamic, 447–448

presentation tier, 458–461

product reviews feature, 667–673

Product table, 408, 410, 452

Product URL, 200

Product.aspx Web Form, 177, 673

Product.aspx.cs file, 221

ProductAttributeValue data table, 182, 184–185

ProductDescriptionLength configuration, 147

ProductDetails struct, 152

ProductID column, 135

ProductID field, 119, 127

ProductRecommendations.ascx Web User Control, 458

ProductReviews.ascx Web User Control, 671, 673

ProductsAdmin.ascx file, 340–342, 344–345, 348

ProductsList Web User Control, 170, 177, 250

ProductsList.ascx file, 167, 189, 193, 226, 265

ProductsList.ascx.cs file, 195

ProductsPerPage configuration, 147

<profile> element, 503

ProfileCommon class, 503, 517, 541

ProfileDataSource control, 508

ProfileWrapper class, 507, 516

PromoDept field name, 127

PromoFront field name, 127

Properties window, 189

ProviderUserKey property, 535

PSCheckFunds class, 566, 593–594, 660, 662–664

PSCheckStock class, 566, 594–595

PSDummy class, 570, 577–578

PSDummy.cs file, 577

PSFinalNotification class, 566, 599, 601

PSInitialNotification class, 566, 591–592

PSInitialNotification.cs file, 591

PSShipGoods class, 566, 597, 599

PSShipOK class, 566, 599

PSStockOK class, 595–596

PSTakePayment class, 566, 596–597, 663–664

purifyUrlRegex member, 212

■Q

Quantity field, 408

query string parameters, 198

querying new data, 133–139

■R

RangeValidator control, 417, 429

RC2 (Ron's Code, Rivest's Cipher) standard, 473

RDBMS (Relational Database Management Systems), 73

recommendations. See product recommendations

records, 62

<redirect> element, 217, 223

Reference column, 532

Reference field, 583, 659

Reference property, 660

Refresh folder, 49

Refresh method, 542, 555

Regex class, 205, 209, 210

RegexOptions value, 211

Register link, 499

registration page, 466

regular expressions, 204–211

RegularExpressions namespace, 212

Relational Database Management Systems (RDBMS), 73

relational databases, 116–120

relationships

    enforcing with FOREIGN KEY constraint, 120–121

    many-to-many relationships, 117–120

    one-to-many relationships, 117–118

RemoveItem method, 382

RemoveProductFromCategory stored procedure, 280, 325–327, 351

Replace method, 210

Representational State Transfer (REST), 675, 678–681

requireSSL attribute, 527

response groups, 679

Response Groups link, 681

REST (Representational State Transfer), 675, 678–681

Review table, 669

reviews feature, 667–673

Rewrite element, 223

<rewriter> element, 204, 217

RightToLeft member, 211

Rijndael standard, 473

risks, e-commerce site, 8–9

Rivest's Cipher (RC2) standard, 473

Rivest-Shamir-Adleman (RSA), 473

RoleGroup Template, 499

Roles class, 502

Ron's Code (RC2) standard, 473

ROW_NUMBER function, 138

RSA (Rivest-Shamir-Adleman), 473

■**S**

SalesRank response group, 681

scalable architecture, 14

search engine optimization

    BalloonShop, 197–198

    HTTP status codes, 216–222

keyword-rich URLs

    for BalloonShop, 200–204

    generating, 211–215

    ISAPI_Rewrite, 199

    overview, 198–199

    UrlRewriter.NET, 199

overview, 197

regular expressions, 205–211

Search Engine Result Pages (SERPs), 216

Search method, 243

SearchBox control, 258

SearchBox.ascx control, 246, 258

SearchCatalog method, 243

searching catalog

    business tier, 243–245

    choosing method for, 225–226

    presentation tier, 246–255

    teaching database to search itself

        FULLTEXT catalog and indexes, 229–232

        full-text feature, 228–229

        improving relevance, 236–238

        overview, 226–227

        SearchCatalog stored procedure, 238–243

        sorting by relevance, 232–235

secret access key, 677

secure connections, setting up, 525–529

Secure Sockets Layer (SSL) connections, 8, 525

SecureCard class, 482, 494–495, 516

SecureCard.cs file, 468

SecureCardException.cs file, 468

SecureLib library, 482

Security page, 41

Security tab, 497

SecurityLib class

    encryption, 472–495

    hashing, 468–472

    overview, 467–468

SecurityLibTester.aspx file, 469

SEH (Structured Exception Handling), 480

Select master page, 51

SELECT statement, 73–74, 82, 133, 135, 137, 185–186, 418

SelectedIndexChanged event handler, 429

SendMail method, 413, 574, 590

serialization attributes, XML, 644

SERPs (Search Engine Result Pages), 216

server-side control, 23

server-side validation, 415

set cookie element, 223

SET IDENTITY INSERT ON statement, 184

SET IDENTITY_INSERT command, 125

set property element, 223

SET ROWCOUNT statement, 418

set status element, 223

SetEditMode method, 442, 632

SetOrderAuthCodeAndReference method, 585, 660

SetOrderDateShipped method, 585–586

SHA1Managed instance, 471

Shared parameter, 264

shipping charges. *See* tax and shipping charges

Shipping table, 548–549

ShippingCost column, 549

ShippingID column, 549–550

ShippingInfo struct, 552

ShippingRegion fields, 508

shippingRegion property, 519

ShippingRegion table, 504

ShippingRegionID column, 549

ShippingType column, 549

shopping cart

    administering, 396–402

    business tier, 375–383

    data tier, 372–375

    PayPal, 270–277

    presentation tier, 383–395

ShoppingCart table, 370–371, 410

ShoppingCartAccess class, 378, 410, 457, 534

ShoppingCart.aspx control, 403

ShoppingCartGetItems stored procedure, 374

ShoppingCartRemoveItem stored procedure, 373

ShoppingCartUpdateItem stored procedure, 374

ShowMessageBox property, 417

Simple Mail Transfer Protocol (SMTP) server, 88

Simple Object Access Protocol (SOAP), 675, 681

Singleline member, 211

site skeleton, 45–53, 104

SiteName configuration, 147

size property, 145

.skin extension, 98

SkinID property, 98

skins, 98

Small response group, 681

SMTP (Simple Mail Transfer Protocol) server, 88

SmtpClient class, 88

SOAP (Simple Object Access Protocol), 675, 681

Source Code area, 53

SourceStage integer property, 572

Split method, 210

SQL (Structured Query Language), 25, 73–76

SQL Server 2008

    BalloonShop project, 39–44

    connecting to, 79–81

    data types, 65

    full-text search feature, 227–228

    management interface, 29

    paging, 138

    using, 25–26

SQL Server 2008 Express Edition, 20, 31–32

SQL Server and Windows Authentication mode, 41

SQL Server Managed Data Provider, 83

SQL Server Management Studio, 44, 188

SQL Server Management Studio Express, 29, 39, 73

SqlConnection class, 80–82

SqlDataSource control, 508, 622

sqlexpr_adv.exe file, 228

SQLEXPRADV_x64_ENU.exe file, 32

SQLEXPRADV_x86_ENU.exe file, 32

SSL (Secure Sockets Layer) connections, 8, 525

SSL certificates, 526

Start Debugging command, 37

Status column, 532

Status int column, 532

Status table, 611

statusDropDown control, 629

stored procedures, 25
  executing, 81–83
  parameterized, 145–146
  saving query as, 76–77
  writing new, 139–144

storing
  customer accounts, 466
  new data, 115–127

StreamReader object, 481

string members, 657

string parameter, 644

StringBuilder object, 592

StringEncryptor class, 474, 482

StringEncryptor.cs file, 468

StringEncryptorException exception, 480–481

Structured Exception Handling (SEH), 480

Structured Query Language (SQL), 25, 73–76

subqueries, 138, 454–455

Substring method, 658

SUM function, 431

SupplierEmail class, 573

symmetric encryption, 472

System Configuration Checker option, 32

System.Collections.Generic namespace, 552

System.Data namespace, 190–191, 684

System.Data.Common namespace, 84, 419

System.Data.SqlClient parameter, 84

SystemException class, 572

System.Math class, 556

System.Security.Cryptography namespace, 473

System.Text namespace, 593

System.Text.RegularExpressions namespace, 209

System.Web.HttpResponse class, 217

System.Web.Mail namespace, 88

System.Web.Security namespace, 590

System.Xml namespace, 684

■T

table joins, 134–136

table relationships. See relationships

table variables, 138–139

tax and shipping charges
  business layer, 552–556
  database modifications, 547–551
  further development, 560–561
  overview, 546–547
  presentation layer, 556–558

Tax table, 548, 557

TaxID int column, 548, 550

TaxInfo struct, 552

TaxPercentage float column, 548

TaxType column, 548

Templates panel, 36

Text data type, 66

text pattern, 205

themes, 98–99

three-tier architecture, 15–20, 24

throw statement, 87

Thumbnail field name, 127

TieButton method, 416

to attribute, 204

ToCategory method, 213–214

ToDepartment method, 103, 212–214

TOP keyword, 138, 452

ToProduct method, 213–214

TotalAmount field, 430

<Transaction> element, 657

TransactionClass class, 647, 657

Transact-SQL (T-SQL), 25, 72–73

Trim function, 215

try block, 87

try-catch construct, 87

try-catch-finally construct, 86

T-SQL (Transact-SQL), 25, 72–73

two-tier architecture, 19

TxnDetailsClass, 647

Type property, 417

■U

UAC (User Account Control), 34

UNION method, 187

unique columns, 64–65

UNIQUE constraint, 120

UniqueIdentifier data type, 66

Unless element, 223

Update method, 434–435, 619

Update Quantities button, 411

UPDATE statement, 75

UpdateCategory stored procedure, 301–305, 321

UpdateDepartment stored procedure, 300

UpdateItem method, 381

UpdateOrder method, 619, 621, 632

UpdateOrderStatus method, 584

UpdateProduct stored procedure, 335

UpdateProfile method, 518

up-selling, 447

url attribute, 204

UrlEncode method, 208

UrlPathEncode method, 215

UrlRewriter method, 200

UrlRewriter.NET tool, 199, 222–223

UrlRewriterV2 folder, 200

UrlRewriterV2\bin\Release\Intelligencia.Url Rewriter.dll assembly, 200

URLs

automatic correction, 218–219

canonicalization, 198

keyword-rich

for BalloonShop, 200–204

generating, 211–215

ISAPI_Rewrite, 199

overview, 198–199

UrlRewriter.NET, 199

rewriting, 198–199

User Account Control (UAC), 34

user profiles, 466, 502–520

userDropDown control, 623–624

UserId field, 623

using statement, 432

Utilities class, 89, 413, 574, 590

utility functions, 565

■V

ValidationSummary control, 416

validator controls, 415

Value parameter, 621

VarBinary data type, 66

VarChar data type, 66, 145

VaryByControl parameter, 264

VaryByCustom parameter, 264

VaryByHeader parameter, 264

VaryByParam parameter, 264

VB .NET, 24

VBScript, 22

Verified bit, 436

Verified field, 408

verified orders, 405

VeriSign, 526

__VEWSTATE hidden form field, 260

View Cart button, 270

View Sites link, 34

ViewState class, 258, 260–262

Visual C# Express, 467

Visual Studio 2008, 24–25

Visual Web Developer 2008, 23, 38

Visual Web Developer 2008 Express Edition,
    20, 24–25, 30

vwdsetup.exe file, 30

W

Web clients, 21–22

Web Forms, 23, 45

Web Install section, 31

Web Management Tools, 33

Web Server Controls, 23

Web servers, 21–22

Web User Controls, 23, 46

web.config file, 39, 200–201, 221, 466, 682

Website Payments Standard Integration
    Guide, 270

Welcome.html document, 53

WHERE clause, 75, 138

Windows Authentication, 33, 41, 466

X

Xml property, 658

You Need the Companion eBook

Your purchase of this book entitles you to buy the companion PDF-version eBook for only $10. Take the weightless companion with you anywhere.

We believe this Apress title will prove so indispensable that you'll want to carry it with you everywhere, which is why we are offering the companion eBook (in PDF format) for $10 to customers who purchase this book now. Convenient and fully searchable, the PDF version of any content-rich, page-heavy Apress book makes a valuable addition to your programming library. You can easily find and copy code—or perform examples by quickly toggling between instructions and the application. Even simultaneously tackling a donut, diet soda, and complex code becomes simplified with hands-free eBooks!

Once you purchase your book, getting the $10 companion eBook is simple:

❶ Visit **www.apress.com/promo/tendollars/**.

❷ Complete a basic registration form to receive a randomly generated question about this title.

❸ Answer the question correctly in 60 seconds, and you will receive a promotional code to redeem for the $10.00 eBook.

2855 TELEGRAPH AVENUE | SUITE 600 | BERKELEY, CA 94705

All Apress eBooks subject to copyright protection. No part may be reproduced or transmitted in any form or by any means, electronic or mechanical, including photocopying, recording, or by any information storage or retrieval system, without the prior written permission of the copyright owner and the publisher. The purchaser may print the work in full or in part for their own noncommercial use. The purchaser may place the eBook title on any of their personal computers for their own personal reading and reference.

Offer valid through 9/09.